LATIN AMERICA:

the struggle with dependency
and beyond

STATES AND SOCIETIES OF THE THIRD WORLD

A Schenkman Series edited by Richard Harris

LATIN AMERICA: THE STRUGGLE WITH DEPENDENCY
AND BEYOND
Edited by Ronald H. Chilcote and Joel C. Edelstein

THE POLITICAL ECONOMY OF AFRICA
Edited by Richard Harris

POLITICS AND MODERNIZATION IN SOUTH AND
SOUTHEAST ASIA
Edited by Robert N. Kearney

POLITICAL ELITES AND POLITICAL DEVELOPMENT IN
THE MIDDLE EAST
Edited by Frank Tachau

LATIN AMERICA:

the struggle with dependency and beyond

edited by
RONALD H. CHILCOTE
and
JOEL C. EDELSTEIN

A Halsted Press Book

Schenkman Publishing Company, Inc.

JOHN WILEY & SONS
New York — London — Sydney — Toronto

Distributed Solely by Halsted Press, a Division
of John Wiley and Sons, Inc., New York

Library of Congress Cataloging in Publication Data

Chilcote, Ronald H.
Latin America: The Struggle with Dependency
and Beyond.

(States and Societies of the Third World)

1. Latin America — Economic conditions — 1945–
— Addresses, essays, lectures. 2. Latin America —
Social conditions — 1945–   — Addresses, essays,
lectures. I. Edelstein, Joel C., joint author.
11. Title
HC125.C488   309. 1'8'003   74-8393
ISBN 0-470-15555-8
ISBN 0-470-15556-6 (pbk)

For the peoples of the Americas who suffer the violent
condition of underdevelopment and for those who struggle against it.
To the reader in the hope that understanding will lead to action.

ACKNOWLEDGEMENTS

To Karen Middlebrook, a student assistant who will soon happily forsake typing the writings of others to pursue her own work in the biological sciences, we extend our sincere thanks for her accurate typing of portions of the introductory chapter, revisions of other chapters, and editorial correspondence nearly equal in length to the book itself. We also acknowledge the skillful work of Linda Jaworski, graphic arts specialist, who prepared the maps under our supervision. For their helpful comments on portions of an early draft of the introductory chapter, we would like to express our gratitude to Harry Cliakakis, Harriet Edelstein, Anthony Galt, Emil Haney Jr., David Osterberg, and Larry J. Smith. On a later draft of the chapter we were especially appreciative of suggestions from Frances Chilcote, Sara Sheehan, and Howard Sherman, as well as students in a graduate seminar on dependency at the University of California, Riverside. We are also deeply grateful for the assistance of Marjory and Donald Bray and Timothy Harding who, together with us, were directly involved in the criticism and dialogue that carried us through four drafts of the introductory chapter. We are, of course, solely responsible for any interpretation, error or omission in this chapter. Finally, we would like to express our thanks to the contributors of this volume for their collaboration and commitment to fulfilling the ambitious goals which we jointly decided to pursue, for their ideas, suggestions for improvement, and constructive criticisms, and for their patience, understanding, and toleration of the innumerable delays, which while exasperating to all, hopefully have resulted in a better book.

RONALD H. CHILCOTE
JOEL C. EDELSTEIN

CONTENTS

PREFACE

This volume is part of a series on "States and Societies of the Third World." The term "Third World" is rather vague. We know what parts of the world are included in it—all the nations of the world except those of North America and Europe, the USSR, China, Australia and New Zealand. However, what the nations of the Third World have in common, why they should be placed in the same category, what the concept implies, are more problematic. The term is sometimes used to refer to countries which are poor, primarily non-white and non-industrial. But among nations regarded as part of the Third World and even within Latin America, some countries are predominantly "white" (Argentina and Uruguay), some have significant industrial centers (Argentina, Brazil and Mexico) and others have a per capita GNP closer to that of non-Third World countries than to most countries of the Third World (e.g., Argentina's per capita income is about average for the Eastern European countries and is about nine times greater than that of Haiti). The common defining characteristic must be found elsewhere.

The term came into use in the 1950's when the world was divided into two hostile camps. This was also a decade when many colonies gained formal independence. Many were admitted to the United Nations and some observers thought that these "new nations" would be a third force in world politics. Of course, not all the "new nations" were "new." Most of the Latin American countries had been formally independent for over 130 years. Some countries such as Thailand had never been under colonial rule. The idea that the Third World countries would act as a political bloc has fallen in the course of time. Unity has simply been less frequent than its opposite.

The concept has also been used to imply that the Third World countries are just now emerging from feudalism and that they have the opportunity to create a new, third path of development "between capitalism and socialism." This idea is no more viable than the others we have mentioned. It is more dangerous because it denies one feature which is shared by the nations of the Third World—their history of economic domination. Each society has been caught up in the expanding international capitalist system. Regardless of formal legal status, the economy of every Third World nation was shaped by the needs of the system's

ix

center. They became exporters of a limited number of primary products and they became dependent on foreign trade to provide all of the products their economies did not produce. Responding to international market forces, they developed the distortions of dependent capitalism. In our understanding, the defining characteristic of the Third World concept is this economic structure which maintains dependency.*

Some nations have thrown off the forces of foreign penetration and the domestic ruling classes which have cooperated with imperialism. Cuba, following this course, has removed the allocation of resources and labor from the control of the market and the profit motive. By eliminating the private ownership of the means of production, it has been possible to institute planning directed toward independent national development. Cubans have acquired a new respect for their own culture and society. The dependent economy inherited from the colonial and neo-colonial period has not yet been overcome. Cuba's need to import and to find markets for its limited variety of exports makes Cuba vulnerable. Thus, Cuba is still a Third World nation. However, the Cuban people are now mobilized to create a sovereign economy on which full political independence can be based.

The problem of Third World peoples to overcome poverty and to achieve dignity lies first in regaining control of their resources. This task requires revolutionary struggle against domestic ruling classes and their foreign supporters. Most Third World countries are still governed by comprador elites, some relatively strong and others which would fall in a matter of months if not supported by imperialist military strength. In Asia and Africa and in the Americas the struggle continues, more advanced in some areas, using different forms and tactics in different contexts. In many countries the counterrevolution has dropped its demo-

* Some leaders of ethnic minority movements in the United States have included their respective ethnic groups in the Third World. We consider this a correct interpretation of the concept, granting that these groups are sufficiently separate from the dominant society to be considered as distinct communities and that dependent economic structures and relationships exist between each minority and the dominant society. The land formerly occupied by native Americans and the territory of the southwest which was once part of Mexico were expropriated in the course of capitalist expansion. Africans were forcibly removed from their homeland and brought into the United States to provide cheap labor. Though today some assimilation occurs, it almost always requires adoption of the dominant culture after the fashion of the assimilationist policies of European colonial powers in Africa and Asia. Contemporary economic relationships are essentially neocolonial. Though there are important differences between the historical experience and contemporary situation of Third World states and ethnic minorities in the United States, they are not central.

cratic façade, placing military regimes in power. The effort to stop the Third World revolution has encouraged similar tendencies in the very center of the system. Nonetheless, the revolution continues and in some nations succeeds. It will surely be the dominant force in the history of the world for the balance of this century.

Until now, there has not been a book which contains studies of sufficient length to explore in some detail the development of underdevelopment in each of several countries. This volume attempts to fill the void, to provide a book suitable for undergraduate and graduate courses concerning Latin American history, economy and politics as well as courses on international relations, modernization and political and economic development.

We believe that previous explanations of underdevelopment have misunderstood its root cause. They have provided justification for government policies and corporate activities which have maintained and enhanced political economic patterns and social structures which produce vast human suffering and which prevent the realization of individual and social potential. A new understanding of underdevelopment has come through an analysis of imperialism and dependence and is clearly taking hold among a growing number of scholars. At scholarly meetings attendance at presentations of this work is large and is increasing. More books and articles are being published and bought. We hope that this volume will contribute to the general acceptance of the new analysis. We are concerned with destroying myth and with bringing about a more correct understanding. Moreover, it is our earnest hope that understanding will lead to action and change toward the complete reorientation of policies of the U.S. government and to modification of U.S. economic and social institutions, change which is necessary if Americans are to play a positive role in the struggle against underdevelopment in the Americas.

While each Latin American country is in many respects unique, there are many ways in which the studies of the present volume might be grouped. Argentina, Brazil, and Mexico are large countries, ranging in population from twenty-five million to over ninety-five million inhabitants. Chile, Cuba and Guatemala have populations under ten million. Mexico and Cuba have experienced revolutions which involved large segments of their respective populations. Brazil and Argentina have been under direct military rule in recent years. Cuba and Chile are in different ways pursuing a socialist path.

We have chosen to place initially Guatemala, Mexico and Argentina because they represent different strains of a pre-1960 Latin America; Guatemala as a more or less traditional alliance of the oligarchy and the military; Mexico as a nation now ruled by a conservative bourgeoisie; and Argentina as a case of unresolved stalemate among forces which· emerged early in this century. Brazil, Chile and Cuba represent new directions: Brazil as a concerted effort toward dependent growth with the U.S. empire; Chile as a nation attempting to gain control of its resources to undertake an independent development effort, and Cuba as an attempt to mobilize itself toward the creation of a new society.

CONTENTS: INTRODUCTION

ALTERNATIVE PERSPECTIVES OF DEVELOPMENT
AND UNDERDEVELOPMENT IN LATIN AMERICA

BY

RONALD H. CHILCOTE

AND

JOEL C. EDELSTEIN

It is costly to be born a Latin American rather than a North American, at least in statistical terms. The average life expectancy in the nations of Latin America is about 54 years compared to about 69 years in the United States. If you had been born a Latin American it would cost you about 15 years or more than one-fifth of your life. As an "average" Latin American, you would receive only a sixth of the schooling you get as an "average" North American—less than two years compared to nearly twelve. The possibility of hunger and starvation would be much greater. A 1968 study (Citizen's Board of Inquiry, 1968:7) estimates that 14 million people suffer from hunger in the United States, about 7 percent of the total population. Some estimates regarding Latin America include as much as three-fourths of the population. As an "average" Latin American, you would be sick much more, and there are proportionately only a third the number of doctors and those are concentrated in the cities away from where most people live. Your income would be only one-tenth that of an "average" North American. The probability that you would witness the death of one of your children in the first year of life would be about four times greater.*

These facts of human existence are beyond dispute. *Why* these social conditions exist and how they can be *changed* are subjects of heated and sometimes bitter arguments. Two alternative explanations have been advanced by observers of Latin America. One suggests that the development of areas like Latin America will come about through outside influence and assistance; this explanation is embraced by the *diffusion model*. The second explanation, incorporated in the *dependency model*, views foreign penetration as the cause of underdevelopment in Latin America and implies that underdeveloped countries can develop only if both their internal structures and their relations with other nations undergo a complete change.

Our objective in this introductory chapter is to explain the essential premises of these two models and to examine their contrasting perspectives in relation to some prevailing assumptions about development and underdevelopment. These models are related to the historical experience in Europe, especially in England and the Iberian countries, as well as in Latin America. From our discussion of the models and the historical

* While these figures provide an accurate presentation of differences in the condition of the "average" Latin American and the "average" North American, a few points of clarification are necessary. The situation in Latin America is probably worse than the figures indicate. Data collection of health and welfare for many areas is poor. Moreover in most cases we have used sources such as the *Statistical Abstract of Latin America* (Ruddle and Hamour, 1970) which rely on the governments themselves and there is an ever present tendency for political reasons to portray things as better than they are. Also, averages are highly misleading. Inequality in both the United States and Latin America is great, but is particularly extreme in Latin America. According to a study by the United Nations Economic Commission for Latin America (1970:376), Latin America's richest 5 percent had a per capita income in 1965 of $2600, less than, but comparable to, the average income in the United States at that time. The poorest 20 percent in Latin America had an income of only $60 per person per year. The average annual per capita income for the bottom four-fifths of Latin America was only $180. For these more than 200 million people, the situation is far worse than for the upper 5 percent who have full access to food, medical care and schooling. Average figures for each country also hide the large differences in the conditions of urban and rural Latin America, particularly in regard to schooling and medical care which are especially lacking in rural areas. In addition to the gross differences within each country which are obscured by aggregate figures, we should not forget the very great differences between countries. We are very uneasy when we refer to "Latin America" as a whole in this essay and we do so only because the qualifications necessary to account for the differences among countries would continually interrupt the train of thought being followed (and would likely double the length of the essay).

interpretation based therein emerge three controversial issues or aspects of class struggle that permeate past and present literature on Latin America: 1) feudalism and dual society; 2) the national bourgeoisie; and 3) the ruling class. We show that polarized positions on these issues are related to one's reliance upon either the diffusion *or* dependency model. We critique three major studies of Latin America to exemplify how these issues have led scholars to different interpretations and conclusions. Then we look briefly at some problems which face societies that attempt to break their dependency with capitalism, and finally, we assess the prospects for the struggle with dependency.

I THE DIFFUSION MODEL

Our initial attention is to the diffusion model, to a critical discussion of the theoretical thrust of the model and its underpinnings. In our examination of the role of history in the diffusionist interpretation of development and underdevelopment, we focus on feudalism and capitalism as forms of economic activity that stimulated a "dual society" with a backward, feudal order on the one hand, and a commercial and industrial bourgeois order on the other. Then we relate the assumptions of the diffusion model to the experience of the United States in Latin America, with a review of overt intervention, Pan Americanism, and economic assistance and penetration. Finally, as a stimulus for further reading we offer a brief synthesis of the literature upon which the model is based.

ASSUMPTIONS OF THE DIFFUSION MODEL

According to the diffusion model, progress will come about through the spread of modernism to backward, archaic, and traditional areas. Through the diffusion of technology and capital, these areas will inescapably evolve from a traditional toward a modern state.

Essentially, the diffusion model sees underdevelopment as a condition which all nations have experienced at some time. While some nations have managed to develop, others have not. In Latin America, according to the model, a feudal structure inherited from the Spanish and Portuguese conquistadores has stifled change. Though modern cities have arisen through contact with the developed world, the countryside remains backward, mired in the unproductive agriculture of large feudal estates. If conditions are to improve, traditional values must be challenged and modern diversified industry must replace current dependence on one or two agricultural products. Change requires the introduction of outside capital because the region is poor. Foreign investment can also bring modern technology and organizational methods to these backward nations—a problem which did not confront feudal England and other early developing nations, but one that becomes especially critical for the late starters on the road to development. However, business requires political stability—and this is a major problem. There is a revolution of rising expectations and the masses are impatient. The middle class, though democratically inclined, has been weak and divided. In these conditions, modernizing military governments appear as the last resort of progress. Hopefully the order they provide can stimulate foreign investment bringing about the modernization of agriculture and industry necessary to create the basis for a new democratic stability. Thus, the diffusion model encourages increased U.S. investment to advance economic development in Latin America and increased North American influence to develop Latin American culture. The diffusion model even endorses the granting of aid to Latin American militaries in the name of democracy.

Within the diffusion model, underdevelopment is signified by either a per capita gross national product below $300 or $400 as a single criterion (see Staley, 1961) or together with other characteristics including illiteracy, political instability, inequality, heirarchy and lack of social mobility, and an economy characterized by the dominance of one or two agricultural or mineral products and by a low level of technology and productivity. A region or a nation-state which manifests all or most of these characteristics is regarded as an underdeveloped area. The more pronounced these features are, the greater the degree of underdevelopment. In these terms, most of the nations of Latin America are clearly underdeveloped. There is no doubt about Guatemala, for example, where the per capita GNP is $328 and 62.1 percent of the population is illiterate. Nor is there any question about the status of Brazil as an underdeveloped nation since annual per capita income is only $337, probably half of the population is illiterate, and one product, coffee, accounts for over 40 percent of foreign exchange earnings. It is less clear that Argentina is an underdeveloped country. Literacy is nearly universal (91 percent); the average annual income is $739; there is a substantial middle class.

The diffusion model uses two criteria to define development. One is national wealth which is measured by a single aggregate figure, the per capita gross national product. The second is the degree of "modernity," a concept which comprises social and political characteristics such as the rate of social mobility; the complexity of the social structure, with emphasis on the progressive role of a "middle class"; the degree of specialization of political and social roles and institutions; national integration; urbanization; and limitations on government power accompanied by the rise of mechanisms for compromise and for the expression of popular will. In the terms of definition employed by the diffusion model, medieval England was underdeveloped. National integration was lacking, poverty and illiteracy were the normal conditions of the serf. Relative to current standards, the feudal economy employed a low level of technology, and productivity was low. Today England is seen as a success story of gradual progress from underdeveloped island to developed nation-state.*

FEUDALISM, CAPITALISM, AND DUAL SOCIETY IN ENGLAND AND LATIN AMERICA

In the discussion below we describe in some detail the early beginnings of development in England, examining the characteristics of feudalism and tracing the transition to capitalism through the growth of commercialization and early industrialization. At the outset, our discussion focuses on England because of the belief, inherent in the diffusion model, that the experience of England serves as an example for the development of backward areas elsewhere. In comparing England to Latin America, we acknowledge that in rural society many characteristics of the early European feudalism seem to be evident in Latin America. Likewise, we also note parallels in the devolpment of urban life in England and Latin America; the emergence of capitalism was the consequence of such considerations as capital for new industry and technology for modern production. And capitalism was accompanied by the rise of a bourgeoisie and a subsequent decline of the feudal lords in England, although in Latin America two societies, one feudal and the other capitalist, tended to prevail. It is with this notion of dual society that we contend in our discussion of the dependency model. Here, however, we are concerned with a diffusionist explanation of dual society. Later we shall identify the contradictions of that explanation.

Feudalism. The diffusion model sees Latin America as feudal and stresses a transformation to capitalism as the key to development. This model uses the transition of Northern European and English feudalism as an example which can and should be followed by contemporary underdeveloped nations. In the English feudal system people were spread across the land on great estates. Technology was at a very primitive level and people produced little more food than they and their children needed to live. By far, the vast majority of the people worked the soil

---

* Throughout the text we make reference to England as a feudal or industrial society. England grew in territory and became Great Britain, but to avoid confusion, we consistently use England to refer to all of Great Britain in recent centuries as well as to England in its original state.

as serfs. A portion of what food that was left over fed the few artisans of the manor who produced manufactured craft articles—tools, arms, and some household items. The serfs were forced by the power and position of the nobles who owned the estates, in a sense were forced by the manorial system itself to produce the surplus and to turn it over to the nobles for their use and for their artisans.

The mentality and the consciousness of the people of the feudal system, of the serf and the nobleman, was very different from our own. The concept of change, the sense of acquiring greater wealth and comfort, of moving around to see the world, ideas and aspirations which dominate our own lives were virtually unknown to the people of the medieval world. Their society was highly structured. If one were born a serf, he or she tilled the soil and belonged to the lord of the manor. The serf's position was fixed by legal custom and could not be changed. There was virtually no movement from one place in the feudal hierarchy to another. One's goal was not to compete for higher positions in society, but to do what one's mother or father did, to till the soil giving part of the produce to one's secular or ecclesiastical lord, to practice the prescribed simple religious duties and to rest on Sundays. One did not expect more of life because one was not aware of more, nor did one ever receive more. Life was simple, fixed, and predictable.

Feudal economies consisted of very simple agricultural structures and in no way resembled the occupations and industries in which the majority of North Americans work. The service sector, composed of teachers, lawyers, office workers, salesmen, bureaucrats hardly existed. This sector forms the economic base for most of what we now call the middle class. While a primitive class of clerks (clerics) and bureaucrats had come to exist as a by-product of the governmental functions of the Universal Church and the incipient monarchies which could be seen as a managerial class, essentially feudal society consisted of two classes—the secular and spiritual lords of the manor and the ecclesiastical estates, and the serfs and artisans who were born to these estates and worked the fields or in the village households that sprang up around the manor.

The responsibilities of the serf included working in the lord's fields and providing a number of other services, and paying rent in cash or in kind for the privilege of farming some land for himself. The arrangements between the serf and his lord, often spelled out in considerable detail (for example, see Cantor, 181–84), were quite extensive, giving the lord power in matters such as marriage of the serf's children.

A serf could not move off the estate without permission. Mobility hardly existed. People spent their whole lives within a few square miles, and seldom met strangers of any kind. It would be unlikely if they would ever meet more than a few hundred people in their lifetime. Traditional codes and customs amounting to the force of law enforced this way of life and completed the bondage.

In this kind of society urban centers were very slow in appearing. Productivity was too low to provide enough surplus to support much urban development. Though there were occasional fairs in which trading occurred, there was not enough produce to create a commercial world out of this simple trade, and transportation was too difficult. The people identified with the immediate locality in which they lived, with the land they farmed and its master.

Interpersonal relationships in feudal society were unlike those which we experience in our daily lives especially as related to economic transactions. In our society, a buyer and a seller usually see each other only in these limited roles. In feudal societies relationships were more personalized. Although the opportunity to buy and sell goods may have been the primary reason for contact, the act of exchange occurred within the context of a long-standing traditional relationship. The dealings between employers and employees today also differ from the more personalized relationship between the lord and the serf.

In feudal societies there was no union to provide a protective barrier for the serf and no bargaining. There was no economic constraint on the lord of the estate. There were no legal remedies for the serf. The lord was the law in his own territory (the baronial or seigneurial courts). The law governing that relationship was rooted in the specific custom and tradition of that area which itself was molded over the centuries by the families of the lords. Two conditions operated to protect the serf from any injurious effects of the lord's arbitrary power. First, the serf and his lord were engaged in more than just a business relationship. In addition to the "employer-employee" or "leasor-lessee" roles, they shared a kind of unequal friendship. The lord was clearly the superior in this relationship, but he had paternalistic responsibilities for the welfare of his serfs. This "responsibility" was sanctioned in custom and operated to some extent as a constraint. The relationship included not only the traditional, mutual obligations but also an exchange of favors between the lord and individual serfs. In our society, the owner of a business and his employees are kept together by money—from the worker's point of view, the boss is a signature on his paycheck. For the owner, the worker is a cost of production, nothing more—and the smaller the paycheck the greater the profit for the owner. In feudal societies the tendency for the lord to use his power to take nearly all that serf produces was mitigated by the personalized character of their relationship.

Also protecting the serf was the limited nature of the motives for the lord to exploit him. The serfs were exploited to finance the crusades, the church and the lords' high level of consumption. However, with only limited trade, there was less reason for the lord to extract a surplus from the serfs. In our own society, production is for the purpose of selling in the market. As long as the businessman can sell, he has an incentive to force his employees to produce as much as possible. The greater the demand for goods, the greater is the motive for increased production. In feudal society, short-term variations in production depended only on the weather—abundance in good years and low yields in times of flood or drought.

Moreover, since most production in feudal society was not the purpose of profit, production costs were not important to the lord. In capitalist society, the profit motive dictates not only maximizing production to meet demand, but also cutting costs by holding down the share of the product received by the workers. The feudal lord had no motive to attempt to force the serf to work the highest number of hours or at the fastest pace feasible, nor to subsist on the least possible portion of his product. (This is not to imply that the life of a serf was a bed of roses. Low productivity made it difficult for the serf to produce much beyond his own needs and, while the demands of the lord were not unlimited, the serf was often pressed severely to meet them.)

The absence of the profit motive had another effect: There was little incentive to try to increase productivity by technological innovation. In addition to increasing production and cutting costs by pressing workers to work longer and harder or to consume less, technological innovation can also achieve these goals by reducing the amount of labor required for a given level of production. Thus, in feudal society change was so slow as to be virtually absent. Production both in agriculture and in crafts was simple, requiring few tools. There was little investment in equipment for production. The values of hard work and saving in order to accumulate more wealth, power or social position had no place in feudalism.

Comparing contemporary Latin America, especially rural society, with early European feudalism, the same individualized, personalistic social relations, generally prevail, and these relations are emphasized in the diffusion model. Peasants, those living on the large farms and plantations, the *latifundia*, and those who work tiny plots of land, the *minifundia*, seem much like feudal serfs. They, too, are subject to the arbitrary power of the *latifundistas*, who comprise only about one percent of the landowners but own as much as 60 percent of the land (Feder, 1971:55). Though the traditions governing the relationship between the landowner and the peasant are not as formalized or detailed as in

European feudalism, their dealings are based on a similar mutual obligation combined with an exchange of favors in a system of patronage. In most areas there are no unions to intervene between them. As in feudal society, there are essentially two classes in rural Latin America, the landowners and the peasants. Except for limited opportunities in the Church and the military, the peasant has virtually no possibility of moving from the class into which he was born. The concept that one can and should advance through hard work and thrift is not established.

Politics in rural society is not characterized by competitive bargaining or negotiation. Power is held by the class of owners. Moreover, even among the latifundistas the give and take of bargaining is precluded by an orientation toward interpersonal relations called *dignidad*. Similar in some respects to the feudal code of chivalry, it places too great an emphasis on honor to provide for regularized confrontation in which one party may lose.

Much of the land is relatively unproductive (Furtado, 1970:114–23). While there are some technologically advanced, capital intensive areas in agriculture which are economically very important, on most agricultural properties investment is low (Feder, 1971:96–103). A study of land use in Argentina, Brazil, Chile, Colombia, Ecuador, Guatemala, and Peru found that 49 percent of land in farms was used for grazing animals without any attempt to grow forage crops (Feder, 1971:105) and the percentage of land dedicated to pasture was increasing. There is only limited use of fertilizers, machinery or other equipment and methods of modern intensive agriculture. This failure to invest capital in land to increase productivity would appear to flow from a feudal concept of land—ownership as a source of prestige and of power over the peasants who live on it instead of the modern, capitalistic idea that land is a factor of production used to earn the maximum possible profit.

Commerce as a Road to Development. In the perspective of the diffusion model, feudal Latin America can and should develop as feudal England did. In England, change occurred when technological progress permitted the creation of an agricultural surplus and its transportation. An increasing urban population could then be supported because the people on the land produced more than they needed to live on and reproduce. Trade grew and so did the proportion of goods produced for sale in the new market. With this initial change, several trends were set in motion.

The new towns and cities became a haven for serfs and artisans who gained an opportunity to escape the manorial system to make a living in the new commerce and manufacturing. In the towns the artisans became small businessmen and sold their crafts for profit. Those who assisted the master craftsmen were bound to the master as apprentices, learning their trade while being tied to the master in essentially the same kind of relationship they had to the lord of the estate. As technology advanced, manufacturing became more complex. The investment in tools became larger. Alongside the master craftsman, there grew a different type of manufacturer, the person who owns and administers the factory but does not work in production. With the coming of the Industrial Revolution, the steps in manufacturing were divided up and thereby simplified. Whereas the apprentice once had to learn over many years all the aspects of producing his craft, he now could do his simple job with hardly any training. The position of apprentice was replaced by the modern role of worker, who became dependent upon his wage to buy the necessities of life which he could no longer produce for himself. Thus, the nature of economic and social relationships changed. The lord-serf and the master-apprentice forms, which involved the participation in many aspects of their lives, which were highly personalized and within which an exchange of favors in a system of patronage took place, the arbitrary power of the lord or master notwithstanding, gave way to the more impersonal and limited relationship of the employer and his employee based on wages. No longer was the worker tied to the land or the household of the master. He was free to sell his labor for the highest wage it would bring in the market.

As trade grew, more agricultural products were sold in the market. Just as the labor of the worker was assigned a price, the status of land changed. Once the only base of power and prestige in society inherited by the lord and passed on to his male children, land became just another factor of production and was subject to sale at a price. It became an investment which had a value in money, a value determined by the profit which could be made through selling what was produced on it. All of the factors of production, land, and labor, and capital, acquired a monetary equivalent and were freed to follow the demands of the market.

In the perspective of the diffusion model, commerce was an essential stimulus in the development of England. Long distance trade in Europe was at its lowest ebb in the 9th and 10th centuries. Capitalism arose out of feudalism through the revival of commerce beginning in the 10th and 11th centuries. Increased trade supplied a motive for creating a larger and more continuous surplus. According to the diffusionist view, the new merchant and artisan classes it created grew and eventually took over existing non-agricultural settlements which had not been centers of economic activity before the increased long distance commerce. Trade was more important than early manufacturing. The struggle against the feudal order was led by the large merchants. They consolidated their control over the towns, and contended with the feudal lords whose interests, according to the interpretation of the diffusionist approach, were opposed to it. Over several centuries feudalism was defeated as the market penetrated the countryside and the political power and the ideology of the new bourgeoisie achieved dominance. These economic, social and political changes arising from the resurgence of long distance trade created conditions in which the industrial revolution and modern capitalist society were born.

The diffusion model perceives the cities of Latin America as the foci of modernization and development, reaching out to the countryside just as the medieval towns did centuries ago. Latin America is the most urbanized area of the world outside of North America and Western Europe. Latin Americans living in urban areas are etimated to comprise 40 to 50 percent of the population. While a portion of this trend is due to population growth within the cities, the rate and scale of migration to urban areas has not been equalled by any other area of the world. During the period 1930–1960, the population of Latin America doubled while the 22 largest cities more than tripled in population (Ruddle and Hamour, 1972:4).

In the major cities one finds tall buildings, superhighways and traffic jams. There are shops where the finest goods from all over the capitalist world can be purchased. In the business district there is an appearance of wealth and modernity which is in sharp contrast with rural poverty and tradition. The streets are filled with businessmen and office workers. In the cities, this new sector seems to represent a society which has moved far beyond the feudalism of the countryside toward a developed capitalist society.

Old ways do persist. Speculation in tangible urban real estate is more attractive than purchasing stocks which is only an abstract representation of wealth. Manufacturing methods and equipment considered obsolete in the United States are employed alongside modern assembly plants. Small workshops in which the owner works in production with his employees continues to operate. At the same time more large factories are built. In the new firms, the managers are hired by the owners and own a small share of the firms they manage. The large work force employed by these factories is organized into unions to bargain for better wages and working conditions. While the cities are ringed by vast slums where residents do not participate in political life, the organized workers and the middle class have an important vote in nations where elections are held.

Not only in political and economic life does the city seem to be the agent of change. Cultural values and orientations, especially among the middle sectors, are changing too. The traditional attitudes about sex roles embodied in *machismo* give men the virtues of aggressiveness and freedom of action while confining women to the houses of their parents or their husbands in dependent passivity. Where once alternatives to the pedestal carried with them social disapproval and the implication of immorality, work outside the home by women has achieved greater acceptance. The practice of dating has made considerable headway against the mores that used to require that an unmarried female be chaperoned at all times. In some countries women's liberation movements have arisen, although their ideologies are directed more toward placing increased limitations and obligations on the male than gaining greater freedom for the female. Conditions of urban life have also made some inroads into the strength of the extended family and in favor of the nuclear family. Requirements of modern economic life have begun to affect the typical casualness with which Latin Americans have regarded the clock. In business the importance of personal relationships, though still great in comparison with North American practice, has lessened in relation to more modern orientations in economic life. Latins have in the past had contempt for North American materialism, giving more emphasis to aristocratic values of the inner person, his personal philosophy and the personality he projects. In a society in which social mobility was virtually absent, the traditional poor were not induced to feel failure in being poor and could maintain a sense of self respect and inner dignity, regardless of social status. However, among the urban middle sector a shift has been underway for some time toward attitudes about work, consumption and getting ahead which are close to orientations prevailing in the United States. Among portions of the middle sector, North American tastes in food and even fads in fashion and popular music have replaced traditional preferences.

A Dual Society in Transition to Capitalism. The picture we have drawn suggests that many nations may be composed of two societies, one feudal and the other capitalist. Such an assumption has led many observors of Latin America to query if this "dual society" is essentially feudal or capitalist? Or is the hinterland feudal while the city is capitalist? The tendency among the followers of the diffusion model is to accept the latter suggestion; to understand the conquest of Indo America by Iberians as a process in which the feudalism of Spain and Portugal was transferred to the New World; to view the cities of Latin America as having been brought into capitalism through commercial contact with more modern nations; and to characterize the countryside as remaining in stagnant feudalism due to isolation from the dynamic forces of capitalism. The prescription called for by this diagnosis of Latin American underdevelopment is clearly the penetration of the hinterland to bring the patient further along the road out of feudalism.

Compared to the countryside, the city is the center of Latin American modernity in political, economic, social and cultural matters. It seems to be the source of the challenge to traditions which have apparently immobilized the resources of the land and the energy of the people. This perception of the cities in relation to the rest of their respective nation relegates the countryside to the status of a peripheral area, which because of its poverty and backwardness is holding back and dragging down the thrust of the vital metropolis within each country. It appears that to achieve the tasks of modernization and development—freeing the rural population from the arbitrary power of the landowners, propelling both land and labor into the realm of the market where they can be effectively employed to bring about economic growth, increasing the middle class to provide upward mobility and reduce the conflict of class polarization, creating expanding industrial capacity not only for prosperity but also as a base for labor unions and modern forms of both political and economic representation—these tasks which nations such as the United States and Western Europe have already substantially accomplished will be undertaken by extending to the countryside the wealth, methods and the modern ideas which are growing in the cities.

This view of the relationship of the city to the countryside includes a parallel interaction between developed and underdeveloped nations. The metropolis—with reference to Latin America, the dominant center is the United States—provides the capital for new industry, the technology and methods of organization necessary for modern production, and a set of values appropriate to developing modern capitalist society. Since the most direct linkage with the periphery, the underdeveloped nations, is with their major cities, it is to be expected that in these cities the seeds of modernization and development will germinate to spread life and fertility even to the most remote areas of the underdeveloped countryside. Just as technological progress brought forth an entirely new form of production and economic organization hundreds of years past in the history of the now developed countries, the capital and technology introduced by these nations into the underdeveloped world are transforming the underdeveloped economies. And just as new economic organization created a new class in Western Europe the growing industrialization of Latin America under the sponsorship of the United States is giving birth to a new middle class of ever increasing importance. In Western Europe an industrial bourgeoisie integrated the nation-state; it created the mechanism for savings, investment and capital accumulation; it struggled against arbitrary power for forms of representative, limited government, and for individual rights in a secular state; and later, it supported labor to build an adequate system of social welfare. The perspective we have described has placed the burden of economic, political and social progress on Latin America's middle sectors, supported by the activities of North American private and governmental agencies.

Thus, according to the diffusion model, the solutions to the problems and conditions of underdevelopment must originate from beyond the borders of Latin America. Development is to be diffused from metropolis to periphery, from the United States to the national urban centers, from this metropolis to regional trading cities, from these centers to their periphery. The process involves the increased integration of the hinterland with its metropolis at each level, a strengthening of the linkages already established. In this view, though the problems are enormous, development following the path first travelled by England centuries ago is underway. But the pace must be accelerated. It is primarily a matter of expanding the introduction of capital and new technology from the developed countries. What is required is the creation of economic and political conditions which can attract the greater participation of foreign enterprise.

DIFFUSION AND THE UNITED STATES IN LATIN AMERICA: THREE PERSPECTIVES

The theoretical assumptions of the diffusion model have had very serious consequences at a level of practice, especially as regards U.S. relations with Latin America. Let us, therefore, examine some of the public manifestations of the view that the United States could bring progress to Latin America. Then we look at some of the consequences of U.S. involvement in Latin America.

The diffusion model has been articulated through several interrelated ideas. Ever since the mid-19th century when John L. O'Sullivan formulated the phrase "manifest destiny" in the advocacy of the United States' territorial expansion, most North American writers have held that solutions to problems must come from the outside. Much of the social and political thought of the past century assumed the existence of a continuous process in which humanity would evolve from savagery to a civilized state. Initially, the condition of the Latin American masses was attributed to racial inferiority. Based on personal transformations of Darwin's theory of evolution, predictions and prescriptions for Latin America called for a takeover by the United States. Those who were regarded as inherently inferior could be improved or reformed only under the rule of those who were naturally superior. Below are some manifestations of this view.

Josiah Strong, Congregational clergyman:

Then this (Anglo-Saxon) race of unequaled energy, with all the majesty of numbers and the might of wealth behind it—the representative, let us hope, of the largest liberty, the purest Christianity, the highest civilization— having developed peculiarly aggressive traits calculated to impress its institutions upon mankind, will spread itself over the earth. If I read not amiss, this powerful race will move down upon Mexico, down upon Central and South America, out upon the islands of the sea, over upon Africa and beyond. And can any one doubt that the result of this competition of races will be the 'survival of the fittest'?

Our Country: Its Possible Future and Its Present Crisis, 1885 (Pratt, 1959:6)

John W. Burgess, founder of the first department of political science in the United States:

. . . by far the larger part of the surface of the globe is inhabited by populations which have not succeeded in establishing civilized states; which have, in fact, no capacity to accomplish such a work; and which must, therefore, remain in a state of barbarism or semi-barbarism, unless the political nations undertake the work of state organization for them. This condition of things authorizes the political nations not only to answer the call of the unpolitical populations for aid and direction, but also to force organization upon them by any means necessary, in their honest judgment, to accomplish this result. There is no human right to the status of barbarism.

Political Science and Comparative Constitution Law, 1890 (Pratt, 1959:9)

President Theodore Roosevelt, in his annual message to Congress, December 6, 1904 (The Roosevelt Corollary to the Monroe Doctrine):

". . . If a nation shows that it knows how to act with reasonable efficiency and decency in social and political matters, if it keeps order and pays its obligations, it need fear no interference from the United States. Chronic wrongdoing, or an impotence which results in a general loosening of the ties of the civilized society, may in America, as elsewhere, ultimately require intervention by some civilized nations, and in the Western Hemisphere, the adherence of the United States to the Monroe Doctrine may force the United States, however reluctantly, in cases of wrongdoing or impotence, to the exercise of the international police power."

Such views reflected policy positions of the United States during the 19th and 20th centuries. These diffusionist views became manifested in the actions of the United States in Latin American affairs. Three tendencies were conspicuous in this period of U.S. dominance: overt intervention; penetration through Pan-Americanism to ensure order; and recent shifts in policy involving multiple strategies ranging from intervention to collaborative programs in which U.S. assistance was to stimulate a "new development" for Latin America. Let us briefly examine each of these tendencies in the context of the diffusion model.

Overt Intervention. On April 28, 1965, U.S. President Lyndon B. Johnson ordered the invasion by four hundred marines of Santo Domingo "to protect the lives and property of U.S. citizens residing in the Dominican Republic." Nearly a century and a half earlier, President James Monroe promulgated the Monroe Doctrine in an annual message to Congress on December 2, 1823. That doctrine challenged the incursion of European powers into the Western hemisphere and established the "principle in which the rights and interests of the United States are involved, that the American continents, by the free and independent condition which they have assumed and maintained, are henceforth not to be considered as subjects for future colonization by any European powers." (For details on the doctrine and contrasting perspectives, see Dozer, 1965.)

According to Mexican economist Alonso Aguilar (1965), the motivations behind the Dominican invasion were the same as those which had led Theodore Roosevelt to provoke a revolt in Panama to seize control of Colombian territory and to build a canal across the isthmus; which had justified Taft's protection of U.S. monopolies that sought raw materials in Latin America; and which had prompted Calvin Coolidge to assert Washington's obligations to protect the rights of U. S. investors there. Even earlier the Doctrine had been applied by President James K. Polk in the 1848 dispute with Mexico that gave the United States extensive Mexican territory.

On numerous other occasions the Doctrine was applied in the hemisphere. For the sake of "American interests," armed intervention was evident in Nicaragua in 1853, 1854, 1857, 1894, 1898, 1899, 1910, 1912 to 1925, and 1926 to 1933; in Cuba in 1906 to 1909, 1912, 1917 to 1922, 1933; and in the Dominican Republic in 1903, 1904, 1914, 1916 to 1924. The Somoza dynasty in Nicaragua and the dictatorships of Fulgencio Batista in Cuba and Rafael Trujillo in the Dominican Republic emerged as a direct result of these occupations. These were regimes whose military forces were able to contain revolutions and protect American interests. Intervention in Panama during 1856, 1865, 1885, 1903 to 1914, 1918 to 1920, and 1925, not only assured political changes resulting in the construction of the canal but also stability for the U.S. economic and military presence in the Canal Zone for several decades thereafter. U.S. involvement was conspicuous elsewhere in the Caribbean and Central America, notably in Haiti (1888, 1891, 1914, 1915–34) in Honduras (1903, 1907, 1911, 1912, 1919, 1924, 1925) and in Guatemala (1920). These events were followed by the establishment in the 1950s of a dictatorship in Haiti under François Duvalier, dominant military rule by the Honduras armed forces, and a C.I.A.-financed coup in Guatemala during 1954. U.S. forces also became involved in the affairs of Mexico (1859, 1866, 1870, 1873, 1876, 1913, 1914 to 1917, 1918 to 1919) and in the South American nations of Uruguay (1855, 1858, 1868); Paraguay (1859); Colombia (1860, 1868, 1873, 1895, 1901, 1902); Argentina (1890); Chile (1891); and Brazil (1894).*

Penetration through Pan-Americanism. The diffusionist interpretation that the United States could bring benefits to Latin America was at least implicitly tied to U.S. involvement in the movement toward Pan-Americanism. Simón Bolívar, the liberator of much of South America, promoted Pan-Americanism at the Congress of Panama in 1826. His vision was the consolidation of the former Spanish colonies "into one great body politic" independent of the United States. Yet the United States was invited to the conference and, although its delegation failed to attend, the principle of U.S. involvement in Latin American affairs had been affirmed. While the Pan-American movement itself languished throughout the 19th century, there occurred unprecedented U.S. expansion in the New World. In addition to the acquisition of territory which today comprises Oregon, Washington, Idaho and parts of Wyoming and Montana as well as Alaska, the United States annexed Texas in 1848 and seized more than half of Mexico's territory.

By the latter half of the century Bolívar's plan of creating a defensive confederation had been abandoned by Latin America. In 1881 James Blaine, Secretary of State under President Garfield, called for a continental conference because "the United States could displace Europe in trade with America." The conference finally took place in 1889, at a time "when the vast domestic market inside the United States began to

* A summary of U.S. intervention abroad was presented on September 17, 1962, by Secretary of State Dean Rusk to a joint meeting of the Committees of Foreign Relations and Armed Services of the U.S. Senate (1962:82–87). Nearly two hundred interventions were listed to show that there was precedent for the use of such force without Congressional authority; Rusk was defending U.S. involvement in the abortive Bay of Pigs invasion by Cuban exiles during April 1961.

be insufficient and the rate of profit began to decline, when the power-ful industrial trusts, the mining and railroad interests, and the banks demanded new spheres of influence . . ." (Aguilar, 1965:38). The Pan-American system emerged to ensure U.S. industrial domination throughout Latin America. With headquarters in Washington, D.C., the inter-American organization offered little resistance to U.S. determina-tion to control the Gulf of Mexico and the Caribbean, especially after the war with Spain in 1898 and intervention in Panama at the turn of the century. Under the Platt Amendment the United States secured the lease of a naval base at Guantánamo, Cuba, thus ensuring a strategic position in the Caribbean. The consequences were analyzed by General Leonard Wood, commander of U.S. forces there:

> Of course, Cuba has been left with little or no independence by the Platt Amendment . . . It cannot enter into certain treaties without our consent, nor secure loans above certain limits, and it must maintain the sanitary con-ditions which have been indicated. All of this makes it evident that Cuba is absolutely in our hands, and I believe that no European government would consider it otherwise: a real dependent of the United States and, as such we should consider it. (Le Riverend, 1967:210)

Panama was "the product of the decision to get the Panama Canal im-mediately, and never before had such quick action been taken. The Panamanian 'revolution' was announced in Washington practically be-fore it broke out . . ." (Aguilar, 1965:48). President Roosevelt pro-claimed: "I took the Canal Zone." Later he justified his action on the mandate of "civilization" to "coerce a nation which by its 'selfish' actions, stood in the way of measures that would benefit the world as a whole" (quoted in Lewis, 1963:78). Such actions became formalized in 1904 in the Roosevelt Corollary to the Monroe Doctrine which called for the intervention by "civilized" states in any disorderly country.

Latin American resentment to Roosevelt's Big Stick policy was clearly evident at subsequent Pan-American conferences. Yet during the first six meetings, from 1889 to 1928 the United States managed to restrict debate on controversial political affairs and to focus discussion on com-mercial matters. (For detailed analysis of this period, see Bemis, 1943). By 1929 direct U.S. investment in Latin America amounted to $3.5 billion, most of which went into railroads and mines. This investment comprised two-fifths of worldwide U.S. investment. (For a detailed analysis of U.S. investment in Latin America, see North American Con-gress on Latin America, 1971.)

The crisis of 1929 and subsequent depression and world war provoked reconsideration of U.S.-Latin American relations. A policy of non-intervention evolved in the Coolidge and Hoover administrations. Hoover ordered the withdrawal of U.S. Marines from Nicaragua and Haiti and repudiated the Roosevelt Corollary. At the same time trade barriers were raised against Latin American products to protect industrial groups in the United States. In 1933 President Franklin D. Roosevelt initiated his Good Neighbor Policy, declaring that the United States was "opposed to armed intervention" and that intervention would be only a joint concern of the whole continent. Such principles were reaffirmed at the Seventh International Conference of American States in Montevideo in December 1933. A series of agreements was reached, providing for mutual cooperation and consultation within the inter-American system and armed against aggression from outside the hemisphere. These agreements were secured in spite of Latin American reaction to U.S. meddling in Cuban affairs that had brought down the Grau San Martín government which followed the Machado dictatorship, thus ushering in the long dictatorial reign of Fulgencio Batista. Once stability and order had been achieved, Roosevelt agreed to the abrogation of the Platt Amendment while retaining the right to the naval base at Guantánamo. Agreements with Cuba, however, resulted in a sharp increase in trade and assured U.S. hegemony over the Cuban economy (see O'Connor, 1970). In fact, such hegemony continued as a pattern throughout Latin America as the Roosevelt administration did not modify the monopolistic structure of the United States. Such a structure assured that "the countries south of Rio Grande remained subjugated to the great power in the north and very soon the illusion vanished that things would change radically" (Aguilar, 1965:69). It was a fact, however, that the inflow of new capital was negligible between 1929 and 1945, this being a consequence of there being little or no surplus capital during the depression and later preoccupation with war production. Frank (1967:28) contends that such conditions resulted in a decline of dependence on the world metropolises and allowed for a temporary spurt in economic development. But, he argues, the Latin American satellites could only be "rechanneled into underdevelopment by the subsequent recuperation and expansion of the metropolis or by the restoration of its active integration with its satellites." Thus, while U. S. investment may not have expanded during the Roosevelt years, it was maintained as a basis for a massive penetration of U.S. capital into Latin America during the post-war years.

The Roosevelt era had initiated multilateral agreements on hemispheric solidarity. A consultative pact signed in 1936 at an inter-American conference in Buenos Aires was partially a response to rising fascism in Europe. At the Eighth International Conference of American States in 1938, the Declaration of Lima reaffirmed the principle of collective defense against all foreign influence in the hemisphere. After the outbreak of world war, the United States established close relations with Latin American military officers and secured a series of military agreements providing for air and naval bases in some 16 Latin American nations.

Such agreements set the precedent for military and economic assistance in the post-war years. Diffusion of this assistance consolidated the U.S. hold on the continent. By 1947 the Rio Treaty of reciprocal assistance obligated the American nations to assist in repulsing armed attacks from within or outside the hemisphere. This led to the establishment of an elaborate defense network as a deterrent to the "Communist" threat. Ensuing developments made clear that the new arrangement was advantageous to U.S. interests in Latin America. During the Ninth International Conference of American States, held in Bogotá in 1948, the popular Colombian liberal Jorge Eliécer Gaitán, was assassinated, probably by terrorists linked to conservative groups; the ensuing spontaneous demonstrations of violence, known as the *bogotazo*, were attributed to a communist "plot." At Caracas the Tenth Conference declared itself against the intervention of international communism. The immediate concern was Guatemala whose government had expropriated banana holdings of the United Fruit Company. U.S. Secretary of State John Foster Dulles argued for action against Guatemala and international communism: "At the start of the conference the Dulles proposal was supported by only six countries, all of which were dictatorships: but other nations bowed reluctantly to Dulles' threats of economic and political retaliation" (Gil, 1971:211). The March 1954 vote in favor (17 to 1) of his declaration was followed by the C.I.A. supported invasion of Guatemala in June. By the end of the month the leftist government of Jacobo Arbenz had fallen.

The Organization of American States was called upon to support U.S. intervention in Latin American affairs during the 1960s, specifically in the abortive C.I.A-backed Bay of Pigs invasion in April 1961, culminating in the expulsion of Cuba from the O.A.S. (Six countries representing three-fourths of Latin America's population abstained—Argentina, Bolivia, Brazil, Chile, Ecuador, and Mexico, but the others fell into line through political and economic pressure.) In April 1965 the United States sent U.S. soldiers and Marines to the Dominican Republic under the pretext of protecting Americans threatened by progressive elements. Without O.A.S. consultation this unilateral action by the Johnson administration was similar to the interventionist era of Teddy Roosevelt. Once U.S. Marines had broken through rebel positions and established order, the O.A.S. met in Washington where a two-thirds vote finally endorsed the U.S. proposal of establishing an inter-American peace force (Chile, Mexico, Ecuador, and Uruguay opposed it and Venezuela abstained, while the Dominican "delegate" was permitted to vote in favor of the resolution).

Aid and the "New Development." Whether involving overt armed intervention or pressures through the O.A.S., U.S. policies of the past few decades have clearly been oriented to economic considerations. Under the Good Neighbor Policy, few gains were made in modest efforts to break down artificial trade barriers which discriminated against Latin American goods and perpetuated a highly protectionist U.S. market. Gil (1971: 167) affirms: "The extension of economic assistance as a conscious governmental policy to help raise standards of living in foreign areas was a novel idea in the 1930s. Much more study and a clear definition of objectives were needed before this policy could be successfully implemented." However, the Export-Import Bank was established in 1934, and after 1940 it became deeply involved in the economies of Latin American nations. In 1944 the World Bank and the International Monetary Fund were created; both institutions would have a decisive impact on the hemisphere. The World Bank offered detailed study, technical assistance, and credit for the implementation of long-range development plans for nations whose economies had been shaped by I.M.F.-supported stabilization and anti-inflationary programs. The I.M.F. insisted on the halting of inflation through price level controls and the elimination of certain direct controls (for elaboration of these programs see David Felix in Hirschman, 1961:81–93).

Following the Second World War and particularly since the rise to power of Fidel Castro in Cuba, the United States moved aggressively on the economic front. Multinational corporations turned to foreign markets and profits, while the U.S. government stimulated the growth of U.S. investments abroad through investment guarantees and tax incentives. At the same time, U.S. foreign aid contributed to "stable" business climate and new markets for the private investor. However, the loss of U.S. investments in Cuba was a major consideration that prompted the United States in 1961 to promote the Alliance for Progress. The Alliance purported to offer a formula of gradual evolution and reform in housing, health, education and other sectors. Publicized as a revolutionary program, it was in fact a façade for old diffusionist strategy. While U.S. Secretary of State Dean Rusk declared that the Alliance "rests on the concept that this hemisphere is part of Western Civilization which we are pledged to defend," his Latin American counterparts made clear that the intentions of the program were to preserve the status quo.

Venezuelan Rómulo Betancourt affirmed that through the Alliance: "We must help the poor . . . in order to save the rich." And the U.S. co-ordinator for the program, Teodoro Moscoso admitted: "In supporting the Alliance, members of the traditional ruling class will have nothing to fear" (Quotes in Aguilar, 1963:31).

The Alliance was a failure for Latin Americans and North Americans alike. In assessing this failure Federico Gil (1971:245) noted that "the new program floundered at first in a swamp of bureaucratic organiza-tion. Administration of the Alliance was entrusted to the Agency for International Development (AID), which was not structured to under-take such an essentially revolutionary task." Indeed AID was established to promote U.S. interests in the region, and clearly these were not revolutionary no matter what visions the Kennedy administration may have had in the early 1960s. As Mexican agricultural economist Edmundo Flores (1963:13) noted in an early critique, the Alliance would face the choice of opposing or favoring revolutionary change: "If, following cur-rent misconceptions, the United States backs the quasi-feudal and mili-taristic governments in power, there will be a pretense of economic de-velopment and *Alianza* funds will be misallocated and wasted without changing the conditions responsible for political unrest and economic stagnation. This will lead eventually to the establishment of military dictatorships of the extreme right."

It was precisely this situation that developed under the Johnson ad-ministration. In March 1964 Johnson's Assistant Secretary of State for Inter-American Affairs, Thomas Mann, was quoted in an off-the-record talk to Latin American diplomats as suggesting that the United States would not in the future take an *a priori* position against governments coming to power through military coups. His statement was affirmation of a policy that had evolved earlier in discussion among specialists of Latin America in American universities, the Rand Corporation, the State Department, and the Pentagon. A conference on militarism, coordinated by Professor John J. Johnson of Stanfard University and sponsored by the Rand Corporation in 1959, was concerned primarily with "those officers who have used armies for extra-military purposes" and "to the question of why military governments have promoted national develop-ment and democratic practices in some countries . . ." (Johnson, 1962: 3–4). Later, Johnson (1964) elaborated upon his proposition that the military in Latin America is "undergoing a social-economic and profes-sional transformation." He believed that the military rather than poli-ticians, bureaucrats, and businessmen, would serve their nations as a modernizing force for change. This view paralleled the development of programs for the training of hundreds of Latin American officers in the

United States or the Panama Canal Zone in the techniques of civic action and counterinsurgency. Subsequently, the United States quickly supported a series of military coups throughout the hemisphere: Argentina, and Peru in 1962; the Dominican Republic, Guatemala, Ecuador and Honduras in 1963; Bolivia and Brazil in 1964. Later military intervention took place again in Argentina and Peru and also in El Salvador, Panama, and Uruguay.

The official U.S. reaction to these events became known as the Mann and Johnson doctrines. The former doctrine endorsed military intervention by the Latin American armed forces. Where a weak or divided Latin American military could not resolve internal instability, the Johnson Doctrine became the order of the day. The conspicuous case was the intervention into the Dominican Republic in 1965. In a message to Congress, Johnson stressed that there was no one else who could ensure "the right of all people to shape their own destinies" and before a labor conference in Washington, he stated: "where Americans go that flag goes with them to protect them." In commenting upon the Dominican intervention a *New York Times* editorial (May 6, 1965) suggested that "the United States gives the appearance of heading toward the unenviable, self-righteous and self-defeating position of world policeman . . . Ours is the most powerful nation on earth, but there are things that even the United States cannot do in this period of history." U.S. troops in the Dominican Republic totalled nearly 20,000—more than half the number in Vietnam at that time. While ultimately the U.S. failure in Vietnam was to ensure the political demise of Johnson and the futility of his doctrine, the Mann Doctrine had signalled the recognition that the Alliance for Progress had also failed. Rather than aid, U.S. policymakers now emphasized trade as the means whereby the United States would strengthen its control over the internal markets of other nations; promote capitalism as the basis for economic development of underdeveloped nations, and maintain stability at any cost. The Nixon administration quickly adopted this thrust as the foundation for its policy toward Latin America. Appropriately, Nixon's initial appointee for Assistant Secretary of State for Inter-American Affairs was Charles A. Meyer, a director of the United Fruit Company, long notorious for its autocratic dealings in the "banana republics", and an executive of Sears Roebuck, which has stores throughout Latin America.

When governments intervene in the affairs of other nations, they rarely explain their actions exclusively in terms of self interest. The United States government has pictured its Latin American policies for the benefit of the North American people as a result of a happy coincidence of North American and Latin American interests. U.S. citizens have been told by the government that their tax dollars are being spent for a policy which protects our national security and interests while bringing economic benefit to the people of the United States—a policy which at the same time promotes national independence, self determination, democracy, economic development and social progress for the peoples of Latin America. As we have seen thus far, the claim that U.S. policy has simultaneously advanced all of these objectives relies on several theories and perceptions of the world which are questionable and others which are clearly false.

Most relevant to the contributors of this volume is the need to seek a new understanding of Latin American underdevelopment and to critique the assertion that the penetration of Latin America by North America's political, economic and cultural influence contributes to Latin American development. This assertion has provided the intellectual underpinnings of U.S. policy. The ideas in the period of Manifest Destiny held that U.S. intervention was often necessary to maintain "civilization." Recent U.S. policy not only reaffirms that credo but also contends that North American penetration is essential to the elimination of underdevelopment.

THE DIFFUSION MODEL IN THE LITERATURE

Some of the traditional ramifications of the diffusion model, especially its impact upon U.S. policy in the interventionist, diplomatic, and economic relations with Latin America have already been noted. American predispositions about manifest destiny, the civilization of mankind, and racial superiority have been clearly manifested in the official documentation justifying U.S. involvement in Latin America; they have also been the concern of many historical and interpretative writings; and, finally, they are deeply embedded in the thought and writing of American social science. It is to this latter body of literature that we briefly turn our attention.

Bodenheimer (now Jonas) (1970B) and Frank (1968B) have provided us with definitive, in-depth critiques of the diffusionist literature on development. Their critiques are supported by James Petras (1965), José Nun (1967) and José Ocampo and Dale Johnson (see Cockcroft, Frank, and Johnson, 1972:399–424). Jonas focused on what she and Sheldon Wolin have called the paradigm-surrogate in contemporary political science. Her discussion, however, is applicable to all social science, and her immediate concern is the extension of misleading analysis to our understanding of Latin America. Jonas directs her discussion to four levels of theory about development: first, the cumulative notion of knowledge and development, that is, stepped up knowledge and accumulation of data which signify a tendency toward modernization just as development is the process of continuous, irreversible, and linear progression from traditional-ism to modernism. This level is exemplified by the emphasis on structural-functionalism in the writing of political scientist Gabriel Almond (Almond and Powell, 1966). While the approach of Almond influenced a prolific literature in comparative politics, it in turn had been based on formula-tions in socioligy: derived from Max Weber's ideal types but rooted in the pattern variables of Talcott Parsons (1951) and some of the work of his followers, Marion Levy (1952) and Robert Merton (1957), Almond's work also was influenced by the early functionalism of anthropologists Bronislaw Malinowski (1954) and A. R. Radcliffe-Brown (1957). Finally, there was the stress on stages of economic development in Walt W. Rostow (1962) and the political science sequel to his work by A. E. K. Organski (1965). A second theoretical level is the preoccupation with stability and orderly change. The emphasis on continuity with past and present and on equilibrium is inherent in the structural-functional literature cited above and the research which attempts to predict future behavior on rational and scientific grounds. Again, Parsons' writing established the foundation for this preoccupation, and he provided the thrust for David Easton (1953 and 1957) whose writing influenced many political scien-tists over the two ensuing decades. At a third level is the belief that modernization and technological society accompany consensus and the end of ideology, as exemplified in Daniel Bell (1960) and Seymour Martin Lipset (1963). Attention to consensus is tied to American con-ceptions of pluralism, to the idea that a developed polity is related to the competition through bargaining and compromise of rival pressure groups, and to the belief that pragmatic coalitions transcend flexible class structure. A fourth level involves the notion that development occurs through the spread of cultural patterns and material benefits from developed to underdeveloped areas and that, likewise, a similar diffusion takes place from the modern to traditional sectors within each under-developed nation. Frank's penetrating examination of the diffusionist literature is similar to that of Jonas, but with attention to three approaches in the literature: the index approach (emphasis on pattern variables and stages of growth); the diffusionist approach as evidenced by the diffusion of capital, technology (including knowledge and skills), and institutions (including values and organizations), and the psychological approach which according to Frank tells us how the ideal type characteristics identified by the first approach and diffused by the second approach "are to be acculturated by the underdeveloped countries if they wish to develop."

While Jonas' fourth level of theory and Frank's third approach stress diffusion, our own introductory synthesis lumps all their concerns into what we have called the diffusion model. Our intention has been to make clear the distinctions between the diffusion and dependency models. Beyond our own analysis and that of Jonas and Frank, however, there exists some provocative and useful literature that critically assesses some of the specifics of the diffusion model. For perspectives on functionalism, see Frank (1966), Szymanski (1972) for a critique on Malinowski, Parsons, and Merton from a Marxist view; and Mills (1961). On development in continuum, see Nun (1967). Thorson (1970) does well in exposing the fallacies of political science efforts to be scientific and determinist as a mechanistic borrowing of biological concepts. A devastating attack on Rostow's stages of growth propositions is offered by Paul Baran and Eric Hobsbawn (1961); supportive of their position is Griffin (1969: 32–37) and Rhodes (1968). For a critique of the end of ideology school there is La Palambara (1966).

II THE DEPENDENCY MODEL

Over the last decade an alternative view has taken shape in the writings of a number of scholars, both Latin American and North American. It finds that rather than being a force for development, foreign penetration has created underdevelopment. Instead of supporting the thrust of U.S. policies, this alternate view asserts the necessity of a complete reversal of action if the United States is to become a positive force for development in Latin America. Dos Santos (1970C:231) offers a generally accepted description of dependency:

> By dependence we mean a situation in which the economy of certain countries is conditioned by the development and expansion of another economy to which the former is subjected. The relation of interdependence between two or more economies, and between these and world trade, assumes the form of dependence when some countries (the dominant ones) can expand and can be self-sustaining, while other countries (the dependent ones) can do this only as a reflection of that expansion, which can have either a positive or a negative effect on their immediate development.

Departing from this notion of dependency, it is now our intention to examine the assumptions underlying the dependency model's interpretation of development and underdevelopment. We do this through a critical assessment of "dualism" as a dominant characteristic of Latin American society and through an analysis of different classes that may dominate over particular societies in Latin America. Finally, using the dependency model as a framework for discussion, we look at the consequences of dependent development in Spain and Latin America.

ASSUMPTIONS OF THE DEPENDENCY MODEL

The dependency model of Latin American underdevelopment identifies contemporary Latin American social and economic structures shaped by economic dependency and it distinguishes underdeveloped Latin America from pre-capitalist England and Europe. Instead of hypothesizing underdevelopment as an original state, it asserts that the now developed countries were never underdeveloped and that contemporary underdevelopment was *created*. Ironically, the very same process (the expansion of capitalism) through which the now developed countries progressed brought about the underdevelopment of many parts of Latin America. The most significant aspect of the colonial heritage is not a system of values or cultural orientations, but economies shaped by the needs of the center of the expanding system. When the center of the system needed to acquire raw materials and to sell finished goods, Latin America responded as both supplier and market. Though the United States has replaced Great Britain as the metropolis and though Latin America imports now include producers' goods to supply manufacturers of consumer goods within Latin America, dependency has not changed. In fact, it has deepened through greater foreign corporate, governmental and foundation penetration of banking, manufacturing, retailing, communications, advertising and education. The results of this penetration have not changed in nature. A higher level of technology and greater economic power are rewarded with higher prices for foreign imports while the prices of Latin American exports follow a long term downward trend. Capital is drained through repatriated profits, interest payments on loans, and fees for royalties, insurance and shipping. Within each country, the pattern of metropolis-periphery relations is replicated; the economic surplus of the countryside is drained into the urban areas through a process of internal colonialism. The countryside is poor not because it is feudal or traditional but because it has enriched the cities. Latin America is underdeveloped because it has supported the development of Western Europe and the United States.

The political result of economic dependency also has not changed. Just as the landed elites and merchants who exported Latin America's wealth pursued their interests in maintaining dependent economic patterns, modern industrial managers and military elites favor foreign interests. They also fear the demands of the masses within their own nations, preferring military dictatorship to nationalistic reform or revolution.

The solution does not lie in increased penetration. More foreign investment does bring an expanded gross national product, but it does not create self-sustaining economic development. Outside control is enhanced.

Outward capital flows increase. Investment decisions continue to be based on plans for improved profitability and balanced development of multinational corporations rather than domestic employment and production needs. Economic growth does not even reduce poverty since few jobs are generated by the new technology, while less advanced domestic competition is eliminated. Development requires the profound alteration of economic, social and political relationships comprehending the overthrow of the market and the mobilization of domestic populations in a nationally oriented effort. Thus, development requires the elimination of foreign penetration which supports the status quo and the creation of a socialist context for development.

While the dependency model agrees that the characteristics employed by the diffusion model to define underdevelopment are *typical* of underdeveloped areas, underdevelopment is *not defined* by them. Instead, the most significant defining characteristic is the economic dependency which has shaped the economies, social structures and political systems of underdeveloped regions and countries, producing the characteristics by which underdevelopment is recognized.

In fact, "growth without development is a frequent experience in the past and present of the now underdeveloped countries" (Cockcroft, Frank, and Johnson, 1972:xv). The dependency model does not measure development by per capita GNP or the indices of modernity. Economic development includes the establishment of economic sovereignty (which does not imply isolation) and a level of productivity and a pattern of distribution which adequately provide for the basic (culturally determined) needs of the entire population, generating a surplus for investment in continued national development. Social and political aspects of development are less clearly stated, but generally include equality, the elimination of alienation and the provision of meaningful work, and forms of social, economic and political organization which enable all members of society to determine the decisions which affect them.

The diffusion and dependency models offer different definitions of underdevelopment. The definition in the diffusion model is ahistorical. It embodies a tacit assumption that underdevelopment is an aboriginal state—that underdeveloped areas have always been underdeveloped. Within the diffusion model, underdevelopment appears as a starting point on the road to development, a condition which has characterized every region and nation-state, from which some have advanced toward development. In contrast, the dependency model understands both underdevelopment and capitalist development (which should not be confused with the conception of development stated above) as the product of the same historical process, the expansion of international capitalism. Through this process the political, economic and military forces of the system's center have penetrated underdeveloped areas, creating development in the metropolis and underdevelopment in the periphery (Frank, 1966A, 1967A). This perspective incorporates the history of the underdeveloped areas, as well as their integration into the expanding system. As expressed by A. G. Frank, ". . . Neither the past nor the present of the underdeveloped countries resembles in any important respect the past of the now developed countries. The now developed countries were never *under*developed, though they may have been *un*developed" (Cockcroft, Frank and Johnson, 1972:3).

The dependency model finds many interpretations of English history and development superficial. The economy of undeveloped feudal England did not respond to an international market. By the time this market had been established as a major force, England was in a position to meet all challenges of its domination of the market. English economic growth, especially decisions regarding investment in both infra-structure and production, was determined by the indigenous elites whose interests were shaped initially by internal conditions. External markets provided incentives for the growth of a diversified industrial economy.

In contrast, from the first moment of European penetration, underdeveloped nations of Latin America were dominated by external elites and markets. These forces created monocultural economies. Infra-structural development was oriented toward agricultural export. Competition from already industrialized countries stifled attempts toward indigenous industrialization, while a configuration of political-economic interests within the host nation resulted in a suppression of national capitalist forces favoring independent development by those benefitting from the existing economic patterns. As the center of an expanding capitalist system, England traded from a position of superiority. Terms of trade were favorable for English goods. England was not burdened with a foreign debt. The English economy has always been owned by the English. Thus, the surplus exploited from English peasants and workers has been invested in the creation of a developing capitalist economy. The overseas expansion of this economy has, initially via Spain and Portugal, appropriated the surplus created by the labor of Latin America (Stein and Stein, 1970).

Isolated and therefore necessarily self-sufficient societies of Indo America became dependent on English goods and markets as a consequence of foreign penetration and the imposition of Iberian elites. The economic and social structures created and perpetuated by dependence have resulted in contemporary societies crucially different from feudal England. Both the capitalist development of England and the underdevelopment of Latin America began with the emergence of English dominance of the wool trade in the late Middle Ages.

The Myth of a Dual Society. Inspite of the existence of feudalistic ideology and social relationships in the countryside, we, along with other advocates of the dependency model, reject the characterization of Latin America as a dual society in transition to capitalism. In brief, the feudal images projected by the huge estates only hide a more important reality —the Latin American economy responds to market influences.

Unlike the English experience on which the diffusion model is based, the market system in Latin America creates underdevelopment rather than development. While the market in England operated to mobilize resources for their most productive use, land and labor are grossly under-utilized in Latin America under the market system. The traditionalism of the countryside is not due to isolation and must not be viewed in isolation. In fact, its poverty and its conservatism are reinforced by its relationship to the city. Moreover, while the growth and expansion of the market in England gave rise to a dynamic entrepreneurial class which took command of society and led the transformation into the industrial revolution, in Latin America the forces of the market system first suppressed and since, have coopted this class. Contrary to the diffusion model, development will not be brought about by intensifying relations between the hinterland and the city, between Latin America and the developed capitalist nations, nor by strengthening the capitalist class. On the contrary, development requires the overthrow of capitalism and imperialism and the creation of a socialist context for development. Because of the complexity of these questions of capitalism, feudalism or dual society, our comments thus far cannot be more than a skeletal statement of our position, an introduction to the discussion which we now pursue.

Economic development requires the investment of an economic surplus to increase future productivity. The surplus must not only be produced and accumulated; it must also be invested. The potential for producing some surplus has existed in virtually all societies. That is, there have been few instances in which a society could not get from its environment more than the minimum (culturally determined) requirements to subsist, if conditions existed which created a reason to do so. Feudal serfs were forced to produce a surplus. The days they labored in the fields of the lord, and the crops and later money which they paid in rent represented such a surplus, since they managed to subsist and reproduce even giving up this portion of their labor and/or their product. The surplus was for the most part consumed by the lord and his household or the nobles or the church heirarchy to whom the lord was a vassal. That part of the surplus not consumed was accumulated. However, it did not contribute to raising productivity. It was not accumulated as an investment, but as ostentatious display in castles and churches which did nothing to bring about economic development.

The rise of commerce in England did lead to the development of an independent capitalist society, but only indirectly. Its direct effect was to accumulate surplus which was invested in expanding trade to accumulate more surplus. Through the process of commercial accumulation, capital was available to invest in altering the process of production. But this most important development required the ascendency of a manufacturing class with the motive and the ideology to do so (Mandel, 1970:95–131).

Commerce does not necessarily result in the growth of a manufacturing class, nor does it necessarily destroy the power or the ideology of the feudal nobility (Hilton, 1952:32–43; Hibbert, 1953:15–27). It provides an incentive for the lord to extract a greater surplus from his serfs so that he can sell it to purchase luxury goods. But this can be accomplished *within* the manorial system, using the position accorded the lord in feudal society to support increased demands on the serf. Ironically, instead of breaking feudal bonds to undertake a system of free labor, traditional relationships and agricultural methods are reinforced with the only changes being greater extraction of surplus from the serfs.

The commercialization of agriculture in this fashion is in accord with the interests of the merchants whose livelihood is made from purchasing agricultural produce from the landed nobility and supplying them with luxury items. However, for a number of reasons, it is incompatible with the growth of manufacturing. First, the introduction of more productive agricultural methods is limited. Any innovation which might threaten the manorial system will be resisted by the lord, who sees such a change correctly as a threat to the social structure on which he relies to expropriate the product of his serfs. The value of the traditional system to the landed nobility also reinforces the conservative predisposition which rejects innovation on ideological grounds. Without great advances in agricultural productivity, the labor supply for the most part remains tied to the land and is not available to work in manufacturing. Moreover, when rent to the lord is in labor or in kind for use of land, the self remains largely outside the money economy. When payment is in money, the self is forced into direct contact with the market by the need to sell his produce to pay his rent. But in the market, he receives little more than what he must pay the lord. In neither case are the serfs able to buy manufactured goods. A potential manufacturing sector is denied an internal market for its products which is essential to its growth.

Thus, the commercial road out of feudalism can result in an apparently dual society. In the towns a more urban life grows. Wealth accumulates from both commercial and financial activity. A "white collar" class of clerks employed in these activities grows. Free artisans produce for the urban market. The life of the towns is founded on buying cheap and selling dear. Its economy supports an ideology different from that of the manor involving speculation and risk. The goal is profit to use in larger transactions to make a still greater profit. Based on the wealth drawn from the countryside, the trading cities become relatively modern prosperous centers of commerce. In the countryside the manorial system remains. Personalistic social relationships are continued. The same productive methods are used. The feudal way of life appears virtually unchanged. The heavy extractions on the serfs made by the landed nobility to get the produce they need to pay for luxury goods keeps the serfs in poverty. What has changed is the motive for production. Dominance of production for consumption by the serf and the household of the lord with random additional demands for taxes and tribute to outside authorities gives way to production for sale to merchants who transport the product far beyond the manor. As a result, decisions arise concerning what will be produced on the estate and in what amounts. These decisions turn on changes in market conditions reflected in the prices and terms brought to the manor by the merchants.

The qualification, an "apparently" dual society, is used because of the crucial importance of the link between the city and the countryside. Examined in isolation, the countryside appears to be poor and traditional simply because, as in the diffusion model, outside agents of change have not yet arrived on the scene. But as explained above, conservatism is reinforced by the opportunity of the landowners to make a profit by using the traditional system to increase exploitation of the serfs or peasants. This is only one aspect of the relationship between the apparently feudal countryside and the city. Let us now turn to other aspects.

What Kind of Bourgeoisie? Both local and long distance trade have existed for thousands of years. Commercial capitalism in England was a prelude to the development of industrial capitalism, but not in Latin America. The apparent dualism as a dominant characteristic of Latin American society could not develop without the existence of a foreign market. That is, the heightened systematic exploitation of the countryside, not through taxation as for example in eighteenth century France, but through extension of the market system, occurs only when a market for agricultural products exists beyond the manor. If demand is in the city, then we can expect the growth of a manufacturing bourgeoisie. To pursue its interests this class must free land and labor for the market and integrate the nation. Increased domestic trade requires that a system of roads be maintained and the nation be unified to provide free right of travel on them. A body of law must be established which provides for the right of property. Policies must be adopted which force unproductive serfs and lords from the estates so that both land and labor may be subject to the efficient allocation of the market. As economic enterprises become larger, mechanisms for joint investment must be established. As manufacturing grows, the new nation requires land and naval military power to develop and protect its international trade. An efficient tax system must be built which can finance these ventures without absorbing all the resources it collects.

If the market for agricultural products is not in the cities but in a foreign nation, then commerce will strengthen the landowners and merchants of the agricultural nation bringing about dominance of an agro-commercial bourgeoisie. This class does not need a good system of roads, except for transport to the sea. It does not require, and in fact is threatened by, a strong central government which raises revenues to finance public projects. And it is not in the interests of this class to carry out developmental tasks which would conflict with and therefore threaten its relationship to the metropolis. Therefore, it rejects policies which would encourage the growth of an independent manufacturing bourgeoisie. Industries grow only in areas which do not conflict with metropolitan competition, and in these fields, manufacturing tends to arise as an extension of agrarian capital, not in opposition to it.

Under the policies of the agro-commercial elite, the agricultural nation acquires the characteristics of a dual society. And it does not develop. Though capital is accumulated in the cities through commerce and finance, it is not applied to production. Therefore, labor does not become more productive. The market for manufactures is confined to luxury goods for the rich and does not grow. The social structure remains static —an upper class of rich urban merchants and "feudal" landowners who rule; a fragmented "middle class" of clerks, bureaucrats, artisans and independent professionals; and a lower class of serfs or peasants in the countryside and various laborers and apprentices in the cities. The countryside is dominated by market forces in an international capitalist economy.

These agricultural nations dominated by an agro-commercial bourgeoisie have been described above as capitalist. Yet they lack a manufacturing bourgeoisie.* These nations and even the large plantations in the countryside produce for an international market. But can a capitalist so-

---

* In the 20th century, Latin America has experienced considerable industrial growth. However, because of the dominance of foreign involvement in this industrialization, a *nationalist* manufacturing bourgeoisie has not been created. We return to this subject later.

ciety arise without a strong nationalist manufacturing bourgeoisie? It is this class which historically in the now developed capitalist countries has been given the role of acting sometimes consciously and at other time unwittingly or even unwillingly as the revolutionary agent of social transformation. It is this class of people, pursuing self interest at times individually and at others collectively, which has used the surplus accumulated from the labor of the producing class, to change the nature of the economy over which it gains power, to alter the way in which that society interacts with nature to gain the means of its subsistence, thereby changing society itself completely. It was asserted above that these nations may be accurately described as capitalist in spite of the absence of this dynamic class. The paradox is resolved with a deceptively simple observation that while a capitalist society cannot exist without a manufacturing bourgeoisie, this class need not be a part of that society. That is, a nation may become capitalist through its integration into another economic system which has already achieved the strength and dynamism by which the capitalism of Western Europe and the United States (and more recently, Japan) have been characterized.

Together these two types of nations, one dominated by a manufacturing bourgeoisie and the other by an agro-commercial bourgeoisie which responds to the demands of the more developed nation, constitute a single system. Just as the underdeveloped nation may appear to consist of two separate societies, this system may appear to be a sort of dual society— one dominant nation, capitalist and developed, and the other dependent nation, feudal and underdeveloped. But this view ignores the linkages described above which, to repeat dos Santos' description of dependence create ". . . . a situation in which the economy of certain countries is conditioned by the development and expansion of another economy to which the former is subjected."

Spain and Latin America: The Consequences of Dependent Development. Even though it had participated in the conquest of Latin America, Spain itself became a dependent nation.

Spain was unable to use the riches extracted from the New World to promote economic development. To do so would have required that the wealth from the colonies find its way into the production process as an investment in the Spanish economy. Had the economic and social basis existed in Spain, this might have occurred. That is, if a manufacturing bourgeoisie had been dominant in Spain in the 16th century, American silver would have paid for the expansion of Spanish industry. The interest in industrial expansion would likely have led this group to unify and consolidate a divided country. The price inflation in Spain caused by the arrival of colonial wealth would have enabled the manufacturers to raise their profits by even more than the increase brought about by expanded production since wages, as occurred in England, would have increased more slowly than prices. When the flow of silver declined in the first half of the 17th century, Spain would have been left with an established industrial economy in a strong competitive position in Europe and the Americas. Even without the flow of precious metals, the nation would likely have proceeded on a course of national development characterized by continuous technological, economic and social change organized by a nationally oriented manufacturing bourgeoisie.

Already an economic dependency of Europe at the time of the conquest, the Spanish Kingdom was divided sharply into three regions. In Castile, a commercial capitalism was already well established. In this context, the wealth of the Americas could not be used for national development. The merchants required a trade monopoly to benefit. By limiting trade to the port of Sevilla, monopoly was achieved. But the conquest thereby became a force to heighten regionalism rather than national integration. An economic pattern based on trading Spanish line, wool and iron ore to England, France, Holland and Italy in return for ironware, steel, nails, textiles and paper was altered only by the addition of precious metals as commodities which the Spanish used for trade. Spanish food, clothing and hardware industries expanded in response to demand from the colonies in the first half of the 16th century, but later were overwhelmed by English, Dutch, French and Northern Italian competition (Stein and Stein, 1970:4–20, 44–53). The prices of Spanish goods were too high to compete with these products due to the price inflation caused by the silver of Peru and Mexico. Though this wealth might have been used to subsidize Spanish manufacturers and though other trade restrictions might have kept out English competition, the interests of the Spanish merchants lay in a pattern of exchanging precious metals for European goods. While the commercial class increasingly became an agent for English capital, its domestic position grew stronger because of the increased role of trade in Spain.

With the decline of silver, Spain's role in the Americas was weakened. Without economic power, Spain could do nothing to hold the colonies. After the boom, nothing had been accumulated. The benefits had gone to other European nations, especially England, which after the wars of independence dropped the Spanish linkage to the Americas and dominated the area directly.

Thus, though a great deal of wealth passed through Spanish ports, little remained when the boom was over. The pattern of economic activity and the technology employed in production remained unchanged.

The export oriented commercial capitalists and the commercial landowners had been strengthened. Their interests lay in fulfilling a narrowly
defined role in an international economic system. They fulfilled that
role and maintained a stagnant status quo in Spain.

It was this same pattern of economic activity with the same combination of ruling interests which was established in the Americas. In a
most fundamental sense these patterns were not "imported" from Spain
any more than feudalism or Latin values were carried across the Atlantic
Ocean. Rather, the conquest occurred at a time of great demand in
Europe for precious metals and for certain plantation crops, especially
sugar. The existence of the metals and of excellent conditions for growing crops led to the creation of economies which fulfilled these demands.
The forces were sufficiently strong to overcome obstacles such as a shortage of labor which could have caused different patterns to arise. While
the conquistadores and those who followed them across the ocean carried
the cultural orientations of the society into which they had been born,
these norms—authoritarianism, hierarchy, machismo, dignidad, and the
concept that physical labor is degrading—were perpetuated because the
Americas were integrated into the expanding capitalist economy centered
in England which came to fulfill a role similar to that of Spain.

The early establishment of mining and plantation agriculture had as
a direct consequence the creation of an essentially two class society with
a narrow elite at the top. This elite, though quickly characterized by
several divisions (peninsulares versus creollos, Liberal versus Conservative, Federalist versus Centralism-Unitaryists, pro-Church versus anti-
Church, etc.), was defined by its relationship to the buyers of its products
and the suppliers of its goods—to Europe. The indirect consequences
of this economic structure and the social class structure which is created
may be seen in cultural orientations as well as in economic policies.

As to the cultural orientations, the values which appeared in both the
Iberian peninsula and in the Americas were appropriate for societies in
which mining and plantation agriculture predominate and in which
ownership of the means of production is highly concentrated. The labor
system requires outright slavery or conditions approximating slavery.
Authoritarianism and hierarchy are characteristic of this type of labor
system and are in fact necessary to it. With virtually no mobility, the
lower classes must accept their position. A fatalistic orientation is encouraged. In this type of economy the social classes are sharply distinguished by whether or not they engage in manual labor. A small elite
can avoid all forms of physical work while the lower classes must participate in manual labor to survive. Physical labor becomes a sign of lower
class status. This sharp class division also leads to a division of women

into the categories of those who are honorable and, therefore, must be isolated from contact with the lower classes and a second category of dishonorable women whom the land owners may appropriate without guilt. The situation of the plantation owner as a dictator on his own land encourages a rejection of settling disputes through courts since arbitration suggests that the latifundista is subordinating himself to the authority of the court. In a sense, he jeopardizes his sovereignty over his domain.

This explanation of the cultural orientations of Latin America as an indirect result of the economic structure of mining and plantation agriculture is strengthened by comparing the Latin American experience with that of North America. The area which is now the United States was conquered by people from northern Europe and England who did not possess the cultural orientations of the Iberians. In the area which is now the northern United States, geography and climate precluded the development of plantation agriculture, and precious metals were not found. The growth of family farms and an economic structure which permitted greater upward social mobility fostered the growth of concepts such as the dignity of work and discouraged authoritarianism and fatalism. The position of women in the family farm unit, though subordinate, was reinforced by the vital economic role they played. The land tenure system did not lead to an avoidance of arbitration and adjudication of disputes. The area in the south of what is now the United States was conquered by people of ethnic and national backbrounds similar to those of the north. However the rise of plantation agriculture, slavery and a two-class system led to a set of cultural orientations quite distinct from those of the north—these attitudes and values of the U.S. south were very similar to those associated with Latin American culture, even though the two areas differed in religion and ethnic and national origins.

The Latin American economies established in the colonial period created a dependence which has still not been broken. Economic activity was oriented toward the production of commercial crops and precious metals for export. Domestic food production and crafts grew up around the mines and were dependent upon the prosperity of mining. Thus the colonial economies required the maintenance of external markets for exports. Exports were necessary to provide foreign exchange to purchase all the products not produced in the colonies, both necessities and luxury goods.

The pattern of dependence based on export of a few raw materials in order to satisfy the need to import all the commodities not produced has remained, with some changes, to the present day.

It is not surprising that England proclaimed an ideology of free trade and sought to penetrate to the furthest reaches of the planet in search of materials, markets and profits. The acceptance of this doctrine of *laissez faire* by Latin American elites, on the other hand, might seem to indicate short-sightedness, incompetence or plain stupidity. However, it must be recognized that the English elite brought about national development in England by following policies that enhanced the individual position of members of its dominant sector. In Latin America, the original establishment of plantation agriculture and mining for export to the metropolis created oligarchies whose members' individual interests coincided with the maintenance and expansion of the trade patterns, even though they prevented development and created dependence. The behavior of elites in England and in the colonies was the same—pursuit of immediate self-interest. The result of self-interest was quite different because of the structural contexts of the respective elites.

For the metropolis, the flow of raw materials constituted fuel for expanding industries. Demand from the colonies for manufactured goods contributed to a market stimulus for metropolitan industrial growth. Profit derived from this trade pattern provided investment capital for the metropolis. Industrial expansion confirmed and strengthened the domestic position of the metropolitan industrial bourgeoisie, assuring the dynamic role of this class in orienting its own society. In dependent societies, each boom strengthened the internal position of the agro-commercial sector of the elite. The temporary prosperity created by the boom further encouraged monocultural tendencies as the demand for the boom product channeled resources into expansion of production in this limited area while the inflation accompanying the boom priced potential domestic manufactures above those of foreign imports. Moreover, in periods of monocultural expansion, the agro-commercial elites receive large profits enabling them to purchase foreign goods. From their perspective, change was unnecessary. Change could even be dangerous, since existing patterns of exploitation of the masses might be disturbed and trade relations with the metropolis could be disrupted.

At various times, particularly in the 20th century during the First World War, the Great Depression, and the Second World War, when the metropolis has been unable to supply manufactured goods and been otherwise preoccupied, the issue of competing with industrial imports and shipping in foreign bottoms has arisen. However, that segment of the bourgeoisie whose interests coincided with independent national development was rarely strong enough to prevail over the agro-commercial sector. The few victories were not permanent, dissolving when the metropolis was able to resume pre-existing patterns.

United States history provides a parallel to the Latin American experience. In the period following our war of independence, the agro-commercial elites of the South argued for a low tariff policy while the North sought to further its industrial aspirations by promoting a protectionist policy. In Latin America, the agro-commercial elites were dominant. What has followed in the two regions raises the question of which nation the rich resources of North America would have developed if the North's protectionism had not ultimately won out in the United States. In any case, economic policies in both hemispheres did not spring from cultural orientations or racial characteristics, but from elite interests shaped by prevailing economic patterns.

The dependency model finds the origins of contemporary underdevelopment in dependence. Not only was England never underdeveloped because it was never dependent, the very same process of expansion of capitalism by which England progressed brought about the underdevelopment of Latin America. The outward reach of the market brought boom periods to the colonies as they were penetrated. In Mexico and Peru it was silver. In Cuba and the northeast coast of South America, it was sugar. In the interior of Brazil, rubber and coffee; in Chile, nitrates and later copper. Each of these boom periods, though different in length and intensity, left virtually nothing behind upon which self-sustaining growth and development could be based. Like the bullion boom in Spain created by exploitation of the colonies, the beneficiaries were the developing, not the dependent nations. The spread of commercial capitalism destroyed existing manufacturing in the colonies and prevented the rise of competition with imported products. Each boom created an inflation which made imported goods cheaper relative to domestic manufactures. Land and other resources were employed in producing the product in demand in the international market. Monocultural economies were created. Infrastructure—roads, railroads, housing and other facilities—was built to permit and facilitate extraction of resources and shipment abroad. Networks of internal communication and transportation were neglected. When the international market for the boom product declined, there remained symbols of past glory such as the magnificent opera house that still stands in Manaus, Brazil, a leftover of the days of the rubber boom.

THE DEPENDENCY MODEL IN THE LITERATURE

The following synthesis is an effort to guide the reader into the recent but rapidly growing literature on dependency. Our attention is to some general efforts at conceptualization, to an examination of precursors who laid the foundation for dependency theory, to a look at contemporary dependency theorists, and finally to attempts at empirical validation of dependency theory.

Among general efforts at conceptualization available in English, there is the brief synthesis by Theotonio Dos Santos (1970C) whose definition we have included in our earlier discussion; he offers historical distinctions among colonial dependence which dominated the economic relations of the Europeans and their colonies; financial industrial dependence which consolidated itself in the rise of imperialism at the end of the 19th century when hegemonic centers expanded their investments abroad in the production of raw materials and agricultural commodities; and the new dependency characterized by the rise of the multinational corporation which invests in industries geared to the internal markets of underdeveloped countries. Another useful general effort is that of Susanne (Bodenheimer) Jonas (1970A) whose definition derives from Dos Santos. Demonstrating that dependency has been a constant in Latin America since the 16th century, Jonas examines the specific characteristics of the international system (prevailing forms of capitalism, the needs of the dominant nations, concentration of capital, and type of international trade) as well as the ties of the dependent nation to the international system. Focusing on her notion of "infrastructure of dependency," she cities two examples: dependent industrialization which is "integrated into and complementary to the needs of foreign economies"; and clientele social classes "which have a vested interest in and profit from the structure of the international system." She argues that while the dependency model provides a framework for analysis of capitalist expansion and its impact on underdeveloped nations, it does not offer reasons for that expansion nor does it make explicit the relation of U.S. state and private capital. Examining alternative theories which explain U.S. relations with Latin America, she finds that contemporary international relations theory and non-Marxist theories of imperialism are insufficient, but that a Marxist theory of imperialism adequately complements the dependency model. A third synthesis of the dependency model is offered by Antonio Murga F (1971) who disparages early efforts to overcome dependency through the acceleration of industrialization by means of import substitution and the creation of heavy industry. He argues that while developmentalists appropriately considered relations between metropolitan and peripheral nations, they erred in considering dependency only as an external expression of economic ties. Dependency involves both external and internal dynamics: "the relations of dependency are the incorporation of the metropolitan structure into that of the peripheral nation." Osvaldo Sunkel (1972) gives a very readable survey from a Latin American view. Fernando Henrique Cardoso (1972) offers an in-depth review of dependency literature, and Juan E. Corradi (1971) has given us an excellent synthesis, available in English. A useful discussion of dependency theory is in Cockcroft, Frank, and Johnson, (1972, especially chapters by Frank: 19–45 and Johnson: 71–111 as well as the introduction: ix–xxix). Finally, for some theoretical perspectives not directly related to Latin America; see the analyses of the Union for Radical Political Economics in Weisskopf (1972) and Emerson (1962).

Dependency theory is largely a Latin American creation and only very recently have some North American specialists of Latin America become interested in it. The dependency model evolved essentially from two schools of thought: one nationalist and sometimes anti-imperialism but non-Marxist whose analysis emanated from economists grouped around the Argentine, Raúl Prebisch, in the Economic Commission for Latin America (ECLA); and the other anti-imperialist and Marxist in orientation whose ideas stemmed from imperialist theory generated by analysis of European expansion during the late 19th century. The ECLA school was shaped by beliefs and principles set forth in its manifesto (see United Nations, 1950). Hirschman (1961) has divided the history of this movement into three phases: from 1950 to 1953 when its ideology was formed, elaborated, and tested; from 1953 until 1958 when intensive studies were made of individual Latin American countries with the objective of proposing plans for their future development; and since 1958 when attention has shifted to the study and promotion of regional intergration through formation of a common market.

Werner Baer (1969) examines the ECLA philosophy which was formulated by Prebisch (1959) and other ECLA-oriented economists (see, for example, Urquidi, 1964). These economists divide the world into an industrial center and a primary producing periphery, both of which, they believe, should benefit from the maximizing of production, income, and consumption. However, Prebisch demonstrates that unrestrained competition tends to result in appropriation to the center of most of the increment in world income. Jonas, Murga, and others affirm that the ECLA thesis correctly linked Latin American underdevelopment to the international economic system, but that the analysis was limited. It fails, for example, to examine the conscious policies and specific needs of the nations of the center; it mistakenly attributes Latin America's backwardness largely to traditional or feudal oligarchies; it inappropriately assumes that development would be promoted by a progressive, nationalist bourgeoisie, an assumption thus far negated by historical experience; and its stress on import substitution has led to greater dependence on the international system and to economic stagnation.

The Marxist school of contemporary dependency theory emerged through general dissatisfaction with the ECLA model, especially with its failure to explain stagnation in Latin America. In the mid-sixties initial efforts to reformulate a model of dependency were promoted by Latin

American social scientists associated with the United Nations Latin American Social and Economic Planning Institute in Santiago. Through internal discussion and reports, this group turned from the ECLA preoccupation with deteriorating trade patterns to investigation of other areas of foreign influence and control which affect Latin American underdevelopment. At the outset they were influenced by external aspects of dependency. Theoretical premises on external dependency had been elaborated with the expansion of Europe and later the United States in the "age of imperialism" (see the excellent historical analysis by Magdoff, 1969). While Magdoff gives us a recent perspective of imperialism, J. A. Hobson's work (1965), published in 1902, focused on British imperialism, and according to Magdoff, "marked an historic turning point in the study of the subject." While Hobson as well as Schumpeter (1951) offered non-Marxist interpretations of imperialism, Hobson in particular deeply influenced Lenin's significant study (1967). And Lenin was definitely an influence upon the dependency theorists of the 1960's (for recent readings on imperialism, see Rhodes, 1970, and Fann and Hodges, 1971). So too was Paul Baran, who together with Paul Sweezy, was widely read throughout Latin America. Baran (1965:11–12) admonished bourgeois economists who obscured the main issue of underdevelopment: "What is decisive is that economic development in underdeveloped countries is profoundly inimical to the dominant interests in the advanced capitalist countries." His clear explication of economic surplus and its backward consequences in capitalist society was linked to monopoly capitalism. Later Baran and Sweezy elaborated on these themes (1966).

The Latin American theorists of dependency were also influenced by the early writing of André Gunder Frank whose ideas focused on the development of underdevelopment (1966A and fully elaborated in 1967A). He emphasized commercial monopoly rather than feudalism and precapitalist forms as the economic means whereby national and regional metropolises exploit and appropriate the economic satellites. Thus capitalism on a world scale produces a developing metropolis and an underdeveloping periphery, and this same process can also be found with nations between a domestic metropolis (say, a capital city) and the surrounding satellite cities and regions. While Latin American advocates of the dependency model were later to find Frank's analysis incomplete (Frank, 1972:1–12), he in turn attempted to move beyond the widespread usage "which has become equally acceptable to bourgeois reformist and Marxist revolutionaries" by giving "an operational definition." Frank's struggle with conceptualization was accompanied by a concern with historical example, and his theory was elaborated in relation to the experience of several countries, especially Brazil, Chile, and Mexico. In this sense he shared the concern of other intellectual precursors to the contemporary dependency school, among whom notable examples are Brazilian Caio Prado Júnior (1969) and Argentine Sergio Bagú (1949) whose incisive historical interpretations of their nations' political economies have become classics in today's literature. Celso Furtado's economic history of Brazil (1963) also is a contribution in this direction.

Contemporary dependency theory has evolved primarily in the writing of social scientists in Brazil, Chile, Mexico, and Peru. A useful, although not exhaustive, effort to critically synthesize some of this literature has been undertaken by Claire Savit Bacha (1971) whose study concentrates on the Brazilian experience. Let us, however, identify some of the major writings for those desiring to explore in some depth the contrasting perspectives of the dependency model.

Most of the theoretical impetus for the study of dependency has been provided by Brazilian social scientists, including Fernando Henrique Cardoso, Francisco C. Weffort, Theotonio Dos Santos, and Helio Jaguaribe. While all these writers focus on dependency, conceptual consensus does not exist among them. Jaguaribe, for example, was the intellectual founder of a school of developmental nationalism in Rio de Janeiro during the 1950's. He argues (1970:25) that Latin America faces three alternatives: dependence, revolution, or autonomy. And he opts for autonomous development through nonrevolutionary change, a position strongly attacked by Frank (1972:183–241) as simply an ECLA strategy "disguised under another name." Likewise, Weffort (1971) in a penetrating critique of the dependency model warns that the concept of dependency runs the risk of being manipulated as an ideological rather than as a scientific construct. Dependency, he argues, could merely become a substitute for already inadequate explanations of underdevelopmentalism. He sees a theoretical ambiguity between "external dependence" and internal "structural dependence." He sees this ambiguity in Cardoso and Faletto (1969), in Frank (1967A), and in Quijano (1970); thus the problem remains, "how to combine external dependency and internal dependency." Finally he questions if dependency theory has not merely replaced imperialist theory. In a detailed rebuttal Cardoso (1971B) argues that Lenin's theory of imperialism is not sufficient as an analytical framework for interpretation of contemporary situations of dependence. With reference to the focus of Santos (1970A, 1970B, 1970C) and his group in Chile which had been analyzing "the new character of dependency," Cardoso makes clear that their work on dependency has served as a critique of analyses of development that separate social and political conditions from economic conditions; that emphasize evolution or stages of growth; and that offer a functionalist theory of development.

In a discussion sensitive to the over-emphasis of theorists to the internal aspects of dependency, Cardoso (see Bonilla and Girling, 1973:7–16) reassesses Lenin's imperialist theories in the light of the advances of contemporary dependency theory. He believes that Lenin's characterizations of imperialism and capitalism, while providing a useful foundation, "are no longer fully adequate to describe and explain the present forms of capital accumulation and external expansion." He then affirms that "it is not difficult to show that development and monopoly penetration in the industrial sectors of dependent economies are not incompatible. . . . there occurs a kind of *dependent capitalist development* in the sectors of the Third World integrated in the new form of monopolistic expansion." He argues that internal structural fragmentation is evident in many Latin American countries, yet that fragmentation results in a connection of "the most 'advanced' parts of their economies (i.e., those most directly linked to the international monopoly capital system) to the international capitalist mode of production." In part this explains the unevenness of capitalist development. For example, the type of development produced by foreign investment "creates a restricted, limited and upper class oriented type of market and society." But then he shows that the amount of foreign capital actually invested in the dependent economies has been decreasing in recent years. The consequences are twofold: 1) "local savings and the reinvestment of profits realized in local markets provide resources for the growth of foreign assets with limited external flow of new capital" and 2) "dependent economies during the period of monopolistic imperialist expansion are *exporting* capital to the dominant economies." It should be clear to the reader that Cardoso is discussing capitalist development (in dependent nations) which "is contradictory, exploitative and generates inequalities." He is not refering to development that involves a redistribution of income and the provision for basic needs of the entire population, and other criteria which we have stressed earlier.

Other theoretical literature focuses on internal and external aspects of dependence. The early work of González Casanova proposed a framework for analysis of internal colonialism (1969 and 1970). This approach was also elaborated by another Mexican sociologist, Rodolfo Stavenhagen (1970). A full discussion of internal colonialism and dependency as related to Blacks, Chicanos, and Puerto Ricans in the United States is elaborated by contributors in Bonilla and Girling (1973:149–234, with a comprehensive bibliography on pp. 251–62). Celso Furtado's recent investigation (1972) concerns external dependency which he conceptualizes: "the process of transplanting consumption patterns, provoked by the industrial revolution and operating through a system of international division of labor imposed by the industrialized countries, gave rise to peripheral capitalism, a capitalism unable to generate innovations, and dependent for transformation upon decisions from the outside." Marcus

Kaplan (1968) has also focused on external dependency. In addition to these sources, Hinkelammert (1970), Ruy Mauro Marini (1969), and Sergio de la Peña (1971) offer assessments of underdevelopment that relate to the concerns of the dependency theorists.

In large part, dependency theory remains to be validated empirically, although commendable efforts at data gathering and documentation have been initiated. For example, the North American Congress on Latin America in its bimonthly *Latin America and Empire Report* has published a series of case studies on the activities of United Fruit in Central America; the Hanna industrial complex and its interests in Brazil; the Rockefeller empire in Latin America; the role of U.S. investment in Chile; and many others. Likewise, a group of researchers under Theotonio Dos Santos at the University of Chile focused attention on the role of foreign corporations in Latin America.

While such studies have exposed the impact of the United States upon underdevelopment in Latin America, there is a need, according to James Petras, "to examine the internal linkage that permits foreign forces to penetrate a country and create a dependent situation . . . . this involves an examination of the relationship between external investors and social classes within a country." This need to tie external dependence to internal class structure has been satisfied in part by Petras' study with Thomas Cook on attitudes of Argentine executives toward foreign investments and U.S. policy (Petras, 1973: Chapter 5). Other important studies that move in this direction are Cardoso's (1971A) investigation of business attitudes in Argentina and Brazil; Dale Johnson's (1967–68) survey industrial managers in Chile; and Armand Mattelart *et al*'s (1970) examination of the ideology of the Chilean dominant class. Orlando Caputo and Roberto Pizzaro study the new forms of imperialism in Chile (1970) while Torres-Rivas (1969), Aníbal Quijano (1971), and López Segrera (1972) offer definitive studies of dependency and internal class structure respectively in Central America, Peru, and Cuba (prior to 1959). Carlos Osmar Bertero (1972) gives us a case study of dependency in the pharmaceutical industry in Brazil.

Finally, the widespread acceptance of dependency theory, including that of non-Marxist observers, has led to other criticisms. Frank Bonilla (Bonilla and Girling, 1973:5–6) states that dependency theory has been "largely silent about what is to become of the national idea . . . dependency theory has failed to come to grips with crucial questions regarding internal differentiation and the sources of political energies reconstitutive of national aims." Specifically, Bonilla believes that these shortcomings are due to "the incomplete and controversial treatment in Marxist analyses of certain key categories—ethnicity, caste, culture, racism and nationalism." While dependency theory has indeed stressed political economic rather than cultural explanations of backwardness, say among ethnic minorities, it would be unfair to deny that the dependency model provides a framework for analysis of the problems of those minorities. In fact, the essays in the Bonilla and Girling collection contribute significantly in this direction. Bonilla also is dubious about the prospects for formalization of dependency theory in a computer model. The validation of dependency theory also was the concern of Tyler and Wogart (1973) who correctly refer to "a dearth of objective and scholarly research." They attempt "a modest empirical test" of some facets of dependency theory and conclude that "the available evidence does not refute the dependency thesis." Moore (1973) provides a diffusionist perspective of foreign investment in dependent Latin America, for while imperialism and dependency have negative consequences, the multinational corporation can bring benefits to underdeveloped Latin America. Such benefits, however, would be based on "the efforts of developmentalist-nationalist governments to bend the activities of multinational corporations to suit the needs of development without withdrawing from the dominant international pattern of trade and investment."

David Ray (1973) attacks Frank and Jonas (Bodenheimer), arguing that Soviet imperialism as well as U.S. imperialism have resulted in dependent relations with the less advanced nations; that foreign investment causes development as well as exploitation; and that the stress on dependence has obscured the need to discuss nondependence alternatives. The first criticism ignores the considerable differences in trade terms, loan agreements, and other considerations that exist in relations among capitalist and among socialist countries, although it cannot be denied that forms of dependency have existed between socialist nations. The second criticism has been dealt with by Cardoso, as described above, since capitalism is likely to promote uneven development, resulting in benefits for ruling classes and exploitation of ruled masses. The third criticism is indeed valid, for the dependency theorists have been less concerned with offering an analysis of revolutionary alternatives than on formulating a framework for critiquing the diffusionist model, as it was described earlier. Our discussion in this introductory essay has not dwelled on revolutionary alternatives, for the country essays that follow do deal somewhat with this problem. We do, however, identify capitalist imperialism as the principal enemy of dependent Latin American nations and we have tried to relate this imperialism to the ruling classes within those nations. Let us, therefore, review our earlier discussion and direct attention to several issues of dependency theory that are evident in an analysis that seeks to relate capitalist imperialism to ruling classes.

III ISSUES OF UNDERDEVELOPMENT AND DEVELOPMENT

The premises of the diffusion and dependency models have been carefully elaborated. Through each model we have examined the impact of feudalism and capitalism on Europe and Latin America. We have traced a story of pre-capitalism, capitalism, and monopoly capitalism in the economic history of Europe and we have referred to the capitalist expansion in the New World as colonialist and imperialist. We have noted that the consequences for Latin America were considerably different than those for Europe. Our discussion has revealed several crucial issues which are evident in a continuing dialogue about Latin American development and underdevelopment: the dual society; the national bourgeoisie; and the ruling class. These issues relate to the nature of social classes in Latin America, to their struggle internally, and to their dependent ties with the outside world. These internal-external relationships are discussed in the specific analysis of the Latin American countries included in the present volume. As an introduction to this analysis, therefore, let us now focus on each of these three issues. In the light of the Latin American experience we briefly summarize our earlier discussion and differentiate the interpretation of each issue as related to the diffusion and dependency models. Later we examine three major books on particular Latin American nations, respectively Mexico, Argentina, and Peru; our intention is to make clear to the reader that different models and conceptualizations lead to different analyses and conclusions. Our hope is that the reader will be encouraged to seek a framework that will offer a clear understanding of development and underdevelopment in Latin America.

THE ISSUE OF DUAL SOCIETY

It might seem odd to the introductory reader that the authors, who have described their central concern as the condition of Latin Americans today, would spend so much time discussing developments hundreds of years and thousands of miles away. Yet, we believe that many journalists and scholars begin with the false assumption that Latin America is a feudal society as England was. This leads to an equally false conclusion that Latin America can and should follow the path first taken by England. We have tried to correct both of these misperceptions through a simple, but careful, review of the most important aspects of feudalism and the different ways in which the diffusion and dependency models interpret these subjects in contemporary Latin America.

Our earlier description focused on feudalism as the formative core of a European civilization based on two classes: the secular and spiritual lords of the manor and the ecclesiastical estates; and the serfs and artisans who were born on these estates and worked in the fields or in the village households that sprang up around the manor. We described the commercial road out of feudalism as resulting in an apparently dual society in which the towns prosper from commercial and financial activity and the countryside appears unchanged. Based on the European example, the diffusion model anticipates a breakdown of this dual society as the landlords demand new luxury goods produced in the towns in exchange for produce which is transported beyond the estate. Production for consumption by the serf and lord gives way to market conditions as reflected in prices and terms brought to the estate by the merchant.

It was also noted above that an apparent feudalism existed in Latin America; whereas the relations between landowner and peasant were not as formalized or detailed as in European feudalism, two classes prevailed with power held by the class of landowners to whom an immobile peasantry remained obligated to a system of patronage. The diffusion model interprets this condition as feudal and separate from the commercialization and industrialization evident in the cities of Latin America. The cities are developing while the rural areas remain underdeveloped, a condition which will be corrected when the capitalism of the urban areas is diffused to the backward rural areas. The dependency model, however, sees a capitalist link between the city and the countryside which accounts for the persistence of and even promotes underdevelopment and an apparent rural "feudalism." This link is characterized by commerce between landowners and merchants who form an agro-commercial bourgeoisie which is subject to market forces of a national and an international capitalist economy. These differences in the diffusionist and dependency interpretations are clearly illustrated in Figure 1.

It may be helpful to the reader to review briefly some of the interpretations of dual society in Latin America. One interpretation is evident among non-Marxist European and U.S. social scientists. Jacques Lambert (1959), the French geographer, exemplifies this tendency. He identified two Brazilian societies: "The dual economy and the dual social structure which accompanies it are neither new nor characteristically Brazilian—they exist in all unequally developed countries." By this analysis Lambert would attribute the poverty of the Brazilian Northeast to its isolation, archaic nature, or feudalism. Following a similar line of thinking but basing his analysis on a mixture of contemporary bourgeois social science and Marxist notions, González Casanova (1970: especially Ch. 5) attempts to relate dual society in Mexico to his idea of internal colonialism: one society dominates and exploits the other (marginal and indigenous) in a colonial relationship which is characteristically internal and not dependent on the international order. A more orthodox position on feudalism has been maintained by the pro-Soviet Communist parties of

Figure 1

Diffusion and Dependency
Interpretations of the Dual Society*

Diffusion Model

Commerce stimulated the development of England. Capitalism grew from feudalism in the 10th and 11th centuries. The struggle with feudal lords was led by the large merchants who consolidated their control over the towns and penetrated the countryside with new markets to establish a bourgeoisie political and economic dominance.

The challenge to feudalism in the Iberian Peninsula was not immediately successful. Thus the conquest of Indo America by Iberians involved the transfer of feudalism to the New World.

A feudal aristocracy evolved in Latin America and was to predominate to the present day. This aristocracy was to impede the development of capitalism and the rise of a progressive national bourgeoisie.

In the cities of Latin America, capitalism was introduced through commercial contact with more modern nations.

Through capital and technology the development of the modern metropolitan nations was diffused to the national urban centers in Latin America. With an acceleration of this process, there would be a breakdown of the two societies through a diffusion from city to countryside, resulting in an integration of the hinterland with the national and international metropoles.

Dependency Model

During the period of American conquest, Spain, like England before it, was a country in transition from feudalism to capitalism, a nation of uneven development combining feudal institutions with a relatively strong bourgeoisie that was dealing with foreign markets.

The discovery, conquest and colonization of America was a natural development for the Iberian countries that had broken their ties with the rural economy of the Middle Ages. The capitalist purpose of the conquest was the exploitation and commercialization of precious metals.

The Iberian countries (especially Spain) conquered America in order to incorporate it within a new system of capitalist production, not to reproduce the European feudal cycle.

Latin American countries were *not* ruled by feudal lords but by a bourgeoisie that had no desire to develop the domestic market and national industry because its basic source of income lay in the export trade.

The market system in Latin America creates underdevelopment rather than development. The poverty of the countryside is reinforced by its relationship to the city and to the outside world. Development can only be brought about with the overthrow of capitalism and imperialism.

* For a fuller statement and critique of the dual society thesis, see Luis Vitale (in Petras and Zeitlin, 1968:34–43).

Latin America and by traditional Marxist-Leninists such as Argentine Rodolfo Puiggrós who steadfastly insist upon a dualist-feudalist framework in order to advocate a revolution in which a progressive bourgeoisie would oppose reactionary landed interests. In assessing such views, Brazilian economists such as the Marxist, Caio Prado Júnior, and the liberal, Celso Furtado, would discount Lambert's interpretation of the Northeast by relating the region's underdevelopment to mercantile and capitalist shifts in an international system that brought prosperity, then depression, as the focus of the Brazilian economy moved from the sugar plantations of the Northeast to the coffee-growing areas of the south. Rodolfo Stavenhagen would recast González Casanova's concept of internal colonialism and relate it to the international order: What Spain signified to the colony, the colony signified to the indigenous communities. According to Stavenhagen (in Petras and Zeitlin, 1968:16), "What is important is not the mere existence of two 'societies' or a 'dual society' . . . but rather the relationships that exist between these two 'worlds' and bind them into a functional whole." And André Gunder Frank, who has carefully negated all arguments in favor of dualism, also has disposed of Puiggrós (Frank, 1969A:331–47). Frank, in turn, has been criticized by Novack (1970) who insists that both capitalism and feudalism were combined in a process of uneven development in Latin America. Colonialism, he argues, exploited pre-capitalist conditions of production for the benefit of the rising capitalist system; pre-capitalist and mercantile relations coexisted on the *encomiendas* and in mines and on the sugar plantations where the products of forced and slave labor were sold on the capitalist market.

The mind boggles at such a plethora of interpretations. The authors of this volume have been concerned with identifying the prevailing thrust of economic life in England, Spain (and to a lesser extent Portugal), as well as Latin America. Some qualification of our interpretation may be in order, however. While we have stressed the feudal beginnings of England, historians now know that development there was evident even before the Middle Ages; many medievalists place emphasis on incipient capitalism rather than feudalism in their analyses of European development. We also know that in Latin America there existed a landed aristocracy which enjoyed the prestige and status characteristic of feudal lords. Andrew Pearce (in Stavenhagen, 1970:15–20) describes the power of this aristocracy as being "maintained *directly* by the acquisition of labor power and its application to the land *without* deep involvement in market relations." He identifies this early pattern as precapitalist but he also makes clear that the estates or rural properties of today are market-oriented, even though they make use of share-tenure and service-tenure labor combined increasingly with wage labor. At the same time the estate "attempts to maintain as much internal subsistence as possible" leaving it "a complicated, rigid structure for which adaptation to modern conditions is extremely difficult." In contrast, the plantation organization of estates was an early response to European market demand for tropical products like sugar, cotton, or coffee. The plantation thus existed to produce for the market and to make profits for its owners; it "came to signify a capitalistic type of agricultural organization in which a large number of unfree laborers were employed under unified direction and control . . ."

The backward agriculture of the past colonial and the present national periods generally has been intimately related to the advanced capitalist sectors of Latin American society. The perpetuation of feudal-like underdevelopment in the backward sectors is seen as a consequence of the repercussions of monopoly in the capitalist areas, with the monopoly maintained by imperialist foreign capital. Our critique of dualism focuses on the *interaction* between these advanced and backward sectors. In spite of the existence of feudal ideology and social relationships in the countryside, we have described this dual society as having already left feudalism behind. In our view, the feudal images projected by the landed estates only hide the more important reality—an economy responding to market influences. Of course, the result is not a dynamic society characterized by continuous growth which we usually associate with capitalism. Capital accumulated in the cities through commerce and finance is not applied to production. Therefore, labor does not become more productive. The market for manufactures is confined to luxury goods for the rich and does not grow. The social structure remains static—an upper class of rich urban merchants and "feudal" landowners who rule; a fragmented "middle class" of clerks, bureaucrats, artisans and independent professionals; and a lower class of serfs in the countryside and various laborers and apprentices in the cities. The countryside is characterized by an essentially capitalist economy but it is not a developed industrialized capitalism. The cities (and therefore, the nation) are capitalist but lack a manufacturing bourgeoisie.

THE ISSUE OF A NATIONAL BOURGEOISIE

The rise of commercialism was followed by industrialization in many parts of Latin America. At the head of this process emerged a "new" manufacturing bourgeoisie which claimed to be progressive in advocating reform and to be enterprising in the promoting of national development. This dynamic segment of the bourgeoisie often manifested nationalist xenophobia or resentment against the imperialism that had permeated the hemisphere. This "new" or "nationalist" bourgeoisie represented a new force in the struggle against the "old" or "international" or "imperialist" bourgeoisie made up of the agro-commercial elite that ruled so long and effectively. Differing interpretations of the role that this national bourgeoisie plays in contemporary Latin America have become a central concern of the diffusion and dependency models. Our effort therefore will be to identify the contrasting perspectives of these two models, as traced in Figure 2. Then we will elaborate upon the contradictions and weaknesses of the thesis that the national bourgeoisie is a revolutionary and a developmental force in Latin America.

Reorienting economic policies toward national development in Latin America requires displacement of the agro-commercial elite and the assumption of power by a leadership committed to undertaking development regardless of the hardships. The diffusion model has looked to the so-called national bourgeoisie, the segment of the capitalist class engaged principally in manufacturing which directed the now developed capitalist nations to empire and capitalism. The national bourgeoisie has been expected to overcome the power of the latifundista class to establish policies toward more intensive land use and economic diversification. It has also been perceived as a source of leadership for social reform and political democracy, holding a preference for constitutionalism displayed by its counterpart in England. With support from the urban middle sector and urban industrial workers, the national bourgeoisie was to chart a democratic course to modernization and development, overturning centuries of "feudal" heirarchy and stagnation.

To cope with the problem of a negative balance of payments, this strategy looks to import substitution to reduce the outflow of foreign exchange now paid for products which could be produced domestically. Import substitution is also expected to build the manufacturing sector, strengthening the domestic position of the national bourgeoisie vis à vis landed interests. The modern urban population is also to be enlarged through industries created by foreign investment. Inflation, a problem general to underdeveloped economies, is to be controlled by monetary stabilization, increasing tax revenues through more effective tax collection methods and decreasing expenditures by cutting social welfare programs. Government enforced wage freezes are also used.

Foreign participation is considered a necessity to provide investment capital and modern technology in agriculture and industry as well as modern organizational methods. The strategy assumes that resultant economic growth, creating a "larger pie" will increase the size of the portion received by the masses. Growth is also expected to alleviate chronic and massive unemployment and underemployment, if population growth can

Figure 2

Diffusion and Dependency Perspectives
of the National Bourgeoisie*

Diffusion Model

The national bourgeoisie is interested in breaking the power and dominion of the landed aristocracy. This is because of a profound conflict of interests between the new and old bourgeoisies (modern commercial and industrial entrepreneurs versus the traditional aristocracy or oligarchy).

In overcoming the power of the landlords, the national bourgeoisie (the manufacturing class) will provide modernization of agriculture and industry. They will lead in the drive for social reforms and political democracy. Imperialist capital will prompt the national bourgeoisie to take an anti-imperialist stand against the alliance of the landowning aristocracy and imperialist foreign interests.

The national bourgeoisie will promote development through the diffusion of technology, capital, and enterprising spirit to the backward areas. Inevitably there will be a transition from traditionalism to modernism.

Dependency Model

Agricultural, financial, and industrial interest are often found in the same economic groups, the same firms, and even in the same families. Thus, the capital of archaic latifundias may be invested by their owners in lucrative enterprise in the cities; or the grand families of the city, associated with foreign capital, may also be the owners of the backward latifundias.

The combined interests of the landowning aristocracy and the urban commercial bourgeoisie will be aligned with the interests of the manufacturing bourgeoisie.

Tied to the dominant class interests and dependent on world imperialism for the manufacture of some goods, for foreign currency, and for foreign capital, the national bourgeoisie has no choice other than to accept its condition as a dependent bourgeoisie.

The diffusion of capital and products to the backward zones results in economic stagnation and decapitalization. This diffusion extends monopolies into the rural areas with negative consequences for balanced development as income becomes concentrated in a class of merchants and middlemen.

be reduced from rates which, except for Argentina, are now above 3 percent a year.

Attracting foreign investment requires economic and political stability. The political strategy has three elements. The assumed democratic lean-

* For a useful discussion of arguments for and against the national bourgeoisie in Latin America, see Stavenhagen (in Petras and Zeitlin, 1968:18–26) and Romeo (in Horowitz, Castro, and Gerassi, 1969:595–606).

ings of the national bourgeoisie and the "middle sector" are to be strengthened by encouraging representative political mechanisms such as political parties while depoliticizing other institutions. A popular theory recognizes modernity in the functional specificity of institutions. In these terms, labor unions should be economic institutions which enable workers to bargain collectively over wages and working conditions, not political organizations seeking to effect national government policies. Schools are to provide education, particularly technical training, not organizational bases for mobilizing the political energies of students and the intelligentsia. The military should be an arm of civilian government, responsible for national defense and internal order as directed by the government. It should not have a political role either as a veto group or as government, itself. The depoliticization of the military is to be accomplished through "professionalization." Providing training and sophisticated weapons has been expected to enhance the role of technical competence within the armed services, diminishing non-professional political inclinations.

The second aspect of the political strategy lies in the capacity of economic growth to provide opportunities for upward mobility. With more jobs for the unemployed and greater opportunities for individual advancement through industrial expansion, the potential for militant opposition is to be undercut. Those who benefit from these opportunities will be satisfied with existing political and economic arrangements and, perhaps more important, those still unemployed or otherwise dissatisfied with their individual situations, will have a reason to hope that they will eventually benefit. Finally, to deal with militant opposition which cannot be coopted, the strategy emphasizes a strengthened military, well-armed and well-trained so that it has morale and the capability to deal with internal dissention.

The emphasis on the national bourgeoisie as challenger of the landed oligarchy whose continued "feudal" stagnation has been maintained by surprisingly divergent perspectives. It appeals to members of the national bourgeoisie, itself, and to U.S. interests for obvious reasons. But it has also been a feature of orthodox Marxist analysis, particularly among Latin American Communist parties. By using this conception (stripped of the acceptance of foreign penetration), the Communist parties have been able to justify policies of cooperating with the national bourgeoisie, following the hope that organized urban workers could help industrial capitalists to create capitalism and the conditions for socialist revolution.

Since the mid-1960s, theories relying on the national bourgeoisie have suffered a decline. They have been betrayed by history. It is now generally accepted that this segment among the Latin American ruling classes has been weak, that monocultural economies did not provide an economic base for a strong national bourgeoisie. In the early 1960s several writers noted that elites who were owners and managers of manufacturing enterprises were also qualitatively different from their English counterparts. Claudio Veliz (1965:1–8) discussing Latin America generally, and Osvaldo Sunkel (in Veliz, 1965:130), writing on Chile, observed that the manufacturing elite had been coopted by the traditional agrarian oligarchy. Dale Johnson's research (Cockcroft, Frank and Johnson, 1972: 165–217) on this group indicated that it lacked self identity and a coherent line of policy. In his study of the development of Argentine industrialization, Gustavo Polit (in Petras and Zeitlin, 1968:399–430) found that the industrialists had never been independent of landed interests, that they had arisen as an extension of agrarian capital. A degree of industrialization has occurred, particularly in Brazil, Mexico, Argentina and to a lesser extent in Chile. However, it has been the result of the disruption of characteristic trade patterns caused by the inability of the metropolis to supply manufactured products in the World Wars and the failure of trade in the Great Depression. These events, rather than a conscious policy of industrialization directed by an independent national bourgeoisie, stimulated import substitution.

The national bourgeoisie has generally been unable to promote economic policies leading to national development. Except in Mexico, it has lacked the power and independence from the agro-commercial elite to establish its dominance. The Mexican bourgeoisie, though eventually coming to power through a process begun with the 1910 revolution has not maintained a level of mobilization of the masses necessary to undertake policies which would break the ties of economic dependence. It has not been in its interests to adopt these measures since its control would thereby be threatened. The Brazilian military coups in 1964, approved by a large segment of the "national" bourgeoisie, dramatically illustrates this point. When it appeared that continued support of the reformist coalition attempting to work out a program of national capitalist development would lead to reform which would damage its interests, the national bourgeoisie became a "consular" bourgeoisie (Jaguaribe in Veliz, 1965: 162–87). It supported military coups which brought to power a policy of submission to international capitalism. It was not a force for national development, nor a social aggregate lacking identity or policy. The Brazilian bourgeoisie (as Dos Santos in his study in this volume shows) has a clear and effectively executed policy to achieve political stability and economic growth as a dominion within the U.S. empire.

The Brazilian experience has also destroyed the assumption that constitutionalism is a dominant value of the national bourgeoisie. In England, the abolition of arbitrary unlimited power of the crown and the establishment of elections transferred power to the national bourgeoisie. The right to vote was initially very restricted. The franchise was extended throughout the population only after the masses had been involved in industrial employment and could be counted on to support the national bourgeoisie against the agrarian elite. In Latin America, however, the manufacturing elite has been in a weak position, but between the *latifundistas* who controlled the vote of the peasants who worked for them and the urban masses pressuring for radical change to solve their desperate problems. While constitutionalism has been favored by the British national bourgeoisie because elections have come out the "right" way, corresponding groups in Latin America have not hesitated to support the overthrow of elected governments which have gone "too far" toward reform.

In Latin America generally, electoral mechanisms for the transfer of power have not been firmly entrenched. Governments highly dependent on a foreign power have commanded little respect. Only in Chile has the ruling class shown enough independence and competence to establish legitimacy for itself and the political system by which it maintains its power. However, even in Chile the bourgeoisie at the end of 1972 was showing itself to be like the others in Latin America. As a headline in the *Wall Street Journal* (October 24, 1972:1) described the situation, "The Bourgeoisie in Chile Battles Allende Policy; A Civil War is Feared. Middle Class Loses Its Faith In Using Electoral Processes; Violent Protests Result."

Military regimes now hold power directly in Brazil, Chile, Peru, Bolivia, Ecuador, Panama, Honduras, and Nicaragua. Since the mid-1960s those who looked to the bourgeoisie and the middle sector to bring about development have turned to the military. (For an analysis of the middle class's dependency on the military, see José Nun in Petras and Zeitlin, 1968:145–85.) Military officers generally come from these segments of the population. Military governments express their perspectives and receive their support. They offer the promise of stability and this encourages foreign economic participation. Moreover, modernization theorists find in military institutions characteristics such as promotion through merit and appreciation of technical competence which justify a high regard for the military as an agent of modernization.

Clearly the national bourgeoisie finds itself in a predicament. Thus far in the Latin American experience the national bourgeoisie has chosen to play a secondary role in the ruling class which dominates national society and is held captive to a network of imperialism. In this role it has relied upon the military for political support and upon U.S. imperialism for economic assistance. If it were to break its dependent relations with other segments of the ruling class and with imperialism, as many observers believe is possible, it would probably be eliminated as a class. A weakened national bourgeoisie could not survive the impetus of revolution in Cuba. In Chile under the Allende regime its prospects were dim. In Peru the military's manipulation has forced some landowners to shift their capital to manufacturing while the regime has nationalized some foreign enterprise. But even in Peru it appears that the emergent national bourgeoisie remains subservient to the dealings of the military with foreign interests and as such it functions more as a dependent than national bourgeoisie.

THE ISSUE OF THE RULING CLASS

Our analysis has stressed the dominance of a ruling order in Latin American society. We have suggested that this order comprises several segments, including the landowning oligarchy or aristocracy, the commercial bourgeoisie, and the manufacturing bourgeoisie; their dominance is assured by a collaborative military. These segments may be old or new, nationalist or internationalist or imperialist, but they all seem to be dependent in some form upon international capitalism and imperialism. The diffusion model would question some of our assumptions. Therefore, we intend to look at the diffusionist interpretation of ruling class and to compare and contrast this interpretation with that of the dependency model as outlined in Figure 3. Finally we turn to a discussion of the implications of ruling class relations with imperialism. Specifically, we look at the impact of the multinational corporations on politics and economics in Latin America.

According to Marx (as summarized in B. T. Bottomore, 1964:24–47), every society beyond the most primitive is characterized by a ruling class and one or more subject classes. The dominant position of this ruling class is explained by its possession of the major means of economic production and of political power. Perpetual conflict is evident between the ruling class and the subject classes. Under feudalism this conflict is obscured somewhat by personal bonds between lord and serf, but under capitalism a radical polarization of classes is encouraged by the sharp divergence of economic interests whereby there is a concentration of wealth by a dominant class and of poverty by the subject classes. Influenced by these assumptions Vilfredo Pareto and Gaetano Mosca offered a modification of Marxian theory. They noted that in every society there is a minority which rules, and they called this minority the governing elite, comprised of those who occupy the posts of political command. Pareto noted that this elite undergoes changes in its membership over time, so he called this a "circulating elite." Subsequent efforts to conceptualize the terms ruling class and elite evolved into two schools of thought and a polemical debate that has preoccupied social scientists since the late fifties. An array of terms, from ruling class and governing class to ruling elite, power elite and circulating or pluralist elite, sometimes obscured an analysis of power.

Bottomore suggests that these different terms might be seen as complementary concepts, which may refer to different types of systems or to different aspects of the same system. There might be, in some societies for example, a ruling class and at the same time elites which represent different interests. There might be societies without a ruling class where a political elite would be in power through administrative or military control rather than through property ownership and inheritance. Likewise, there might be societies ruled by several elites among which there would be no cohesive group of powerful individuals or families.

In working toward a conceptualization of who rules in Latin America, it should be noted that "class" is an economic term and "rule" is a political term; that is a ruling class is an economic class that rules politically. Nichols (1972:35–69), after carefully reviewing the literature on power in the United States, concludes that there is a directorial class that rules politically. This class is "an upper class which is socio-economically distinct, continuous, and cohesive, and which controls the corporate economy of America." It shares common interests: maintenance of capitalism and maintenance of monopolistic power and its benefits. With its control over the corporations and financial institutions, it dominates the economy. Further, it appears to dominate the government because it occupies key positions at the executive center of the state; it finances the electoral process; it controls the national media. As to Latin America, Stavenhagen (in Petras and Zeitlin, 1968:23–25) notes that such terms as "middle class" or "national bourgeoisie" are often euphemisms for "ruling class." Some authors, he argues, find these terms less embarrassing or neutral, yet their analysis often is directed to the power structure of entrepreneurs, financiers, and industrialists at the apex of society. Another problem is that the middle class is usually economically and socially dependent upon the upper strata of Latin American society; they are tied to the ruling class, they are conservative, they defend the status quo, and they seek individual privileges.

We referred earlier to two interpretations of power. One utilizes the concept of ruling class, in the tradition of Marx and the elaboration of Nichols. In Spanish or Portuguese this concept is translated as *clase dominante,* dominant class; this terminology suggests an analysis of rulers and exploiters, on the one hand, and of ruled and exploited, on the other. It should be clear in our discussion above that we do not refer only to a monolithic ruling class, but to a class of varied interests which tends to become cohesive under capitalism and which tends to be intimately related to imperialism. As noted in Figure 3, a ruling class tends to be unified in a closed system with a broad scope of authority and concentrated power. The other interpretation views power as pluralist and is based partially on the formulations of Mosca and Pareto. According to the pluralist position, there are multiple groups in society which represent distinct interests and orientations and which interact with each other. These groups accept a set of rules regarding social change and they tend toward compromise in representing the views not of any single group but of the more varied interests of society. Competing elites are evident in a pluralist framework. Pluralism, then, conceives a more or less diffuse distribution of power within a socio-political framework.

Figure 3

Diffusion and Dependency Perspectives
of the Ruling Class*

Characteristic	Diffusion Model (Pluralism)	Dependency Model (Ruling Class)
Power	Dispersed with many centers	Concentrated and unified
Scope of Authority	Specialized, narrow	Wide, general
System	Open	Closed
Base	Dispersion of Interests	Coincidence of interests
Outlook and Interest	Diverse, competitive	Unified, cooperative
Recruitment	Achievement	By ascription (birth, wealth, etc.)
Duration of Control	Short	Long
Loss of Tenure	Incompetence	Decline in wealth
Consequences	No group favored over the other; Decline in politics as self-interest; Elites somewhat autonomous but encourage foreign capital and technology	Enhancement of interests of corporations and financial institutions, armed forces, and executive; Increased dependence on foreign interests; loss of democracy

* These differences are based on the categories in William Kornhauser (in Domhoff and Ballard, 1968:50) and those suggested by Sara Sheehan, a Teaching Assistant at the University of California, Riverside.

What are the consequences for Latin America, according to these two interpretations of power? The diffusionist notions of pluralism suggest that no group is favored. Interests are dispersed and competing elite groups are able to function independently of foreign interests; the national bourgeoisie would be such a group. At the same time it is assumed that capital, technology, and knowhow of the advanced nations, within certain limitations, can be diffused to less developed nations just as the modern urban metropolises can influence the backward hinterland of Latin America. In contrast, the dependency model sees in Latin America an ever increasing consolidation of interests—among corporations and financial institutions, the armed forces, and the executive branch of government. These institutions reinforce the ruling class interests of the agro-commercial and industrial bourgeoisies. In turn there is increased dependence on, and collaboration with, imperialist interests. We have already elaborated on these relationships, but let us briefly examine the impact of foreign activity on Latin America. In particular we note the recent expansion and penetration of multinational enterprise throughout the hemisphere.

Import substituting for industrialization has not created a basis for sustained growth. Moreover, growth has not "trickled down" to the masses. The ruling class has not shown itself to be democratic. The industrial bourgeoisie has been transformed into an agent of foreign capital, playing a functional role similar to that of the agro-commercial elites which it has joined or defeated. As for development, it has failed. However, it has succeeded in maintaining and increasing the availability of Latin America as a field of operations for foreign corporations, particularly the multinationals.

Earlier in this century, foreign activity was limited to plantation agriculture and utilities. In recent years, a major movement into manufacturing, banking and retailing has occurred. Discussing this development, the Chilean economist, Osvaldo Sunkel, cites a study of the operations of 187 trans-national corporations in Latin America (Vaupel and Curham, 1969) which shows that while in 1945 there were seventy-four of these firms with manufacturing subsidiaries in the region, in 1967 the number of their subsidiaries in the region had increased from 182 to 950, and the total number of subsidiaries from 452 to 1,924. Sunkel notes that this process accelerated in the mid-1950s but in the late 1960s, "it reach(ed) the stage of the wholesale process of buying up local firms and integrating affiliates closely with headquarters and with each other" (Sunkel, 1972:523). He observes a characteristic pattern of expansion:

> . . . first, they export their finished products; then they establish sales organizations abroad; they then proceed to allow foreign producers to use their

licenses and patents to manufacture the product locally; finally, they buy off the local producer and establish a partially or wholly owned subsidiary. (Sunkel, 1972:521)

This process removes still more decisions from the scrutiny and possible control of the host country since international trade takes the form of intra-firm transfers within the multinationals. And since the multinationals integrate their own activities and tend to cooperate with each other, the change also represents the introduction of foreign monopoly power throughout the host country's economy, where earlier it was restricted to the export of primary agricultural and mineral products. Along with this trend, foreign influence in areas such as advertising, communications and education has also increased.

If the growth of foreign participation brought a corresponding increase in the importation of foreign capital, the argument in favor of the multinational firm as an agent of development might be more plausible. However, figures for the period 1960–1964 indicate that only 4 percent of "foreign" investment represented capital actually transferred to Latin America from the United States (Frank, 1969:2, 9). The period 1963–1968 was little better with a real foreign contribution of only 9 percent (Sunkel, 1972:526). Thus, the growth in foreign holdings in Latin America has been generated primarily by the investment of profits produced within the host country. Poverty is general throughout Latin America, but it is not because of an inability to produce wealth. While a portion of the profits of foreign enterprises is reinvested, repatriation of the balance denies the people of Latin America use of capital which they have produced. Between 1950 and 1965, income on foreign investment transferred to the United States ($11,300 million) exceeded U.S. investment in Latin America ($3,800 million) by $7,500 million (Magdoff, 1969:198, 202).

Repatriation of profits is only one channel for capital drain. Repayment of loans is another. Granting of loans became a part of U.S. policy in 1934 when the Export-Import Bank was started to provide Latin American countries with credit to purchase North American goods. It was a program designed to get our economy out of its stagnation, not to help Latin America. Loan payments have now surpassed new loans. It is estimated that they will equal 130 percent of loans by 1977 if current patterns continue (Anderson, 1970:6). Loan payments now absorb a significant portion of the foreign exchange earnings of many countries. A variety of other charges for shipping, insurance, licenses and royalties account for still more capital flowing north. The situation is further exacerbated by the continuous drop in the amount of industrial imports which Latin American primary products will buy on the market due to the long term increase in prices of the former coupled with the decline in prices of the latter.

Inter-American economic relationships are characterized by exploitation in the simple meaning that Latin Americans do not receive the benefit of what they produce. The economic patterns are "natural" in the sense that market relationships always benefit superior technology and economic power. However, it is worthwhile to note that international trade had its origins in piracy and plunder. Robbery has been regarded as a legitimate way of making a living from at least the time of Aristotle. Expeditions for trade and for conquest have not been clearly distinguished. Privateers have been protected and contracted by established governments from early times to the association of the British and French monarchies with privateers (Mandel, 1968:83). Over the centuries more subtle instruments of coercion have supplemented military power to maintain trade in which one "partner" is understandably reluctant to participate. In addition to aid to favorable regimes and military establishments, the United States provides experts in counterinsurgency and "public safety" (which has included training in torture methods). The CIA engages in bribing politicians and journalists. A program sponsored by U.S. corporations, the government and the AFL-CIO trains Latin American labor leaders and keeps them on the payroll for extended periods after they have returned home. Economic controls which will be mentioned below are also employed.

All of this activity functions to maintain the nations of Latin America as an area open to the operation of foreign corporations for the extraction of resources, the export of U.S. products and the profits derived from a variety of business activities carried on within the host countries—in other words, to maintain capitalism and capitalist regimes which are most cooperative with foreign corporations. It is a political policy of domination which, combined with economic activities and programs which affect Latin American culture, maintain Latin America within a North American empire. We have noted the penetration of U.S. firms and some aspects of decapitalization because they represent a heavy burden on efforts to develop. However we do not wish to suggest that the domestic capitalists would act in a manner more beneficial to the Latin American masses if the multinationals permitted them greater opportunity to function. The multinationals are part of the imperialist system: indeed, they are the chief actors in both Latin America and the United States. But the problem is the inability of dependent capitalism to mobilize and direct the energies of the people and the resources of Latin America to meet basic needs. The political role of imperialism in maintaining dependent capitalism is as important as the direct economic exploitation in which the multinationals engage.

While dependent capitalism does not satisfy the needs of the majority of Latin Americans, the system does tend to coopt many groups, operating spontaneously to maintain itself. The bourgeoisie, for the most part unable to compete, is integrated into foreign enterprise. Since the technology of industrial production is capital intensive and does not create much employment, industrial workers have not grown as a proportion of the labor force. In this century, manufacturing output as a portion of the domestic product has grown from 11 to 23 percent while the proportion of industrial workers in the labor force has remained constant at 14 percent (Frank, 1969a:4, 9). In relation to the masses of peasants and urban unemployed, the industrial workers are a privileged group. Both salaried workers and organized labor are generally caught in a race against persistent inflation. But they are fearful of change of a revolutionary nature which would favor the marginals and which could bring retaliation from foreign interests. The very poverty of urban marginals and the precarious existence of poor peasants serve as a means of control, incapacitating them from acting as a political force for change.

In spite of the systematic forces supportive of the status quo and in spite of imperialist manipulation, change is occurring. When it reaches the level of governmental change, brought about by armed struggle or by election, the multinational corporations and the U.S. government react strongly. The full repertoire of economic warfare has been employed against Cuba. Even armed intervention was tried. The failure of these attempts to bring down the Cuban government over more than fourteen years and the increasing acceptance of Cuba by other Latin American nations have begun to open the possibility that the United States government will resign itself to the existence of a socialist Cuba.

In Chile, Salvador Allende was elected to the presidency in 1970, leading a coalition committed to fundamental change. Many of the government's measures to stop the capital outflow and to establish a planned economy (including the nationalization of the copper mines, Chile's largest source of export earnings) have been supported by nearly all segments of the population. The distortions of dependent capitalism place Chile in a vulnerable position. Chile is an agricultural country of approximately ten million people which physically bears a resemblance to California. Yet since the 1960s Chile has spent over $120 million a year to import food. Foreign exchange is also required to purchase industrial equipment, spare parts and medicine. And more than 30 percent of Chile's annual foreign exchange earnings must be used to service a

foreign debt of over four billion dollars inherited from previous governments. An inability to purchase equipment and spare parts would damage
the economy and engender unemployment. Political unrest would also be
encouraged if food could not be imported, especially at a time when large
landowners are sabotaging domestic agricultural production as an act of
resistance to the government. In this critical situation, the U.S. government and the multinational corporations have attempted to overthrow
the Chilean government through economic warfare. In a speech before
the United Nations General Assembly in December 1972, President Al-
ende enumerated the most important consequences:

* Cessation of about $80 million in loans annually which had been
  granted by the World Bank and the Inter-American Development
  Bank.
* Cessation of about $50 million in loans annually which had been
  granted by the U.S. Agency for International Development.
* Suspension of short-term credit to finance foreign trade which had
  been available from private U.S. banks amounting to $220 million.
* Halting of credit normally available from the Export-Import Bank
  to purchase U.S. goods.
* Blocking of short-term operations with private banks in Western
  Europe, mainly based on payment for copper, resulting in more than
  $20 million in credit lines not being renewed, and in the suspension
  of financial negotiations for more than $200 million.
* Blockage (by Kennecott Copper) of payments on Chilean copper
  sold in France, Holland and Sweden. French courts did place an
  embargo on payments temporarily.

In addition to these economic reprisals, Allende cited the efforts of the
giant International Telephone and Telegraph, known widely through the
publication of secret ITT memoranda in 1972, to overthrow the Chilean
government by political subversion.

The expansion of such multinational firms is now the most significant
economic phenomenon in the capitalist world. Growing at an annual
rate of ten percent in the period 1950–1970, they now withdraw over
$1,700 million a year from the Third World, nearly two thirds of this
from Latin America. In the underdeveloped nations, they often act in
concert, creating an oligopolistic base of economic and political power.
Their policies in both underdeveloped and developed countries are directed to achieve maximum profitability over the entire range of their
respective empires, not for the benefit of any of the nations in which
they operate. Even the developed countries have not brought them under
control. The multinationals have been able to defy attempts to merely

require detailed reporting on their activities to host governments. In the United States, a Senate subcommittee under the chairmanship of Senator Frank Church is undertaking an investigation of the multinationals. But movements to challenge them have had to confront vast concentrations of power. The strength of the oil industry is now known to all, and also the fact that it contributed over $5 million to the Republican Party in the 1972 presidential election campaign.

Development in Latin America, understood to include political and economic independence, requires that existing political and economic relationships undergo radical change. It is clear that the power of U.S. corporations engaged in foreign activities will resist this change. Profit rates on U.S. operations in Latin America are far higher than profits on domestic investment. Control of Latin American resources through ownership and lack of competition among the limited number of purchasers of Latin American products result in high profits on imports to the United States. North American exporters to Latin America enjoy monopoly power in many areas, resulting in high prices. Moreover, operations of U.S. business within other nations are growing at a much higher rate than domestic business. Socialism in Latin America would likely mean an end to all direct private foreign investment. Profits on trade would be reduced since the monopoly and monopsony power of the multinationals would be broken. Foreign control of Latin American resources and markets, a goal often as important as immediate profits to North American firms would be ended.

CONFLICTING PERSPECTIVES OF DIFFUSIONISM AND DEPENDENCY: CASE STUDIES OF MEXICO, ARGENTINA, AND PERU

A further understanding of the above three issues may be gained through critical examination of interpretative analysis of particular Latin American nations. For this purpose, we have selected three important studies available in English and written by three major social scientists from Latin America: Pablo González Casanova of the University of Mexico whose contribution, *Democracy in Mexico*, generally has been considered a classic in its own right; José Luis Imaz of the University of Buenos Aires whose *Los que mandan* has been received as a pioneer work and best seller in Argentina; and Aníbal Quijano of the University of San Marcos whose *Nationalism and Capitalism in Peru: A Study in Neo-Imperialism* has served as a major critique of the developmental nationalist policies of the Peruvian military junta in power after October 1968. Each of these works focuses on the issues of dual society, the role of the bourgeoisie, and the impact of a ruling class, yet each draws upon different methodology and conceptualization resulting in different conclusions about the prospects for development and underdevelopment in the respective countries. Undoubtedly, revelation of these contrasting perspectives is instructive to the student, for interpretations and findings are closely tied to whichever model (diffusion or dependency) has been stressed by the author. Our discussion will demonstrate that the studies by González Casanova and Imaz are largely diffusionist in orientation whereas Quijano's work is cast within a critique of Peruvian dependency.

MEXICO AND GONZALEZ CASANOVA

González Casanova's study of Mexico is interwoven with assumptions, factual information, and statistical data. First, he deals with the structure of power, examining constitutional government in theory and in practice as well as differentiating between formal and actual power. Then, he relates social and political structure. Next, he examines political decisions in the light of economic development. Finally, he assesses the future of democracy in Mexico, offering, first a "Marxist" analysis, than a "sociological" analysis. Let us synthesize his line of argument:

1. The polity in Mexico is unbalanced with a hierarchical concentration of power flowing downward from the presidency to the executive branch to the central government. At the same time there is the pluralist influence of competing elite groups or bases of power, including the regional and local *caudillos* or *caciques* (chiefs or bosses), army, clergy, latifundists, and national and foreign entrepreneurs.

2. Even though foreign capitalist influence in Mexico is extensive (more than half of the four hundred most powerful enterprises are either under foreign control or have strong foreign participation), the nation remains stable with a strategy of national independency and development. In the face of international pressures, Mexico continues its policy of liberation and nationalization (evidenced by the takeover of the petroleum industry in the late thirties and the more recent purchase of power utilities) as well as its independent international policy based on nationalist traditions (exemplified by refusal to accept military pacts with the United States or to break diplomatic relations with Cuba).

3. The state is the largest entrepreneur, providing stability and rational utilization of resources within a free enterprise framework. With its economic power reinforced by the concentration of political power in a presidentalist regime, the state controls external pressures of inequality, negotiates with the large monopolies, and promotes the "takeoff" of national development.

4. Mexican society is dualist: the dominant society consists of the Spanish, Creoles, and Ladinos and is characterized by a high degree of participation; the other is marginal and dominated, and consists of the Indian. One society dominates and exploits the other in a colonial relationship called internal colonialism. While internal colonialism is similar to the colonialist relationship between nations, it is directly related to the internal relations of the two societies: the participant and marginal, the haves and have-nots. While the marginal Indian populations reveal the "residue" of a colonial society, internal colonialism is not explained by Mexico's past foreign colonialism or by the nation's dependency on foreign powers. Internal colonialism, however, is evident where a ruling center or metropolis exercises a monopoly over the peripheral Indian community's commerce and credit *or* where social classes of the dominant society exploit the Indian population through "a combination of capitalism, feudalism, slavery, forced and salaried labor, share farming and peonage, and demand for free services." The cultural alignment of dominant and dominated populations is a reflection of prejudice and discrimination as well as colonial types of exploitation and control.

5. The large majority of Mexicans are outside the ruling class. But within the ruling class are lawyers, bureaucrats and others who manipulate the people through the political parties. The parties, however, reflect the disconformity of different sectors of the ruling class and the more advanced strata. The ruling class and these conformist sectors do not view the democratization of institutions as an urgent necessity. Instead stability, control, and cooptation are favored, and protest is discouraged.

6. Mexico is "pre-capitalist" and "pre-democratic" because of its internal colonialism. A bourgeois democracy and a fully developed capitalist system must be achieved. Further, conditions of socialism do not exist. Thus the ruling class must join with the proletariat to mold a progressive bourgeoisie and to put an end to internal colonization. This will be achieved through capitalist development. National integration will incorporate all classes, including the ruling class which will join the others in an evolving democracy. Employing our earlier criteria, it is clear that González Casanova has generally taken a *diffusionist position because he acknowledges the existence of feudalism and a dual society; he advocates the formation of a national bourgeoisie; and he analyzes the ruling class in terms of pluralist elite which exercises decision-making which is independent of foreign influences.* He sees remnants of feudalism or semi-feudalism in the marginal populations. Further evidence that Mexico is pre-capitalist, in his view, is that there are two societies, nearly mutually exclusive one from the other. One is dominant and participating with access to salaried labor, to credits and investments, and with an

ability to manifest demands through organization of the political economy —indicators of an evolving democracy. The other society, dominated and marginal, is isolated; it has no organizations, no rights, and no intermediaries through which it can pressure for resolution of its problems. A kind of ruling class duminates over the participating society; its decisions favoring stability and the status quo ensure its economic well-being. In turn, the stable participating society is held together by a highly centralized institutional framework within which a pluralism of interests is represented by different power groups. An expansion of these democratic, tendencies along with the evolution of capitalism will break down the existing dichotomy of societies and classes. National integration will be achieved through the molding of a new bourgeoisie which will confront foreign domination and ensure a controlled internal capitalist growth. Mexican development in the form of political democracy and economic progress will thus occur under the leadership of a national bourgeoisie which will absorb both the proletariat and the ruling class.

In contrast to this diffusionist perspective, the dependency model would interpret Mexican political economic history in a different context: feudalism probably never existed in any dominant form, and there was no dual society; a national bourgeoisie was not fully evolved and in any event could not have successfully promoted significant autonomous development; and the ruling class, while comprised of many diversified segments and politically nationalistic, nevertheless economically, culturally, and socially had much in common with its foreign counterparts and therefore could not function independently in the interests of the nation. In rebutting the interpretation of González Casanova, Frank (1969A, Ch. 20), argues that since "the arrival of Cortés a single and integral society was rapidly formed—totally integrated, furthermore, into the world system of mercantile expansion and capitalist development." He demonstrates that the so-called marginal areas were once integrated with the more advanced center around Mexico City. Indeed the core of the regional and national market was tied to the world economy—tied to worldwide demand for gold and silver. But reduction in production of these commodities, coupled with a simultaneous demand for luxury goods by the prosperous classes, produced an economic depression and a decline in the outlying areas—the consequence was uneven development. Further, the prevailing metropolis-satellite relationships acknowledged by González Casanova preclude an existence of a dual society; the Indians were never outside the market economy, although they are poor, dominated, and discriminated against. Thus, internal colonialism exists but in a different form. The emphasis of González Casanova on political, social, and cultural relations ignores the fact that internal colonialism also has economic ramifications. Its ties are to the outside world. Capitalism in Mexico ensures that nation's integration into the world economic order while generating capitalist underdevelopment at home.

ARGENTINA AND IMAZ

Imaz deals almost exclusively with a detailed analysis of who rules in Argentina. Like González Casanova, Imaz speaks of a ruling class, and his ruling class has a variety of power bases—in the executive branch of government, the armed forces, the land owners, entrepreneurs, church, and professional politicians; and he even has a chapter on labor leaders. His focus on elites is particularly useful since the question of power in Argentina often has been obscured by interpretations that examine populism as manifested by Peronismo and the organized labor movement or through the Radical Party as responses to industrialization in the early twentieth century. The question of power has been clouded also by stress on an apparent pluralism in the Argentine multi-party system. Then too, military intervention on numerous occasions since 1930 has resulted in misleading interpretations. Let us briefly examine the argument in Imaz' *Los que mandan* and then determine to what extent his conclusions are related to diffusionist or dependency perspectives.

1. Imaz believes that "a complete ruling class" existed under General Agustín P. Justo from 1936 to 1943. This ruling class was a socially cohesive group restricted by such membership criteria as personal relationships, family position, and club affiliations. One belonged in government by right of ascription and the foremost criterion for high office was business ability or legal capacity. This ruling class operated at top and intermediate levels of government and its dominance via machine politics was assured by electoral fraud and the apolitical stance of the armed forces.

2. While there must always be an elite in the sense of individuals who command, Imaz affirms that today there is no longer a ruling elite in Argentina. There is a "nominal" elite, an aggregate of individuals who hold the highest positions and head the basic institutions, but there is no real elite or group of individuals who "act in concert, lead the community, direct it with a view to achieving certain ends and objectives, and accept approximately similar normative frameworks."

3. This nominal elite is still largely the "old" elite of large landowners that ruled until 1943 and regained control in 1956 after the fall of Juan Perón, and it has continued in that position. In hopes of obtaining the backing of the old elite, the holders of political power usually have surrendered control over the economic and financial system. Thus the upper

class maintains control of certain strategic economic and governmental sectors. Judges and diplomats usually are recruited from their ranks as well.

4. The old elite permitted a "circulation of elites" which presented them with difficulties as a "new" upper class became inflexible in the face of reform. While the "old" members extended the voting franchise to the whole population, the "new" members resisted such change, a crisis ensued, thereby provoking their replacement by a completely different group led by the Peronistas.

5. The entrepreneurial elite comprises members of the well-to-do bourgeoisie, foreigners serving their native corporations as managers or representatives, and immigrants of humble origins. They seem not to have been active in public life nor does their economic prestige seem to ensure them a place in the upper class. The power of the foreign entrepreneurs is limited because they fail to identify with the national interests. In general, the entrepreneurial elite lacks unity due to diversity of interests, personal and group conflicts, and different national origins.

6. These weaknesses among the landowning and entrepreneurial elites have produced a leadership crisis: "a whole generation of leaders has failed" as a consequence of an evolving complex society and the lack of a base for ruling a modern nation-state. This base can only be built with the escape from Argentina's present pre-capitalist stage of development.

Clearly there are important differences between Imaz and González Casanova. The latter advocates the formation of a national bourgeoisie, the former a ruling class. Does Imaz' orientation therefore move him away from the weaknesses in diffusionist interpretations? We think not, for a number of reasons. First, Imaz, like González Casanova, places Argentina in a pre-capitalist stage of development. Capitalism in the hands of competent leadership will lead Argentina toward modernization; the prescription is growth by stages, through an evolutionary process. His position implies that a cohesive ruling group will be able to exercise independent decisions leading Argentina along the path of development. While Imaz is aware of foreign influence upon the Argentine political economy, he tends to underestimate its significance. Nowhere does he discuss the possible collusion of domestic clientele classes and foreign elites; nor does he offer insights into the obstacles created by foreign capital: for example, decapitalization caused by high profit remuneration or interference in politics such as that advocated by ITT to prevent Chilean President Salvador Allende from taking office in 1970. As is true of González Casanova's analysis, Imaz' emphasis upon a contemporary pre-capitalist society suggests the possibility of a dual society;

dominant and marginal, elites and masses, and so on; but he does not explore this conceptualization. Nor does he discuss in detail the meaning of pre-capitalism; one can only infer that he assumes the existence of a feudal society. His stress on political power perhaps has unconsciously led him to skirt this important question. Then too, Imaz' concept of elite is confusing. The English translation of his work jumps from ruling class to governing elite to circulating elite; the ruling class of one historical period becomes a nominal elite in another time. In an appendix, Imaz acknowledges his preference for the use of "ruling categories" rather than "ruling class." It is clear that Imaz intended to deal not with classes but with groups at an elite level. His pluralistic framework stresses functionalism and specialization as a society modernizes. He expresses this diffusionist ideal (suggested by Max Weber and later emphasized by Talcott Parsons): "The more modern, the freer, the more pluralistic the society, the more varied the aspects and the more complex the number of interests, ideologies, and world views to be articulated." Finally, Imaz is distressed at the failure of leadership, essentially in the middle class whose prospects are not good: "the great majority of producers have ended by abdicating in favor of large landed interests." The middle sectors are weak and unstable. Factionalism in Argentine politics and weaknesses in the economy produce destabilizing and anti-democratic tendencies within the middle sectors; thus military rule occasionally is necessary to stabilize society. Yet he despairs of the fact that "neither the middle classes nor the army is acting in a vacuum but within the frame of a dominant culture that is still controlled by the traditional upper class." Somehow, while not explicitly advocated, we sense that Imaz is counting on the rise to power of a new bourgeoisie to fill the vacuum left by the nominal elite and the weakened middle class. He may label it a new ruling class, but it sounds suspiciously like the national bourgeoisie envisaged by González Casanova.

We conclude therefore that *Imaz' argument is essentially diffusionist: his notion of elite is diffused in pluralistic politics; his identification of Argentina as pre-capitalist suggests a dual society; and his advocacy of a new class implies some sort of technocratic, modern-oriented, and centralized ruling group that will lead Argentina along a continuum of development.* It is our feeling that if Imaz were to incorporate a critique of dependency into his discussion, that his analysis would be more focused, new questions might be raised, and new interpretations be offered. For example, his analysis concerns power, primarily as a political phenomenon and only cursorily does it examine the relationship of industrial to agrarian interests, their linkages and their impact on political and economic decisions. While we are not certain that his interpretation incorporates the notion of a dual society, likewise we have few clues as to any interaction between rural and urban life. One problem is that these diverse interests are examined within institutional frameworks such as agrarian and industrial societies. Yet he offers some provocative facts: of 82 family groups with land of more than 25,000 acres, 56 bear names of members of the upper class of the city of Buenos Aires. Large property owning families also tend to control agricultural corporations. The old oligarchy participated in establishing the industrial union and the industrial bank. Viewing Argentina within the context of dependency theory might have led to investigation of the impact of foreign influence upon the domestic political economy. To suggest, as does Imaz, that the managers of the great foreign corporations do not identify with the country where they live because decisions are made elsewhere by their boards of directors may be misleading; at least his evidence is inconclusive. Other analyses might have examined the interrelationships between middle and upper classes. Then too, there might have been some discussion of the military and industrial interests; the military is known to be involved in industrial enterprise. To what extent is this a consequence of middle class instability?—of collaboration between classes? We agree that Imaz' book is provocative and interesting. It definitely is a contribution to an understanding of Argentina. Yet its shortcomings lie with vague conceptualization, a diffusionist emphasis on elites and classes, and a framework resulting in some weak conclusions.

PERU AND QUIJANO

The military regime which came to power in Peru in 1968 has been involved in restructuring the country along lines advocated explicitly by González Casanova and implicitly by Imaz: that is, molding a cohesive national bourgeoisie which, guided by the state, will promote development while containing the dominance of foreign economic and political influence. Aníbal Quijano carefully analyzes recent events in Peru and offers criticism which shatters the illusion that the regime's objectives will readily be achieved in the near future. Like González Casanova and Imaz, Quijano examines the strengths and weaknesses of the social class structure in his country, but he also relates the nature of class relations to the outside world. *His analytical framework is based on the dependency model. He is not concerned with a dual society but instead places emphasis upon the interrelationships among social classes within Peru and upon their relations with interests outside the country. He sees the Peruvian military regime as guided by an ideology of class reconciliation (combining interests of workers and capitalist enterprise) and of limited nationalism within an imperialist order; and he concludes that in the absence of any ability to fight for independent power or historic national interests a small nationalist bourgeoisie is unlikely to be capable of eliminating imperialist domination.* Let us examine his argument in more detail, and then assess its usefulness.

1. Quijano begins by relating conditions in Peru to the general situation in Latin America. Presently in Latin America, imperialist domination is characterized by two overlapping and contradictory models: one being "traditional imperialism," with the United States as the hegemonic power operating through enterprises totally controlled by foreign capital, and the other, in effect since the Second World War, "consisting of a progressive shift in the axis of domination from agro-extractive sectors to the urban-industrial sector." This shift accompanied economic, political, and social changes; the power of the old oligarchies declined but did not disappear; new groups such as white collar workers and the petty bourgeoisie began to assert their demands; and an industrial proletariat expanded in the cities and peasant movements emerged in the countryside. These changes produced "the crisis of oligarchic hegemony," that is, the actions of the new bourgeoisie became moderate and indecisive in the face of an oligarchy whose bases of power were declining too slowly while at the same time threatened by a popular revolution. There ensued a crisis of legitimacy of bourgeois domination, a fragmentation of power which could be controlled generally only by the armed forces which was well-organized and held decisive power.

2. In Peru, before the 1950s, foreign domination over the economy was held through control of agro-extractive resources. Thereafter foreign penetration of mining increased and capital began to flow into industrial production. Since this "erratic and mixed" process was dependent on foreign capital, "it exemplifies a combination of old and new patterns of imperialist control: the appearance of new imperialist bourgeois interests with different ties to native bourgeois groups over and above those already existing between foreign capital and the agricultural and cattle-raising sectors of the native bourgeoisie." Thus ended the era of domination based on "the alliance between the native landholding-commercial bourgeoisie and the imperialist bourgeoisie."

3. After coming to power in 1968, the military junta tried to end foreign control of production in agricultural exports as well as in mining and petroleum while simultaneously strengthening the role of foreign and domestic capital in the urban-industrial sector. By expropriating the property of landholders and making payment in an amount which must be invested in a new industrial plant, the regime's policy was "to convert agrarian capitalists into industrial capitalists." The state would control

"basic industry" and private companies (generally international and supranational monopolies) would control manufacturing. The new arrangement would not eliminate dependency, however. The state becomes stronger, more efficient, and better organized, but its ties to a network of "imperialist" monopolies "presupposes that it is less national than before."

4. The Peruvian ruling class has always been a dependent bourgeoisie, but the recent reforms of the military junta have made it a less homogeneous bourgeoisie, the consequence of declining power in the landholding sector and the growing importance of the urban industrial groups. Quijano breaks this class into groups: an upper landholding bourgeoisie, residing along the coast and responsible for agricultural exports and not directly under the control of foreign companies; a middle level landholding bourgeoisie, located in the Sierra and owners of agricultural resources producing for the domestic market, an upper industrial bourgeoisie wholly dependent on foreign investment, and a middle level industrial bourgeoisie, diversified with meager financial resources. Financial and family ties bind these sectors together and the landholding sector played a large role in banking and commerce, industry, mining, and petroleum.

5. The regime proclaims the new order will replace capitalism and at the same time preclude socialism; they describe this order as "nationalist," "humanist," and "communitarian." However, the new order has strengthened state capitalism in basic industry and in trade of agro-extractive products. Large autonomous state enterprises control these areas. The new order has also strengthened the dependent bourgeoisie which nevertheless remains in alliance with the "imperialist bourgeoisie" and "subordinate to the more decisive alliance between the latter and the state." Quijano concludes "that there is absolutely no question here of eliminating imperialist investment . . . under the formal limits established by the law, the margins of imperialist participation are sufficient to assure it a dominant position in the country's economy, even though it may be subject to state supervision."

Our identification of Quijano's argument offers only a glimpse at his sophisticated analysis, and although our discussion is not conclusive, it should be immediately clear to the reader that his analytic framework, closely tied to theory that posits a dependent relationship to the outside world, offers in-depth perspectives not usually generated in diffusionist-oriented analysis. Rather than reiterating the belief of many scholars that two societies persist in Peru (feudal and capitalist, agrarian and industrial, oligarchic and bourgeois), interrelationships between these sectors are carefully identified and empirically verified. Rather than assuming that the consolidation of a national bourgeoisie will resolve Peru's developmental problems, he examines its weaknesses and contradictions.

Rather than interpreting domination as the consequence of a monolithic ruling class, he reveals the diversified nature of this class and identifies the bonds between the different elements. Rather than assuming that development is the natural consequence of a regime that professes national independence, he looks carefully at economic policy that reinforces dependent relations with outside nations. Thus, internal conditions are directly related to external influences, and the contradictions of the military regime are clearly exposed.

Our discussion thus far has tried to establish the usefulness of the dependency model as a critique of the old and new political economic orders in Latin America. The assumption has been that most of Latin America is bound by its dependent relationship to the capitalist world, to the United States in particular. We have argued that dependency as a reflection of imperialism has contributed to the persistence of underdevelopment in Latin America. What then are the prospects for nations that strive to break their dependent relations with the outside world? In recent times, only three nations have moved in such a direction. The efforts of Peru have already been discounted by Quijano. Chile, in a transition from capitalism to socialism, has made considerable advances by gaining control over most of the foreign held interests, but with the ouster of the Allende government these may be invalid. Cuba is perhaps the most interesting example of a nation that has broken its dependent ties to the capitalist world. Having broken these ties, Cuba has attempted to solve some of its problems of underdevelopment. Its concerns involved the elimination of individual alienation and the building of a collectivity. Indeed, Cuba found itself building a new society.

IV

BEYOND DEPENDENCY: TOWARD A CLASSLESS SOCIETY

The following discussion is purposely tentative and brief. It is our intention to direct the reader to a series of important concerns to which societies attempting to break with dependency must address themselves. It is our belief that the struggle must be toward the ideals of a classless society, involving at least four fundamental problems: alienation, consumption, work incentives, and the formation of the "new person" in a collectivity. We address ourselves to each of these problems, and where relevant, we make reference to the experience of the Cuban revolution.

Alienation. In a work familiar to students of the American scene, Herbert Marcuse (1968:7) has identified the distinguishing feature of advanced industrial society as the "effective suffocation of those needs which demand liberation—liberation also from that which is tolerable and rewarding and comfortable—while it sustains and absolves the destructive power and repressive function of the affluent society." Among these needs are "the overwhelming need for the production and consumption of waste; the need for stupefying work where it is no longer a real necessity; the need for modes of relaxation which soothe and prolong this stupefication; the need for maintaining such deceptive liberties as free competition at administered prices, a free press which censors itself, free choices between brands and gadgets." For Marcuse, liberty becomes "a powerful instrument of domination." At the root of his discussion is an explanation for the condition of alienation that exists not only among advanced industrial societies, but among less advanced societies as well. Karl Marx put it well when he described work as external to the worker who "does not fulfill himself in his work but denies himself, has a feeling of misery rather than well being, does not develop freely his mental and physical energies but is physically exhausted and mentally debased." Alienation from work, says Marx, is characterized by the worker who "does not belong to himself but to another person" (Quotes in Fromm, 1961:98–99). Specifically, alienation takes many forms. Often the worker is powerless, unable to control the work process or to attain self-fulfillment and self-expression. The worker is unable to influence policies of management, and unable to control conditions of employment. Then too work is often meaningless where tasks are specialized and standardized (on an assembly line where the worker has no sense of the total production process). The worker is often isolated by division of labor (uprooted from local organization or membership in a community). Finally, the worker is alienated from himself by the work process which he finds boring—there is little possibility for personal growth.

Alienation does not disappear with a definitive break in dependent relations with the capitalist world, as was the case in Cuba's estrangement from the United States in the early sixties. Nor does alienation disappear automatically with the nationalization of the principal means of production, shifting from private ownership to ownership by the state, as was also the case in Cuba and among some other nations advocating socialism. According to Belgian economist Ernest Mandel (1968, II:680), alienation "disappears only when individuals feel *consciously and spontaneously* the owners of the products of their labour and the masters of their conditions of labour." This is achieved by eliminating the social divisions of labor through abolishment of routine work, active participation of people in the management of their society, and human solidarity. In effect the traditional sense of labor would be eliminated gradually through a process of the humanization of people in a "continual enrichment of everything human, an all-round development of all facets of humanity." This process would also evolve new understanding of the commodity, of value, of money, and of classes.

Changing Patterns of Consumption. Ideally, the problem of alienation would be resolved through a new understanding of "a classless egalitarian society, a society of abundance for all, a society in which everyone would be free and able to develop as a whole human being" (Huberman and Sweezy, 1969:155). But how do we achieve such a society? Even in a country as rich as the United States, it would not be possible to provide for the entire population the consumer products available to a wealthy minority.

A central theme of the Cuban Revolution is anti-consumerism. In opposition to the concept of success as individual advancement, the goal of the revolution is a classless society in which each person contributes to society and benefits as development is achieved. Individual material payment as an incentive to work is de-emphasized in favor of the satisfaction of contributing to national development. Recognizing that an underdeveloped country cannot provide more than basic necessities for its population while creating and·investing surplus for future development, the revolution is committed to assuring at least a minimally sufficient material standard of living for the entire population. While income differences are still rather large, luxury consumer goods are not available for purchase. Cubans travel by bus, not by private automobile. Economic gains are not distributed to a few in the form of super consumption. Instead, an increasing variety of goods and services (local telephone calls, admission to sports events, housing) are made available either free or without reference to income. Rather than being subjected to wave after wave of radio and television messages designed to create intense desire for individual products and consumption in general, Cubans are encouraged to find satisfaction in contributing to their society.

The anti-consumerism of the Cuban Revolution is directly related to the desire to eliminate vestiges of the hierarchical class structure that prevailed prior to 1959. The Cuban leadership moved quickly to eliminate the availability of luxury goods, even to those who had money to buy them. At the outset of the revolution, class disparities were lessened by the provision of new jobs, guaranteed prices, and higher rural wages —measures which increased the demand for many consumer goods such as milk and meat. A rationing system was imposed to assure an equitable distribution of needed resources among the people, and the government increased investment, eventually up to a third of national income in the attempt to restructure the economy for diversification and increased production. There was also an increase in the allocation of needed resources among the people, especially in education (through the literacy program of 1961 and expansion of school programs at all levels) and in health (through expansion of medical facilities and services), and in other services such as recreation and cultural activities. This allocation was accompanied by a reallocation of resources, especially from the city to countryside where rural conditions were improved through agrarian reform. (For detailed analysis of changing patterns of consumption in Cuba, see Barkin, 1972.)

Work Incentives. Changing consumption patterns were accompanied by a deemphasis on efficiency, a value which in capitalist societies like the United States or in socialist societies like the Soviet Union takes precedence over values of life (the building of a dam in a beautiful valley, for instance, might be considered economically more significant than the preservation of an aesthetic value). Likewise, equitable distribution of scarce resources to all people rather than to those who could afford them tended to undermine the belief of some people that hard work and maximized production would assure access to more things. Under such circumstances it was difficult for privileged groups and classes to dominate Cuban society.

These anti-elitist policies were related to a decision to deemphasize material incentives in favor of moral incentives, an approach originally advocated by Ché Guevara and formally adopted by Fidel Castro in a speech of August 26, 1966. Workers would contribute to the development of the nation rather than produce for their own personal gain. Monetary and other material incentives such as extra pay, vacations, and the like, would be reduced and eventually eliminated in favor of titles, awards and special recognition. Education and emulation campaigns would encourage workers to aspire to *conciencia*, the conscious commitment to the revolution itself. The stress was on "a nonmarket decentralist mode of resource allocation based on feelings of group solidarity as manifested in the socially approved competition for social status based on prizes and titles of all kinds" (Bernardo, 1970–1971:119). The new work ethic was the worker's desire to serve society, not himself. This relentless pursuit of egalitarianism necessitated personal sacrifices, including reduced consumption for those who had been well off and increased production. It was accompanied by a change in the motivations of people, by a new outlook which accepted the proposition that money does not determine choices about life, including the quality of life, food, clothing, and other material benefits. With money no longer a major determinant in assuring access to education and culture, education became available to the masses of Cubans at all levels. Education in the school was mixed with work in the field, a sort of combination of theory and practice signifying action and involvement in everyday affairs. Furthermore, the objective was to mix people (country and city people, old and young, bureaucrats and field workers, and so on) directly in the production process. Rather than being a competent cane cutter, the Cuban farmer would also understand how sugar actually reaches the dinner table. Motivations to work were based on considerations other than income. One's personal investment was in a cause, the development of Cuba. Cubans seemed determined to do something about alienation. Their work had to be an expression or enjoyment of themselves. They would receive benefits of their production. They would establish a society with no top or bottom. (For perhaps the best discussion of this thrust in Cuban society see Bernardo, 1970–1971 and 1970.)

The New Person in the Collectivity. Elimination of alienation, modification of consumption patterns, and promotion of moral incentives in the drive toward an egalitarian and classless society have been closely related to the formation of the "new" person. Such a concern has preoccupied some observers of socialist society outside Cuba. Among the rapidly growing studies on the subject are works by Polish philosophers Leszek Kolakowski (1968) and Adam Schaff (1965), and John Gurley has focused on the question as related to China (1970).

In Cuba, Ché Guevara helped to initiate discussion on the role of woman and man in a collective society:

> It is not a question of how many kilograms of meat are eaten or how many times a year someone may go on holiday to the seashore or how many pretty imported things can be bought with present wages. It is rather that the individual feels greater fulfillment, that he has greater inner wealth and many more responsibilities. In our country the individual knows that the glorious period in which it has fallen to him to live is one of sacrifice; he is familiar with sacrifice. (Guevara, 1967:42–43)

This view was reinforced by Fidel Castro in his March 13, 1968, speech in which he announced the nationalization of small commercial establishments, affirming that "the concept of a higher society, implies a man devoid of those feelings [of individualism]; a man who has overcome such instincts at any cost; placing, above everything, his sense of solidarity and brotherhood among men (see Silverman, 1971, for various Cuban views on this question as related to the other concerns we have discussed above). Cuba is pursuing the formulation of what we shall call the "new person" as the basis for the collective society. In theory the characteristics of this new person have been suggested by a black observer, Dan Aldridge (1969); his ideas are useful in assessing the impact of the concept upon Cuban and any other society. According to Aldridge, the development of the new person is the primary task of the revolution: "Our revolution must produce the most politically conscious and socially responsible human being possible." As to the character of that human being:

1. He is "completely devoid of all vestiges of selfishness, individuality, egotism, and 'me-firstness.'"
2. His individual development, his energy and work "lead him to tasks for the benefit of the collective."
3. His basis of morality is the struggle against injustice: "His human sensibilities have been developed to the point where he can deal efficiently with everyday problems. His social sensibilities have been developed to the point where he is willing to struggle against the exploitation of man by man and the division of society into classes."
4. He is willing to fight to the death in the daily political struggle. He understands what the struggle is and he is not afraid.
5. He is "rebellious, heroic, and studious." He continuously analyzes problems and seeks their solutions. He is disciplined. He understands that the revolution has rights: the right to exist, the right to advance, the right to triumph.

It has not been our intention here to demonstrate that the notion of the new person is a reality in Cuba today, but to suggest a framework for understanding a central thrust of a contemporary revolution that, first, has broken successfully with a dominant capitalist system that had shaped Cuba's dependent relations with the outside world and, second, is striving to formulate a new humanistic and collective order. In this regard, the Cuban Revolution is certainly unique to Latin America. A precedent has been established in the struggle with dependency. But what of the rest of Latin America? What are the prospects?

V PROSPECTS FOR THE STRUGGLE AGAINST DEPENDENCY

Development in Latin America, understood to include political and economic independence, requires that existing political and economic relationships undergo radical change. It is clear that the power of U.S. corporations engaged in foreign activities will resist this change. Profit rates on U.S. operations in Latin America are far higher than profits on domestic investment. Control of Latin American resources through

ownership and lack of competition among the limited number of purchasers of Latin American products result in high profits on imports to
the United States. North American exporters to Latin America enjoy
monopoly power in many areas, resulting in high prices. Moreover,
operations of North American business within other nations is growing
at a much higher rate than domestic business.

Socialism in Latin America would likely mean an end to all direct
private foreign investment. Profits on trade would be reduced since the
monopoly and monopsony power of the multinational corporations would
be broken. Foreign control of Latin American resources and markets, a
goal often as important as immediate profits to North American firms
would be out of the question, even if limited or indirect participation
were permitted. Nevertheless, even concern for the loss of opportunities
for future growth and super profits did not cause the corporations to put
their resources into a struggle to maintain the status quo; the prospect
of nationalization of existing holdings would itself be sufficient.

The U.S. economy is characterized by oligopoly. In virtually all major
industries over 80 percent of production is carried out by three or four
firms. The largest domestic corporations are also dominant in foreign
investment and in production of military equipment used to maintain
the imperial system, areas which are even more concentrated than domestic enterprise in general.

In capitalist systems, economic power is the source of political power.
Electoral campaigns require resources available only to those who have
the support of a significant segment of the owners of corporate wealth.
The pursuit of profit and growth is the normal (and unavoidable) behavior of the capitalist firm. Since U.S. policy, particularly foreign policy,
is determined by a corporate consensus in favor of maintaining and
expanding foreign operations, imperialism must be viewed as a natural
product of our political economic system.

Nonetheless, change can come about. Though the particular ways in
which socialist governments achieved power in Chile and Cuba are not
likely to be repeated, other Latin American nations may break out of
the imperialist system. Also, we may speculate that change will arise
within the United States in response to economic recession and unemployment and dissatisfaction with the existing system's ability to deal with
severe social and environmental problems. In the latter case, change in
U.S. relations with Latin America would be part of defeating corporate
power toward a broader restructuring of North American society. Even
though imperialism is a systematic property of the monopoly capitalist
system, it is useful to consider the implications of an end of empire for
the U.S. economy and the North American people.

In *The Age of Imperialism,* one of the most valuable books on the subject, Harry Magdoff (1969) states:

"Students frequently put the question: Is imperialism necessary? . . . . Such a question is off the mark. Imperialism is not a matter of choice for a capitalist society; it is the way of life for such a society." (1969:26)

We agree in the sense that the class in power benefits from imperialism and will not willingly yield. But if, in spite of the exercise of U.S. power, revolution throughout Latin America were successful, what would the consequences be? While lower corporate profits would directly affect owners of corporate stock and bonds, over 80 percent of corporate stock and 88.5 percent of corporate bonds are owned by a group consisting of only 1.6 percent of the North American population (Lundberg, 1968: 13). This group is so wealthy that its ability to consume would be affected little if at all by a lower return on investment.

For the overwhelming majority of North Americans, the implications of socialism in Latin America are unclear. The major problem of the U.S. economy is a tendency toward stagnation—unemployment and unused plant capacity (Baran and Sweezy, 1966: *passim*). Because of the lack of price competition, cost cutting technological advances in the United States have resulted in higher profits for the large corporations because they have not been forced by competition to pass savings onto workers and consumers. These surplus profits are available for investment, but a demand sufficient to provide profitable investment opportunities to absorb surplus is not generated spontaneously. Although government spending, motivational advertising and waste serve to stimulate demand and to absorb some of the surplus, the economy is characterized by a persistent tendency toward stagnation.

Exports provide one possibility for absorbing production which U.S. workers cannot buy. Purchase of this excess abroad opens up opportunities for investment and jobs within the United States. Those who argue the importance of imperialism to the United States point to purchases of U.S. products in the Third World as one way in which our economy benefits. Opponents of this perspective respond that exports are insignificant (less than 5 percent) in relation to the U.S. GNP. However, the appropriateness of comparing exports to GNP is in dispute, since the Gross National Product includes government expenditures, personal and professional services, trade, and activities of banks, real estate firms, and stock brokers. In relation to the output of U.S. farms, factories and mines, exports are far more significant.

Regardless of how significant exports are for the economy now, the future of exports to a socialist Latin America represents an equally important question. Trade with Cuba was stopped by the U.S. government in an attempt to undermine the revolutionary government. The United States has engaged in trade and even provided military assistance to at least nominally socialist countries (e.g., Yugoslavia) for many years. Recent arrangements with the Soviet Union and openings toward China should destroy any lingering doubt about the possibility of trade with socialist nations. Though loss of U.S. monopoly power would result in lower profits on exports, and though some industries, such as shipping which might not be able to operate at competitive rates, would be destroyed, Latin America would still be in need of much that is produced in the United States. Of course, we are not suggesting that prevailing trade patterns would continue forever. Lower prices in Latin America for U.S. goods would be one benefit of the overthrow of imperialist penetration and the resultant savings would be important in the Latin American development effort. As these efforts succeed eventual diversification of production would require a drastic change in trade patterns. The U.S. economy has been oriented to appropriating primary products from other nations and exporting finished goods. As the nations of Latin America escaped from dependence on selling these resources to acquire what they cannot presently manufacture, the U.S. economy would have to be shaped to match the new situation. However, initially development must be built on the distorted economies created in the imperialist period. In the course of development, needs for industrial equipment and other sophisticated products increase. Higher prices for Latin American exports would enable these nations to purchase more foreign products. The U.S. economy would benefit from this market to the extent that goods could be offered at prices competitive with those of other industrial nations.

It is easy to see the relationship of North American exports to employment levels in the United States. The impact of eliminating restraints on competition for internal U.S. markets is equally clear. North American political and economic power has been used to prevent competition of foreign manufacturers with U.S. enterprise. While most primary products can now be imported duty free into the United States if they are in a raw or unprocessed state, a wide variety of tariffs and restrictions are in effect on the same products if they have been processed. Other ways of restricting competitive imports are also employed. For example, the U.S. government pressured Brazil (reportedly through threats to cut Brazil's aid allocation) to impose an export tax on Brazilian powdered coffee. Using cheap broken coffee beans, Brazil had been able to take over about 14 percent of the U.S. instant-coffee market. Political pressure was thus used to destroy the advantage of Brazilian producers (Magdoff, 1969:163).

The effect of radical change in inter-American economic patterns on markets for U.S. goods both in Latin America and in the United States is of direct significance because demand is important for the U.S. economy. Sufficient surplus for investment is continuously generated. An additional potential for creating surplus exists, requiring only a growth in demand which would make additional investment profitable. Predictions regarding the impact of radical change on internal and Latin American markets for U.S. goods requires a weighing of the factors discussed above.

Two other areas require consideration and both are still more problematic. First, what would be the domestic effect of the loss of the opportunity for direct private foreign investment? Opportunities for foreign investment have been viewed as an escape valve for surplus capital. However, while initial investment usually creates a net capital outflow and absorption of excess capital, today the growth of U.S. holdings abroad is financed by profits earned on foreign operations and by capital raised locally in the host country and abroad from government loans and from foreign private banks. As we noted above, repatriated profits are far larger than new investments of U.S. capital going abroad. Thus, foreign investment aggregates the problem of surplus capital in the United States. Two other considerations are worthy of note. Though profit on foreign operations is equal to more than 25 percent of profit on domestic enterprise, U.S. capital invested abroad is well under 10 percent of domestic investment. Second, while direct private investment would likely not be permitted by socialist governments in Latin America, the development efforts of these nations would probably provide vast opportunities for long term, low interest untied loans.

Finally, the impact on the U.S. economy of loss of control of Latin American mineral resources must be considered. In the twentieth century the United States has become an importer of both rare and common minerals. The United States does not have some minerals and supplies of others have been reduced or exhausted. At the same time, requirements of our economy have increased. Consequently, U.S. imports of iron ore equal more than 40 percent of domestic production, of oil about a third of domestic production and imports of lead and zinc more than 130 percent of domestic production. Regarding strategic materials such as chromium, nickel, columbium and cobalt, dependence on imports is still greater. Most of these minerals are imported from the Third World, but not from Latin America. If confronted with socialist governments throughout the Third World, it is likely that the United States could continue to acquire these materials though at somewhat higher prices than currently are paid, at least in the immediate period of Third World development. Higher prices for imported minerals would also stimulate domestic production from low grade ore reserves which exist within the United States but which are not currently profitable due to the availability of cheap foreign high grade ore. Longer range considerations regarding resources are more problematic. We will touch upon this subject below.

The impact of the rise of socialism and the end of imperialism in Latin America exhibits a commanding importance of foreign operations for North American corporate owners. We observed that change would only come with the defeat of corporate, financial power, either through successful revolution in the nations of Latin America or through radical political change within the United States. In all probability the process of being forced out of Latin America by revolutionary movements and governments would bring about very significant political change. However, assuming no dramatic change, a weighing of the considerations discussed above does not yield a clear projection of how the material standard of living for the non-stock owning majority of North Americans would be affected by revolution in Latin America.

If the end of empire were brought about by or associated with the defeat of corporate power within the U.S., a majority of North Americans would benefit. In terms of material standard of living, the poorest 60 percent of the population which now receives approximately one third of the total personal income would benefit from income redistribution to a greater extent than they would lose from any negative consequences to the economy. Moreover, change in the United States would open possibilities for marked improvement in the quality of life. In this regard, instead of suppressing change in Latin America we could benefit greatly from observing and learning Latin American experimentation.

In spite of the process of underdevelopment, some social practices (for example, conjugal visits for prison inmates) only recently introduced as progressive innovations in the United States have been in use in Latin America for many years. Rather than pressing materialistic values and practices on the rest of the hemisphere exemplified by current efforts of North American advertising and communications firms, we might find value in the greater emphasis in Latin America on aesthetic and personal philosophical concerns. Both traditional and revolutionary Latin America are making contributions to the arts. For example, in recent years the Latin American novel has achieved a place alongside the French novel in the view of many critics. Clearly, current superiority in technology and wealth should not prevent the United States from being open to the values and achievements of Latin American societies.

Earlier the evolution of modern society was examined in terms of the growth of role-playing behavior and an increase in social mobility. In recent years many young people in the United States have been repulsed by role-playing and have attempted to establish community and openness as a basis of interpersonal relations. The demands of conformity, specialization, and participation in often meaningless work which success requires have been rejected in favor of spontaniety and commitment. At the center of this cultural tendency is a rejection of consumerism, an avoidance of unnecessary material goods and a refusal to be defined by one's possessions.

In his article on "Outwitting the 'Developed' Countries," Ivan Illich (1969:20–21) argues that Latin America must avoid the preoccupation with unnecessary goods and unnecessarily sophisticated products if dependence is to be overcome:

> U.S. trucks can do more lasting damage than U.S. tanks. It is easier to create mass demand for the former than for the latter. Only a minority needs heavy weapons, while a majority can become dependent on unrealistic levels of supply for such productive machines as modern trucks. Once the Third World has become a mass market for the goods, products, and processes which are designed by the rich for themselves, the discrepancy between demand for these Western artifacts and the supply will increase indefinitely . . . .

> Each car which Brazil puts on the road denies fifty good people transportation by bus. Each merchandised refrigerator reduces the chance of building a community freezer. Every dollar spent in Latin America on doctors and hospitals costs a hundred lives, ... Had each dollar been spent on providing safe drinking water, a hundred lives could have been saved. Each dollar spent on schooling means more privileges for the few at the cost of the many; at best it increases the number of those who, before dropping out, have been taught that those who stay longer have earned the right to more power, wealth, and prestige. What such schooling does is to teach the schooled the superiority of the better schooled . . . . . (1969:20–21)

While the United States is more able to provide material goods for mass consumption, a different life style less dominated by the striving for these commodities could well provide greater satisfaction and more meaningful lives for North Americans. Moreover, there are indications that natural resources such as minerals are not sufficiently abundant in the earth's crust, even allowing for technological innovation, to provide the consumption level of North America for even half of the world's population. (Eyre, 1971: *passim*) The prospect of unlimited economic growth for the United States is seriously in question. It would appear that as demand for a finite quantity of resources reaches the limits of supply, consumption in the United States will be at the expense of Third World development more directly than ever before. Increasing military force will be required to ensure the extraction of resources. Even if current consumption patterns continue, assuming that the Third World is prevented from industrializing, the viability of consumerism as a way of life is in doubt. In 1965, the United States, Europe, the USSR, Japan and South Africa used over 90 percent of world metallic copper production. U.S. industries alone consumed half the world production of aluminum, a quarter of the smelted copper, about 40 percent of the lead, over 36 percent of the nickel and zinc, and about 33 percent of the chromium. Even with control of Third World reserves and with technological innovations and some greater effort at recycling, inadequate resources or environmental pollution caused by expanded industrial production may well place limits on U.S. economic growth.

Earlier it was noted that in Cuba an effort is being made to eliminate the role of consumption as a central motivating force in favor of other values. Though for the population as a whole this goal will not be achieved in the near future, it represents one alternative to the sense of meaninglessness common in the United States and to the danger of environmental crisis through pollution or resource depletions. Cubans can pursue this course because the government has its political base in the masses of workers and peasants. The situation in the United States is far different. As a rich country, it does not need to make demands on its population which the Cuban development effort requires. However, under the control of a ruling class based on the economic power of ownership, with its population already dominated by the consumerist ethos, and with an economic system which demands mass consumption, most North Americans are not at present in a position to use lessons which the Cuban experience may offer. Nonetheless, Latin America will likely show us a variety of alternatives to our present structures and institutions. The very existence of these alternatives will be a challenge and a force for change.

RONALD H. CHILCOTE is Associate Professor of Political Science at the University of California, Riverside. Since completing his Ph.D. at Stanford University, 1965, he has focused his research and teaching concerns upon the third world and more specifically in Brazil and Portuguese Africa. He is the author of numerous monographs and articles in scholarly journals, including *Portuguese Africa* (Englewood Cliffs: Prentice Hall, 1967); *Protest and Resistance in Angola and Brazil* (Berkeley and Los Angeles: University of California Press, 1972); and *The Brazilian Communist Party: Conflict and Integration, 1922 to 1970* (New York: Oxford University Press, 1974). His current research, based on field work since 1969, involves a comparative study of ruling class power, underdevelopment, and dependency in six provincial communities of Latin America (Brazil, Chile, and Mexico).

JOEL C. EDELSTEIN currently teaches in the Concentration in Modernization Processes at the University of Wisconsin-Green Bay, offering courses on U.S. and Latin American political economy. He has published articles on these subjects in scholarly and popular journals in the United States, Mexico and Canada. He is a founder of the Union of Radical Latin Americanists, an organization of scholars devoted to influencing both the Latin American studies profession and U.S. foreign policy, and has served as editor of the *URLA Newsletter*. He earned a B.A. and an M.A. at the New School for Social Research and is currently completing a Ph.D. in political science at the University of California at Riverside, writing a dissertation on the development theory of the Cuban Revolution.

CHAPTER 1

GUATEMALA

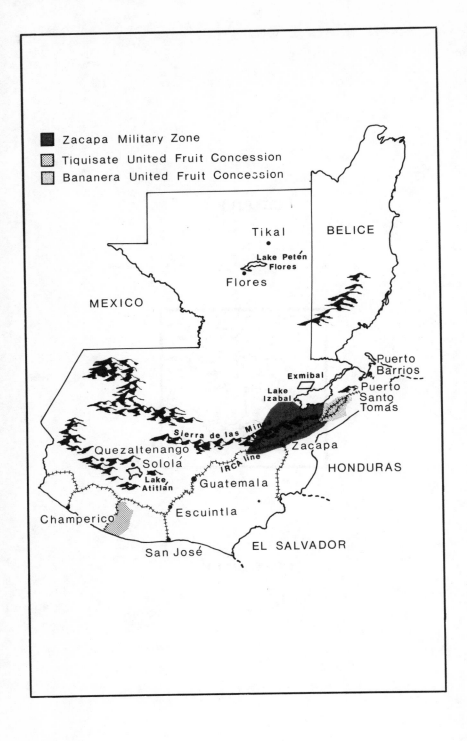

CONTENTS

GUATEMALA: LAND OF ETERNAL STRUGGLE

APOLITICAL INTELLECTUALS

One day
the apolitical
intellectuals
of my country
will be interrogated
by the simplest
of our people.

They will be asked
what they did
when their nation died out
slowly,
like a sweet fire,
small and alone.

No one will ask them
about their dress,
their long siestas
after lunch,
no one will want to know
about their sterile combats
with "the idea
of the nothing."
No one will care about
their higher financial learning.
They won't be questioned
on Greek mythology
or regarding their self-disgust
when someone within them
begins to die
the coward's death.

They'll be asked nothing
about their absurd
justifications
born in the shadow
of the total lie.

On that day
the simple men will come,
those who had no place
in the books and poems
of the apolitical intellectuals,
but daily delivered
their bread and milk,
their tortillas and eggs,
those who mended their clothes,
those who drove their cars,
who cared for their dogs and gardens
and worked for them,
                    and they'll ask:
"What did you do when the poor
suffered, when tenderness
and life
burned out in them?"

Apolitical intellectuals
of my sweet country,
you will not be able to answer.
A vulture of silence
will eat your gut.
Your own misery
will pick at your soul,
and you'll be mute
in your shame.

       — OTTO RENÉ CASTILLO*

* (Otto René Castillo, a Guatemalan poet, was tortured, imprisoned, and then exiled, as a result of his organizing activities at the national University of San Carlos. After studying abroad, he returned to Guatemala in 1966 and joined the FAR (Armed Rebel Forces). In March, 1967, his guerrilla group was ambushed and captured. After four days Castillo was put to death, and his body incinerated.)

I saw them bury a dead child
in a cardboard box
(This is true, and I don't forget it.)
On the box there was a stamp:
"General Electric Company.
Progress is our Best Product" . . .

       — Luis Alfredo Arrango
        in *Papel y Tusa*
        (Guatemala: 1967)

GUATEMALA: LAND OF ETERNAL STRUGGLE*

BY

SUSANNE JONAS**

INTRODUCTION

In the Cold War consciousness of middle America, the discovery and history of any small, underdeveloped, non-European nation dates back to the revelation that it is being threatened or taken over by International Communism. Thus Vietnam was discovered sometime after 1954, Brazil in 1964, the Dominican Republic in 1965, and so on. By this chronology, Guatemala is one of the older countries. In the early summer of 1954, the American public was informed that a valiant fraction of the Guatemalan Army, supported by the besieged propertied classes, saved Guatemala (and by implication, all Latin America) from International Communism, and reestablished a solid, stable, anti-Communist regime.

This moment of Guatemalan history and the aftermath of institutionalized violence during the 1960's have placed the country permanently on the Cold War map. In order to justify continual U.S. intervention there since 1954, State Department publicists and their social science cohorts have produced an official mythology about Guatemala which systematically distorts the causes of the country's underdevelopment and instability. Our task here is to clear away these misconceptions, and to take the first steps toward understanding the development of underdevelopment in Guatemala.

The point of departure for such an understanding must be the recognition that contemporary Guatemalan underdevelopment is the product of a 450-year process, beginning with the Spanish conquest. The colonial

* This title is inspired by the slogan of Guatemalan tourism—"Guatemala: Land of Eternal Spring."
** Susanne Jonas (Bodenheimer)

experience and the evolution of dependent capitalism since the sixteenth century set the stage for contemporary U.S. imperialism in Guatemala. As a result of these historical experiences, capitalist underdevelopment and U.S. imperialism are more accentuated and obvious, with fewer mitigating conditions, in Guatemala (and the rest of Central America) than in other Latin American countries. Guatemala provides, at the same time, a clear example of the contradictions inherent within dependent capitalism, and within the accompanying oppression on the basis of class, race, and sex.

INDIGENOUS GUATEMALA: PRE-HISTORIC SOCIETY

'GUATEMALA: LAND OF THE MAYAN GODS'

> . . . always there is the Indian, in his hand-woven costumes, whose patterns and colors follow dictates of custom that harken back to the pre-conquest glory of Mayan culture. . . . Wherever one goes in Guatemala there are reminders of Mayan culture. (*Latin American Report,* Feb. 1957:10, 14)
>
> But for really fabulous ruins, nothing can compare with the Mayan cities which dot Guatemala. . . . Tikal is one of the dozen wonders . . . in the Western hemisphere. (tourist ad.)
>
> Maya civilization, I believe, was the product of Maya character. But there was another essential ingredient—a creative minority with the imagination and mental energy to start Maya lowland civilization on its course and keep it on that course for several hundred years. (Thompson, 1954:268)

International business magazines, tourist advertisements, and textbooks all have bombarded us with an image of Guatemala based on the exotic glory yet simultaneously the pre-civilized backwardness of the country's Maya Indian origins. Romantic idealization (of the elites) and often unconscious racist denigration (of the masses) feed into each other to mystify the Guatemalan past and present. The dominant theme is a fascination with the pre-hispanic Mayan "culture" defined narrowly as "high culture," the achievements of the elites (calendars, religious monuments, art, etc.) and viewed in isolation from its roots in economic, social, and political structure. (Who would presume to understand European feudalism merely by studying Gothic architecture?) This leads, furthermore, to a perception of pre-hispanic society as homogeneous, rather than complex and socially stratified, and as static over time until the Spanish conquest, rather than dynamic and changing. It presents pre-hispanic society, in short, as folklore, rather than as history. There are several reasons for this one-sided perspective. First, with the exception of a few Mayan chronicles, Guatemala's history has been written by the conquerors and their descendants, who have redefined "culture" to suit their own interests and their own Western "culture." Second, the complexities of pre-hispanic socio-economic structure, particularly the life of the masses, have been ignored or denied because so little is known about them.

Although we are hampered here by the lack of precise information about pre-hispanic Guatemalan society and its evolution, we may call attention to a few of its most salient aspects. By almost any criterion, it would be difficult to view pre-hispanic Guatemalan society as "primitive" or "underdeveloped"—particularly in comparison with Western Europe during the same era. The material well-being of the Indians was far better before the Spanish conquest than at any time since. Most significantly, starvation and malnutrition as chronic conditions of the Indian population, as they are today, were unknown. The staple of the Mayan diet, corn, was supplemented by beans, vegetables, fruits, roots, cacao, spices and occasionally meat to make a nutritionally adequate diet (Behar, 1968:116; Wolf, 1959:63–6). Due to the custom of prolonged lactation, young children were generally strong and healthy. Compared with the diet of the average Europeans of the era, the Maya ate well (von Hagen, 1960:56); and in general, despite occasional severe famines due to drought, etc., the pre-hispanic Indians "did not have serious [nutritional] problems and were well adapted to their environmental circumstances and degree of cultural and technological development" (Behar, 1968:116). A principal reason was the population's access to sufficient land for cultivation of food—unlike today's Indians, who often must buy even their corn (to say nothing of the less nutritious refined foods), since the best land has been appropriated by a tiny minority of the population and is used to produce cash crops for export, rather than food for Guatemalans. The Indians had developed advanced medicinal treatments for illness; moreover, they did not suffer from many of the most severe diseases and epidemics which the Spaniards brought in the sixteenth century. Thus, the "integration" of the Indians into "Western culture" has been a calamity for them.

The economic basis of the society was agriculture—in cotton as well as foodstuffs. Both the land ownership patterns and the techniques of cultivation were varied. Although the concept of "private property" was alien, individual holdings (based on land *use* rather than owenrship) and concentration of wealth existed side-by-side with communal lands, worked communally or parcelled out to individuals (Guzman & Herbert, 1970:16–17; De Landa, 1937:38). (The traditions of communal property and mutual assistance remain alive in Indian regions.) Cultivation techniques varied from "slash and burn" to two-field and sophisticated intensive land use. The surplus from good seasons was stored and saved in anticipation of droughts, etc. The technology was unevenly developed, ranging from the use of irrigation and fertilizer in farming to the absence of the wheel and of domesticated animals as a work force. In addition to agriculture, the Indians engaged in metallurgy, weaving, and other artisan trades, small family "industry" (e.g., dye). In short theirs was a very diversified productive structure.

The social structure of pre-hispanic Guatemala was at least as complex as that of medieval Europe. Far from resembling primitive egalitarian communalism, it was based on a complex division of labor and specialization—including peasants, artisans, merchants, priests, and warriors. Nor did these groups coexist in equality; as we shall see, during each period Mayan society was dominated by a privileged elite, which supported itself and its "achievements" through the labor and tribute of the peasant masses. In addition to the clear division between "nobles" and commoners, there developed a limited form of slavery—private property in human labor—and a slave trade. The condition of "slavery" was somewhat flexible, insofar as it was not hereditary, and slaves could own property and work their way out of servitude (Wolf, 1959:144, 189; von Hagen, 1960:135). Nevertheless, these socio-economic cleavages, the nucleus of a proto-class society,[1] gave rise to conflicts of interest, in some cases so severe as to provoke violent struggles. Cutting across the "class" divisions, it is generally believed, was some sort of organization by clans, which served as administrative units for organizing the work and tribute payments of the commoners and whose chiefs constituted an elite. These social divisions were complemented by a marked cleavage between city and countryside. Although the particular function of the cities changed over time, the urban nuclei were generally centers of certain political, administrative, religious and military activities. In short, their functions were defined in terms of the needs of the dominant elites, not of the commoners, most of whom lived in surrounding areas.

Within this general framework, pre-hispanic society in Guatemala underwent considerable evolution. Guatemala's pre-conquest history is intimately linked to that of Mexico, since it was settled by the same Indian populations (primarily Maya) and passed through many of the same stages of development. We shall deal with two periods: the so-called "classic period" from 300 A.D. to 900 A.D. and the so-called "period of decline" from about 900 A.D. to 1524. The first major civilization in

---

[1] Whether or not this can be considered a "class" society, strictly speaking, is difficult to determine, in the absence of detailed information about the (land) property relations. Many aspects of pre-hispanic Indian society closely resembled class society, and there can be no doubt as to its socially stratified, hierarchical nature.

what is currently Guatemalan territory was centered in the Petén (lower Yucatán peninsula). Here Mayan civilization is said to have reached its height. The ruling elite during this so-called "classic" period was the priesthood. Although the source of the priests' power is generally believed to have been ideological (i.e., based on their monopoly over access to the gods and thus over men's lives), they also exercised important economic functions. These functions included control of the religious calendar which regulated agricultural activities; distribution of the agricultural surplus; allocation of land; and trade expeditions and markets.

The relation between priests and commoners was fundamental to the "classic" or "theocratic" society—most notably, its "culture." So much has been made of that "culture" in the standard works on Mayan civilization that, rather than describing it, we need only attempt to place it in its proper perspective. The art and architecture (pyramids, temples, etc.) of the "classic" period were clear expressions of the differentiation between elite and commoner—of the domination exercised by the elite for the construction of monuments to itself, based on the physical labor of the peasants. The rise of "classic" art, moreover, destroyed an earlier tradition of popular figurine art:

> The common folk are thus robbed of their ability to portray their deities or supernatural principles on their own. In contrast, the art of the tombs and temples acquires great rigor, severity, and austerity, in contrast to the more exuberant art of the folk (Wolf, 1959:84).

Similarly, the hierarchy of theocratic society was reflected in the nature of the cities and their relation to the surrounding areas where the people lived. The cities, such as Tikal, served primarily as religious ceremonial centers, and as the locus of economic and political power concentrated in the hands of the priesthood. Insofar as the Maya lowlands during the "classic" period were a "loose federation of autonomous city states" (Thompson, 1954:81), the inter-city relations were relations among elites. This imbalance "between holy town and hinterland"—not unlike that imbalance today—meant that "ultimately the towns grew wealthy and splendid because the countryside labored and produced" (Wolf, 1959: 108).

The degree to which theocratic society was based on domination by an elite, even exploitation of the masses, is suggested by the way in which that society "fell" around the tenth century. Numerous explanations have been given, ranging from theories about exhaustion of the soil and declining agricultural productivity to epidemics to inter-elite power struggles. Least explored has been an equally likely theory: a revolt of the peasants, who had for centuries borne the burden of a ruling class and its "parasitic ceremonial centers." Evidence for this hypothesis has been found in the ruins of the religious monuments and stellae in such theocratic centers as Tikal, smashed deliberately *not* by the Spanish armies, but several hundred years earlier by the masses—"a sort of razing of the Bastille" (Thompson, 1954:89). Wolf (1959:108-9) suggests that what occurred was a typical rebellion of the periphery, where "the controls of government and religion tend to be at their weakest [and where] the forces of dissatisfaction can easily gain both strength and organization" against the (religious) center; Thompson attributes the likelihood of a series of peasant revolts to the "oppressive system of conscription or virtual slavery by which the pyramids and buildings were erected" (Thompson, 1942: 15-16), "the evergrowing demands [on the peasants] for service in construction work and in the production of food for an increasing number of non-producers," or "exotic religious developments" (Thompson, 1954: 87).

From the tenth century on, "Petén cities could no longer count on food deliveries from the highlands" (Wolf, 1959:110; also Thompson, 1954: 86). The abandonment of the major theocratic cities did not, however, signify the disappearance or "decline" of Mayan civilization. As the Petén lost its earlier preeminence, the center of gravity in Guatemala shifted toward the western highlands. Sometime after the tenth century two Mayan tribes, the Quiché and the Cakchiquel, arrived on Guatemalan territory. Originating in Mexican territory to the north, these tribes had wandered for centuries before settling in the Guatemalan highlands and subduing the smaller tribes already living there (possibly including descendants of the Maya of the earlier Petén empire) (*Popol Vuh*, 1950:72). Eventually, during the fourteenth century, the Quiché consolidated their political hegemony over the entire area, primarily through military conquest, and established their capital at Utatlán in the western Guatemalan highlands. For the duration of the Quiché empire, the neighboring tribes paid regular tribute. In the second half of the fifteenth century, the Quiché king Quikab was deposed in a revolt led by his own sons, probably stemming from dissatisfaction with the king's demand for tribute (*Annals of the Cakchiquel*, 1953:94). The Cakchiquel took advantage of this situation to settle apart from the Quiché in the Lake Atitlán area. The ensuing rivalry between the two peoples led to a series of wars which greatly weakened the Quiché (*Annals . . . ,* 1953:17), and resulted in their loss of hegemony. This was the situation on the eve of the Spanish conquest.

Although the available information about this period of Guatemalan history is even sketchier than that about the "classical" Maya era, it can generally be summarized as a period of "warfare and military expansion on the one hand, intensive agriculture and the appropriation of surpluses through tribute payments on the other" (Wolf, 1959:117). The peasants were no freer than before; Guatemala on the eve of the conquest was a complex, stratified—proto-class—society, with all the attendant social tensions. Given the continual intertribal rivalry, the dominant elites were now the warriors, whose hegemony left an imprint very different from that of the priests. At the top of the hierarchy was a hereditary king who, at the peak of the Quiché empire, ruled the entire area. (When independent, the Cakchiquel elected their king.)

The thrust toward centralization of power gave rise to a council of officials (heads of the twenty-four main families) to advise the king, and an incipient bureaucracy to collect tribute (in service as well as produce) etc.—all of whom enjoyed special privileges, such as exemption from tribute. The cities reflected the new social stratification: "surrounded by deep ravines and reinforced by ramparts," they were more like fortresses than ceremonial centers (although they still housed temples) and, according to one interpretation, were evolving toward "multi-functional cities" (Guzmán & Herbert, 1970:21–2)—but still oriented to the needs of the dominant classes.

Not only the internal organization of each "urban" center, but also the relations among these centers became more complex. Most significant in strengthening the material base was a great increase in trade. Rivers as well as roads became principal arteries of commerce, not only within Guatemala but also with the Mexicans to the north. (These very roads, linking the Guatemalan highlands with both coasts, were later used by the Spanish in their conquest of Guatemala.) The increase in trade was "simultaneously the cause and the result of numerous wars for control and defense of the routes of commerce." The growing importance of commerce gave rise to a class of merchants who "lived in the cities, organized fairs upon returning from their trips, were exempt from paying tribute and had special privileges"—and who were organized into guilds (Guzmán & Herbert, 1970:14–16). Nominally religious festivals provided opportunities for commercial markets and fairs. Thus the city evolved as a locus of material accumulation and of the consolidation of power by new elites.

This combination of war and trade at the material base had two other side effects. First, the intense commercial traffic created the need for a unit of exchange. Since money itself was unknown, such goods as cacao, beans, feathers of the quetzal bird, and jade were used. (The cacao came from lands conquered by the Quiché from other tribes.) Second, the wars produced captives, who were frequently used and traded as slaves for agricultural and domestic labor.

Thus, since the end of the "classic" period, pre-hispanic society had undergone a considerable change—but not a "decline" or "decay," as many experts regard it.[2] In fact, the material base appears to have developed considerably during this period. To the extent that there was any "decline," it was a decline in the fortunes and high culture of a particular ruling class (Thompson's priestly "creative minority"), and its replacement by another ruling class, with the consequent shift in the nature of the political economy. In short, what the Spaniards found in 1524 was a society in transition and evolution—in its form (not substance), not totally unlike the evolution occurring in Europe. (One theory is that it was evolving toward a modified slave society, [Flores, 1968:3; Martínez, 1970:536].) Had it not been interrupted by the Spanish conquest, it might well have developed—though in a different direction—into a society as sophisticated as Western Europe.

This point is important for our understanding not only of pre-hispanic society *per se,* but also of subsequent Guatemalan history. It is not surprising that the notion of a "decline" dates back to the accounts given by the Spanish conquerors: for if the Mayan glory were "dead" by 1500, then the genocide and human misery wrought by the conquest, while deplorable, could be justified as the triumph of and necessary price for civilization, development and progress—rather than as outright military conquest. To define the "rise" and "fall" of Mayan civilization in terms of its high culture, furthermore, is to forget that during the epoch of "glory" as well as that of "decline" the masses labored to the benefit of a tiny elite. Nevertheless at no time before the conquest did the Indians suffer the systematic material deprivation that has become chronic since 1524. The reason is rather simple: prior to 1524, Guatemalan society was not integrated into a world market which systematically channeled its surplus (and even its subsistence) into the pockets of a foreign ruling class—and which systematically maintained Guatemala in a subordinate position. Thus *underdevelopment* as we know it today did not exist in Guatemala prior to 1524, but is the direct outcome of the conquest and the integration of Guatemala into an expanding world capitalism.

---

2 Typical examples of this attitude are the following: "Recent excavations . . . have underlined the cultural impoverishment of [the post-classic] militaristic regime" (Thompson, 1954:121); "When the Spanish embarked upon the conquest of . . . America, these [Indian] peoples were in full decadence" and "Grand civilizations had existed in remote epochs, as illustrated by the monumental ruins, civilizations which had disappeared. . ." (Villacorta, cited in Guzmán & Herbert, 1970:6).

COLONIAL GUATEMALA: OCCUPIED COUNTRY

THE ARRIVAL OF "WESTERN CIVILIZATION"

Several years before the Spanish conquerors reached Guatemala in 1524, their arrival in America was heralded to the Guatemalan Indians by a raging epidemic (possibly smallpox) originating in the Spanish army in Mexico. As described in the *Annals of the Cakchiquel* (1953:155–6):

> It happened that during the twenty-fifth year 1520 the plague began, oh, my sons! First they became ill of a cough, they suffered from nosebleeds and illness of the bladder. It was truly terrible, the number of dead there were in that period. . . . [In 1521] the people could not in any way control the sickness. . . . Great was the stench of the dead. After our fathers and grandfathers succumbed, half of the people fled to the fields. The dogs and vultures devoured the bodies. The mortality was terrible. . . . So we became [orphans] when we were young. All of us were thus. We were born to die.

The Indians' low resistance to the new disease combined with its psychological impact rendered it a principal ally of the conquerors. In the wake of the epidemic arrived the Spanish army, led by Cortés' brash, adventurous lieutenant Pedro de Alvarado. (One previous Spanish attempt to conquer Central America in 1509 had been foiled by the Indians.) Alvarado's instructions from Cortés had been to pacify the natives without bloodshed if possible, convert them to Christianity and explain to them the "advantages" of submission (Mata, 1969:112). They were met, however, by fierce resistance from an alliance of Indian tribes headed by the Quiché, determined to defend their territory. After a series of bloody battles, which evidenced the superior military force of the Spaniards, the Quiché attempted to trick Alvarado, inviting him and his army into their capital, Utatlán, to negotiate, but with the intention of ambushing and killing them. When he realized the trick, Alvarado captured all the Quiché nobles and burned the entire capital. After the fall of the Quiché, Alvarado set about subduing the other tribes. Everywhere the Indians resisted—in El Salvador, south of Guatemala, so vigorously that the Spanish were forced to maintain an occupation army, and even this did not prevent a major uprising in 1526.

The only temporary exception were the Cakchiquel, whose leaders (probably because of their lond-standing rivalry with the Quiché) submitted peacefully and allied with the Spanish. No sooner was Guatemala "pacified" in 1524, however, when the Cakchiquel, appalled by the Spaniards' harsh treatment and exorbitant demands for tribute, launched the greatest uprising of all. They were eventually joined by other tribes and the "nearly general uprising" was not definitively subdued until 1530 (*Annals,*

1953:123–9). Significantly, while the Cakchiquel leaders had initially offered peaceful submission, the people initiated the uprising (Lujan, 1968:129).

What the army left undone was accomplished by soldiers of God. During the 1530's the northern provinces today known as Alta and Baja Verapaz were peacefully brought under Spanish control by Dominican friars (although the Indians revolted in 1556). This left only the Indian island outpost of Tayasal (near the ancient site of Tikal) in the Petén. The first group of Christian missionaries to Tayasal, in 1622, was killed by the Indians and subsequent expeditions were driven back. Only in 1697 was the Spanish army finally able to take possession of the city by force. The very existence of this independent realm, according to one observer (von Hagen, 1960:211), "encouraged rebellion among the other Maya living under the Spanish yoke." Indeed the colonial era was marked by sporadic Indian revolts.

The total cost of the conquest in human (Indian) lives is difficult to determine: although Las Casas' figure of four to five million Indian deaths in Guatemala between 1524 and 1540 is doubtless a numerical exaggeration, it is accurate in spirit (Jones, 1940:267; Cardoza y Aragón, 1965:283). Who or what was responsible for this catastrophe? It would be difficult to overlook completely the personal role of Pedro de Alvarado, whose cruelty and avarice (which included using child labor to exact tribute, burning Indians alive, and raping the wives of Indian nobles) were such that the *Spanish* government initiated criminal proceedings against him in 1529. But he was not alone: as we shall see, each group in the entourage of the conquest made its own contribution to the depopulation (of natives) of Guatemala. But the human cost of the conquest extended far beyond the number of lives lost; it represented the violent clash of two socio-economic systems and two cultures. In order to understand the various dimensions of this confrontation, we must review briefly who were the conquerors, and what was the nature of the society from which they came.

The conquerors were a diverse group of men, representing various Spanish interests. In the forefront, of course, was the army, sent by the Spanish Crown, but searching for wealth—specifically for gold. Accompanying or following close behind them were the missionaries, whose task was to save souls—and to strengthen the economic and political position of the Church. Less visible in the conquest itself, but no less important, was a nascent class in Spain which directed and financed the conquest, and whose interests were increasingly heeded by the Crown: the mercantile bourgeoisie. The conquest, beyond its military phase, was not strictly speaking a state enterprise; rather, it was a venture of private economic interests which had obtained Royal permission to carry to the New World their search, initially for new trade routes, and subsequently for new markets and sources of raw materials. The relation between the Crown and private interests was formalized through *capitulaciones* or contracts under which the Crown authorized the private enterprise to operate, in return for Royal political hegemony over the inhabitants and a certain percentage of the wealth discovered in precious metals, etc. (Mata, 1969:103).

This "partnership" grew out of the particular conditions in Spain by the end of the fifteenth century. Spain had never been a typically feudal country, and the several centuries of war against the Moslems hastened the consolidation of power by a central authority against the feudal lords and nobles. Particularly the areas affected by the war were populated by a free peasantry. Meanwhile, the cities saw the rise of a commercial bourgeoisie whose fortunes were linked to the discovery of new foreign markets and trade routes as well as to investment in incipient Spanish industry. This class required state protection, both against the remnants of an autonomous nobility with its own interests (extensive agriculture) within Spain, and against a competing bourgeoisie in the northern European countries. Even at its height, the Spanish empire was not a stable center of the expanding capitalist economy of Europe. By the end of the sixteenth century, Spain's domestic turmoil and defensive position in Europe were to give the Crown a particular interest in maintaining close control over the wealth obtained in the colonies. It was as part of the exanding mercantile capitalist economy of Europe that the Spaniards viewed their American holdings and established the institutions of a dependent capitalism which were to shape the Latin American political economy.

THE COLONIAL BASIS OF DEPENDENCY AND UNDERDEVELOPMENT

The conquest marked a change in all aspects of the relations among men and women in Guatemala. A diversified economic base, land ownership, and accumulation of wealth were not new to Guatemala, but took on new and changing forms. Exploitation of man and woman by man had existed before the conquest, but acquired a basically different dynamic. In the colonial experience, which lasted three hundred years (1524 to 1821), we find the seeds of contemporary Guatemalan underdevelopment and dependency.

The basic new fact of Guatemalan life after 1524 was that economic, social and political priorities were henceforth determined by needs and interests of a foreign power—more specifically, of the dominant classes of Spain, which in turn were shaped by Spain's subordinate position in the expanding capitalism of Western Europe. As is still true today, some of these interests came to be articulated by the upper classes living in Guatemala, thus giving the false appearance of expressing legitimately "Guatemalan" interests; neither then nor today have they represented the aspirations or needs of the Guatemalan masses. Nevertheless, the fact that one sector of the incipient international bourgeoisie resided in Guatemala during the colonial period and became the *criollo* elite, created certain conflicts and instabilities which culminated in the severing of the formal colonial relation.

In at least one respect Guatemala (and the rest of Central America, all of which was included in the colonial Captaincy-General of Guatemala) disappointed the conquerors: there were no large deposits of gold or silver. For the first few decades the Spanish attempted to milk the nearly dry cow by demanding that the Indians produce gold from the river beds; subsequently they engaged in small-scale mining for jewelry and money, one-fifth of which had to be remitted as tribute to the Spanish Crown. But eventually they had to abandon their gold-lined dreams, particularly after Indian labor in the mines was formally prohibited and since the Indians frequently refused to disclose the location of mineral resources (Solórzano, 1963:99). The land remained, however, the primary source of wealth in colonial Guatemala—not so much for what it contained as for what it could be made to produce for export.

The first act which defined the nature of colonial relations was the Spaniards' appropriation of the Indians' land—and of an Indian labor force to work the land. The reliance on cheap Indian labor obviated the need for introducing more efficient and productive methods of agriculture (Melville & Melville, 1971:16). For some time after the conquest the principal crop was cacao, used as a unit of exchange (including Indian tribute to the Crown) and a principal export. During the course of the seventeenth century, however, the Spanish government decided to transfer large-scale cacao-growing to Guayaquil and Venezuela, thereby precipitating a marked decline in Guatemalan cacao production.

Meanwhile, the beginnings of a textile industry in Europe had created a demand for another product of the Guatemalan soil: indigo (*añil*), the base of blue dye. As a crop, an industry and an export, *añil* dominated the colonial economy and financed the bulk of Guatemala's imports for over two hundred years. Other crops included sugar cane (grown on great plantations, worked by imported black slaves), corn, cattle-raising, and on a smaller scale, cotton and tobacco. From the very outset, the Spanish colonists controlled all but subsistence agriculture. These agricultural crops—nearly all of them for export to Europe or consumption by the *criollo* bourgeoisie—were supplemented by related industries:

the elaboration of *añil*, leather, metal- and wood-working, weaving and so on. Any industry which might compete with Spanish goods was, of course, banned.

Many of these productive activities had existed before as well as after the conquest, but they were now part of a system which defined wealth not in terms of its direct use to producers or buyers, but in terms of capitalist accumulation, "capital multiplying miraculously in the process of exchange" (Wolf, 1959:176). Moreover, they were now geared to the demands of a foreign economy, which was part of the international capitalist market. This dependent relation to Spain had several important implications for Guatemala. First, it meant that the vascillations of the Spanish economy—particularly the depression of the seventeenth century —reverberated sharply, ultimately producing a serious depression in the Guatemalan economy. Second, it established the complementary nature of the Guatemalan economy: production based on Spanish rather than Guatemalan needs, and varying with the ups and downs of the international market. Third, it meant that commerce was no longer simply a question of exchanging a surplus in one type of goods for other necessities for consumption, but rather of generating wealth to support the activities of the Spanish state and to enrich the merchant class in Spain and its counterpart in the colony.

The particular forms of colonial dependency in Guatemala were shaped by the fact that Spain was on the defensive, attempting to protect her colonies from encroachment by other European powers. Spanish control could only be guaranteed through a monopoly over colonial trade, concentrated in one Spanish port (Sevilla until 1717, then Cádiz) to ensure collection of customs duties for revenue to the state, and formalized through such institutions as the Board of Trade (*Casa de Contratación*), the merchant guild in Sevilla (*Consulado de Comercio*), and escorts for merchant ships. First in Sevilla, later in Cádiz, there was a "division of role" between the state and oligopolistic Spanish private interests:

> While the state took responsibility and some profit from the creation and maintenance of the political and economic superstructure in the colonies, the merchants . . . controlled effectively the flow of trade and commission fees. The crown sometimes conferred upon the merchant guild, often a large creditor, the functions of government in customs collection and decision-making in affairs affecting its interests. . . . (Stein & Stein, 1970:49)

At the other end of the trade route, colonial trade and prices were controlled through officially designated ports, so that all goods entering or leaving Guatemala passed through the Mexican port of Veracruz. Within Guatemala, despite the lack of a *Consulado* until the end of the eighteenth century, a small group of merchants with close ties to the guild in

Sevilla functioned as a human gateway to the international market. Not only trade with Europe but also among the colonies was closely regulated from Spain; since the colonies served Spain not only as a source of raw materials but also as a market for Spanish manufactured goods, it obviously would not do to allow the colonies to supply each other in such necessities as cloth. The trade which Guatemala had enjoyed with Mexico before the conquest was now prohibited. Scarcity and high prices of manufactured goods were among the obvious results of these policies.

But even this elaborate, highly structured system of controls was not sufficient to maintain a closed trade circuit. The incursions by other interested parties took various forms: Dutch, French and British merchants soon discovered the opportunities for contraband in the American ports; as early as the sixteenth century, piracy was common on the high seas and in the colonial ports which the Spanish Armada could no longer protect militarily; during the seventeenth and eighteenth centuries, the British operated from their Caribbean island and mainland possessions. Increasing pressuring from European competitors led in the eighteenth century to Spanish acceptance of liberalized trade. Internationally the demise of the Spanish monopoly was acknowledged by implicit acceptance of the doctrine of free trade and the concession of commercial privileges to England in the 1713 Treaty of Utrecht—just one more reminder that Spain was a subordinate or intermediate link in an international market increasingly dominated by private interests in northern Europe.

In fact, the Spanish monopoly had never been very complete, given that "by 1700, [Spanish merchant] guild members were for the most part mere fronts for Genoese, French, Dutch and English resident and non-resident merchants" (Stein & Stein, 1970:17), and that colonial wealth had increasingly flowed not *to* Spain but *through* Spain into the pockets of northern European merchants and incipient industrialists. Only in the latter part of the eighteenth century did Spain attempt to regain control by reforming (liberalizing) trade with the colonies to combat the flourishing contraband trade and by simultaneously strengthening protectionist legislation. In Guatemala the Spanish struggle against British interests culminated in a proxy war in the 1780's, between Guatemalan forces and British-armed and trained Jamaican "Zambos" (Indian-Negroes), who were temporarily defeated in 1787. Meanwhile, within Guatemala, pressure had also been building up for a loosening of controls, and in 1744 a limited trade (in goods produced in the colonies) was authorized with Mexico, Peru and Chile. Nevertheless, in 1778, eighty-five percent of the value of all imported goods still came from Spain (Floyd, 1961:91).

Trade was not Spain's only means of milking Guatemala. Closely related were the monetary controls which overvalued Spanish currency in the colony and resulted in a chronic monetary crisis in Guatemala. Money as such barely existed outside the capital city, and cacao remained an important unit of exchange. Metal currency was scarce, due to the lack of large-scale mining and of a mint in Guatemala, the irregularity of foreign trade, and the remittance of what little there was to Spain as tribute. In addition, Guatemala became the dumping ground for worthless *pesos* from other colonies. For two hundred years Guatemalan petitions to rectify this situation were ignored; lacking large gold and silver deposits, Guatemala was hardly of primary concern to the Spanish Crown. Only in 1731 did the Crown authorize a *casa de moneda* (mint) in Guatemala, but even after it began operations the problem remained acute, and the scarce "good money" continued to flow out of the colony.

Finally, to underwrite its colonial expenses and European wars, the Crown imposed an elaborate series of taxes—on imports and exports (*alcabala*), production, sales, stamped paper, salaries of public officials (a kind of income tax) and sale of public office. Additional revenue for the royal treasury came from state monopolies on gunpowder, tobacco and liquor. A special tax, consisting of one-tenth of agricultural production (*diezmo*) was collected by the Royal Treasury on behalf of the Church. Aside from tribute paid by Indians (see below), these taxes became the cause of considerable discontent among all groups affected in Guatemala—to the extent that one royal customs official was the subject of several assassination plots (Solórzano, 1963:160).

Thus for the Spanish Crown and the privileged Spanish merchants, Guatemala was not a colony to be developed, but a source of wealth for the peninsula. It was almost a case of *planned underdevelopment,* with all the familiar characteristics: mono-export, decapitalization, scarcity, high prices, etc. Those who came to settle in Guatemala were no less interested in exploiting the colony for their own profit; but because they occupied a somewhat different position in the economic system, they developed a different set of interests which eventually came into conflict with those of their cousins in Spain.

The kingpin of colonial society was the land tenure system established by the Spanish conquest: the expropriation of the land from the Indian by foreign interests and the denial of his property rights; its increasing concentration (particularly of the best land) in the hands of a minority (e.g., by 1819 one family was producing one-sixth of all Guatemalan indigo (Smith, 1959:186) although indigo was mainly grown on numerous small and medium-sized farms); and its privatization (Guzmán & Herbert, 1970:62). The large privately-owned estates or *haciendas* were organized for commercial production of a large export crop for profit. From the outset they were part of the international capitalist economy;

thus the decision to produce *añil* rather than food, for example, was made in response to technological innovations in British textile factories, rather than to the nutritional requirements of the local population. Furthermore, the *hacienda* involved vast expanses of unused land: "Inefficient in its use of land, . . . [the *hacienda*] was yet greedy for it" (Wolf, 1959:205). Complementary to the large tracts of good land appropriated by the *criollos* were Indian communities—not the natural groupings of the pre-hispanic era, but social units created by and for the benefit of the con-querors. Within these communities the land was parceled out to be worked individually by the Indians in their "time off" from the *hacienda*. Thus was born the *latifundia-minifundia* system which even today dominates the Guatemalan political economy.

The *hacienda* was a peculiar capitalist institution in that it required only a limited amount of capital. Its basic resource was Indian labor:

> [The *hacienda*] needed and wanted more land not to raise more crops, but to take land from the Indians in order to force them to leave their holdings and to become dependent on the *hacienda* for land and work. . . . Like the slave plantation [it] was a system designed to produce goods by marshaling human beings regardless of their qualities and involvements as persons. . . . (Wolf, 1959:205, 207)

Despite some personal ties between Indian peons and *criollo* landowners the Indians became fundamentally a factor of production no less essential to the *hacienda* economy than is the machine in a modern factory. It was in this relation to the Indians that the *criollos* acquired their new identity *qua criollo*. They came from diverse socio-economic backgrounds in Spain, including the middle and working classes (Martínez, 1970:121–2); it was *in* Guatemala, in relation to the Indian labor supply, that they became *hacienda,* ranching or merchant entrepreneurs. Both literally and figuratively, it was by denying the humanity of the Indians that the *criollos* asserted their dominance—though certainly, from the perspective of the international bourgeoisie, a relative dominance. The racist con-tent of the *criollo* ideology was based not only on a sense of racial supe-riority and a need to justify their parasitic non-productive existence, but also on their need for a captive labor force in order to reap profit from the land.

This exploitative relation between *criollo* and Indian was formalized through an array of institutions which "replaced" the initial slavery: *encomienda, repartimiento, mandamiento,* debt peonage and even salaried labor. Through the *encomienda* the Spanish Crown granted to the *criollo* who had obtained land a certain number of Indians to work his land and to pay him in money, produce or personal service, in exchange for "protection" of their rights and a "Christian education."(!) Under the *repartimiento* (conscription), the Indians were compelled to perform a certain type of labor for a designated master (including mining and construction of public works) or to "sell" their produce to the *criollo* in exchange for a pittance (wine, a shirt or a machete).

With the abolition of the grossest forms of slavery, subterfuges were developed such as the *mandamiento,* under which a certain number of Indians in a village were ordered by magistrates to work for *criollos* or in construction of public works at very low pay. A subsequent disguise was advance payment of wages, maintaining the worker in constant debt to his employer, hence tied to the land in virtual slavery. (The only modification in the *repartimiento* during the eighteenth century was a change for the worse for the Indians: instead of working on the *hacienda* in weekly shifts, they had to work entire seasons—precisely the seasons when they would have had to cultivate their own land [Martínez, 1970: 506ff.]. What clearer evidence is needed that even the Indian communities existed not for the welfare of the Indians, but only as a convenience to the *criollos,* a place to get rid of the Indians when they were not needed on the *hacienda?*)

Formal slavery, once outlawed for Indians, reappeared for blacks imported from Africa—not only on the land, but also in mines, indigo works and sugar mills. The very need to import Africans was a telling commentary—less on humanitarian concern for the Indians than on the demographic disaster wrought by colonialism. The colonial slave trade itself, legal from mid-sixteenth to mid-seventeenth century, was a "capitalist enterprise, organized with large amounts of capital" (Vitale, 1968: 37) and served as a "formidable motor of capitalist accumulation" in Europe (Bagú, 1969:43, 53). Since the blacks could buy their freedom, and since they posed a constant threat of rebellion, however, colonial authorities never allowed them to become a significant labor force in Guatemala. Indian women were subjected to special forms of exploitation: as the conquerors' sexual objects (rape), as subjects of tribute, and as slaves or forced labor e.g., they were physically shut in corrals to make thread out of cotton, or to weave cloth for tribute (Jones, 1940:18; Martínez, 1970:526).

Whatever the marginal differences among these forms of forced labor, they were in reality variations on one theme and served common purposes: to guarantee the permanent conquest and subjection of the Indians and to compel the Indians to produce an economic surplus, to be ap-

The Middle American Indians had known a kind of limited slavery in which slaves had been permitted to own property, call some of their time their own,

propriated by the *criollos* and channeled into the world market. This was a slavery very different from that of pre-conquest society:

and in which the children of slaves were free. They were confronted now with a new, unlimited slavery in which a human being was treated as a mere commodity, to be sold to mines, sugar mills, and farms, and to be used as an expendable resource (Wolf, 1959:189).

Though apparently "feudal" in some of their characteristics (e.g., payment of *criollo* lords in kind, work without salary), these forms of forced labor differed substantially from medieval serfdom. The colonial bourgeoisie saw in them the organization of a capitalist labor force. Moreover, they were geared not to a closed, self-sufficient estate, but to an export economy, integrally tied to the world market.[3]

But these very forms of organizing the work force were irrational in that once the Indians had been deprived of their land, they could be maintained only by coercion and terror. Violent abuse of the Indians was not the exception but the rule, not incidental but essential to making the system stick. These chronic abuses were largely responsible for a crisis in the labor supply; hence the need arose to import Africans. In human terms, the cumulative effect was disastrous: an estimated two-thirds to six-sevenths of the Indian population in Central America and Mexico died between 1519 and 1650 (Batres, 1949:65; Wolf, 1959:30–1, 195–6). The Indians were cut off from their land, hence from their previous food supply, indicative of the "growing imbalance between man and land" (Wolf, 1959:199). Disease epidemics introduced by the Spanish—smallpox, typhoid, measles and malaria—ravaged the Indian population throughout the colonial era. The tropical lowland indigo works to which the Indians were shipped carried special health hazards, notably fatal bites by diseased flies (Smith, 1959:185).

In response to this situation, the Crown, with the sanction of the Church, issued regulatory legislation. The "New Laws" of 1542 legally eliminated personal service as payment to *encomenderos,* permitting them only to collect tribute with special licenses. In addition, the Laws abolished hereditary *encomiendas,* restricted their number, provided for punishment of abuses of the Indians, and made the Indians royal subjects. This legislation, which was vigorously protested by landowners, has led many scholars to view the Crown and the Church as humanitarian "protectors" or "defenders" of the Indians. However, compliance with these regulations, as with subsequent bans on debt slavery etc., was lax

3 Thus colonial Guatemala was neither fully "feudal" nor "capitalist" in the classical European sense; rather, the colonial order in Guatemala was a projection of European capitalism, although some of its principal characteristics appeared to resemble those of feudalism (Martínez, 1970:618–620. Flores Alvarado, 1971:69).

and the Crown eventually acquiesced in the most blatant violations. In a sense the Crown *had* to tolerate these violations, insofar as land and a free hand with the labor force were the only incentives for inducing Spanish migration to Guatemala. By 1784 conscription from Indian villages was officially permitted. Moreover, the point of these laws was not to free the Indians, but to make them direct subjects of the Crown rather than of the landowners. In this sense, the "welfare" (survival or non-extermination) of the Indians became a pawn in the evolving latent struggle of the Crown against the *criollos*. Finally, Royal and Church policies were designed to extract economic gain from the Indians through direct taxation ("tribute") and were in many respects as harmful as the practices of the *hacendados*. In order to facilitate the collection of these taxes (as well as the concentration of labor power and of souls for conversion to Christianity), they forced the Indians into the *reducciones* or "communities"—when necessary, burning the scattered villages and lands where the Indians had previously lived.

As the overt ally of the Crown, the Church had more than a spiritual interest in the colonial enterprise, which it legitimated. Besides the "contributions from the faithful" (*diezmos* or compulsory taxes), missions of the Church, as well as the Jesuit orders (whose interests were linked to those of the *criollo* bourgeoisie until their expulsion in 1767) were exempt from tax obligations. In addition they were the first big moneylenders in the colony and were sizable landowners—Dominicans in Vera-paz, Franciscans in Occidente, and Jesuits in the valleys of Guatemala and Amatitlan (Guzmán & Herbert, 1970:67). By 1700 ecclesiastical interests owned five of the eight largest sugar mills. Rather than standing in the way of the *criollos,* the Church became the "right arm of the ruling class" (Cardoza y Aragon, 1965:281). While deploring the most flagrant cruelties, it provided the institutional and ideological underpinning which made possible the pacification of the Indians. With the exception of individual clerics such as Bartolomé de las Casas, who seriously defended the Indians, the priests who wrote sympathetically about the culture of the Indians were "applied anthropologists"; their task was "to make colonial rule enduring" (Stein & Stein, 1970:117). If the *hacendado* saw in the Indians nothing more than a factor of production, the priest saw a mass of savages, who needed a spiritual opiate and social control in their Christian *cofradias*. It was indeed a strange form of salvation, in that it was part of a concerted effort to negate the history and culture of the Indians.

But the efforts of Christianity and civilization to stamp out "pagan" values and culture, in conjunction with the imposition of an exploitative labor system, were by no means wholly successful. The Indians discovered numerous forms of resistance and self-defense. Aside from violent armed uprisings which punctuated the colonial era (at least five during the eighteenth century) and were quelled only by military force, there were several incidents of Church burnings and violent attacks on missionaries —notably in Verapaz, the province which the Dominicans were said to have "peacefully" subdued (Zavala, 1945:49–50). Another defense was the Indians' abandonment of the "communities" into which they had been concentrated, fleeing to the mountains, the forests, or to clandestine refuges in marginal areas (Martínez, 1970:102–3, 557–63; Solórzano, 1963:31). More generalized was the deliberate maintenance of their own religious traditions and conscious rejection of some elements of Christianity, as is still evident today in such Indian towns as Chichicastenango. And what the Spanish regarded as their "laziness" was in reality, a conscious refusal to work hard under intolerable conditions. Culturally, then, the conquest was never consummated.

The situation of the old Indian elite was somewhat different. Having lost their role as an autonomous ruling class in the Indian community, many of the nobles accepted the opportunity for cooptation and privilege offered by the Spanish. While some became agents of the Spanish in collecting tribute and marshaling the labor force (for which they were well paid), others moved to the towns to learn the ways of Western civilization. One outcome of the latter trend was some racial intermixing, giving rise to a new element, the *ladino*. Far more important as the origin of the Guatemalan *ladino,* however, was the conquerors' violent rape of Indian women.

The *ladino* "identity" is one of the most elusive elements of Guatemalan society. Originating historically and socially in an act of class violence, the *ladinos* were best defined as not *criollo* yet not Indian, as having no roots in either class. Alienated from their own history, seeking always to enter the exclusive world of the *criollos,* they easily adopted the capitalist *criollo* values of competition, individualism and accumulation of wealth. Their extreme alienation (self-denial) and individualism contrasted markedly with the surviving Indian values of community and communal labor, and their sense of belonging to a social class. Lacking any social consciousness or cohesiveness, the *ladinos* were unable to organize themselves for any resistance against or pressure upon the *criollos*— much less to join forces with the Indians (Guzmán & Herbert, 1970: 107ff.; Martínez, 1970: ch. 6; Stein & Stein, 1970:64; Wolf, 1959: 236ff.). As we shall see, these characteristics of the *ladinos,* forged during the colonial era, have had a profound effect on subsequent Guatemalan history. Economically, the *ladinos* were neither slaves (like the Indians) nor property-owners (like the *criollos*), but landless free laborers, initially in a constant struggle for survival. Systematically denied access to land in the countryside, the majority worked on the *haciendas* for a salary or rented land, and were exempt from the tribute imposed on the Indians.

Equally important for the future of Guatemala was their development in the colonial towns. From the very outset the urban *ladinos* did not constitute a cohesive social class: occupying different positions in the economic structure, they could not develop common interests, much less any sense of class solidarity. At the bottom of the urban heap were the *plebe*, the marginal poor: struggling artisans, salaried but exploited workers in shops or mills, or unemployed. This unemployment, the existence of a variable mass possessing nothing other than labor power and seeking work, was a typically capitalist feature of colonial society. The displacement of small artisanry by imported industrial goods and the general precariousness of the colonial Guatemalan economy swelled the ranks of the unemployed in the urban slums. One step above them were the artisans, including all who provided goods and services (in addition to "artisans," strictly speaking, also millers, tanners, innkeepers, salesmen, druggists, cobblers, carpenters, etc.), whose economic prospects were limited but somewhat more secure. In the capital they were organized into guilds—less to protect their own interests than to assure their conformity to regulations and prices dictated by the municipal government. The artisan sector was rent by several cleavages—between those who did and those who did not have work, between masters and apprentices, between productive (weavers, etc.) and non-productive (barbers, surgeons, etc.), between users of local versus imported raw materials, etc.—such that no common interests among them could possibly develop.

The cities also saw the rise of an upper middle stratum of *ladinos,* the embryo of a petty bourgeoisie, including small producers and manufacturers, professionals, intellectuals, small merchants harmed by monopoly —in short, those groups which, together with their rural counterparts (small and medium landowners), found their economic advance and entry into the *criollo* elite blocked by the colonial structure (Martínez, 1970: ch. 6). In no sense, thus, did the cities belong to the *ladinos*. In theory the cities were governed by royal officials through the *ayuntamientos* or municipal councils. But in practice, patronage and sale of public office led to lax law enforcement and a corrupt bureaucracy, subservient to private interests (Stein & Stein, 1970:68-80). The colonial cities developed as class institutions, instruments of the *criollo* bourgeoisie. Specifically, they served the *criollos* as centers of exchange and commerce (and the link to the metropolitan market), of political hegemony, and of recreation and wealthy living. They were founded "as a requirement

for the consolidation of the empire" (Martínez, 1970:304). Like everything else in colónial society, they were the product of Indian and *ladino*
labor for the *criollo*.

Nor were all cities of equal status in the colonial political economy.
Heading the urban hierarchy was the capital city (although it moved
several times, as a result of natural disasters). Above all, the capital was
the center of the economically dominant class in the colony: the merchants. This dominance was not shared by *all* engaged in commerce; a
tiny group, principally representatives of the great monopolistic merchant
houses in Sevilla and later Cádiz (many of whom still considered themselves Spanish) controlled domestic as well as international trade. (In the
early seventeenth century, five merchants were each worth at least 500,000
ducats (Woodward, 1966:3).) They controlled indigo prices, thus becoming the principal beneficiaries of the indigo trade. They channeled
some of the profits into loans to smaller indigo growers who were forced
to mortgage their crops (especially in the provinces outside Guatemala),
gradually replacing the Church as bankers, until the establishment of the
Indigo Growers' Society in the 1780's. Provincial growers and cattle
raisers all were beholden to the Guatemalan merchants, the suppliers of
goods and credit. Politically and socially, too, the merchants were in
command.

Perhaps more than any other group in colonial Guatemala, the merchants acted as a *class:* their stands, particularly on the crucial issues of
trade, were determined not by principles (e.g., for or against liberalization of trade), but by their own economic interests, narrowly defined, at
any given moment. During the seventeenth and eighteenth centuries, for
example, they repeatedly petitioned the Crown to authorize a *Consulado
de Comercio* for Guatemala (liberalization); once the *Consulado* was
established in 1793, they vigorously fought against the opening up of new
ports which would compete with Santo Tomás de Castilla (preservation
of monopoly). They opposed any move to strengthen the autonomy of
the indigo growers. They (unsuccessfully) resisted the campaign of the
municipal government to open up their ranks to smaller merchants, and
continually asserted the autonomy of the *Consulado* from official supervision. They felt no responsibility to the general well-being of the colony:

> While the Crown intended the *Consulado* to serve as an agency for general
> commercial development and improvements at a time when the economy of
> the colony was faltering, the merchants of Guatemala hoped to use the privi-
> leges and prestige of the *Consulado* to further their own special class interests
> (Woodward, 1966:8).

To the extent that they contributed anything to construction of roads or port facilities, it was strictly for their own benefit. Here was the embryo of a truly dependent bourgeoisie—dominant within Guatemala, yet totally dependent on the international market, with interests diametrically opposed to whatever might have brought genuine development to the country. More than any other class, they personified the integration of the dependent capitalist economy into an international system designed to meet the needs of the ascendant European burogeoisie.

THE CONSOLIDATION OF UNDERDEVELOPMENT, 1821–1871

"INDEPENDENCE"—FOR WHOM?

By the 1820's, Spanish colonial policy had established in Guatemala (Central America) the basic syndrome of capitalist underdevelopment—mono-export, extreme concentration of wealth juxtaposed with extreme poverty, decapitalization (channeling of the economic surplus abroad, or into the pockets of a tiny minority within Guatemala which was tied to overseas interests), and lack of transportation and port facilities. The downward spiral in the economy was both evidenced and reinforced by the contraction of the indigo base. Following the brief eighteenth century economic boom and expansion in trade (when Guatemala was the world's largest indigo producer), both production and exports declined in the last years of the century and after 1800. Principal causes were inadequate transportation facilities and high taxes which weakened Guatemala's competitive position internationally; competition from more efficiently produced indigo from British colonies (in 1810 the British East India Company dumped 5.5 million pounds on the world market); locust plagues affecting production after 1800; and Spain's war with England, which greatly reduced Guatemala's indigo exports (Beeson, 1964; Floyd, 1965; Smith, 1959; Woodward, 1965a). In short, the lifeline of the colonial Guatemalan economy was being cut by external events and by the very process of Guatemalan underdevelopment. Meanwhile, the public treasury remained empty, so that even normal operating expenses of the colony could be financed only through the accumulation of a sizeable debt.

This disastrous economic impoverishment could not fail to have unstabilizing social consequences: proletarianization within the lower strata and discontent within the upper class. In the cities a growing number of *ladino* artisans joined the ranks of the marginally or un-employed *plebe*, particularly after the great earthquake of 1773 destroyed the capital. This unemployment was a direct result of the low demand for goods and services, a reflection of a large mass without purchasing power. The situation of poor *ladinos* (to say nothing of Indians) in the countryside was even more precarious: denied access to land by *criollos* and by royal policies, they were forced to work on the *haciendas* for a pittance.

Meanwhile, various currents of discontent developed into conflicts among the *criollos:* first between the older *criollo* aristocracy and the newer immigrants from Spain who challenged their economic supremacy and displaced them (Martínez, 1970:104); second between the *criollos* and the colonial bureaucracy—as manifested politically in the interminable jurisdictional and political battles between the royal *Audiencia* (supreme colonial authority) and the *criollo*-dominated *ayuntamientos* (municipal governments), for example, over taxes and controls of the Indian population, its services and tribute; third, between merchants and landowners (e.g., over the "profiteering" merchants' control of indigo prices and all foreign and domestic trade); and fourth, between Guatemala City, the stronghold of the merchant monopoly and Spanish rule, and the "provinces," particularly El Salvador. None of these conflicts of interest were new; they reflected the contradictions which had been structured into colonial society. By the beginning of the nineteenth century, however, they were aggravated by the economic depression and played into a movement for independence. The crystallization of that movement, however, was triggered by external events.

Spain's economic, political and military decline in Europe, beginning in the sixteenth century, culminated with the Napoleonic invasion of 1808, followed by several years of Anglo-French war for control of Spain. Even before the French had been driven out of Spain, a constituent assembly *(Cortés)* was convened in unoccupied Cádiz in 1812 to write a liberal constitution, based on the principles of economic liberalism, free trade, private property and certain political guarantees. The 1812 constitution was discarded two years later with the restoration of the Spanish (Bourbon) monarchy, and was only reinstated through a successful military rebellion in 1820.

This turmoil in the metropolis was bound to have repercussions in Central America. The vacillations of authority in Spain gave the *criollos* an opportunity to defy the Spanish bureaucracy in Central America—a challenge which on several occasions erupted into armed uprisings, riots, and plots, particularly in the "provinces": most notably in El Salvador (1811, 1814) and in Nicaragua (1811). Even in conservative Guatemala, the 1813 "conspiracy of Belén" plotted to capture Spanish colonial authorities, liberate Nicaraguan political prisoners jailed in Guatemala, initiate a military uprising and declare independence.

The response of the Spanish colonial authorities was a dual, "carrot-stick" policy. On the one hand, particularly after the appointment in 1811 of the absolutist anti-reformist José Bustamente as Captain-General, severe repressive measures were taken against "subversive" forces (e.g., suppression of agitational newspapers, imprisonment or exile of pro-independence leaders). On the other hand, a concerted effort was made to quiet unrest through concessions, particularly since the 1812 constitution had granted limited Central American representation in the *Cortés*, abolished tribute and some royal monopolies, and permitted free trade. These concessions were called into question by the Bourbon restoration of 1814, but it was too late to return to the *status quo ante*. Slowly, from 1814 to 1820, the pro-independence movement gathered momentum. But only after the declaration of independence in Mexico did the Central Americans follow suit on September 15, 1821. The Spanish Crown, weakened by internal instability and having already accepted *de facto* the independence of the more important colonies, offered no resistance.

Who were the architects of Central American independence, and how did they finally come together? By September 15, 1821, overt opposition to independence came only from the Church hierarchy and representatives of the Spanish Crown itself. Pro-independence sentiment had by no means, however, appeared in all sectors of the population simultaneously or for the same reasons; rather, it coalesced around a temporary coalition of groups, each motivated by its own interests. A large sector of *criollo latifundistas* (especially in the indigo-growing areas) saw independence as a means of eliminating impediments to their advancement: regulations on their treatment of Indian labor, burdensome taxes, and the exclusive royal-merchant monopoly which had kept down their prices and cut them off from free market competition. Their interests were served by the doctrines of economic liberalism of the ascendant industrial bourgeoisie in Europe: free enterprise and competition, elimination of the state monopolies and of state intervention which had been the backbone of mercantile capitalism, and free trade. "Free trade" and elimination of Spanish control were also primary concerns of the French and British agents, sent by their governments to help "liberate" Central America from Spain (ultimately, of course, to establish their own dominion over the region's resources and markets).

The pro-independence coalition also included the primarily *ladino* upper middle strata, descendants of displaced or impoverished *criollo* landowners, small and medium growers, the smaller merchants who had been excluded from the *Consulado* clique, intellectuals, teachers, students, professionals, artisans, office-workers, the lower ranks of the military and the clergy and a few urbanized Indians—in short, the embryo of a petty bourgeoisie (Martínez, 1970:322–48). Some of these groups—particularly the intellectuals and students clustered around the University, lower level clergy, and women who became propagandists for independence (Mata, 1969:292)—were influenced by the intellectual currents of the

French Enlightenment, and the examples of the French and American Revolutions and ultimately of the Mexican War of Independence. More to the point, these groups all shared a profound frustration induced by economic factors, notably the royal taxes and the general impoverishment of the colony.

Meanwhile, discontent was also brewing among the Indians, who had never fully accepted the conquest. By the beginning of the nineteenth century this discontent focused on the issue of royal tribute—particularly after the abolition of the tribute in 1811 and its subsequent reimposition in 1814. Violent uprisings materialized and were subdued only by military force in Coban in 1803 (which threatened to spread to all Verapaz), in Sololá in 1813, and throughout Chiquimula and Sacapulas from 1818 to 1820. In July, 1820, Quiché-populated Totonicapán erupted into a full-scale revolt, directed primarily against the immediate oppressors, the local officials who administered tribute and forced labor. For one month the area was ruled by an Indian king, Atanasio Tzul, under a new constitution which eliminated tribute. Once again a sizeable contingent of the Spanish army was required to subdue the area. While this and previous Indian revolts were not motivated directly by a desire for independence from Spain (indeed their spirit was as much anti-*ladino* and anti-*criollo* as anti-Spanish), they fed into the pro-independence ferment (Contreras, 1962:57ff., 64) and, as we shall see, were crucial in influencing the actions of the *criollos*.

Not surprisingly, the last to support the movement for independence were the privileged merchants of Guatemala City. Until the very end, they had everything to gain by maintaining their commercial monopoly with Spain and opposing the campaign for free trade. Nevertheless, when Independence was finally declared in 1821, they supported the move— perhaps because it promised "a brighter economic future without altering the basic social structure" (Woodward, 1966:xiv); perhaps because of a conflict of interest with colonial authorities over opening new ports (Woodward, 1966:65–66); perhaps because they wanted no part of Spain under the liberal 1812 constitution, restored in 1820; perhaps because they understood that their future lay in controlling an independent Guatemala (since they could not prevent it). Even more important, they "reluctantly accepted independence as an alternative to possible civil war" (Woodward, 1965a:563). And in this they were not alone. Fear of popular uprisings—by Indians, *ladinos,* or both—remained uppermost in the minds of the *criollos*. For this reason, they sanctioned the repressive Bustamente regime until 1818. For this reason, too, they finally led the independence movement—less as a matter of principle than to maintain order, and to prevent social revolution. The revolt in Totonicapán may well have been the final evidence of the danger of revolution. The Declaration of Independence itself was quite explicit: Independence had been declared

> to prevent the consequences to be feared in case the people themselves might proclaim it; . . . the Ayuntamientos, responsible for the preservation of order and tranquility, should take the most active measures to maintain it undisturbed in the entire Capital and surrounding villages (Mata, 1969:280–2).

It is frequently said that Central American independence was an achievement of the *criollos* alone. Insofar as *ladinos* and Indians participated in various phases of the movement, and insofar as their participation forced the *criollos* to take up the cry for independence, this was not the case. In several important respects, however, independence *was* a movement of the *criollos*. First, regardless of the social origins of the movement, the *criollos* quickly gained control and remained the dominant force. Second, independence became a vehicle for maintaining their class privilege and defending their interests against popular aspirations. Third, it left intact the economic and social structure of the colonial era, and opened the curtain on *neo-colonialism* in Guatemala. The intention of the *criollo* bourgeoisie was, no doubt, to eliminate Spanish rule in order to usurp it for themselves. That they were unable to do so in the post-independence era, that Spain's place was taken by other foreign interests, remains one of the fundamental contradictions of a neo-colonial and dependent capitalist society. In this sense, even the *criollos* were actors in a mere "pantomime" of independence (Flores, 1968:10).

THE LIBERAL EXPERIMENT

It did not take long for the true nature of the Central American "independence" movement and its internal conflicts to become clear. Even within the coalition favoring independence from Spain, there was a strong feeling that Central America was not ready for total independence. Conveniently for them, the *criollo* military leader of independent Mexico, Augustín Iturbide, who, supported by the Mexican clergy and aristocracy, had just had himself declared Emperor, shared their sentiments and "invited" Central America to annex itself to Mexico. Until a decision could be made, the last Spanish Captain-General, Gabino Gaínza, remained the head of the government. When the Central American representatives met in January 1822 to determine the region's future status, most of the Guatemalan delegates favored annexation, while the other provinces initially opposed it. Shortly thereafter, Iturbide sent expeditionary troops into Central America to "convince" the other Central American states to become part of the Mexican Empire, meeting resistance only in El Salvador. The commander of the Mexican forces in Central America, Vicente Filísola, became the head of the Central American government and remained so until the overthrow of Iturbide in March 1823. Finally in July 1823, a new constituent assembly convened to declare the "absolute" independence of the United Provinces of Central America.

Although the entire two-year incident had the air of a political farce, it indicated several significant aspects of Guatemala's past and future. First, the majority of the *criollos* favored independence from Spain in 1821, annexation to Mexico in 1822, and separation from Mexico in 1823, all for the same reason. The determining consideration on all three occasions was the preservation of order and stability, regardless of the implications for sovereignty. Thus, having no army of their own, when street fights between political factions and general unrest erupted after Independence, the Guatemalan *criollos* saw annexation to a militarist monarchy as offering the best hope of security. A year later, with Iturbide's ouster and the establishment of a republic in Mexico, the *criollos* lost faith in Mexican "stability" as a guarantor of their own, and decided to separate from Mexico. Second, annexation became a pawn of opposing interests within Central America. While the conservative *criollos* in Guatemala City viewed it as a means of preserving Guatemalan hegemony, "provincials," even in the Guatemalan city of Quezaltenango saw an opportunity to break free of economic and political domination by Guatemala City.

Neither side paid much attention to the fact that Iturbide was using these divisions within Guatemala (and within all Central America) to maintain his own temporary power and to exploit the region economically. The result was disastrous. As of Independence in 1821, the Guatemalan treasury contained only sixty *reales,* and a deficit of more than three million *pesos,* which was considerably increased during the Mexican occupation (Bauer, 1966:43) since Central America had to finance the exploits of Filísola's army. What little hard (gold and silver) currency there was flowed out to Mexico, aggravating the shortage in Guatemala. While the Mexican government imposed new taxes and duties, Filísola appropriated local community savings—a practice which even the Spanish authorities had never attempted. Thus the bill for Mexican-guaranteed law and order for the *criollos* was paid by the Guatemalan people.

The period following annexation to Mexico was one of civil war and continual jockeying for power between competing political factions of the Central American bourgeoisie. It began with the convening of a Constituent Assembly to draft a constitution and accompanying legislation. While invoking the principle of universal suffrage, the Assembly set up a complicated electoral college system at both the Central American and the state levels; it abolished the special privileges of the Church and clergy (leading the Dominicans to protest, upon being deprived "of [their] property through the liberation of eight hundred slaves which [they] legitimately owned" [cited in Cardoza y Aragón, 1965:306]); it guaranteed certain civil rights; it abolished slavery and government monopolies, and institutionalized the principles of free contract of labor, *laissez-faire* and free trade.

Although the Central American delegates were able to hammer out a compromise constitution, the underlying cleavages soon became evident. On the one hand there was disagreement over the nature of the Central American "union"—between centralists particularly in Guatemala City, favoring strong central authority, and federalists, mainly *provincianos,* favoring more local autonomy. Parallel to this division was the rift between Conservatives and Liberals. This division had its roots in the pre-independence era, although the parties finally crystallized only in the 1820's. The Conservatives represented *latifundistas,* the monopolistic *Consulado* merchant clique, the established Church and some artisan sectors, and were based largely in Guatemala City. Conservatism stood for centralization in Central America, state-protected commercial monopolies (many of the merchants attempted to maintain the traditional relationship with Cádiz even after Independence (Woodward, 1965a: 564)), preservation of colonial structure and privileges, including those of the Church—and, coincidentally, defense of certain lower-class interests threatened by the Liberals.

The Liberals represented *criollo latifundistas,* among them some of the "best families," and the incipient *ladino* petty bourgeoisie, including small and medium landowners, intellectuals, and ideological pro-Independence activists. Liberalism stood for federalism in Central America, opposition to the Mexican annexation, free trade, *laissez-faire,* political liberalism in the Cádiz tradition, and certain "developmental" reforms of the colonial structure which would benefit their particular interests. While including important *ladino* middle sectors, the Liberal Party was dominated by *criollos,* who, for all their "progressive" principles, acted in their own self-interest (Woodward, 1965a:557). Rhetorically, the differences between the two parties seemed great; but in the end, both were parties of the *criollo* bourgeoisie, and neither showed the slightest concern for the Indians.

Given the minor differences between the parties in practice, and the ease with which many *criollos,* even leaders, shifted from one to the other, the bitterness of the struggle between them from 1823 to 1831 seems ironic. From 1826 to 1829 the power struggle erupted into open civil war—not only between the parties, but also between Guatemalan and Central American governments. Only in 1831 did the Liberals consolidate their military and political power, with Francisco Morazán in Central America and Mariano Gálvez in Guatemala. A militant Liberal, Morazán expelled the bastions of the Church, as well as the leading Conservatives, and maintained strong leadership until 1838.

The ultimate impossibility of preserving the Central American unit stemmed not only from the profound regional rivalries and resentments against Guatemala City, but also from the economic underdevelopment of the region, as manifested specifically in the chronically empty federal treasury (Smith, 1963). As the old sources of revenue (tobacco and other monopolies, customs duties, forced loans) declined and only Guatemala contributed state funds, the federal government turned to borrowing. Between 1821 and 1831 the public debt had already increased by fifty percent (Smith, 1963:494). Domestic financial support came from a group of "progressive" Guatemalan merchants. In 1824 a contract was signed with the British house of Barclay, Herring and Richardson for the sale of Central American bonds in London. The face value of the loan was over seven million *pesos,* but the real value was five million *pesos* (one million pounds), at six percent (later eight percent) interest, with the income of the federation as collateral. In fact, Central America received only 325,000 *pesos* (used to cover back salaries and budget deficit), but was in debt for nearly one million *pesos.* When the Barclay house went bankrupt in 1826, further negotiations were begun with Reid, Irving and Company, but came to nought. The foregin debt totaled £163,000 when it went into default in 1828 and was assumed by the individual states, five-twelfths (£68,000) as Guatemala's portion. This was the origin of the famous *deuda inglesa* which was not finally resolved until 1966–67 and was frequently used by British interests as an instrument of diplomatic pressure.

Guatemalans got their first taste of Liberalism during the 1831–8 regime of an upper class *criollo* intellectual and financier who had begun his political career as a Conservative, Mariano Gálvez. He is generally remembered for his "progressive" legislation and his abortive attempt to change the social and economic basis of Guatemala forty years before Liberalism finally took hold. Central to his program were political-administrative reforms, anti-clerical measures, secularization of marriage and divorce, and promotion of education at all levels. In the economic sphere, he stimuated cochineal (red dye), coffee, sugar, several factories, various infrastructure projects, and an "agrarian reform." Auspicious though it seemed, however, the Liberal experiment proved contradictory and failed in the end—as we may understand by focusing on a few key aspects.

Recognizing Guatemala's colonial legacy of underdevelopment, Gálvez attempted to create the prerequisites for economic development: legislation to facilitate and rationalize exploitation of the land, and communication and transportation networks. The "agrarian reform" legislation created mechanisms for the transfer into private hands of unused public land and land formerly held by the Church, and for the determination of property boundaries. Large estates already owned by *latifundistas* were left intact. Numerous Indian communities, however, were "legally" deprived of their communal properties without compensation, as privileged *ladinos* claimed title to their lands. Thus "progress" encroached upon the only enclave which colonialism had left the Indians, and the principal beneficiaries of this agrarian policy were the ascendant *ladino* landowners.

The other plank of Gálvez's land policy was a massive colonization scheme to open up the vast areas of unused public land, particularly in the northeastern part of the country. Here again, private interests were to be the agents of development—not Guatemalans, but foreign (British) enterprises, contracted by the government to settle the land conceded to them in perpetuity as their property. (Federal legislation of 1824 had authorized unrestricted immigration on very favorable terms.) These concessions were most generous. In return for the obligation of colonizing the land with foreign immigrants and developing infrastructure, the companies obtained free and exclusive use of all resources on their property, guarantees to immigrants of all the rights of Guatemalan citizens, and a series of special privileges, notably exemption from almost all taxes, export and import duties, and from military service, for twenty years. Cheap Indian labor was an added incentive. The inspiration for this incredible scheme was Gálvez's belief in the necessity of foreign capital and technology to develop Guatemala's productive structure, infrastructure and commerce with Europe—his search for a short-cut to development—and his rather racist desire to "Europeanize" Guatemala, to "civilize" the local population through the noble example of the European immigrants (Griffith, 1965:284).

If the motivation for the venture was "idealistic" given the Liberal mentality, the reality was absurd. Gálvez readily found takers for the offer:

Within a period of six months in 1834 the government of Guatemala approved a series of colonization agreements that stripped the state of virtually its entire public domain. The concessions granted away virtually all the unoccupied public lands contained within the three great northern departments that comprised about three-fourths of the total area of the state (Griffith, 1965:32).

One company alone, the Eastern Coast of Central America Commercial and Agricultural Company, received fifteen million acres—more than half of Guatemala. The crowning touch in this colossal giveaway was that none of the British companies had the slightest interest in or intention of developing Guatemala. Their business was land speculation—fraudulent, at that. Furthermore, their financial base in London was so shaky that the whole venture never got off the ground. The few immigrant communities and infrastructure projects they initiated soon collapsed. Guatemala was left with nothing—less than nothing, since the companies had taken advantage of the unlimited logging rights in the concession areas. Unfortunately, in his haste to attract foreigners, Gálvez had been rather careless about assuring benefits to Guatemala: thus the companies took full and immediate advantage of their rights (exploitation of the mahogany resources) while virtually ignoring their contractual obligations. That Gálvez should have expected monopolistic foreign enterprise to develop Guatemala indicates a basic contradiction of the Liberal mentality. Nor was the incident unique; it became almost a *model* for Guatemalan "development" (e.g., by United Fruit Company after the consolidation of Liberalism in 1871, and in some respects for the contemporary Alliance for Progress).

Colonization was only one aspect of the growing British economic grip on Guatemala. For all Gálvez's "reforms," Guatemala remained an export-oriented economy, totally dependent on the world market. As mercantile capitalism gave way to industrial capitalism in Europe, commercial monopoly was replaced by the doctrine of free trade, and Spain by England as the metropolis. "Free trade" after 1821 turned out to be a guise for the British monopoly over Guatemalan exports and imports. The exports—primarily cochineal, indigo and cotton—were transported in British ships to service the industrial revolution and textile boom in England. By 1839, ninety percent of all imports (primarily luxuries for the urban elite) were British or came to Central America via England. The great influx of expensive British manufactures resulted in the outflow of silver and gold currency, aggravating the monetary crisis, and in a negative trade balance. Through this commercial nexus and the *deuda inglesa,* Guatemala was drawn into the empire of the pound sterling. Two British houses with subsidiary agencies in Guatemala monopolized Guatemalan commerce (Arriola, 1961:188-9). Guatemalan merchants quickly allied with these lucrative import-export interests. Indicative of the primacy of foreign trade over domestic, the cost of transport between Guatemala City and the Atlantic coast was over ten times greater than between Liverpool and Belice (Arriola, 1961:191)—a situation typical of dependent capitalism, which builds links to the world market at the expense of internal development. Having the only deep-water port in Central America, British-controlled Belice became the gateway for nearly all trade with Europe.

Although Belice was primarily important for its mahogany resources and as the base for British commercial operations in Central America, at times it appeared a potential beachhead for territorial expansion, particularly in the concessions adjacent to Belice. At least for the British pro-consul in Guatemala, the concessions provided an easy means of making all Guatemala "subservient to British influence without requiring on the part of England the trouble and expense of its direct government" (Chatfield, cited in Griffith, 1965:54). Furthermore, on various occasions the British determination to thwart a resurgence of Spanish hegemony via the Holy Alliance, and later to counter U.S. ambitions through strategic control of the Caribbean took concrete forms: temporary occupation of the island of Roatán and other areas of the Central American coast, initiatives for a British-controlled canal in Nicaragua, refusal to recognize Central American states as sovereign entities, and unofficial expansionary moves by Belice authorities (Van Aken, 1962). Nevertheless, Central America was primarily a commercial appendage for England; thus, Central American prosperity rose and fell with that of England (Naylor, 1960:371). In Guatemala, as throughout Latin America, "[the] English had been the major factor in the destruction of Iberian imperialism; on its ruins they erected the informal imperialism of free trade and investments" (Stein & Stein, 1970:155).

The same propensity in Gálvez's imported liberalism which led him to trust in the civilizing influence of British immigrants inspired another disastrous experiment: the adoption in 1837 of the penal code drawn up by Edward Livingston for the North American state of Louisiana (where it was rejected), guaranteeing protection of civil liberties (including jury trials and *habeas corpus*) (Rodríguez, 1955). Barely three months after being adopted in Guatemala, it was discarded. Unrest and a severe cholera epidemic in the provinces was met with a quarantine. This "emergency" served as an excuse for suspension of constitutional guarantees, imposition of martial law, and burning of villages in the affected areas, and for Gálvez's assumption of dictatorial powers. It now became clear that the urban Liberals had intended the Code as a protection of their own rights, but not for the largely Indian provinces: after all, how could the "backward," uneducated Indians be entrusted with jury decisions? (Rodríguez, 1955:20)

In fact, Gálvez's Liberalism had never been very "liberal" toward the Indians. Aside from encroachment on their land and the implementation of repressive measures in Indian areas, Gálvez institutionalized acculturation through compulsory primary education—to the extent that children of recalcitrant Indian parents would be considered "orphans" and taken into state custody (Arriola, 1961:171-2). A major effort was made to abolish Indian *traje* (native dress). In the name of humanism, the Indians were now being stripped of their few remaining means of communal identification and survival. The universal two *peso* head tax instituted by Gálvez was reminisent of colonial tribute. Although Gálvez abolished the 1829 anti-vagrancy (forced labor) law and established free contract of labor, the latter principle was consistently violated, and Indian conscripts were assigned to construction of roads and prisons (Smith, 1963: 508; Karnes, 1961:75-6). Thus it is not surprising that the movement to overthrow Gálvez gained strong support in the Indian provinces, where unrest began in 1837.

Although the Gálvez regime was finally toppled in January 1838 by the armed guerrilla movement in Mita (in eastern Guatemala), led by Rafael Carrera, the move had a broad popular base, and was preceded by uprisings throughout the country. The Indians, acting in their own interests (*not* out of ignorance), had every reason to oppose Gálvez. Poor *ladinos* in the eastern provinces also had numerous grievances. The colonization venture—particularly its preferential treatment of foreigners and cession of unlimited logging rights and of the best land in Guatemala—made him an easy target for widespread nationalism, and caused active unrest in eastern Guatemala. Gálvez's concentration of power in Guatemala City and his alliance with powerful merchants added to resentment in the provinces, which was additionally aggravated by the restrictive "anticholera" measures. The bulwarks of Conservatism, particularly the Church, capitalized on the unrest. No less important, Gálvez's former supporters among the Liberal intelligentsia deserted him after he began backtracking on his own legislation, took two Conservatives into his Cabinet, and assumed dictatorial powers in 1837.

Shortly after the fall of Gálvez, the Central American federation dissolved. This dual collapse represented a temporary setback of the ascendant *ladino* petty bourgeoisie (intellectuals, professionals, medium landowners—and merchants, when it was in their interests), which formed the backbone of Liberalism, but was as yet too weak to consolidate its power. Aside from the strong coalition of opposing forces, its weakness stemmed from the contradictions of the situation and within the Liberal movement itself: the persistence of the colonial economic base, and the need to rely on foreign interests and vested Guatemalan private interests. The result was that the Liberal model of "development"—"a prosperous and wealthy bourgeoisie, possessing and protected by a poor government, dedicated principally to mere police functions" (Bauer, 1966:56)— deepened underdevelopment in Guatemala.

LA DICTADURA CRIOLLA

What began as a popular uprising was quickly taken over by the Conservative *criollo* elite. Its leader, Carrera, generally described by historians as a "semi-literate Indian" (only Indians are illiterate!), was at least seventy percent Spanish by origin (Jones, 1934:42). Even in the minds of his Conservative supporters, Carrera's occupation of Guatemala City was enough to conjure up images of mob violence and anarchy, so he was bribed to disperse his forces while the merchants organized a militia to protect their property. By the time Carrera returned to the capital in April 1839 to assume power, he had built a solid alliance with the Conservatives. The Church, the *criollo latifundistas* and the *Consulado* merchants all became his close advisers.

Given the Conservatives' overriding concern with order and stability, their first task was to subdue the Indian provinces of Quezaltenango, Totonicapán and Sololá, which had taken advantage of the chaos in 1838 to secede from Guatemala and gain federal recognition as a separate *Estado de los Altos* (Highland State). The principal motivation was the desire, championed by Liberals, for local autonomy against Guatemala City domination. Only through the existence of the federal Central American government could this sixth state survive: shortly after the federation collapsed, Carrera's forces brought the area back into Guatemala. Two subsequent attempts to establish the autonomous state and constant uprisings in other Indian areas throughout the 1840's, often fomented by the Liberal opposition, were subdued by military force. Only after Carrera's renunciation in 1848 and return to power in 1849 was order established. To guarantee the government's ability to pacify future insurgencies, formal military and police forces were strengthened, and the 1851 constitution centralized authority in the Presidency. In 1855 Carrera was made President for life.

In some respects the twenty-six year Carrera regime represented a restoration of the pre-Liberal era. Most of the Liberal legislation was rescinded. The Church obtained most of its old privileges, notably *diezmos,* much of its property, and control over education; in 1852 relations were formalized with the Vatican. The *Consulado de Comercio* was revived, as was the companion *Sociedad Económica de Amigos*. Both were controlled by the established mercantile bourgeoisie in Guatemala City, and, as quasi-governmental institutions, were entrusted with collecting state revenues, formulating economic policy and stimulating new areas of production (including coffee) and infrastructure (roads, etc.). Despite their close cooperation, they differed slightly in approach. While the *Sociedad* evidenced some interest in fomenting long-range development and education, the *Consulado* continued to service the very specific interests of the old Guatemala City mercantile clique: maintenance of their monopolistic position in trade, construction of roads and ports essential to their particular operations (e.g., the *Consulado* refused to work on roads which might benefit competing merchants in Quezaltenango), and unwillingness to sponsor risky new projects in mining, etc. (Woodward, 1966).

Despite the revival of some colonial institutions, the Conservatives could not turn the clock back. In some respects their regime was more a continuation of than a break with Liberalism. For one thing, after the decline of indigo, the chief export throughout both regimes was the red dye, cochineal. The switch to cochineal in the early nineteenth century had been financed primarily by the Guatemala City merchants, who retained control of credit for its cultivation. Requiring no large amounts of land, capital investment, or labor, cochineal was cultivated primarily by small *ladino* growers. As one of Carrera's advisers summarized its effects:

> It was a factor of development for the nation, helping to consolidate internal peace, since it employed the class of *mestizos* which, without a means of satisfying aspirations and with disdain for the manual labor of honest and industrious people, appears to be in America an enemy of public tranquility. (Enrique Palacios, cited in Solórzano, 1963:312)

Like indigo, cochineal was grown for export, thus depending on world market demand. The invention of cheap chemical dyes in the 1850's brought a quick end to the Guatemalan cochineal industry. The decline of cochineal stimulated interest in diversification: primarily in sugar, cotton, and coffee. Sugar enjoyed a brief export boom to California during the 1860's. With the outbreak of the Civil War in the United States and the secession and blockade of the southern (cotton) states, world market demand and prices for cotton rose. British interests needing alternative cotton sources, as well as the Guatemalan government seeking new exports, provided incentives to cotton growers in Guatemala. The end of the American Civil War halted the short-lived cotton boom—another example of the precariousness of a dependent capitalist economy, fluctuating with the whims of the world market. This was compounded by an insect plague in Guatemala. Significantly, the Guatemalan textile industry, which had supplied the domestic market in colonial times, had been wiped out by cheaper British textile imports after independence (Woodward, 1964:88; Solórzano, 1963:302, Piedra-Santa, 1971:7).

Although Carrera had risen to power on the crest of a strong wave of "nationalism," foreign economic and political influence continued during his regime. Despite the colonization fiasco of the 1830's, the Conservative regime re-validated the concessions to British companies and pushed several new schemes; in 1842 a contract was signed with a Belgian colonization company, on more or less the same terms as the earlier British concessions, and with the same disastrous results; an 1868 decree offered all the by now standard incentives to individual immigrants. U.S. interest in settling blacks in tropical areas, however, was rebuffed: "white immigrants would be welcome, but not negroes" (Jones, 1940:171). Several contracts were signed with foreign companies for construction of roads, bridges and ports; most of the projects failed and had to be completed by the Guatemalan government and the *Consulado*. Popular suspicion of foreign interests remained active. For example, the influential *Consulado* opposed construction of the Santo Tomás port by a British company, arguing that the terms were not favorable to Guatemala (i.e., to the merchants' monopolistic interests) and that it might stimulate popular unrest (although a majority in the *Consulado* subsequently favored contracting a Belgian company to do the job).

Trade remained a major nexus between Guatemala and Britain. By this time, important British interests had been incorporated into the merchant elite, consolidating a Guatemala-London axis not unlike the colonial link with Sevilla and Cádiz. Although Carrera greatly reduced the public debt and raised funds through merchant loans and colonial-style taxes, the fiscal situation remained precarious. Turning once again to foreign sources, Carrera contracted a Swiss bank to found a bank with exclusive issue rights, but opposition from vested lending interests stopped the project. New British loans were signed in 1856 for £100,000 (to refund the unsettled *deuda inglesa*), and in 1869 for £500,000, revenue from customs duties serving as the guarantee in both cases.

Although British interests remained primarily commercial, the line between commerce and political-territorial expansion was often blurred. Carrera proved most amenable to British machinations, carried out principally by agent Frederick Chatfield, and even participated in a plan to request a British "protectorate" over Central America (cf. Rodríguez,

1965:73ff.; Karnes, 1961:112ff.). On several occasions British men-of-war appeared off the coast to remind Central Americans of their financial obligations and to assure the "rights" of British merchants. With Belice as a *de facto* foothold in Central America, England occupied several areas including the Bay Islands and Mosquito Shore.

British apprehensions over U.S. intentions in Central America (beginning with the 1823 Monroe Doctrine) deepened after the proclamation of "Manifest Destiny" and the defeat of Mexico in the late 1840's. During the mid-century California "Gold Rush," Central America assumed additional importance for the U.S. as a transit route. The "encounter of the two imperialisms" (Cardoza y Aragón, 1965:298) was played out through the intermittent Central American wars between the Conservative regimes (including Carrera's), supported by England, and the Liberal regimes (El Salvador and Honduras), supported by the United States. Competing Anglo-American interests in a Nicaraguan canal were temporarily resolved in the 1850 Clayton-Bulwer Treaty, in which both agreed to "respect" Central American sovereignty, and that any canal should not be controlled or fortified by either nation. Tensions were renewed with the expedition of the American adventurer, William Walker, who "conquered" Nicaragua and received U.S. diplomatic recognition. Although the Central American governments attempted to oust Walker, only the combined efforts of England and the American railroad baron, Cornelius Vanderbilt (whose Nicaraguan transit company had been confiscated by Walker), were successful. The 1856 Dallas-Clarendon Treaty between England and the United States formalized Walker's retreat from Nicaragua, and Britain's from various Central American enclaves—except that the United States (without consulting Guatemala) recognized British rights and the doubling of British territorial holdings in Belice. Only three years later, when it was a *fait accompli,* did England sign a convention with Guatemala, formalizing British sovereignty and the new boundaries in Belice, and providing for British construction of highway or river communications between Guatemala City and the Atlantic coast near Belice—a provision which the British never fulfilled, thus giving Guatemala grounds for its denunciation of the treaty and current claims on Belice.

The Carrera period is generally evaluated as a kind of regression in Guatemalan history—the "dark" era between the Liberal regimes of Gálvez and Barrios. In fact, however, most of the underlying forces remained continuous from 1821 to 1871. Ultimately "development" under the highly educated, "progressive" *criollo,* Gálvez, was not strikingly different from the "reaction" under the illiterate, proletarian *"caudillo,"* Carrera.

THE LIBERAL REFORM: "MODERNIZATION" AND DENATIONALIZATION, 1871–1944

By the 1860's political independence had made very little structural difference in Guatemala. The colonial economy and class structure had taken new forms, but in essence remained intact. Gálvez attempted to provide an opening for an ascendant rural *ladino* upper middle class; but the political economy of cochineal was an insufficient base for their consolidation of power. Carrera, while ostensibly representing a strange coalition of *criollos*, poor *ladinos* and Indians, all threatened by this rising class, was in fact forced to nourish the ascendant *ladino* (rural upper middle) class, since it provided Guatemala's main export. What the Liberals had been unable to accomplish by legislation and the Conservatives had been unable to prevent—the definitive rise to power of a new class—was made possible by developments outside Guatemala.

It is characteristic of dependent capitalism, whose lifeline is its exports, regulated by foreign rather than domestic interests, that fundamental change originates from shifts in the world market. In this case the stimulus came from the expansion of world capitalism, generated by the consolidation of the Industrial Revolution in Europe and the United States, the attendant growth of prosperity and international commerce, and the monopolistic concentration of wealth. This expansion took three concrete forms which, although not simultaneous, converged in the second half of the nineteenth century to reshape the process of underdevelopment in Guatemala: the rising demand for coffee; the generation of surplus capital in the industrial nations, seeking new investment outlets; and the definitive rise of the United States as a world power.

(1) *Coffee:* Greater prosperity, changing tastes, technological advances and lower transport (railroad and steamship) costs in the world's centers created a new demand for coffee; conversely, Europe and the United States needed markets for their manufactured goods, and would therefore profit by strengthening commercial ties with the underdeveloped areas. For Guatemala this signified a shift from a mono-export economy based on cochineal to one based primarily on coffee. Although coffee had been grown and promoted sporadically a century earlier, it took hold only with the stimulus from the world market and the recognition by the Guatemalan bourgeoisie that coffee offered the only salvation from chronic economic stagnation.

The spread of coffee had several important implications. First, it provided an opening for adjustments in the Guatemalan power structure, culminating in the triumph of Liberalism. Second, large-scale production of coffee necessitated basic reforms in four areas: (a) *land tenure:* whereas indigo and cochineal had been grown by thousands of small and medium producers, coffee required large expanses of land, with ownership concentrated in a relatively small group; (b) *infrastructure,* particularly transport and port facilities; (c) *credit* for initial investment and working capital (plus a series of fiscal incentives); (d) *labor:* coffee, unlike cochineal, required large concentrations of cheap labor power. These reforms would require legislative and financial support for private enterprise from the state. Taken together they added up to a significant modification (but not transformation) of the colonial institutions and class relations. Third, to the extent that Guatemala came to depend on coffee for foreign exchange earnings (50 percent by 1871 (Woodward, 1966:51), 92 percent by 1880 (Mosk, 1955:12), 76.6 percent by 1929 (Wickiezer, 1943:22)), the entire Guatemalan economy was regulated by the fluctuations in world demand and prices for coffee.

The dramatic increase in demand, particularly from the United States after the 1870's, provided the initial stimulus. Periodic crises in the world market, stemming from the policies of Brazil (the major coffee exporter), or economic conditions and price manipulations in the great financial and consumption centers, reverberated sharply in Guatemala. The entire Guatemalan economy reflected the 1896–7 financial panic and drop in coffee prices, followed by twelve years of generally low prices; the 1909–13 rise in prices and subsequent slump before World War I; the dislocations in world trade and eventual loss of the German market caused by the War; the subsequent increased dependence on the United States market (while Germany consumed 61 percent of Guatemalan coffee exports in 1900 and .5 percent in 1920, the United States rose from 19 percent in 1900 to 83 percent in 1920 (Ukers, 1922:192)); and finally the crash of October, 1929, which drove coffee prices during the 1930's down to half of the 1929 level. For Guatemala, as we shall see, these fluctuations brought periodic unemployment, food crises, monetary chaos and a chronic shortage of public revenues. The only significant departure from coffee—the banana enclave—diversified but did not essentially change the political economy of mono-export.

(2) *Imperialism:* The consolidation of monopoly capitalism—the concentration of production and capital in a few hands—generated capital surpluses in Europe and the U.S. which needed outlets in profitable investment abroad. The evolution of capitalism from its competitive to its monopoly stage during the last quarter of the nineteenth century, the intensification of its global expansion through the export of capital as well as commodities, and the increasing control over raw materials resources throughout the world formed the bases for imperialism, in the

specific sense of the word.[4] For the underdeveloped countries such as Guatemala, imperialism combined with the previously established commercial ties to the world market to accelerate and deepen the evolution of dependent capitalism. Its specific forms in Guatemala were monopolistic, foreign private investment, stronger financial links to foreign interests, and continual, if often subtle, political intervention. As a result of the shift from the earlier British "free trade imperialism" to the formal imperialism of direct foreign (German, British and especially U.S.) control over important productive sectors of the economy, new ties were created to the world market, new areas of the Guatemalan political economy were penetrated by foreign capital, and the alliance between the privileged Guatemalan bourgeoisie and privileged foreign interests was consolidated.

(3) *Definitive rise of the United States:* After the 1870's Britain was forced into a defensive posture, both world-wide and in Guatemala, principally *vis-à-vis* the United States. For several decades after the 1870's, Central America was an arena of competition among British, German and U.S. interests; but particularly after the World War, which reduced German influence and weakened England, American interests penetrated all spheres of Guatemalan life. More than a mere displacement of British hegemony, U.S. ascendancy signified a reinforcement and a shift in the nature of Guatemalan dependency and underdevelopment.

THE POLITICAL ECONOMY OF COFFEE

The shift to a coffee economy made possible and necessary an adjustment of the social order inherited from the colonial era. Specifically, the ruling class, previously the preserve of a tiny *criollo* elite, was forced to expand, to include the *ladino* upper middle class. This class, and principally its rural sector, frustrated since Independence, now found in coffee the economic base for its rise to power. (Significant support came also from urban commercial interests.) Their ascendance, concretized in the triumph of Liberalism in 1871, did not *displace* the old *criollo* elite, but rather was a successful challenge of the *exclusive* power previously held by the old *criollos*. The *cafeteleros* (large-scale coffee growers) were "enemies who wished to attain equality with the *criollos* with respect to the possibilities of obtaining land and controlling the Indians to exploit them" (Martínez, 1970:577). Their interest, therefore, was not in totally

[4] According to Lenin's classical definition: "Imperialism is capitalism in that stage of development in which the dominance of monopolies and finance [banking merged with industrial] capital has established itself; in which the export of capital has acquired pronounced importance; in which the division of the world among the international trusts has begun; in which the division of all territories of the globe among the biggest capitalist powers has been completed" (Lenin, 1965:106).

restructuring, but in modifying and expanding the bases of Guatemalan wealth, through reforms to meet *their* needs.

Historically this readjustment began with the death of Carrera in 1865, followed by six years of Conservative rule, facing constant political-military challenges by the Liberals. The insurgents finally won in 1871 (with a good deal of assistance from the Liberal regime in Mexico), led by two strongmen: Miguel Garcia Granados (born in Spain and rooted in the cosmopolitan mercantile *criollo* bourgeoisie and in the Liberal intelligentsia) and Justo Rufino Barrios (a moderately wealthy and upwardly mobile provincial grower). After Garcia Granados' brief rule, Barrios became President from 1873 to 1885. He was succeeded by a series of Liberal regimes: M. Lisandro Barillas (1886–92) and J. M. Reyna Barrios (1892–8), both military generals; M. Estrada Cabrera, who took power in 1898 after Reyna Barrios' assassination, and maintained his rule through "re-election" and a police state until he was forced to resign in 1920; a brief "democratic" interlude in 1921, quickly overthrown and followed by several transitional regimes; and finally the fourteen-year rule (1931–44) of the military dictator, Jorge Ubico.

Characteristic of all these regimes was the Liberal ideology: a firm positivist belief in material "progress"—which, although disguised rhetorically as "national progress," meant in reality the advancement of the bourgeoisie; a more active role for the state in protecting and subsidizing, but never regulating or restricting, private enterprise; and an open door to foreign interests. (In Barrios' words, "One of the principal and most urgent needs is to bring foreign capital and great currents of honest, intelligent and industrious immigrants to exploit the vast resources of this country." [Guzmán & Herbert, 1970:72].) The political expression of increased and centralized state power was dictatorship, repression and generalized terror for all but the ruling class.

The principal task of the Liberals was an "agrarian reform" which would facilitate a new accumulation of wealth. The first move was the nationalization of all lands belonging to the Church and monasteries; also appropriated were lands belonging to small holders, municipal *ejidos,* and communal holdings in Indian villages. These lands, plus vast uncultivated state holdings, were divided up and sold cheaply or granted to private interests. Complementary legislation facilitated property inheritance, land transactions, property evaluation, surveys and settlement of disputes, established an ownership register, and suppressed restrictive taxes (e.g., *diezmos*). Occasional measures to limit the size of holdings were not seriously applied (Piedra-Santa, 1971:40). By 1926, concentration of land tenure was such that only 7.3 percent of the population owned property (Jones, 1940:176). Thus the Liberal reforms strengthened the bases of a *latifundismo*, tightly integrated into the world market.

Who gained from this massive land redistribution? The principal Guatemalan beneficiaries were previously medium growers, who became *latifundistas* by virtue of their ability to buy or negotiate with the government for land. No less important, foreign interests were encouraged to take advantage of the new legislation. Various colonization laws attempted to induce European and American immigration, always under privileged conditions reminiscent of those offered by Gálvez in the 1830's (free passage, housing, medical care, land, labor and exemption from taxes, export-import duties and military duty, etc.). The individual immigrants who came quickly rose into the ranks of the Guatemalan bourgeoisie. From the very outset, coffee growing, processing and trade had been largely financed by foreign (mainly German) interests; particularly during crises in coffee prices, Guatemalan producers were often forced to sell out to their creditors. By 1914 nearly half of the coffee was produced on foreign (mainly German)-owned land (Jones, 1940:206–7), thus depriving Guatemala of a good share of its potential export earnings. Even after World War I and through the 1930's, this proportion did not change, as Germans regained much of their property expropriated during the war. By 1931 foreigners (including foreign corporations, such as United Fruit Company) owned more than thirty percent of all land under cultivation, their average holding being twenty-five times the size of average national holdings (Jones, 1940:178).

The losers, as always, were the lower classes and the state itself. The state presided over its own impoverishment through the policy of parceling out most cultivable public lands to private interests. Legislation requiring titles to private property legitimated the appropriation of municipal and Indian communal holdings, particularly those deemed "uncultivated" (in reality lying fallow to increase their fertility). Only a few half-hearted attempts were made to restore land to some communities. One group of Indians came from Nahualá to voice their protest to the President in the 1890's:

> "You have ordered us to leave our lands so that coffee can be grown. . . . [These lands] have always been ours. We have paid for them three times [under Presidents Carrera, Cerna and Barrios]. We have the money now. How much do you want for our own lands this time?" (Melville & Melville, 1971:21)

The lower classes also suffered from another effect of the "land reform"; since the best lands had been appropriated for specialized and commercial export crops, principally coffee, the growing of food for domestic consumption was relegated primarily to the uneconomic *minifundias*. The result was to convert Guatemala, for the first time by 1900, into an importer of food staples, to drive up prices for those staples, and to create serious food shortages, especially in periods of crisis when imports were restricted (e.g., 1907). The various campaigns for agricultural diversification, both in staple foods and in new exports (sugar, bananas, rubber, etc.), only reinforced the takeover of large-scale production by foreign interests, and in any case did very little to alleviate the problem.

The full potential of the "land reform" could not be realized without concomitant advances in infrastructure—not primarily in services for the Guatemalan people, but in strengthened ties to the world market. Particularly lacking were facilities for transporting and shipping coffee. Port, railroad and communications construction were begun and initially financed with Guatemalan resources; but the financing as well as the construction contracts soon passed into the hands of foreign, predominantly American, enterprises. A similar pattern of "modernization" and denationalization prevailed for other public works—water systems, hospitals, telegraph, etc.

Particlarly given the instability of coffee prices, credit for heavy initial investments (in machinery, etc.) and working capital remained a chronic problem for coffee producers. Although the *Consulado* was suppressed after 1871, capital remained the monopoly of export-import intermediaries, who were ultimately dependent on foreign buyers. Their usurious (high interest, short-term) loans often forced producers to sell coffee at prices dictated by the exporters and to mortgage their crops, with dual results. On the one hand, the new coffee *latifundistas,* particularly those who ran the *beneficios* or processing plants, established their own banking institutions. By 1895 six commercial banks were operating. What began as a conflict between *cafeteleros* and export-import interests resulted in their integration: while the wealthiest *cafeteleros* began to export their own coffee, many export-import firms became producers as they took over the farms of their debtors. The latter pattern was especially common among foreigners who, unlike Guatemalans, had direct access to the European and American banks (for credit) and coffee markets. On the other hand, lack of credit forced small and medium producers to sell out to the *latifundista-beneficio*-financial-mercantile interests, thus accentuating the disappearance of small farms, the concentration of land ownership and the proletarianization of the countryside.

The benefits of the Reform to the newly privileged *ladinos* were predicated upon forging new chains for the Indians. The Liberal governments took it upon themselves to guarantee the permanent supply of cheap labor required by the new *cafeteleros* and foreign investors. The land reform itself contributed to this end. As during the conquest, the Indians were dispossessed of their land, the more easily to be converted into a cheap and captive labor force. Indian villages which had been left intact during the colonial era were shattered, as their inhabitants were forced to migrate from the highlands to the previously unpopulated coffee-growing areas near the coast. Official legislation defined the categories of forced labor: debt slavery was revived in the form of *colonos,* peons tied to *fincas* (plantations) through hereditary debt to the *finqueros.* Under the *habilitación* system, designed to recruit seasonal labor under "contract," agents of particular *fincas* came to the villages to lend money to the Indians; to pay off the debt, the Indians were "contracted" to work on the *fincas,* particularly during harvest. (Although these Indians were theoretically "freely" contracted wage laborers, the *finqueros* had no contractual obligations, leaving large numbers of Indians unemployed during periods of low coffee prices.) In a revival of the colonial *mandamientos, jefes políticos* (local officials) maintained registers or lists of Indians available for work at the request of *finqueros.*

The state, too, used these registers to recruit its labor force for military service and construction of public works: e.g., under the *vialidad* system, Indians who could not pay a two *peso* head tax (i.e., almost all Indians) were compelled to work for two weeks (later one month) a year on road construction. Thus the state used Indian labor to meet the coffee-growers' needs for roads, ports, and other "public" works. Finally, vagrancy laws required *all* Indians—not just those in debt—to work at least 150 days a year and to carry a *libreto* (card) showing the number of days they had worked. While eliminating debt slavery, the 1934 vagrancy law was in reality a more systematic form of forced labor.

The full power of the state was applied to enforce these regulations. In 1934 the Labor Department officially became an adjunct of the National Police. Those who resisted their "obligation" to do useful work, by periodically revolting or leaving the *fincas,* were jailed. The registers of local authorities followed the Indians everywhere, restricting their movement from one village to another. In short, Liberalism subjected the Indians to the institutionalized violence of a police state. Their situation worsened steadily, as new laws patched up the few remaining "loopholes" and perfected "contracts" as the new disguise for forced labor.[5] This

[5] These forms of forced wage labor (as opposed to classical "free" wage labor) have frequently been interpreted as feudal relations of production ("serfdom"). Despite their patrimonial and compulsory aspects, however, there existed a great "social and cultural gulf" between *finqueros* and workers, accentuated by the high rate of absentee ownership (Hoyt, 1955:34–5). Moreover, these labor forms were part of a capitalist structure of production for the world market; they signified *not* the "survival of feudalism" (in fact, Guatemala was never "feudal"), but rather the more complete penetration of world capitalism to all levels of Guatemalan society.

exploitative and brutal face of the Liberal state was not incidental but essential to its "generous" face (concessions, protection and subsidies to the Guatemalan bourgeoisie and foreign interests). Once again, the human price of "modernization" and of further integration into the world market was paid by the Indians.

Although most obvious in regard to the economic base (land and labor relations of coffee), the two faces of Liberalism were revealed also in the state's extension of authority in superstructural programs. On the one hand, the Liberal state took responsibility for reforms and modernization in areas previously neglected or left to the clergy. Special stimulus was given to the secularization, expansion and standardization of education at all levels—although shortage of public funds limited education for the masses, and by 1921 the illiteracy rate was still 86.8 percent (Jones, 1940: 337). With an eye toward removing threats to and consolidating their own authority, the Liberal regimes greatly reduced the power of the Church through nationalization of its holdings, elimination of its special privileges, expulsion of clergy and religious orders (which were fomenting opposition in the East), freedom of religion and secularization of education, marriage, etc. Administrative reforms centralized and increased the efficiency of national and local government, concentrating authority in the Presidency and the executive bureaucracy.

But the dark face of political "modernization" was terror. Particularly during the Estrada Cabrera and Ubico dictatorships, the apparatus of repression was perfected: a larger, stronger, and professional army and *Guardia Civil* (accompanied by the founding of the professional training school, *Escuela Politécnica,* in 1873 and the institution of compulsory military service) ; reorganization and training of the police, with the aid of a New York expert; Presidential power to declare martial law; antisedition legislation; and a network of secret informers. Liberal practice made a mockery of Liberal ideals: *continuismo* (rigged re-elections) vs. the principle of "free elections"; absolute Presidential authority vs. the constitutional principle of "separation of powers"; martial law, censorship and suppression of political opposition vs. Liberalism's traditional "individual guarantees." Yet these political realities were the *sine qua non* to guarantee a tranquil and stable climate for the material advance of the Guatemalan bourgeoisie and foreign capital.

THE AGE OF IMPERIALISM IN GUATEMALA— STAGE ONE

The strengthening of the bourgeoisie and the state within Guatemala during the Liberal era was in many respects only relative. The absolute beneficiaries of Liberalism were not Guatemalans at all, but foreign—

primarily U.S.—interests. The vehicles of Guatemala's definitive entry into the orbit of the U.S. were private investment, loans, trade and political intervention. By the 1930's, U.S. interests were no longer a series of "foreign influences," but had become part and parcel of domestic Guatemalan life, reinforcing the structures of a dependent capitalism.

Direct (private) U.S. investment after the 1870's did not have to force its way into Guatemala; it was *invited* in and given every possible favor by the Liberal regimes. Barrios sounded the keynote:

> I am not like many Central Americans who believe that the North American intervention in such enterprises is dangerous for the integrity and independence of Central America. . . . What more should we wish than that the country as a whole should profit in all ways with this [U.S.] powerful influence destroying the ignorance of the masses who now neither serve nor produce, redeeming them with the stimulus of work, and making them understand their rights and duties (quoted in Jones, 1940:250).

Although foreign investors hastened to take advantage of the Liberal incentive legislation in various sectors, by far the most important single investments were three U.S. monopolies, in agriculture for export (United Fruit) and in public services (International Railways of Central America, Electric Bond and Share).

At the end of World War I, Guatemala faced total darkness. The nation's electrical facilities, constructed by German interests, had been intervened and nationalized during the War under U.S. supervision. In 1919 the Guatemalan *Intendente* (supervisor), Daniel Hodgson, an American citizen, warned the government that the nation's electricity would have to be suspended (and *that* would mean total chaos), due to the shortage of electrical equipment and spare parts which, in the postwar era, were available only from the U.S. For some time the U.S. War Trade Board refused to authorize a license for export of these materials from the U.S. Pleas by Guatemalan officials to release the equipment were of no avail in Washington. Then, miraculously, the War Trade Board authorized shipment of the equipment—but only after licensing the U.S. monopoly, Electric Bond and Share (EBS), to negotiate the purchase of the nationalized Guatemalan electrical facilities. Under these pressures (and particularly since the U.S. Ambassador was considered the "custodian of enemy goods in Guatemala"), the Guatemalan government had to do business with EBS. The 1919 contract stipulated EBS rental of the facilities for 10 years, at $40,000 a year. The ink was hardly dry when it was violated: the EBS representative, H. W. Catlin, secretly (without the required public bidding and without authorization) bought 495 shares (out of 600) at one-third their real value and in 1920 illegally "sold" them to Central American Power Company, an EBS subsidiary. Meanwhile, in 1920, without government authorization, he ceded the initial rental contract to another subsidiary, American Foreign Power Co., which was not even licensed to operate in Guatemala.

These maneuvers resulted in EBS acquisition of the installations in 1922 (in violation of the Guatemalan Constitution and of the rental concession, which prevented sale of the enterprise for 10 years), and in the continual raising of electricity rates in Guatemala. The 1922 contract gave EBS an unchallengeable monopoly, free reign over rates and a series of special privileges for fifty years. These and subsequent changes of the company's legal status in Guatemala were designed to avoid U.S. as well as Guatemalan taxes and U.S. anti-trust (holding company) legislation, and to stimulate "new investment." By the 1940's the EBS subsidiary American Foreign Power owned 81.8 percent of the stock of *Empresa Eléctrica Guatemalteca* (EEG) (as it was now called), leaving the remaining 18.2 percent in the hands of the most cooperative Guatemalan bourgeoisie. All of the company's accounting was done in New York, so that Guatemalan authorities were unable to keep track of the financial irregularities and of undeclared profits remitted to EBS in the U.S. (partly through a $50,000 a year "technical service" contract with another EBS subsidiary). Exorbitant rates and bad service became permanent features of Guatemalan electricity. The various maneuvers by EBS had, of course, made a farce of the Guatemalan Constitution and laws.

The rise of the banana-railroad empire in Guatemala, which can only be sketched in its barest outlines here, began indirectly in the late nineteenth century. (The best sources are: Bauer, 1956; Kepner & Soothill, 1967; León Aragon, 1950; for the Company's point of view, see May & Plaza, 1958). Several rail lines from the Pacific to the capital were begun by U.S. contractors (in association with Guatemalan citizens), financed internally or by public foreign loans. (The main lines were: San José-Guatemala and Pan American [both built by the U.S.-owned Guatemala Central Railroad Company] and Champerico-Retalhuleu and Ocos [both eventually bought out by that company].) Although the contracts were always favorable to foreign interests (tax exemptions, subsidies, concessions of land surrounding the tracks, etc.), the lines were owned and principally financed by Guatemala. The Northern Railroad, from Puerto Barrios on the Atlantic to the capital, was undertaken initially by a series of U.S. companies, but eventually by the government and financed through internal taxes. When it was two-thirds completed, in 1904, the government signed a concession with the U.S.-based Guatemala Railroad Company, whereby the latter took over the completed portion and undertook construction of the remaining sixty miles. In exchange, the company received, in addition to all the standard privileges, incentives and guarantees, a great deal of land, the right to operate the entire line for ninety-nine years and virtual ownership of Puerto Barrios itself. The head of the Guatemala Railroad Company, Minor C. Keith, was already a railroad baron in Costa Rica, and just happened to be vice president of United Fruit. In 1912 the Company changed its name to International Railways of Central America (IRCA) and with Guatemalan governmental approval took over *all* existing railroad lines in Guatemala (including the Pacific lines, of which it had not constructed an inch).

By a contract of 1908, IRCA was to have built a line from Zacapa to the El Salvador border—which it failed to do until a second contract was signed in 1923 for the same line. One clause in the 1923 contract entitled the government to half of the net profits on this new line, but this was annulled in a 1936 agreement. The 1923 contract also enabled IRCA to standardize and consolidate the contracts for all its holdings, thereby extending the excessive privileges of the 1904 and 1908 contracts to all its holdings, many of whose initial contracts had been less favorable. By 1930 IRCA owned the major Atlantic port and 887 miles of railroad in Guatemala and El Salvador—virtually every mile in Guatemala, including the large sections financed by the Guatemalan people. Thus, the opening wedge of a mere sixty miles on the Northern Railroad had given IRCA monopolistic control over land transportation in Guatemala.

Meanwhile, in 1901, the Boston-based United Fruit Company (UF) had secured a contract to transport Guatemalan mail from Puerto Barrios to the United States in its shipping line, the Great White Fleet. "On the side" the contract also premitted UF to buy bananas from Guatemalan producers through individual contracts, at fixed prices; it could then transport the bananas in the Great White Fleet to guaranteed U.S. markets. Not until 1924 did UF get a formal land concession around the Motagua River to grow bananas. How, then, did UF manage to produce a high percentage of the bananas it exported from 1901 to 1924? Through a series of maneuvers and manipulations of contracts with individual growers, the Company had ruined and forced many of them to sell out to UF: 1) by rejecting large quantities of bananas, thereby causing great losses to growers, and keeping prices high in the U.S. markets; 2) by producing more efficiently and cheaply, as monopolies are able to do; 3) by controlling scarce water resources; 4) by controlling transport to the U.S. through its Great White Fleet; 5) by monopolizing railroad transport within Guatemala, as well as the major Atlantic port, via its virtual subsidiary IRCA; 6) by having access to the Rio Motagua lands ceded to IRCA in its 1904 contract. The key, of course, was the interrelation between UF and IRCA; coincidentally, the same Minor Keith who was president of IRCA from 1911 to 1929 was vice president of UF from 1899 to 1921. Thus, the 1924 contract, renting UF thirty square kilometers of the best Guatemalan land for twenty-five years at $6,000 (later $14,000) a year and formalizing its operations on previously acquired lands, merely legalized a *de facto* monopoly. Subsequent contracts prolonged and even extended UF's empire, always on unbelievably favorable terms.

On the Pacific coast a small company had been contracted to construct port facilities. In 1929 UF, fearing competition for its Atlantic port, and seeking a foothold on the Pacific coast, forced the smaller company to sell its concession and its lands to a UF subsidiary, Compania Agrícola de Guatemala (CAG). The CAG already had a 1928 contract to construct a "modern" Pacific port, which it had rescinded in 1929 (once the competitor was out of the way) and renewed in 1930. That the entire port construction was nothing more than a pretext for UF to eliminate its rival and to gain land for its Pacific banana plantations became clear in 1936, when a new agreement with the government formally cancelled the Company's obligation to build the port. The determining consideration, which deprived Guatemala of a modern Pacific port and retarded the region's development, was IRCA's monopoly on rail transport from the coffee-growing areas to the Atlantic and its desire to channel all trade through the Company port, Puerto Barrios.[6] Thus, in the words of the Company's apologists, the 1936 agreement, plus UF's simultaneous payment of IRCA's debts, was a "lifesaver for IRCA" (May & Plaza, 1958: 167). This was neither the first nor the last time the Company defaulted on its obligations to Guatemala.

If IRCA and UF ignored their obligations, they used—and misused—their privileges, subsidies and guarantees (which can only be summarized here) to the point of absurdity: unlimited use for twenty-five to ninety-nine years of much of the best land in Guatemala, and of all Guatemala's resources (water, forests, etc.); exemption from stamp, port, and other taxes, from duties on *all* imports (including items like food for their commissaries, as well as construction materials), and from all but an insignificant export tax (1 cent, later two cents per *racimo* of bananas,

[6] The incredible hell-hole created by the Company in Puerto Barrios was graphically described by a journalist of the 1930's: "Puerto Barrios, boom banana port, epitomizes the haste and cruelty and bleeding rawness of the process . . . in Puerto Barrios the conglomerate ugliness of raw-product exploitation is spewed forth into the glaring torrid sunlight. . . . Yes, Puerto Barrios is an achievement in ugliness in a natural setting of beauty . . . . [always] a group thumping the marimba, 'Yes, we have no bananas' " (Beals, 1932:144–6).

so that bananas contributed 1.9 percent of their total export value compared with 8.7 percent for coffee) (Kepner & Soothill, 1967:213); unlimited profit remittances, thus further depriving Guatemala of the potential balance of payment benefits; freedom to construct telegraph and related networks and to extend their operations into new, unrelated areas; virtual non-regulation of railroad rates; protection of the railroad against competition, thus assuring its monopoly; annual government subsidies of $5,000 to $12,000 to IRCA; liberty to import foreign workers, who would then be exempt from many of the duties of Guatemalan citizens; and virtual secrecy of their accounting records, giving the companies a *carte blanche* for endless manipulations of records for purposes of tax evasion.

The monopoly over production and "public services" was staggering, particularly given the relationship between UF and IRCA. Through Minor Keith and other interlocking directors, this relationship had been cemented long before the 1936 formal agreement, whereby UF acquired forty-three percent of IRCA stock and openly invested in rail cars. It was evidenced also in IRCA's discriminatory rates: bananas were transported much more cheaply than other produce, and UF bananas more cheaply than those of independent growers. IRCA rates to transport coffee (grown near the Pacific) to Pacific ports were more than double the rates per mile to the Company-owned Puerto Barrios, on the Atlantic, which was also the base for UF's Great White Fleet (Kepner & Soothill, 1967:162). The vertical integration, monopolistic at every stage, was complete: from banana lands (and all the necessary installations for company towns) to the IRCA lines, the port facilities, the shipping fleet, and the Fruit Dispatch Company for banana transport and distribution within the U.S. In fact, the Company diversified far beyond what was needed for its banana operations: other subsidiaries included the Tropical Radio and Telegraph Co. (initially constructed by Guatemalans and operated by the government), other transport and shipping lines and numerous (non-banana) food industries. It was, in short, an incipient conglomerate.

Within the Guatemalan context, the empire became the prototypical enclave or "state within a state": an autonomous entity (with even its own schools, commissaries and hospitals), contributing negatively to the local economy (since it exported far more capital than it invested), and making decisions in response to the needs of its Boston directors. Yet, by virtue of sheer financial power, the Company was able to exert more influence on the Guatemalan government than any internal pressure group and to deprive the state of control over the resources necessary for development. Indeed, its numerous tax exemptions, subsidies and excessive profit remittances added up to a significant impoverishment of the Guatemalan public sector, and a general decapitalization of the nation. While the strategists of this monumental rip-off remained in Boston, it could not have been achieved without the collaboration of a pliant, dependent Guatemalan bourgeoisie and its government. That bourgeoisie's perception of total compatibility between its interests and those of the U.S. monopolies, and the Guatemalan state's complicity in its own impoverishment, were fundamental to the Liberal mentality. For the entire strategy was predicated on the assumption that the future of "development" lay in tighter integration into the capitalist world market, rather than the creation of a strong domestic market based on mass purchasing power; and if foreign monopolies held the key to that integration, so be it.

Guatemala's intensified integration into the world market—increasingly into the U.S. sphere—took other forms as well. Continued vulnerability to the frequently fluctuating world prices of one or two agricultural exports contributed to a chronic monetary and financial crisis. Periodic declines in the value of export earnings combined with other factors to depress the exchange value of the local currency. The depreciation of Guatemalan currency and the resulting inflation were compounded by Estrada Cabrera's decision, shortly before 1900, to permit private banks (from which the government had been borrowing heavily) to issue unsecured, irredeemable paper bills. The results were increased monetary instability, virtual control of the monetary system by the private banks and twenty-five years of serious inflation. What prolonged the monetary chaos and inflation was their profitability to powerful Guatemalan and foreign interests. The principal beneficiaries were producers for export (primarily the coffee and banana interests)—who sold in a gold market, while paying for services (including wages) in worthless paper money—and the related complex of private bankers, foreign financial interests and speculators. The losers were producers for domestic consumption, generally small growers, and above all, salary- and wage-earners, squeezed between low wages and rising prices. Vested domestic and foreign interests, given free reign by the state, enjoyed their bonanza until 1923, when the first reforms were made: stabilization of the exchange rate, elimination of the worthless paper bills, establishment of a monetary reserve and of the *quetzal* as a monetary unit on a par with the U.S. dollar, and in 1926 of a state bank backed by gold reserves.

Meanwhile, the public revenues had been depleted by the government's dependence on unreliable export earnings and by its loss of revenue through tax exemptions and subsidies to vested interests. Lacking funds with which to finance its ambitious "modernization" program (e.g., in railroads) and to pay off old debts, the government resorted once again to foreign borrowing. This expedient did not resolve, but aggravated, the problem. New loans were added to the *deuda inglesa* inherited from the post-Independence era. When coffee prices were low, the Liberal governments defaulted on debt repayments, setting off a vicious cycle of compounded interest, elaborate refunding schemes, and overt political pressure by several European governments on behalf of their bondholders (threatening seizure of Guatemalan ports, sending warships, etc.) in 1902 and again in 1912. Although saved by World War I from the more odious pressures (e.g., customs receivership), Guatemala was forced to pledge customs income, the coffee export tax, sugar tax, liquor tax, consular invoice tax, and profits from railways, electricity plants, banks and the match monopoly—in short, nearly all sources of income—as security for these loans (Jones, 1934:158). The mortgage of public revenues to debt service was chronic; the only question was which of the irate bondholders had priority. Repayment of the foreign debt ($16.4 million by 1930) continued to drain what little foreign exchange there was until the 1930's when Ubico settled a large portion of it.

The U.S., worried that these unpaid debts to competing claimants might serve as a pretext for *European* intervention in Guatemala, after 1900 encouraged participation by American banking syndicates in refunding schemes. In the 1920's New York displaced London as the principal market for Guatemalan bonds. The pound sterling was gradually replaced by the dollar in government bonds and in loans for infrastructure projects. Financial dependency on the U.S. was complemented by commercial dependency, particularly after World War I and the decline of trade with Germany: by 1922–23, 60–62 percent of all Guatemalan imports came from the U.S. and 67–77 percent of all exports went to the U.S. (Young, 1925:43–4).

As American corporations and bondholders acquired increasing interests in Guatemala, Washington became more determined to preserve "stability" there and throughout the area. (U.S. direct investment had risen from $6 million in 1897 to $58.8 million in 1929 (Torres, 1969: 111), including investment in mining, food processing, etc., as well as the three monopolies.) Asserting that the projected Panama Canal "puts these Central American countries in the front yard of the U.S." (Secretary of State Elihu Root, quoted in Munro, 1964:155), the United States became the champion and the overseer of various "peacekeeping" schemes. The United States took a leading role in arbitrating the boundary dispute between Guatemala and Honduras—a dispute which, although dating back to the 1820's, had been dormant until conflicting claims to the land by the United Fruit Company in Guatemala and the Cuyamel banana-railroad interests in Honduras resulted in armed confrontations in the late 1920's. (Before a border settlement was reached, UF won its claims by buying out Cuyamel in 1929.) The intermittent wars and interventions among the Central American countries, interspersed with abortive attempts at reviving a Central American union and the "peacekeeping" agreements of 1907 and 1923, all served as pretexts for U.S. intervention. The United States sent warships "to protect American citizens and property" in 1885 after Barrios declared his intention to unify Central America by force, and again in 1906. (Karnes, 1961:160, 186). Ironically, Barrios had made every conceivable effort to obtain U.S. support for his ambitions in Central America, offering even to assist U.S. acquisition of territory in Central America and a canal concession in Nicaragua (Rippy, 1940).) Symbolic of U.S. tutelage over Central American affairs was the Washington Conference of 1923, presumably convened to work out *Central American* affairs: an American chairman presiding over an agenda set by the U.S. relegated the Central Americans to the status of "secondary partners" (Karnes, 1961:223ff.)

Equally effective in protecting American interests was Washington's manipulation of Guatemala's internal politics. His signature of the 1901 and 1904 concessions with UF and IRCA guaranteed Estrada Cabrera U.S. support for reelection, while his refusal to cede electrical facilities to EBS in 1919 resulted in U.S. acquiescence in his ouster. When his successor remained firm against EBS, the United States permitted his overthrow in 1921, and recognized the unconstitutional but more cooperative (with EBS and IRCA) Orrellana regime—although the U.S. sponsored Agreement of 1907 prohibited recognition of *golpista* regimes. During the 1930 power shuffle, the United States refused to recognize "undesirable" candidates, while maneuvering for the eventual "election" of Jorge Ubico (who had begun his career by working closely with the Rockefeller Foundation, and in whom the State Department had been actively interested since the demise of Estrada Cabrera in 1919). Ubico's cooperation with U.S. corporations "won him special concessions for Guatemalan coffee in the U.S. market" (Rodríguez, 1965:130), and U.S. support for his "reelection" in 1936, which coincided with contract revisions and additional privileges to UF and IRCA (Munro, 1964; Krehm, 1957; Bauer, 1966).[7]

---

[7] By the 1920's American ambassadors were operating as pro-consuls, as described by an American journalist who interviewed one during the 1930's: "[Ambassador Geissler's] influence had succeeded in convincing [President] Orellana to ratify the Washington 1923 treaties, to revise a railway concession . . . to replace the French officers training the Guatemalan army with American officers. . . As an evidence of the pernicious Mexican influence, Geissler pointed out the new labor law of Guatemala. Fortunately the government had brought it to him for

The unchecked advance of American penetration reveals as much about Guatemalan Liberalism as about the undoubtedly imperialist ambitions of the U.S. corporations and government. The groundwork for imperialism had been laid in the evolution of a dependent capitalism in Guatemala. Given the historical and social roots of Liberalism, whatever "modernization" and "development" of the material base it might promote would change only the modalities but not the basic nature of Guatemala's relation to the world market. The ruling class of Liberalism, primarily the coffee-export-import oligarchy, had evolved as a dependent bourgeoisie, tightly aligned with foreign interests, owing its hegemony within Guatemala to this alliance and to its function in relation to the world market. Therefore, the Liberals accepted Guatemala's role in the international division of labor as a simple provider of coffee and bananas for European and U.S. consumers. Therefore, too, they permitted the monopolistic banana export enclave to manipulate the Guatemalan economy in accordance with the interests of corporate and financial directors in Boston. Having ceded so much to private U.S. interests, they were hardly in a position to resist official U.S. "protection" of those interests.

Eagerly welcoming monopolistic foreign investors, following the latest fashions in London, Paris and New York, alienated from the social necessities of Guatemala, the new bourgeoisie obtained state power not in order to transform the nation's neo-colonial structure but rather to profit by it, to make room for themselves. In this sense, the Reform signified a re-formation of colonial class relations, permitting merely the incorporation of the *cafeteleros* and their urban counterparts within the dominant *criollo* bourgeoisie. In no sense could the Reform be considered a *"ladino"* movement, particularly since it did nothing for the *ladino* proletariat; rather it was the logical expression of the *ladino cafetereros'* aspiration to become *criollos*. Their very ascendancy, in fact, was based on the general underdevelopment of Guatemala—as evidenced by their manipulation of the monetary system, and, even more clearly, by their development of new, more "perfect," more violent mechanisms for exploiting the Indian labor force.

As the tool of a dependent bourgeoisie, the Liberal state collaborated in its own impoverishment—through its economic and monetary policies, through the concessions, subsidies and tax exemptions to foreign monopolies, through the latter's unrestricted remittance of profits, and through

---

prior consideration. . . The worst features had been ironed out before passage. . . The State Department had been obliged to warn the Guatemalan government not to accept loans from Schwartz [local] banking interests" (Beals, 1932:75–6).

the personal fortunes built by the rulers themselves. Liberalism produced, furthermore, the paradox of the "strong" state which, in fact, voluntarily yielded all control over national resources and production to private interests, and whose only real function was the protection of those private interests and the preservation of law and order. In the name of "development," Liberalism reinforced capitalist underdevelopment for the nation as a whole, in order that a tiny minority might preserve its privileges.

THE LITTLE REVOLUTION THAT COULDN'T

Seventy years of Liberalism had deepened the dependent capitalism of mono-export in Guatemala and had left the nation perpetually on the brink of crisis. The underlying internal instabilities were finally revealed, and the collapse of the Liberal order was triggered, however, by external events: the contraction of world capitalism in the 1929 crash and depression of the 1930's, followed by World War II.

The shock of the 1929 crash was transmitted to the Guatemalan economy, as always, via the sector most closely linked to the world market, the coffee export sector. During the 1930's coffee prices fell to less than half of the 1929 level. Whatever possibilities might have existed for a recuperation of prices in the late 1930's were shattered by the Brazilian price war of 1937. The advent of World War II effectively foreclosed Guatemalan access to European markets, greatly increasing dependence on the United States (27.1 percent of coffee exports went to the United States in 1930–4, 51 percent in 1935–9, 90.4 percent in 1940–4 (Torres, 1969:140)) and enabling the United States to set prices almost unilaterally. Low prices, combined with a decreased volume of exports, resulted in a significant loss of export earnings. Aside from Guatemala's reduced import capacity, the supply of manufactured imports was cut off during the Depression and the War. The crisis in the foreign trade sector was translated into general and prolonged economic stagnation: drastically reduced state expenditures; rising unemployment, both rural and urban; and loss of property by smaller producers, driving many of them into the subsistence sector. This stagnation was a logical expression of the contradictions inherent in an economy regulated by its foreign trade sector.

Nevertheless, the major contraction in world capitalism, specifically in U.S. expansion abroad, presented potential opportunities for Latin American countries to alter the previously established international division of labor. In fact, the larger South American nations took advantage of the hiatus in imperialism to diversify production, to reduce their dependence on manufactured imports, and to broaden their domestic market through import-substituting industrialization. But the Ubico regime, instead of seeking alternatives, attempted to shore up a faltering system, to reinforce the *status quo*. No measures were taken to alleviate the serious unemployment in all sectors of the economy. Rather than stimulating new areas of production, Ubico adopted deflationary policies: restriction of bank credit, of public investment, and of budget expenditures (i.e., a forty percent cut in salaries of the bureaucracy). The deflationary thrust was so extreme that despite the sharp decline in public income, the state treasury maintained a budget surplus from 1933–34 through the entire World War. (cf. Torres, 1969:127ff.) Diversification efforts were initiated only during World War II by the U.S., in need of reliable and nearby sources of rubber, essential oils, vegetable fibres and other strategic materials. Nor did Ubico take advantage of the outflow (*dis*investment) of foreign capital to establish national control over key sectors of the economy; instead, new contracts extended the privileges of the U.S. monopolies.

Why was the state incapable of taking the necessary initiatives to rationalize and modernize Guatemalan capitalism? The crucial factor was the social base of Liberalism and of the Ubico regime, specifically the *cafetelero*-export-import oligarchy allied with U.S. monopolies. Pushed to the wall by the repercussions of the world economic crisis, this Guatemalan bourgeoisie could not conceive of alternative solutions, such as import-substituting industrialization and the expansion of the domestic market. Industrial investment would have entailed risks which they were not prepared to take. Moreover, such innovations were bound to release new social forces and to alter the Guatemalan power structure—a prospect which horrified the Guatemalan bourgeoisie. Their response therefore was to secure state cooperation in protecting their specific interests, in facilitating exploitation of the Indian labor force, and in maintaining law and order. Thus the 1930's brought lower wages and new repressive labor legislation (e.g., the anti-vagrancy law of 1934 and a 1944 law permitting *finqueros* to shoot trespassers seeking food, etc.).

These policies were enforced politically by censorship, secret police, and brute military force directed against increasing social tensions and workers' revolts. In 1933, for example, the government executed one hundred labor leaders, students and members of the political opposition. This authoritarian solution was "a way of making the popular sectors— including . . . peasants, urban workers, employees and bureaucrats, small property owners, merchants and artisans—pay the price of the economic contraction" (Torres, 1969:142). It represented the last stand of a desperate dependent bourgeoisie. The inability and unwillingness of the *cafeteleros* to resolve the crisis of dependent capitalism by stimulating national development—in short, to act as a national bourgeoisie—revealed not their strength but their weakness.

As is generally the case for those defending an intolerable *status quo*, their violent defense combined with internal and external contradictions to destroy the very stability they sought. Even their dependence on the U.S. backfired: the catalyst for change came from that metropolis, now parading as a "Good Neighbor," during World War II. The United States enforced the liquidation of the sizeable German coffee, banking and merchant interests in Guatemala, even sending FBI agents to carry out the expropriations and interning German Guatemalans in American camps. Thus Ubico and the *cafeteleros* were deprived of their strongest allies. The legitimacy of the regime was further challenged by the known pro-fascist sympathies of Ubico and the concrete ties to German interests of many of his close advisers and Cabinet Ministers. Thousands of U.S. troops were stationed in Guatemala, presumably to defend the Panama Canal—and to keep Ubico in line with Allies. Moreover, American anti-fascist propaganda provided an ideological base for Ubico's opponents. Freedom of speech and worship, freedom from fear and want, were now in fashion, and clashed strikingly with the political realities of *Ubiquismo*. By 1944 the certain defeat of fascism by bourgeois democracy—the dénouement of inter-imperialist rivalry—had created within Guatemala a new opening for a broad frontal attack on the Ubico dictatorship and the oligarchy it represented.

The crisis came to a head in June, 1944, two months after popular pressure had ousted the dictatorship in neighboring El Salvador. What began as a student strike, demanding University autonomy from government control, mushroomed into a general strike in Guatemala City, after the government denied the students' demands, suspended constitutional guarantees, and fired on anti-government demonstrators, killing one. Within a week the general strike and continual anti-government demonstrations forced Ubico to resign. He appointed a military triumvirate which maneuvered the "election" of Federico Ponce as Provisional President. After promising a few token concessions, the Ponce regime consolidated its power, kept on many *Ubiquistas* in high positions, and stepped up the level of repression. Discontent spread: workers throughout the country, and even army officers, protested that their wages and salaries had never been lower. The political opposition, feeling the brunt of the terror, and recognizing that Ponce had no intention of holding elections, finally opted for armed revolt. On October 20, 1944, armed students and workers joined the dissident military officers to oust Ponce. The interim *Junta Revolucionaria,* headed by two army officers, Francisco

Arana and Jacobo Arbenz, and a civilian, Jorge Toriello, held congressional and presidential elections. On March 15, 1945, Juan José Arévalo became President, having received eighty-five percent of the (literate male) vote.

Who were the October Revolutionaries? The dominant force was the urban petty bourgeoisie, generally educated but frustrated by the absence of political liberty and of opportunities for economic advancement. The movement was spearheaded by a generation of university students mostly of "middle-class origins," who perceived themselves as "classless" and as "spokesmen of the Guatemalan people," offering workers and peasants "a party which would *take into account* their needs and concerns." (Villamar, 1969:55–61) (emphasis added) The coalition also included intellectuals and professionals (e.g., lawyers); small businessmen and merchants, whose economic prospects had been limited; and underpaid public employees, including teachers and junior army officers. These groups were joined by progressive, nationalistic property-owners who had been out of favor with Ubico (many of whom had participated in the 1920 ouster of Estrada Cabrera).

The movement was also supported by a limited number of politicized peasants, and by the incipient proletariat, both rural (primarily banana workers) and urban (impoverished artisans and workers in the few factories). The role of the Indian labor force was marginal in the October movement itself. Nevertheless, general unrest among the Indians had undermined the stability of the Ubico and Ponce regimes; as in 1821, rebellious Indians demanding land and food in Patzicia in October, 1944, had to be subdued by troops and machine guns. But the plight of the Indians was hardly the chief concern of the October Revolutionaries. Even the organized workers were clearly junior partners in the movement, and their interests were secondary. What made the Revolutionary coalition possible was the desire of nearly every sector of the population, excluding only the tiny coffee bourgeoisie and foreign interests, to overthrow Ubico and establish a constitutional bourgeois democratic order. Beyond that, however, the needs of the various classes were by no means identical, nor even compatible. As the Revolution took power, its broad social base could not be preserved intact. The big question for the future of the Revolution was: whose hands would guide it, and for what ends?

"SPIRITUAL SOCIALISM" IN POWER

The first Revolutionary President, Arévalo, was an intellectual and educator. Despite his claims of belonging to no political party or social class (Martz, 1959:29), he was clearly of petty bourgeois origins. His ideological orientation was a rather *sui generis* "spiritual socialism." It was "socialist" only in being inspired by a concern for humanitarian ideals, human dignity and public welfare . His idealism, the standard fare of social democrats, opposed both Liberal individualism and Marxian socialism as "materialist." Leaving aside the details of his ideology (see Díaz, 1958: ch. III), what was Arévalo's program for Guatemala?

The first task of Arévalo, and of the new Constitution adopted a few days before he took office, was to establish political democracy. "Universal" suffrage was granted to all adults except illiterate women—76.1 percent of women and 95.2 percent of Indian women as of 1950 (Arias, 1962:8, 11). Freedom of speech, press, etc., were guaranteed. Political parties could be organized and function freely—all but the Communist and other "foreign or international" parties. Thus, after the seventy year Liberal dictatorship which had excluded all politics, elections might have real contenders, offering real alternatives to the people. Political power was decentralized, as the University, municipalities, armed forces and other institutions were made autonomous.

The Arévalo government devoted one-third of state expenditures (Bauer, 1956:27) to an ambitious social welfare program, with emphasis on construction of schools, hospitals and housing. The educational system was reorganized and reformed at all levels. A national literacy campaign worked mainly with *ladinos,* although attention was later given to Indian males (Inman, 1951:22). Public health programs focused on sanitation, nutrition, immunization and an extensive system of hospitals and clinics. Full social security coverage was provided for workers. In these and other areas the Arévalo government received considerable technical assistance from the United Nations and other international agencies and from the U.S.

This badly needed social legislation would have been meaningless, however, in the absence of an organized labor movement. The Guatemalan labor force as of 1945 was ninety percent rural, consisting mainly of unorganized, unprotected Indian coffee workers. The only rural force recognizable as a modern proletariat, concentrated at the point of production, with the germ of collective consciousness and a history of spontaneous strikes before 1945, were the 15,000 workers on the two United Fruit plantations. In the cities, too, the largest proletarian concentrations were in the Company's railroad (5,500 IRCA employees) and port installations. The "industrial proletariat," working principally in light industry —textile, food processing and beer factories—constituted 1.7 percent of the economically active population, complemented by an artisan semi-proletariat (Bush, 1950: II, 2ff.). Wage levels as of 1945 were unbelievably low: an average Q6.08 (=$6.08, with one Guatemalan Quetzal equalling one American dollar) per week for the few industrial workers

(Q 4.59 for women), and Q 2.00 weekly in agriculture (Guerra, 1969:31 —although other estimates gives figures as low as Q.25–.50 daily in the cities and Q.07–.10 daily in the countryside). The weakness and lack of organization of the work force before 1945 were the result of its very structure—few large concentrations of freely contracted labor—and of the deliberately repressive policies of the pre-Revolutionary regimes (prohibiting unions, except for docile, government-controlled "mutualist" organizations, shooting any serious organizers, and banning and helping smash virtually all strikes).

With the advent of the Revolution, for the first time in Guatemalan history, legislation was passed to *protect,* rather than to further exploit, labor. The 1945 Constitution abolished the vagrancy laws and all forms of forced labor, and laid the foundations for labor legislation. The 1947 Labor Code defined basic rights: compulsory labor-management contracts; minimum wages (in principle, although no figure was specified); equal pay for equal work; decent working conditions; social security coverage; right to strike; and right to organize unions. Nevertheless, the government retained the power to recognize (or refuse to recognize) specific unions, to arbitrate labor disputes through a network of courts, and to dissolve "illegal" unions (including those which served "foreign interests" or engaged openly in politics). Thus at least some of the workers obtained legal mechanisms for redress of grievances and gradual wage increases.

Urban, banana and railroad workers quickly began to organize to secure their rights under the Labor Code. During the Arévalo government, several important labor confederations emerged, representing diverse political positions, and engaging in considerable ideological and factional struggles. The leadership was predominantly petty bourgeois, and the objectives were primarily *revindicalista,* oriented toward immediate improvement of working conditions. By 1950 a number of collective pacts and limited gains had been achieved, despite strong opposition from organized employers.

The majority of the rural ninety percent of the proletariat did not fare as well. Rural wages rose little or not at all. The 1947 Code made no provision for unionization on *fincas* employing fewer that five hundred workers. A 1948 amendment permitted their organization, but peasant unions were required to have at least 50 initial members, two-thirds of whom had to be literate. These unions attempted to enforce implementation of the Labor Code, minimum wage requirements, and prohibition of earlier forms of exploitation in the *campo* (countryside). Even so, the Arévalo government made no attempt to facilitate rural unionization, and on some occasions obstructed it. More important, even in the face of consistent pressure from the principal rural labor confederation, Arévalo was not prepared to make the basic structural change in the *campo,* an agrarian reform.

Guatemala's heritage of underdevelopment left no doubt as to the necessity for changes in the nation's productive base. Arévalo initiated a program of *fomento,* or investment promotion, directed mainly toward diversification of the economic base. A principal agency was the Instituto de Fomento de la Producción (INFOP), which, together with the newly created state bank, Banco de Guatemala, provided credit for agricultural diversification. The 1947 Industrial Promotion Law gave incentives for private industrial investment, especially elaboration of Guatemalan resources. Financing for these and other programs was facilitated through the rationalization of the banking system under the Banco de Guatemala. Although these measures were crucial in creating new jobs and diversifying production, the real test of Arévalo's intention to transform the structure of the Guatemalan economy arose with respect to two critical areas: foreign enclaves and land tenure. It was in these areas that throughgoing social change would require encroachment upon deeply entrenched interests.

The approach to foreign investments was to leave them intact, but to begin regulating their operations in accordance with national interests. Concretely, the government attempted to limit EEG (but not IRCA) rates, and to gain compliance with the new labor legislation. IRCA was forced to accept a collective pact. The government insisted that UF submit to arbitration of wage disputes, both in the fields and in Puerto Barrios—although the Company employed numerous forms of pressure (locking out workers, and suspending shipping operations, thus paralyzing the economy (Inman, 1951:51-2)), and won both cases in the end. By 1950, thus, little headway had been made toward *effective* restriction of the power or even the privileges of the three foreign monopolies. With respect to future foreign investment, new laws stipulated that exploitation of Guatemalan resources (especially oil) should be undertaken by the state, by Guatemalan companies "whose capital is predominantly national" or by foreign contractors under government direction. In industry, foreign investors would be welcomed on the same terms as nationals.

Arévalo's agrarian program was implemented in fits and starts. Most of the former German plantations, expropriated during the War, remained under government administration as *fincas nacionales,* to be rented out to individuals, cooperatives or joint stock companies. The 115 *fincas* (primarily in coffee), employing 21,400 workers on a free contract basis (Bush, 1950: II, 44), provided an opportunity for experimentation and diversification. Other government programs promoted and gave state support to consumer, producer and credit cooperatives, provided agricultural credit and technical assistance, and initiated a colonization experiment in the Petén. The 1949 Law of Forced Rentals was designed to stop the widespread *finquero* practice of kicking peasants off land formerly rented to them: under the new law, *finqueros* were required to continue renting those lands, at limited rates, for at least two years. In practice, this law hit small landowners far more than the big *finqueros*. Thus, by 1951, the power and property of the *finqueros* remained virtually untouched. Although the Constitution had recognized the "social function of private property," "prohibited" *latifundias* and permitted expropriation of private property in the public interest, in fact there were no expropriations. This is not surprising, given Arévalo's assessment of the problem:

> In Guatemala there is no agrarian problem; rather, the peasants are psychologically and politically constrained from working the land. The government will create for them the need to work, *but without harming any other class.* (cited in Guerra, 1969:34; emphasis added)

Power structure be damned; it was simply a question of educating the peasants.

All in all, Arévalo's program was one of moderate reforms. Certainly, as one American observer pointed out in 1950, they were "not as radical as those of the New Deal in the U.S. or the Labor Government in Great Britain" (Inman, 1951:10). In no sense could it be considered a social revolution, since the basic structural problems had not been resolved. Conditions for the working class had improved and, far more important, labor had been granted the right to organize to demand change. But Arévalo had managed to avoid taking drastic measures for direct redistribution of income and resources. Nor had the proletariat achieved any independent power: the petty bourgeoisie remained in command, making concessions to the bourgeoisie where necessary, leaving intact their economic power and their potential return to political power.

NATIONAL CAPITALISM ON TRIAL

By 1949 the scramble for the 1950 elections was in full swing. Francisco Arana and Jacobo Arbenz had announced their Presidential candidacies. The right wing opposition saw in Arana (head of the armed forces) their last hope of turning back the Revolution. Minister of Defense Arbenz had strong support from organized labor and two of the three Revolutionary parties. In the highly charged atmosphere of July, 1949, Arana was mysteriously assassinated.[8] The assassination touched off a military uprising led by supporters of Arana. Students and organized workers took to the streets to defeat the rightist insurgents, with arms distributed by the government. All observers agree that this popular volunteer militia was decisive in maintaining Arévalo in power (Bush, 1950:IV, 14; Inman, 1951:17; Suslow cited in Melville & Melville, 1971:36). With order re-established, the campaign continued, interrupted by one more abortive rightist military coup, led by Colonel Carlos Castillo Armas.

In the newly established environment of bourgeois democracy, several political parties had formed, split and finally coalesced into three major currents. Opponents of the Revolution found their candidate in Miguel Ydígoras Fuentes, an old *Ubiquista*. The more moderate elements within the Revolutionary coalition supported Jorge Garcia Granados, from one of Guatemala's oldest "best families," diplomat and drafter of the 1945 Constitution. Arbenz was backed by organized labor, peasants and the more radical groups within the petty bourgeoisie, including two of the three Revolutionary parties and the Communists. The election, universally acknowledged to be honest, gave Arbenz an overwhelming majority: sixty-three percent of the total vote, seventy-seven percent of the votes of the illiterate (males), who were voting (by public, not secret, ballot) for the first time in Guatemalan history.

Upon taking power in 1951, Arbenz clarified his objectives:

> ... first, to convert [Guatemala] from a dependent nation with a semi-colonial economy to an economically independent country; second, to transform our nation from a backward nation with a predominantly feudal economy to a modern capitalist country; and third, to accomplish this transformation in a manner that brings the greatest possible elevation of the living standard of the great masses of the people (Arbenz Inaugural Speech, cited in Díaz, 1958: 267).

In short, the new President envisioned a capitalist development—but a national and independent capitalism, a break from the dependent capitalism (which he called "feudalism") of the past, and significant redistribution of income. Guatemalan dependency could never be overcome so long as all manufactured, construction and capital goods (as well as food) were imported. The strategy, thus, was import-substituting indus-

---

[8] Although many "experts" glibly implicate Arbenz in the assassination, no sound evidence was found; some even speculate that Arana supporters committed the deed to discredit Arbenz (Melville & Melville, 1971:42). In any case, several on-the-scene American observers reported persistent rumors that Arana had been involved in a plot to take power by force (Inman, 1951:11; Bush, 1950:IV, 11–12); if so, it was the twenty-third known attempt to overthrow Arévalo.

trialization, utilizing and transforming national resources—standard U.N. strategy for Latin American development during the 1950's. In fact, Arbenz equated industrialization with Guatemala's transformation into a capitalist nation. Clearly, private enterprise was to be encouraged; Arbenz demonstrated his commitment to the capitalist road by adopting some of the key recommendations of the high-level 1950 World Bank Mission to Guatemala—hardly a socialist outfit! In order to construct even a modern capitalist economy, however, the Arbenz government would have to confront the two great entrenched interests left intact by Arévalo: the foreign monopolies and the landed oligarchy.

New foreign investors would be welcome, so long as they respected Guatemalan sovereignty (e.g., complied with national labor legislation, paid taxes). They would have to refrain from demanding special privileges above and beyond the incentives granted to national investors, from creating monopolies, particularly in natural resources, and from intervening in national politics. But what about the three U.S. monopolies already firmly established in Guatemala? Arbenz's strategy was to limit their previously unchecked power in the Guatemalan economy—not by nationalizing them, but by competing with them and forcing their compliance with national laws. Thus he undertook three great construction projects: a government-run hydroelectric plant, Jurún-Marinalá, which would provide cheaper and better service than EEG; a highway to the Atlantic, to compete with IRCA's expensive monopoly on transport (according to the World Bank, IRCA's rates for all but UF bananas were the highest in the world);[9] and a new Atlantic port, Santo Tomás, to compete with UF's Puerto Barrios.

The game got somewhat rougher as Arbenz evidenced his intention to enforce Guatemalan laws and court rulings. In 1953 the government seized IRCA's assets on the grounds of non-payment of taxes. UF refused to submit to government arbitration of a 1951 wage dispute; the Company also demanded renewal of its previous labor contract for three years, as well as government guarantees protecting it from any possible tax increase, devaluation, or exchange controls. When Arbenz refused to give in and countered with his own demands on the Company, UF curtailed

[9] The issue of IRCA rates was finally brought to a head in the United States around 1950, when the American minority shareholders of IRCA sued the majority owner, UF, claiming that IRCA undercharged UF and overcharged for all other transport. The case was settled in 1960, when a New York Court of Appeals made UF pay $4,531,055 for losses to IRCA through December, 1955. A separate civil anti-trust suit by the U.S. government forced UF to divest itself of all stock ownership in IRCA and to stop other monopolistic practices. Nationalistic Guatemalans, of course, had been trying unsuccessfully to make that point for decades.

its shipping services (thus cutting off Guatemalan trade) and laid off 4000 workers. In response to these pressure tactics, Arbenz confiscated 26,000 acres from UF, as a guarantee for payment of back wages. Nevertheless, in the end, the Company won renewal of the old labor contract in exchange for $650,000 in back wages. As always, UF had resisted the wage increase on the grounds that its wages were already three times those of other Guatemalan workers; but, it has been pointed out, "three times nothing was hardly the solution that labor leaders were seeking" (Rodríguez, 1965:153).

All previous conflicts were a mere warm-up, however, for the storm unleashed by the 1952 agrarian reform law. The precondition for capitalist import-substituting industrialization, Arbenz recognized, was expansion of the domestic market, of mass purchasing power. And the key to the latter, in a nation whose work force was ninety percent rural, was necessarily an agrarian reform. Abolition of forced labor and organization of rural workers were important first steps, but did not resolve the underlying problem of land ownership. Clearly it would be necessary to give the land back to the peasants, to reverse the long process of underdevelopment set in motion by the Spanish conquerors. Since the Liberal Reform had assured the appropriation of all good land by a minority of private owners, no serious agrarian reform could avoid a confrontation with vested interests. An agrarian reform presented, thus, the first possibility of transforming the colonial base of production, and the first serious threat to the Guatemalan and foreign bourgeoisie.

The Arbenz government proceeded cautiously, making careful studies of the land tenure situation and consulting all groups affected (including the *finqueros'* Asociación General de Agricultores) regarding possible reform plans.[10] In the meantime, a 1951 law amended Arévalo's Law of Forced Rental, lowering rents and extending its application to all unused lands. The Agrarian Reform Law itself was finally approved by Congress in June, 1952. The law provided for the expropriation of holdings over 223 acres, particularly idle lands, and their distribution to eligible recipients. Peasants would receive the land in lots not exceeding 42.5 acres, either in ownership or in use for life, and would pay for it at a rate of three percent or five percent of annual production. Compensation would

---

[10] The 1950 Census had revealed that 57 percent of the peasants held no land at all. While 88 percent of farms (*minifundias*) covered 14.3 percent of cultivable land, 2.1 percent of *fincas* covered more than 70 percent. (Twenty-two *finqueros* held 1.3 million acres, or 13.4 percent). *Latifundistas* were keeping 60 percent of their lands idle. The average daily wage of rural workers was 26 cents as opposed to Q1.80 for urban commercial workers (cited in Cardoza y Aragon, 1955:98–9; Díaz, 1958:212; CIDA, 1965:58).

be made through twenty-five year government bonds at three percent interest, the value of the land being determined by the *finqueros'* 1952 valuations for tax purposes. The law would be implemented by agrarian committees (the majortiy of members, for a change, representing peasants) ; all appeals would be handled directly by the President. Aside from these expropriations, land from state-owned *fincas nacionales* would also be distributed. Far from being an attack on private property or capitalism, the law was intended "to liquidate feudal property . . . in order to develop capitalist methods of production in agriculture . . . and to prepare the path for Guatemala's industrialization" (Agrarian Reform Law, cited in Cardoza y Aragón, 1955-85). It was far more moderate than both the Mexican agrarian reform which preceded it and the Cuban reform a few years later.

The government began in 1952 by distributing 107 *fincas nacionales*— many of them, because of their size and their operations of scale, to peasant cooperatives. In January, 1953, the expropriations began. The general objective (sometimes violated in practice) was to eliminate the *fincas* with large expanses of unused land, respecting the integrity of well-worked holdings of any size (CIDA, 1965:43). By June, 1954, 1002 plantations covering 2.7 million acres had been affected (although only 55 percent of that was actually taken, constituting 16.3 percent of available privately owned idle lands), worth Q8,345,544 in indemnization bonds. Approximately 100,000 peasant families received land, as well as credit and technical assistance from new state agencies. Rural social services were vastly improved, as the Indians for the first time since 1524, became the beneficiaries of government policies and graduated from the subsistence economy.

The process did not go smoothly, however. *Finqueros* objected to nearly every aspect of the law—from the Presidential appeal to the amount of compensation to the composition of agrarian committees (how could they be asked to submit to committees dominated by barefoot, illiterate peasants!) to the very idea of expropriation. These objections often took the form of violent retaliations against the peasants. Impatient peasants, in turn, (who, after all, had waited over four hundred years for an opportunity like this) sometimes took initiatives before settlement of the legal formalities; spontaneous land invasions and occupations and peasant violence were not uncommon. Nor did they always discriminate between *latifundistas* and small land-owners. These problems, which created a division between the landless and the small owners, were symptomatic of a general weakness of this structural reform: that it was not accompanied by any deliberate attempt to transform mass consciousness, to build an awareness of who was and who was not the immediate class enemy. Similarly, no serious effort was made to incorporate, educate, or mobilize peasant women in conjunction with the agrarian reform. These were shortcomings of a potentially revolutionary change directed from above by the petty bourgeoisie.

As the largest landowner in Guatemala, UF could hardly expect to retain its holdings intact. Of its over 550,000 acres, no more than fifteen percent were under cultivation. (The Company maintained it needed "large reserves" to combat the effect of banana diseases.) In several decrees, the government expropriated from UF a total of almost 400,000 acres, offering Q 1,185,115 in compensation (Paredes, 1964:30). The Company, backed by the U.S. State Department, claimed the property and damages for the Pacific holdings alone were worth nearly $16 million. The issue was important, not only because of the $15 million difference, but because it provoked the climax of a long-brewing crisis.

THE METROPOLIS RESPONDS

Initial relations between the Arévalo government and Washington were cordial. World War II had given the United States an opportunity to reduce the influence of the competing German interests; and certainly a pro-American petty bourgeois reformist government could be tolerated, so long as it respected long-standing U.S. interests in Guatemala. Thus during the first few years, U.S. technical experts and cultural missions actively assisted Arévalo. Since Arévalo was receptive to foreign capital, U.S. private investment in Guatemala increased from $86.9 million in 1943 to $105.9 million in 1950. But the honeymoon was short-lived. When UF's violations of the Labor Code became a major issue, the U.S. Ambassador "suggested" that the Code be altered, since it "discriminated" against UF (Bauer, 1956:41). Instead of capitulating to pressure and lending its assistance to the Company's violent strike-breaking measures as in the past, the government contested the Company's claims and insisted on a legal settlement of the dispute. Nevertheless, throughout the bitter two-year dispute, the Arévalo government never threatened confiscation of UF property, and even dismissed a Cabinet Minister who suggested such a step.

As nationalism grew in Guatemala, Arévalo was forced to cancel a contract with the U.S. educational mission. The 1949 petroleum law virtually closed the door to several U.S. oil trusts (including Standard Oil of Ohio), despite U.S. Ambassador Patterson's open pressure on their behalf. Patterson further strained relations by arrogantly telling Arévalo to fire several Cabinet Ministers, as well as seventeen "Communists" in the government. When he carried his involvement with the opposition beyond cocktail parties to the point of attending clandestine meetings plotting Arévalo's overthrow, the government informed Washington that it could not guarantee his safety and demanded his recall. By this time Arévalo was being denounced as pro-Communist in the U.S. press and Congress. As one eminent American noted, "the campaign against Guatemala" in principal U.S. media (including *Reader's Digest,* the *New York Herald Tribune,* the *New York Times* and Associated Press) "is too unanimous to have come about by mere chance" (Inman, 1951:iii, 48 & *passim*). UF's friends and other vigilant anti-Communists in the Senate (Senators Lodge, Brewster and Pepper) and in the House (Boston Representative McCormack) supported the Company's claims and echoed the charges of Communism or Communist "inclinations" in the Arévalo government.[11]

The situation deteriorated after 1951. The U.S. opposed and refused aid for Arbenz's highway to the Atlantic (which would end IRCA's transport monopoly). Further difficulties with UF, stemming from labor disputes and the expropriations, culminated in Washington's formal claims against the government on behalf of UF. By this time the U.S. and UF had allies within Guatemala. Arbenz's agrarian reform had polarized public opinion and shattered the Revolutionary coalition of 1944. Urban and rural labor and the majority of the Indian peasants, along with the nationalistic sectors of the petty bourgeoisie, were firmly committed to the Revolution. Opposing it were the *finqueros* and non-landed dependent bourgeoisie tied to U.S. interests, the Catholic Church, and many of the petty bourgeois professionals and military officers who had participated in the Revolution of 1944.

The rest of the story is well known. By early 1954 the government had discovered clear evidence of the plots for its overthrow, which had been rife for more than a year, both within and outside Guatemala. One such plot involving neighboring Central American governments, had led to an armed uprising in Salamá in March, 1953, and resulted in Guatemalan withdrawal from the Organization of Central American States in April, 1953. In January, 1954, the government intercepted conspiratorial correspondence between two of the principal plotters, Castillo Armas and Ydígoras. At the March Inter-American Conference of the Organization

11 Arévalo's disillusionment and bitterness over these attacks were reflected in his final speech as President: ("I came to understand how the great commercial newspapers and broadcasters [distort] the meaning of . . . 'democracy,' 'dignity' and 'liberty' . . . and how, according to certain unwritten . . . international norms, small countries have no right to sovereignty. . ." cited in Díaz, 1958:123) and in his famous writings after 1954 (*Anti-Kommunism in Latin America, The Shark and the Sardines*). Yet by the late 1960's and early 1970's, he served as ambassador for the counter-revolutionary Méndez and Arana regimes.

of American States (OAS) in Caracas, the U.S. twisted enough arms to secure passage of a resolution, clearly directed against Guatemala, for hemispheric unity and mutual defense against "Communist aggression," in effect giving the U.S. a free hand to intervene in any country where such a "menace" existed. (Only Guatemala opposed the resolution, with Mexico and Argentina abstaining.) The Latin American delegates vigorously applauded Guatemalan Foreign Minister Toriello's brilliant speech in defense of Guatemala, while capitulating to U.S. threats of withdrawing aid.

Meanwhile, the U.S. was laying the groundwork for the operation through its team of ambassadors in Central America. Heading the team was the new (since October, 1953) Ambassador to Guatemala, John Peurifoy, a tough, expert anti-Communist trouble-shooter, renowned for his role in making Greece "safe for democracy." (Peurifoy went along with the definition of Communism as "a religion . . . originated in hell, with the assistance of Satan and all the evil forces." [Melville & Melville, 1971:98]) In January, 1954, he was quoted as saying,

> Public opinion in the U.S. might force us to take some measures to prevent Guatemala from falling into the lap of international communism. We cannot permit a Soviet republic to be established between Texas and the Panama Canal. (Travis and Magil, 1954:6)

In May Washington found its pretext for open hostilities against Guatemala, when a shipment of Czechoslovakian arms arrived in Puerto Barrios on the Swedish ship *Alfhem*. (Arbenz had bought the arms from Czechoslovakia only after the U.S. had imposed an embargo on arms to Guatemala from all U.S. "allies" since 1948, and had vigorously blocked all attempts to buy them from "free world" sources, even seizing a shipment of Swiss arms to Guatemala in New York.) In response the U.S. stepped up arms shipments to the reactionary Honduran and Nicaraguan regimes —and to Guatemalan exiles in those countries who were preparing Arbenz's overthrow. Actually, these exiles had been organizing the "Liberation" movement since early 1952. In early 1953, the CIA had made contact with them, choosing Carlos Castillo Armas (a graduate of the U.S. Command and General Staff College at Ft. Leavenworth, Kansas) as their leader, and providing funds for training, equipment and payment of a mercenary army. In May, 1954, U.S. Secretary of State John Foster Dulles (of the law firm Sullivan and Cromwell, which handled UF affairs, and who is said to have written drafts of UF's 1930 and 1936 Guatemalan contracts) openly denounced Guatemala. The U.S. press and Congress added many voices to the anti-Communist crusade. The CIA stepped up its psychological warfare in Guatemala through "Radio Liberty" broadcasts.

Isolated on the diplomatic front, having irrefutable evidence of the invasion conspiracy, the Arbenz government declared a state of seige in early June and took strong action against known collaborators. But these measures came too late. On June 18 Castillo Armas' mercenary force (160–200 men) invaded Guatemala from Honduras; instead of proceeding to Guatemala City for a battle, they stopped just over the border in Esquipulas. All observers agree that militarily the invasion was a fiasco —or would have been, had it not been backed up by the CIA's aerial operations. (Even in Washington, the success of the operation was by no means taken for granted.)

The day after the invasion, Guatemala lodged a formal protest against Honduran and Nicaraguan aggression to the U.N. Security Council. But U.S. delegate and head of the Security Council, Henry Cabot Lodge (an important UF stockholder) ruled that it was not a case of international aggression but of internal "civil war," and therefore of no concern to the Security Council. After the Security Council refused to consider the Guatemalan case, the matter was referred to the U.S.-dominated OAS, which had condemned Guatemala in March and which, according to Guatemalan Foreign Minister Toriello (1955:182) might well have prepared a collective intervention in Guatemala if the U.S. had not acted first.

Meanwhile, CIA planes, manned by American pilots, began a regular bombardment of the capital and other cities, to demoralize the Arbenz government. Arbenz lost his nerve as the chiefs of the armed forces defected or refused to defend the government. On June 27, Arbenz resigned, turning over the government to three "loyal" military officers. At this point U.S. Ambassador Peurifoy refused to accept Arbenz's replacement by the regular Army officers, and began maneuvering for the installation of Castillo Armas, the CIA favorite, as President. On July 3 Castillo Armas entered Guatemala City in Peurifoy's U.S. Embassy plane. After becoming President on July 8, Castillo Armas lost no time in beginning an "anti-Communist" witch hunt, and proceeded with the liquidation of the Guatemalan Revolution.

Any doubts as to the U.S. role in "liberating" Guatemala were subsequently dispelled by President Eisenhower himself, by several Congressmen, by CIA-hired participants and by diplomats (see Wise and Ross, 1964:ch. 11; also Eisenhower, 1963; Toriello, 1955; Cardoza y Aragón, 1955). Relying on "Liberation" sources, one expert estimates that the United States spent $7 million on the operation, to finance costs of training, equipment and salaries for the mercenaries, training bases outside

Guatemala, and training in psychological warfare in the United States (Cehelsky, 1967:58). The U.S.-sponsored invasion of Guatemala came only days after the U.S. installed another dictator, halfway around the world: South Viet Nam's Ngo Dinh Diem. The supposed reason for overt U.S. intervention in Guatemala was to destroy the Communist menace there. Therefore, it is important to determine whether, in fact, such a menace existed and whether, in fact, this was the motivation for the intervention.

"Communism in Guatemala" is one of the most controversial non-issues in Cold War history. Arévalo's "spiritual socialism" was explicitly and unequivocally anti-Communist (e.g., "Communism is contrary to human nature" (cited in Inman, 1951:38)). His actions bore out his words: suppression of the Marxist labor school Claridad; exile of Communist agitators; refusal to legalize the Communist Party; dismissal of several government officials associated with the Communist newspaper and a general "housecleaning"; loyalty to the U.S. with regard to Korea. Nor was he an innocent "dupe" of the Communists; as reported by S. G. Inman (1951:2), an impeccable American anti-Communist, Arévalo said:

> We know exactly who the communists are and what they are doing. At any time that they become a real menace to our national or inter-American safety, we will grab them and put them in jail so quickly they will hardly know what has happened.

That Arévalo was widely denounced in the U.S. as a Communist or fellow traveler is nothing short of incredible. Washington's failure to clarify the issue was an early sign of bad faith toward even an essentially pro-American but nationalist government.

The case of the Arbenz government was more complicated. It is true that Arbenz legalized the Communist Party as the Partido Guatemalteco de Trabajo (PGT) in 1951, and that the PGT subsequently held four out of fifty-six seats in Congress. It is true that the PGT had close ties to and worked within the labor and peasant confederations. It is true that several Marxists held important government positions, particularly related to implementation of the Agrarian Reform Law. It is true that, as he was deserted by many 1944 Revolutionaries, Arbenz eventually needed Communist support for his more radical (but still capitalist) measures. But these facts hardly substantiated the conclusion that Guatemala under Arbenz presented a "Communist threat" to the U.S.—even in the heyday of the international Cold War and McCarthyism in the United States. To evaluate the Arbenz government in terms of the Communist numbers game, as so many State Department apologists and Cold

War scholars have done (e.g., James, 1954; Schneider, 1958; Martz, 1956; La Charité, 1964), is to distort its nature. The prominence of this non-issue, furthermore, obscures the *real* and disturbing problems of the Guatemalan Revolution: why was the United States unable to tolerate the nationalistic capitalist policies of the Revolution? Why did the U.S. intervention succeed? Or, to put it another way, what were the internal contradictions of the Revolution that incapacitated its resistance to imperialism?

The U.S. could not tolerate the Guatemalan Revolution essentially because even a nationalistic independent capitalism directly threatened existing U.S. interests there and called into question the feasibility of maintaining the area as a "safe" preserve for future investments. In the post-war era of expansion, U.S. investors could not afford to rely on an unpredictable national bourgeoisie. Having rid Guatemala of rival European interests during World War II and consolidated Guatemala within its sphere as a market for capital and commodity exports and a source of raw materials, the U.S. was not about to let go easily—particularly since the expanding monopolistic corporations were well represented in Washington. More specifically, the interests of United Fruit, as well as the Company's (at least indirect) participation, were central to the intervention.[12] Behind "anti-Communism" as the motivation, then, lay opposition to *any* regime which might make trouble for U.S. capital. No less important, U.S. interests were threatened by the mobilization of workers and peasants, and their potential for independent action in the future.

[12] If ever there was a clear-cut case of U.S. policy being shaped by direct ties of public officials to private interests, the Guatemalan affair is that case. To mention a few of the details:
—Secretary of State John Foster Dulles was a senior partner in Sullivan and Cromwell, UF's law firm, and had personally helped draw up UF's 1930 and 1936 contracts in Guatemala.
—CIA Chief Allen Dulles (John Foster's brother), had also been with Sullivan and Cromwell.
—Dulles' predecessor as head of the CIA, Walter Bedell Smith, became a Director of UF in 1955.
—Henry Cabot Lodge, U.S. Ambassador to the U.N., was a major UF stockholder and had been on the Company's board.
—John Moors Cabot, Assistant Secretary of State for Inter-American Affairs, was also a major UF stockholder.
—Thomas Dudley Cabot (brother of John M.), also a high State Department official, was a director of First National Bank of Boston (UF's bank, and with interlocking directors); he was only one of several high officials in the Eisenhower Administration with ties to that bank.
—Spruille Braden, ex-Assistant Secretary of State for Latin America who publicly urged armed U.S. intervention in Guatemala in March, 1953, December, 1953

But why was the Revolution so vulnerable to U.S. intervention? The obvious reason was the overwhelming power of the United States brought to bear against it, in contrast with the near absence of support from the socialist bloc. More fundamental, however, in several important respects, it was *not* a revolution: first, in that its structural changes were incomplete; and, second, in that its class base was inadequate to sustain a revolution or to permit the development of a revolutionary consciousness. Any evaluation of the structural reforms must keep in mind, of course, the historical context. To reverse a heritage of more than four hundred years of dependent capitalism and underdevelopment within ten years —particularly during ten years of active expansion by U.S. capital—was, to be sure, a monumental task. Nevertheless, Cuba (learning, perhaps, from the Guatemalan experience), faced with essentially the same obstacles, came much closer to succeeding in the first ten years of its Revolution. The Guatemalan Revolutionary governments made no break from the economy of mono-export (coffee alone was 80% of all exports in 1952) nor from the economic grip of the United States. While disavowing a restrictive bilateral trade treaty with the United States and initiating protectionist policies, the Revolutionary governments never managed to define a clear alternative foreign trade policy. By 1952–3, 85.2% of Guatemalan coffee exports and 83.2% of all exports still went to the United States while 62.9% of all imports originated there (Cardoza y Aragón, 1955:101). Nor did the Revolutionary government definitively eliminate the influence of the great U.S. monopolies.

The failure to alter Guatemala's fundamental relation to the capitalist world market and specifically to the United States was related to the very objectives of the Revolution. Its leaders attempted not to eliminate capi-

---

and May, 1954 speeches, was simultaneously chief of public relations for UF.
—H. Christian Sonne, chairman of the National Planning Association (which published a major book attacking the Arbenz government and a few years later published the major work defending UF operations in Latin America) was director of a leading corporation operating in Guatemala (Travis and Magil, 1954:21).
—At the Guatemalan end, Juan Córdova Cerna, an organizer of the Salamá uprising of 1953, and the liaison between Castillo Armas and the CIA in the "Liberation" itself (Cehelsky, 1967:64–5), was a legal advisor to UF.
—Finally, future President Ydígoras, a principal "Liberation" plotter, in a by-now famous passage in his memoirs, told how he was approached by an ex-UF executive and two CIA agents regarding participation in overthrowing Arbenz; he refused because their conditions included promises by Ydígoras "to favor the United Fruit Co. and the International Railways of Central America; to destroy the railroad workers labor union; . . . to establish a strong-arm government on the style of Ubico. . ." (Ydígoras, 1963:49–50).

talist structures, but to modernize and stabilize capitalism in Guatemala. Private enterprise was respected and even encouraged in new areas; foreign capital was welcomed so long as it respected Guatemalan sovereignty. Even the agrarian reform was capitalist in nature, and was undertaken without the other necessary structural changes. Armed with the vision of overcoming "feudalism," the Revolutionaries (including the Communists) did not comprehend that Guatemalan underdevelopment and dependency were *capitalist;* that national capitalism was an insufficient basis for fighting imperialism; that in a country where underdevelopment was the legacy of four hundred years of integration into the international capitalist system, capitalism was *necessarily* dependent; and that, therefore, the precondition for breaking out of that legacy of dependency as an internal structural condition would have to be an anti-capitalist transformation of Guatemalan society.

These shortcomings were directly related to the urban petty bourgeois class base of the Revolution. The old entrenched bourgeoisie openly opposed the Revolution from the very beginning, continually plotted against it, and were only too glad to collaborate with their U.S. allies in overthrowing it. That they were able to do so reflected the degree to which their power as a *class* had not been destroyed. They and the right-wing "Liberation" activists were, however, a tiny minority, whose motivations were clear. More problematic was the position of those who did not actively collaborate in overthrowing the Revolution. The "modern" bourgeoisie created by the Revolution and its diversification programs, and initially oriented toward the Guatemalan rather than the international market—the new cotton, banking and industrial bourgeoisie, for example—was far more concerned with its own economic advance than with national development. It could easily make its peace with the older bourgeoisie and foreign interests. This group (including many Revolutionary military officers who acquired property) as well as a number of cabinet ministers in the Revolutionary governments revealed its nature as a new sector of the dependent bourgeoisie by not defending the Revolution and by being easily integrated into the rightist, pro-imperialist post-1954 coalition. So much for the "national bourgeoisie."

Similarly, the majority of the urban petty bourgeoisie—professionals, teachers, employees of the state or private enterprise, small and medium property owners, military officers,—initial supporters of the Revolution, eventually collaborated with or acquiesced in its destruction. Their alienation from the Revolutionary process was not, as is often said, because Arbenz "betrayed" it, but because they never wanted a real revolution to begin with. Having made a break with the old bourgeoisie in 1944, these groups needed popular support to come to power. Nevertheless, as a class they remained more interested in consolidating their own political and economic power than in sharing it with the masses. Their motivations, typical of a dependent consciousness, were opportunism, or the desire to promote their own careers through the Revolution, and fear of any alliance which might entail an independent power base for the proletariat and peasantry and a consequent weakening of petty bourgeois hegemony. Thus, after the peasants began taking initiatives, they became skeptical of the agrarian reform and (particularly the military, perceiving a threat to its monopoly on armed force) were horrified by the prospect of a popular militia. And thus, with the fall of the Revolution, the majority were easily incorporated into the counter-revolution. The small sector of the petty bourgeoisie which had been radicalized by contact with the masses and continued to struggle after 1954 was only the exception that proved the rule.

Without question, the Revolution brought real gains to the male proletariat and peasants: improvement in wages and working conditions, social welfare and the right to organize on behalf of their own interests. Under Arbenz the unified labor movement even achieved a certain measure of influence, as did the peasant confederation in regard to the agrarian reform. Their unions, nevertheless, were dominated by a petty bourgeois leadership. Their gains were insecure, insofar as they were conceded by a class which, for the most part, feared their independent power. As expressed by one peasant, "It wasn't we who were in the government; it was Colonel Arbenz, who was merely a friend of ours." A certain degree of class consciousness grew naturally out of the process of organizing, but certainly there was no concerted effort to instill a revolutionary or anti-capitalist consciousness.

Finally, the Revolution did very little for two crucial groups: Indians (*as Indians*) and women (*as women*). To be sure, the Indians obtained full rights as citizens, benefitted from the social welfare legislation, the abolition of forced labor, and the agrarian reform, and in isolated instances even began to participate actively in local politics (Marina, 1968: 96–7). But the Revolution made little headway with their special problems (beyond studying those problems) and provided no basis for their massive, independent, mobilization and politicization *as Indians*. For women, particularly Indian women, the record was worse. The Constitution made some provisions for formal equality (equal wages for equal work) and social welfare, while denying illiterate women the vote. The Alianaza Feminina organized women in support of the Revolution, but its predominantly petty bourgeois leadership limited its mass appeal, especially among the disenfranchised Indian women. Since the Revolution failed to mobilize women or to change their concrete situation *as women,* their continuing conservatism or apathy and their disinterest in defending the Revolution is not surprising. Certainly the experience of the Revolution made clear to Indians and to women that they could never be given their equality and freedom by an urban, *ladino* male petty bourgeoisie, but would have to demand it.

The final overthrow of the Revolution was merely the concrete expression of these latent contradictions. Clearly the petty bourgeoisie, even the Revolutionary sector, would risk nothing to defend it. Colonel Arbenz, on whom the final decision rested, was of the petty bourgeoisie (military), yet had created an alliance with organized labor and peasants. At the critical moment, however, he wavered and (unlike even Arévalo in 1950) relied on his military colleagues rather than on the masses. Around the country, peasants who had benefitted by the agrarian reform clamored for arms to stop the invasion, and in several towns improvised peasant and worker militias, unarmed or armed with machetes, sticks and shotguns, resisted. But the military refused to arm the people. And Arbenz, lacking faith in the popular will or ability to defend the Revolution, and demoralized by the lack of support from his military colleagues, resigned and turned over the government to those very colleagues. They, in turn, were interested only in saving their own skins, and were easily persuaded to permit the triumph of the counter-revolution. Nor, with individual exceptions, did the "sophisticated" petty bourgeois political party leaders, immobilized by internal divisions, offer strong support for resistance. In a real sense, then, Arbenz's vacillation and precipitous resignation epitomized the incapicity of an entire *class* to lead the struggle against underdevelopment and imperialism. The U.S. and the Guatemalan bourgeoisie succeeded because they were able to take advantage of this internal contradiction, which limited the possibilities for a lasting revolution.

THE AGE OF IMPERIALISM IN GUATEMALA— STAGE TWO, 1954–1971

The results of the 1954 CIA-sponsored overthrow in Guatemala are not just history, they are the daily inheritance of Guatemala's destitute. (Melville & Melville, 1971:289)

Safely installed in the Presidency, thanks to the maneuvering of the U.S. Embassy, Castillo Armas proceeded with the main business of the Counter-Revolution: the liquidation of the Revolution and of those who had made it. The government immediately suspended all constitutional guarantees and embarked upon a drastic witch hunt, headed by the former secret police chief under Ubico. Hundreds of political and labor leaders exiled themselves with diplomatic asylum, and many more without it. By conservative estimates, nine thousand were imprisoned and many tortured under the government's virtually unlimited powers of arrest. The official Committee of National Defense against Communism was charged with ferreting out and summarily arresting "Communists" and their sympathizers. A thorough "house-cleaning" in the government bureaucracy resulted in hundreds of firings. But the special targets were United Fruit union organizers and Indian village leaders. The "Preventive Penal Law against Communism" legislated the death penalty for a broad range of "crimes," thus effectively gutting the protective labor legislation of the Revolution. In the countryside scores of peasants were murdered outright. Needless to say, the label of "Communist" was used by the witch hunters against thousands of non-Communist supporters of the Revolution.

Aside from the persecution of individuals, all traces of popular organization were destroyed. The political parties of the Revolution were dissolved (although the PGT remained alive underground). The Castillo Armas regime canceled the registration of 533 unions and amended the Labor Code so as to make effective unionization impossible. Peasant and labor unions were disbanded—including those of UF and IRCA, at the insistence of the companies. In the first year of the "Liberation" the labor movement was reduced from 100,000 to 27,000 (cited in Sloan, 1968:48). Even Serafino Romualdi, Inter-American representative of the (pro-"Liberation") American Federation of Labor, was shocked by the excesses against the entire labor movement in the name of cleaning out the Communists.

While the prisons filled up and the death tolls mounted, simultaneous measures annulled the progressive economic and social legislation of the Revolution. A few of the Revolutionary measures—the Bank of Guatemala, social security legislation, the abolition of forced labor—were retained. By and large, however, Castillo Armas was obsessed with rooting out the programs of the Revolution, particularly those benefitting the lower class. Executive orders repealed the Law of Forced Rental and the 1952 Agrarian Reform Law. 99.6% of all land expropriated under the law was returned to its former owners, including UF. Virtually all beneficiaries of the agrarian reform were dispossessed, and all cooperatives dissolved. Literacy programs, branded tools of Communist indoctrination, were suspended, and hundreds of rural teachers fired. The government ordered the burning and proscription of "subversive" books such as the novels of Guatemalan Miguel Angel Asturias, the writings of Arévalo and other Revolutionaries, Dostoyevsky, and Victor Hugo's *Les Miserables*. The Church, which openly identified with the "Liberation," was restored its pre-1871 privileges, and an open invitation was extended to foreign missionaries.

In place of the nationalistic economic legislation of the Revolution, the Counter-Revolution granted new concessions and privileges to foreign capital. Revolutionary legislation taxing profits remitted abroad was repealed. Suits pending against IRCA and EEG were cancelled. The government returned its land to UF and signed a new contract, although the Company subsequently turned over 100,000 acres to the government and agreed to pay thirty percent taxes on profits. The new Petroleum Code of 1955, replacing that of Arévalo, provided for the cession of subsoil rights to foreign oil companies, and even permitted them to maintain their concessions as unused reserves: at least eight of the largest U.S. oil companies took advantage of this give-away measure, initially drawn up in English and only subsequently translated into Spanish.

Overseeing all of the above was the U.S. Embassy, which obligingly provided the witch-hunters with lists of "Communists" to be eliminated, and the bureaucrats with "ideas" for legislation. During the Castillo Armas years alone, the U.S. poured in $80 million in grant funds, not counting military assistance, and maintained a tight grip on the "development" programs of the Counter-Revolution. Such was the nature of Dulles' "glorious victory" over the people of Guatemala.

THE FOUNDATIONS OF THE COUNTER-REVOLUTION

In some respects the "Liberationists" wished to turn the clock back, to revive the pre-1944 *status quo ante*. In reality, however, such a reversion was not feasible, primarily because of certain definitive changes in the post-war international context. These changes, no less than internal events, redefined Guatemala's position in the international system and profoundly affected the country's evolution after 1954.

Briefly, the principal relevant shifts in the international capitalist division of labor after World War II were the following:

(1) the post-war overseas expansion of (primarily U.S.-based) corporations. Chief characteristics of this new thrust toward investment abroad have been the increasingly monopolistic concentration of capital and resources in fewer units, horizontal and vertical integration in corporate operations, diversification of investments from agricultural and extractive to manufacturing, and multi-nationalization of operations (though not of control over capital);

(2) a more active role of the U.S. government in stimulating and protecting these investors and in maintaining a "favorable (stable) investment climate" in Latin America;

(3) long-range instability and decline in world market prices of traditional Latin American agricultural exports such as coffee; also, changing demand patterns in the advanced capitalist nations for goods which could be produced in Latin America;

(4) definitive hegemony of the U.S. vis-à-vis Latin America;

(5) politically, the Cold War, anti-Communism, and the internationalization of McCarthyism; for Latin America after the Cuban Revolution came to power in 1959, this aspect of U.S. policy took the form of the Alliance for Progress and an extensive counterinsurgency campaign.

In short, changing needs in the metropolis (U.S.) required, on the one hand, that Guatemala supply certain new commodities and services, and on the other hand that Guatemala expand as a market for goods produced by U.S. corporations. Under these conditions, Guatemala's traditional economic and social structure, essentially that of (coffee) mono-export, could not be maintained intact, but had to be modernized. Specifically for Guatemala's economy this implied two basic adjustments: diversification of agricultural production, particularly for export, and import-substituting industrialization. Given the necessity for these changes, the question was how, under whose leadership, and for whose benefit they would be made.

The first steps toward modernization were taken by the governments of the Revolution. Under post-war international conditions, however, nationalistic independent capitalism was necessarily perceived as too unpredictable, hence an intolerable threat to U.S. interests. Once the Revolutionary route had been blocked, the only alternative was the redefinition and intensification of Guatemalan dependency vis-a-vis the international capitalist system and its dominant power, the United States, and a tighter integration of the Guatemalan economy into that system. Although this dependency is centuries old, its specific manifestations have been altered in accordance with the new forms of foreign penetration of the economy. Concretely, the intensification of dependency has meant that the key to Guatemala's evolution since 1954 has been the country's relation to the United States and U.S. private interests. From this perspective, the increase in U.S. influence over this or that policy or in private U.S. investments are manifestations of a more pervasive and total dependency relation, conditioning all facets and processes of Guatemalan society. The very priorities and policies of Guatemalan development have been set in response to foreign rather than national needs—specifically, the need to maintain favorable conditions for private U.S. investment.

More than anything else, the "Liberation" and the Counter-Revolution represented, in response to the needs of the metropolis, a change in the class composition of the ruling coalition. The nature of this coalition demonstrated the necessity of modifying the forms of the pre-Revolutionary power structure, while reviving its essence. The "Liberation" signified, first, the return to power of the traditional landed and mercantile bourgeoisie—those groups which had supported Ubico and which at no point had been incorporated into the Revolutionary coalition. Given the modernization of Guatemala's productive structure which began during the Revolution and was continued after 1954, however, the traditional agro-export bourgeoisie represented far too narrow a base to wield power by itself. While receiving a new lease on life and retaining their hold over the older agricultural export sectors, the *finqueros* had to incorporate and ally with new social groups, and to venture into non-traditional productive activities.

Allied with the agro-export bourgeoisie was a more "modern" bourgeoisie, in part the product of the Revolution itself. The efforts of the Arévalo and Arbenz regimes to diversify production and to expand exports had generated a new class of property-owners—especially cotton-growers benefitted by INFOP incentives (including some of Arbenz' closest advisers) and industrialists. Despite its initially progressive political stance, this "Revolutionary" bourgeoisie has adopted the conservative, defensive stance and values of the older bourgeoisie, and has behaved since 1954 as a "modernized descendant of the old coffee oligarchy." (Torres, 1969:151). Also included were property-owners from the "Generation of 1920," veterans of the movement to oust Estrada Cabrera—some of whom, while initially supporting the Revolution, later became leading "Liberationists." The majority of the "new" industrial-financial bourgeoisie, however, has acquired its property base *since* rather than during the Revolution. Rooted in the post-1954 diversification of the economy, this sector owes its position to, and has benefitted from, the nation's dependency vis-à-vis the U.S. Particularly for the industrial bourgeoisie, the junior partner of foreign interests, the Revolutionary path of non-dependent capitalism was never a real option.

The very nature of the economic diversification has spurred concrete conflicts of interest among these various sectors of the bourgeoisie. Most obvious was the conflict between the traditional importers of manufactured consumer goods, whose interests lay in low tariffs, and the newer producers of those goods, who required a highly protective tariff wall. These potentially divisive conflicts were partially avoided or resolved through the integration or fusion of the two groups. It has been quite common, for example, for former importers of manufactured goods to associate themselves with local or foreign interests setting up factories to produce these goods. Similarly, a significant number of the largest land-owners who formerly only grew certain crops have expanded into industrial processing and manufacturing of those crops (e.g., cotton growers expanding into production of cottonseed oil and its various by-products) and into new agricultural fields. Meanwhile, certain groups within the industrial bourgeoisie began to acquire land, thus bringing their interests in line with those of the older *finqueros*. In short, the power structure of the Counter-Revolution, like that of the 1871 Reform, signified an expansion of the oligarchy, without altering its essence or relation to the majority of the Guatemalan people.

Characteristic of the entire bourgeoisie, both "old" and "new," has been its dependent relation to foreign interests. Particularly since 1954, the *Guatemalan* social base of power has been so narrow, as a result of the deliberate exclusion of all popular sectors, that the bourgeoisie has required an alliance with foreign capital. Owing its domestic dominance to economic, political, and military support from abroad, the Guatemalan bourgeoisie "belongs" more organically to the international bourgeoisie than to Guatemalan society. In exchange for foreign support, this local bourgeoisie behaves as an "intermediary," carries out certain functions on behalf of foreign interests, and has become "the social base required by foreign capital to operate effectively" (Torres, 1971:275). As concrete manifestations of their clientele status, many Guatemalan industrialists, for example, are junior partners in foreign-controlled enterprises. Rather than fighting foreign encroachment, they have followed the path of least resistance and most immediate profits, selling out to foreign interests, often remaining associated as minority shareholders. In this sense, foreign capital constitutes the only *real* Guatemalan bourgeoisie.

The other critical force in the Counter-Revolution has been the male urban *ladino* petty bourgeoisie—including various groups which had participated actively in making the Revolution. The "Liberation" gave expression to a profound split within the ranks of the petty bourgeoisie. A small minority continued to defend the nationalistic values of the Revolution. Carrying this stance to its logical conclusion, some groups, particularly in the University, became the base of support for (and occasionally participants in) the guerrilla struggle. But the opportunistic majority has defined its function as servicing the bourgeoisie, newly returned to power.

In order to understand the behavior and orientation of the petty bourgeoisie since 1954, we must briefly recall its origins. Specifically, how was it possible that the very class which formed the backbone of the Revolution was so quickly integrated into the "Liberation?" The majority of the petty bourgeoisie, alienated by the progressive radicalization of the Revolution, and instinctively fearful of the independent organized power of the working class and peasants over which it had no control, turned to the bourgeoisie for security. Moreover, the primary motivation of the petty bourgeoisie in making the Revolution had been to break out of the frustration of the economic depression and lack of opportunities under Ubico. Essentially the same motivation which, under particular historical conditions, gave them a progressive role in 1944, led them ten years later to acquiesce in the most conservative and repressive measures of the Counter-Revolution.

Furthermore, a sizeable sector of the petty bourgeoisie, both before and after 1954, was rooted in the expansion of Guatemala's productive structure. Agricultural diversification and industrialization produced a need for lawyers, accountants, engineers, and other university-trained professionals. In the post-1954 balance of power, the straightest road for their advance lay in taking advantage of the new opportunities to service private Guatemalan and international capital. A small number of them even succeeded in bridging the gap between service to the bourgeoisie and membership in the bourgeoisie. This is the case, for example, of high military officers who have acquired land, and lawyers for monopolistic foreign coporations and the largest Guatemalan interests, who also have a material interest in those enterprises.

Another principal sector of the petty bourgeoisie is the public bureaucracy. Rooted initially in the expansion of state services during the Revolution, this bureaucracy is ultimately, if less directly, tied to *private* Guatemalan and foreign interests. Primary motivations for the technocrats are careerism and aspirations for upward mobility, a stake in the existing order, fear of losing their jobs, and hence strong tendencies toward conformism (Weaver, 1970). These rather typical bureaucratic attitudes were no doubt reinforced in the Guatemalan case by the trauma of 1954: those who managed to escape the witch hunt and maintain their jobs (an estimated 70%) could easily be neutralized and incorporated into the new order.

Aside from the University (as the training-ground for professionals) and the bureaucracy, several other petty bourgeois institutions—the Church and the military officer corps—were important as vehicles for foreign influence and anti-Communism, while simultaneously providing individuals with channels of social ascent. In reward for its unequivocal support of the "Liberation" (Archbishop Rossell counted Castillo Armas as a "martyr of authentic anti-Communism"), the Church was fully re-established after 1954. Among other things, the Church was granted the right to teach religion in public schools, civil recognition for religious marriages, *de jure* recognition of the Church (which allowed it to own property for the first time since 1871), tax exemption on its properties, and autonomy for the Catholic university. In addition to its traditional function of educating the children of the elite, the Church has played an important role in pacifying the lower classes, particularly the Indians; as the Archbishop told the slum-dwellers of Guatemala City, "You, the humble ones of this colony, are the most cherished by me; . . . where there is poverty, there is happiness." (Melville & Melville, 1971:252). Eighty-five percent of the clergy are foreign and are financed from abroad (Adams, 1970:289). Their work in community development has, however, produced certain contradictions among the clergy, as we shall see.

With respect to the army, although its base is eighty-nine percent Indian, it is controlled by a *ladino* officer corps whose principal ties are to the Guatemalan bourgeoisie, and to the U.S., which provides training. The role of the military in the Counter-Revolution has been to serve the bourgeoisie, not only through armed protection of its property, but also · through the role of the military in Guatemalan politics (see below).

While the preceeding sketch of the Guatemalan petty bourgeoisie is necessarily general, it helps explain the behavior of that class since 1954 —specifically, its opportunism, its cooptability, its readiness to abandon the short-lived alliance with the working class and peasants, to provide the instruments for exploiting those classes. The decision of the petty bourgeoisie to consolidate its position vis-à-vis the bourgeoisie, which necessarily implied the total exclusion of all popular forces, is the key to the social base and the "development" strategy of the Counter-Revolution.

THE "DEVELOPMENT" STRATEGY OF THE COUNTER-REVOLUTION: MODERNIZATION OF DEPENDENCY

The modernization of Guatemalan economic and social structure necessitated by post-war conditions provided a certain continuity between the Revolution and Counter-Revolution. The class base and the relation to the U.S. were so drastically altered after 1954, however, as to cause a sharp break with the policies of the Revolution. Specifically, given the class composition of the post-1954 governments, Guatemala's modernization has aggravated the already serious social inequalities, maldistribution of income, and concentration of wealth in the hands of a tiny minority. Furthermore, being carried out by a dependent bourgeoisie, under the tutelage of the U.S., the process has deepened Guatemala's dependency vis-à-vis the U.S. Aside from its specific manifestations such as the sharp increase in private U.S. investments, this dependency has been expressed in two general, all-pervasive ways. First, the entire "development" strategy has been formulated in the United States and transmitted through U.S. foreign aid agencies advising Guatemalan government officials and financing specific programs.

Second, since the cornerstone of the entire policy has been that foreign

(U.S.) private investment is *the* key to economic growth, the corollary is that all development policies should be geared to the creation of a "favorable climate" for such investment, i.e., of conditions which would attract U.S. investors to Guatemala. Specifically, a favorable investment climate has implied such measures as: orthodox fiscal policies; restrictive labor legislation, incentives (AID investment guarantees, industrial promotion laws, etc.); absence of any legislation restricting, regulating, or even orienting foreign investment (e.g. reserving certain sectors of the economy for national investors or the state); absurdly low tax rates; expansion of the market (through regional integration); government provision of basic infrastructure to service foreign investors; and political stability.

Industrialization, foreign investment, and the Central American Common Market: Central to the "development" strategy of the Counter-Revolution has been the deliberate policy of industrialization. As a means of import substitution, this policy was a carry-over from the Revolution. After 1954, however, there were two fundamental changes. First, while Arbenz had understood the crucial link between successful industrialization based on an expanded domestic market (mass purchasing power) and agrarian (and other structural, redistributive) reforms, the post-1954 regimes have attempted to industrialize without making those reforms. What made this appear feasible was the movement, since 1960, toward Central American economic integration. The Central American Common Market has relieved the immediate pressure for basic social transformation: the consumer base could now be enlarged by combing Guatemala's middle- and upper-class consumer base with those of the other Central American nations, thus obviating the immediate need to raise the living standards of the Guatemalan masses. Thus, in post-1954 Guatemala, regional integration has been the inseparable twin of industrialization. The second major difference was that, whereas industrialization under the Revolution had been fundamentally a policy of economic nationalism and liberation from Guatemala's traditional dependence on the advanced capitalist nations, since 1954 it has been a channel for denationalization of Guatemalan property and resources, specifically through the dramatic take-over of industry by foreign (U.S.) capital.

A salient feature of Guatemalan industrialization has been the deliberate refusal of the governments to restrict or regulate such crucial factors as the composition of capital in key sectors, priority sectors for investment, and profit remittances of foreign corporations. The relevant legislation, such as it is, indiscriminately encourages all investment in all sectors by any investor. The Industrial Promotion Law of 1959, replacing a far more restrictive and sensible law of 1947, offers generous fiscal incentives in the form of exemptions from income taxes and from duties on machinery and raw material imports. The indiscriminate application of the measure has led to a sharp loss of revenue to the state, and has rewarded the utilization of imported, rather than local, raw materials. In 1965 these tariff exemptions were nearly 20% of total tariff receipts. By 1968 the state had lost nearly sixty million dollars as a result of those exemptions. The main beneficiaries have been the large, often monopolistic corporations which least need such subsidies. The systematic abuse of this legislation led one economist to conclude that "the cost of industrial promotion in Guatemala has served almost exclusively to finance profits" (Pimentel, 1969:58). Counterproductive as this is for the purposes of national development, it makes good sense, within a policy of industrialization based very heavily on foreign investment, which demands such incentives as the price of locating its plants in Guatemala.

Another symptom of the anti-developmental policy and the resulting concentration of resources is the pattern of bank credit to industry. One study done in the Bank of Guatemala demonstrated that in 1967, two thirds of bank credits to industry went to fourteen percent of firms receiving credit at all (around six percent of all firms) (Bank of Guatemala, 1970:54). Moreover, regional inequalities have been accentuated: as of 1968, sixty-nine percent of all industry was located in and around the capital city.

Even more significant is the failure of industrialization to alleviate Guatemala's serious unemployment problem. Whereas the value added from manufacturing more than tripled between 1950 and 1969 and its contribution to gross domestic product rose from 10 percent in 1950 to nearly 14 percent in 1970 (Rosenthal, 1971:23b), industrial employment as a percent of overall employment remained at about 11.5 percent from 1950 to 1964 (Fletcher et al, 1970:11–14). The ratio of industrial to total non-agricultural employment actually declined between 1925 and 1960. The problem is particularly serious, given the high migration to the cities, which stems in turn from growing rural unemployment: from 1950 to 1962 industrial employment rose an average of 1.5 percent a year, while the urban population increased at an annual rate of 5.1 percent. One source (Gordon, 1971:152) estimates that industry is creating only 1500 new jobs annually.

Industrial technology, particularly in the "non-traditional" sectors, has been capital- rather than labor-intensive, often using sophisticated machinery to do the job which might have employed tens or hundreds of workers. Once again, the reason is directly related to the extraordinarily high proportion of foreign capital: foreign corporations are far less interested in Guatemala's unemployment problem than in cheaply using the technologies already developed elsewhere. For basically the same reason, a high percent of Guatemalan "industry" involves little more than assembling or mixing imported components, and therefore contributes almost nothing to the Guatemalan economy.

To take another indicator: what is billed as import-substituting industrialization, and should therefore be presumed to contribute to resolving Guatemala's balance of payments problems, has in fact aggravated the deficit. Instead of importing the finished product, as was formerly the case, producers based in Guatemala now import most of the components —duty-free, at that. The composition of imports has changed, but the dependence on them has increased. In this sense, industrialization has turned out to be little more than a glorified form of commerce. Finally, the inefficiency and high level of protection of Guatemalan industry has resulted in higher rather than lower prices for Guatemalan consumers.

In summary, by almost any meaningful indicator, Guatemalan industrialization is artificial. In order to understand why this is true, one need only drive out of the capital on the Carreterra (Highway) Roosevelt, past a string of shiny, modern "factories," mainly drug and chemical companies—Upjohn, Hoechst, Abbott, Miles Overseas, Eli Lilly, and so on. Most of these plants employ fewer than fifty (of whom half are in executive or administrative positions), import everything but the water and air used in mixing, enjoy full benefits of the Industrial Promotion Law and unrestricted profit remittances. In short, a principal reason why industrialization has contributed very little to Guatemalan development is that it has become the province of foreign investors—one 1968 study estimates that more than sixty-two percent of all major manufacturing establishments are controlled by foreigners (Bechtol, 1968:25–6); and that all basic decisions are based on maximizing profits to the parent corporations. What differentiates Guatemalan industrialization today from that of the relatively more advanced South American nations is an historical circumstance: in Chile and Brazil, for example, the process began at a time when the advanced capitalist nations were preoccupied with a domestic depression and a world war, and thus began under national control; in Central America, by contrast, since the 1960's was a period of expansion by U.S. capital, industrialization has been dominated by foreign interests from the very outset.

In this sense, industrialization cannot be considered a process organic to the Guatemalan economy; rather, it is part of a shift in the overseas strategy of U.S.-based multinational corporations which has been superimposed upon Guatemala. In part, this shift represents an attempt to reduce the visibility of U.S. corporations as targets of nationalism, to

eliminate the risks involved, for example, in direct agricultural investment, to get around protectionist tariff walls and maintain areas like
Guatemala as markets. This shift has also affected the methods of control: in addition to majority or total ownership of subsidiaries, U.S.-based
corporations maintain control though minority participation, "technical
assistance" contracts, manufacturing licenses, and a host of sophisticated
financial and managerial manipulations. The net effect, however, is
greater rather than lesser penetration of the economy by foreign capital.
Whereas U.S. investment in Guatemala at the end of World War II had
been concentrated in the three monopolistic enclaves in agriculture and
public utilities, the investors of the 1960's are spread over a wide range
of productive activities and dominate the central economic process, industrialization. By 1969 17.4% of U.S. private investment and 34.5% of all
foreign investment was in manufacturing (as compared with .8% and
10% respectively in the early 1960's) (Rosenthal, 1971:108a, 109a).

The movement of foreign investment into new areas has occurred, concretely, in two ways: first, through new investment by companies which
previously had no investment in Guatemala (e.g., Coca Cola, Monsanto,
Texaco, W. R. Grace, International Nickel, Eli Lilly, and so on), and
second, through diversification by the older investors. An example of the
latter trend has been United Fruit, which, shortly after helping bring
down the Arbenz government, began to sell its lands and to pull out of
banana growing; while retaining control over the less risky and visible
marketing of bananas, UF moved into new agricultural export products
(e.g. African palm oil) and a number of food processing operations. Of
the other two old monopolies, IRCA's installations were taken over by
the government in 1968, after a protracted dispute over the Company's
refusal to pay salaries and after the Company had extracted further subsidies and loans from the government; EEG, also a violator of numerous
Guatemalan taxes and laws, was negotiating a good deal for "nationalization" of its assets in 1972.[13]

In quantitative terms, foreign investment doubled, from $137.6 million
in 1959 to $286.25 million in 1969, although other calculations put the

[13] The way in which Guatemala's three old monopolies phased out of their operations since the 1960's is an instructive sign of the changing times and tactics.
After losing an anti-trust suit in the U.S. in 1958, UF began unloading most of its
remaining lands in Guatemala. As the Company closed down its Tiquisate operation, 2500 workers were fired. The workers' union attempted to purchase the
lands from the Company, but were told it had already been sold to twelve "former
employees" of the Company—very high-level employees, including the (American)
manager and his relatives, as it turned out (Melville & Melville, 1971:179–80).

By 1970 the U.S.-based Del Monte made a bid to acquire the remainder of UF's banana holdings in Guatemala for more than $10 million. Although Guatemalan law prohibited the sale of the UF holdings to foreign interests, Del Monte finally purchased those holdings in 1972 for over $20 million.

By this time UF was quite a different operation than during its heyday in Guatemala. It had acquired diverse holdings in processed foods, meat and real estate, as well as expanding and diversifying its growing operations; and the old UF had merged with other corporations to become the giant United Brands conglomerate (annual sales $1.425 billion). Under a new UF "Associate Producer" program, UF leases its lands to local growers from whom it buys bananas, thus reducing the risk to itself, and lowering its profile in Central America (Tobis, 1971). UF's "modern look" did not end its exploitative practices: the Bank of Guatemala claims that UF undervalued inter-country banana sales (in comparison with world prices) up to 20–40% of the value of total banana exports between 1960 and 1970, so as to pay lower taxes (transfer pricing) (Rosenthal, 1971:66).

IRCA's installations were taken over by the Guatemalan government in December, 1968 after the company claimed it was "insolvent," and unable to run the railroad any longer. This rescue operation cost the Guatemalan public at least $31 million, which IRCA owed but did not pay. The $31 million—in unpaid salaries to IRCA employees (causing a strike in 1968), government loans and government-guaranteed loans, etc.—was far more than the IRCA assets were worth (Calderón, 1969:30–31). Furthermore, the Company's claims of bankruptcy had been called into serious question when IRCA's former representative, Carlos Rafael López Estrada, testified, on the basis of the Company's books, that IRCA's parent company in the U.S. had abundant resources (Bauer, 1970:156).

EEG had remained a subsidiary of AMFORP, part of the Morgan-controlled Electric Bond and Share empire. In August, 1969, Electric Bond and Share (now called Ebasco Industries) was acquired by Boise Cascade—which also has extensive investments in Guatemala in paper products. In Guatemala, EEG continued to provide inadequate service—the government found it necessary to create a public Instituto Nacional de Electrificación in 1959, with exclusive rights for adding to Guatemala's generating capacity—and to violate numerous national laws (tax laws, rate regulations, etc.) and its own concession. From 1931 to 1970 it had remitted $47 million in profits (Comisión Técnica, 1971).

EEG's planned exit from Guatemala in 1972 followed a wave of previous nationalizations, beginning with the loss of some properties in Argentina under the Peron government and continuing with the loss of its half ownership of the Cuban electric company in 1960 and other nationalizations in Brazil. The company saw the handwriting on the wall and responded with a twofold strategy: a) sell out to local governments and get a bigger yield on the interest from government purchase notes than it had from the income on the utility business (profits had been restricted by government pressure to keep public utility rates low); then b) gradually reinvest the proceeds of the sale in even more profitable non-utility enterprises in Latin America. This formula with some variations has been successfully applied by AMFORP as it has negotiated the sales (for $400 million plus) of its utilities operations in seven countries. Having done such good business in other countries, EEG was naturally willing to negotiate such a deal with Guatemala. (The government had already acquired old—some claim obsolete—installations in EEG's generating system in 1967.) As in other countries, AMFORP did negotiate a profitable $18 million withdrawal from Guatemala.

latter figure at $207. million (Rosenthal, 1971:89). By 1970, eighty-six percent of this investment came from U.S. firms and their subsidiaries in Panama and the Bahamas. The very term "U.S. investment" is quite misleading, however, insofar as the net effect for Guatemala is a capital outflow rather than inflow. For one thing, of the total foreign direct investment over the period 1962–9, only around half represented new capital inflows, the other half coming from reinvested profits, local bank loans, etc. Some corporations, such as W. R. Grace, have had a deliberate policy of mobilizing local bank capital rather than ploughing in U.S. dollars. Moreover, a high proportion of profits (39% in 1962, 45.5% in 1968 and 42% in 1969) is remitted to parent corporations (Rosenthal, 1971:88a), with adverse effects for Guatemala's economy and balance of payments. Nor have foreign corporations played the "innovative" role of opening up new fields where cautious local capitalists would not venture; rather, many have moved into traditional fields, frequently displacing and ruining smaller locally-owned industries. For example, a Guatemalan who once employed thirty people in a flourishing Quezaltenango shoe factory can now be found in a small storefront with one assistant, repairing shoes, while a Goodyear subsidiary dominates the market for shoes (Bechtol, 1969:96). To cite another example, at least seven U.S. corporate giants (including General Mills, Pillsbury, Purina, Coca Cola, C.P.C.) have bought out Guatemalan food industries.

In addition to their natural advantages, by virtue of sheer size and more sophisticated technology, U.S. corporations have been granted special privileges not available to local investors. Chief among these has been the investment guarantee program of the U.S. government Agency for International Development (AID): under this program, U.S. firms are insured against losses from inconvertibility (inability to convert local currency into dollars for remittance), expropriation, war, revolution and insurrection, thus providing a hedge against risk in politically unstable areas like Guatemala. In the event of expropriation, etc., AID would compensate the company and then settle accounts with the Guatemalan government, thus elevating a dispute between a U.S. firm and the Guatemalan government to an international dispute between the two governments. (The program has been so heavily criticized in Guatemala that Guatemalan officials have actually applied it in only a few cases, despite dozens of applications from U.S. firms.) Regardless of these privileges and advantages, U.S. investors have accepted no responsibilities in Guatemala—to the extent that when market conditions took a turn for the worse in 1970, several U.S. firms decided unilaterally to close down their Guatemalan installations, without any provision for the workers left jobless or the other effects on the nation. Even under normal conditions, foreign corporations employ a mere 2 percent of the work force (Calderón, 1969:52). On all counts, then, virtually unregulated foreign investment has served less as an instrument for development in Guatemala than as a means of channelling the country's wealth abroad.

The disproportionate importance of foreign investment is directly related to the historical circumstance that Guatemala is industrializing during an era of unprecedented expansion by capital in the advanced industrial nations. This process has been shaped by the needs of monopolistic corporate (mainly U.S.-based) interests, particularly the need for markets large enough to be "economic"—which, in Central America has necessarily meant the pooling of the five national markets. This is not to suggest that the Central American Common Market (CACM) was simply a scheme imposed by U.S. corporations on Central America. Nevertheless, once having accepted the idea that foreign investment was the necessary basis for industrialization and the cornerstone for any "development" policy, the Guatemalan and other Central American governments had to go ahead with the CACM in order to attract foreign investors to a market of scale. Moreover, the common market has provided even greater advantages for foreign over local investors, since the former have the capital and technology to undertake projects which are beyond the capacity of local firms.

Although space is lacking here for a detailed discussion, a few words must be said about the CACM—if only because Guatemala's development since 1960 has been affected by the integration process, and because it exhibits some of the very same problems that have plagued Guatemala. The basic premise of the integration movement—that each of the five Central American economies is unviably small by itself—is clearly valid. But the impact of Central American integration, as of industrialization, depends on who is in control of the process, and for whose benefit.

The initial discussions during the 1950's among the Central Americans, held under the auspices of the United Nations Economic Commission for Latin America (ECLA) office in Mexico, were seriously concerned with defining a rational industrialization policy and achieving balanced growth within the region. The key to this approach was careful planning, coordination, and deliberate policies designed to overcome the historical inequalities within the region. In those early years, the United States, from the sidelines, viewed Central American integration initiatives with great skepticism, particularly insofar as it might challenge U.S. dominance and insofar as ECLA was regarded as having dangerously "statist" or "socialistic" views. By the end of the 1950's, however, recognizing that if they could not prevent integration, they could at least profit from it, Washington and Wall Street ended their diplomatic boycott of Central American integration. Through generous financing of the integration organisms, particularly the Central American Bank for Economic Integration, the United States has been able, subtly, to exercise a decisive influence over the particular strategies and institutions of integration. In place of the "statist" ECLA approach, the United States pushed a line of free enterprise and investment decisions based purely on market considerations, and violently opposed UN-sponsored schemes for planned industrialization.

As a result, "balanced regional growth" has become an impossibility, since foreign investors have flocked, as always, to the relatively more developed areas (Guatemala and El Salvador), leaving particularly Honduras with a very low proportion of the region's industry. The not-too-surprising outcome of this built-in problem was Honduras' 1970 decision to pull out of the CACM, at least temporarily, charging that both the Honduran private sector and the government were paying for the benefits of Central American integration to the Guatemalan and Salvadoran private sector and to foreign interests. Indeed it was true that, aside from the U.S.-based corporations, Guatemalan private interests have been the main beneficiaries of the CACM: by 1969, Guatemala enjoyed thirty-two percent of the region's foreign investment (as compared with 12% in Nicaragua) (Rosenthal, 1971:87b) and by 1970 was the only nation whose trade balance was positive with all of the other Central American nations.

Thus the CACM crisis of the early 1970's was simply the logical outcome of the unresolved contradictions structured into the CACM by virtue of the domination of foreign capital and a recalcitrant, dependent Central American bourgeoisie. For foreign corporations, it was simply a mechanism for creating new investment opportunities and a market large enough to be worth their while. For the regional bourgeoisie, it made possibly the indefinite postponement of basic structural reforms within each country. In contrast with the initial ECLA strategy of state planning and rationalizing of the integration process, in practice Central American integration has meant state protection of an increasingly irrational social and economic structure. What the 1970 crisis has made clear, however, is the frailty and precariousness of integration based on such irrationalities.

Agriculture: More than a decade of industrialization, foreign investment, and regional integration clearly failed to alter Guatemala's basic position in the world market. As seen above, "import-substituting industrialization" has merely changed the composition of imports, while increasing the dependence on imports, particularly raw materials imports, thus giving rise to a chronic deficit in the nation's trade balance. (The only time in recent history that Guatemala's balance of trade with the United States was positive was for three years under Arbenz.) In order to finance a constantly rising level of imports, Guatemala has had to generate more export earnings. Thus the country remains a supplier of raw materials (agricultural and, more recently mineral), but the composition has changed considerably since World War II.

A basic fact of Guatemalan life since World War II has been the continual fluctuation and, after the mid-1950's, the long-range decline in coffee prices, and the introduction of quotas by the coffee importing nations. In 1965 Guatemala's export earnings from coffee were no greater than in 1956, although exports were fifty percent more (Galeano, 1967: 141). Given the instability of world coffee prices, the need for diversification of exports, hence of agriculture, became clear. It remained to be seen how this diversification would be carried out, under whose auspices, and for whose benefit. The key was who controlled the land, and their relation to the world market. In agriculture, no less than in industry, diversification and modernization of production did not generate national development; rather, it resulted in the use of the nation's resources in accordance with the needs of foreign interests, the progressive denationalization of ownership, and the increased concentration of wealth in the hands of a minority.

As seen above, a basic policy of the "Liberation" and the Counter-Revolution was the annulment of the 1952 agrarian reform law, the return of lands expropriated under it to their former owners, and the dispossession of virtually all beneficiaries. From the very beginning the U.S. has been anxious to demonstrate that the client governments were committed to their own brand of "agrarian reform"—particularly after this became the mark of good behavior under the Alliance for Progress. The governments of Castillo Armas and his successors, with a good deal of advice and support from AID, have made a big show of initiating their own agrarian reform programs, including distribution of uncultivated state-owned lands and provision of credit and technical assistance. But for all the rhetoric and fanfare and the millions of dollars in U.S. aid, these "reforms" are little more than cruel deception of landless peasants, insofar as the *latifundia,* which occupy the best land, remain intact.

First, these colonization programs have in no way resembled a true agrarian reform, since colonization has meant opening up of virgin lands —generally inaccessible and/or unusable—owned by the State, to avoid tampering with privately-owned unused but fertile lands. The government campaign during the late 1960's to relieve pressure on fertile Pacific

Coast land by resettling peasants in the jungles of the Petén have been expensive and disastrous, as a result of such factors as the poor quality of the land, its inaccessibility and lack of marketing facilities (Fletcher, 1970:139). Second, even these weak laws have been full of loopholes and mechanisms for defense of *latifundistas*. Third, while various agricultural credit institutions were established, in fact by 1967, ninety percent of all bank credit was being monopolized by big growers of coffee, cotton and sugar for export (Griffin, 1970:13; Guzmán & Herbert, 1970:85).

Fourth, the amount of land distributed to ·the landless has been miniscule. From 1955 to 1966 an average of less than five hundred families were settled each year under government programs (Fletcher, 1970: 138). Between 1961 and 1967 under the Alliance for Progress, only .7 percent of the rural population (.4 percent of the total population) was resettled (Hanson, 1968:54). Even according to official (overly favorable) figures, by 1967 only 22,000 families had received 400,000–500,000 acres of land—as compared with 100,000 peasants who had received 1.5 million acres in less than two years under Arbenz (Gordon, 1971:150). Thus, according to the 1964 census, the land tenure situation had barely changed from that of 1950, before Arbenz' reform: while 87.4 percent of landowners (*minifundistas*) possessed nineteen percent of the land, 2.1 percent of landowners (*latifundistas*) controlled sixty-two percent (Fletcher, 1970:59). 16.5 percent of the rural population was landless; the average salary of *hacienda* workers was seventy-seven dollars a year (Torres, 1971:198, 216). During the 1950's one percent of landowners were foreign, controlling twenty-five percent of the land under cultivation (Monteforte, 1959:424). One often-cited justification for the skewed structure of ownership is that large holdings are more efficient; in fact, studies have shown that large holdings in Guatemala produce only one-fourth the yield per acre compared with small farms (Torres, 1971:225). Finally, while *minifundistas* use all of their cultivable land, *latifundistas* leave 60.7 percent of their arable land unused (Amaro, 1970:313).

Despite this inefficiency, the tiny class of *latifundistas* which controls and monopolizes Guatemala's best lands and resources has also gained increasing control over the market. Small landholders or *minifundistas* have been squeezed out altogether or forced onto the worst lands. Small producers have been progressively less able to compete in selling their products or even to survive at a subsistence level *as producers*. For many of them, the only alternative has been to enter the labor market, i.e. to become salaried workers. Thus, the outcome of modern capitalism in the Guatemalan countryside has been the proletarianization of the peasantry (Flores Alvarado, 1971).

Given this land tenure system, the modernization of the rural sector—the expansion of credit institutions, the abolition of forced labor, mechanization, and diversification of production—has benefitted a tiny rural bourgeoisie. The specific decisions affecting agricultural diversification have been made by this bourgeoisie, which is largely the traditional *cafetelero* oligarchy, expanding into new areas of production. Most important was whether Guatemala's best lands would be used to meet national needs (food) or those of the world market (exports); Guatemala's *finqueros* clearly opted for the latter. According to 1964 figures, while per capita agricultural production in 1963–4 was 141 percent of that in 1952, per capita food production in 1964 was only 101 percent of that in 1952 (Adams, 1970:152). Both in 1950 and in 1967, only 38 percent of the value of agricultural production was for internal consumption, the rest being for export (Guzmán and Herbert, 1970:77). Guatemala's food shortages have worsened, to the point that the two basic staple grains (wheat and corn) have had to be imported, primarily from the United States. Beef is being exported, while Guatemalans remain meatless and protein-deficient. The reason is not that Guatemala could not feed its population, but rather that importers in the advanced capitalist nations can pay more for coffee, cotton, sugar, and beef than starving Indians can pay for corn and beans. So long as the land is controlled by the bourgeoisie, the decision will always be based on profit, not on Guatemalan needs (T. Bodenheimer, 1971).

In line with the country's traditional dependence on the world market, agricultural diversification has been shaped by demand in that market. During World War II the United States stimulated growing of certain strategic commodities such as rubber and citronella oil. Since then, all major exports, with the exception of cotton, have gone mainly to the United States. By 1965 coffee alone still accounted for 47.4% of exports, while coffee and cotton amounted to 67.5%. (The main new feature has been the rising proportion of intra-CACM trade.) But despite the shift in their composition, Guatemala remains in 1971 nearly as dependent as in 1571 on a few agricultural exports, and the economy still follows the ups and downs of world market prices (and U.S. quotas) for those commodities.

Nickel: In February, 1971, after ten years of negotiations, the Guatemalan government signed a contract with Empresa Explotaciones y Exploraciones Mineras de Izabal, S.A. (EXMIBAL). Under the contract, EXMIBAL, a subsidiary of (Canada-based but U.S.-controlled) International Nickel Co. (INCO), with twenty percent ownership by Hanna Mining Co., was granted the right to mine Guatemala's sizeable nickel resources in Izabal province and to export sixty million pounds of nickel annually for the next 40 years. As always, the impetus for the project, which promised a major shift in the Guatemalan political economy for the 1970's and beyond, came not from within the country but from world market conditions.

Ever since the late nineteenth century, nickel has been a strategic metal, particularly in alloys with iron and steel or non-ferrous metals. Forty percent of all nickel is used for stainless steel. Its qualities of strength, hardness, ductility, resistance to corrosion, and maintenance of strength at extreme temperatures have made it crucial for military and defense purposes, especially in the modern age of high-speed aircraft and missiles. After the Korean War, in 1954, the Defense Department reported that nickel "comes closest to being a true 'war metal'." The United States, which now consumes one third of world annual nickel production, has been stockpiling nickel since 1950. Primary sources during the 1950's were Canada and Cuba. By the early 1960's, two factors affected the U.S. market: after the Cuban Revolution took power, Cuban nickel (the largest reserves in the world) was cut off to the U.S. market; and the war in Vietnam sharply increased U.S. consumption. Throughout the 1960's free world demand skyrocketed, doubling from 1959 to 1966, and growing at an annual rate of eighteen percent from 1963 to 1967. The late 1960's witnessed an extreme nickel shortage, particularly in the second half of 1969 during a four-month strike at INCO's Canadian facility. Only in 1971 did the shortage end, bringing a fall in prices (Carter & Goff, 1971).

The other unusual feature of the world nickel market is the extent to which it is dominated by one company: INCO. As *Forbes* magazine (Dec. 1, 1967) summarized its position,

> Of all industrial empires forged by J. P. Morgan at the turn of the century, there is only one that still remains unchallenged master of an unregulated industry—(INCO). . . . How has INCO, almost alone among the great Morgan companies, been able to fulfill its founder's dreams of continued market power? One reason is that INCO was smart enough—and lucky enough—to escape the long arm of the U.S. trustbusters. In 1928, 17 years after the great wave of monopoly smashing started in the U.S., INCO quietly domiciled itself in Canada . . . a sanctuary from high taxes and the threat of anti-trust.

Although located in Canada, INCO is sixty percent owned by Americans and is run from Wall Street. A 100% vertically integrated near-monopoly, by 1971 INCO still controlled fifty-four percent of the capitalist world nickel market (down from seventy-five percent a decade earlier), and thus exercised virtually total control over nickel prices. In order to maintain its dominance, and to end its dependence on Canadian mines, with their susceptibility to strikes and other uncertainties, INCO launched an unparalleled expansion program in the underdeveloped world. The Guatemalan concession was one facet of this expansion program. Guatemala is important to INCO not only as an additional nickel source under the Company's control, but also because of the lower labor costs than in Canada, and because of Guatemala's laterite or surface deposits, amenable to strip mining (as opposed to the more complex and expensive underground mines in Canada).

Negotiations with the Guatemalan government began in the 1960's after Hanna completed initial exploration from 1957 to 1960 in the Lake Izabal area. The joint INCO-Hanna subsidiary, EXMIBAL, was formed in 1960 and received a forty year mining concession in 1965. A new mining code had already been adopted in Guatemala and was very favorable to foreign investors. It had been drawn up by a Peruvian mining technician who was employed by INCO. The final contract was not signed with the Guatemalan government, however, until February, 1971. During that time the projected investment quadrupled, from $60. million to $250. million (the largest single project in the country, doubling all previous U.S. investment there). The protracted period of secret negotiations was due partially to INCO's desire to be assured of favorable market conditions. Even more important was the strong opposition to the project from certain sectors of the Guatemalan population, which forced the government at least to bargain for better terms than the Company had initially attempted to impose. Some of the chief features and issues in the negotiations were the following:

1. perhaps the most important apparent "victory" for Guatemala (initially opposed by INCO) is the government's thirty percent participation in the authorized capital ($50. million) of EXMIBAL. As a minority stockholder, however, the Guatemalan government cannot control the Company's basic policy decisions or machinations;

2. early in the negotiations INCO planned to export nickel from Guatemala in impure form, for further refining in Europe (its final destination) to avoid European Common Market tariffs. Such a plan would have deprived the Guatemalan economy of jobs, foreign exchange, and other benefits. By 1971, however, INCO agreed to refine the nickel to ninety-eight percent purity *in* Guatemala. In any case, the refining process would be cheaper in Guatemala;

3. EXMIBAL is committed to the vague obligation of "gradually substituting" imports of raw materials, fuel, and services by Central American goods and services, but there are no specific obligations. And what appears to be a positive contribution to the Guatemalan economy and

use of resources in Guatemala may in fact be of benefit to other U.S. corporations there—as for example with a Chevron-Shell joint venture in Guatemala which will be importing crude oil from Venezuela for processing in Guatemala and sale to EXMIBAL for diesel fuel;

4. no less vague are the clauses requiring rehabilitation of mined areas and other ecological precautions by the Company;

5. the Guatemalan government is footing the bill for some of the principal infrastructure requirements, particularly improvements in port facilities at Santo Tomás de Castilla. To finance the work, the government had to get a $4.55 million loan from the U.S. Export-Import Bank at five and one-half percent interest;

6. after the initial construction phase, EXMIBAL will employ around 1200. On the grounds of special manpower requirements, EXMIBAL is exempt from the law requiring that ninety percent of all employees in any enterprise be Guatemalans—in exchange for which the firm promises to train a certain number of middle- and lower-level personnel;

7. EXMIBAL has won its contention that, as a "transformation industry," it qualifies for the generous benefits (tax and import duty exemptions) of the Industrial Promotion Law. Having received its classification under the Law, EXMIBAL's maximum tax rate will be 33.6 percent. Other tax-related issues revolve around EXMIBAL's definition of the value of the nickel at the mouth of the mine;

8. most controversial have been INCO's attempts to gain privileged treatment for foreign exchange generated by nickel exports, and to violate Guatemala's mild foreign exchange legislation. Specifically, INCO has insisted that it be permitted to maintain all its dollar earnings abroad, not even registering these with the Bank of Guatemala, in accordance with national monetary laws. (Guatemalan law does not regulate the *amount* of profit remittances, but only requires that they first be registered in the Bank.) INCO's excuse was that the U.S. Export-Import Bank (EXIM-Bank) and other agencies lending money to INCO for the Guatemalan operation were insisting on full repayment of their loans ($70. million from EXIM-Bank alone) within seven years, and thus had to be assured of the immediate availability of dollars—a most unusual provision, since EXIM-Bank loans are often repayable after fifteen to twenty years. The final contract permits INCO to accumulate dollars abroad for debt service, stipulating only that the operation must produce a net balance of payments benefit (however small) to Guatemala, i.e., that profit remittances cannot exceed foreign exchange generated. Despite this paper assurance, knowledgeable experts have raised serious questions as to the long-range balance of payments (and tax) benefits to Guatemala.

The preceeding are only some of the highlights and disputed points of the EXMIBAL investment. Even this brief review should make clear that if the contract had gone through on INCO's terms, it would have been a throw-back to the old United Fruit concessions, making EXMIBAL a privileged state within a state, while profoundly affecting Guatemala's economy and ecology. That certain gains were made for Guatemala during the nearly ten years of negotiations was thanks not to the government's vigilance for the national interest, but rather to the vigorous campaign of opposition and criticism from the University and from other progressive sectors. (Perhaps it was no coincidence that the final contract was signed while Guatemala was under strict state of siege, banning all political activity and free speech.) Even in its somewhat improved form, the contract leaves Guatemala little control over many aspects of INCO's operations.

But the final chapter of the EXMIBAL story has yet to be written. Even after the contract was signed, INCO did not proceed with its investment, claiming now it lacked $80. million of the necessary financing. Knowledgeable observers suspect that INCO's stalling tactics are designed: a) to pressure the Guatemalan government into granting a guarantee of the investment, which the government has thus far refused to do; or b) to wait with the investment for more favorable world market conditions. The great nickel shortage and sky-high prices of the 1960's finally ended and during 1971, as part of the general recession in the industrial nations, sales and prices fell sharply. INCO's response was to cut back production and employment by seven percent, then by fifteen percent, with further cut-backs for 1972. Only in mid-1973 did INCO begin construction of its plant in Guatemala, in accordance with the company's global plans.

Ascendancy of the private sector and the dependent state: Implicit within the strategy of the Counter-Revolution has been a definite conception of the role of the state vis-à-vis private interests. In its own domain the private sector has enjoyed almost total freedom from state regulation or interference. Moreover, private interests have acquired increasing access to and control over "public" policies.

This ascendancy of the private sector has had several concrete manifestations. First, it has become evident in the proliferation of private sector interest and pressure groups since 1954. The traditionally strong agricultural groups, particularly the *cafeteleros,* had been organized to some extent before the Revolution, but it was only after 1954 that the newly emerging sectors (e.g., cotton and sugar growers and industrialists) as well as the older commercial groups began to organize formally for more aggressive protection of their interests. Castillo Armas accelerated the process by creating a Council on Private Initiative. Succeeding governments have actively and, as a matter of policy, promoted the formation of these ruling class interest groups.

The various pressure groups are organized within three more general associations: the older Asociación General de Agricultores (AGA), the Cámara de Comercio, and, after 1959, the Cámara de Industria (and a smaller Asociación de Banqueros). An umbrella Coordinating Committee, CACIF, purports to represent the entire private sector on matters of common interest. The functions of these groups include general lobbying and protection of Guatemalan and foreign investors against strikes and permissive labor legislation, against competing producers in other countries, against new state taxes and other bothersome impositions. Increasingly the AGA and the Cámaras have come to expect Guatemalan governments to consult with them on all measures which might affect them and, in fact, on all important policy matters. This is especially the case of the industrialists in all questions related to Central American integration—to the extent that by 1971 it was taken for granted that the Cámara de Industria would have its representatives at all inter-governmental negotiations. True to the dependent character of the Guatemalan bourgeoisie, these organizations (with the exception of the bankers) have not been used in defense against takeovers of Guatemalan enterprise by foreign interests. On the contrary, foreign investors are included within these associations and are very influential in some of them. (Bryant, 1967a; 1967b; Adams, 1970: Ch. 6).

A second manifestation of the internal hold of private interests over the public domain since 1954 is related to personnel in the legislatures, Cabinets, and major government positions. Generally the Guatemalan bourgeoisie has preferred not to hold key positions in the Ministries, etc., but rather to rule indirectly, through their spokesmen and humble servants in the petty bourgeoisie, particularly lawyers and military officers. This has proved a lucrative means of upward economic and social mobility for the petty bourgeoisie, as well as a useful service to the bourgeoisie and foreign interests.

Third, particularly since the 1960's and the Alliance for Progress, the state has assumed a redefined and more active role—not, however, to exercise real planning and control over "development" policies, but rather to protect and subsidize the private sector in new ways. Unlike the extreme conservatives who oppose any state initiatives, the newer industrial bourgeoisie has understood how to take advantage of "state intervention" to promote their own welfare and profits. For example, while leaving all productive sectors of the economy in the private domain, the state has assumed responsibility for those areas which are insufficiently profitable to attract private enterprise. Using the rhetoric of "development" and "planning," the state has expended a good portion of its scarce domestic resources and incurred a growing foreign debt in order to service the needs of the private sector, and particularly of foreign investors, for roads, utilities, communications facilities, and so on.

In subsidizing the operations of private capital, the state has contributed to its own impoverishment. Public or state investment remains at a very low level of two and one-half to three percent of gross domestic product, as a result of insufficient public savings and the state's inability to marshal private sector savings. From 1946 to 1962 there was a private capital flight of $65.9 million (Torres, 1971:247). In order to finance even a low level of state expenditures, the public internal and foreign debt has been substantially increased: total public debt rose from $88.3 million in 1961 to $182 million in 1968 (Amaro, 1970:120). Even more dramatic is the bad state of Guatemala's public revenue, which fluctuates between six and eight and one-half percent of gross domestic product— an unusually low proportion, by international standards—and actually declined between 1965 and 1967 (Best, 1969:45). Of total tax revenues, only 15.4 percent came from direct (income and property) taxes in 1967. During the 1960's the property tax provided only 2–3 percent of government revenue (as compared with 5.3 percent in 1933–4). Direct taxes on enterprises provided .6 percent of national income in 1950, .8 percent in 1966 (Best, 1969:52, 68, 117–18); one factor has been the excessively generous Industrial Promotion Law (as a result of which the government had lost $60. million by 1968).

The one attempt of the government to reform the tax structure failed miserably. Soon after coming to power, the Méndez Montenegro government in 1966–7 tried to push through a tax reform which would have dealt with the serious financial crisis by moderately increasing property taxes; when this failed, Congress passed a progressive sales tax penalizing luxury consumption, but this too was repealed after a few weeks. The opposition from the Guatemalan bourgeoisie was so intense that, in addition to not getting the measures adopted, the Méndez government was forced to dismiss its reformist Finance Minister in March, 1968, faced talk of a coup, and never again dared to take any developmental initiatives or to tamper with the privileges of the bourgeoisie. Since 1967, all efforts have focused on safer but ineffective policies of "improving administration and collection" of existing taxes, leaving intact the tax structure, and leaving the burden on middle- and lower-income groups. Colonel Arana based his 1970 Presidential campaign partly on a promise

to the bourgeoisie of "no new taxes." Thus Guatemala's tax performance
and structure remain nearly the worst in Latin America and in the entire
underdeveloped world.

Meanwhile, even the traditional sources of government revenue have
declined. Legislation in 1963 reduced the coffee export tax by 50 percent;
government receipts from export taxes (mainly coffee) *declined* from
$14. million in 1955–6 to $6.4 million in 1963–4, from 17.6 percent to
6.5 percent of total revenues (Griffin, 1970:7–9). By 1970 coffee interests were campaigning for further reduction, if not total elimination,
of export taxes. Meanwhile, import duties have also fallen off, as a result
of the Central American customs union and the Industrial Promotion
Law.

Given this chronic impoverishment, the Guatemalan state has renounced any serious role in developmental planning or reforms. While
modernizing its institutional apparatus and taking on new functions, it
has become more rather than less subservient to the Guatemalan and
international bourgeoisie, and is virtually powerless to move against them.
The dependency of the state vis-à-vis the bourgeoisie directly affects the
nature of Guatemalan politics, as we shall see. Its principal function
being to subsidize and protect dependent industrialization and to attract
foreign investment, the state can make no pretensions to represent truly
national interests or to meet the needs of the people, and thus faces a
permanent crisis of legitimacy.

THE POLITICS OF TERROR AND RESISTANCE

Just as the Revolution had entailed a redefinition of politics, so too the
Counter-Revolution carried certain implications about the possible forms
of politics. The two political imperatives of the Counter-Revolution
were: the maintenance of a favorable (stable) climate for foreign investment; and the elimination of all traces of popular or lower class organization and the prevention of any such mobilization in the future.
Politics became the business of protecting the interests of the Guatemalan
and international bourgeoisie.

Given these political imperatives, theoretically there were several possible approaches. The witch hunters of the "Liberation" and their political descendants have favored outright repression. The liberals, including Alliance for Progress reformers, hoped to accomplish the same goals,
but through less drastic means—to preserve the semblance of normal
politics. During the initial stages of the "Liberation," Castillo Armas
dispensed with the trappings of normal politics. Soon thereafter an
attempt was made to return to and maintain the forms of bourgeois
democratic politics (elections, political parties, constitutional guarantees,

etc.). In a situation such as Guatemala's under the Counter-Revolution, however, even normal political activity was incompatible with stability; thus it became necessary to pervert those forms.

When they have taken place at all, elections have been a dubious indicator of "democracy":

> The electoral laws are violated, evaded, or occasionally just ignored. Electoral fraud . . . is a normal occurrence in Guatemala . . . . electoral abnormalities are common in rural areas controlled by either the government or large landowners. Moreover, the power structure manipulates the electoral laws, in such a way that no party which threatens the interests of the military, the landowners, or the capitalists is allowed to participate. (Sloan, 1970:81)

Castillo Armas' "election" in a Ubico-style plebiscite in 1954, in which he received ninety-nine percent of the vote, was only the beginning. The 1957 Presidential election, following Castillo Armas' assassination (by one of his own guards), was so overtly fraudulent that it was annulled. A new election in 1958 gave the Presidency to Gen. Miguel Ydígoras Fuentes, a corrupt *Ubiquista* with close ties to Dominican dictator Trujillo. His even more reactionary opponent, Cruz Salazar, was bribed by the CIA ($200,000.) to concede to Ydígoras (Cehelsky 1967:123–5). This and subsequent elections in 1959 were characterized by intimidation, bribery, and numerous irregularities (Sloan, 1970). The Presidential election scheduled for 1963 was preempted by a U.S.-supported military coup led by Colonel Enrique Peralta Azurdia, to prevent the candidacy and anticipated victory of ex-President Arévalo.

The 1966 election, following three years of *de facto* military rule, is generally thought to have been honest, and was even won by an opposition candidate and civilian reformer, Julio César Méndez Montenegro. The real fraud came only later: although his election was a clear mandate for structural change (campaigning as the "Third Government of the Revolution"), Méndez was permitted to take office only after literally signing a pact with the army, guaranteeing it a free hand in counterinsurgency, autonomy in such matters as selection of the Defense Minister, Chief of Staff, budgets, etc., and promising to exclude "radicals" from the government, but not to retire too many generals. The Méndez government's capitulation to United States and Guatemalan right-wing military pressures clearly constituted a betrayal of the election mandate. Finally, the 1970 election of rightist Colonel Carlos Arana Osorio, while superficially free of gross fraud, was held under conditions of extreme terror.

Even the apparently less fraudulent elections in Guatemala since 1954 can hardly be characterized as "free." First, physical intimidation, threatened firings, and bribery have become institutionalized techniques for securing votes, especially in the countryside. Second, there is no room for real alternatives. Even so moderate a reformer as Arévalo could not be tolerated. All political parties to the left of center have been excluded from legal participation in elections. The PGT (Communist Party) remains illegal by definition. Several smaller leftist parties, most notably the Unidad Revolucionaria Democrática, have been kept out by means of a 1963 law requiring parties to have fifty thousand members and at least twenty percent of them literate, with government officials deciding whether or not a party's membership rolls are valid. The Christian Democrats, initially an ultra-rightist party, came under the control of younger, more progressive leadership in the late 1960's, and was finally able to run candidates in the 1970 election. Whatever possibilities existed that the Partido Revolucionario might play a truly progressive role were squelched in the late 1950's when its high-handed leader, Mario Méndez Montenegro, purged the entire left wing of the Party.

There is no need to present here a catalogue of political parties and coalitions, insofar as the differences among them in practice are marginal (aside from the somewhat left-of-center Christian Democrats). While the rhetoric and the campaign appeal vary considerably, from the reformist, social democratic image of the Partido Revolucionario (PR) (Méndez' party) to the openly fascist appeal of the Movimiento de Liberación Nacional (MLN), political descendant of the "Liberation," in practice all governments since 1954 have devoted their efforts to maintenance of upper class privileges and police-state law and order. Moreover, the top-down functioning and ruling class base are common to all of these parties and governments. To the extent that there is any differentiation, it reflects the different factions and tendencies *within* the bourgeoisie.

Thus, the existence of competing political parties and the occurrence of elections should not obscure the fact that, in the context of post-Revolutionary Guatemala, "politics," as normally defined, offers the people no real alternatives. Given the Counter-Revolution's political imperatives of maintaining stability and excluding the working class, normal political activity would pose a serious threat. (In case there had been any doubt, this became clear in the coup of 1963 to prevent the fair election of Arévalo.) Thus, Guatemala has experienced an abolition of real politics, behind a facade of pseudo-parliamentary procedures. The political process has become a mere farce, acted out by the U.S. Embassy, the Guatemalan bourgeoisie and petty bourgeoisie—while, to the Indians and the entire working class, the difference between PR's Méndez and MLN's Arana is imperceptible. The extent of popular disillusion with electoral politics is indicated by the high rate of voter abstention: of those registered, only fifty percent voted in 1966, less than sixty percent in 1970; and of those *eligible* to vote, only around twenty-five to twenty-six percent actually voted in those years (Amaro, 1970:242). In the words of the late guerrilla leader, Yon Sosa,

> The electoral path is barred in Guatemala, not only because the bourgeoisie cannot provide democratic elections and continue to remain in power. It is also barred because the workers and peasants do not believe in elections. . . . (cited in Sloan, 1970:91)

Complementing the distortion of bourgeois democratic institutions has been the militarization of politics since 1954—not only during periods of overt military rule (1963–6) but also as an integral feature of "civilian" governments. Nearly all Guatemala's constitutionally elected presidents since 1954 have come from a military background and had firm military support. In order to take office, the major exception, Méndez Montenegro, was forced in 1966 to sign the famous pact with the army, whereby he subsequently ruled with his hands tied behind his back. During long periods of supposedly civilian rule—e.g., the last year of the Ydígoras regime, and nearly the entire Méndez government—effective power remained in the hands of the military. To take another indicator: the increase of defense expenditures per member of the armed forces between 1955 and 1965 was greater in Guatemala than in any other Latin American country. Official defense expenditures reached eleven percent of annual government spending by 1965 (Adams, 1970:147)—seventeen percent for defense plus internal security—as compared with two percent to the University. These figures do not even count the unofficial extra allotments for defense which in 1970 nearly *doubled* the military budget.

At the local level—particularly during states of siege, which have been as much the rule as the exception—politics is generally run by the Commander of the Military Zone. Most important are the ubiquitous *comisionados militares,* quasi-military representatives of the army reserve in each town, most of whom are former army personnel. In the summer of 1965, in Jutiapa province, the network included 971 *comisionados* and agents (Durston, 1966). Their functions go far beyond recruitment for military service and the normal maintenance of law and order, to include extensive intelligence (spying) on the local population and other policing functions, and responsibility for development programs, as part of "civic action" (see below). During states of siege, the *comisionados,* who are often selected by, hence beholden to, the local bourgeoisie, become the ultimate regional authorities. Finally, under military rule, even the courts have been militarized.

Thus, in a very real sense, the military has become the arbiter of Guatemalan politics—the only force which can hold the system together. Symbolic of the evolution of politics as an extension of armed force has been the spectacular career of Colonel Arana, rising from chief of counterinsurgency operations in Zacapa in 1966 to the Presidency in 1970. Nevertheless, at a deeper level, the political power of the Guatemalan military does not reside in the military, but is, rather, an expression of the class alliance underlying the Counter-Revolution. On the one hand, the militarization of politics permits the Guatemalan and international bourgeoisie to rule indirectly and poses no challenge to their interests. On the other hand, it reflects the incorporation of the dependent petty bourgeoisie into the ruling coalition. Given the insecurity of the petty bourgeoisie and its fear of the masses, it is incapable of governing alone and must rely on the military. In this sense, the top-down, authoritarian mentality and style of the military coincides with the imperative of the Counter-Revolution to exclude popular participation. For the officer corps, meanwhile, this role serves their own goals of upward mobility: being well connected with the local and national elites, military officers enjoy special privileges, in addition to their regular access to the commissaries, subsidized housing, and other fringe benefits. It is principally this petty bourgeois consciousness which establishes the officers' identification with the *finqueros* and the United States and which has thus far precluded any generalized Peruvianization within the military.

A further aspect of the politics of the Counter-Revolution has been the abolition of bourgeois democratic legality and the prevalence of outright terror. During the nine years from 1963 through 1971 (108 months), Guatemala spent forty-eight months, or nearly half, under states of siege, prevention, or alarm—all of which have entailed to a greater or lesser degree the abrogation of constitutional guarantees and liberties. Freedoms of speech, assembly, press, etc. have been honored more in the breach than in the observance. The omnipresence of soldiers bearing machine guns has turned the capital into a garrison city. The jails are chronically filled with citizens arrested, often without warrant, and for no specific crime.

But this chain of states of siege has involved far more than the virtual abolition of citizens' rights. More ominously, it has provided a backdrop for widespread right-wing/official terror, under the guise of maintaining public order and combatting a leftist guerrilla insurgency. Beginning with the witch hunt of 1954, the governments of the Counter-Revolution have condoned, and at times carried out, the physical elimination of all existing or potential members of the political opposition. The more fortunate dissidents have joined the large community of Guatemalan exiles living abroad. A more sinister fate has been assassination. Principal engineers of the terror, particularly since 1966, have been a series of rightist vigilante groups, the most famous being the *MANO Blanca* ("White Hand"), and more recently, *Ojo por Ojo* ("An Eye for an Eye"). Although allegedly clandestine and beyond official control, these groups have operated with total impunity, are generally known to have a strong base in the armed and police forces, and have been used in government counter-insurgency operations. They are financed by the Guatemalan bourgeoisie. Their tactics range from publication of names and photos of their intended victims and threatening letters, to brutal assassination, nearly always accompanied by torture. Typical of the integration between official forces and the terrorist Right has been the daily experience of hundreds of victims, last seen after being picked up by police or army vehicles; generally they disappear for several weeks (while friends and relatives search for them in the jails), and finally their corpses are found, tortured and mutilated, in some ditch or dry river bed.

A special target of these rightist groups has been that small sector of the petty bourgeoisie—professionals, university students and professors—which maintains its identification with the Revolution of 1944–54 and its alliance with the masses. (Also included are some moderate leftists who, although active in the Revolution, have not participated in politics since 1954.) Some faculties of the national University of San Carlos (regarded by the bourgeoisie as a Communist breeding-ground) have been virtually gutted by the terror. So numerous have been the rightist/official actions and political assassinations, particularly since 1966, that only a few specifics can be mentioned here. In May, 1966, twenty-eight intellectuals and students being held as "guerrillas" were executed (without trial) by government firing squad, and their bodies sewn into burlap bags and dropped into the ocean from Army transport planes. (Details were revealed by former police agents in July, 1966.) In January, 1968, the body of Rogelia Cruz Martínez, a former Miss Guatemala, known to have leftist sympathies, was found stabbed, beaten, raped, poisoned, brutally tortured, and left naked for the vultures. In March, 1968, in broad daylight, the *MANO Blanca* kidnapped Archbishop Casariego, hoping the deed would be blamed on the Left and would provoke a military coup. And in January, 1971, following a series of similar right-wing murders, moderate leftist Congressman and prominent law professor, universally respected, Adolfo Mijangos—paralyzed from the waist down—was shot to death in his wheelchair.

Nevertheless, although some individuals and groups within the petty bourgeoisie have been marked for elimination by the Right, the brunt of the terror has been borne by the working class and the peasants, particularly in the zones of guerrilla activity. It is the countless number of unnamed peasants which brings the death toll of the rightist terror to an estimated seven thousand from 1966 to 1970 alone (although a precise body count is impossible to obtain). The systematic demobilization of the working class and peasants has been accomplished only through violence. The labor movement has been decimated: its ranks declined, according to the U.S. Bureau of Labor Statistics, from over 100,000 members under Arbenz to 16,000 by 1962 (Gordon, 1971:150). During states of siege, even normal union activities (e.g., collective bargaining), have been greatly restricted or prohibited. Property-owners, both urban and rural, have taken advantage of states of emergency and siege to get rid of troublesome organizers. In the late 1960's a law was passed giving *finqueros* the right to consider themselves authorities of the law and to shoot any "guerrilla suspects"—in effect giving them a legal weapon against trespassers on their land and other nuisances. On numerous occasions Guatemalan or foreign *finqueros* (including United Fruit) have received assistance from the army in evicting peasants from land which they had occupied, often for years. (For specific cases, see Melville & Melville, 1971). Such evictions have often entailed the firing of workers and murder of organizers. In addition to overt force, the law has consistently been used to deprive peasants of their rights. "Law and order" in the countryside has become indistinguishable from rightist terror, which is unmistakeably the terror of the bourgeoisie. To the peasants, however, death by violence is nothing new; the fierce repression of the Counter-Revolution is merely an extension of the institutionalized, daily violence of Guatemalan life from hunger, disease, and infant mortality.

Aside from the thousands of deaths, the protracted violence takes its psychological toll on the living in Guatemala. The population is maintained in a permanent state of fear and uncertainty. The generalization and apparent indiscriminateness of the violence, the steady stream of political assassinations in broad daylight, the tales of torture by the *MANO,* the blurring of the distinction between official repression and terror perpetrated by "clandestine" rightist groups, the omnipresence of police and machine guns in the streets—all these are aspects of the psychological war which is necessary to the political strategy of the Counter-Revolution. That strategy must be to wipe out from the collective mind of the Guatemalan people the memory of the Revolution; to stamp out the popular desires which produced that Revolution; and to physically eliminate the moderate leftists who made and still symbolize that Revolution. Thus, what is justified by the government as "counter-insurgency" or "pacification" is in fact the government's only way of attempting to assure the permanent demobilization of the populace, in order to provide foreign investors with the stability they demand and to maintain the privileges of the Guatemalan bourgeoisie.

Under these circumstances of psychological as well as physical warfare, electoral politics has been a useless means of expression and participation, and all serious political responses have been formulated outside electoral channels. Popular resistance has taken many forms, some of them almost unrecognizable as resistance. A generalized *culture of resistance* has evolved in response to the magnitude of the repression and the frequency of states of siege, when overt political demonstrations, organizing and propaganda activities are banned. In this culture the oral media of popular songs, myths, and jokes are used to ridicule or criticize. Students stage an annual "Huelga de Dolores," a spoof/critique of current events. A funeral may be turned into an event of popular protest—as happened with Mijangos' funeral in January 1971. Even the mass newspapers may carry sharp ridicule or criticism, but always disguised as reportage. During calmer periods and occasionally during states of siege, leaflets appear throughout the capital—their source remaining untraceable. Thus the culture of resistance is a partial substitute for politics, in unifying the people and breaking down the isolation and alienation created by the terror.

At the more obvious level, peasant land invasions, increasingly frequent during the 1960's, have assumed a profound political significance—as did an Indian uprising in Comalapa in 1968. Less overtly "political," yet important as a form of popular resistance, has been the rising level of spontaneous violence in the Guatemalan countryside. The urban proletariat has been too small and weak to wage a continual struggle. The capital-intensive nature of industrialization has limited the size of the industrial proletariat. The smashing of the labor movement in 1954, and the severe persecution of militant organizers and the lack of access to legal protections since, have left a mere 1.2% of the proletariat organized. Of that tiny proportion, many have been organized into the non-militant unions affiliated with the Inter-American network of the AFL-CIO—the only unions relatively free from government repressions: they constitute a privileged "labor aristocracy" whose objective interests are closer to those of the petty bouregoisie than of the working class. Nevertheless, a few major labor strikes have been very important. Of particular significance was the 1973 teachers' strike which mobilized thousands of teachers and generated the first massive street demonstrations since 1962 and which served as a catalyst for militancy in other sectors of the working class.

Meanwhile, certain forms of resistance have developed within the institutions of the urban petty bourgeoisie. There have been several revolts in the armed forces, beginning with the cadets' uprising of August, 1954, an attack on a contingent of Castillo Armas' privileged "Liberation Army." (A precedent was the abortive revolt by cadets againsts the Estrada Cabrera dictatorship.) This was followed by the "Colonels' Conspiracy" of January, 1955, and a series of civilian-military plots against Castillo Armas, culminating in his assassination in July, 1957. The famous abortive military revolt of November 13, 1960 was designed to overthrow Ydígoras and was inspired largely by resentment against U.S. use of Guatemalan soil as a training base for foreign (Cuban exile) troops for the Bay of Pigs invasion. Some estimate that up to eighty percent of the officer corps was involved in plotting, though not in carrying out, the November 13 revolt (Buttrey, 1967:23). These incidents have led one observer (Cehelsky: Ch. VII) to conclude that, if the army never accepted the Revolution, neither did it accept the "Liberation." Nevertheless, although some individual military officers later joined the revolutionary movement, the military uprisings as such never transcended their petty bourgeois inspiration.

Similar resistance has come from another sector of the petty bourgeoisie: university intellectuals. University students staged a series of demonstrations in June, 1956, which were put down by armed force. In the spring of 1962, following allegations of fraud in the 1961 Congressional elections, the students, with considerable support from the working class and from opposition parties, again took to the streets for two months of demonstrations, clashes, and strikes—the first mass struggle since the fall of Arbenz. A general strike was declared in the capital. Several thousand women in the *Frente de Mujeres Guatemaltecas* marched through the streets in April, 1962, to protest the shooting of law students by the government. The University has remained a thorn in the government's side, at least at the level of verbal protest; but the rhetoric has not been consistently translated into action. Even within the Church, there has been considerable protest, from foreign as well as Guatemalan clergy. At the end of 1967 several Americans from the Catholic Maryknoll order were expelled from Guatemala for their collaboration with a Christian guerrilla movement; in 1971 the (American) Episcopal Bishop was expelled for circulating a petition critical of the Arana regime.

Finally, the traditional petty bourgeois Left, centered partly around the PGT, has remained a source of resistance. Its persistent expressions of nationalism and opposition to sell-out measures such as the EXMIBAL contract have been crucial, and have on several occasions forced the hand of the government (e.g. in not conceding many foreign investment guarantees). Nevertheless, the majority of these progressive forces have retained their middle- or upper-class identity—to the extent that, during the Christmas season, some of the "leading leftists" attend the parties of their political enemies in the ruling class, at the Guatemala Country Club. And in the long run, the petty bourgeois base of the traditional Left now, as during the Revolution, is too narrow to impell a generalized struggle.

A number of leftists from the petty bourgeoisie (from the PGT, the military, the University) have given up their class privileges to join with the lower class in the guerrilla struggle. Their ideological origins were nationalism and reformism. Following the abortive November 13, 1960 uprising, a number of the participants—most notably, Luis Turcois Lima (trained in the U.S. Army Ranger School at Ft. Benning, Georgia) and Marco Antonio Yon Sosa (trained at the U.S.-run Ft. Gulick in the Panama Canal Zone)—took refuge among the peasants. It was here that their radicalization began:

> There were no facilities for holding organized discussions and making decisions; but in Guatemala, as in Honduras and El Salvador, all the peasants helped and protected the rebels, tried to influence them and win them to their side. The peasants' motive was not only to offer their solidarity but also to win allies and leaders in their struggle for the land. . . . Many of the rebels did not respond, but the effort was not in vain; the influence was felt by some, although not immediately. Yon Sosa and Alejandro de León and their *compañeros* did not jump to conclusions; but, little by little, the peasants won them over. (Gilly, 1965:16)

Learning from the people over several years' time, they came to understand the class basis of the political struggle against the existing order, and evolved from a nationalist and reformist perspective to an explicitly socialist program, demanding, above all, land for the peasants.

Contrary to the myth widely disseminated by U.S. social scientists attempting to debunk the guerrilla movement, the principal base during its rural phase was not among frustrated, adventurist students from Guatemala City. Rather, it lay among the peasants politicized by the systemic violence which has kept them from the land and the repression necessary to enforce that system. A study of one guerrilla column in 1963 showed its composition to be fifty-nine percent peasants and only two percent students (Aguilera, 1970:123). During the intense rural phase, until 1968, the main base was in Izabal and Zacapa (*ladino* areas); the guerrillas had made significant inroads there by 1966, when the counter-attack began in earnest (directed by Colonel Arana and with massive U.S. assistance). Since 1968 the focus has been in urban areas, particularly the capital, although rural efforts have also been renewed.

Armed guerrilla actions have included assaults on army and police stations (to obtain weapons), bank robberies and kidnappings of the bourgeoisie (to obtain funds), and of diplomats—including the kidnap and/or killing of two U.S. military advisers, a U.S. labor attaché, U.S. Ambassador Mein, and German Ambassador von Spreti. These and other armed actions of the guerrillas have been very directed and discriminate, *and hence in no way comparable to the chronic and indiscriminate rightist violence.* Crucially important have been the guerrillas' political education through "armed propaganda" (whereby they occupy peasant villages temporarily, explain their programs and organize a resistance within the villages) (Galeano, 1969:31), and provision of essential services to the peasants.

As of 1971, it was clear that the guerrilla movement had not definitively challenged the ruling class, and had been severely reduced. In addition to military setback, the guerrillas had suffered some defections from their ranks to the forces of repression, and were at least partially isolated from their popular base. There are several reasons for these setbacks. First, as a result of their very success in threatening established authority, the guerrillas were pursued with the most sophisticated and brutal technology available to Guatemalan and U.S. security forces (see below); by the late 1960's the movement had not yet built up sufficient strength to withstand a counter-attack of this magnitude. Moreover, given U.S. determination to prevent "another Cuba," no matter what the price in bloodshed, U.S. intervention was too massive to be defeated in one country alone, much less in a country the size of Guatemala (unless, as in Vietnam, it had had decades of experience in waging a war of national liberation).

Second, the movement was affected by certain realities about the Guatemalan masses: the weakness and lack of organization of the proletariat (as described above); and the division of the lower class between Indians and *ladinos*. A remaining heritage of the colonial experience is that poor *ladinos* often alleviate their own miserable situation by exploiting the Indians "below" them. In certain regions, for example, small *ladino* middlemen and money-lenders make their living off small Indian farmers. In addition, the *ladinos* have historically evidenced a certain prejudice against the Indians. The Indians, in turn, have developed a mistrust of the relatively privileged *ladinos* who are often their nearest and most visible, though not their ultimate, oppressors. The Indians are also divided from poor *ladinos* by differing traditions and attitudes— most notably, the *ladino* appreciation of private property, as opposed to the Indian traditions of communal lands, collective work on the land, and mutual assistance (Marina, 1968:99–101). Although these Indian-*ladino* antagonisms have become a weapon of the bourgeoisie to keep the proletariat divided, they have deep historical roots; until they are overcome, no definitive class challenge to bourgeois rule can succeed.

Aside from (although related to) these "objective conditions" have been certain failings of the male, *ladino* and largely petty bourgeois leadership of the guerrilla movement—all of which are manifestations of the imperfect relationship of that leadership to the mass base. The movement has been greatly weakened by factionalism at the leadership level. The main groups are the Fuerzas Armadas Rebeldes (FAR), which evolved principally out of the PGT but broke with the Party in early 1968; and the Movimiento Revolucionario 13 de Noviembre (MR-13), which was heavily influenced by Trotskyists, and only broke with them in 1966, when it was discovered that they were sending funds raised in Guatemala to the Fourth International headquarters abroad. FAR's grievances against the PGT were related to the Party's support of Méndez in the 1966 election and its attempt to subordinate the guerrillas to Party leadership. But most important,

> After four years of fighting, this is the balance sheet: 300 revolutionaries fallen in combat, 3000 men of the people murdered by Julio César Méndez Montenegro's regime. The PGT (its ruling clique) supplied the ideas, and the FAR the dead. (cited in Gott, 1971:109)

Relations between FAR and MR-13 have fluctuated from rivalry to unity.

Equally important, the primarily *ladino* male leadership has been plagued by one of the same limitations that characterized the Revolutionary leadership: an inability to incorporate fully Guatemala's two majorities: Indians and women. A unified class struggle waged jointly by Indians and *ladinos* requires that the movement overcome the divisions created by the colonial heritage, which the bourgeoisie has always been able to turn to its own advantage. Ultimately this means that the urban *ladino* leadership ally with an authentic Indian leadership. By 1970 the Indians had been mobilized and incorporated into the struggle, particularly at the leadership level, only in isolated instances; but new efforts in predominantly Indian zones were beginning.

Finally, what Wolf (1959:239) identifies as the typically *ladina* "urge for personal vindication through power" is most visibly expressed in male-female relationships. *Machismo,* or male oppression of women, has hampered the guerrillas from being able to mobilize the entire population for resistance. To be sure, some women have been involved in the movement; but this is no substitute for confidence in the revolutionary potential of women and concrete programs based on the needs of (especially Indian) women, which necessarily implies a transformation of the *macho* consciousness.

Despite these limitations, there can be no doubt—indeed there was none in the minds of the Guatemalan and North American organizers of the counter-insurgency—as to the lasting importance of the guerrilla movement. Within Guatemala it has clearly altered the terms of the struggle and posed the first possibility of a socialist revolution there. And despite the serious setbacks suffered by the end of the 1960's, the counter-insurgents were unable to extinguish the movement permanently, much less to pacify the country. By the early 1970's, there were signs that the movement, far from being liquidated, was learning from past weaknesses and was developing a much broader base. Moreover, the experience of the Guatemalan guerrillas has been crucial for all Latin America. Those who went to the mountains of Izabal and Zacapa in the early 1960's had no models to follow. Their advances by 1966 became an example and a symbol for all Latin America; their shortcomings were part of a collective learning experience for the entire continent.

THE LONG ARM OF THE UNITED STATES

While unsuccessful thus far in overthrowing the existing order, the forces of popular resistance have, nevertheless, maintained the country in a state of permanent unrest, and have created a situation which Guatemalan security forces are unable to handle. Thus it has been necessary for the United States, the ultimate guarantor of the Counter-Revolution, to assume a direct role in administering the "pacification" of Guatemala. At times this tutelary role has involved overt U.S. intervention. The first such occasion since 1954 arose in 1963, in response to Arévalo's anticipated electoral victory: the Kennedy Administration deliberately instigated the overthrow of Ydígoras to prevent the election (*Miami Herald,* Dec. 24, 1966).

Far more significant has been the constant direct involvement of the U.S. in combatting the Guatemalan insurgency. An early stage was U.S. use of Guatemala as a training ground for the 1961 Bay of Pigs invasion of Cuba. Specifically, President Ydígoras' close adviser, Roberto Alejos Arzú, donated his *finca*, "La Helvetia," in Retalhuleu for the cause; amid vigorous denials by the government, unmistakeable traces of the operation were discovered (training and prison camps, mysterious planes, etc.). According to one account (*Miami Herald,* Dec. 24, 1966), Ydígoras' price for cooperation included: cancellation of an unpaid debt of $1.8 million, the remnant of a CIA loan to Castillo Armas for the 1954 invasion; a higher sugar quota; and Washington's support of the

Guatemalan position in the dispute over Belice. But the presence of the U.S. base and the Cuban trainees proved useful to Ydígoras in other ways. Former Batista thugs were integrated into Guatemalan security forces. When the Nov. 13 rebels took the garrison in Zacapa, the government used Cuban exile mercenary pilots from the Retalhuleu base to bomb and retake the garrison (Aguilera, 1970:131; Buttrey, 1967:24).

Although formal U.S. counter-insurgency assistance began as early as 1960, soon after the Nov. 13 uprising, the program became massive in 1966 when the guerrilla movement had become a real threat in Izabal and Zacapa. During the 1966–8 campaign in that area, after the Guatemalan army proved incapable of containing the insurgency, U.S. training, bomber planes, napalm, radar detection devices, and other sophisticated technology were decisive in smashing it. Although it is categorically denied by official U.S. sources, the presence of U.S. Green Berets (estimates range from several hundred to one thousand) has been documented by careful observers, and even acknowledged by a high Guatemalan police official (Munson, 1967; Geyer, 1966). Numerous travelers to Guatemala have reported encounters with Green Berets in such places as the bar of the luxurious Hotel Biltmore in the capital. Observers have also noted a striking resemblance between torture techniques now used by Guatemalan security forces and those used by Green Berets in Vietnam. Several Americans have died mysteriously in the mountainous guerrilla zone; the secrecy surrounding their deaths was linked to United States and Guatemalan government efforts to cover up the active combat role of U.S. Special Forces "advisers." In addition, U.S. aerial counter-insurgency operations (napalm raids) were carried out from U.S. bases in Panama.

Training in the use of the U.S.-provided hardware (including planes, napalm, etc.) has also been extensive: the ratio of U.S. military advisers to local army forces is higher for Guatemala than for any other Latin American country. Since 1964, Guatemalan security efforts have been coordinated with those of the neighboring countries through the U.S.-sponsored Central American Defense Council (CONDECA). The Guatemalan police, as well, have received generous U.S. ("public safety") assistance. Aside from a steady flow of helicopters, paddy wagons (ridiculed in Guatemala as *perreras* or dog-catchers' wagons), radio communications equipment, etc., a special gift of the Alliance for Progress in 1967 was fifty-four radio police cars, blessed by the Archbishop. Extensive training in riot control, intelligence and surveillance, and fingerprinting has been provided to over three hundred Guatemalan police personnel in the United States and to 32,000 locally by U.S. public safety advisers; and $400,000 of AID funds was donated for a new police academy. This training is accompanied by a healthy dose of anti-Communist, pro-U.S. indoctrination. The full extent of U.S. expenditures on training and equipping the Guatemalan military and police is impossible to determine without access to classified information; certainly it is far more than the official figures of $4.2 million for public safety and an average of $1.5 million (but up to $3. million) per year of military assistance, not counting U.S. arms sales.

Complementing this very big "stick" of U.S. security assistance is the "carrot" of "civic action" programs. The inspiration for civic action is to "win the hearts and minds" of the Guatemalan people through the provision of basic services in guerrilla zones. The goal is to "improve military-civilian rapport," to build a favorable image of the forces of repression, and to gain peasant cooperation in catching guerrillas. As the U.S. Army's *Military Review* (Jan., 1969) enthusiastically described it,

> Twenty-one tiny Guatemalan youngsters were seated at the long, low table. They were busy. They were eating their noon meal, a nourishing stew of chicken, rice, carrots, potatoes, and green beans in chicken broth. These children, many so listless and weak from malnutrition and parasites they could barely feed themselves, had been brought to the Uzumatlán Nutritional Center for care and feeding under the Guatemalan Government's nutritional program. The Uzumatlán Center is one of two such centers being financed by the Guatemalan Army. There are similar centers located throughout the country. . . .

Specific efforts have focused on provision of hot lunches for school children (though the food must travel under armed escort!) and medicines, literacy courses, mobile medical units, construction of wells, schools, roads, bridges, and so on. Much of this is done through civilian "philanthropic" agencies such as CARE. Civic action teams are also needed to hide the more violent aspects of pacification (e.g. by filling in bomb craters). The essentially pacificatory (rather than developmental) objective of this military social work is evidenced by the complaints of peasants throughout Guatemala that they cannot get even the most elementary services unless there exists a clear "guerrilla threat" in their region. And even in the chosen areas, civic action cannot really meet the needs of the people, since the basic intent is not structural change but public relations.

Despite the evidence of a very active and direct intervention in Guatemalan affairs since 1954, the U.S. prefers to maintain a low profile and to run the show from behind the scene. The principal mechanism for this more subtle but continual intervention is the $360. million in economic aid funds since 1954, channeled not only through U.S. government agencies but also through U.S.-dominated multilateral organizations (principally the Inter-American Development Bank and the World Bank). U.S. aid was initially designed to ensure the survival of the

Castillo Armas regime. For this purpose the U.S. poured in approximately $80. million in non-repayable grants from 1954 to 1957—more U.S. aid per capita than to all the rest of Latin America at the time. Exactly how this money was spent is nearly impossible to determine, but reports persist that much of it ended up in the private pockets of "Liberation" politicians.

In the 1960's under Alliance for Progress "developmentalism," the pattern changed somewhat: although grants were used several times to prevent the total bankruptcy of the Ydígoras regime, most of the aid has come as loans. Until 1966, the aid program was relatively small, partly because of the maverick military anti-Americanism of the Peralta regime. But in Méndez Montenegro the Alliance for Progress had its model government: a civilian, reformist facade, eager to finance "development projects" through foreign loans, yet backed up by a strong, anti-Communist military. Thus, whereas Guatemala had received a total of $40. million in loans by the beginning of 1966, the total by mid-1970 was $152.5 million: 74 percent of *all* foreign loans between 1960 and 1970 were signed during the Méndez regime (CNPE, 1970:184).

One result was that Guatemala's foreign public debt from these loans increased by 60 percent between 1964 and 1968, and rose from 28.4 percent of total public debt in 1961 to 41.5 percent in 1968 (Calderón, 1969: 100; Amaro, 1970:120). Service payments on the foreign public debt increased from $2. million in 1959 to $26.8 million in 1969. By 1969 service payments on total foreign debt (including profit remittances from foreign private investment) reached 41 percent of all export earnings (CNPE, 1970:191)—although another source calculates the figure at 51 percent (Calderón, 1969:100–1),—in any case, a figure high enough to seriously reduce the country's capacity to import. (Nearly all loans must be repaid in dollars.) If "foreign aid" is used, then, to alleviate Guatemala's immediate fiscal crisis (as a substitute for tax reform), in the longer run, it merely aggravates the chronic fiscal and balance of payments problems.

More significant than the amount of the foreign debt is the use of aid to serve United States rather than Guatemalan interests. Specifically, the aid program has been a means of providing for the needs of U.S.-based corporations and of maintaining a "favorable climate" for U.S. investment. Direct services of U.S. aid to U.S. corporate investors in Guatemala have included such items as the following: AID financing of up to 50 percent of the cost of pre-investment studies undertaken by U.S. firms; AID's provision of information and advice to prospective investors regarding labor, taxes, and other conditions in Guatemala; publicly financed training programs, both within and outside the universities, for managers, skilled labor and other manpower needed by U.S. subsidiaries—thus saving them the expenses for such training; loans on exceptionally concessional terms to U.S. firms which could easily afford commercial terms; loans to the Guatemalan government for infrastructure projects which have often been of more benefit to U.S. corporations than to the local population (e.g., the EXIM-Bank loan for port improvements at Santo Tomás de Castilla, which will primarily service EXMIBAL); AID's investment guarantee program (see above); preference to U.S. firms for supervising, engineering, construction, and accounting contracts related to aid-financed infrastructure projects; and special conditions attached to loans to benefit U.S. corporations (e.g., a World Bank loan for one hydroelectric project was conditioned on certain agreements with EEG) (Galeano, 1969:110–11).

No less important has been the function of aid in creating a hospitable climate for U.S. investment. This implies, first, the enhancement of a suitable ideological climate, specifically by promoting the ideology of free enterprise and anti-Communism through the mass media and educational institutions; by penetrating indigenous grass-roots organizations or establishing parallel institutions, and instituting training programs for labor and peasant leaders; by "depoliticizing" (i.e., countering the prevalent leftist orientation in) the universities through training and "reform" programs. Second, it implies the use of aid to create a stable, predictable political environment or even to reward or punish particular policies. For example: Ydígoras was generously rewarded for his cooperation in the Bay of Pigs invasion. In 1955, under direct orders from President Eisenhower, the World Bank had to violate its own policy of not lending to nations which are delinquent in debt repayments (as Guatemala was with the *deuda inglesa*) by making an $18.2 million loan for highway construction in Guatemala, as a reward to Castillo Armas.[14] Third, there have been military uses of aid: certain roads have been financed, for example, largely for their value in counter-insurgency.

Most important has been the use of aid to promote policies conducive to long-range planning efforts of foreign (U.S.) corporations. Such policies have included special incentives, tax holidays, absence of exchange controls or profit remittance regulations, orthodox fiscal policies, etc. The principal mechanism for influencing policy has been to send in aid "experts" or advisers to supervise or directly administer aid projects (and hence all related policies) from within Guatemalan government

[14] Although Ubico offered to settle the debt in 1944, some bond-holders did not present their claims in time; the British government used its influence in the World Bank to prevent all other Bank loans to Guatemala until a final settlement was made in 1966.

ministries and agencies. Symbolic of this colonial relation was the AID-contracted Klein and Saks mission which virtually made policy from its office in the Presidential Palace during the late 1950's. In many situations it has not even been necessary for AID or international aid agencies to dictate policy; merely by making funds available for certain types of projects rather than others, they are able to channel development policy. Similarly, these agencies have used their funds to shape the specific nature of key institutions such as the Secretariat of the National Economic Planning Council (in its initial stages) and the Central American Bank for Economic Integration. (Nevertheless, U.S. influence can backfire when carried too far: in the early 1960's several high AID officials were accused of meddling in Guatemalan affairs and in two cases were firmly told to leave the country.)

Although the principal function of aid is to protect the expansion of private U.S. capital, there has been a sincere desire among some aid personnel for reform and development. Alliance officials insisted, for example, that Ydígoras pass a (mild) income tax law in 1962; a significant faction in U.S. policy circles favored Méndez Montenegro's abortive tax reform in 1967; and some even talked of the need for an agrarian reform. In practice, however, they have always been willing to settle for less and have abstained from applying real pressure for reform. A $23. million rural sector loan from AID required a reorganization of the Ministry of Agriculture, creation of new credit institutions, cooperatives, and an elaborate structure for improving marketing—everything but an agrarian refrom. Far from forcing structural change, the stop-gap measures of the Alliance have actually relieved the pressure for it, especially for tax reform. In this sense the Alliance has been an *alternative* to real development. And regardless of the reformist intentions of some aid functionaries, the context within which they operate—specifically, the firm alliance between the U.S. government and the Guatemalan bourgeoisie—makes such reform virtually impossible.

CONCLUSION: GUNS AND HUNGER

The convulsions of contemporary Guatemala are no passing phenomenon, but rather the logical culmination of the 450-year process of capitalist underdevelopment. More specifically, the current situation is a direct outcome of the inability of the ruling classes in the United States and Guatemala to tolerate the only serious attempt to build a non-dependent capitalism, the 1944–54 Revolution. But history cannot be unwritten; the experience of the Revolution cannot be erased. Hence the attempt to reverse it and to impose the Counter-Revolution is based on illusion.

The principal characteristics of the Counter-Revolution—increased dependency vis-à-vis the United States, growing concentration of wealth within the bourgeoisie and conversely the marginalization of the lower classes, and terror—are inherently contradictory and destabilizing. These conditions can be altered not by "nationalist capitalism," which rests on an alliance of the buorgeoisie with the petty bourgeoisie, but only by a break with 450 years of dependent capitalism and a socialist transformation of the existing order, based on the needs and the will of the Guatemalan people.

Increased dependency vis-à-vis the U.S. precludes development based on an expanded domestic market. Initially the strategists of the Counter-Revolution attempted to circumvent this imperative through regional integration of markets; but the very same domination by U.S. capital and priorities which prevents an independent capitalism in Guatemala eventually led to the crisis and breakdown of the CACM. Moreover, national development is inconceivable in Guatemala so long as the economic surplus (profits) generated by production is channeled out of the country to the U.S.—in short, so long as Guatemala is being *de*capitalized. This is, of course, no accident; it is inevitably the case when a country's "development" is geared toward meeting the needs of foreign interests rather than those of its own population. Finally, dependent industrialization has restricted the expansion of the Guatemalan consumer market which is a necessary condition for the expansion of the U.S. corporations themselves. Thus foreign capital has created the conditions which ultimately limit its own opportunities in Guatemala.

The fruit of this continuing process of dependency and underdevelopment, deepened by the policies of the Counter-Revolution, is the negative redistribution of income since 1954. Although reliable figures are unobtainable, one study (cited in Adams, 1970:383) revealed the following:

	1950		1962	
	Percent of pop.	Percent of GNP	Percent of pop.	Percent of GNP
1. Subsistence economy	71.3	24.	72.7	21.9
2. Commercial economy	28.7	76.	27.3	78.1
a. Low income	21.1	24.2	20.	20.9
b. Medium and high income	7.6	51.8	7.3	57.2
total 1 and 2a	92.4	48.2	92.7	42.8

Even more dramatic are the worsening conditions in the countryside, where, ultimately, Guatemala's problems must be resolved. The annual per capita income of subsistence farmers and agricultural laborers—two thirds of the population—*fell* from $87. in 1950 to $83. in 1968, with prices six percent higher. Meanwhile, per capita income rose thirty percent during that period for the top seven percent of the population (Gordon, 1971:152). Numerous studies confirm that farm workers were worse off by 1960 than under the Revolution (CIDA, 1965:90; Whetten, 1962:105; Adams, 1970:401).

The principal outlets for the rural landless and unemployed have been land invasions and migration to the cities. Throughout the 1960's land invasions had to be countered by forceful evictions. Migration to Guatemala City swelled the *barrancas,* the shanty-towns in the capital's mud-paved ravines (only a few minutes' bus ride from and in full view of the modern, bustling downtown), where the majority of the inhabitants are unemployed or marginally employed, shining shoes or selling gum or lottery tickets. Between 1950 and 1964, unemployment rose from fifty-six percent to seventy percent of the total urban population (Cohen, 1969: II, 14). Between 1950 and 1962 the employable urban population increased seven times faster than the number of urban employed (Adams, 1970:425). This geometric rise in the reserve army of the unemployed has created pressures which the half-hearted measures of the Counter-Revolution and the Alliance for Progress could in no way contain. Nor is this the only indicator of worsening conditions:

> There is little doubt that as far as the majority of the people are concerned, conditions in Guatemala are slowly deteriorating. . . . [In addition to rising unemployment] the housing deficit is becoming worse. The pupil:teacher ratio is rising, as is the ratio of students to schools; at the same time, the proportion of pupils remaining in schools is falling. Finally illiteracy is increasing. . . . At the present pace of regress Guatemala will soon catch up with Haiti and become the most illiterate nation in the Western Hemisphere. By most indications Guatemala has embarked on a process of steady under-development. (Griffin, 1970:16)

The progressive marginalization of the lower classes and the continuing concentration of wealth by the elite are far too extreme in contemporary Guatemala to be resolved through moderate evolutionary measures.

The political correlate of this situation is permanent and institutionalized unrest. Firmly in the hands of the bourgeoisie, the government is unable to respond by making the necessary reforms. This was symbolized by one observer's description of President Arana in 1971:

> Meanwhile, Arana hops about the country by helicopter, dedicating schools, opening roads, expressing his shock at the conditions of life of the workers on the coffee *fincas* owned by his right-wing supporters. (SFRC, 1971:4)

Since the government can make no claim to meeting popular needs, its legitimacy is open to constant challenge. The only means of containing the pressures for social change has been generalized repression. But this very process, whereby the brutal face of the Counter-Revolution is permanently unmasked, contains its own contradictions. While striking fear into the hearts of the population, the process of the repression has also politicized and radicalized various sectors. Thousands of peasants, particularly in the guerrilla zones, have been impelled from apathy to resistance after witnessing the arrest or murder of their relatives by official forces, or personally experiencing the repression. Similarly, as seen above, the terror has generated resistance within the very petty bourgeois institutions—the Church and the military—designed to hold the system together. The government has even been forced to move against dissenters within the very class it is supposed to protect—as, for example, in the case of one ruling class politician who has been jailed and tortured numerous times since 1954 for his opposition to rightist government policies. The very logic of its own domination has created serious cracks in the unity of the ruling class.

Thus, while the pressures for change are building up, the safety valves are being closed off. The very magnitude of the brutality, which brings Guatemalan underdevelopment into the lives of the entire population, breeds polarization and politicization at all levels. The realization that time is on the side of the people forces the government to respond with ever-increasing repression, as the only means of maintaining bourgeois hegemony. In reality, however, this violence is not an assertion of authority, but a holding action, an operation of weakness and desperation, a reminder that all apparent "solutions" are illusory and, at best, provisional.

You have a gun
And I am hungry.

You have a gun
because
I am hungry.

You have a gun
Therefore
I am hungry.

You can have a gun
you can have a thousand bullets and even another thousand,

you can waste them all on my poor body,
you can kill me one, two, three, two thousand, seven thousand times
but in the long run
I will always be better armed than you
if you have a gun
and I
only hunger.

—"Arms," by Manuel José Arce (Guatemala: 1970)

SUSANNE JONAS (BODENHEIMER) is a staff member of the North American Congress on Latin America (NACLA), a U.S.-based research collective which documents the operations of U.S. corporations, government agencies and other interests in Latin America. She is also completing her Ph.D. in political science at the University of California, Berkeley. She has traveled in and studied various Latin American countries. Her most recent work has focused on Guatemala and Central America. She has written numerous articles, both scholarly and journalistic, on Latin America, for magazines in the U.S. and in Latin America.

STATISTICS

Area: 108,889 km.² (42,042 mi.²), slightly smaller than the state of Tennessee

Population: 5.2 million (1970)

Population Growth Rate: 3.1 percent per year

Birth Rate: 42.4 births per 1000 inhabitants in 1964

Infant Mortality Rate: 91.5 deaths per 1000 live births in 1966

Capital City: Guatemala City

Degree of Urbanization: 31.9 percent urban in 1970 (24.1 percent in 1950)

Literacy Rate: 36.7 percent or lower (one of the lowest in Latin America) of population over seven years old

Degree of Unionization: 1.2 percent of workers

Social Security Coverage: 7 percent of population (21 percent of economically active population)

Unemployment: in 1970, 100,000 in cities, 500,000 rural

Housing: housing shortage of 800,000 units, at least; by 1964 only 29.5 percent of houses had running water, 22 percent had electricity, and 30.6 percent had toilets (this situation is one of the worst in all Latin America)

Health: 2.5 physicians per 10,000 population (one-sixth the ratio for the U.S.); 2.5 hospital beds per 1000 inhabitants (no improvement since 1950)

Malnutrition: 75 percent of all Guatemalan children under 5 years old are malnourished

Racial/Cultural Composition: in 1964, 58.6 percent *ladino,* 41.4 percent Indian, (53.6 percent Indian in 1950)

Per Capita Gross National Product: $293. in 1968

Rate of Increase of Per Capita GNP: 1.7 percent (Alliance for Progress "target:" 2.5 percent)

Income Distribution: there is no scientific study of income distribution in Guatemala; the only available figures show the following:

	1950		1964	
	Percent of population	Percent of GNP	Percent of population	Percent of GNP
Subsistence Economy	71.3	24.	72.7	21.9
Commercial Economy	28.7	76.	27.3	78.1
Low income	21.1	24.2	20.	20.9
Medium and high income	7.6	51.8	7.3	57.2
Total 1 and 2a	92.4	48.2	92.7	42.8

Another indicator is that, while the national average per capita income in 1965 was $286., the average per capita income of the poorest 75% of the population was $70. a year, or less than 20 cents a day per person.

Degree of Concentration in Land Tenure: (figures from 1964 Census) :

Size of farm	Percent of owners	Percent of farmland
micro-finca (less than 1 manzana*)	20.4	1.
sub-familiar (1–10 manzanas)	67.	18.
familiar (10–64 manzanas)	10.5	19.
medium mulifamiliar (1–20 caballerías*)	2.	36.
large multifamiliar	.1	26.

* 1 manzana = 1.7 acres
  1 caballería = 64.4 manzanas = 109.8 acres

Direct Taxes as Percent of Total Tax Revenue: 15–16 percent

Budget Expenditures: for education and culture: 16 percent
for defense and internal security: 17 percent

Dependence on Main Exports: in 1967, 34.5 percent of export earnings came from coffee, and 16 percent from cotton

Trade Deficit: in 1969, $17.6 million

Foreign Public Debt: $75.7 million in 1968

Foreign Debt (Public and Private): $387. million by 1967

Service Payments on Foreign Debt as Percent of Export Earnings: 41 percent (some estimate 51 percent)

Foreign Private Investment: $286.25 million in 1969 (not counting EXMIBAL)

Major Governments Since 1930:

Jorge Ubico (1931–1944) : came to power, and maintained power through rigged "elections"

Juan José Arévalo (1945–1951) : elected

Jacobo Arbenz (1951–1954) : elected

Carlos Castillo Armas (1954–1957) : came to power through CIA-supported and -engineered coup overthrowing Arbenz

Miguel Ydígoras Fuentes (1958–1963) : elected, after assassination of Castillos Armas, in election of dubious honesty

Enrique Peralta Azurdia (1963–1966) : came to power through military coup, overthrowing Ydígoras, to prevent 1963 election

Julio César Méndez Montenegro (1966–1970) : elected

Carlos Arana Osorio (1970–1974) : elected

CHAPTER 2

GULF OF MEXICO

PACIFIC OCEAN

MEXICO

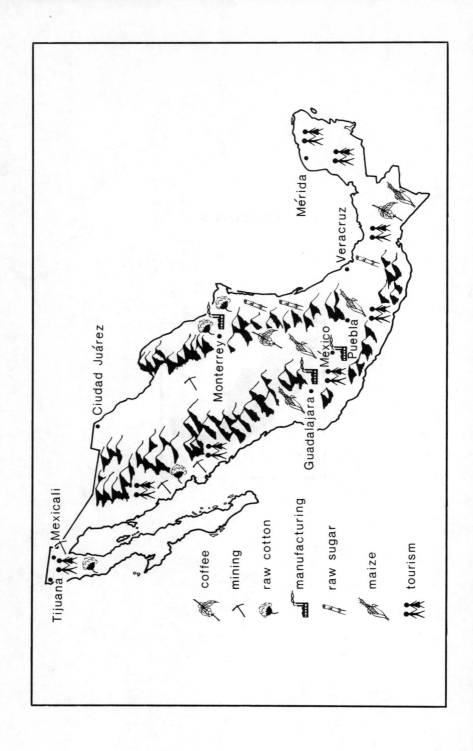

Tijuana

Mexicali

Ciudad Juárez

Mérida

Veracruz

Monterrey

México

Puebla

Guadalajara

coffee

mining

raw cotton

manufacturing

raw sugar

maize

tourism

CONTENTS

MEXICO

"I come for gold, not to till the land like a peasant" — Hernán Cortés

De los campos los burgueses se adueñaron
Explotando los veneros que en el subsuelo encontraron
Mientras tanto los millones de pesos al extranjero
Se llevaban los patronos con escarnio verdadero. (corrido mexicano)

— The bourgeoisie made themselves lords of the countryside
    Exploiting there the veins they found in the subsoil
    Meanwhile the bosses took abroad
    The millions of pesos with true scoffing. (Mexican revolutionary song)

Cárdenas es como el sol
Brilla sobre todo
Pero calienta a nadie. (dicho mexicano)

— Cárdenas is like the sun
    He shines upon everyone
    But warms no one. (Mexican saying)

A U.S. company that puts its money into Mexico can be confident of avoiding most of the problems which customarily unnerve foreign investors elsewhere in Latin America. The country has gone for decades without a revolutionary change in government, the dangers of sudden expropriation are minimal, and the currency is stable. (*Fortune*, April, 1965)

". . . two, three, many Topelejos" (student slogan during 1968 revolt, referring to peasant-controlled liberated zone outside of Mexico City, and modelled after Ché Guevara's slogan, ". . . two, three, many Vietnams")

MEXICO

BY

JAMES D. COCKCROFT

INTRODUCTION

In spite of much propaganda to the contrary, and in spite of an uniquely rich cultural heritage, Mexico is not that much different from the rest of Latin America when it comes to the problems of underdevelopment. The majority of the population lives in conditions of grinding poverty, while an economic and political elite lives off the profits of the labor of the working class, half of which is rural. Nevertheless, Mexico has experienced more economic development than most Latin American countries and has a good potential for sustained economic growth with relatively equitable distribution of its benefits among the people.

It has become fashionable in most textbooks on Third World developing countries to refer to Mexico as an example of "balanced growth," worthy of the emulation of her poorer neighbors in Latin America and cousins in Asia, Africa, and the Middle East. In point of fact, Mexico does share certain structural characteristics with countries like Brazil (until the 1964 military coup), India, Algeria, Kenya, Ghana, Tanzania, and Egypt. It has a "mixed" economy, characterized by a strong state and centralized bureaucracy, national ownership of most of the natural resources needed for industrial production, a growing industrial base, and rapidly increasing urbanization. However, Mexico's economy, like that of the other countries mentioned, is far from "balanced"; its growth is by spurts and sputters rather than sustained; and its development has been malformed and limited. Most importantly Mexico suffers continued economic dependence upon a foreign metropolis, yesterday Spain and Great Britain, today, the United States.

Many commentators, Mexican and foreign alike, believe that Mexico's evolution in the twentieth century represents a form of economic development which is uniquely Mexican, or *sui generis*. Where else can one find peasant revolutionaries like Emiliano Zapata, or charismatic leaders like Lázaro Cárdenas, the President who nationalized oil in 1938? Where else has such an unique combination of state intervention and lucrative private enterprise, working in cooperation rather than conflict, survived for such a long period of time without the usual conditions of instability and frequent revolutions or palace coups? The answer is: many places, from India to Guinea, Egypt to Brazil, Ghana to Argentina, with obvious differences in chronology and culture. Narciso Bassols, former Mexican Secretary of Education (1932–1934), may have been right when he described the highly touted *sui generis* thesis in 1937 as one propagated by "Mexican conservatives and even by some revolutionary members of the government and the official party" to throw up "pure camouflage . . . an essentially reactionary attempt to isolate the Mexican masses from the exploited peoples of the rest of the world" (cited in Ashby, 1967:23).

Indeed, far from being deemed unique in the annals of economic development or revolutionary change, Mexico has come to be recognized, especially by admirers of its economic policies, as some kind of "model" for social change, some kind of "middle way" between Socialism and Capitalism which can readily be adapted to other societies undergoing the trials of "development." Governments in Guatemala, Venezuela, Brazil, Argentina, Chile, Bolivia, and now Peru, for example, have all, at one time or another since Cárdenas, consciously steered their development policies in the Mexican direction, with about the same degree of success in terms of economic growth rates, degree of labor unionization, amount of poverty and corruption, degree of foreign economic control, and preservation and strengthening of monopolistic corporate firms and the elite families who run them. Advocates of the Alliance for Progress have championed the Mexican way as the American way—that is, the "inter-American" way, as it is now euphemistically called. It is precisely because the Mexican example is not *sui generis* that it commands so much attention today, and deservedly so.

In 1967, Latin American representatives to the Organization of American States approved "the Protocol of Buenos Aires," which reads remarkably like an official statement from any one of Mexico's last seven Presidents. The Protocol calls for "mobilization of our own national resources . . . with adequate planning," "price stability in harmony with sustained development and the achievement of social justice," "modernization of rural life and effective reforms which lead to equitable regimes and efficient land tenure," "just salaries," "rapid eradication of illiteracy," "adequate nutrition," "adequate housing for all sectors of the population," all these things and more by means of the "promotion of private initiative and investment in harmony with the action of the public sector" (cited in Aguilar, 1967:124). Such is the Mexican model, and such, increasingly, is the model for all Latin America and much of the Third World as a whole, with full U.S. approval and encouragement. Why?

To answer this question it is necessary to review the entire history of Mexico in terms of the process of its underdevelopment, class structure, and relationship to other parts of the world. Only then will we understand Mexico's problems today, its condition of limited development, prolonged underdevelopment rather than autonomous self-sustained development, and continuing misdevelopment.

DEVELOPMENT OF UNDERDEVELOPMENT

Mexico's condition of limited development, prolonged underdevelopment, and economic dependence upon a foreign, capitalist metropolis, derives from its first contact with Europe. Hernán Cortés did not find Mexico in a state of underdevelopment—quite the contrary. He and other *conquistadores* were bedazzled by the wealth, prosperity, architecture, flourishing marketplaces, strength, beauty, dignity, and intelligence of the Aztec and Mayan Indians they encountered. Viewing the Indian treasures, Cortés informed the Indians: "We Spaniards are troubled by a disease of the heart for which the specific remedy is gold."

Mexico's Indian civilizations included advanced techniques of agriculture, architecture, artisanry, commerce, and social organization. Aztec feats included terracing, irrigation, floating gardens (*chinampa*), medical cures with local flora, pyramids (Teotihuacán—pre-Aztec), temples, weaving, pottery, and exquisite metal-work, especially in gold. The Aztecs organized the peasants into *calpullis*—a type of village estate farmed communally. Peasants were permitted to own land and did not have to submit to the judicial authority of village nobles who headed the *calpulli*. Aztec civilization included a highly developed priesthood, as well as an autonomous merchant class. Finally, the Aztecs had a strong, centralized state linking far-flung Indian communities and conquered tribes to the Emperor.

While it is true that the Aztecs engaged in human sacrifice, the deaths caused in this way were not unlike those caused by the Old World's Catholic Crusades and Inquisition—all were inspired by religious fanaticism and material greed. And although the Aztecs collected tribute from the peoples they conquered, slavery as a system was not of essential importance. The sons of slaves were allowed to be freemen, slaves could own other slaves, and the Aztec system was far less rigid than Old World practices of slavery, which, after the Conquest of Mexico, were imported to the New World as well. As for the supposed "primitiveness" or "cultural backwardness" of the Indians, they learned Latin and theology so well in the Spanish schools that, after ten years, they became the tutors of the sons of the *conquistadores*.

Mexico's highest Indian civilization was the Mayan (Classic Period, 325–925 A.D.), extending from the highlands of today's Guatemala to the semi-arid frontier zones of Yucatán. The Mayan civilization was one of city-states, with government in the hands of a small class of priests and nobles. Mayans were especially creative in architectural sculpture, mural art, painting, hieroglyphic writing, and mathematics, where they developed the concept of zero. In astronomy, the Mayans could accurately chart the course of such planets as Venus, without a telescope. They had a chronology and calendar that defined the 365-day solar year more accurately than was to be done a thousand years later under Pope Gregory in 1582.

In brief, Mexico was not underdeveloped when the Spaniards arrived. In many areas, it was developed and more advanced than Old World civilizations, while in others it was not so far advanced or even behind (for example, it did not have the wheel, the horse, or anything approaching the military technology of the *conquistadores*). But it did *not* become underdeveloped until after the Conquest, and because of the Conquest.

From the Spanish Conquest to the present, the colonization of Mexico has meant the exploitation of people, the destruction of great cultures, and the development of underdevelopment by the expanding forces of mercantilism and capitalism. The high Indian civilizations of Mexico, already weakened by internal strife and decay, were thoroughly smashed by the Spaniards. Those Indians not killed outright, died from overwork or disease. Six-sevenths of the Indian population was wiped out between 1519 and 1650, many falling victim to diseases imported by the Spaniards or slave-ships (smallpox, typhoid fever, measles, malaria, yellow fever).

Spain's mercantile drive for wealth in the New World was an important force in the transition from feudalism to capitalism on a world basis. As Cortés remarked: "I come for gold, not to till the land like a peasant." Mexico's gold and silver fed the coffers of Spanish mercantilism; Mexico's ports connected the trade routes of Asia and Europe; and Mexico's internal class structure was shaped by this dependent relationship vis-à-vis Spain.

The Manila galleon carried Mexican silver from Acapulco to the East Indies in exchange for the silks and spices which Europe coveted. In the words of Adam Smith: "The silver of the new continent seems in this manner to be one of the principal commodities by which the commerce between the two extremities of the old one is carried on, and it is by means of it, in great measure, that these distant parts of the world are connected with one another" (cited in Cockcroft *et al.*, 1972:Ch. II, 4). Every aspect of culture revolved around this development of mercantile capitalism, including religion. As Bishop Mota y Escobar remarked: "where there are no Indians, there is no silver" and "Where there is no silver, the gospel does not enter" (Frank, 1969:233–34).

Emerging from feudalism into mercantile capitalism, Spain was in no mood to transfer to her colonial territories feudal modes of organization which might create an autonomous nobility free from the Crown's control. Nor were the *conquistadores* anxious to become mere feudal barons. Cortés was representative of the nascent capitalist spirit of the time. His twenty-five thousand-square-mile estate in Oaxaca was netting his son eighty thousand gold pesos a year in Indian tributes by 1569, when the Crown confiscated it and other estates of the *conquistadores* to prevent too independent an ownership class from developing in Mexico. The Cortés estate also included a nascent silk industry based on the mulberry tree, two sugar mills, wheat, fruit, horses, cattle, sheep and corrals for the mules Cortés bred in Tehuántepec to service the mines to the North.

As Eric Wolf has pointed out, the conquering Spaniard "became a mining entrepreneur, a producer of commercial crops, a rancher, a merchant," in brief, a capitalist, not a feudal lord. With the introduction into silver-mining of the patio process in 1555, permitting profitable exploitation of low-grade ores, these entrepreneurs firmly established "the technology of large-scale capitalist mining" by the end of the sixteenth century (Wolf, 1959:176–78).

To service the flourishing mining centers, commercial agriculture was developed: mules and horses to transport the wealth; sugar and maize (corn) to feed the labor force that produced it. Grinding and processing mills sprang up on the large estates (*haciendas*) like factories in the field. In the words of that astute observer of colonial Mexico, the German geographer Alexander von Humboldt:

Trips through the Andes highlands or the mountainous part of Mexico offer the most obvious examples of the beneficent influence of the mines on agriculture. Without the establishments formed for the working of the mines, how many places would have remained unpopulated, how much land uncultivated, in the four districts of Guanajuato, Zacatecas, San Luis Potosí, and Durango. . . . The foundation of a city follows immediately after the discovery of a large mine. . . . Haciendas are established nearby; the scarcity of foodstuffs and the high prices caused by consumer competition favors agricultural products, compensates the grower for the deprivations of life in the mountains.

In this way, arising only out of the desire for profit . . . a mine . . . is very quickly linked up with lands long under cultivation . . . (Frank, 1969, 235–6).

In addition, Mexican agriculture was integrated into the import-export flow of goods for Europe: European manufactures for Mexican indigo, cochineal, silk, cacao, cotton, hides, tallow, leather goods, wool, sugar.

Thus, most of Mexico's economy came to revolve around trade with Europe, especially in the mining sector with the emergence of world-famous cities like Guanajuato, Zacatecas, San Luis Potosí, and Pachuca, the present capital of the state of Hidalgo. These areas boomed in the sixteenth century, declined in the seventeenth, and rose again in the eighteenth. Today they are representative of Mexico's most underdeveloped regions, characterized by *caciquismo* (bossism), a corrupt spoils system, fanatic Catholicism and anti-Communism, and abject poverty. Far from suffering from centuries of neglect and isolation from the market economy (feudalism), these areas became systematically *under*developed through their colonization and subjugation by the Spaniards, their maximal integration into the world-wide capitalist market economy, and their subsequent abandonment once the capitalists had exhausted their natural wealth, labor supply, and surrounding countryside soils. In this way, mercantilism and nascent capitalism led to the underdevelopment of Mexico (Frank, 1969:322–3).

Characteristic of mercantilism was the strong role assigned to the state and the corporation, with specific limitations set upon individuals. The Spanish Crown demanded its *quinto real* (Royal Fifth) of the wealth found in Mexico. Similarly, it placed restrictions upon the *conquistadores* and their descendants so as to prohibit an autonomous economic rival class of miners and landowners from developing. To assert ultimate control over both the colonists and the Indian masses, the Crown declared them all its vassals. While in practice the *conquistadores* enslaved the Indians, the Crown quickly introduced the *encomienda* system which "commended" to the Spaniards the Indians' souls and labor, but not their land, in exchange for which the Spaniards were to provide religious instruction. The colonists thus had to have royal permission, through the *encomienda,* to lay hands on Indian labor.

In the second half of the sixteenth century, this system was replaced by the *repartimiento* (forced labor) and, by the end of the century, a "free" labor system. Colonists now had to hire Indian labor at a royal labor exchange at the same price paid by other colonists competing for the same precious labor-producing commodity, the Indian. Ultimately, in the second half of the sixteenth century, it was these "free" laborers, bought in the marketplace of competitive supply and demand, regulated by the Crown, that furnished the labor for the mines in Northern Mexico.

As Gibson has pointed out, the Crown sought in every way to create a "free" labor force, adequately paid in wages—further evidence that capitalism, not feudalism, was the driving force of the colonization of Mexico. (Gibson, 1964:228; cited by Aguilar, 1968:30). The northward expansion itself, in terms of financial investment and profits, "was the work of great capitalists, grown rich in mining, stock-raising, and commercial agriculture." (Wolf, 1959:194).

Influential as mercantilism was in the development of the Mexican economy in colonial times, it was more important as a midwife in the birth of capitalism. Most of the appropriation of wealth in Mexico was done by private individuals and partnerships. As Frank has noted, "It was they who financed the entire enterprise and it was they who received the profits, including a good part of the royal share, which went to the Genoese, Dutch, and German bankers who were financing the Spanish king (who was also the German emperor)" (Frank, 1969:243). Directly and indirectly, New World mineral wealth financed much of the early development of capitalism in all of Europe.

Because the New World was from the outset intended to be a source of valuable mineral wealth and raw materials for the homeland (Europe) and not a primary producer in its own right, Spain set restrictions upon the development of manufacturing in Mexico. Periodically in the colonial period, Spain outlawed production of olive oil, wine, silken goods, and textiles. The only independent manufacture to develop in Mexico was wool and cotton textiles. *Obrajes,* primitive industrial sweatshops utilizing spinning wheels, reels, horizontal looms, water-driven machinery, and the forced labor of the Indians, were established in Mexico but never allowed to out-compete European manufactures. From Spain came iron, mercury, arms, paper, fine cloth, wine, books, olive oil, while Mexico sent back silver, gold, sugar, wool, leather, tallow, cochineal, cacao, and indigo. This pattern of trade—primary goods for manufactured goods—has not radically altered to this day, except that now Mexico's main trading partner is the United States, and industrial equipment and producers' goods have replaced manufactured goods as Mexico's major import.

INDIAN AND AFRICAN RESISTANCE

Ultimately, economic exploitation of Mexico depended upon one item: the Indian. "The conquerors wanted Indian labor, the Crown Indian subjects, the friars Indian souls" (Wolf, 1959:195). For the Indian, the Conquest and subsequent colonization of Mexico was a near-total disaster. Those Indians not dying in combat or from disease, met early deaths from starvation or overwork. By importing sheep and plows, the Spaniards further reduced Indian lands—the sheep ruining the landscape with their root-killing grazing, and the plows requiring more land per unit of food produced. In addition, Spaniards took Indian lands to provide wheat for the white man. Also, Spaniards monopolized the sources of water. In brief, starvation set in for the Indians. Most of the Spaniards were male and did not hesitate to take Indian women for their companions, a process which led ultimately to the majority of today's Mexicans being *mestizo* and only 11 percent full-blooded Indian.

Under the Azetc and Mayan ruling classes, the Indians had been exploited, but at least they shared a common religion and culture and had some autonomy. The Spanish Conquest, however, lacked a common purpose and common language and provided little or no autonomy so far as the Indian was concerned. It not only replaced intensive seed-planting with extensive, plow-and-livestock agriculture; "it also sacrificed men to the production of objects intended to serve no end beyond the maximization of profit and glory of the individual conqueror" (Wolf, 1959:200). The only way in which the Indian finally succeeded in overcoming this new and strange exploitation he suffered in the minepits and on the *haciendas* of the colonists was by transferring as much of his old religious identity as he could to the new and strange Catholic Church with its exotic rituals, some of which resembled those of the sun-god whom he earlier had honored. Otherwise, the Conquest for the Indian was a biological disaster, a spiritual trauma, and economically a change for the worse. It was the start of underdevelopment.

Not that the Indians accepted their subjugation passively. On the contrary, divided though they were between regions and factions, Mexico's Indians put up stiff resistance against the Spaniards, and have been resisting their white, and later *mestizo,* overlords ever since. In a series of bloody battles, the Spaniards had to destroy the beautiful and prosperous city of Tenochtitlán (today's Mexico City) in order to capture it. One of the few gains of the 1910 Revolution was the renaissance in Indian culture and national respect paid to the Indian heritage. Hardly anywhere in Mexico today can one find a statue of Cortés, or even more than an occasional one of Moctezuma, the Aztec Emperor who submitted to Cortés' deceitful negotiations and thereby sacrificed the lives of many of his people and, eventually, his own. On the other hand, statues of Cuauhtémoc, Moctezuma's nephew who fought to the death against the Spaniards, are to be seen everywhere. The Mexican word for treason is "malinchismo," after the Indian mistress and translator of Cortés, Malinche, who betrayed her people.

In addition to the Aztec resistance, prominent cases of Indian resistance and revolt over subsequent centuries included those of the Huastecans, the Mayans, the Mixtons, the Indians of Tehuántepec and Hidalgo, and the Yaquis. The Haustecan tribes along the Panuco River (Vera-cruz, Hidalgo, San Luis Potosí) bitterly opposed the Spaniards. Thou-sands were burned alive by the Spaniards, more were captured and sent to the Caribbean as slaves, while others held out and fought guerrilla actions against the invaders for over two hundred years. In fact, as late as the mid-nineteenth century, some of these Huastecan Indians were secure in their own communities, practicing a self-declared anarchism (*Rebelión y plan* . . . , 1956). Serious Indian revolts occurred in the Huasteca during the last decades of the Díaz regime, and these Indians helped win the Mexican Revolution of 1910 (Cockcroft, 1968:53, 156).

Mayan tribes in Yucatán held off the Spaniards for years. Montejo finally seized the northern tip of Yucatán only after burning alive chief-tains, cutting off the arms and legs of male prisoners and hanging or drowning the women. In 1761, the Mayans rose up under the leadership of Jacinto Cano against excessive tributes, and in 1848 the Indians fought in a long and savage revolt against the domination of whites in the famous Caste War of Yucatán (Reed, 1964).

The Mixton Rebellion of 1541 in the Zacatecas-Jalisco area of Western Mexico led to the death of the conquistador Alvarado and prolonged guerrilla warfare by the Indians. Tepic miners revolted in 1598, and again the Tepics rose in revolt under Mariano in 1801. As late as the Presidency of Porfirio Díaz (1877–1911), the Indians of this region took refuge in the Sierra de Nayarit, from whence they launched forays against white landowners.

In 1680, the Indians of Tehuántepec revolted and took control of much of the Isthmus for eight years. To this day, these Indians are known for their independence and dignity. In the 1860's, the Indians of Hidalgo State and the central plateau rallied behind the leadership of Julio López and seized the lands to farm for themselves. Yaqui Indians in Sonora held off much of the white man's advance until the twentieth century. Yaqui revolts in 1900 threatened the Díaz regime and were brutally re-pressed, the captured warriors being sent as slaves to harvest tobacco crops in Oaxaca. Similarly, Africans brought to Mexico aboard the slave ships resisted subjugation. In the eighteenth century, the African leader Yangas led his followers in a revolt in Veracruz State that was so success-ful that the rebels were given their freedom and permitted to found a village called San Lorenzo de los Negros, under their own rule. The most successful and noble Independence guerrilla-peasant leader was the Afro-Indian Juan Alvarez, who lived to sign the 1857 Constitution amidst much pomp and circumstance (Alvarez since has been relegated to his-tory's footnotes by *mestizo* and white authors).

Even *mestizos* joined these underdog revolts in many of the cities, where the so-called "rioting of the rabble" known as *tumultos* became a commonplace during the colonial period. Often the *creoles,* native-born Mexicans of Spanish descent, were terrorized by these uprisings, while sometimes they used them to threaten the *gachupines* (their rivals for power—native Spaniards in control of the bureaucracy and commerce). In every case, the Indians, Africans, and *mestizos* moved against the symbols of wealth and oppression by looting stores and destroying the gibbet and the stock.

COLONIAL CLASS STRUCTURE

Mexico's class structure was conditioned and shaped by the incursions of mercantile capitalism. In broadest terms, it took the form of a large, highly exploited working class, mainly Indian but increasingly Mestizo, and a small commercial and productive bourgeoisie, mainly white and Creole, which appropriated the fruits of the proletariat's labor.

From the outset, this commercial bourgeoisie was subordinate to the Crown and the European bourgeoisie, remitting the major part of any economic surplus to the metropolis in Spain. What it did not remit to Spain, Mexico's bourgeoisie reinvested to develop the export productive apparatus, or to import capital goods for the same end, or to purchase luxury items for the bourgeoisie's own consumption. As Frank has noted

> rational capitalist behavior of the colonial bourgeoisie automatically made the dependent development of underdevelopment in Latin America into a self-reinforcing part of the historical process of world capitalist development. . . . Thanks to foreign trade and finance, the economic and political interests of the mining, agricultural, and commercial bourgeoisie did not lie with internal development. (Frank, 1969:377; Cockcroft *et al.,* 1972:Ch. 2)

On the contrary, the very nature and condition of the bourgeoisie in Mexico led it to further the process of underdevelopment. What few efforts were made toward autonomous development, as in the case of the textile *obrajes,* were held in check by the Crown's restrictions and by the merchandising monopoly held by the Casa de Contratación in Seville and the numerous Consulados established in Mexico to regulate and control all foreign trade. Not even primary products were permitted to develop too far, if the Crown felt that too strong a colonial bourgeoisie might result. For example, cacao was a major export crop in early colonial Mexico, but by the eighteenth century Spain had shifted its trade quotas and investment opportunities for cacao to Venezuela, leading to the demise of cacao as a money-earner in Mexico and its ascent to the position of leading export in Venezuela. This tragic misdevelopment for both Mexico and Venezuela, like the rest of underdevelopment and the lopsided class system, derived from the advent of European capitalism and its development at the expense of the natives of the New World.

No significant middle class developed during the colonial period of Mexican history. Most mestizos became debt peons along with the Indians and joined in the *tumultos*. Some mestizo parish priests, minor officials, lawyers and other professionals emerged as a recognizable middle group spawned by the flourishing universities and schools in the eighteenth century, but for most of the literate mestizos government patronage or enlistment in the Army were the only means of achieving wealth. Mestizos as a class lacked either class cohesion or class consciousness. They had neither a legitimate Indian identity, even though many of them were peasants, nor a Creole identity, even though a few of them entered commercial ranks with the expanded free trade provisions of Crown decrees toward the end of the eighteenth century. Nor did mestizos comprise a racial group as such, since a mestizo who worked on an *ejido* (Indian communal landholding) or private plot of land was automatically considered an "Indian." Mestizos had to forge their own identity, which was not easy to do since they were divided among themselves between middle-class and proletarian. Since middle-class mestizos did not have middle-class aspirations, but rather aspired to upper-class values, wealth, rank, and status, there never emerged in colonial Mexico either a cohesive middle class or a racially conscious mestizo group.

Most Mexicans were peasants, miners, carriers, and workers, that is, proletarians. The major portion of the working class was the peasantry, attached to the *haciendas*. The *hacienda* system of agriculture, or *latifundismo* (system of land tenure based on a few large estates), was not a feudal import from Spain. Rather, it was the product of the colonists' need to increase production and employ a means of exploiting labor more efficient than that provided by the *encomienda* or the *repartimiento*. The *hacienda*, like the cattle ranch and mining enterprise, was preeminently a commercial venture. To succeed, it depended upon a readily available cheap labor supply and a market for its products. As we have seen, the *hacienda* received its impetus as a productive adjunct of the mining industry. As more and more Indians died, as labor became more scarce, and as the market for agriculture expanded to include not only supplies for the mines and the cities that rose up nearby but also export crops, the landowner devised an ingenious system of debt peonage to tie peasants to the *hacienda*. Simultaneously, the *hacendados* applied concerted pressure on the communal landholdings of the Indians (*ejidos*), hoping by their reduction to increase available labor supply.

On a "free" labor market, it became less difficult to ensnare the Indians in a system of loans, *tiendas de raya* (company stores on the *haciendas*, replete with the chit system), share-cropping, tenant-farming, and, in sum, debt peonage. As Chevalier has noted, "the best way to get 'free' workers was to take away their communal lands" (Chevalier, 1956, cited by Aguilar, 1968, 35). And the best way to keep them on the *hacienda* was to tie them down with debts, passed on to their offspring; use of force, as with whippings, rapes, and other forms of intimidation; and development over the years of a master-slave style of human relationships.

In the course of the decline of mining in the seventeenth century, a century which became known world-wide as the century of "depression," the commercial and productive bourgeoisie of Mexico shifted much of its capital into agriculture. Given the rising costs of mining and the rising prices of food, this was a rational decision—agriculture was more profitable. However, epidemics having wrecked havoc on the Indian population, labor was ever more scarce, and so the beourgeoisie launched its full-scale assault on the *ejidos* of the Indians to release needed hands to farm the expanding *haciendas*. Lauro Viadas, Director-General of the Ministry of Agriculture under Porfirio Díaz and a well-known *científico* ("scientific one"— as the Díaz braintrusters were known), accurately described the logic of the situation when he wrote:

> Agriculture is, before and above all else, a business, and in every business the amount and safety of the profits are what determine the character of the enterprise. . . . If the large rural properties continue to exist it is because they are the logical consequences of the state of evolution of agriculture in our country, and they will have to continue to exist for the same reason, in spite of the firmest and best-intentioned plans, as long as those obstacles which hamper our agrarian progress are not removed. Large-scale agriculture asserts itself and excludes small-scale family agriculture; it takes possession of the land, attracted, and I would say strongly attracted, by economic advantages that spring from the two following causes: (1) The high price of the means of livelihood. . . . The high price of these goods leads first to a high profit for the growers and subsequently, a high price for arable land, which places it within the reach only of capitalist entrepreneurs. (2) The cheapness of labor, which reduces, relatively if not absolutely, the cost of production and produces, thereby, the above-mentioned effect of raising agricultural profits . . . (Frank, 1969, 238).

In brief, Mexico's working class was highly exploited by a small but strong commercial, agrarian, and productive bourgeoisie. At first, especially in mining and agriculture, Indians supplied the labor, generated the capital, and provided the necessary technology and social organization. Eventually, Indians, mestizos, and even occasional poor whites became subjugated into a rigid class system of rich bourgeoisie over poor proletariat, with the fruits of the vast majority of labor immediately appropriated by the bourgeoisie.

But no matter how many centuries the system endured, it was never stable. The bourgeoisie, dependent upon Spain, was resentful of its lack of autonomy and terrified by the repeated outbursts of revolt from below (Indian revolts and *tumultos*). The War of Independence, 1810–1821, grew out of these tensions, as did subsequent civil wars in "independent" Mexico.

INDEPENDENCE; BRITISH ASCENDANCY

Ever since the defeat of the Spanish Armada in 1588, Spain had suffered the increasing military and economic competition of the rest of Europe's emerging capitalist powers, especially Britain and France. Contraband trade alone in the New World posed a serious threat to Spain's nominal economic hegemony. In an effort to increase the flow of goods, outcompete European rivals, offset the inroads of smuggling, and assuage the rising discontent of Creole traders discriminated against by the Spanish monopoly, the Crown issued a series of Free-Trade Acts (1765, 1778, 1789). These Acts reduced and equalized duties for Veracruz, Buenos Aires, and other major ports, while opening channels through which foreign traders could legitimately operate and by means of which Mexican traders could now trade with other parts of Latin America.

In 1796, Spain, bogged down in war with Britain, authorized the right for Creoles to ship their own goods in their own bottoms to Spain and back. In practice, neutral nations were also allowed to engage in this shipping, so that by the first half of 1799, of thirty foreign ships landing at Veracruz, twenty-five were of U.S. registry. Leading Mexican trading houses appointed agents in U.S. cities, and U.S. merchants did likewise at Veracruz. More importantly, Mexican Creoles greedily eyed the expanding marketplace of Britain and looked with favor upon selling their goods to the British.

Much of the Caribbean was already *de facto,* if not yet *de jure,* British. By 1810, British traders were solidifying commercial relations with all of "Spanish" America, while Creole spokesmen for Independence like Miranda and Bolívar were counting upon British and U.S. funds and guns. The "liberal" tie that united British and Creole commercial and political interests was not the liberalism of Jacobin ideologues and Black, proletarian insurgents (who smashed the British and French armies in Santo Domingo and Haiti); rather, it was the liberalism of free trade—economic liberalism—the key doctrine in the transition from mercantilism to capitalism world-wide. From the viewpoint of the industrializing and colonizing British bourgeoisie, the words to be spoken in 1824 by Foreign Minister George Canning would sum things up: "The nail is driven. Spanish America is free, and if we do not mismanage our affairs sadly, she is English."

In Mexico, Creoles saw their chance for greater economic strength and political autonomy from the mother country when Spain was subjugated by Napoleon's armies and became bogged down in war and civil turmoil. The free-trade years from 1778 to 1808 had already set the Creole bourgeoisie in motion towards greater self-assertion. Those years had produced an increase in trade competition, a decline in import prices, growing and diversified consumption of foreign manufactures, and a sizeable rise in agricultural and mining production and value. Most significant of all, there developed within the commercial and productive bourgeoisie an ascendant stratum of Creole landowners and merchants (producers of primary goods and exporters), anxious to solidify and extend their recent economic gains and to seize corresponding political power.

Creoles resented the monopoly of power held by the *gachupines*. Father Hidalgo, the priest who initiated the War of Independence with his "grito de Dolores" in 1810, had been assigned an unimportant parish merely, he thought, because he was a Creole. He blamed all his and Mexico's problems on the *gachupines,* and compensated his hurt feelings by reading foreign books, raising forbidden grapes, pressing out forbidden wine, planting forbidden mulberry trees, and spinning forbidden silk. (Simpson, 1941:186) Another Creole complaint was having to pay for and even join the armies of Spain in her endless European wars. As Fray Servando Teresa de Mier observed:

> . . . as Spain is unable to protect her commerce and unwilling to allow others to export our products and us to import theirs, and has deprived us of factories and industries, the European war is more cruel for us than for her, and is ultimately waged with our money. We simply need to stay neutral to be happy. (Humphreys, 1966, 27)

Although having ample cause for revolt against Spain, the Creoles were by their nature a conservative class of landowners, miners, and merchants. As Humboldt observed in 1803, the increase in Mexican wealth in the last three decades of the eighteenth century had heightened economic inequalities within colonial society. Higher food prices meant greater riches for the *hacendados* and poverty for the masses, as well as a deepening of the division between higher and lower clergy. More and more peasants surrendered their lands to the expanding *hacienda* system; more and more unemployed persons crowded into the already socially tense cities. Humboldt therefore predicted an "explosion of social conflict" (Florescano, 1969, 193–5, cited by Frank, 1971 MS., 19).

Ultimately, the Creoles declared for Independence not because of Spanish tyranny but because of the loosening of Spain's control over her colonies and the threatened usurption of power from below by Indians and Mestizos. Creoles had long objected to the protection the Crown had offered Indians and Indian lands, wanting instead to extend their *haciendas* as they were to do *after* Independence to the point of taking away almost *all* of the Indians' lands. As the Creole "Liberator" of South America, Simón Bolívar, put it in his famous "Letter from Jamaica" of 1815, the Creoles' grievance against Spain was not so much Spain's intolerance of democracy as Spain's refusal to permit Creoles enough authority to preserve some respect among the Indians and Mestizos, who threatened to disrupt all America with Revolution: "we have been deprived of an active tyranny, since we have not been permitted to exercise its functions" (Humphreys, 1966:263). In other words, the Creoles had been kept from the highest offices of government in Spanish America, and thereby deprived from exercising the tyranny that was so necessary to avoid the chaos and disorder of revolution from below.

The Guatemalan Act of Independence of September 15, 1821, argued that Independence had been declared "to prevent the consequences that would be fearful in the event that the people should proclaim it." In Mexico that same year, the Creoles, behind Iturbide, joined the fight for Independence in order to put down the previous decade's struggle by the Indians and Mestizos for a thorough-going social revolution. Thus, for Creoles, Independence was a necessary step in a dramatic and never-ending class war between wealthy elites and the rising agrarian and urban masses, with the Creoles seizing power in order to better repress revolt from below.

Class war in Mexico had been heightened by the social reform measures of the Congress of Chilpancingo, 1813, led by the priest Morelos, who foresaw the breaking up of all *haciendas* and issued political proclamations condemning "all the rich, Creoles and *gachupines*" (Aguilar, 1968:69). The Congress promised higher wages for the poor, abolished government monopolies, sales taxes and tributes, and introduced an income tax. Though the Congress also guaranteed the virtues and rights of private property, Creole landholders feared Morelos, his Indian followers, and their revolutionary ideas, even as they had feared the massive and bloody rampage through central Mexico of Hidalgo's Indian and mestizo followers three years earlier. Spain's General Calleja armed the

Creoles to fight Morelos' guerrillas, and in 1815 Morelos was defrocked and executed.

In 1820, a military coup in Spain overthrew Ferdinand and momentarily re-introduced the Liberal Cadiz Constitution of 1812. Creoles in Mexico, still threatened from below, now saw loyalty to Spain as unwise, since the Liberal provisions of the Cadiz Constitution included laws protecting Indians and Indian lands and thereby increased the threat to bourgeois class hegemony. Even the *gachupines* preferred seizing independence to living with such a constitution, and so Iturbide—one of Calleja's best generals in earlier battles against the proletarian armies of Morelos and Juan Alvarez (Afro-Indian peasant guerrilla who succeeded Morelos)—tricked Guerrero, a guerrilla leader of the South, into an alliance for independence from Spain. On September 27, 1821, Mexico City fell to Iturbide, who shortly thereafter proclaimed himself Emperor of "independent" Mexico.

This political independence from Spain did not automatically bring economic independence from Britain and other European nations, to whom Mexico owed a debt of seventy-six million pesos. Mexico would not have a balanced budget until 1894. Mexico's bourgeoisie had wrested state power from Spain not only to prevent the masses from doing it first, nor merely to deflect the course of revolt from below from its actual target, the bourgeoisie itself. The winning of independence also meant for the Mexican bourgeoisie the elimination of rival commercial intermediaries and Spanish monopolists precisely as a step toward the strengthening of trade relations with Britain "as producers and exporters of primary products and importers of cheap English manufactures." (Cockcroft *et al.*, 1972:Ch. II, 14). In effect, independence gained with the armed support of the masses led to a strengthened Mexican bourgeoisie, politically free from Spain and dominant over the masses, and economically more entrenched and secure as primary producers and exporters. Independence also meant a sharpening of class differences between rich and poor, and the Mexican bourgeoisie's continued dependence upon foreign bourgeoisies. The historical process of Mexico's underdevelopment and internal class conflict thus continued.

POST-INDEPENDENCE

FOREIGN TROOPS

After independence, Mexico faced the accumulated problems of underdevelopment and colonialism: a highly skewed class system, a huge foreign debt, a nation ravaged by war and near famine, most of the mining system flooded or wrecked, and, of course, little domestic capital with which to launch a full-scale development program. Where could Mexico get its much-needed capital? From the army, the Church, or the *hacendados*—that is, the government could cut back the payroll for the generals (which accounted for most public expenditure), could confiscate the properties of the Church, or could tax the wealth of the Creole bourgeoisie. This, of course, the army, Church, and bourgeoisie would not permit, and so the government relied on two other sources: foreign capital, and domestic money-lenders known as *agiotistas*. This allowed the economic life of the country to pick up, but to the profit again of the few, based upon the fruits of the labor of the many. Henry Bamford Parkes has summarized the post-Independence "development" program as follows:

> The *agiotista* lent money to the government for short terms and at high rates of interest, receiving in return a mortgage on government property or on the customs duties. When the mortgages fell due, the *agiotistas* collected their profits, the revenues shrank, and the government usually succumbed to revolution. . . . Mexico began to mortgage herself to foreign bankers and industrialists. . . . The mines were reopened and new agricultural commodities developed, but a large proportion of the profits went into the pockets of foreign investors; and whenever revolution interrupted the flow of dividends, there was the threat of a foreign intervention. (Parkes, 1938, 179)

And intervene the foreigners did. Until the start of the long, brutal dictatorship of Porfirio Díaz, when almost the entire Mexican economy would be delivered to foreigners lock, stock, and barrel, Mexico suffered foreign invasions and military occupation on the average of one out of every six years, *not* counting the twenty-five year occupation of what is today's Texas. In 1823, Americans began to colonize northern Mexico (today's Texas). In 1829, the Spanish briefly invaded Tampico. In 1835–1836, Americans in Texas led a bloody and successful secession from Mexico. In 1838, the French invaded Veracruz during the so-called Pastry War, which ended only upon Mexico's guaranteeing payment of a 600,000 peso debt owed the French.

From 1846 to 1848, the Americans invaded Mexico obstensibly to force Mexico to pay off a multi-million dollar debt owed Americans who had lost properties during the War of Independence and subsequent Mexican civil wars, but in actuality to seize almost half of Mexico's territory as part of the United States' "manifest destiny," that is, imperialism. All Mexico got out of the Treaty of Guadalupe Hidalgo was fifteen million dollars to tank up its drained treasury, while the United States not only picked up some of the wealthiest territory of Mexico but also increased the wealth of U.S. railmen, farmers, and land tycoons by systematically violating treaty provisions guaranteeing the property and civil rights of those Mexicans remaining at their homesites in today's Southwestern United States.

In less than two generations after the War of 1848, almost twenty million acres were lost by Mexican-American citizens in the Southwest. This trend of swindle and thievery, with no fair judicial recourse, has continued to the present for the approximately fifteen million Mexican-Americans, or "Chicanos" as they now call themselves, residing in the Southwestern states covered by the Treaty of Guadalupe Hidalgo. For generations, Chicanos throughout the United States have been resisting the systematic subjugation that conquest, exploitation, and racism have been imposing upon them. Today, the Chicano movement in the United States has it own political party, its own youth militia, many outstanding leaders, a strong women's liberation section, and a growing consciousness of its roots in "la raza," or the race of Mexicans who have resisted subjugation since early times ("la raza" also refers to the human race, struggling to be free). Expressions of solidarity have become increasingly common between militant Chicano farm workers, welfare mothers, war veterans, and youth in the United States, and rebellious peasants, slum-dwellers, and students in Mexico. The strength of the Chicano movement is reflected in the savage repression it has evoked. Non-violent mass demonstrations have been broken up by gun-fire, resulting in the killing and wounding of scores of Chicanos, especially in Los Angeles. At least one confessed police agent has confirmed plots to assassinate Cesar Chavez, leader of the striking farm workers. In New Mexico, there has emerged a militant Chicano movement to reclaim the lands stolen from Chicanos after the Treaty of Guadalupe Hidalgo. The original leader of this land movement, Reies López Tijerina, won his own trial by defending himself without a lawyer in one case but was eventually sent to jail anyhow. Upon his release, López Tijerina had the sad and delicate duty of making public to his people at a Chicano and Puerto Rican conference, with prior permission from his wife, the nightmarish details of how police had repeatedly intimidated his wife and family while he was in jail, ending in their rape of his wife and her near-total nervous breakdown, as well as his own. Less publicized is the daily suffering of the Chicano people in general, who suffer such brutalities on a regular basis in their impoverished rural and urban "barrios." In a real and not rhetorical way, however, the Chicanos are discovering their true history, their identity with "la raza," and they are forging a new unity among themselves and with other oppressed races and classes, especially among the poor in the United States.

The 1854 Gadsden Purchase finished this imperial expansion of the United States, won by war, and provided Mexico's needy treasury with yet further stop-gap funds. In 1861, a tripartite agreement for intervention was signed by England, France, and Spain, with Spanish troops landing at Veracruz. Finally, from 1862 to 1867, French troops occupied Mexico, set up the emperorship of Archduke Maximilian of Austria, and fought a series of battles against patriot forces led by the Zapotec Indian Benito Juárez, before succumbing to defeat.

FREE TRADE

Even if sectors of Mexico's dependent bourgeoisie had wanted to industrialize and establish relatively autonomous economic development—and there are indications that a few of the bourgeoisie did at first in fact so desire—it is questionable whether they would have been able to, given the colonial heritage of misdevelopment, foreign debt, and technological lag. Mexican agricultural, mining, and commercial interests had a vested interest in maintaining the export economy structure. Tariffs to protect nascent industrialization efforts held no attraction for them, since they benefited from the free trade of their primary goods for Europe's manufactured goods.

As for the foreign bourgeoisie, consolidation and extension of their power on a global basis depended upon preventing autonomous Latin American industrial development, while completely opening up the world's markets through "free" trade. The foreign bourgeoisie sided with Mexico's *hacendados,* miners, and exporters, against whatever industrial interests emerged. Given Mexico's foreign debt and budgetary deficits after the War of Independence, and its balance-of-payments deficit which worsened with more free trade, it became an easy matter for foreigners to take over the financing of Mexican "development." The landing of troops was the ultimate guarantee. Foreign loans, comparable to today's foreign "aid," followed by collection of debts and acquisition of land and properties in payment, further increased the flow of capital out of Mexico to the developing capitalist countries. Finally, currency devaluations and inflation, then as today, "benefited the native and foreign merchants and property owners at the expense of those whose labor produced the wealth, robbing artisans, workers, and peasants not only of their real income but also of their small landed and other property" (Cockcroft et al., 1972:Ch. 2, p. 18). By 1867, Mexico's foreign debt had soared to 375 million pesos and its domestic debt to seventy-nine million pesos, while public income still had not reached twenty million pesos (Cumberland, 1968:147; Aguilar, 1968, 195).

Occasional elements of the bourgeoisie resisted these trends in vain.

The Liberal Estevan de Antuñano and the Conservative Lucas Alamán began respectable textile industries in Puebla and Orizaba with modern machinery. To finance and stimulate the new industry Alamán founded the Banco del Avio. An occasional government laid the first few miles of railroad track in Mexico. But the viscissitudes of foreign interventions, civil wars, and internal politics repeatedly brought such independent efforts to a halt. The economy increasingly passed into the hands of foreigners, while the major forces within the Mexican bourgeoisie actively encouraged the process. As Mariano Otero observed in 1842: "trade was no more than the passive instrument of foreign industry and commerce . . . and today those cabinets, in everything submissive to the mercantile spirit, are profoundly interested in keeping us in a state of misery or backwardness from which foreign commerce draws all the advantages" (cited in Frank, 1971 MS., 51–2).

Foreign capitalists invested in rehabilitating the mines and predominated in drawing off the profits from the increased mineral production that followed. Mexico depended more than ever upon silver and gold for her export earnings (86 percent in 1872—Cumberland, 1968:171), while hides, sisal and ixtle led the way in agricultural exports, followed by coffee. England and the United States accounted for about 70 percent of Mexico's trade by 1870. By 1890, on the eve of the Díaz Government's final transferal of the remainder of the core of the Mexican economy to foreign capitalists, the Liberal Matias Romero was able to express his satisfaction to the Chamber of Deputies "on seeing foreigners as owners of high finance, of credit institutions, of the electric power plants, of the telegraphs, of the railroads and all those things which signify culture and the progress of Mexico" (Cumberland, 1968:196).

Such dedication to all things foreign by the Mexican bourgeoisie and their political spokesmen was manifested in all areas of culture. Even during the war against the French, members of the upper class were so enamored of French customs and manners that they more than earned the nickname *"afrancesados,"* or "Frenchified ones." Education was for the elite, not the masses, and had much to do with the cultural "superstructure" which reflected the material "infrastructure" of Mexican society. In 1879, instruction of English became mandatory because, in the words of Mexican educator Ezequiel Chávez, "it was believed necessary . . . given the growing union between the Anglo-American people and our people" (Vázquez de Knauth, 1970:55). Justo Sierra, Secretary of Public Instruction under Porfirio Díaz, encouraged the "saxonization" of Mexico and more immigration to solve the nation's problems. A national Normal School was not created until 1887, and from then until 1919 almost all Mexican textbooks became the private business of Appleton Publishing

Company of New York and U.S. authors. By 1911, illiteracy still plagued 84 percent of the population. Today, *Selecciones del Reader's Digest* has the largest circulation of any magazine in Mexico, and U.S. fashions are mimicked by the bourgeoisie as devotedly as ever they imitated the French. So profound an effect does this type of cultural imperialism have upon Mexicans, that many youth are psychologically driven toward consumption of U.S.-style goods and fashions, as for example, contemporary rock and pop music. In spite of their own nationalism and their own bountiful culture, Mexicans often find themselves imitating and aspiring to the values and goals of the historically hated "gringo." This type of behavior is called *pochismo*. In the lexicon of the new nationalism, there is no greater insult than to be called a *pocho*. This new nationalism is becoming acutely aware of the class-based roots of *pochismo* in Mexican history.

Even at the height of the civil war between Liberals and Conservatives, bourgeois forces of both sides often sought out foreign assistance rather than resist it. Juárez, a Liberal and the closest thing to a true nationalist Mexico had produced since Morelos and Alvarez, in 1858 was willing and anxious to cede free passage through Baja California and Tehuántepec to the United States in exchange for U.S. recognition of his government (McLane-Ocampo Treaty). The Conservatives, for their part, played a key role in inviting and supporting the French military occupation.

There were some legitimate grounds for Liberals opposing Conservatives, especially as represented by the Catholic Church. The Church-owned *Juzgado* was Mexico's principal banking institution from colonial times until its abolition in 1861. Because it demanded that loans be secured by real estate, the Church came to exercise considerable control over land in Mexico (Costeloe, 1967). Special privileges, or *fueros,* excusing clergymen and the military from normal civil procedures, further angered Liberals in government, who preferred to draw funds from the Church or cut military budgets before dipping into their own well-lined pockets. In 1855, Liberals passed the Ley Juárez abolishing these *fueros.* And in 1856 the Ley Lerdo forbade any corporation from owning land, but assured the Church that it would be paid for any lands claimed under the law, with the government receiving a cut of the transfer price. These anti-clerical laws were institutionalized in Articles 26 and 27 of the Liberal 1857 Constitution.

LIBERAL REFORM

The Liberal Reform against the Conservatives reflected an ideological struggle within the bourgeoisie, joined by few except for some Mestizos and middle-class professionals who took sides as much out of a system of political pay-offs known as *empleomanía* (or job hunger) and self-advancement as out of moral commitment. Mexico's rural proletariat fought in the battles of the Liberal-Conservative civil war with only dim hopes of repossessing the lands that had been stolen from them over the years. Some peasants were sincere Catholics, fighting for the Virgin of Guadalupe even as they had done under Hidalgo against the Spaniards. Others were sincere nationalists, driving out the haughty priests and, later, even haughtier French. But for the bourgeois Liberal landowners and businessmen, the Liberal Reform, especially the agrarian reform, stimulated by rising agrarian-export and land prices since 1851, was pre-eminently an economic aggression in their own interest which "served to accelerate the very economic process that had stimulated it in the first place. Once in power, the Liberals associated themselves ever more with the trade and foreign capital of the developing imperialist metropolis, which was (and is) their natural ally" (Cockcroft et al., 1972:Ch. 2, p. 21). And it was an aggression not only against the Church but more importantly against the Indians.

Under the new Liberal laws, *ejidos* qualified as corporately held property as much as did Church lands. Consequently, Liberal bureaucrats, ambitious merchants and money-lenders, land speculators, and big landowners moved in under the protection of the Liberal Reform and bought up or confiscated huge quantities of Indian communal lands. The 5 percent *alcabala,* or marketing tax, made it impossible for the average peasant to compete against these land sharks. Land monopolization in the hands of a wealthy few was furthered by the "vacant land" decrees issued by Juárez to raise funds for fighting the French invaders. In four years, some 4.5 million acres of prime land, much of it belonging to Indians who could not prove title, passed into the hands of the *latifundistas* at about two and a half cents an acre (Cockcroft, 1968:28; Cumberland, 1968:165). The Creole landholders finally were able to achieve what not even the colonial elites had been able to do: take over the vast majority of Indian land.

An occasional Liberal was nationalist enough to warn against this crime against the people. For example, Ponciano Arriaga told the delegates to the constitutional convention of 1857 that Article 27 would inevitably produce "monopolistic capitalism." His proposal to break up the *latifundia* was unanimously rejected by the delegates. Arriaga correctly perceived that under Article 27, "laboring citizens are condemned to be mere passive instruments of production for the exclusive profit of the capitalist" (Cockcroft, 1968:28–29). Ideologically, the Liberals waved the flag of anti-feudalism to combat such voices of reason, but other Mexicans, including many of the constitutional delegates themselves, had long since recognized the situation as Mariano Otero had described it in 1842:

> When it has been said to us very seriously that we have an aristocracy, when we have been exhorted to bring it up to date and we have been told of the European nobility and the feudal clergy, no one has known what he was talking about; words have miserably been mistaken for things, and an error in language has brought about one in politics . . . . the Mexican aristocracy was not at all similar to the European: it was . . . a parody . . . and the individuals that composed it . . . lived indolently upon capital, enjoying their profits. (Aguilar, 1968:73)

In fact, the Liberals had a credo which extended beyond their sanctimonious anti-feudalism and incorporated the very ingredients of their own class interests: free labor (to favor foreign immigration), free non-corporate land, private property, private industry, freedom of religion, free secular education, and freedom of trade and investment (which furthered the Mexican bourgeoisie's embrace of foreign capital). Here too Arriaga voiced a realistic warning:

> Upon decreeing freedom of trade, industry, and other franchises, great concessions are made to foreigners, scarcely reflecting upon the impossibility of our industry and crafts competing with the foreigners, given three centuries of delay, monopoly, and servitude that have weighed upon the Mexican people (Aguilar, 1968, 153).

The Mexican clergy and military, together with more traditional-minded landowners and businessmen tied to them, found themselves on the losing side against a rising Liberal tide led by a surprisingly large number of landholders, businessmen, and industrialists, and many artisans and professionals.

Foreign capitalists were not indifferent to this titanic struggle. With the United States bogged down in its own civil war, England, France, and Spain agreed to intervene in Mexico, an act which Karl Marx described as "one of the most monstrous enterprises ever registered in the annals of international history" (cited in Aguilar, 1968:179). When the French assumed the burden of the intervention, Napoleon wrote General Forey:

> if a stable government is established there with the help of France . . . we will have established our beneficent influence in the center of America, and such influence, upon creating immediate avenues for our commerce, will procure for us indispensable primary materials for our industry . . . (Aguilar, 1968:188)

The crowning irony for the Conservatives who sought the aid of the French is that Maximilian carried out the policies of the Liberals insofar as education, land, property, and freedom of thought and commerce were concerned. Thus, the French occupation furthered the causes of capitalism, national and international, even while provoking the Mexican national consciousness enough to generate Juárez's overthrow of Maximilian. Indeed, the departure of the French furthered the power of the now-triumphant Liberal bourgeoisie in Mexico, who proceeded consciously to increase their own power at the expense of the Church and the proletariat and to the joint profit of themselves and the foreign (increasingly U.S.) capitalists.

Insofar as "independent" Mexico ever had a chance to generate its own autonomous economic development, it probably had its best opportunity with the incipient banking and industrialization program of the early 1830's. But after that, as we have seen, the agrarian, mining, and export bourgeoisie reasserted itself and furthered the underdevelopment of Mexico and its dependence upon foreign capital.

PORFIRIATO: IMPERIALISM'S "BARBAROUS MEXICO"

To sustain itself in power, Mexico's bourgeoisie had to resort to dictatorship. That it did so in the name of Liberalism only confirms the economic foundation of that ideology. The thirty-five year reign of Porfirio Díaz, known as the Porfiriato, witnessed the most concentrated period of railroad construction and industrialization that Mexico was ever to experience, with the possible exception of the post-1940 period. Although Mexicans often contributed to the economic growth of the Porfiriato, especially in the form of initial capital and labor, foreigners dominated and eventually took over the nation's economy.

As early as 1900, the railroad grid of modern Mexico was in great part completed and in the hands of foreigners. It linked the rich mining areas of the North to the key Gulf ports and Texas border-towns. Representing the majority of foreign capital in Mexico was U.S. capital, of which 83 percent was in rails and mining. The Guggenheims developed a near total monopoly of the metallurgical industry. By 1910, the United States was receiving 77 percent of Mexico's mineral exports. Aided by key loans from Mexican businessmen, Edward L. Doheny carved out an oil empire for himself along the Gulf Coast. By 1910, foreigners owned from one-seventh to one-fifth of Mexico's land surface. Most commercial establishments and industries were also foreign-owned, although here again Mexican businessmen occasionally participated. The informal alliance between Mexico's bourgeoisie and foreign businessmen was a logical continuation and outgrowth of Mexico's history of underdevelopment. Confronted with periodic economic slumps and the need for more capital and new machinery, Mexican businessmen "had to work with whatever was available. Their needs happened to occur in an economically 'underdeveloped' country at a time of rapid U.S. expansion around the world. It was only natural that they resorted to collaboration with U.S. investors, when the goals of both nations' upper bourgeoisies had so much in common: economic expansion, industrialization, and profit" (Cockcroft, 1968:23, *passim.*).

In the countryside, land monopolization continued at a brisk pace, abetted by the *baldío* laws of 1883 and 1894 which provided for the surveying and sale of vacant lands. According to the 1910 census, eighty percent of the population depended upon agricultural wages. Of rural family heads, 96.6 percent held no land whatsoever. As Rosenzweig has observed, this was a *"latifundista* agriculture, oriented toward the market . . . and employment of wage labor." (Rosenzweig *et al.,* 1965:315). Díaz's top advisors described the countryside in terms of "capitalist agriculture," farmed by a "rural proletariat." According to Lauro Viadas, Director-General of Agriculture under Díaz, the growing concentration of land in the hands of a few, the rising cost of food staples, the low cost of labor and consequent "reduced production costs and increased profits," were all symptomatic of "capitalist agriculture lacking a non-capitalist farmer element" (cited in Cockcroft, 1968:31–32).

Barbaric social relations characterized Mexico, leading one observor to describe Mexico as "Barbarous Mexico" (Turner, 1910). Such relations, however, were not the result of "feudalism" or "traditionalism." On the contrary, they reflected the uneven and combined development of modern, capitalist forms of production with harsh, dictatorial social and political forms of control over the populace. A strong army, combined with a rural police force known as the *Rurales,* squashed the repeated efforts of peasants to take back what was rightfully theirs. The countryside resembled not so much the feudal manor as the company store, and, given the foreign takeover of the economy, Mexico as a whole was not so much a nation as a non-nation, not so much a company store as a company country.

Introduction of modern machinery and transportation further capitalized agriculture. This was true both in the North (Cockcroft, 1968:Ch. 1; Couturier, 1968) and in the South. For example, Morelos, the home state of Emiliano Zapata, a small landholder who himself lost his lands to the encroaching capitalists, became one vast "network of rural factories. By 1908 the seventeen owners of the thirty-six major haciendas in the state owned over 25 percent of its total surface. . . . Investment in

irrigation works probably went as high as that in milling machinery. . . .
After Hawaii and Puerto Rico, Morelos was the most productive cane-
sugar region in the world" (Womack, 1969:49–50).

The analysis of this "capitalist" agriculture provided by Díaz's agrarian
experts was confirmed by Madero's Sub-Secretary of State and Director-
General of Agriculture when they wrote:

> land was worth more and labor less each day, and the poor felt their misery
> grow to the extent that the landholders enrichened themselves. Capitalist
> organization turned out to be, then, the most effective means of augmenting
> slavery and the misery of the people and the inequality ruling between poor
> and rich, so that each day the poor and the wealthy grew more and more
> so. . . . Increased profits, deriving from the monopolization of productive
> lands seized from the hands of the peons who worked them, that increase is
> an inducement for capitalist exploitation . . . . monopoly of land inevitably
> leads to the reduction of day-wages. . . . Thus we have singled out the ab-
> jectly low day-wages as one of the factors fomenting capitalist exploitation
> and consolidating capitalist farming. . . . The banking organization, frankly
> privileged and with an irresistible political and social potency . . . [and] the
> railroad organization effectively helped to consolidate latifundism and agrarian
> slavery. . . . The governmental work of the dictatorship of General Díaz was
> that of systematically organizing the capitalist regime. (González Roa and
> Covarrubias, 1917, 88, 55, 58, 71, cited in Frank, 1971:MS., 31)

Mexico's landholding elite, then, was not an isolated, feudal one. Rather,
the *latifundistas* held overlapping economic investments in land, industry,
commerce, banking, transportation, and mining. This domestic bourgeoisie, however, did not hold ultimate economic power. The single most
important economic group in Mexico was a *foreign* bourgeoisie. This led
to conflicts within the Mexican bourgeoisie between the advantages accruing to them from their relationships with foreigners and their natural
desires for greater independence (nationalism). When proletarian pressures from below were combined with petty-bourgeois intellectual and
political leadership, as in the Precursor revolts of 1906 and 1908, an
ideology incorporating elements of nationalism, anarchism, and socialism
began to emerge. Mexico's bourgeoisie once again faced a struggle for
survival in the face of the heightened class contradictions of Mexican
society.

U. S. INFLUENCE AND MISDEVELOPED REVOLUTION

The prevalence in 1910 of a capitalistic social structure, dominated by
bourgeois families dependent in varying degrees upon foreign capital,
makes it impossible to conclude that the Mexican Revolution was a

classically bourgeois (antifeudal) revolution. The dynamics of Mexico's uneven and combined development during the Porfiriato implied what, in effect, came to pass: an explosive confrontation between proletarians and capitalists, with heavy anti-foreigner overtones.

When the Revolution of 1910 opened the floodgates of civil war, enlightened members of the Mexican bourgeoisie faced many ostensible "enemies" or rivals: foreign capitalists, foreign troops (Veracruz, 1914, the Pershing mission, 1916), aroused workers and peasants, and, most obvious of all, the conservative, dictatorial, corrupt, and inflexible segments of the bourgeois class itself, exemplified by the Científicos, Díaz's *caballada* (or herd of tame horses, as the dictator called his legislators), and the most reactionary of the *hacendados,* industrialists, financiers, and merchants. From the viewpoint of an enlightened Mexican landholder-businessman, the years 1910, 1913, and 1915 were ones of crisis calling for flexibility, broadmindedness, a number of unfulfillable promises, willingness to make some concessions, strong leadership in bourgeois hands to prevent "the proletarian rabble" from taking over, influence with key generals of the Army, support of U. S. business, arms, and diplomatic interests—in brief, political opportunism and muscle.

In bourgeois terms, what was needed was civilian rule, civil law, civil behavior, backed up with adequate military force—the orderly processes of bourgeois "democratic" politics, from which, as Francisco I. Madero said in his campaign of 1910, all good things would eventually flow to all men. Madero epitomized the naivete, faith, and idealism of this bourgeois vision, as well as the bourgeois political leader's willingness to engage in unprincipled opportunism, as in the case of his unfulfilled promises of agrarian reform. A personal friend of Díaz's Finance Minister and from a family with economic interests in land, ranching, mining, iron and steel, banking, textiles, and so on, Madero was the ideal representative of the bourgeoisie in its hour of need. Together with Venustiano Carranza, whose economic and political background he shared but whose hardheadedness he lacked, Madero represented the most enlightened elements of the bourgeois class in the years of strife following the outbreak of the 1910 Revolution.

Proletarians constituted the major force of the Revolution. Most of them were peasants, in part tied to the *haciendas* in a form of debt peonage, but in ever larger part migratory and wage-oriented, moving from harvest to harvest, and from farm to factory, over huge expanses of territory not unlike migrant farm workers today (Peña, 1964:116–138). There existed also a burgeoning, militant, anarchist and socialist-oriented urban and industrial proletariat, with its roots in the large-scale, anti-imperialist mine, textile, and rail strikes of 1906–1908, ranging from

Cananea in the Northwest to Orizaba and Río Blanco in the Southeast. Many of the urban industrial workers, operating out of shoe factories, breweries, smelters, and generally small and medium industry, organized themselves into the Anarchist-oriented Casa del Obrero Mundial, which became especially influential in Mexico City (Cockcroft, 1968:134–145, 223–229).

These urban workers, however, were often isolated from their rural counterparts, who, under Emiliano Zapata and Pancho Villa, had taken up arms in a full-scale war against first the army of Díaz and eventually that of Victoriano Huerta (the general who, with the help of the American Ambassador, helped plot the assassination of Madero in 1913, and then emerged as President). The driving force of the Revolution was the peasantry, and even it was divided by geographical and regional differences. Zapata's forces tended to stick to the South and to agrarian issues. Not that they lacked a proletarian consciousness—on the contrary, whenever they could, the Zapatistas seized all the means of production: fields, mills, rail stations, and distilleries. They set up liberated zones. As Womack has shown, theirs was a classic "people's war." No single force could defeat their combination of guerrilla warfare and popular participation and support. First Díaz, then Huerta, and finally Carranza launched scorched-earth wars of terror against the Zapatistas, killing all civilians; but in the end, only trickery and assassination could take Zapata's life and leave his movement divided and without a leader in 1919.

To the North, Villa's forces were less homogeneous than those of Zapata. Absorbing much of the Madero bureaucracy and developing a large, more modern-style army, the Villistas controlled and administered immense expanses of territory. Their top ranks included more cowboy caudillos (*charros* and *rancheros*), petty-bourgeois store managers and tradesmen, and middle-class bureaucrats than communal peasant farmers (*ejidatarios*), while their foot-soldiers were usually miners, migrant farm laborers, rail workers, and unemployed. Even though Villa sided with Zapata from 1914 to 1915 against the northern *latifundista* Carranza, the expectations of the Villistas were often more commercial than those of the Zapatistas. Also, Villa depended in large part on the United States for guns and ammunition, which he obtained in exchange for cattle and cash. Consequently, many U. S. properties in the North which paid taxes to Villa, such as those of the American Smelting and Refining Company or those of William Randolph Hearst, were not only left alone by Villa's troops but were actually protected from seizure by land-hungry peasants.

Two other factors became crucial in the misdevelopment of the Mexican Revolution: the role of the urban, industrial proletariat, and the role of the United States. Carranza's "Constitutionalist" forces contained such left-leaning figures as Alvaro Obregón, as well as proletarian foot-soldiers. Carranza was enlightened enough to decree progressive agrarian reform and labor laws in late 1914 and early 1915, laws which might attract further proletarian support. Obregón went further. Acting without Carranza's approval, he offered Mexico City's hungry and repressed workers of the Casa del Obrero Mundial—relatively cut off from the peasant armies of the interior—food, money, supplies, and the granting of their basic demands, in exchange for their forming "red battalions" to go North with Obregón to defeat Villa. This opportune alliance between the urban working class, with its Anarcho-Syndicalist and increasingly Socialist ideology, on the one hand, and the enlightened bourgeoisie as represented by Obregón, with its willingness to make concessions to the proletariat when necessary, on the other hand, broke the back of the theretofore relatively unified workers' and peasants' thrust of the Revolution. That Carranza's progressive decrees were mere window-dressing for continued bourgeois class rule was shown a year later when, in order to crush the 1916 general strike, the "First Chief" decreed the death penalty for anyone "disturbing the public order." Then, as President (1917–1920), Carranza failed to implement any serious agrarian reform.

Also contributing to the military and class setback of the proletariat was the aid given Carranza by the United States, whose investors composed the main segment of the dominant foreign bourgeoisie in 1911. U. S. investments in Mexico were estimated to be more than those of the Mexican bourgeoisie and twice as large as all the rest of foreign investment (U. S. Congress, *Investigation of Mexican Affairs,* 1920, cited in Nearing and Freeman, 1969:85). Moreover, U. S. control and interest in oil resources in Mexico, which by 1921 accounted for almost 24% of the world's total oil production, led to heavy U. S. intervention in the internal affairs of the Mexican Revolution . The United States controlled 70 percent of Mexican oil production, Great Britain 27 percent. Between 1910 and 1920, Mexican production shot up from ten million barrels to almost two hundred million. The stakes were high, and the United States, oil interests and government knew it.

Standard Oil Company, and the Mexican Petroleum Company (Doheny) which it later absorbed, had backed Madero, in retaliation against Díaz's having encouraged the British El Aguila Oil Company headed by Weetman D. Pearson. Gustavo Madero, the new President's brother, held shares in Doheny's company. When Huerta replaced Madero, Pearson floated "the loan that kept Huerta in power" (Meyer, 1968:87). President Wilson recalled the American Ambassador who, distrustful of Madero's talk of reforms, had helped bring Huerta to power, and sent in his stead John Lind as his confidential agent in Mexico. Lind tried vainly to deal with Huerta by suggesting that U. S. bankers might provide an immediate loan in exchange for new elections. Huerta, now allied with British oil interests, balked. President Wilson withheld U. S. recognition from the Huerta regime, established a financial blockade and arms embargo against Mexico, and proceeded to help overthrow Huerta. Secretary of State Bryan cabled to U. S. representatives in Mexico on November 24, 1913, the U. S. policy "to isolate General Huerta entirely, to cut him off from foreign sympathy and aid and from domestic credit, whether moral or material, and to force him out," resorting, if necessary, "to use less peaceful means to put him out," (*U. S. Foreign Relations,* 1914, 444, cited in Nearing and Freeman, 1969:97–98).

Then, on February 3, 1914, Wilson lifted the arms embargo in order to rush in material aid for Carranza. In April, claiming that it must prevent a German munitions ship[1] from landing and delivering its cargo to Huerta's forces, the United States sent in marines and bluejackets to occupy and control Veracruz. The wife of the American Charge d'Affaires in Mexico City noted at the time: "With the taking of Vera Cruz, through whose customs a full fourth of the total imports come, Huerta is out a million pesos a month, more or less. We are certainly isolating and weakening him at a great rate. 'Might is right.' We can begin to teach it in the schools." (O'Shaughnessy, 1916:290). Meanwhile, Doheny, as he later told a Senate Committee, provided Carranza hundreds of thousands of dollars worth of credit and military equipment, while refusing to pay federal taxes to Huerta. President Wilson wired U. S. delegates at the Niagara Conference concerning U. S. occupation of Mexican territory that should the conferees fail to agree to the U. S. program, "then the settlement must come by arms, either ours or those of the Constitutionalists" (*U. S. Foreign Relations,* 1914, 510, cited in Nearing and Freeman, 1969:110). Confronted with blockade, embargo, foreign troop occupation and aid to his enemies, Huerta swiftly succumbed to the advancing forces of Villa, Obregón, Zapata, and Carranza.

But the role of the United States did not end there. As the class lines separating Carranza from Villa and Zapata became clear, the United States shifted its support to Carranza, providing his faction with arms and granting it diplomatic recognition in October, 1915. As Secretary of

---

[1] Actually, the arms and munitions were U.S.-made, purchased in the United States by Huerta agents, and shipped via Europe to decoy U.S. federal authorities. The fact that they ended up on a German steamer of the American-Hamburg line was coincidental and not originally planned. No matter—Wilson needed a pretext for asserting U.S. power in determining the course of events inside Mexico (Meyer, 1970).

State Robert Lansing wrote in his private notes at the time, acknowledging Carranza as the least of the evils who might be won over with dollar diplomacy: "The real problem Carranza will have to face is financial. He has no credit; his paper money is worthless; his source of revenue uncertain; and his soldiers without pay. We can help him in this . . ." (cited in Smith, 1963, 576).

The bonded debt of Mexico had been in default since 1913, and U. S., British, and French investors held most of the Mexican bonds. From here on out, the United States conditioned any further loans to Mexico upon prior U. S. diplomatic recognition. The State Department huddled with Thomas W. Lamont, senior partner of J. P. Morgan and Company, and worked out a plan for an international bankers' committee to handle bond and investment guarantee negotiations with Mexico. According to specific instructions of the State Department, the bankers' committee "shall be under the leadership of American bankers and that the policy of the United States Government regarding Mexico [shall] be the dominating influence in the operations of this group." As Leon J. Canova of the Department's Division of Mexican Affairs put it: "We hold the whip handle at the present time. We are the bankers of the world and have advanced large sums to England." (Smith, 1963:580–581). President Wilson was more blunt:

> Do you know the significance of this single fact that within the last year or two we have . . . ceased to be a debtor nation and have become a creditor nation. . . . We have got to finance the world in some important degree, and those who finance the world must understand it and rule it with their spirits and with their minds (cited in Nearing and Freeman, 1969:273).

In addition, the United States cut off arms to Villa and Zapata. In retaliation, Villa launched raids against U. S. citizens, some of which brought him across the border. The United States responded with a large-scale military buildup along the border and an invasion force led by General Pershing. Finally, the United States threatened armed force against Zapata as well, intimidating many of the Zapatistas into seeking amnesties from Carranza and into laying down their arms (Womack, 1969:300–317, 346–351). Thus, even as foreign conquest and control had led to Mexico's economic underdevelopment and thereby helped generate its colonial class structure in the first place, so did foreign economic, diplomatic, and military power abet the misdevelopment of the Mexican Revolution by helping the bourgeoisie to control, check, or throw back the aroused masses.

Nearly two million Mexicans were killed or died during the fighting of the 1910–1917 Revolution. Ideological concessions to workers and peasants in the 1917 Constitution, along with attrition and exhaustion, contributed to the gradual re-establishment of "peace," that is, relatively stabilized bourgeois rule acknowledging the proletariat's needs. Article 27 of the new Constitution provided for agrarian reform and the nation's ownership of all minerals and subsoils, including oil. Article 123 gave labor various guarantees of security and income, including the right to form unions and to conduct "legal" strikes. Carranza wisely signed the radical Constitution, even though he opposed most of its progressive articles; not to accept it would have meant renewed civil war. But as President, Carranza ruled with a firm hand, and the long years of class war had produced only a misdeveloped revolution, not a successful one. The main results of the bloodshed were: "a defeated peasantry, a crippled and dependent labor movement, a wounded but victorious bourgeoisie, and, for a divided Mexican people, a paper triumph—the 1917 Constitution" (Cockcroft, 1968:235).

Ever since 1917, the class war has continued to ebb and flow, while foreign economic and diplomatic pressures have continued unabated. Mexican leaders after 1917, with few exceptions, confined their revolutionary posture mostly to verbiage, being in no position, politically or financially, to expropriate much of anything. U.S. and British oil companies sucked out the nation's largest source of wealth, petroleum, ruling Gulf Coast oil towns with their own police force, or "white guards." Until it could receive some form of guarantee against expropriation of oil, which Article 27 certainly implied, the United States refused to grant diplomatic recognition to the government of Obregón (1920–1923). The oil companies were thus seen by Mexicans as colonial intrusions, and their refusal to budge from the privileged positions granted them by Díaz, a refusal buttressed by the U.S. Government, led most Mexicans to view them as a force retarding Mexico's efforts to assert her sovereignty over her social and economic life in accord with a progressive constitution.

Obregón, while taxing the oil industry, had assured Washington all along that Article 27 was not retroactive and therefore would not affect properties already granted foreign oil interests, but Washington wanted the guarantee in writing. Thomas W. Lamont of the international bankers' committee helped smooth the way for a settlement by negotiating an agreement with the Obregón government concerning Mexico's burdensome external debt, which Mexico's war-torn economy would default on repeatedly over the next fifteen years. The debt was estimated at three times what it had been in 1911, *not* counting an additional $1 billion in private foreign claims (Smith, 1967; Parkes, 1938:378; Cumberland, 1968:256). Then Mexico and the United States signed the Bucareli Agreements which reaffirmed the non-retroactive clause governing Article

27 while obliging Mexico to pay compensation for damages to U.S. property incurred during the Revolution. The United States promptly followed with diplomatic recognition of Obregón's government, August 30, 1923.

This was convenient for Obregón, who found his power threatened by rebellious generals nominally led by his former Treasury Secretary Adolfo de la Huerta. Two things saved Obregón's government from being overthrown in a renewed civil war: U.S. munitions provided Obregón after the signing of the Bucareli Agreements, and the support of militant peasants whose interests had been represented in Obregón's Congress by an agrarian political party led by the former braintruster of Zapata, Antonia Díaz Soto y Gama. In addition, the Confederación Regional Obrera Mexicana (CROM), Mexico's largest labor organization, backed Obregón, although the strong-arm tactics of CROM's corrupt labor boss Luis Morones alienated many worthy followers. Finally, the United States sent the cruiser U.S. Richmond to blockade the port of Tampico to prevent anti-Obregón forces from receiving arms. On June 12, 1925, Secretary of State Kellog issued a frank statement summarizing Mexico's condition of economic and political dependence:

> . . . it must remain very clear that this Government will continue maintaining the present government in Mexico only so long as it protects American lives and the rights of Americans and lives up to its international agreements and obligations. The Mexican government now stands in judgment before the world . . . (cited in Meyer, 1968:81).

Obregón's hand-picked successor, Plutarco Elías Calles, ordered the owners of oil fields to exchange their titles for fifty-year leases, dating from the time of acquisition. U.S. oil magnates clamored for intervention, but U.S. public opinion was lukewarm after the military humiliation Villa had dealt Pershing and in light of the more recent Teapot Dome oil scandals, which had involved such leading U.S. oil figures in Mexico as Doheny and Albert B. Fall. In 1927, President Calvin Coolidge dispatched a new ambassador to Mexico, Dwight Morrow of—who else?—J. P. Morgan and Company. Within two months of Morrow's suave, low-keyed negotiations with Calles, the Mexican Supreme Court declared Calles' earlier oil legislation to be unconstitutional and foreigners who had acquired subsoil rights before 1917 to be entitled to perpetual concessions. Once again, the oil belonged to the oil companies, as it always had.

While the U.S. and Mexican financial and political elites thus wheeled and dealed, militant proletarian pressures from below began once more to mount. Striking oil workers would finally force a showdown with foreign oil companies, in 1938. Prior to that, however, Mexico's bourgeois, so-called "revolutionary" leaders were modernizing, but not decreasing, Mexico's dependent relationship with foreign capital: they were emphasizing economic growth instead of equality or social welfare, national pride without the essentials of national sovereignty, and the formation of an autonomous middle class at the expense of most of the working population. While the great mural, sculpting, and literary renaissance of the early 1920's, subsidized by the government under Secretary of Education José Vasconcelos, gave new recognition to the Indian and the artist, it added to the nationalistic atmosphere in which the new leaders of Mexico 'were able to continue old-style policies with new-style rhetoric.

Finance Minister Alberto Pani led a group of developmentalists in setting up the National Bank of Mexico and encouraging controls on foreign capital, not as part of an inevitable revolution or "a utopic socialistic levelling" but in order to stimulate private enterprise and "the formation and encouragement of an autonomous Middle Class" (cited in Smith, 1969, 150). By means of the Lamont-Pani Agreement of 1925, foreign bankers accepted the new National Bank in exchange for Mexican commitment to return the National Railways of Mexico, nationalized under Díaz, to private management. Ambassador Morrow helped bring about a settlement of the Cristero Revolt in the late 1920's, caused by enraged clerics' dissatisfaction with enforcement of anti-clerical provisions of the 1917 Constitution, especially obligatory secular education. Morrow persuaded Calles that domestic stability, a slowdown in agrarian reform, guarantees for private property and investments, and cooperation between foreign and Mexican capital were the keys to Mexico's future prosperity. Calles himself, after asserting that Mexico's interests "can be satisfied only within the limits set up by the present so-called capitalist system," promised "to safeguard the interests of foreign capitalists who invest in Mexico" and in 1930 publicly declared the agrarian reform "a failure" (cited in Wilkie, 1967:62). Morrow, outfitting his home in Cuernavaca with Mexican handicrafts and commissioning famous muralist Diego Rivera to paint a fresco in the local town hall, catered to Mexican national pride while re-negotiating Mexico's foreign debt in 1928–1929. His partner in J. P. Morgan and Company, Lamont, was delighted, since he saw long-range stability in Mexico as the key to increased profits, as he wrote J. P. Morgan on January 16, 1928:

> This is the best chance that we have had yet. Heretofore the committee agreements have been temporarily designed to get as much money for the bondholders as could be legitimately secured. Now we have something more permanent to look forward to for the bondholders. It will be of immeasur-

able value to have Dwight helping along constructively in this way. (cited in Smith, 1969:162)

In 1930, however, Lamont and the bankers' committee, made more insecure by the world Depression and fearful that Morrow would compromise *too* much with the Mexican Government, withdrew their support for Morrow's efforts to settle all U.S. debt claims. In addition, Mexico's major class—the rural proletariat—stepped up its demands for agrarian reform at the very time when Calles and Morrow were seeking to cut back on social welfare in order to reduce the nation's budgetary deficit. In 1931, Mexico went off the gold standard and the value of the peso declined. Foreign bondholders did not achieve a settlement until 1943, but by their patience they had achieved a longer, more secure, and more profitable future than had the oil magnates. "Today Mexican bonds are sold on Wall Street, and in Mexico the offices of major U.S. banking firms greet one on almost every corner" (Smith, 1969:166).

DEPENDENT STATE CAPITALISM

According to a study of 2,040 companies with the largest incomes in Mexico, made by economist José Luis Ceceña, foreign capital controls 36 percent of the income of the largest four hundred companies and strongly participates in another 18 percent, while Mexican private capital controls only 21 percent and the Mexican government 25 percent. Another calculation based on an average of incomes of the largest one hundred, two hundred, three hundred and four hundred companies, respectively, yielded similar results—in both, more than 50 percent of the companies' income was either controlled or strongly participated in by foreign capital (Gonzalez Casanova, 1965, 207–208). The government's sector of economic involvement is almost totally in the infrastructure: energy, fuel, transportation, communications, and pump-priming investments during recessions. As economist Alonso Aguilar, paraphrasing a Mexican banker, felicitously describes the state's economic role: "it is the duty of the state humbly to set the table, and the job of private enterprise to eat what it finds there" (Aguilar, 1967:65). Mexican private capital, most of it in light industry, tourism, and consumer goods, is monopolistic, that is, highly concentrated in the hands of a few families and thus oligarchic. About 6 percent of Mexico's non-foreign manufacturing firms account for 94 percent of those firms' fixed capital, 90 percent of their value of production, and 70 percent of their employed personnel, while 1.8 percent of non-foreign commercial firms absorb 73 percent of such firms' capital and 63.9 percent of their income (Aguilar, 1967:27–28). In broad outline, then, the Mexican economy is one of state capitalism, preponderantly dependent upon a foreign bourgeoisie and conducive to favorable investment conditions for both foreign and national capitalists.

In terms of national economic and political planning, five interrelated goals seem to dominate the Mexican polity: Mexicanization (51 percent or more Mexican ownership in select corporations), investment (infrastructure, industry), economic growth, public welfare, and political stability. Favoring of one goal, for example public welfare, can have a negative effect on another (investment) while advancing a third (political stability—Anderson and Cockcroft, 1966). In a developing society faced with scarce resources, increased dependence upon foreign loans and investment, rapid population growth, 44 percent of the population rural and impoverished, more than 25 percent of urban areas wretched slums, and with such contradictory goals, it is virtually impossible to overcome the patterns of underdevelopment and misdevelopment analyzed in this chapter, unless the power of the bourgeoisie is usurped by the majority class. That is the problem today, and that was the problem in the 1930's, when closer to 75 percent of the population was rural, 67 percent illiterate, and the present fast rate of population growth began.

While the roots of Mexico's overall crisis go back to the Spanish Conquest, implementation of its contemporary developmentalist goal-structure derives mainly from the six-year presidency of Lázaro Cárdenas, 1934–1940. Cárdenas's populist policies and nationalization of select industries did much to avert renewed civil war, assuage proletarian unrest, and establish dependent state capitalism on a firm basis. With the power of the U.S. capitalist metropolis momentarily weakened by Depression and internal labor strikes, and the Mexican bourgeoisie in turn challenged by economic crisis and rising proletarian militancy, Cárdenas, gifted with great political entrepreneurship, found it possible to help create and manipulate labor and peasant political constituencies while introducing Mexico's first (and last) large-scale social reforms since those of the armed peasants of 1913–1915. Under Cárdenas, two times more land was distributed to peasants than under all the preceding regimes combined; illiteracy was reduced by about 7 percent; federal price controls were introduced; organized labor emerged as a major political force capable of mounting relatively successful strikes (when the government permitted); the government established its role in labor-management relations; the petroleum and rail industries were nationalized; and today's single political party, initiated in 1929, took its present normative form of three sectors: labor, peasant, and popular ("middle class," bureaucrats, lawyers, although under Cárdenas there was also a strong military sector, which merged with the popular sector in 1940). However, such populism as that of Cárdenas is bound to be a mere episode in history so long as the economic position of the bourgeoisie is left intact. "And in 'mixed economies,' one has left bourgeois economic power intact, in spite of much rhetoric to the contrary" (Cockcroft et al., 1970: 197–98).

In spite of the revolutionary language of the Cárdenas government, available evidence indicates that the continuing model for Mexico's political leadership was one of capitalism, industrial growth, modern technological agriculture, and the preservation of private property and various foreign and domestic private economic interests, with whatever state assistance and regulation necessary (Ashby, 1967; Brown, 1964; Cornelius, 1970; González Navarro, 1965; López Aparicio, 1952; Michaels, 1966, 1970; Nathan, 1952; Reynolds, 1970; Wilkie, 1967, 1969). The major change under Cárdenas was not a turn from capitalism to socialism, but rather was the strengthening of national industrial interests at the expense of comprador-bourgeois elements and foreign monopolists, and the increased regulation of capitalism by the state so that the depressed economy might move forward and private ownership might be preserved, not overthrown. In this latter sense, that of preserving capitalism, Cárdenas served, intentionally or not, the same interests in Mexico that Franklin D. Roosevelt served in the United States—and in some instances in like fashion. In fact, Roosevelt's Ambassador to Mexico, Josephus Daniels, brought to Mexico the message of the New Deal even before Cárdenas took office: "he came to talk of social reform, education, and the welfare of the masses . . . Mexico was free to develop an ideology of social revolution" (Wilkie, 1967:70). The silver purchase program of 1934, by means of which the United States bought huge quantities of Mexican silver, lent further support to Mexico's economic development plans. The United States, the country representing the largest segment of foreign investment in Mexico, thus gave its initial approval to reformism as President Cárdenas took office (although later developments would show how disturbed the United States could become when its own interests were directly affected by Cárdenas's acts of nationalism).

None of this is intended to suggest that Cárdenas was not a genuine reformer, or that he did not genuinely want to improve the lot of the masses. Rather, it is to describe what, in fact, the effects of his policies were. That Cárdenas was able to accomplish the reforms he did is a tribute to his leadership abilities, as well as a result of conditions prevailing inside Mexico at the time.

The essence of those prevailing conditions was that no single class was in ascendance, conscious of itself and asserting class power. Even though so many of the landed oligarchs had interlocking urban investments, the

Mexican bourgeoisie contained conflicting landed and industrial interests. The bourgeoisie also included *comprador* elements whose interests were tied to foreigners unlike those of independent-minded national industrialists. Most importantly, the bourgeoisie had evolved historically in a dependent manner, and its crisis in the 1930's was umbilically linked to the larger global crisis of the metropolitan bourgeoisies of the United States and Europe.

Inside Mexico, other classes posed a threat to this dependent, ununited, misnamed 'national' bourgeoisie—including relatively directionless petty bourgeois elements and, more critically, workers and peasants who constituted a burgeoning revolutionary threat from below, although the workers' dependence on the state undercut the autonomy of that threat. In this situation, where no single class was able to assert its hegemony, the state emerged as a natural arbitrer and central power, as well as an agency of reform. Populism flourished in this period because of the developmentalist state's (and Cárdenas's) need for support among the popular classes, as well as the bourgeoisie's need to meet some of the demands of the masses as a "lesser evil" to the alternative of outright revolution. In the midst of this vertiable whirlpool of conflicting interests and emotions, the state apparatus and the brilliant leadership of Cárdenas became pivotal in shaping the destiny of Mexico.

Ironically, key spokesmen for bourgeois sectors became so perplexed as to view short-run radical reforms as threats to their survival rather than as long-run guarantees of their utimate hegemony, and, in the short run, much of Cárdenas's policy did constitute a kind of threat to the bourgeoisie *as it had grown accustomed to functioning.* The key question, therefore, became one of how much power the state, in introducing the developmentalist policies of the 1930's, would permit the working classes to exercise.

Workers' and peasants' vastly increased influence upon key economic institutions—such as railroads and certain sectors of agriculture and industry—could lead, ultimately, to workers' and peasants' control over the state, unless their economic penetration of these other institutions was shaped, if not controlled, from the outset by the state. Cárdenas provided that kind of top-down control, by introducing, and then staffing with state bureaucrats, the reforms in agriculture and industry which permitted in the first instance workers' increased involvement in the mechanisms and institutions of economic power. The use of the state as the key power resource in the 1930's, rather than the use of a single, united class (such as the proletariat *or* the bourgeoisie), combined with the continued dependence of the Mexican economy on external conditions (accumulated foreign debt, agreements with foreign bondholders, world-wide depression), meant that Mexico was unable to generate either a thorough-going revolution from below or an independent "nationalist-bourgeois" industrialization program from above for autonomous economic development. These inadequacies in turn had been conditioned historically by the development of Mexico's class structure and economic dependence previously described.

With eventual metropolitan recovery from depression and war, and increased concentration of capital in the hands of a decreasing number of giant monopolies, U.S. capital made its presence felt more strongly than ever before in the Mexican economy, sometimes directly, other times through the use of transnational corporations. The use of the state for relatively independent development efforts, and the causes for that use, receded after 1944. Government activities were increasingly integrated with the policies of U.S.-based transnational corporations, while the Mexican bourgeoisie associated itself with foreign capital rather than risk 'going it alone.'

During the Cárdenas era, the major challenge to state-regulated capitalism, fixed firmly within the Western capitalist sphere of operation, was neither the revolutionary example of the Soviet Union, nor the organizational activities of the Mexican Communist Party. Nor was it the Communist-sounding statements or actions of organized labor's main leader, Vicente Lombardo Toledano, who actually was opposed by the Communist Party of Mexico. Rather, the major challenge to state-regulated capitalism was the continued threat from below, from the peasants and workers. The number of strikes went up from 13 in 1933 to 642 in 1935 (one unofficial estimate exceeds 1,000 for first half of 1935)—not only in industry and mining, but also in agriculture. In the Laguna district in north-central Mexico, where capitalist agriculture prevailed and had received its impetus from progressive farmers like Madero at the turn of the century, there occurred in 1935 alone some 104 strikes by farm workers (Ashby, 1963:152). It was precisely in sectors badly disrupted by strikes that the Cárdenas Administration took its most famous revolutionary measures—land distribution in the Laguna, oil expropriation, nationalizing of the railroads. Since many of these strikes occurred before Cárdenas formed his alliance with organized labor's Confederación de Trabajadores de México (CTM), and since many of them continued after that alliance and even in opposition to Cárdenas's pleas for return to work, it is hard to argue that Cárdenas fomented the labor movement rather than the working class itself providing the necessary impetus.

By recognizing labor's right to strike and abetting the development of the CTM through government assistance and juridical decisions against recalcitrant private corporations, and yet declaring a number of strikes "illegal" in order to maintain political stability, Cárdenas employed a policy of carrot-and-stick towards labor which made the development of state-regulated capitalism possible. For Cárdenas to have completely sided with labor in Mexico's continued class war would have meant overthrowing capitalism or, at a minimum, unleashing another blood-letting civil war like that of 1910–1917. If Cárdenas had sided with the ownership classes completely against labor, on the other hand, then armed uprisings similar to those of 1910 likely would have occurred. Cárdenas steered a middle course, avoiding a bloody civil war, preserving relative political stability (relative to the alternatives), and solidifying Mexico's system of state-regulated capitalism. Cárdenas's statements during his regime ranged from calls for socialism, to denials that he sought socialism; from outright support of workers on strike, to denial of their right to strike; from appearing at demonstrations of the workers as one of them, to sending the troops to quell them. This was not socialism,[2] but political entrepreneurship. The one consistent ideological theme under Cárdenas which helped make it work was that his government was "liberal, democratic, and nationalist." Symptomatic of the skills which Cárdenas brought to bear on Mexico's problems was his success in healing the long rift between the government and the Catholic Church. Cárdenas appointed the pro-Catholic Saturnino Cedillo Secretary of Agriculture in his second cabinet and declared "the era of Church persecution" as terminated; the Church supported his nationalization of oil; and his successor, Manuel Avila Camacho, repealed the "socialist" reform of education outright, while becoming the first President since Díaz to declare himself a believer in the Catholic faith.

The crisis of the 1930's (or today) was not only one of class war. There also existed then, as today, new younger leaders with reformist ideas anxious to step into positions occupied by ageing members of the

[2] The constitutional reform of October, 1934, two months before Cárdenas took office, which made public education "socialistic," derived from the traditional distinction in Spanish and Latin American thought between "socialist, or rational," on the one hand, and "clerical, or religious," on the other. It was conceived in government documents as "education to community responsibility" (Cornelius, 1970, 24). A key figure in this intellectual heritage was Spanish pedagogue Francisco Ferrer Guardia, who founded the Escuela Moderna in Barcelona, 1901, and co-founded with a group of Anarchists the International League for Rational Education of Children, 1907. Ferrer Guardia was executed in 1909 by the Spanish Government, as an alleged chief of the anti-monarchist revolutionary movement. European Anarchists made his case a *cause célèbre,* as did Mexican Anarchists who headed the Precursor Movement against Díaz. After Díaz's overthrow, organized labor's Casa del Obrero Mundial set up workers' schools modelled on Ferrer Guardia's principles (Cockcroft, 1968, 175, 223).

ruling elite. These younger "radicals" rewrote Calles' Six-Year Plan at the Convention of Querétaro in 1933, and President Abelardo Rodríguez, himself a tool of Calles' political machine, found it expedient to implement much of the Six-Year Plan before Cárdenas took office, as in the case of the 1933 minimum wage bill (Wilkie, 1967:70–71).

The question on economic policy for Cárdenas, then, was not whether reformism would be permitted in Mexico. The green light had already been given on that score by both the American ambassador and the previous Mexican president and political boss. Cárdenas himself had noted as early as December, 1935, that "The United States will not intervene in our internal affairs, first, because of its Good Neighbor Policy . . . and second, because it is profoundly concerned with meeting the problems that have arisen within its own territory" (cited in Cornelius, 1970:84). The question politically for Cárdenas, however, became one of how much power Calles was willing to surrender to him and the younger reformers who composed his team.

If Cárdenas were to become, in modern parlance, "his own man," or "captain of his own team," then he would have to challenge the powerful Calles machine, with its control of the national political party and bureaucracy, its connections with big business and old-guard labor leadership (CROM), its friendliness with the foreign investment community, and its influence in the Army (where Cárdenas, himself a General, also had some support). Where could Cárdenas turn? Historically, new leaders had turned to organized labor—Obregón had turned to the Casa del Obrero Mundial in 1915 and to the CROM in 1920, as had Calles in later years. As it happened, a new labor movement was available to Cárdenas: the forerunner of today's CTM, the Confederación General de Obreros y Campesinos de Mexico, led by ex-professor Lombardo Toledano.

The CROM had lost many of its major unions (printers, iron and metalworkers, and textile), as rank-and-file workers had become disillusioned with the corruption of its leadership and the failure of Calles to pay off in social-welfare benefits. In the first year of the Cárdenas regime (1934–1935), a rash of strikes broke out against such companies as the Mexican Tramways Company (Canadian-owned), Huasteca Petroleum Company (Standard Oil), San Rafael Paper Company (Spanish-French capital), and the Mexican Telephone and Telegraph Company (American Telephone and Telegraph sister company, in which Calles held a large number of stock shares). These strikes were in the tradition of labor militancy against foreign capital, which dated back to the inception of the labor movement under Díaz.

Labor was not yet enamored of Cárdenas. In a major speech at the end of his election campaign, Cárdenas had sanctioned collective bargaining, a minimum wage, and other welfare measures commonly recommended in the advanced capitalist countries of the time. He had favored small private landholdings over communal holdings. He had emphasized the protection of private property, although acknowledging the existence of the class struggle—"an essential within the capitalist regime" —and promising support for the working class. Under these circumstances, "the labor movement did not rush to support Cárdenas" (Ashby, 1967, 24). On the contrary, the labor movement launched a series of strikes.

On June 11, 1935, Calles red-baited the union leaders, especially Lombardo Toledano, and denounced all strikers as engaging in unpatriotic behavior equivalent to "treason." He challenged the new President to restore order or suffer the consequences. Cárdenas responded on June 13 with a statement mid-way between labor's demands and Calles' adamant opposition. Cárdenas viewed some of labor's demands as justified and felt that by granting some of labor's wishes the economic situation might be made "more stable," assuming that concessions to labor were granted "within the economic possibilities of the capitalist sector." To reassure business, Cárdenas warned that "in no case will the President of the Republic permit excesses of any kind or acts that involve transgressions of the law or unnecessary agitations" (cited in Ashby, 1967:27). The working class—led by the strikers, independent unions like the Railway Workers and the Electricians, and new leaders like Lombardo Toledano, whom Cárdenas supported in his drive to replace the pro-Calles CROM—responded to Calles' attacks by threatening a general strike, branding Calles a traitor to the Revolution, and forming the National Committee for Proletarian Defense, which in February of 1936 would be reconstituted with Cárdenas's support as the CTM. This new labor coalition applauded Cárdenas's June 13 statement, and from that moment on "the labor movement was wedded to Cárdenas, and he, in turn, to the labor movement . . . but the government kept, always, the upper hand" (Ashby, 1967:273).

Meanwhile, Cárdenas made sweeping changes in the party and government bureaucracy and in the military. He won rank-and-file soldier support and maneuvered the generals into a position of neutrality. Noting the Army's ambivalence and awed by the sight of thousands of workers in the streets supporting Cárdenas and threatening a general strike, many political figures pragmatically shifted their support from Calles to Cárdenas.

Overcome by this newly fashioned labor-government alliance, Calles and CROM's Morones were put to rout, or, more exactly, deported

(April, 1936). Once again, new political leadership in Mexico had met the rising demands of workers part-way, and, in so doing, had replaced the older, more recalcitrant leadership, even as Obregón and Calles had done against the Carranza camp in 1919–1924. Once again it was the actions of the working class, through large-scale strikes and demonstrations, that had precipitated the changes. And once again, the new government leadership moved in to help meet some of labor's demands and to bend the labor movement back "within the economic possibilities of the capitalist sector."

As Cárdenas hedged on the right of either workers or the state to take over factories where productive machinery was inactive or where owners disobeyed labor laws or court decisions, the working class grew impatient and stepped up its pace of strikes. When in February of 1936 the nation's largest industrial (and conservative) center, Monterrey, became immobilized by strikes, President Cárdenas issued his famous "Fourteen Points" statement. He encouraged workers to form a "united front," with which the government would deal "to the exclusion of minority groups which might choose to continue" (e.g. CROM). He warned industrialists that, should they cease production in the factories "because of the demands of the unions," then the factories could rightfully be turned over "to their laborers or to the government" (·a warning against employers' use of the shut-down and lockout). On the other hand, Cárdenas encouraged employers also "to associate themselves into a united front," which they rapidly did in the form of Chambers of Commerce and Industry. He applauded further growth of industries, since the government "depends upon their prosperity for its income through taxation." And he urged businessmen "not to continue provoking agitations," because "this would bring on civil warfare." In brief, Cárdenas made it clear that he favored the right to organize for both business and labor, so long as serious disruption, or "civil warfare," did not occur (Ashby, 1967:34–5). As Professor Arnaldo Córdova is showing in works in progress, Cárdenas' policies were those of "corporativism"—state control and regulation over many, separate, organized socio-economic groups.

In March, 1936, in the face of strident protests by certain big businessmen, some of whom insisted on the right to shut down a factory where labor trouble occurred, Cárdenas repeated that he had no intention of nationalizing all industry. He assured a delegation of bankers and industrialists that even in the most extreme cases of uncooperative behavior by big business, "the most that could happen would be that certain branches be withdrawn from the sphere of private interest to become social service" (cited in Ashby, 1967:37). Moreover, Cárdenas used the phrase "socialization of the means of production" to mean government regulation of *privately*-owned productive property, the kind of regulation that was introduced in many advanced capitalist countries during the Depression. As Ashby points out, the Cárdenas government aimed "to develop private industry," not to nationalize it, and "to keep on fairly good terms with its powerful capitalist neighbor of the North" (Ashby, 1967:56).

And in most cases, this is precisely what the Cárdenas government did. While encouraging *ejido* agriculture where efficient and practical, Cárdenas by no means liquidated agrarian capitalism. In fact, between 1930 and 1940, the number of privately-owned farms increased by 44 percent. Moreover, in 1940 "at least 60 percent of the peasants eligible to receive land had either inadequate plots or no land of their own, and over 50 percent of the nation's cultivable land still lay in estates of more than 5,000 hectares" (Cornelius, 1970:92). While many of the nation's earlier, traditional *hacendados* had been killed during the 1910–1917 Revolution or had gone into exile, others had survived to rebuild and expand their estates, their ranks swelled by so-called "revolutionary land-lords who had taken advantage of the turmoil and confusion of the early period of armed struggle to amass huge estates for themselves" (Cornelius, 1970:6). Numerous "revolutionary" generals and politicians became large landholders. Cárdenas had to tread lightly in threatening the interests of these *latifundistas,* although he did not hesitate to form peasant militias and even to send in troops when regional caciques allied with conservatives and foreign oil interests in an effort to stop his "atheistic, Bolshevik reforms," as in the case of the swiftly repressed Cedillo revolt of mid-1938 in San Luis Potosí.

In general, though, Cárdenas respected the spirit of Article 27 of the 1917 Constitution, which protected private property. In order to ameliorate momentarily a prolonged worker-employer conflict in the big sugar-growing area of Los Mochis, Sinaloa, he distributed lands to the workers in 1938. Yet he left the properties of the principal producer, the United Sugar Company, *untouched,* and refused to concede any wage increases to the workers (Ashby, 1967, 104–106). In the areas of the most radical land-distribution program, the Laguna and Yucatán, the largest and most prosperous private landholdings were protected. In the Yucatán, "Cárdenas left the henequen-processing plants in the hands of the old land-owners who by using them were still able to control the peasants" (Michaels, 1970:63). Even after the formation of collective *ejidos* in the Laguna region, 1936, less than 10 percent of all *ejido* farmers in Mexico worked on a collective basis. In fact, the best one-third of the Laguna lands, with more than two-thirds of the artesian wells, reportedly remained untouched by the agrarian reform. The most productive

Laguna lands remained in the hands of twelve corporations, 70 percent of them foreign-owned. These corporations had in earlier decades, especially after the victory of Carranza's Constitutionalists against the peasant revolutionaries of the region, developed "capitalism in the region" by means of "the modernization of working methods by the use of tractors and other farm machinery" (Ashby, 1967:151, 164–5). Because of widespread unemployment, partially caused by this continued mechanization of agriculture, and because of the monopoly on good lands, water, and credit enjoyed by the corporate capitalists of Mexico's countryside, many *ejidatarios* were forced to hire themselves out to the corporate farmers as peons and even to rent their own *ejido* land out to the *latifundistas* and then work it for them. Often, in the turbulent countryside, the peasants' only allies in seeking agrarian reform were school teachers, more than two hundred of whom were shot down by the hired *pistoleros* of the large landholders (Raby, 1968). Some eight hundred thousand people were still living on *haciendas* in 1940, when the government itself acknowledged that "despite the agrarian transformation carried out up to the present, and the division of the great landed properties effected by the Government with the purpose of creating small proprietorship, with regard to the concentration of landed property Mexico continues to be fundamentally a country of great estates" (cited in Raby, 1970: 365).

Although the government-sponsored National Bank of Ejidal Credit was a progressive step towards alleviating the peasants' plight, the employees of the Bank often were the personnel of the old private banks, in sympathy with the *latifundistas*. Corruption in the Ejidal Bank has since become such common knowledge in Mexico that many peasants actually prefer to obtain their credit from private corporate farmers, however exploitive and usurious the rates of interest.

Because of the combined turmoil of the countryside and workers' strikes in the cities, food production plummeted and prices skyrocketed. "The government sought to solve the agrarian crisis by curtailing land reform after 1937. It hoped that this curtailment might give security to Mexico's still large class of private landowners who would return to developing their lands" (Michaels, 1970:65). In May of 1938 the government opened the Office of Small Property, which was given the power to issue certificates of exemption from seizure.

Consistent with his politics of corporativism, Cárdenas prevented peasant organizations—which he earlier helped develop by political appointments at every level—from affiliating with the CTM, as he also did in the cases of bank employees' unions, public employees' unions, and teacher unions. As Lyle Brown points out, "There was no doubt that Cárdenas desired separately organized labor and peasant confederations that would look to him for support and over which he would exercise such control as might be necessary to keep them functioning in harmony with the objectives of his administration. . . . Both the Communists and Lombardo Toledano spoke of the importance of uniting peasant and labor groups in a great proletarian organization, but Cárdenas was too shrewd a politician to allow such a development" (Brown, 1964:211). Cárdenas organized close to two hundred thousand peasants into peasant militias, in main part to defend the agrarian reform and offset any threat of a coup d'etat by the Army. He also formed some workers' militias, under the control of the Defense Ministry, for similar purposes. As Cornelius has observed, however:

> Although Cárdenas specified that peasants receiving arms would be organized into reserve units trained and supervised by regular army officers, it was clear that the idea of an armed peasantry as a counterweight to the Revolutionary generals—and, conceivably, to *Lombardista* labor leaders, should they get out of control—was not far from the center of his thinking." (Cornelius, 1970: 66–67)

The overall effect of Cárdenas's corporativist policies was "to pacify the countryside" and channel working-class discontent "into officially-sanctioned strike activity" (Cornelius, 1970:78).

Professor Eyler N. Simpson correctly ascertained in 1936–1937, when the *ejido* appeared to be "Mexico's way out," that the mixed system of *ejido* and continued private ownership of the best lands could never resolve Mexico's long-standing agrarian problem: "The Revolution will have fulfilled itself if and when Mexico has been transformed from a land of privately-owned, individualistic haciendas and *ranchos* into a land of socialized *ejidos*, and not before" (Simpson, 1937, 512–3, 518). In fact, Cárdenas's agrarian reform policies, while arousing the enthusiasm of millions of Mexicans at the time and granting the peasant a dignity he had not felt since the days of Zapata, served in the long run to preserve and stimulate the private system of farming for commercial profit. Firstly, responding to the mounting pressure of striking peasants of the Laguna and other regions, Cárdenas used agrarian reform to avoid impending agricultural paralysis and disruption. Secondly, in the Laguna, Yucatán, Sonora-Sinaloa, and Baja California regions, where *ejidos* have enjoyed their greatest strength alongside the better equipped private properties of the commercial farmers, capitalist agriculture for export has had its greatest boom in the 1940–1965 period. Thus, civil war and disruption were avoided by agrarian reform, while capitalist production increased manyfold. Whetten maintains that, by granting the peasants some of their demands for land, Cárdenas's agrarian reform prevented "international communism" from making headway in Mexico, and further "forced private landholders to farm their remaining lands much more efficiently in order to make a living, thus helping to increase agricultural production at a faster rate than the increase in population" (Whetten, 1948:6). It is no coincidence that *neo-latifundismo,* the current form of monopoly agriculture in Mexico, flourishes best in precisely those areas of Cárdenas's much-disputed agrarian reform (Stavenhagen, 1968; González Navarro, 1965; Ashby, 1967:178).

A recent book on *neo-latifundism* and exploitation verifies this analysis:

The impact of foreign demand appears clearly in the following statistics: in 1940 agricultural products were about 10.3% of total exports, whereas in 1945 this proportion was nearly 21%. . . . After 1940 when, during the war, American demand for Mexican agricultural products increases again: (1) Agricultural development depends more on external forces (demand and supply of inputs) than on the domestic market; (2) The best lands, the irrigated ones and the other resources, like capital, labor, credit and physical inputs, begin to concentrate themselves in certain regions and in the hands of a few owners; (3) That growth opens the doors to foreign capital, which begins the process of control of national agriculture; (4) Agrarian products begin to constitute the base of Mexico's trade balance, on the side of exports . . . ; (5) The economic policy of the country, and especially the monetary and fiscal policy, far from contributing to the elimination of the miserable living conditions of the rural population and liberating it from exploitation, support the monopolization of the land and the exploitation of human labor; (6) This same policy helps generate the grave inequality in distribution of income. These tendencies become even stronger in the last decade . . . . "encouraged" by the Korean War, the international market maintained attractive prices on principal export crops: cotton, coffee, and tomatoes. . . . It is necessary to emphasize, then, that the minifundium really constitutes 86% of the units of production. . . . In 1960, two percent of the farms accounted for 70.1% of the value of sales. To get an idea of the acute degree of concentration suffered in agriculture, it is well to note that in the United States 10% of the farms generated 40% of the sales, and it is said that this already is a high degree of concentration.

This means that agriculture is a wonderful business for a very few people, while the large majority of the working population lives under very poor conditions. More than 55% of the farms counted by the census had sales below 1,000 pesos [80 dollars] in 1960. . . . Between 1950 and 1960 . . . the number of those employed in agriculture who do not manage their own farming increases by 60%, rising from 2 million to more than 3.3 million. This means that in 1960 the agricultural population without land is greater in absolute numbers than in 1930 and also than in 1910, and that it now accounts for more than half of the total agricultural population . . . . the agricultural problem in Mexico is today more complex and in some respects undoubtedly more serious, than when the Army of the South launched into battle under the flag of Emiliano Zapata more than half a century ago. The concentration of land and of other productive resources in new forms and the foreign control exercised by Anderson Clayton and Company are facts that converge and join each other in one single fact: the increasing exploitation of the enormous masses of peasants. . . . The neo-latifundism is not an isolated phenomenon and cannot be attributed to circumstantial factors: the peculiarities of a landowner, the dishonesty of some official, the lack of adequate personnel of this or that government department. Neo-latifundism is simply the natural result of the present structure of power, that is, of the class structure in the country. (Stavenhagen, 1968: back cover, 19, 30–31, 75–78, 86–87)

Further statistics could be cited to confirm this picture, such as the fact that by 1950, 85 percent of all tractors were on private farms, and by 1957, 60 percent of agrarian production was for export. Meanwhile, about eight hundred thousand farm workers a year joined the stream of *braceros* going to the United States in quest of survival wages during the 1950's. Francois Chevalier has summarized present reality in historical perspective:

> The majority of *ejidos* possess only non-irrigated land on which essential foodstuffs are cultivated, especially the traditional crop, maize. Above all, these *ejidos* do not have access to credit, and the result is greater dependence on moneylenders. These may be capitalists from outside the *ejido,* or local shopkeepers or farmers who are more enterprising or thrifty than the others. Here the danger of seizure of the plots, even of complete ruin and elimination of the *ejidatarios,* is greater than elsewhere. The situation is comparable to that in certain ancient Indian communities which, at the end of the nineteenth or the beginning of the twentieth century, were literally dispersed or destroyed by the penetration and incursions of mestizos who—since they were much more economically advanced than the Indians—rapidly took over all the land (Chevalier, 1967:182).

Even as the Liberal Reform of 1857 furthered the monopoly control of land and wealth by a dependent national bourgeoisie allied with a foreign bourgeoisie, so the agrarian reform of 1935–1936 abetted this same (mis) development.

In only one major area did the Cárdenas government move against foreign capital: petroleum. An unyielding attitude by the oil companies forced Cárdenas's hand, as did a long-term, intermittent strike by oil workers between 1936 and 1938. The oil companies had already sucked out most of the oil wealth to be had. Production had peaked in 1921, and by 1937 Mexican oil accounted for only 3 percent of Standard Oil of New Jersey world production. Of main concern to the companies and their governments was the *example* such nationalization would set in other more critical areas: Venezuela, the Middle East, and other foreign investment in Mexico. Incensed by the oil expropriation, Secretary of State Hull wired Ambassador Daniels on March 26, 1938: "Re-examine commercial relations with Mexico—to defer continuation of monthly silver purchase arrangements with Mexico 'til further notice" (Department of State, 1938:729). Huge indemnities were demanded, with the Mexican Government eventually paying over $200 million to the companies. The United States and Great Britain cut off all marketing facilities for Mexican oil, forcing Mexico to turn to the Axis powers for its oil trade. World War II and the Axis threat helped bring the United States to terms with Mexico, with corresponding economic benefits, as we have seen, for the bourgeoisies involved.

Once again, class strife raging inside Mexico and international conflicts among the world's strongest bourgeoisies contributed to Mexico's ability to take a progressive, if small, step towards economic autonomy. A neo-Fascist ideology called Sinarquismo was making inroads among Mexico's peasants still untouched by agrarian reform, middle-class people suffering from inflation, and ultra-reactionary clerical and business figures. Supporters of Sinarquismo numbered nearly a half million by 1940, some of them reportedly organized into paramilitary units. In addition, the working class was growing disillusioned with Cárdenas's ambivalent policies on strikes, failure to curb inflation, and possible succumbing to a power play by more conservative Army generals. Peasants noted the cutback in agrarian reform in 1937, as well as corruption among bureaucrats running the reform. The time was ripe for a bold action against a common enemy, such as foreign economic interests, which would unify public opinion.

Although Cárdenas's own sense of national pride, the oil companies' recalcitrance (they passed up Cárdenas's last-minute acceptance of their wage proposals by insisting on having it in writing—an insult to the President of Mexico), and the militant strike posture of the oil workers sufficed to bring about expropriation, the tremendous propaganada campaign that followed, during which the nation's poorest women contributed their last bits of cheap jewelry to the national indemnity fund, reflected the President's political savvy in assuaging class conflict and rallying the entire nation behind a patriotic cause. Cárdenas followed the oil expropriation with reorganization of the national political party, formation of a national peasant organization, and suppression of the Cedillo revolt. Similar acts of Latin American nationalism and policies of reformism under similar circumstances of crisis for the foreign metropolis (the Southeast Asian War, U.S. economic crisis) and internal unrest (student revolts, guerrilla warfare) could be observed in Peru, Bolivia, and Chile in 1971.

Cárdenas immediately assured other foreign investors that "the case of oil was exceptional and its solution would not be applied to other private investments in the country. He promised to protect all businesses and investments so long as they benefitted the nation·and conformed to Mexican laws" (Michaels, 1968:73).

That Cárdenas had no intention of going any further than necessary in resolving these crises, or of undermining the long-run developmentalist goals "within the economic possibilities of the capitalist sector," was swiftly proven by his anti-labor actions immediately following the expropriation of oil. In late 1938, Cárdenas broke a mineworkers' strike directed in main part against Anaconda Copper Company. He discharged workers who engaged in a sit-down and assured the companies that further expropriation would not occur . From 1938 to 1940, he discouraged strikes and was especially critical of the oil and railroad workers whose continued strikes and militancy caused him to refuse their demands and expound upon "the necessity of ending extreme situations which would endanger the collective interests" (cited in Michaels, 1970:70). In 1938, only 13,435 workers struck, in 1939, only 14,486, and in 1940, only 19,784, compared to 145,000 in 1935, 113,885 in 1936 and 61,732 in 1937. In 1940 oil and rail workers were still on strike. The oil workers objecting to Cárdenas's plan to reorganize the industry, pulled out of the CTM, which still supported the government. Cárdenas responded by sending federal troops to break a strike at the Atzapotzalco refinery (Michaels, 1970:68; Gonzalez Casanova, 1965:183).

Cárdenas also encouraged private investment by allowing the government's major development corporation, the Nacional Financiera, founded in 1934, to borrow from the Central Bank "to underwrite private investments and . . . provide initial capital for industrial enterprises" (Michaels, 1970:71). As Wilkie has noted: "the basis for rapid industrialization was firmly established when Cárdenas left office. In fact, the volume of manufacturing production increased about as fast during the Cárdenas era as it did during the Avila Camacho epoch" (Wilkie, 1967:265). By 1940, 87 percent of Mexico's trade was with the United States. One of Cárdenas's last speeches, in February, 1940, spelled out his ideology and overall bourgeois developmentalist goals:

> There is not a communist government in Mexico. Our constitution is democratic and liberal. True, it has some moderately socialistic features such as those concerning national territory and relationships between capital and labor, yet they are no more radical than those of other democratic countries and of some which retain monarchial institutions. It is not necessary for us to rely on the ideologies or ideals of other countries, but rather to adhere more closely and with a greater sense of justice and liberty to our own prin-

ciples and to the vital needs of Mexico at this time. (cited in Michaels, 1970: 78–79)

Cárdenas accepted the moderate Avila Camacho as his successor precisely in order to carry out the next decade's industrial development program, or, in the words of his last major public address, September 15, 1940, the task of "unification, peace, and work." Incoming Presidents ever since have echoed these themes, with today's President Luis Echeverría, suspected by some to have links with the CIA, introducing the slogan that Mexico will move neither right nor left, but "upward and forward."

In sum, Cárdenas's reforms were made possible by the relaxation of foreign pressure brought about by Depression and war and an increase in Mexican proletarian militancy. The reforms served to introduce sufficient structural change to avert civil war, strengthen state-regulated capitalism, provide for greater national integration, with the office of the Presidency sacrosanct, and furnish a social, economic, and ideological basis for rapid industrial growth and capitalist development of Mexico between 1940 and 1960. Cárdenas's program closed the gap between workers' expectations and government performance, which in no small part permitted the intense exploitation of workers, especially peasants, that fired the high GNP rates of subsequent years. While industrial production went up 120% between 1940 and 1960 and agrarian production increased 100 percent, average real income for workers declined 6 percent and the minimum agrarian wage in real value dropped 45 percent (González Casanova, 1965:130). In other words, economic growth continued for the benefit of the few to the cost of the many. According to Navarette, from 65 percent to 70 percent of the Mexican population has had no share in the benefits of economic development (Navarette, 1967); according to González Casanova, from 50 percent to 70 percent of the population is "marginal" (González Casanova, 1965). While harsh on Cárdenas, the bitter statement of a railway brakeman in Mariano Azuela's novel *La nueva burguesía* undoubtedly reflects the feeling of many Mexicans then, as today:

> Isn't it true, Campillo, that the only thing that Mexico has to thank Cárdenas for is that the cost of living is five times higher than it was when he came into power? . . . and how many thousands are dying of hunger because there is no work? (cited in Michaels, 1970:57).[3]

[3] The author gratefully acknowledges the criticism of many readers for their suggestions concerning the Cárdenas era. Professor David L. Raby was especially helpful in attacking some of my interpretations, which I have modified in certain instances. Since completing this chapter, I had the opportunity to be Visiting Profes-

U.S. CONTROL OF THE ECONOMY

Stimulated by increased U.S. demands for food and primary materials during World War II and the Korean War, the Mexican economy showed substantial GNP growth rates after 1940, often over 6 percent a year. The Mexican Government cooperated in an economic development program which, from 1940 to the present, has provided tax incentives for private industry, free remittance of profits abroad, a cheap and well disciplined labor force, and state pump-priming of the economy and development of the infrastructure.

Presidents Avila Camacho and Miguel Alemán retained the populist rhetoric of Cárdena's development program, while re-negotiating Mexico's foreign debts and shifting emphasis in the goal-structure to favor Investment and the private sector. They and most of their successors channeled funds and political muscle out of Public Welfare and into light industry, durable consumer goods, roads, hotels, private commercial agriculture, middle-class education, and limitations on agrarian reform and labor's right to strike. Today's corrupt CTM chief Fidel Velázquez replaced Lombardo Toledano, as organized labor's leaders "came increasingly from middle-class backgrounds and came to reflect middle-class preferences, aspirations, and values" (Cornelius, 1970:99). First the threat of Fascism and then U.S. wartime needs benefitted Mexico's foreign trade which, from a post-1916 low reached in 1932, multiplied almost ten times by the end of 1946, as exports doubled during World War II. Because of the War, the United States was unable to export to Mexico its usual quantity of manufactured goods, and so Mexico engaged in intensive import-substitution, as industrial production increased 35 percent. To finance its war production, the United States purchased much Mexican silver. Ostensibly in return for Mexican support for the Allies, but also to further penetrate and influence the Mexican economy, the United States advanced large credits for Mexican industry, then stepped in with its own large-scale investment right after the War, buying out many of Mexico's nascent industries. U.S. direct investment in Mexico started to rise sharply in 1946. In sum, after 1940, Economic Growth took precedence over Public Welfare in the overall goal-structure, and government policy became technocratic, centralized, and bureaucratic, building on the populist rhetoric and corporativist structure of the

sor at UNAM (Mexico's National University), where I discovered the brilliant work of Professor Arnaldo Córdova on "corporativism" under Cárdenas, as well as other works in progress by Córdova, Jorge Basurto, Salvador Hernández, and other Mexican scholars on the Cárdenas era. These works are more complete than my analysis, while not incompatible with it in any major way.

Cárdenas era. The United States strongly influenced and encouraged these developments.

Once again, Mexico threw open its doors to foreign investors. Direct foreign investment increased from $449 million in 1940 to $1.6 billion in 1958, half of it in manufacturing and commerce. From 1950 to 1970, U.S. direct investment went from $286 million to over $2.2 billion. Of this, according to Banco de México statistics in 1970, manufacturing absorbed 74 percent, commerce 15 percent, mining and metallurgical industry 6 percent, agriculture 1 percent, and others 4 percent. By 1970, U.S. investors accounted for 79 percent of all foreign investment. Moreover, the 1940–1960 period saw foreign investors taking *out* of Mexico more capital than they put in, a trend which continues unabated, as Table 1 indicates for 1955–1965, a representative period.

TABLE 1 FOREIGN INVESTMENT IN MEXICO
(thousands of dollars)

Year	New Direct Foreign Investments	Total Net Foreign Income on Investments*	Reinvested Profits
1955	84,926	79,611	12,479
1956	83,325	120,113	29,142
1957	101,024	117,233	29,046
1958	62,833	122,592	26,045
1959	65,581	128,621	16,152
1960	62,466	141,566	10,570
1961	81,826	148,067	25,178
1962	74,871	159,344	36,190
1963	76,090	182,907	34,363
1964	83,075	242,202	56,339
1965	110.058	234,928	73,493

*Profits remitted abroad and profits reinvested, interest, royalties, and other payments.

Source: Banco de México, as reported in Secretaría de Industria y Comercio (1967).

In this decade alone, foreign investors, on new direct investments of $886 million, made an income of almost $1.7 billion, of which they reinvested less than 20 percent in Mexico. This "suction-pump effect" of foreign investment taking capital out of Mexico, combined with increased foreign credits, declining conditions of trade (Mexico pays more for imports, sells at lesser prices its exports), periodic flight of capital (one-third of the nation's monetary reserves in 1961), and accumulated underdevelopment, has led to Mexico's progressive indebtedness, economic dependence, and what González Casanova has correctly termed "decapitalization" (1965, 120). Payments of the foreign debt alone absorb almost 50 percent of Mexico's export earnings (Table 2).

TABLE 2 MEXICO'S DEBT PAYMENTS AND FOREIGN TRADE
(millions of dollars)

YEAR	PAYMENTS OF INTEREST AND AMORTIZATIONS	IMPORTS	EXPORT EARNINGS	EXPORTS AS PERCENT OF IMPORTS
1965	522	1,560	1,114	71
1966	539	1,605	1,186	74
1967	560	1,748	1,104	63
1968	551	1,960	1,181	60

Sources: Nacional Financiera (1968); The Economist Intelligence Unit (1970); Banco Nacional de Comercio Exterior (1968).

Chronic balance-of-trade deficits, incurred to sustain the consumer appetites of the Mexican bourgeoisie, derive from Mexico's dependence on the United States as its major trading "partner" (the U.S. Government restricts Mexican exports of tomatoes, textiles, shoes, etc.).

The United States now holds effective control of the Mexican economy, in spite of Mexico's policy of "Mexicanization," or 51 percent Mexican control of select industries determined by the executive branch of government. Many firms remain 100 percent foreign-owned—General Motors, Chrysler, Ford, General Electric, Admiral Corp., Monsanto Chemical Co., and Anderson-Clayton, among others. U.S. business spokesmen often applaud Mexicanization as part of a healthy, stabilizing, and profitable trend in Latin America towards "multi-national corporations," which continue to be dominated by U.S. interests but, by involving Latin American capitalists, disguise continued U.S. penetration and takeover of the economies. Furthermore, as the *New York Times* recently pointed out (September 19, 1971), Mexicanization "is now seen as guaranteeing foreign investors against expropriation." U.S. corporations finance 70% of their investments with Mexican capital, make their profits on cheap Mexican labor, sell their goods at exhorbitant prices directly in Mexico or abroad through the Latin American Free Trade Association (LAFTA) and Central American Common Market, and remit the bulk of their profits to the United States.[4] Further diluting the effect of "Mexicanization" is

[4] Mexico's rapidly growing favorable trade balance with LAFTA reflects both this trend and the fact that Mexico has had a headstart on poorer Latin American countries which have not had the kind of state-supported reformist measures and economic planning that Mexico has had since 1936. When compared to Guatemala, Mexico may be a prosperous, even booming colony—but none the less a colony

the use of Mexican names to front for U.S. investors; corruption and bribery; and economic pressure applied by foreign investors and creditors. Another factor which strengthens foreign control of Mexicanized companies is the concentration of stock ownership in the hands of one or two foreign companies and the dispersal of Mexican participation among the larger number of very junior partners.

Part of the United States' increased control of the Mexican economy derived from its huge advantages over Mexico in technology and capital reserves. While Mexican industrial output (dominated by foreigners) increased five times between 1940 and 1965, imports of foreign, mainly U.S. capital goods, industrial parts, and replacement parts increased 12.5 times (Aguilar, 1967:115). In other words, Mexico's development program has increased the country's reliance upon capital imports, foreign investment, and "loans," while not dealing with the ever-growing unfavorable trade balance.

Exemplar of predominant U.S. economic influence in Mexico is the role of Anderson Clayton in agriculture, which "ranks 10th among Mexican companies based on net earnings which in 1967 were about 3.5 million dollars; by sales, it ranks second" (NACLA, 1968:33). Cotton is Mexico's leading export, and Anderson Clayton controls the marketing and profits. Also, Anderson Clayton controls the production process and schedule of Mexican cotton by providing over $200 million annually in credits (or nearly twice the amount of *all* loans to Mexico's *ejidatarios* from the national Ejido Bank). Anderson Clayton also controls cotton production in the countries with which Mexico must compete: Brazil and the United States. A one-cent drop in world market prices of cotton costs Mexico $9 million in export earnings; and Anderson Clayton periodically engages in cotton "dumping" to remind Mexico who is in control (Stavenhagen, 1968).

In recent years, Anderson-Clayton stopped financing cultivation of cotton, as costs and risks rose. The Mexican Government assumed this role, but Anderson-Clayton still processed the cotton, and has now branched out into Mexican production of cattle feed, chocolates, planting seeds, edible oils, and insecticides. Other U.S. corporations have joined Anderson-Clayton in effectively taking over Mexico's agribusiness, from production and sale of machinery and fertilizers to the processing and merchandising of agricultural goods. This is especially evident in the food

---

for that. In work in progress, Professor David Barkin of the Department of Economics, Lehman College, Bronx, New York, shows how Mexican economic dependence on the United States is even more severe in the 1970's. Prof. Barkin shows particularly well U.S. penetration of Mexican banking.

processing industry, one of Mexico's biggest, where United Fruit Company's 1967 purchase of Clement Jacques, "one of Mexico's oldest food preserves companies . . . alarmed some observers in part because of United Fruit's propensity for overthrowing uncooperative governments" (NACLA, 1968:32). However, Mexico is not Guatemala, and United Fruit is not Anderson-Clayton.

Even in the fast-growing area of petrochemicals, normally limited to Mexican control since the 1938 nationalization decree, the United States has moved in with economic muscle. A 1959 "Regulation of the Petroleum Law" act has opened the doors to various U.S. concerns in so-called "secondary" petrochemicals, including unrestricted areas of investment like pharmaceuticals, paints, and synthetic fibers, all U.S.-controlled today. U.S. companies have invested almost $200 million in Mexican chemical operations. One U.S. company, the Pan American Sulphur Co. (PASCO), produces 75 percent of all Mexico's sulphur output. Mexico ranks second in world production and export of sulphur, after the United States. World demand for sulphur, an important ingredient in agricultural fertilizers, exceeds world supply. Consequently, Mexican sulphur, now a major Mexican export, is a multi-million dollar industry. "Mexicanization," as is customary, works to PASCO's advantage, as suggested by a *Wall Street Journal* article: "higher export quotas, higher sulphur prices and lower taxes that would result from the 'Mexicanization' might triple profits." As one U.S. chemical company executive exuded: "It's a millionaire's Klondike" (cited in NACLA, 1968:37). In May of 1972, the Mexican Government announced the "Mexicanization" of PASCO. Twenty percent of the company's stock was left in private hands and, according to a report in the *New York Times* financial pages, "the Americans were not unhappy."

But the main area into which recent foreign capital has flowed has been manufacturing industry. Traditionally, as we have seen, Mexico imported manufactured goods and exported primary goods. However, structural changes made under Cárdenas provided a basis for Mexican industrialization. The unbalanced class structure in Mexico, uneven income distribution, and existing demand structure led Mexico to concentrate on light industry and durable consumer goods, mainly for the high-income market and middle-class consumer needs (food, drink, clothing, housing, private cars, household goods and appliances, etc.). Mexico's industrialization program did not free Mexico from foreign dependence, in part because it did not focus on industrial equipment and producers' goods, which it increasingly had to import from abroad just to keep the import-substitution process going. By 1968, capital goods (mostly U.S.) represented 50 percent of all imports and raw materials for industrial production another 32 percent. Mexico was the sixth top buyer of U.S. goods in the world. (The Economist Intelligence Unit, 1970:19). Thus, as Reynolds has noted, import-substitution turned out to be import-intensive (Reynolds, 1970:252).

Moreover, most Mexican industries have become controlled (e.g. cement, textiles, automotive, cigarettes, tires, food processing, synthetic fibers, etc.) or strongly influenced (petrochemicals, iron and steel, etc.) by foreign capitalists. Manufactures as a percentage of total Mexican exports have increased from 11 percent in 1960 to 22.5 percent in 1968, but half of these items are sugar and tinned and prepared fruits, and most of them are again foreign-dominated. What has happened is that U.S. investors are now not only sending obsolete machinery at high prices to Mexico to be assembled there with cheap labor, as in the boom days of Mexico's wasteful, expensive, and irrational development of its automotive industry (Fenster, 1969). They are now also investing in original production plants inside Mexico itself, using reinvested profits or Mexican capital and cheap labor to produce and sell finished goods right there, pocketing exhorbitant profits, and tying into the flow of trade of "Mexican" manufactured goods to other Latin American countries through LAFTA and the Central American Common Market. From a U.S. businessman's point of view, why bother with taxes, trade regulations, quotas, tariffs, and middlemen expenses when, instead of exporting manufactured goods to Mexico, you can begin to produce them right there, at lower costs and higher profits—and simultaneously maintain and increase export profits and favorable trade balances with Mexico by replacing the export of U.S. finished goods with the export of U.S. capital goods and industrial supplies and equipment?

In addition, U.S. companies are setting up labor-intensive assembly plants across the border to take advantage of the Mexican Government's elimination of import duties and latest stop-gap measure to ameliorate unemployment: provision of jobs through American companies, now that the *bracero* program for agrarian workers has been terminated. The Mexican Secretary of Industry and Commerce has stated the goal: "Our idea is to offer an alternative to Hong Kong, Japan and Puerto Rico for free enterprise" (cited in NACLA, 1968:37). Besides traditional U.S. manufacturers like GM, Dupont, Dow Chemical, and so on, such diversified concerns as Transitron Electronic Corp., Litton Industries, Fairchild Camera, Hughes Aircraft Co., and Lockheed Aircraft, most of them among the top twenty subsidized clients of the Pentagon, have now moved into Mexico.

U.S. control of the economy is further manifested in banking. Mexico's major banking institution is the industrial development bank Nacional

Financiera, a "mixed" body with the government holding majority shares. With total assets of $76.3 million, Nacional Financiera extends 72 percent of its loans to the infrastructure and only 7 percent to basic industry (mostly iron-steel, including private companies). It cooperates with both the Mexican Government, whose top financial officials are usually drawn from Nacional Financiera's Board of Directors, and private capital, including foreign investors to whom it often makes loans. U.S. bankers are very influential in Mexico's economy, directly through branch offices inside Mexico and indirectly through purchases of Mexican bonds, including those of Nacional Financiera. Since its inception in 1934, Nacional Financiera has received $4.8 billion in foreign financing, mostly U.S. capital channelled through international loan agencies like the World Bank, Export-Import Bank, AID, and Inter-American Development Bank. Well over half of Nacional Financiera's resources come from foreign loans. Among the world biggest financial institutions which have extended credits to Nacional Financiera are the following: Bank of America, Prudential Insurance Co., Manufacturers Hanover Trust, Irving Trust Co., Chase Manhattan Bank, Chemical Bank, New York Trust Co., Girard Trust Corn Exchange Bank, First National City Bank of New York, Bank of Tokyo, Institute Mobilaire Italiane, and Barclay's Bank, Ltd. (Brandenburg, 1964; Nacional Financiera, 1969; Houk, 1967).

TABLE 3 DISTRIBUTION OF MEXICO'S ECONOMICALLY ACTIVE POPULATION

	1950		1970	
	'000	PERCENT OF TOTAL	'000	PERCENT OF TOTAL
Agriculture, forestry, fishing	4,824	58.3	5,132	39.5
Manufacturing	973	11.8	2,174	16.7
Construction	225	2.7	571	4.4
Petroleum & mining	97	1.2	180	1.4
Public services (electricity)	25	0.3	53	0.4
Transport & communications	211	2.6	369	2.8
Commerce & finance	684	8.3	198	9.2
Services, including government	879	10.6		
Other	355	4.3		
(Other Services)			3,317	25.6
Total labor force	8,273	100.0	12,994	100.0

Source: Population censuses of 1950 and 1970, as reported in Nacional Financiera (1970).

TABLE 4 ORIGIN OF MEXICO'S GROSS NATIONAL PRODUCT (1950 PRICES, BILLIONS OF PESOS)

	1950	PERCENT	1968	PERCENT
Agriculture, forestry, hunting & fishing	9.2	22.4	18.7	15.7
Mining & quarrying*	1.2	2.9	1.8	1.4
Manufacturing	9.6	23.3	33.0	27.2
Construction	1.3	3.2	4.9	3.9
Electricity, gas & water	0.4	1.0	1.9	1.7
Transport, storage & communication	2.0	4.9	4.9	4.2
Wholesale & retail trade	10.8	26.3	31.9	26.3
Public Administration & defence	1.3	3.1	3.2	2.7
Petroleum	. . . .	. . . .	3.9	3.2
Services	5.3	12.9	18.2	13.7
Total	41.1	100.0	122.4	100.0

*In 1950, including petroleum.

Source: Banco de México, as reported in The Economist Intelligence Unit (1970).

Tables 3 and 4 reflect the low productivity of agriculture and growing importance of manufacture; Mexico suffers from uneven economic development and uneven distribution of labor. On the one hand, 40 percent of the labor force is in agriculture, which accounts for only 16 percent of production. On the other hand, only 17 percent of the economically active population is in manufacturing, which generates over 27 percent of GNP. Allowing for a shift in production shares from mining to manufacturing between 1910 and the present, the picture of unbalanced and unequal distribution of labor and income today resembles in its proportions that of 1910, when agriculture accounted for 67 percent of employment and only 24 percent of production, mining and manufacturing 15 percent of the employed and 23 percent of production. Given the structural imbalances of the Mexican economy over historical time, with foreign capital dominating not only in industry but also in banking and agriculture, and given the collaborationist policies of labor's CTM with the national and foreign bourgeoisies, it is unlikely that this picture of misdevelopment will change short of another revolution—that is, a successful one.

When labor has chosen to rebel, as in the years 1958–1959, 1960, and 1962, when over sixty thousand workers struck, the national government has intervened and the U.S. Government has rushed in foreign "aid." Army troops were used to quell the crippling transportation strike of 1958–1959, as they were used to put down striking students in 1968. The government helped stimulate a recovery from the 1958 recession, provoked by the U.S. recession, by granting four-month tax exemptions on reinvested profits and procuring fresh foreign loans. In the first two years of the Kennedy Administration, 1961–1962, the United States committed $615.8 million in loans to Mexico.

One scholar has estimated that "no more than 200 or 300 foreign companies and 600 to 800 Mexican ones—many of them "Mexican" only in quotation marks—dominate the major part of the nation's capital . . . . two thousand families, strictly speaking, constitute the Mexican oligarchy" (Aguilar, 1967, 35). Citing official government figures for 1960, the same author proceeds to note the human labor and poverty base on which these oligarchs and their foreign counterparts build their economic empire:

—More than one million persons who speak only Indian dialects;
—Approximately two million peasants without land;
—More than three million children between six and fourteen years old who receive no education;
—4.6 million workers who, between 1948 and 1957, tried to enter the United States illegally;
—About five million Mexicans who walk barefoot and approximately 12.7 million who generally use no shoes;
—More than five million families whose monthly income is less than a thousand pesos ($80);
—Approximately 4.3 million houses, and twenty-four million people living in them, lacking water service;
—More than eight million persons who do not eat meat, fish, milk, or eggs; and more than ten million who do not eat bread;
—Almost ten million workers who do not belong to unions;
—Approximately eleven million illiterates. (Aguilar, 1967:84)

A further indication of Mexican poverty is the steady infant mortality rate of the last decade, around sixty-six per thousand annually, one of the highest in the Western Hemisphere. In other words, grinding poverty: bad housing, bad clothing, bad diets, minimal education, and inadequate income for the majority of the population. This misdevelopment is the "miracle of Mexican development" which commentators in both Mexico and the United States boast about when citing the high GNP growth rates Mexico has experienced since 1940.

Instead, the historic relationship between Mexico's dependent bourgeoisie and foreign capitalists has been developed toward a new miracle of imperialistic development. The remarkable influx of U.S. investment in Mexico, combined with the cultural imperialism manifested by the tourist industry, establishment of U.S. universities inside Mexico, and wide circulation of U.S. magazines, films, and television programs, "represents the success U.S. corporations have had in extending the border of the United States to include Mexico. The Mexicans are left with the unsolved political dilemmas of unemployment, unproductive agriculture, and depleted raw materials; the U.S. corporations reap the advantages of cheap labor and profits" (NACLA, 1968:38)—to say nothing, we might add, of the advantage of the beaches of Acapulco, where jets fly daily from New York and other American cities.

IDEOLOGY, COOPTATION, AND COERCION

Insofar as Mexico has developed further economically than many other Latin American countries, it is because it did not become bogged down in its stage of "enclave economy," epitomized from the Conquest through the Porfiriato. The 1910 Revolution and Cárdenas Reform loosened foreign controls over the economy sufficiently to permit the Mexican bourgeoisie to assert influence and control over key parts of the economy, especially in minerals and infrastructure, with the result that today Mexico can share in the fruits of imperialism over less fortunate Latin American countries, especially in Central America. Paradoxically, however, Mexico's economy, far from emerging into autonomous, sustained growth, has become increasingly stagnant, underproductive, and dependent upon the imperial metropolis. This is because the underlying structure of the economy and social system was, far from being challenged and altered, preserved and strengthened by means of the defeat of the peasants and workers in the 1910 Revolution and the granting of concessions to them in the 1930's. Since then, a complex and sophisticated system of carrot-and-stick rewards and punishments for the proletariat has emerged to provide conditions of political "stability" for the continuing aggrandizement of the bourgeoisie and its senior foreign partners. This system has been particularly effective because of the development of an appealing and persuasive "revolutionary" ideology based on the ideals and figures of Juárez, Madero, Villa, Zapata, Carranza, and Cárdenas.

How Mexico's centralized one-party political system actually works is a mystery so profound that every six years the greatest public excitement is generated around the question: "Who will be the PRI's candidate?" —not "Who are the nominees?" or "Which way will the three sectors of the PRI swing in their application of power?" Then, in the elections, the question is not "Who will win?" That has already been decided with the announcement of the PRI candidate's name, since the PRI counts the votes. Although minority parties are granted seats in Congress and sometimes run presidential candidates, an impressive majority of votes inevitably is tabulated for the PRI. Voter apathy is widespread, as even by official count one-third of the electorate abstained in 1970.

A normative model of "democratic" politics emerged under Cárdenas and has since become institutionalized. Peasants, workers, and the "middle class" are often under the impression that they *are* represented by the PRI through their respective three sectors in the party, even though all power rests with the PRI's national executive committee in Mexico's corporativist system. Also, each sector depends upon the PRI for political and welfare payoffs. Mexicans are cynical about this system and have a descriptive notion of it which conflicts with the normative model. In other words, they see through it and are disturbed by, although at times complicitous in, the widespread corruption which it generates (Castellanos, 1969). It is precisely this which underlies most of Mexico's recent institutional political crisis, which exploded with the student revolt and massacre of 1968:[5]

> "Political ritual serves to blur these contradictions, and to dramatize the moral conception of the system. The contradictions beween normative and descriptive models of a political system contribute to periodic, large-scale confrontations between specific groups or coalitions and the military or police" (Cockcroft, 1970:207).

The normative model of popular participation in the PRI and the revolutionary heritage of workers' and peasants' struggles are taught at every level of Mexican society, not only in the schools, where 75 percent of the population over age twenty-five have attended for less than four years anyway, but also in the government-controlled and privately owned press and in the political and social organizations, including workshops and farms. Such intense socialization serves to pacify the majority of the populace, make people proud of the nation and their earlier contributions to its development, sensitize them to the bloodshed and violence which those contributions entailed, persuade people that another civil war must be avoided at all costs, and in general assure people that the earlier goals are still being sought after, however gradually, and will be attained if the people work hard and maintain peace.

There are two reasons why this socialization and its corresponding ideology are becoming increasingly ineffective. First, the socialization process contains within it a number of revolutionary examples and sentiments which contribute to the gap between the normative model and

[5] On October 2, 1968, some fourteen thousand police and army units surrounded a peaceful rally of about ten thousand people in the Plaza of Three Cultures at Tlatelolco in Mexico City. Rally organizers, anticipating trouble, decided to cancel a scheduled march, but before they could disperse the crowd, the army and police opened fire with their automatic weapons. Conservative estimates showed forty-nine dead and five hundred wounded, but most observers on the scene estimate that five hundred were killed, twenty-five hundred wounded, and fifteen hundred, mostly students, arrested. Six members of the National Strike Committee were killed, as were women and children, in the massacre.

what people see all around them. Second, there exists within society sharp class cleavages and areas of tension which have been generated by not only the history of Mexican underdevelopment and foreign influence but also the increasing inability of the political system to pay off its constituents at a level that meets their expectations.

Mexico's class system is almost as sharply skewed today as it was in 1910, except that the middle class has experienced considerable numerical growth since then. A glance at the distribution-of-income figures at the beginning of this chapter makes the point. On an income basis, at least 65 percent of the population qualify as lower-class, while up to 20 percent qualify as upper-class. From 15 percent to 20 percent may be considered to be "middle-class." However, closer examination of Mexican society suggests that much of the middle class is in fact a poorly paid and struggling white-collar working class; that lines between classes are blurred; that cleavages exist within classes; and that the major gap in the social structure is between rich and poor, with much of the middle class falling on the poor side, even as was the case in 1910.

As throughout Mexican history, the class structure is conditioned by Mexico's dependent relationship upon a foreign metropolis. Thus, today, Mexico's bourgeoisie is neither autonomous, nationalist, nor progressive. Known popularly as "the coyotes" or "the oligarchy," the bourgeoisie is, like the Revolution whose rhetoric it echoes, so misdeveloped as to constitute the single most effective force for smoothing the way for increased underdevelopment and economic dependence upon the imperial metropolis.

Traditionally, two sectors of the bourgeoisie have represented different ideological emphases and goals within the dependent relationship with foreign capital. Some, generally smaller manufacturers organized into the National Chamber of Transformation Industry, have argued for high protective tariffs against foreign competition. Others, representing larger firms, usually "mixed" or foreign, and organized into the more powerful Confederation of Chambers of Industry, have argued for a minimum of import controls, thus encouraging or abetting the actual trends of foreign takeover of the economy with handsome profits for those Mexican capitalists who cooperate. In recent years, these two ideological positions have tended to merge into one, which ritualistically expresses nationalistic and independent sentiments but allows and encourages the process of misdevelopment and increased dependence to continue, in what one economist has described, approvingly, as an "alliance for profits" (Reynolds, 1970).

Like the bourgeoisies in Brazil and Argentina, the Mexican bourgeoisie is increasingly willing to resort to military repression to protect itself against rising protests from below of oppressed classes which oppose the "oligarchs" and their economic or political policies. When not resorting to armed force, the bourgeoisie employs nationalistic and "revolutionary" ideology to perpetuate its control and the nation's dependence. Anti-Communism has come to supplement, if not supplant, this ideological weaponry. Politically, the slogan of Cárdenas's Party of the Mexican Revolution, "For a Workers' Democracy," has been replaced by that of today's Institutional Revolutionary Party (PRI), "Democracy and Social Justice"—a "directed democracy" at that! Among some of the contemporary slogans are: "national economic development," a "consumers' economy," "fulfillment of the goals of the Revolution," "Order and Progress" (the campaign slogan of Gustavo Diaz Ordaz in 1964 and the motto of the thirty-year dictatorship of General Porfirio Diaz) . . . . and "One Road Only: Mexico," the last-mentioned a none-too-subtle swipe at Castroism and Communism. Thus, for example, student rebels are accused of being controlled by "outside agitators" from Havana, Peking, and Paris (Moscow being spared this dignity, at least until the spring of 1971, apparently because of the Mexican Communist Party's cooperation with the "Mexican way"); workers on strike are said to be "unpatriotic" or disruptive of the "harmony between businessmen and workers"; and Oscar Lewis's books on the "culture of poverty" in Mexico elicit the bourgeoisie's call for banning Lewis from the country since he clearly reflects "Yankee biases," is "anti-Mexican," and fails to realize "we've had a revolution here." This use of Mexico's history of revolution and nationalism to deny the possibility of internal faults, combined with the institutionalized practice of making the central government, especially the Presidency, sacrosanct and therefore beyond criticism, produces the phony kind of "intellectual freedom" that so many observors of Mexico have noted. One is "free" to denounce economic injustice and to call for revolution in other Latin American countries, but one must refrain from attacking the Mexican Government.

The more independent sector of the bourgeoisie, which in the 1930's and early 1940's tolerated or encouraged a 'populist' alliance with unionized workers against foreign monopolies and began to develop national manufacturing of its own, has by now become either out-competed or bought out by more affluent and technologically better equipped foreign capitalists. Today, this sector is well integrated into the junior partner-senior partner relationship between the Mexican bourgeoisie and the foreign bourgeoisie and, for its part, imposes a low-wage scale upon the working class, holds strikes down to a minimum, and enforces a regressive tax system which hurts the middle class as well as the lower class, while barely touching the wealthy elite.

Although part of the bourgeoisie draws much of its wealth from commercial agricultural production, which, stimulated by U.S. demand and the Mexican Government's large investments in roads, dams, electrification projects, and modern equipment, has increased six times since 1940, there is neither a *latifundista* class nor a rural bourgeoisie *as such*. So integrated have today's *neo-latifundistas* become with urban bankers, industrialists, exporters-importers, and real estate men, often one-in-the-same, and so active have they become in the tertiary sector based in the cities as merchants, owners of businesses, public functionaries, professionals, and, most of all, speculators in urban real estate and construction, that one sociologist has described them as a "rural-urban bourgeoisie" (Stavenhagen, 1968). The Mexican bourgeoisie gains its status and power by means of capital accumulation rather than ownership of land and exercises its hegemonic power inside Mexico from its position of monopolistic control of commerce, the distribution of goods and services, and national and regional political power. Non-foreign ownership of the means of production is concentrated in single families and groups of families, some of which hold national monopolies, and others of which constitute strong regional monopolies (Stavenhagen, 1968; Brandenburg, 1964; Aguilar, 1967; NACLA, 1968).

Politically, the bourgeoisie shares its power with a growing but small segment of the middle class. Officially, the middle class constitutes one of the three sectors of the PRI and is organized into the Confederación Nacional de Organizaciones Populares (CNOP). Through a complex system of influence-peddling, corruption, the "mordida" ("little bite," or bribe), provision of government housing and social security benefits, distribution of seats in Congress and local óffices, the possibility of promotions within the huge state bureaucracy, cooptation of dissident intellectuals and professionals by means of lucrative or prestigious appointments in government ministries or the education system, and, in many cases, provision of high-status jobs with an income adequate for employing domestic servants and buying fancy, American-looking consumer goods, the upper portions of the middle class have come to share the dominant values and conservative political role of the bourgeoisie. The same political system and its mythology of providing for the people "have given to the lower middle class and even to some people in the lower class the feeling that it is possible for them to better themselves, but within the system and according to its rules." (Hernández, 1970:42) However, there is a significant gap in status and income between high-level bureaucrats and professionals, on the one hand, and the vast majority of the middle class, mostly bureaucrats and low-paid professionals, on the other hand. As Hernández points out:

"The fact remains that, although individual mobility by individuals is permitted, mobility as a group is not, because such mobility in Mexico would radically alter the shape of the political pyramid. Consequently, if any group pressure begins to build up anywhere in the politico-economic system, sharp measures are taken in order to counteract those trends." (Hernández, 1970: 42)

Most of the middle class has developed as a result of the rapid growth of production and employment in the tertiary sector of the economy, which in the last three decades, has shown far higher per-capita-production growth rates than either agriculture or industry. Industry is capital-intensive, for the most part, so that the increased urbanization Mexico has experienced in the last thirty years has not seen many rural migrants becoming industrial workers (vertical mobility) but rather household servants, launderwomen, prostitutes, lottery salesmen, errand boys, street vendors, lumpenproletarian slumdwellers, and so on (horizontal mobility). Many of these migrants show up in per-capita production figures for the tertiary sector. The more productive middle-class part of the tertiary sector itself is highly skewed between a small and relatively affluent top layer and a broad, austere-living bottom layer (including the petty bourgeoisie of small shopkeepers), hard pressed by inflation and the wage-price squeeze. That this is the case is again reflected in the income-distribution figures, where we observe that 80 percent of the economically active population have been receiving either declining real income or not enough to meet the minimum needed for food, clothing, and housing, and, in comparison with the top 20 percent of the population, have been receiving a lower portion of total personal income than in the past, or else making only insignificant gains.

Portions of this broad bottom layer of the middle class participated in the public demonstrations of 1968 against the government, as a surprisingly large number of government employees came out of the office buildings in Mexico City to join the hundreds of thousands of protesting marchers. Besides feeling longstanding grievances deriving from their having plateaued at too low a level of prosperity to meet their expectations, many civil servants were indignant and bitter at the spectacle of their government spending large sums of money for the pleasure of foreigners, hiking Olympic prices beyond their ability to pay, officially asking them not to take vacations during the Olympic games, and then shooting and killing hundreds of students and non-students, men, women, and children, at the Plaza of Three Cultures on October 2, after so many of them had marched and protested silently, non-violently, and with great "dignidad" (an especially sensitive word in the Mexican lexicon— "dignity").

The rural middle class, smaller than that in the cities, also tends to be divided between affluent and austere. All of rural society, even within classes, is highly stratified, with each upper-most layer tending to exploit the layers immediately below it. For example, small private farmers who do not qualify as large landholders are generally at the mercy of the rural (-urban) bourgeoisie for credits, supplies, and political and social status, and yet in turn exploit less prosperous small farmers and *ejidatarios* who often become their labor force at planting and harvest time. Similarly, the few prosperous *ejidatarios* whose income and standard of living make them "middle-class" exploit their less prosperous brothers and sisters and the landless work force. However, most independent farmers are poor and fall on the austere side of the intra-middle-class divide. Two-thirds of private farms are smaller than five hectares in size and account for only 1.3 percent of the total land held by private farmers. In other words, they are small subsistence farms at best and quite unlike the prosperous middle-class "family farming" which some earlier advocates of agrarian reform envisioned (Stavenhagen, 1968:16). Only a small portion of the rural population, many of them middlemen and in the tertiary sector, reach the affluent side of the middle class, and they are usually mestizo, not Indian, men, not women, and often are connected with foreign or Mexican capitalist employers or else government banks and regional political machines. The more acquisitive of them soon qualify as a "bureaucratic bourgeoisie," linked on an income level, as well as in other ways, including corruption, to "the oligarchy." They are the rural counterparts to the urban "bureaucratic bourgeoisie," that is, the highest echelons of the state and corporate bureaucracy.

As in the case of other Latin American countries, although on a smaller scale, there is a significant brain drain from Mexico to advanced capitalist countries, especially the United States. Between 1966 and 1968, about 20 percent of all graduates in engineering left Mexico, while from 1961 to 1965, some 8 percent of all medical-school graduates went to the United States. The Rockefeller Foundation spent $2 million in Mexican projects in 1967, much of the money going to scholarships and professional training (NACLA, 1968). The drain of income and skills caused by this out-migration of professionals contributes to Mexico's underdevelopment. Those not emigrating often limit their services to the wealthy elite and private, often foreign, corporations. Mexico suffers extreme shortages in all areas of skilled labor, from engineers to skilled workmen.

In addition to political, economic, and social differences separating a small, affluent middle class and the upper class from the austere lower middle class and the proletariat, there exist gross differences in the standards of living between the city and the countryside, which have led one scholar to refer to Mexico's "lopsided revolution" (González Navarro, 1965). As per capita income and other statistics indicate, the countryside is much worse off than the cities. A 1963 survey revealed that 65 percent of the average expenses for an urban family and 84 percent for a peasant family go to basic food supplies, in either case an indication of poverty (Aguilar, 1967:109). Underemployment affects much of the rural populace. According to one front-page story of a local newspaper in Saltillo, Coahuila, in early 1971, statistics indicated that of fifteen million laborers in Mexico some six million are unemployed. There are no official figures on unemployment in Mexico, but estimates range as high as between thirty and forty percent. Two-thirds of these unemployed are in the countryside. Even allowing for error in any and all statistics, the anticipated growth in Mexico's population by another twenty million over the next decade is, at best, ominous in terms of likely increased mass unemployment. Over half the economically active population in agriculture has no land whatsoever. Rural poverty is so abject and the number of landless peasants is growing so rapidly that land invasions have become commonplace, leading to the coining of the word "paracaidista," or "parachutist," for one who moves onto a piece of [neo-latifundista] land to farm it for himself.

When peasants have massed and collectivized these land invasions for self-survival, they have usually been driven back off the land by the Army or the landholders' hired *pistoleros*. In many respects, the poverty, violence, internal migration, and class warfare in rural Mexico are as intense today as they were at the end of the Díaz regime. One independent peasant leader, his pregnant wife, and his three sons were murdered near their home by soldiers in 1962 to set an example for other peasants who might think of following his example. Although that incident received national publicity, there are scores of other such incidents which receive no publicity whatsoever. The official peasant organization Confederación Nacional Campesina (CNC), founded during the Cárdenas administration, usually condemns or denies the occurrence of these land invasions, but this only serves to widen the gap between CNC leaders and rank-and-file members. Yet the incorporation of many Mexican peasants, especially the *ejidatarios*, into the CNC has led to their political control by the government, upon which *ejidatarios* in turn depend for credits. As in the case of the CTM for urban labor, so with the CNC—the PRI's sectoral organization is a corporativist device for preventing working-class constituencies from acting as independent pressure groups or from uniting with each other, and thereby contributes no small amount to Mexico's fragile "stability."

Much of the agrarian problem derives from the "counter-agrarian-reform" of President Miguel Alemán in 1946, when limitations on size of landholdings were relaxed to favor capitalist agriculture. Legal sizes of landholdings were extended to a range of from 100 to 300 hectares, depending on climatic and other conditions, while legal protection from undue confiscation was assured all private landholders; in addition, incentives were granted them for improving their farming techniques. Former Secretary of Education Narciso Bassols complained in 1947: "our disagreement does not have to do with guarantees for truly small properties but rather with the mask behind which such nomenclature tends to allow the nationwide multiplication of forms of land monopolization and capitalist exploitation of land, with the evils which that fatally causes in the subsistence farming of a peonage system" (cited in Stavenhagen, 1968: 71–72). It is perhaps no coincidence that Alemán has engaged in many business ventures with U.S. capitalists, including the Continental Hilton Hotel in Mexico City.

Ever since Alemán's regime, *ejidatarios* have grown poorer and more disheartened. Most of their lands are grazing lands and forests; most *ejidos* have little or no irrigation; and most *ejidos* have split up into functionally, if not legally, tiny private parcels. Any semblance of "communal" farming could disappear altogether in the near future. In the few cases of *ejidos* having well irrigated lands, normally for export crops, the *ejidatarios* are as productive as any of their competitors. In general, however, *ejidatarios* have been forced—through their relegation to the bottom of the agrarian heap with the landless, the refusal of banks to advance them credits, the National Ejidal Bank's taking over of their lands and labor-power in commercial crops, the corruption of civil servants, the emergence of compromised *ejidal* caciques linked with outside interests, and their own poverty—to rent out their parcels and/or join the majority of the rural population as *de facto* landless peasants, underemployed day laborers, and migrant farm workers. Of those peasants who still hold land, whether a tiny parcel of an *ejido*, or a private plot, about 85 percent qualify as impoverished *minifundistas*—subsistence farmers not able even to make enough income off their land to feed their own families (Stavenhagen, 1968: 26). Adding the 3.3 million landless peasants (1960 census) to their numbers, we may safely conclude that a very small percentage indeed of the rural populace benefits from the impressive production statistics of Mexico's booming agribusiness, or *neo-latifundismo*.

Landless peasants are not organized in any significant way, except as day laborers or migrant workers trucked like cattle from time to time and place to place. The CNC is reluctant to organize them, and some CNC members consider them troublemakers of the worst kind. Occasional radical peasant leaders try organizing them, which often leads to serious confrontations in the countryside. Such independent peasant leaders, when not murdered, are usually incarcerated indefinitely. Others, like Jacinto López of the late Lombardo Toledano's small Socialist party, which cooperates with the PRI ordinarily, are coopted by promises to their constituencies and a seat in Congress. Peasant leagues are easily coopted once their leaders are coopted, since they typically have "a shortage of personnel who can become effective leaders, and, often, due to an authoritarian organization structure, the leaders can bring the membership with them" (Cockcroft, 1970:202). On the other hand, the government lacks the resources with which to pay off coopted peasants, short of a complete agrarian reform. Lopez, for this reason, or because of his followers' disillusionment or his personal dissatisfaction with being a national congressman, resigned in 1969 from Lombardo Toledano's party to lead a new, independent agrarian movement. He died shortly thereafter.

Many of the landless may be viewed as a marginal underclass and a "reserve army of the unemployed." Others, together with *ejidatarios* and private *minifundistas,* may be viewed as internal colonies, especially in Southern and Eastern Mexico, serving the sub-metropolises (e.g. provincial capitals) and the metropolitan centers (e.g. Mexico City and major U.S. cities). These internal colonies are often further exploited along racial lines, mestizos over Indians.

With the increased migration to the cities, the size of the urban proletariat has grown considerably since the days of Cárdenas. Employed, unionized workers in the CTM politically, if not economically, constitute a "labor aristocracy," especially in their leadership ranks. Younger, rank-and-file union members are increasingly fed up with the older, corrupt CTM leadership, however, and some CTM members joined the student demonstrations of 1968 against their leaders' commands. A vast number of employed workers are not even unionized. A significant portion of the working class is underemployed or unemployed and constitutes a lumpenproletariat, still unorganized but, together with the rural poor, representing the kind of social dynamite observed in the *tumultos* of colonial times. From 1950 to the present, of all segments of the Mexican population, the poorest 20 percent have suffered by far the most substantial decline in real income, while income distribution generally has grown increasingly unequal. Separated, except for kinship ties, from rural families from which they have migrated, the majority of Mexico's urban workers seem unable to act alone to change the system which oppresses them. If Mexico is to change for the better, urban workers will have to form coalitions with other groups—rural workers, disgruntled lower-middle-class elements, and, perhaps, students.

As shown in 1968, there is a growing tendency in Mexico for youth, especially students, to draw together as a group having a kind of "class consciousness" of its own which transcends class lines as otherwise manifested by income levels, type of employment, and society's ascribed status. For example, in 1968, the student movement erupted at first because of internal squabbles among students. But these conflicts were quickly surpassed by unprecedented student unity across class lines when the police and Army intervened. Students at the National University, who come from upper- and middle-class families, united with students from vocational high schools, who come from the working class and against whom the Army struck its most severe blows. Younger workers and peasants, as well as bureaucrats, eventually joined in this expanding coalition across class lines.

What united young people, including growing numbers of young clergy, was a shared value system—extending to even a sense of international youth community—which exalts honesty, freedom, and sharing, as opposed to the hypocrisy, authoritarianism, and selfishness of the social system in which they live. Socialized and educated in an inspiring nationalistic mythology of Juárez, Zapata, and Cárdenas, Mexican youth "see their leaders following policies which are diametrically opposed to the professed ideals. . . . The trouble with the students is that they believe in the ideals they have been taught, and many of them want to rescue these ideals from their 'safe' entombment as statues, names of plazas and boulevards, and neon-lit slogans on walls" (NACLA, 1968:5). In a personally freer situation than peasants or workers, and conscious of the dangers of cooptation, students are not easily coopted. If a leader is coopted, he is quickly condemned by other students, many of whom are qualified to take his place.

As in the case of the problem of poverty, so in the case of Mexican youth—one of the world's highest population growth rates is exacerbating structural imbalances in a way which makes it harder and harder for young Mexicans to get jobs. For National University students, there is not sufficient rotation of elites to permit them all to join the already crowded upper branches of the establishment. On the contrary, they are beginning to emerge as a potential "counter-elite"; some of them, in fact, declass themselves to become full-time revolutionary organizers. Poorly paid graduates of the vocational schools are faced with a rising cost of living and a fixed role which they are programmed to fulfill but which does not satisfy them either materially or spiritually. Robert F. Smith suggests that vocational students may harbor resentment too because of their having their expectations in the midst of growing opulence shattered by reality and a "new awareness of deprivation" (NACLA, 1968:5). It was perhaps no coincidence that the October 2 massacre occurred at the site of a large, low-income housing project, surrounded by slums, at a time when workers were marching into the Plaza of Three Cultures to join the students, when the revolt had spread to almost all the provinces, when peasants had kicked out government authorities at Topelejo (thus, the slogan, "two, three, many Topelejos")—in brief, at a time when not only the holding of the Olympic Games but also the survival of the government itself was threatened by a nascent multi-class coalition.

What, then, are the prospects for the future development of Mexico? As we have seen since 1959, the ruling bourgeoisie will resort to force to suppress significant student, peasant, worker, or multi-class protest. The Mexican Army, well supplied by the international arms market led by the United States, represents a serious obstacle to development. In addition to its repressive role, the Army constitutes a political power bloc in its own right. In fact, there exist two parallel structures of political power and influence in Mexico: the PRI, and the military. With isolated exceptions, the head of the PRI has always been selected from the officer corps of the Army. Almost one-fifth of the Cabinet was composed of military men during the last Presidency. In addition, Mexico is divided into various *zonas militares,* which receive their orders from the Secretary of Defense. No state governor is permitted to give orders to the "jefe" of the *zona militar,* who has relative autonomy of power, especially in matters of "social unrest."

A third power bloc which has emerged under the auspices of the state political machinery is the panoply of secret-service and police agencies, intelligence networks, and paramilitary units, linked traditionally to the Secretary of the Interior (Gobernación), who has become President in the last two national elections. The reputed connection between the Secretaries of the Interior and Foreign Relations and the CIA was cause for an international scandal recently when the Cubans exposed an alleged CIA agent working in the Mexican Embassy in Havana. At the time, today's President Echeverría was Secretary of the Interior and was seriously implicated in the case, much to the detriment of his bid for the Presidency. Early in 1971 the new President unveiled a "Communist plot" to overthrow the government, linked to training centers in Moscow and North Korea, but many Mexicans suspected that the "plot," if any, was as likely one of the CIA engineered to slow up the Soviet Union's trade offensive in Latin America and to justify continued jailing of Mexican leftists. When a few months later thousands of students and workers took to the streets to insist once again on basic political rights and the release of all political prisoners, eleven were murdered and over two hundred wounded in what reporters on the scene described as a combined armed attack by the police and a right-wing terrorist group known as "los Halcones," or, "the Hawks." Thirty-five of the demonstrators "disappeared."

The parallels to the 1968 massacre were obvious to all, except for one thing. Now an overtly fascistic group, the Hawks, working for the government and paid by it, recruited from "lumpen" elements, and trained in the most savage techniques of beating, torturing, and killing, was being given free reign to terrorize the populace. This group is suspected by many to be the inspiration of the CIA, as are other such groups in the rest of Latin America which emerged as exceedingly strong and ruthless forces throughout the 1960's. In operation throughout Mexico, the Hawks have been especially active in the Mexico City area—as have other similar para-military, right-wing goon squads. The CIA and the FBI are allowed to function in Mexico, and not only at the international airport to harass travellers to Cuba. The FBI operates in Mexico City and the provinces as well. All these forces of surveillance and murder do not yet operate in the monolithic fashion that they do in military dictatorships like those of Haiti, the Dominican Republic, Guatemala, Brazil, or Chile, but they are available to deter independent Mexican efforts at reform and development. They certainly give the lie to Mexican claims of independence from the United States.

Needs are growing in the basic areas of food, health, education, and housing. Urbanization and industrialization have served the goals of an oligarchy, but have not provided sufficient "trickle-down" benefits to the masses. Two-thirds of industry operates at a level below capacity. Yet the infrastructure and industrial bases for development exist in Mexico at a level beyond other Latin American countries. Similarly, although most of Mexico is arid or semi-arid land divided by jagged mountains and unpredictable volcanoes, and the population growth rate is a serious obstacle to development, there exist relatively abundant natural resources —oil, coal, and innumerable valuable minerals. Technologically, Mexico still suffers a growing gap vis-a-vis the United States—but then, too much technology creates problems of its own, as has become evident with the present ecological crisis. As serious an obstacle to development as almost any other is widespread alienation among the Mexican people, produced by the many misdevelopments described in this chapter, especially poverty, corruption, the gap between promise and performance, and foreign influence. Particularly serious is the alienation caused by an institutionalized tradition of male supremacy, which not only perpetuates the oppression of half the population, women, but also creates commonly acknowledged problems in the psyches of men, caricatured in the popular comic book of the 1960's "Los Supermachos" ("The Supervirile Ones").

Mexico is in a state of prolonged crisis. The PRI itself is suffering many internal divisions, difficult to understand because of the secrecy of its "inner circles." Until 1971, there were over a hundred known political prisoners (including famous novelist José Revueltas), many of whom had been tortured, shot upon, and generally harassed. Heavy sentences handed them of up to 16 years, in an unconstitutional manner, caused the prestigious Rector of the National University, sociologist Pablo González Casanova, a known friend of President Echeverría, to ask for an immediate amnesty. By mid-1971, many of these prisoners, including Revueltas, had been released. Rector González Casanova, who was later replaced, viewed total amnesty as a necessary step to "strengthen the faith and confidence of the citizens in the present legal system."

But such faith is rapidly fading, and with good reason. After the massacre of students and other demonstrators on June 10, 1971, by the Hawks and police, the Mayor of Mexico City and the Police Chief resigned. Later, a new president of the PRI was named—an old-time liberal and intellectual. The press played up these and other changes as evidence of President Echeverría's declared policy of a "democratic opening" (*apertura democrática*). However, there accompanied these changes a series of military sweeps in the countryside against guerrilla bands and land-grabbing peasants, in addition to renewed goon-squad attacks in the cities. The southern zone of Mexico and the northern area of Guatemala had already become, in effect, an international free-fire military theatre of operations for the Armed Forces of Mexico, Guatemala, and the United States (including Green Berets), and the technology of another Vietnam War, including napalm (Mexico has its own napalm factory). In an incident that has yet to attract the world attention it should, Guatemalan guerrilla leader Yon Sosa was killed by Mexican soldiers.

In early 1972, the Mexican Government announced the death of guerrilla leader Genaro Vázquez Rojas, who had established liberated zones in parts of southwestern-central Mexico and had established a strong peasant following. While the last of Mexico's political prisoners from the 1950's and 1960's were being released, literally hundreds of new political prisoners were being rounded up by government authorities and thrown into jail without any pretense to "due process of law." The very phrase *"democratic* opening" spoke volumes about the previous nature of the Mexican political system—and whatever the opening, the jailhouse doors were clanging noisily behind it.

Forces for change and development are gravitating towards the development of another revolutionary upheaval, whether through widespread strikes and protests or through armed guerrilla warfare, or some combination of the two. A number of states have experienced localized and sporadic guerrilla warfare over the last dozen years. Urban guerrillas, some of them linked with rural forces, have engaged in a number of recent bank robberies and kidnappings, and have succeeded in getting some political prisoners released and out of the country. It is not likely, however that either guerrilla warfare or largescale striking and protesting alone will change Mexico successfully over the short run. The struggle will be long, arduous, and, in time, massive. The United States, as well as the Mexican bourgeoisie, will not permit "another Cuba."

So long as the United States remains bogged down in the Southeast Asian War, the Mexican bourgeoisie could seek to perpetuate its hegemony and assuage popular unrest through a new introduction of Cárdenas-style reforms, as President Echeverría has sought to do through his much-proclaimed and little-fulfilled "democratic opening." Even that stop-gap measure for sustaining misdevelopment is not likely to succeed over the long haul, given the extent to which the economy and culture have become tied to the metropolis and given Mexico's previous experiences with such "revolutions from above." Precisely because Mexico has had an earlier, bloody revolutionary uprising, out of which has emerged the present panoply of socialization, cooptation, political corporativism and overall goal structure, Mexico's condition of limited development and economic dependence can be perpetuated for some time to come.

The student revolt of 1968 may have initiated a new phase of Mexican history. On the negative side, it has provoked a rising wave of neo-Fascist hysteria and official repression on a scale unprecedented in recent times. Not even in the days of Díaz did a single massacre occur to parallel that of the Plaza of Three Cultures. On the positive side, Mexicans seemed in 1968 to be discovering new forms for expressing solidarity and mutual support, rather than mutual exploitation. Their profound sense of alienation and hopelessness, at first an obstacle to development, showed signs of becoming a source of energy directed away from knifings and homicide (one of the highest rates in the world) and toward individual fulfillment through collective effort. But in the future, that collective effort will not likely be the one about which the government preaches so much.

If Mexico is to really develop, that effort will have to be directed against the government. More importantly, it will have to be directed against the ruling bourgeoisie and those middle-class elements who cooperate with it. It will have to be a mass effort built upon some kind of truly nationalist and revolutionary ideology, of which Mexico already has an abundance. Ultimately, as throughout Latin America, the effort of the Mexican people will have to take on international proportions if it is to confront the final source of modern-day Third World underdevelopment: U.S. imperialism. The struggle to develop Mexico, then, as in the rest of the Third World, will be a very difficult and prolonged one.

JAMES D. COCKCROFT is Associate Professor of Sociology at Livingston College, Rutgers University. Before completing his Ph.D. in Latin American Studies at Stanford University, 1966, Dr. Cockcroft lived four years in Latin American (Colombia and Mexico). He is the author of *Intellectual Precursors of the Mexican Revolution* (Austin: The University of Texas Press, 1968; Mexico City: Siglo Veintiuno Editores, S.A., 1971) and, with André Gunder Frank and Dale L. Johnson, *Dependence and Underdevelopment: Latin America's Political Economy* (Buenos Aires: Ediciones Signos, 1970; New York: Anchor Books, 1972). He has published widely in scholarly journals here and in Latin America, and is presently doing research on comparative revolution, including Cuba, where he visited in 1969, and on the multi-national corporations and the "new imperialism."

STATISTICS

Area: 760,373 square miles.

Population: 48.3 million, of which 46 percent are under fourteen years of age.

Birth Rate: 44.2 per one thousand inhabitants (or 3.5 percent population increase per annum).

Infant Mortality Rate: 60.7 per one thousand liveborn.

Capital City: Mexico City.

Percent of urbanization: 56.5 percent of the 1970 population.

Literacy rate: 62 percent of the population over six years of age; 73 percent of males and 76 percent of females over age twenty-five have less than four years of education (1960).

Per capita GNP: 2 percent per annum, or $266 per annum, (1960–1970 at constant 1950 prices).

Degree of land concentration: Private farms of more than five hectares in size account of 46 percent of net agrarian income but only 7 percent of the population economically active in agriculture. Of all private farms, 3 percent are over two hundred hectares in size and account for 84 percent of land held by private farmers. Two-thirds are smaller than five hectares and account for only 1.3 percent of private land. *Ejidos,* of which over 90 percent are non-collective ones composed of individual holdings, constitute 43 percent of cultivated land. Of all land holdings, private and *ejidal,* 82 percent account for 13 percent of cultivated area. The *minifundium* (five hectares or less—an estimated half of such farms are one hectare or less) accounts for 86 percent of all agrarian units of production. Of approximately six million rural workers, one and one-half million (mostly *ejidatarios*) work their own lands, three million are landless and sell their labor power or are unemployed, and one and one-half million privately hold from .1 to 5.0 hectares of land. About 10 percent of farms absorb 94.4 percent of capital destined for machinery and equipment, while 90 percent of farms account for 5.6 percent of capital for machinery and equipment. Two percent of farms receive 70.1 percent of the value of agrarian sales. (Source: 1960 Census)

Newspapers per one thousand inhabitants: One hundred (but 47 percent of families do not read a newspaper—1964 circulation figures).

Distribution of Income: In 1957, 65 percent of families received 25 percent of total personal income ("lower class"); 19 percent of families received 18 percent of income ("middle class") ; 11 percent of families received 20 percent of income ("well-to-do class") ; 5 percent of families received 37 percent of income ("wealthy class") ; breaking this last figure down further, 2.3 percent of families received 24 percent of income ("oligarchy") (Source: Navarrete, 1967).

Per capita income in 1960 was $120 (rural) and $504 (urban). Surveys in 1956 and 1961–1962 disclosed that 67 percent and 80 percent of families (respectively) received less income than the minimum required for food, clothing, and housing needs. A 1963 study by the Bank of Mexico revealed that 29.2 percent of families received 6.1 percent of income, while 1.8 percent of families received 15.5 percent of income. About 30 percent of the total labor force is underemployed (Source: González Casanova, 1965).

A study by the Bureau of Statistics of the Mexican Government showed 31 percent of the economically active population receiving no wage increment between 1960 and 1965, while other wage increases were so slight that a total of 81 percent of the economically active population either suffered declines in real income or no significant gains (Source: Aguilar, 1967).)

Mexico's income distribution is less equal than that of India or Puerto Rico. The lowest 70 percent of the population has received a declining share of total disposable income between 1950 (31.6 percent) and 1963 (29.5 percent). The top 5 percent of the population has also received a declining share, although in 1963 it still absorbed 27 percent of total income. However, the next 15 percent just below this highest group has received an increasing share of total income, up from 20 percent in 1950 to 32 percent in 1963. The next 30 percent of the population has increased its share of income only 4 percent between 1950 and 1963. The implications of these figures are that families in the lowest 80 percent of the population have been either receiving a declining share of total income between 1950 and 1963 or receiving such a slight increase as to amount to no significant gains. On the other hand, the top 20 percent of families have either gained significantly or else suffered such a decline as to not significantly undercut their "top-dog" position (Source: Reynolds, 1970).

Racial Composition: Census data specify only Indian (in terms of spoken language), and 11 percent of the population is thus defined as Indian. Based on assorted cultural criteria, 70 percent of the population is Mestizo, 29 percent Indian, and 1 percent White, although enough Mestizos consider themselves culturally "White" to elevate this last figure to as high as 15 percent.

Percent of Government Budget for education: 12.8 percent (1967).

Percent of Government Budget for military: 4.5 percent (1967).

Percent of Foreign Exchange derived from largest export: Food products (sugar, coffee, meat, fruits and vegetables, shrimp), 35 percent (1968); cotton, 10 percent (1968, down from 23 percent in 1962).

Tourism (*net*, allowing for Mexican tourists taking money out) matches in foreign-exchange earnings all the above items combined (1968). After tourism, the second largest foreign-exchange earner is border trade (twelve-mile free trade zone along U.S. border). Of all trade, 65 percent is with the United States, from where come 85 percent of tourists to Mexico.

Trade Balance: Minus $779.4 million, mostly with the United States (1968). Of Mexico's imports, 80 percent are capital goods and primary materials for industrial production. Mexico has a $34.4 million favorable trade balance with the Latin American Free Trade Association (1969).

Foreign Debt: $3.5 billion (1970, almost double that of 1965), of which 60 percent is to be amortized over next eleven years. Payments of interest and amortizations equals almost 50 percent of export earnings.

Foreign Investment: U.S. investment in Mexico is $1.2 billion (1966), or 78 percent of all foreign investment (1957). Foreign capital, mainly U.S., controls, directly or indirectly, over 50 percent of the income of the four hundred largest companies (Sources: González Casanova, 1965; NACLA, 1968).

List of Presidents, 1930–1970. *

1930–1932	Pascual Ortiz Rubio
1932–1934	Abelardo L. Rodríguez
1934–1940	Lázaro Cárdenas
1940–1946	Manuel Avila Camacho
1946–1952	Miguel Alemán
1952–1958	Adolfo Ruiz Cortines
1958–1964	Adolfo López Mateos
1964–1970	Gustavo Díaz Ordaz
1970–	Luis Echeverría

* Except for the second President listed, who was appointed by ex-President (1924–1928) Plutarco Elías Calles, political boss of Mexico from 1928 to 1934, all Presidents were elected as candidates of the single official political party in Mexico, founded in 1929, which also counted the ballots.

CHAPTER 3

ARGENTINA

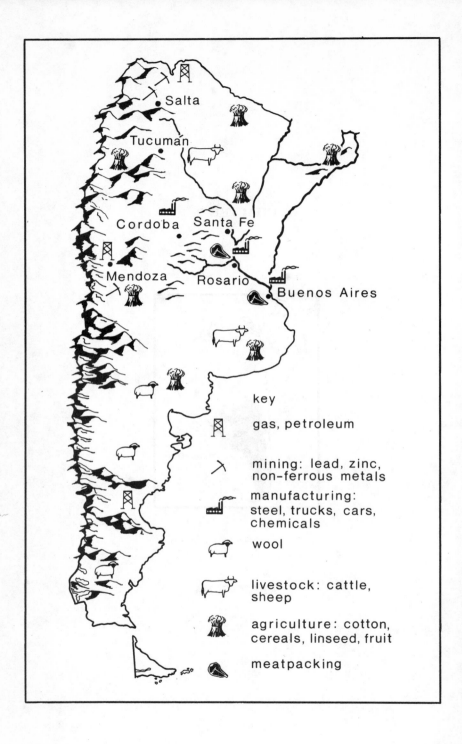

Salta

Tucuman

Cordoba   Santa Fe

Mendoza   Rosario

Buenos Aires

key

gas, petroleum

mining: lead, zinc,
non-ferrous metals

manufacturing:
steel, trucks, cars,
chemicals

wool

livestock: cattle,
sheep

agriculture: cotton,
cereals, linseed, fruit

meatpacking

CONTENTS

ARGENTINA

In a rock-stratum are embedded crystals of a mineral. Clefts and cracks occur, water filters in, and the crystals are gradually washed out so that in due course only their hollow mould remains. Then come volcanic outbursts which explode the mountain; molten masses pour in, stiffen, and crystallize out in their turn. But these are not free to do so in their own special forms. They must fill up the spaces that they find available. Thus there arise distorted forms, crystals whose inner structure contradicts their external shape, stones of one kind presenting the appearance of stones of another kind. The mineralogists call this phenomenon *Pseudomorphosis*.

By the term "historical pseudomorphosis" I propose to designate those cases in which an older alien Culture lies so massively over the land that a young Culture, born in this land, cannot get its breath and fails not only to achieve pure and specific expression-forms, but even to develop fully its own self-consciousness. All that wells up from the depths of the young soul is cast in the old moulds, young feelings stiffen in senile works, and instead of rearing itself up in its own creative power, it can only hate the distant power with a hate that grows to be monstrous.

Oswald Spengler, The Decline of the West,
Volume II, Chapter VII.

Una sociedad donde la mayoría es obligada por la minoría a sentirse minoría.

Luis Felipe Noé, Una sociedad colonial avanzada.

ARGENTINA

BY

JUAN EUGENIO CORRADI

INTRODUCTION

Argentines have always prided themselves in being "different" from their Latin American brethren. They are white, European, urbanized, well fed. Ortega y Gasset thought he had perceived in them an imperialist vocation, though he warned that Argentine grandeur rested more on promise than on accomplishment. He should have known: centuries before, Spanish grandeur had come to naught.

For decades Argentines believed they were a chosen people. *"Dios es argentino,"* they boasted. Chosen they were, but not by deities. British imperialism had elected the *pampas*—those open spaces they must have seemed from London—to supply it with foodstuffs. Argentina became a pampered, informal colony. Cattle multiplied, wheat ripened under the sun, immigrants arrived on the shores of the River Plate to gather the harvests, railways and ports gave up loads of produce to the world. Thus it seemed natural to Argentines to be exempted from the fate of their subcontinent—poverty. They did not know the laws of their well-being. Heedless of the artificiality of good fortune, they became prime exceptionalists and even tried to show others the light.

But circumstances changed in the world and Argentina was left behind. Argentines found to their amazement that they had little or no control over the forces that once made them prosperous. That is to say, they found that they were dependent. Before, they thought an elastic pie would get forever larger and everybody would have his share. Now there was less room. They suffered dictatorship and exclusion. Finally, grudgingly, they began supplying themselves with what the world had given them till then. National enterprise began replacing imports from the industrial metropolises. And so industrialists and workers appeared on the scene. The old Argentina refused to concede defeat, however. It clung to privilege with force, corruption, and fraud. Where one form of economic existence had prevailed, two modes of production now struggled for supremacy: the agrarian and the industrial. They made a compromise, and from their dubious wedlock came something misshapen:

a society in which an incomplete industrial system needed funds from an inefficient agro-pecuarian* structure. The creature could not grow without a constant protection from the State. As the different members of this body—classes, interest groups, etc.—were exhausted, the State began to maneuver and compensate for their weakness. So the slender body gave rise to Caesar's head, that paid off now one sector, now another. Just as the old agrarian Argentina had paid off a sizeable middle class during the apogee of exports, the new Argentina paid off the working class when international prosperity shone briefly during World War II. Caesarism turned into populism—a revolution on the cheap. Perónism added much but destroyed little: it was accretion not creation. The cumbersome system collapsed when exceptional international circumstances ceased to be and funds to underwrite the payoffs ran out.

Thereafter Argentines tried to dismantle what they had built and they could not. They tried to set the clock back and it didn't work. They tried cannibalism, but every major group was too strong to be wiped out. These once-arrogant people came to see failure as their central historical experience: failure to develop by themselves, failure to have confidence in each other, failure to understand the sources of their misery. A country of immense material promise, human diversity, and a spectacular past found that after all it was not that "different." Its more industrialized economy had fallen prey to stagnation; its resources ended up in foreign hands; its elites engaged in a type of politics that Argentines had scorned as suitable only for tropical republics. Dependency, stagnation, apathy, and political decay have been bitter staples for these erstwhile exceptionalists.

In some, the counsel of despair produced a preoccupation with explaining their experience as a failure unique to their circumstance. To others there is nothing unique to Argentina. But they view its failures *sub specie aeternitatis,* as containing lessons for all mankind, and for the advanced nations of the West more than for the others. It is, however, *sub specie temporis* and *sub specie regionis* that Argentine phenomena require explanation. Argentina is one of the most industrialized major countries in the Third World, but it belongs to that world. Its population is urban in a proportion higher than that in most European countries. The proletariat is highly organized and comprises two-thirds of the work force. This singular configuration has created forms of behavior and institutions not to be found commonly throughout the underdeveloped world, but Argentina remains a peripheral capitalist society, a non-metropolitan country, a Latin American nation. In their own ways Argentines will have to struggle against the same evils that beset other

* Pertaining to land and cattle

sister nations in order to do better than they actually do and find a path to rational development.

I. THE COLONIAL HERITAGE

THE UNEVEN DEVELOPMENT OF METROPOLISES: SPAIN

Argentine underdevelopment and international dependency have their roots in the colonial period, in the specific manner in which Spanish mercantilism affected the River Plate region. Spain's search for precious metals led to the colonization of Latin America. Different regions developed at different rates according to their ability to service the requirements of the mother country for natural resources and labor. During the fifteenth century, the displacement of international commerce from the Eastern Mediterranean to the Atlantic fostered the supremacy of the maritime powers on the Ocean and the Northern Sea. The discovery of the American continent—both a result and a catalyst of the world's commercial revolution—faced those powers with the challenge of directly organizing production by articulating capital and labor. The colonial territories were transformed into appendices of a system designed to pump wealth into royal treasuries. There were different means of funnelling the colonial surplus into metropolitan centers: royal enterprises managed by functionaries, indirect methods, such as taxation, and the participation of royal capital in private enterprises. The system rested on mercantilism and monopoly.

An important consequence of the agrarian and limited level of development of metropolitan economies was the restriction of exchange with the colonies to exotic comestibles, precious metals, and a few raw materials. Precarious means of transportation limited trade to products of high value and small volume.

The availability of natural resources and the accessibility to maritime routes of trade patterned settlement and colonization. The existence of exploitable labor was an essential consideration, and its supply was rendered more flexible by a large slave trade. The rigid pattern of centralization that characterized the metropolitan society was extended to the colonies. It prevented the formation of any class with strong local roots which would be tied more to local markets than to metropolitan interests. The situation in Latin America was the opposite of what existed in the New England colonies. Whereas in the latter production was organized by autonomous settlers in small and medium-sized enterprises geared to dynamic local markets and the division of labor became fairly complex, in most of Latin America, large-scale monolithic enterprises utilizing slave or servile labor and under the management of merchants and landowners with links to the royal bureaucracy, yielded a very different social and political order, characterized by rigid social stratification and external dependency. Under this system, economic growth increased the wealth of the metropolitan treasury and the colonial elites, but did not diversify the productive structure and did not develop the colonial economy.

Despite the creation of a vast overseas empire in the sixteenth century and its control of those areas until 1824, Spain itself was an economic dependency of Europe. From 1500 to 1700, Spain and Portugal expanded overseas, creating in turn dependent areas without much positive feedback. In the course of that process they failed to modernize their internal social and economic structures (Stein and Stein, 1970, Part One).

That failure was not, however, an historical accident. Nor was it the product of a peculiar system of values. At the onset of its colonial experience, Spain was an imperfectly organized nation, an economy oriented to the export of a few primary products, a society lacking a dynamic bourgeoisie. Centuries of territorial expansion, the Reconquest, the struggle against Moslem culture, had strengthened the role of a militant aristocracy and the church. The exploitation of the colonies made the restructuring of the Spanish semi-feudal, land-based, aristocratic economy and society unnecessary. The mercantilist expansion overseas in fact contributed to the development and entrenchment of the Spanish aristocracy, the bureaucracy, the service sector, and the church. As the economy—under the impact of capitalism—came to rest on foreign and colonial commerce, Spanish domestic manufacture contracted, raw materials were exported and returned as manufactured goods for domestic consumption and re-export to the colonies, while colonial gold and silver flowed to England to compensate for the deficit in the balance of trade. The acquisition of empire resulted in the proliferation of the patrimonial political structure. The military establishment was impressive, but Spain did not consolidate the economic and political bases of its might. Trade with the colonies was a monopoly benefiting the Crown and supporting large numbers of parasitic merchants. In fact Spain was the first "Latin American" nation in terms of most economic and social indicators. So acute was its dependency on other capitalist powers that by 1700 Spanish guild members were often frontmen for foreign merchants.

The aversion to manual labor, the importance of family connections, and the aristocratic life-style in general which so characterized Spanish culture cannot be tautologically derived from an alleged value system or national character. Nor can Spanish "feudalism" be explained solely in terms of its own social and political structure. These features of society are better understood in terms of the uneven development of capitalism, that is in terms of world-wide networks of dependency, conceived as a complex chain of metropolis-satellite relations in which each satellite "serves as an instrument to suck capital or economic surplus out of its own satellites and to channel part of this surplus to the world metropolis of which all are satellites" (Frank, 1969, 6). The colonial expansion not only laid the foundation of Latin American underdevelopment, it simultaneously reinforced the subordination of Spain and Portugal to the dominant capitalist economies of England, Holland, and France. Thus Western European, Iberian, and Ibero-American economies were interlocked by 1700. England became the dominant center of world capitalism—a process greatly accelerated by the industrial revolution. Spain, like Portugal, became an appendage of its colonies in America. The latter began to gravitate in the British orbit.

THE UNEVEN DEVELOPMENT OF COLONIES: ARGENTINA

From 1500 to 1700, Spain developed a colonial mining sector to maintain its economy and international position. Mexico and Peru became the main poles of colonial development in the fifteenth century. This development took place through private entrepreneurship in which miners, merchants, and the state collaborated and shared the profits. Miners and merchants in America, merchants in Seville, and ultimately the bourgeoisie of Western Europe reaped the benefits accruing from the extraction of gold and silver and from the exploitation of Indian labor. Those benefits also paid for the administrative costs of empire and went to ecclesiastical and secular officials. The export orientation of Latin American economies was shaped during this period. Large estates with a relatively immobile labor force, devoted to agriculture and ranching, were the principal sub-sectors of the mining nuclei. On the ruins of pre-conquest agrarian societies, the Spaniards built a mining export sector and a supportive *hacienda* system with catastrophic consequences for the native populations. Disease, overwork, and culture shock were the price paid by those people for the remolding of communal societies along profit-oriented lines.

The colonial world was characterized by a striking contrast between the main export and production centers and the backward peripheral regions. In the former, the growth of services and the concentration of labor, the royal bureaucracies and their personnel produced a civilization of administrative cities, military garrisons, and busy export trade. In the peripheral regions, far away from established trade routes and deprived of the natural resources coveted at the time, scattered and poor populations barely made a living on subsistence crops and subsidiary production for the more dynamic regions. The territory of Argentina belonged during most of the colonial period to these imperial backwaters. The predominance of the Pacific port of Lima-Callao in the export of Peruvian gold and silver impeded the emergence of Buenos Aires as a commercial center until nearly two centuries after it was founded (1536–1580).

The provinces—later the vice-royalty—of the *Río de la Plata* were among the less adapted of all Spanish colonies in America to the commercial and economic policies of the Spanish imperium. They counted among the last territories to be added to the colonial empire. They were removed from the already established highways of transatlantic commerce, poor in readily exploitable mineral wealth, and thinly populated by nomadic band societies. During most of the colonial period, the pulse of economic life in Argentina was faint indeed. The great *pampa* region was given over mainly to the hunting of wild cattle, an activity that could not be properly called stock-raising, since no systematic effort was made to improve the breeds or to commercialize the produce. In the colonial *estancias* cattle were hunted and slaughtered mostly for their hides, the only good that could be shipped to export markets. Tallow was also exported, and a certain amount of salted beef was sent to the West Indies and Brazil. Eventually, sheep-raising developed and some wool was exported. Here and there corn and wheat were raised, but flour had to be imported to feed the population of this *finisterre*. Despite the increase in the military and strategic importance of Buenos Aires, which in the eighteenth century led to the creation of a vice-royalty on the River Plate, the economy of Argentina remained rustic and picturesque, yet hardly productive. In point of fact, the socio-economic configuration of Argentina was, throughout the colonial period and well into the nineteenth century, the opposite of what it looks today. As men travelled from the Eastern seaboard towards the northwest, as they approached the silver mines of Potosí, they met with increasing activity and prosperity. Raising mules and producing foodstuffs for the mines of Upper Peru gave impulse to the local economies. But this stimulus barely reached the grasslands of the littoral. There self-sufficiency and economic stagnation prevailed. The large landed estate—the *latifundium* —was the dominant form of property. The fiscal and political needs of the Crown in this region of scarce resources resulted in large land grants to individuals.

Though land ownership was concentrated early in a few hands, land values remained very low until the nineteenth century, when cattle breeding and grain culture in the *pampas* came to meet the needs of European industrial capitalism.

From the beginning, the basic interests of the River Plate territory were sacrificed to the interests of the Lima merchants and to those of the royal treasury. Mercantilist policies imposed the total prohibition of commerce. An open port on the shores of the River Plate would have made the whole territory east of the Andes commercially a tributary to Buenos Aires. Hence, if those markets were to be preserved for the commerce of Lima, it was essential that Buenos Aires be prevented from developing into a transit point for imports from Europe. Moreover, from the standpoint of royal fiscal policy, the concession of trading privileges to Buenos Aires had to result in the loss of revenue through contraband and a negative balance of trade. Thus Buenos Aires was closed to all overseas traffic until well past the middle of the eighteenth century. It was also isolated from internal markets by tariff walls, that is, internal, or so-called "dry" customs, and restrictions on the flow of specie. The Argentine economy was all but strangled. In order to survive, the colony waged a surreptitious struggle against those policies, mostly through contraband. As the population and wealth of the colony grew those restrictions were challenged more often and more openly.

The administrative and commercial reforms undertaken by the Bourbons in the eighteenth century liberalized or altogether abolished many of the restrictive measures and opened the gates to the economic development of the *Río de la Plata,* and especially of Buenos Aires. The territories were at last in a position to utilize the advantages of the more direct route to markets through the port of Buenos Aires. Import prices fell and export prices rose. The province and the city of Buenos Aires were visibly at the head of the economic expansion of the eighteenth century. The province of Buenos Aires, and generally the *pampa,* was the most important producer of exportable commodities. The city now became the only port of a vast territory, the terminus and transit point of a large interprovincial and overseas commerce.

Yet Spain could not meet the challenge opened by the economic development of its colonies. It simply lacked the economic capacity to absorb all of the colony's produce and to satisfy the latter's growing demand for manufactures at a reasonable price. Spain functioned as an onerous intermediary between the River Plate and other countries, particularly England, which rapidly became the largest consumer of the colony's produce as well as the main supplier of commodities. The Spanish liberal reforms of the eighteenth century were bound to remain an empty gesture so long as Spain's economic advance continued to lag behind that of Western Europe and North America. Even the economic development of the colonies had outgrown the half-hearted liberalism of the Bourbons. Argentina, and Spanish America in general, were ready for a new pattern of dependency—a neo-colonial pact with the new industrial powers.

Technically, the solution was opening the port of Buenos Aires to all commerce. However, such liberalization of trade was hard to achieve without breaking the unity of the Empire. Opening the port was a direct threat to the merchant-monopolists, who, together with the crown officials formed the upper crust of colonial society. Conversely, "free trade" would directly benefit the non-monopolist merchants and the land-owning cattle breeders. The latter became an interest group standing for free trade and its preservation through political independence. Their opponents included not only the *peninsulares* and the monopolists of Buenos Aires, but also the producers of the interior provinces who had been protected by the isolation of Buenos Aires from internal and external markets.

II. NATION-BUILDING AND THE NEO-COLONIAL ORDER

INDEPENDENCE AND NEO-COLONIALISM

By the end of the eighteenth century, when the vice-royalty of the *Río de la Plata*—comprising what is now Argentina, Uruguay, Paraguay, and Bolivia—achieved economic importance, the Spanish Empire was subservient to British capitalism. Spain had regressed from first to third-rate power status. English vessels not only carried goods to Spain for domestic sale and re-export to the colonies, but began to penetrate the Spanish dominions directly. France—a less dynamic power—was also competing for control of the trade with the Iberian world. Interested in preventing the collapse of Spain, in 1700 France succeeded in placing a Bourbon king on the Spanish throne. This event inaugurated a period of bureaucratic reform designed to prop the tottering imperium. These reforms, far from constituting a "bourgeois revolution" represented a variety of defensive modernization which failed nonetheless to protect the empire from the massive encroachment of British capitalism. Those efforts most likely belong in the same historical category as the flurry of reforms under the dowager empress in early twentieth-century China. They came to naught as the end of eighteenth century approached. Spain entered a severe crisis, not just economic but political and military as well. It culminated with the collapse of central authority before the Napoleonic armies in 1808. On the other hand, Britain's industrialization demanded raw materials for production and a direct access to Latin American markets. The growing economic potential of the River Plate region had already prompted British interest, and in 1806 and 1807 the Buenos Aires *estancieros* and merchants repelled two British invasions, without aid from Spain. When Napoleon occupied Spain and placed his brother on the throne, Argentines seized the opportunity to force upon the kingless viceroy a document granting them free trade with England. This act amounted to a declaration of economic independence, or rather a shift toward a new type of dependency. It was soon followed by political independence. In 1810 the Buenos Aires liberals set up an autonomous governing junta. Six years later the *de facto* independence was ratified by a national congress. Representative government and independence were the ideological rallying cries of the *porteño* coalition of merchants and landowners.

A question that has troubled Argentines since at least the nineteenth century is this: why did two once-colonial areas, the United States and Argentina, develop so differently after independence? The question has often received fantastic answers.

By 1870 the United States had emerged as perhaps the second industrial nation of the world, while Argentina became a major producer of staples and foodstuffs for Europe. The compartive question is especially poignant since the environment in which the English settled was similar in important ways to that of the first Iberian colonists in the *Río de la Plata*. In both cases settlers hoped to discover mines of precious metals. Yet no mines were found. Even if they had been found, labor to operate them was not readily available, for West Europeans in the River Plate region as well as in North America did not have to confront or incorporate substantial Indian cultures. They pushed aside the nomadic Amerindian inhabitants, killed most of them, and isoalted the survivors on unproductive lands. True, Indians and the offsprings of unions between Spaniards and Indians formed a substantial sector of the early colonial population of Argentina. Since then, however, successive waves of immigration absorbed most of the *mestizos* and drove the Indians into remote parts of the national territory. The Indian of Argentina ultimately remained as unincorporated and forgotten as the Indian of the United States. At present, the combined Indian and mestizo population constitutes less than three percent of the national total. Agriculture was unknown among the Indians of Argentina except in the Northwestern part of the territory, where some rudimentary cultivation was practiced. Almost all of the indigenous groups were nomadic and depended on hunting and gathering as their primary means of subsistence. The population remained scattered in small groups.

The indigenous cultures were almost immediately changed by contact with the Spaniards who arrived in the sixteenth century. The most important factor in the change was the acquisition of horses that had escaped from Spanish settlements. The introduction of the horse created greater mobility and ease in hunting, which led to the formation of larger bands of as many as one hundred to five hundred people. They frequently raided European settlements well into the nineteenth century. Contact between Indians and Spaniards was primarily hostile. Sustained exposure to Western culture and techniques resulted in the defeat of the native populations and in the loss of their cultural identity. Those who were not killed in the final decades of the nineteenth century were driven into remote parts of the frontier provinces, and their former lands were converted into farms and estates.

In the 1830's, Juan Manual de Rosas, a *caudillo* who achieved control of Argentina for near a quarter of a century and paved the way for national unity, opened vast territories for settlement at the expense of the Indian population. Pushing the Indians out of the *pampas* was the historical equivalent of enclosures in Argentina. (Centuries before, the transformation of fields into grasslands for grazing sheep, as a result of the development of the wool industry, had thrown thousands of English peasants off their lands and condemned them to starvation.) And in 1879, General Roca, another Argentine strongman, finally "pacified" the Indians with the help of the railroad, the telegraph, and the Remington rifle. Genocide was carried out in several one-sided campaigns.

In seeking a basis for comparing U.S. and Argentine development, analysts are frequently led back to the European culture complexes from which English and Iberian colonists migrated and from which they borrowed their images of social organization. A "social heredity" thesis has been developed along these lines suggesting that, in contrast to Spain, English settlers in North America came from a modernizing England which generally treated literacy, tolerance, individual rights, entrepreneurial initiative, and capital accumulation as inseparable elements of the process of growth. There is some truth to these assertions, but they fail to provide an adequate explanation of different patterns of colonial development. For instance, they fail to account for the structural differences between the Northern and Southern settlements in the United States.

A more satisfying account stresses the so-called external factors in development differentials. Thus, due to limited agricultural possibilities on the Eastern seaboard, the Northern English colonies developed shipbuilding and mercantile occupations, while the Southern colonies created an export-oriented agriculture based upon slave labor—a structure not dissimilar to the Brazilian sugar estates of the seventeenth century, which became the prototype of plantation economies in the

Americas. In other regions of Ibero-America, production was organized on the basis of servile Indian labor in the mines. But throughout the Americas, North and South, settlement was guided by essentially the same capitalist goals. The difference lies rather in the outcome of the same capitalist input upon different natural and social environments, and in the feedback of colonial developments on metropolitan societies.

Of great significance for the development of the United States was the growth of trade with the ex-metropolis. By contrast, the Spanish colonies found neither trade nor financial assistance in their metropolis, itself economically weak and dependent. The growth and diversification of the colonial economies in Latin America was not accompanied by a parallel development of the mother country. The forces making for underdevelopment were at work on both sides of the Atlantic; on the one side the decline of the mother country; on the other, the distortion of the colonial economy—and capitalist dependency at both ends.

We can now reformulate the comparative question: why did Argentina develop in such a way that its post-colonial relations with the capitalist world became subordinate rather than complementary? Why did the River Plate region fail to play the historic role which the North played in U.S. development—a financial center for other agricultural regions and a supplier of manufacturers?

Indeed the similarities between the Northern colonies and the River Plate were many. Both regions were modern colonies as defined by Marx (Marx, *Capital*, I, 25). Both were characterized by a lack of mineral wealth and exploitable native labor. Capitalism was established in both regions. Population grew at a rapid rate in both. Both areas initiated an independence movement. There was, however, one crucial difference. The New England colonies had little fertile land—only forests providing timber for shipbuilding and a sea which was far more hospitable to economic enterprise than the land. To the West lay vast territories suitable for appropriation by a landowning class which could have been capable of living off agrarian rent. But by the time the Western frontier was opened, a society of small capitalists had firmly entrenched itself on the coast. This prevented the early concentration of landownership and the establishment of an agrarian aristocracy. Land in North America would eventually become accessible to ownership by independent settlers and immigrants.

The vast natural prairies of the River Plate, on the other hand, were initially accessible to Spanish colonists, who proceeded to appropriate enormous tracts of land and simply sat back while the natural multiplication of cattle increased their value. This class of landowners became the nucleus of an export-oriented agrarian bourgeoisie. Land rent became the historical substitute of primitive accumulation on the *pampas*: it was capitalist accumulation on the cheap. The landed bourgeoisie thus established a civilization of hides and beef, based much less on the productive labor of man than on the lavishness of nature and the demand of foreign markets. Dependency and misdevelopment were the prices that Argentina paid for the effortless enrichment of its ruling class. Cattle ranching, which was to become the backbone of the Argentina economy, was a productive activity that required little human intervention. At the beginning of the nineteenth century, one foreman and ten peons could look after ten thousand heads of cattle on the *pampas*. Cattle multiplied at a fabulous rate in the mild climate. It is therefore wrong to charge Spain with the responsibility of an allegedly feudal colonization by way of explaining Argentine underdevelopment. The fact was that the natural wealth of the *pampas* stimulated the growth of a certain neo-colonial capitalism with few labor and capital needs, oriented to the outside world and oblivious of the internal market. There was not an ounce of feudalism in this, but many pounds of beef.

CAPITALISM AND CLASS CONFLICT IN THE NINETEENTH CENTURY

The growing disparity in the rate of economic development between the various parts of the Spanish empire was accompanied by a weakening of the bonds that held them together. The political and social unity of the metropolis and the colonies, on the one hand, and of the several colonial administrative areas, on the other, became increasingly tenuous on account of that uneven development. These processes led to the independence of the Latin American colonies. In the River Plate, the groups which benefited most from the Revolution of 1810 were those connected to the grazing industry, overseas commerce, and the portion of inter-colonial trade which emanated from or passed through Buenos Aires.

Political independence opened the country to foreign trade, broadening the market for hides and other cattle products. Land appreciated in value, and cattle owners flourished. Commerce followed in the wake of grazing. The volume of trade increased and its terms became more advantageous than hitherto. The benefits were reaped by the merchant class of Buenos Aires.

The interior provinces, however, suffered from free trade. They had achieved economic integration and self-sufficiency behind the protective shield of Spain's commercial and administrative policies. They had attained a crude industrial development catering to the internal market.

After emancipation they could not withstand foreign competition. The Revolution of 1810 accelerated the economic deterioration of the interior. The provinces could only survive economically under conditions of fairly broad political autonomy as a defense against the economic encroachment of European manufactures pushed by Buenos Aires. Economic self-defense stood behind the federalist conception of state organization sponsored by the interior provinces.

The economic problem became a political contest in which *federales* fought *unitarios*, pitting states rights against Buenos Aires centralization. The program of centralization expressed the interests of those concerned with the expansion of overseas and domestic commerce: the merchants of the city port. They wanted to make internal markets accessible to foreign goods.

The cattle breeders of the province of Buenos Aires, on the other hand, relegated commerce to a subordinate position. They were interested primarily in the expansion of their industry. They wanted to monopolize for the province the economic gains of the Revolution and viewed with suspicion any attempt to nationalize the port of Buenos Aires and its revenues. These cattle interests sponsored a federalism which was not—as with the interior provinces—the expression of economic self-defense. Their federalism represented rather the particularistic supremacy of the most privileged province in the Union.

These deep economic cleavages made effective national organization nearly impossible for decades after the formal proclamation on Independence in 1816. Factionalism and political confusion were rampant. It was impossible to determine a new pattern of social and economic relationships and to anticipate a unified political structure. Moreover, the mobilization of the lower strata of the population, now demanding a share of the new order, upset the calculations of the commercial and intellectual elites.

At the beginning of the struggle for independence, the creole elite as a group preferred monarchical institutions, provided economic policy was modified. It finally chose a republican structure. Internal conflict was not resolved, however, by agreement on a republic. There still remained crucial issues: what kind of a republic: federal (decentralized) or unitary (centralized), presidential or parliamentary, popular or elitist, democratic or aristocratic, liberal or conservative? The conflict over political organization mirrored sharp differences over the existing and future structure of society, over access to and distribution of power, and over the course of economic change. At stake was the issue of who would inherit the revolution.

Not only was the elite divided along economic lines of cleavage:

for the first time the rural population, the *gauchos* and the farmers, as well as the middle and lower classes in the cities had entered the political arena. The nation plunged into a series of civil wars. At the root of these wars stood the central trend in the economic development of independent Argentina: the shift of the economic center of gravity from the interior towards the sea coast brought about by the rapid expansion of the latter and the simultaneous retrogression of the former.

The uneven character of the economic development resulted in a self-perpetuating inequality. The country became divided into poor and rich provinces. The interior provinces were forced to relinquish ever larger portions of the national income to Buenos Aires and other provinces of the East, which were quick to utilize their geographical advantage and superior capital means. In short, as Argentina became caught in the web of neo-colonial relations after independence, the flow of wealth was redirected towards the seacoast in what amounted to a process of internal colonialism. The satellization of the interior took place by a rather circuitous route: Argentina successively fell under the sway of premature centralization (unitarism) which overestimated the potentialities of the national economy, went through a period of civil wars and provincial autonomy, came under the hegemony of Buenos Aires, and was finally unified as a nation under the supremacy of the *pampa* and the city-port.

The half century after independence featured a triadic conflict between Buenos Aires, the Western provinces, and the riparian provinces of the East. The substance of conflict was bare. The revolution had linked the economy of the country to overseas markets at the same time that it separated the interior from areas of which in the colonial era it formed an integral part. So the economy of the interior was not only exposed to the devastating competition of overseas industries in the Eastern markets, but was also deprived of those markets in which European competition was least effective, namely Bolivia and Peru, which after independence remained outside Argentina. In order to offset the injurious commercial liberalism of Buenos Aires and prevent irreparable loss, the Western provinces sought political autonomy and interprovincial trade by means of regional treaties. They thus fought for a type of loose political organization that would guarantee their autonomy and at the same time stabilize interprovincial relations. Such was the programatic core of Argentine federalism: a movement that sought the redistribution of national income in favor of the interior and a better balanced national economy (Burgin, 1946, Chap. V).

The provinces of the Littoral, especially Santa Fe and Entre Ríos, resembled Buenos Aires in that they produced hides, meats, and other by-products of the cattle-breeding industry. Like Buenos Aires, these provinces depended upon foreign markets for a considerable part of their income. Thus, whereas the Revolution of 1810 went too far for the Western provinces, it did not go far enough for the Littoral. Economic reform had not gone beyond the opening of Buenos Aires to foreign commerce. These provinces rebelled against the stifling supremacy of Buenos Aires, which had monopolized the economic gains of the revolution. They wanted direct contact with foreign markets—a practicable program, since the rivers of the Littoral were accessible to oceangoing vessels. This bitter rivalry added much to civil strife in the decades following independence. The conflict took place not only between *unitarios* and *federales,* but also among the latter.

The unitary party represented the interests of a small and articulate class of wealthy merchants and intellectuals sponsoring free trade and liberalism. The *federales,* on the other hand, were concerned primarily with local interests, which varied from region to region. Therefore, they basically agreed on the desirability of home rule and on curtailing the powers of the central government, but seriously disagreed on a number of other issues. For instance, Buenos Aires federalists resisted the nationalization of customs revenues and their distribution *pro rata* among the provinces. They equally opposed opening the rivers of the Littoral to foreign navigation. The country was finally pacified under the dictatorship of Rosas, who became governor of Buenos Aires in 1829.

Rosas would, in contemporary terminology, be termed a despotic but also modernizing "nation-builder." He prepared the ground for economic and political reorganization of the country. He was a strong representative of the cattle breeding industry of the province of Buenos Aires—a Buenos Aires federalist. He presided over the federal reorganization of the country, which gave regional hegemony to the stronger provinces, such as Santa Fe in the Littoral and Córdoba in the Interior, and made Buenos Aires, as the strongest province, the arbiter of Argentine development.

Rosas' governorship represented not the unitary program of the merchant and intellectual elites of the city, but the power of the Buenos Aires cattle industry. The *unitarios* had been in power until then. They had hoped that with the help of foreign capital and European political institutions the country could be rapidly modernized. Their policies were rather premature and hardly corresponded to the social and economic realities of the time. They provoked the resentment of the interior and the suspicion of the cattle breeders of Buenos Aires. The latter instead proclaimed the principle of economic and political autonomy of the provinces, but insisted upon complete freedom in shaping the economy of Buenos Aires. This became Rosas' program.

For most interior provinces Rosas' government represented the continuation of the economic status quo. Buenos Aires continued to exercise control over the country's economy, it kept internal ports closed to overseas trade, and appropriated the nation's customs revenues. Thus, Rosas' federalism expressed the hegemonic interest of the most powerful province. Provincial federalism, on the other hand, expressed the desire of the interior to bring Buenos Aires under the federal control of the provinces.

The economy of Buenos Aires rested solidly upon large-scale cattle breeding and foreign commerce. Abundance of cheap land and free access to foreign markets were essential to the economic development of the province. The federalist party of Buenos Aires, represented by Rosas, rose to its position of leadership on a program of defense of the economic and financial interests of the province. It was basically opposed to the nationalization of customs revenues, the opening of the river ports to overseas traffic, and the protection of domestic industries in the Interior. Hence the tensions between Buenos Aires and the rest of the country continued under Rosas.

Buenos Aires federalism under Rosas was preferable to the rule of the *unitarios,* as far as the interior provinces were concerned. But it was still a selfish and domineering regime. Unlike the *unitarios,* Rosas formally recognized the principle of autonomy for the provinces. Moreover, his administration was extremely popular in Buenos Aires.

Rosas established a dictatorial regime by 1835, which, unhampered by parliamentary procedure, proceeded to take swift action restoring the economy of the province of Buenos Aires, shattered by wars, revolutions, and drought. His regime was very popular not only among the landowners and the *gauchos* in the countryside, but also among the meat producers, the artisans, and the small merchants in the city. But it was essentially a program of isolation from, and political domination over, the rest of the country, injurious to the most vital interests of other regions of Argentina. In order to realize such a program, Rosas needed the undivided support of his whole province, and lacking that, unlimited authority and power to use and dispose of the province's political and financial resources. His methods were contrary to the liberal tradition of the independentist elite, but they were in accord with the practices of the times. Post-independent political structures in Latin America shared by that time the same basic elements: strong executives and wide discretionary power. It was the period of unifying autocracies, which are usually associated with the early phases of political modernization.

THE LANDED BOURGEOISIE

Rosas seldom went beyond the confines of the immediate interests of the province and the class he represented. This was the class that would shape Argentine dependent development. Buenos Aires pursued an independent economic course. It disposed of the produce of its pastoral industries in foreign markets, and in those markets it satisfied its demand for manufactures and foodstuffs. Ever since the opening of Buenos Aires to foreign trade the province had been drawn into the orbit of the European and the North American economy. The province of Buenos Aires, home of the Argentine landed elite, found its place in the world market and was determined to keep it at all costs. It was a dependency of Europe and it satellized—when it did not altogether ignore—the rest of the nation.

Rosas was above all concerned with the prosperity of the pastoral industries. The central problem was the growing scarcity of free land. Twenty years after the opening of Buenos Aires to foreign trade, grazing was rapidly approaching the limits of profitable expansion. Cattle breeders were pushing southward into Indian territory in search for cheap land. Territorial expansion through military conquest of Indian land became the basic policies of Rosas and the ranchers. Within one year alone, Rosas brought under military control vast territories until then inhabited by Indian bands. He pushed the Indians south of the Río Colorado in La Pampa and Neuquén Provinces, opening up a territory which extended to the west as far as the Andes, and as far as Cape Horn, to the south. Some six thousand Indians were killed during the campaign.

Once control over Indian territory was secured, the government proceeded to transfer large tracts to private owners. Many Argentine *belles familles* can trace their origins to the land grabbers of that time (Oddone, 1967, V, VI). Why did Argentina not become a nation of farmers instead of producing this capitalist "aristocracy" of cattle barons? Here again, a glance at comparative economic opportunities yields some answers that do not hinge on the metaphysics of value systems and Spanish heritages.

In the days following independence, enterprising elites laid plans to populate the *pampa*, to expand the area under grain cultivation, and to make the province and the country agriculturally self-sustaining. Governments subsidized immigration, relying on private initiative and fertile soil. These considerations were deemed sufficient to insure prosperity to agriculture just as they insured the continued expansion of cattle breeding. But it soon became clear that domestic agriculture had none of the economic advantages which grazing enjoyed. Agriculture called for proportionately larger investments of labor, which was notoriously scarce and expensive. Secondly, methods of cultivation were primitive, and the yield was low in spite of the excellent quality of the soil. Machinery and agricultural implements were required. Thirdly, the high cost of transportation forced the farmer to move closer to cities where land prices were higher. Finally, unlike the cattle breeder, the farmer had to contend with an often ruinous foreign competition. The domestic market was small, and because foreign wheat and flour were usually of superior quality, domestic farmers had small chance to survive. Agriculture therefore continued to occupy a minor position in the expanding economy of the *pampas*. It only became important much later, when a landed cattle aristocracy was already well entrenched. Agriculture then developed on the basis of tenancy and share-cropping arrangements. The early and natural flow of capital into ranching produced something approaching a land monopoly and a powerful landed stratum. One must be careful not to assume that either of these traits was proof of institutionalized feudalism. A scholar not suspect of Marxist leanings puts it bluntly: "Argentine agro-pecuarian enterprise is free capitalist enterprise and always has been since the revolution and even earlier" (Ferns, 1969,124).

Public land was not only sold at low prices and in enormous tracts: it was also simply given away by the government in the form of land grants to friends and hangers-on. By 1840, Rosas had "liberated" public lands, assuring the pastoral industry a plentiful supply at reasonable prices, and had extended the southern frontiers of the province. Argentina became a paradise for *estancieros* and *saladeristas*: cattle breeders, meat and hide producers were the group that derived the greatest benefits from this regime.

Cattle breeding and meat production were export-oriented activities. A policy of economic laissez-faire suited these interests best. Their markets were abroad, and from abroad came goods against which the artisans, farmers, and wine producers of the interior could not compete. Thus large-scale merchants, cattle breeders, and meat producers were free traders, while producers who did not depend upon foreign trade fought unsuccessfully for protectionism. Industrial protection and economic nationalism were time and again sacrificed. Domestic manufacture seldom received an adequate stimulus. It never gained a foothold in post-colonial Argentina. Ranching was by far the most attractive investment, geared to a foreign rather than to a domestic market.

The economic greatness of Buenos Aires and with it the strength of the nation for many years to come derived from the soil. Buenos Aires did not raise the standard of economic revolt against Spain in the name of industrialization on the European pattern. Economic revolution and Argentine capitalism germinated on the pastures of the *pampa,* among cattle breeders. They were the class which ultimately propelled the economic growth of Argentina, and subordinated the rest of the country to its interests. Their role would change in the course of the nineteenth century from that of a particularistic pressure group in one province to that of a national ruling class—*la oligarquía.*

The Rosas regime consolidated the power of this class and prepared the ground for national unification. Rosas fell when his policies had outlived their usefulness and their historic role. The mounting resentment of other provinces and the mounting costs of his heavy-handed rule brought about his demise in 1852.

THE IMPERIALISM OF FREE TRADE

After the fall of Rosas, a liberal aristocratic Argentina was born which was the heyday of its glory on the eve of World War I, collapsed in 1930, and has been in agony since then.

Rosas was overthrown by a coalition of cattle interests of the Littoral and liberal bourgeois intellectuals, eager to work out a constitution and to establish a policy of modernization. The single most diverse issue was the place of the city and the province of Buenos Aires with respect to the rest of the country. The issue was finally settled in 1880 when the city of Buenos Aires was separated administratively and politically from its province, converted into a national capital, and so became the hub of Argentine society as a whole.

Underlying that issue was the relative position and power of the mercantile and financial interests with respect to the landed interest. It has been speculatively suggested (Ferns, 1960, 314) that, if Buenos Aires had succeeded in keeping its political independence, it would have been possible for its class of financiers and entrepreneurs to undertake their own independent capital accumulation and become, in other words, the nucleus of a national and industrial bourgeoisie. The province of Buenos Aires probably had enough resources and people, and the use of the harbor of Buenos Aires was intensive enough, to warrant the supposition that private and public internal capital accumulation and reinvestment could have taken place.

As it was, the landed interest under the leadership of provincial politicians prevailed. These were not national financial and industrial entrepreneurs but a class of modernizing landlord-liberals devoted to rapid economic growth of the market opportunities for ranching, sheep breeding, and grain farming, to the import of capital to develop the infrastructure of railways, docks, and commercial facilities, to the increased supply of labor through immigration, and to the further expansion of the frontier by building railways and applying the final solution to the Indian problem. They came to be known as the "generation of 1880" the first truly national ruling class.

The capital requirements of their project of modernization were so large that both the landowners and their governments became debtors of international finance capital: the governments to build railways and ports; the landlords to fence their land, dig wells, install Australian tanks and windmills, buy farm machinery, and acquire high-grade breeding stock. From the beginning, the British capitalists were the largest foreign investment interest. British diplomacy during this foothold period unerringly supported the more daring projects of national political integration, that is, the integration of Buenos Aires in the republic, and equally supported the more grandiose projects of economic expansion they knew were well beyond the capacities of Argentine capital.

In the end, saddled with a vast foreign investment, Argentina was obliged to export or go bankrupt, and this meant concentration upon a limited range of exportable staple products with all the social, political, moral, and intellectual consequences of acute dependency. An American rural sociologist put it this way:

A society depending almost altogether on an extensive production of cheap raw products is a slave of export markets, on the one hand, and the exploitation of its lower classes, on the other hand. It is, therefore, socially unhealthy, both domestically and internationally. (Taylor, 1948, 207)

The generation of 1880—a debtor ruling class—had the political power to assert its interest and to ensure its well-being. As opposed to other Latin American "enclave" economies, in Argentina the upper class secured the control over the principal means of production, even though the financing and commercialization of the produce were largely in foreign hands (Cardoso and Faletto, 1969,42-47). There was a certain degree of political autonomy amidst economic dependence. The dominant Argentine interests and their creditors often compromised with each other, shifting the burden of the compromises to wage workers, the middle strata, and the non-owning classes generally. Dependency was continuously negotiated.

And so modernization took rapid hold on the pampas. Within a generation, the social life of the country was altered. A striking feature of this change was the expansion of grain production which led to the emergence of Argentina as a major supplier of grain for industrial markets. Lands formerly idle or used for wild pasturage were converted to the tillage of wheat, corn, alfalfa, and flax. Crop acreage and production went up. Livestock products became a basic pillar of Argentine specialization in foodstuff production. Here again, technological innovations led to a marked increase in productivity. Successful experiments with refrigerated shipping led to the establishment of freezing plants to prepare meat for overseas markets. Since the demand for better grades of meat could hardly be provided by the wild or semi-wild cattle of the *estancias,* a true stock-raising industry was developed. Improved breeds were imported from Europe, and care and vigilance of these refined breeds led to the consolidation and rationalization of property rights. The application of new business techniques was eminently compatible with the existing system of *latifundia* and with the social order it had produced. In fact, the new wave of capitalism— now in its imperialist stage—on the *pampas* came to reinforce the pattern of land tenure and consolidate the power of the landed bourgeoisie. The developing livestock industry led to fencing cattle in ranches rather than to letting it graze on the open range. Further enclosures were made necessary by the intermingling of crop lands and cattle ranches. Much of the cultivation of crop lands on the ranches was carried out by tenants. Tenancy had been largely unknown in Argentina before. But now the growing world demand, the new dependency, the rationalization of production, and the inflow of external migrants rapidly changed the situation (Jefferson, 1926). Immigrants and their descendants became the nucleus of a class of tenant farmers, as share-cropping and other rental arrangements were worked out in order to develop agriculture in a context of super-concentration of property and rising land values.

Perhaps the most revealing feature of the whole process was the development of the railroad system, initiated around 1885. By 1914 most of the trunk lines across the *pampas* had been completed and a network of feeder and branch lines had been created. The radial pattern of the railroad lines expressed their true economic function: all of the major lines spread out from the capital city like spokes from the hub of a great wheel. There was little cross-linkage between internal points, since the vast majority of the goods carried by rail were destined for the capital city for shipment overseas. The peculiarity of the rail network helped Buenos Aires maintain economic and political hegemony over the nation, for the sake of export goods (Scalabrini Ortiz, 1964).

In this way the new Argentine economy was the product of technical advances in manufacturing and transportation which originated in the capitalist metropolises, and of an international system characterized by freedom of trade, movements of capital to the "open spaces," and large labor migrations. The modernization of Argentina, and perhaps even the nation itself, came about as the result of foreign needs and was implemented by railroads, steamships, and refrigerated shipping.

Until the closing days of the nineteenth century, the Argentine economy operated under a system of paper currency. Price inflation was a constant feature. None of the non-owning classes had any political power in this society, so they had scant means of resisting the effects of prices rising faster than incomes. There were, however, countervailing factors: labor—especially skilled labor—was scarce, and this factor pushed wages upward. If the upper classes used the hammer of inflation too harshly, then mass immigration simply ceased to come to Argentina. Thus compromises had to be devised with the lower classes as well as with the imperialist interests. The upshot for several decades was a moderately open, modernizing society. Variety, in people and opinion, was progressively tolerated. Social mobility was high. The world conjunction was favorable, and Argentina enjoyed natural advantages.

Historians discern four stages in the development of what is sometimes called, apologetically, "the free, open society of the landlord-liberals" (Ferns, 1969, 98): 1) an initial stage of integration into the international capitalist division of labor, completed in the 1860's; 2) a critical stage connected with the financial crisis of 1890-1896; 3) a "golden age" of high prosperity from the Boer War to World War I; and 4) a stage of maturity which ended with the international crisis of 1929. In brief, the first stage involved national political unification and the choice of dependent development through foreign investment over autonomous accumulation. This period set the foundations of national indebtedness since development of export agriculture and stock raising was financed from abroad. Argentine wealth was land. Investment in railways, or generally in joint-stock enterprises was foreign, and heavily British.

The flow of foreign capital began as a sustained process in the 1860's and continued almost uninterruptedly until 1890. The intensity of this flow was such that in 1888 to 1889 near half of the new issues in the London capital market were made on behalf of enterprises in Argentina and nearly a quarter of a million immigrants from Europe entered the country. During all this time more goods were flowing into Argentina than were being exported. In 1890 a crisis developed; the important London banking firm of Baring Brothers was threatened with bankruptcy on account of their Argentine accounts. The Argentine economy was simply not producing enough to satisfy all the demands on it. Such crises were familiar in the capitalist world before the first World War. In the Middle and Far East, as well as in other countries of Latin America, those crises led to gunboat diplomacy, that is, to a direct political and military intervention by the imperialist powers in order to administer the community so that foreign capitalists could be paid. The United States frequently behaved in such fashion vis-à-vis their southern neighbors.

In 1890, Argentine dependency on Britain had reached such intensity that the repudiation of debts was considered unacceptable to the landed bourgeoisie, tied as it was to the international market for commodities and capital. Having ruled out autarky, this class turned to the United States as an alternate potential money-lender. The result was disappointing: The Americans wanted to expand their share of Argentine markets but were unwilling to open up their own to Argentine produce. Moreover, they demanded special legislation to protect their interests, and they even wanted a naval base. This type of big stick imperialism from which other Latin American republics suffered so much was far less attractive to the Argentine beef aristrocracy than the subtler and more intelligent manipulations of Lord Rothschild. The British banking establishment offered better terms. Argentine agro-pecuarian production promised a growth of such magnitude that the country's mortgage of its future did not alarm the avant-garde of the London banking community. And indeed Argentine production of wheat, linseed, wool, mutton, and beef did expand enormously. The price of Argentine exports began to rise, the country resumed interest and debt service payments, and foreign investment was resumed in the late 1890's.

The crisis was overcome before the outbreak of the Spanish-American and the Boer Wars. The golden age of Argentina then dawned. Argentina entered the twentieth century enraptured in a dream of unlimited prosperity. To cite Victor Hugo: "situated in the moon, kingdom of dream, province of illusion, capital Soap-Bubble" (*Les Misérables. Saint Denis,* VIII, Chap. 3). Such was the mood of the times. Exports multiplied at a fascinating pace. The landed bourgeoisie and its commercial allies grew enormously rich and adopted a veneer of French culture and English manners.

LIBERALISM AND PROSPERITY

Internationally, Argentine dependent modernization hinged on a world market for foodstuffs unrestrained by tariffs, quotas, and controls. Between 1896 and 1914, the price of foodstuffs improved markedly, while the prices of industrial products tended to fall. Argentina bought competitively certain advantages in the international conjuncture but was to pay dearly for them in the long run. That favorable conjuncture began to change after World War I, was never restored to a state so favorable to Argentina as it had been before, and turned against the country after 1930.

Internally, two main factors made economic growth possible: a large supply of good land, and the availability of a large immigrant labor force.

We have already seen how, from revolutionary times onward, land in Argentina was distributed in large blocks to a small number of families. These possessed estates often as large as entire English counties. In 1914, 78.34 percent of all land was in farms which were more than 1,000 hectares (2,470 acres) in size. According to the census of that year there were 2,958 properties of 5,000 to 10,000 hectares (12,350 to 24,700 acres); 1,474 from 10,000 to 25,000 hectares (24,700 to 61,750 acres); and 485 with more than 25,000 hectares (61,750 acres). Some were more than 100,000 hectares (247,000 acres) (Taylor, 1948, 185; Oddone, 1967, 182-186). In the more remote National Territories, fewer than 2,000 persons owned as much land as Italy, Belgium, Holland, and Denmark combined (Oddone, 1967, 273)!

To briefly sketch the social history of the Argentine *latifundia*: some of them came into existence by free land gifts in a long period when land had little value, and the competition for landownership and use was slight; some of them came into existence much later—some as late as a few generations ago. Profitable cattle production made that land valuable, and so rich cattlemen became the nucleus of the upper class. Later they were joined by rich sheepmen, sugar-plantation owners, and some rich owners of cereal farms.

The history of tenancy, on the other hand, is the story of hundreds of thousands of European immigrants pouring into the country after land that had become so valuable that owners would seldom release titles to it for colonization purposes. They instead colonized it with tenants, or else employed wage labor.

The relationship between the agrarian classes changed with economic development. During the initial period of paper currency and loose credit policies (before the Baring crisis), inflation benefited landowners and working farmers and oppressed wage earners, since prices rose faster than wages. After the crisis, tighter credit and deflationary policies alienated renting farmers from landowners. The system of land rental and share-cropping worked smoothly as long as land was freely available and the international prices of produce rose faster than the prices of goods consumed by farmers and ranchers. When the external market situation changed and land became less available, tensions erupted between the landowning class and the tenant farmers. The latter swung towards the opposition parties after 1912 (Cortés Conde & Gallo, 1967, III).

Argentina became one of the principal absorbers of European immigration before the First World War. Yet neither the expulsion from Europe nor the attraction of the New World reveal the whole story. Given the prevailing ownership structure, the immigrants could hardly be expected to "take root" in the soil. Had it not been for the initial concentration of rural property, immigration could well have yielded a more egalitarian social system, based on family medium and small holdings as an offshoot of European societies. Historically, such systems have developed either by way of land reform or revolution, or through the colonization of farmlands carried out under governments in which landlords did not have a prevailing interest. One could speculate that such agrarian structure could have made agricultural diversification much easier when the impact of external demand ceased and when industries began to require a regular supply for the city markets. As it was, Argentina developed a feeble system of tenancy. It is worth mentioning that nearly half of the immigrants who arrived in Argentina in the period of massive intercontinental migrations returned to their lands of origin.

And yet the people of no nation—with the possible exception of the United States—are more thoroughly the offspring of European immigrants than the Argentines. The magnitude and impact of European immigration after 1853 has been so great as literally to remake the ethnic composition of the country. Between 1890 and 1914 over four million foreigners poured into the country. Many returned home after a brief stay, but immigration left a residue of about 2.4 million to settle permanently. By the eve of World War I, close to a third of the population had been born abroad, which gave Argentina the distinction of a higher proportion of immigrants to total population than any other major country (Germani, 1962, 197; Solberg, 1970, 35–37).

The movement of immigrants and emigrants into and out of Argentina was uneven over the years of recorded data, which began to be collected in 1857. The broad outline of the economic and political forces which attracted and repelled them is fairly well known. There were three crests and three troughs of immigration, matched to some extent by trends in emigration. The increase in the flow of immigrants was modest and consistent until about 1880. Then it began to grow by leaps and bounds. The number of immigrants increased from 26,000 in 1880 to almost 219,000 in 1889 (Taylor, 1948, 91). Immigration declined and emigration rose during the years of crisis and political instability 1890–1895. Then the upward trend recovered, and from 1904 until the outbreak of World War I hundreds of thousands of immigrants poured into the country each year, reaching high points in 1910 and 1912. It was during this period that seasonal workers moved back and forth between the harvests of Southern Europe and Argentina. They were called *golondrinas*, or swallows, because they migrated annually. In that way, Italian and Spanish laborers met a peak requirement at times of harvest without putting a strain on the system of Argentine *latifundia*. Gradually the mechanization of wheat harvesting diminished the migration of these "swallows." But out of the flux there were thousands who after a season or two chose to stay in Argentina. The First World War provoked a sharp decline in immigration. The third and last high tide began in 1920, and lasted until the *debacle* of 1930. With the Great Depression the process came to an end. External immigration, which shaped Argentine society in the era of agrarian prosperity, gave way to internal migration from the provinces to Buenos Aires as an essential component of industrial development.

Italians first, and then Spaniards, composed more than three-fourths of the immigrant contingents. French, Poles, Russians, Ottomans, Germans and Austro-Hungarians trailed behind. Reflecting the trend toward the near-monopoly of landownership by the native bourgeoisie, agriculturists constituted a steadily diminishing proportion of all immigrants. Day laborers, merchants, and mechanics constituted steadily increasing percentages and concentrated in the cities (Beyhaut et al., 1965, 85–123). This explains a unique and probably one of the most significant facts about population development in Argentina. The center of population moved toward the coast rather than toward the interior. The majority of the people in a predominantly agricultural country came to live in cities: over-urbanization in an agrarian society. Ecological disequilibrium resulted in a fan-shaped distribution of natural resources and population, with the hub of the fan located approximately at the city of Buenos Aires—an icon of outward growth and dependency.

Immigration provided a mass of laborers, some qualified personnel, and a small number of entrepreneurs. However, the characteristics of Argentine economic expansion, under British international control and under circumstances which left the basic agro-export structure unchanged, tended to channel entrepreneurial initiative away from industrial activity and into commercial and speculative ventures while increasing urbanization very fast. The upshot was a distorted social structure. Under the continued dominance of the landed bourgeoisie the social mobility of the newcomers ended up inflating a disproportionately large tertiary sector, characterized by a large number of unproductive activities. Immigration, therefore, furthered modernization but left intact the productive structure of society.

Several decades of prosperity seemed to support the development schemes of the "generation of 1880." Facts and figures seemed to justify the euphoria of the ruling class: population grew at a rate of 3.2 percent a year between 1869 and 1929; productivity rose at an average of nearly 5 percent; total capital increased at a similar yearly rate; income per capita jumped from 2,308 *pesos* (at constant 1950 prices) in 1900-04 to 3,207 *pesos* in 1925-29 (Ferns, 1969, 121). The national censuses of 1869, 1895, and 1914 reveal impressive changes: The 1.9 million residents of 1869 were joined as of 1914 by 5.9 million immigrants, of whom 3.2 million became permanent residents. The land under cultivation increased from 1.5 million hectares in 1872 to 25 million hectares in 1914. The railroad network was 35,800 km. long in 1914. British investment in Argentina increased from 5 million pounds in 1865 to 365 million in 1913. The city of Buenos Aires grew by 786 percent between 1869 and 1914. White collar workers represented 6 percent of the working population in 1869; by 1914 they were 21 percent—some 595,000 middle-class individuals, concentrated mostly in Buenos Aires, in a nation with no significant industrial base (Merkx, 1968, 79–93)! As wealth increased, politics were liberalized.

Argentina could even afford to misrepresent itself before other Latin American republics as a champion of the weak against Yankee imperialism. In 1890, the first Pan American conference was held in Washington. On the agenda was a project for the creation of a Pan American customs union, promoted by the United States on the maxim "America for the Americans." Argentina strongly opposed the project with the maxim "America for humanity." In those days U.S. imperialism had already begun to parade under the banner of Pan-Americanism. Argentina's universalism, on the other hand, expressed the confident defense of her dependency on England. The ideological conflict persisted until after World War II (Whitaker, 154, Chap. 5).

As the century came to a close, political parties of the middle class —notably the *Unión Cívica Radical,* or Radical Civic Union—emerged, trade unions developed, and the groundwork was laid for universal manhood suffrage. This period has been widely interpreted as one of development toward democratic gradualism. Such interpretation is made superficially reasonable by the fact that economic growth was followed by a decade and a half of domestic rule. *Post hoc, ergo propter hoc* arguments are treacherous: there are deeper reasons to suspect that the boundary conditions of Argentine democratization were narrow.

The first point to be made is that the process of change in Argentine society during the early part of the twentieth century can in no way be seriously described as "the passing of traditional society." Argentine underdevelopment is a concrete historical process through which societies that have already achieved a high level of development have not necessarily passed.

"Traditionalism" and "modernity" are terms that fail to describe Argentine social change. Argentina had been a dynamic capitalist society for at least half a century. The landowning class had long made the transition to commercial agriculture, in the nineteeth century. Landowners had been quick to exploit expanding export markets for their crops and to link Argentina to world capitalism. The landed bourgeoisie had called for, and received, capital and labor from abroad. Massive immigration, concomitant rapid urbanization, and even some subsidiary industrialization indeed changed Argentine society. But it was a different type of change from that which is typically construed by social scientists when they write about "transitional" societies in which "traditional" patterns are weakened. These metaphors are rooted in the specific historical experience of the European transition from feudalism to capitalism. They tend to hypostatize the internal change of past societies. There industrialization involved the transformation of peasants into industrial workers. The increasing hegemony of the bourgeoisie reflected the mobility of indigenous classes and the growth among them of role distributions based on achievement. Not so in peripheral capitalist societies like Argentina. Here modernization was not an internal transformation. It was rather a change induced by the development of a world-wide capitalist division of labor that pushed certain countries into the role of agro-pecuarian exporters. It then grafted onto the agribusiness nucleus an urban, semi-industrial, service-oriented society, literally from the outside, by means of external financing and foreign immigration.

Society thus came to be organized around a dependent export sector. After massive immigration and rapid urbanization, the productive structure of society remained basically the same. Modernization was superstructural, pseudomorphic.

An analogous situation existed in politics. New political parties—notably the *Unión Cívica Radical*—representing the growing urban middle sectors and some marginal agrarian groups, entered politics, as it were, from the outside. These parties embodied the demands of outsiders who had not been integrated into the land-based authority structure. Their strength was neither a consequence of the weakened power of the dominant class nor the manifestation of a superior mode of production. Their participation in politics dependent instead on the prosperity and self-confidence of the class of landlord-liberals. After 1930, when that prosperity and self-confidence were undermined by events beyond anybody's control in Argentina, the landed bourgeoisie did not hesitate to close the political system on the tacit rule of privilege: "last hired, first fired."

THE MIDDLE CLASS IN POWER

As export development reached sufficient magnitude, a middle class emerged which did not challenge the existing economic order, but demanded political participation and equality, i.e., the extension of citizenship.

The word "pseudomorphic" describes the processes of modernization associated with export development, because Argentina became a bourgeois society before becoming an industrial nation. Historically, middle-class societies have been associated with the Industrial Revolution. In Argentina, however, the structure and the fabric of bourgeois-democratic society was superimposed on agro-pecuarian foundations. The growth of an urban middle class resulted here from the international division of labor, which permitted Argentina to import modern superstructures and join them to a dependent, non-industrial mode of production.

At the time of these developments, the Argentine government was still the preserve of the landed elite. It was an oligarchy: "A government resting on a valuation of property, in which the rich have power and the poor man is deprived of it" ("Plato, *The Republic, Book VIII*, 550-C). With the growth of the new middle class came demands for opening the system through popular suffrage. Moreover, in times of crisis, such as the Baring crisis of 1890, members of the oligarchy were not above recruiting allies from the middle class. It was such a coalition that founded the *Unión Cívica* in 1890. Shortly thereafter middle-class members seceded and formed the *Unión Cívica Radical*—Argentina's first modern political party.

The *Unión Cívica Radical* never represented a united, coherent class, but was rather an aggregation of disparate groups and individuals. Initially, it was more representative of the old middle class, which was largely creole and in which independent farmers were heavily represented. It eventually came to encompass the new middle class which was drawn mainly from the descendants of Spanish and Italian immigrants—the growing white-collar strata of clerks and bureaucrats, and the petit-bourgeoisie of shopkeepers. The leadership of the party was dominated by landed interests not closely tied to world markets. Hipólito Yrigoyen, the party leader who became president of Argentina in 1916 and again in 1928, was himself a marginal landowner.

The party's heterogeneous class composition and the general prosperity of the nation prevented it from articulating a serious challenge to the established economic order. The basic demand of the radicals was popular suffrage. The rest was mostly a lofty-sounding and vague ideology.

Under Yrigoyen's leadership the radicals abstained from electoral participation at the time—electoral politics was rigged and merely a façade for oligarchic control—and twice launched revolts. Radicals frequently conspired with the military in the hope of inducing officers to attempt a coup. The oligarchy became increasingly concerned about such tactics and the more enlightened elements of the elite finally granted universal manhood suffrage in 1912. The radicals returned to electoral politics. In 1916 Yrigoyen was elected to the presidency.

Once in power, *Radicalismo* operated well within the limits of the status quo in a manner acceptable to the dominant landed interests. *Radicalismo* generally eschewed serious reference to economic problems, in part to avoid cleavages among its heterogeneous constituency. Radical economic policies supported the establishment. The radical program sought the extension of political participation and the redistribution of the benefits of export development. In brief, it sought to extend both geographically and socially the institutional structure of agrarian Argentina.

The same programatic and ideological ambivalence was characteristic of other middle-class parties, such as *La Liga del Sur,* which later became the *Partido Demócrata Progresista,* a party based in the province of Santa Fe. Moral indignation and the concern over formal democracy consumed a large amount of the political energy available to the middle-class parties. The political trajectory of these parties, their programs and ideologies, were determined by the process of economic expansion. They called for more participation, for the end of economic abuses and political corruption. But they expressed a fundamental consensus about the content and direction of economic growth. Middle-class insurgency erupted during the periodic crises to which the economic system was subjected. Those crises produced spontaneous "explosions" of middle-class anger, prompted some reforms, and then subsided. A closer scrutiny of the main middle-class subgroups shows their incapacity to formulate alternatives in the field of economic policy.

The industrial sector was too weak to formulate alternative economic policies. Moreover, the middle-class parties did not really represent this sector and did not incorporate its demands in their programs. The commercial sector was in a similar position: commercial capital was largely concentrated in import-export trade which depended on the agro-pecuarian sector. The rest was scattered among small merchants and shopkeepers—most of them Spanish and Italian immigrants. These groups were nonpolitical: their main motive for migration had been to improve their economic lot by acquiring money or property—something they could try without applying for Argentine citizenship. The rural middle class fought for better grain prices and lower rents, but never challenged the tenure system. In brief, the middle sectors had economic interests in many ways parallel to the interests they opposed, namely, the big landlords, meat packers, and ranchers.

That basic economic consensus extended even below the strata of farmers, shopkeepers, and white-collar workers. For instance, after the stabilization of the currency around the turn of the century, a certain coincidence of interest developed among wage-workers and the big exporters. Labor leaders and working class parties, especially the socialists, became strong advocates of price stability, which they associated with free trade. They thus opposed any policy that aimed at industrial protection. Strikes and agitation, which were frequent after 1900, were aimed at obtaining better working conditions and higher wages in the industrial plants but they in no way represented a challenge to the export establishment.

This is not to minimize the radicalism and militancy of the working class movement. Two political currents provided leadership to the proletariat during the export period. One was anarcho-syndicalism, which was very influential in the strikes before 1916. The other was the Socialist Party, founded in 1896, which espoused reformist policies.

As a consequence of immigration, European ideas about trade unions, socialism, and anarchism flourished among the railway employees, the workers in the processing and milling enterprises, in the building industry, in the ports, and among the numerous groups of waiters and servants who supplied the services demanded by the wealthy. Strikes and anarchist violence were common events, especially around 1905. In 1909 there was a general strike in which a clash between demonstrators and troops resulted in four dead and forty-five wounded. Later that year the chief of police of Buenos Aires, Colonel Falcón, was blown to bits by a bomb. Anarchism flourished when larger industrial concentrations began to replace artisan shops, drawing more and more handicraftsmen into the ranks of the proletariat. Anarchism thus expressed the radicalization of a vanishing stratum of the working class. The evolution of the working-class organizations reflects that trend. The first workers' societies were established along immigrant-ethnic lines. By 1891, the movement had a short-lived central federation, the *Federación de Trabajadores de la Región Argentina*. The next organization, the *Federación Obrera Argentina* (FOA), founded in 1904, was crushed, but reorganized itself as the *Federación Obrera Regional Argentina* (FORA). This new central union was controlled by anarchists and syndicalists.

The socialists, who had created the *Unión Central de Trabajadores* (UCT), eventually came to dominate the working class movement, superseding the anarcho-syndicalist period. However, as the economy expanded and social mobility increased, their own constituency became more "middle-class". Their position as a working class party began to deteriorate, and they suffered several defections. The most significant of these, in 1918, led to the formation of the International Socialist Party, which joined the Third International and was a forerunner of the Argentine Communist Party.

The organization of labor was part of the continuing capitalist consolidation of the economy. So was its systematic repression. Anarchist militancy was met by the ruling class with the Law of Residence, passed in 1902, and the Law of Social Defense, passed in 1910, which empowered the government to deal directly with immigrant leaders by deportation. Troops were frequently used against demonstrations. In this, the middle-class government of the *radicales* fared no better than its conservative opponents. In 1919, a metalworkers' strike in Buenos Aires became the nucleus of a series of solidarity strikes in the rest of Argentina. Soldiers were called out, and for a whole week the strikes were forcibly put down. This came to be known as the "Tragic Week" of January 1919. In 1920 to 1921, some two thousand workers were massacred in Patagonia by the military.

RADICALISMO AND THE CONSOLIDATION OF THE EXPORT ECONOMY

The growth of exports stimulated the development of subsidiary industries, many of them concentrated in foreign hands. The meat-packing industry was the nucleus of subsidiary industrialization. American investments prevailed in this sector, followed by British and local capital. In 1927, the United States controlled over half of meat exports, Britain over a third, and Argentine interests the rest. In the commercial sector, firms like Bunge & Born—founded by Belgian financiers with worldwide connections—controlled flour mills, chemical and industrial firms, and loan associations. They virtually monopolized the export of grain, and, being middlemen for other products, they also came to control the available foreign exchange.

Banking, however, was under national control, which allowed the landed bourgeoisie independently to finance production. In other words, the landed bourgeoisie controlled production and local financing, while European and American interests controlled the packing and commercialization of the export produce.

The Argentine economy continued to specialize in the export of meats and cereals. The area under cultivation in grains and forage increased fourfold between 1900 and 1929, always under elite control. Cereal exports grew even faster than meat exports. In 1925, the Argentine contribution to total world export was: maize, 66 percent; flax, 72 percent; oats, 32 percent; wheat, 20 percent; and meat, 50 percent (Daniels, 1970, II, 2).

As long as the economy continued to expand, *radicalismo* did not pose a threat to the dominant classes. The system could sustain substantial reforms and extended political participation. Oligarchic control was loosened. Before 1912, the oligarchy had retained control of the essential offices of the state upon the management of the electoral machinery and the political use of the police and the armed forces to get their own people to the polls and to count the ballots in their favor. In 1912 the Saenz-Peña Law, forced through a reluctant congress by an enlightened president, provided for a compulsory, secret ballot to be conducted by the armed forces. The latter would act as a neutral agency in the preparation of the voters list from the registry of all male citizens obliged to enrol under the law of compulsory military service. They were charged with the duty of seeing that all voted secretly and only once, and that the votes were counted impartially. Genuine elections were at last possible as a means of selecting the members of the formal power structure. These political reforms brought radical and socialist representatives to Congress, and in 1916 they brought Yrigoyen to the presidency.

The radicals came to power in the middle of World War I. To their credit, they stuck to a policy of strict neutrality. They also nationalized the petroleum industry. But the war created other opportunities as well: high prices for Argentine products were offset by the reduction of capital flows and by a rise in the price of imports. Scarcity and high prices gave an advantage to national industries. Yrigoyen's administration did not seize the opportunity to consolidate the advantages by tariff protection and other similar measures. Surpluses were used to reduce foreign indebtedness rather than to increase domestic capital.

If economically the radical regime was unimaginative, socially it was sometimes repressive. When peace came to Europe with its wake of revolutionary unrest, Yrigoyen struck at the working class in what was one of the worst periods of repression and official violence in Argentine labor history before 1955. Yrigoyen left the Argentine economy almost exactly as he found it: dependent on the big export industries and foreign markets. His shortcomings were not, however, accidental. Rather, they expressed the "middle-mass" consciousness of store-owners, clerks, and employees of public utilities, for whom *"radicalismo* is a sentiment, not a program," as the saying went.

The hegemony of the landed bourgeoisie was never questioned. Not only did the landed elite ultimately determine economic policy; the landed oligarchs held a majority in the senate, and were often appointed to cabinet posts. Marcelo T. de Alvear, the second top leader of the *Radicales* who succeeded Yrigoyen in 1922, was himself a member of the old "aristocracy." Again, he did nothing to change *laissez-faire* economic policies.

The undisputed economic hegemony of the landed elite throughout this period of middle-class government is even more clearly revealed by the vicissitudes of the Argentine socialist movement. That movement was born in the 1880's when inflation devoured the incomes of the incipient working class. With the subsequent expansion of Argentine exports, the favorable terms of trade stabilized the currency. Thus, the success of the elite's economic program won for them the support of the socialists, who from then on sought reform and not revolution. Social mobility also contributed to the bourgeois tendencies of the socialists. Eventually they became junior partners of the establishment. These are the historical roots of a spectacle that would puzzle some observers in 1945, when socialists and communists demonstrated against Perón in the company of reactionary landlords.

Yrigoyen was re-elected in 1928. One year later the great economic depression engulfed the capitalist world. As prices of grain and meat fell, Argentina's gold stocks flowed abroad to pay for imports into the country. In order to protect gold holdings, the government suspended the free conversion of paper *pesos* into gold. The price of imported manufactured goods did not fall as that of Argentine exports on account of the sudden contraction of industrial production in the metropolitan countries. This diminished the goods and services available to the mass of the people. Customs revenues fell and the state, devoid of other tax resources, could not meet its payments to the inumerable beneficiaries of the political patronage system that the *radicales* had carefully cultivated. Everybody was more or less worse off.

The economic malaise soon became a social and political crisis. The international crisis awakened authoritarian and reactionary trends among the landed upper class that found its economic basis threatened and therefore turned to political levers to preserve its rule. They called on the military to overthrow the government.

On September 6, 1930, General José Felix Uriburu deposed the president and proclaimed martial law, striking down a decade and a half of democratic rule and, more generally, a liberal system that had endured for sixty-eight years. Uriburu was an officer with landed, conservative family connections. He was inspired by European fascism, which he misunderstood as an aristocratic movement. He was backed in this venture not only by the landed elite, but also by anti-Yrigoyen radicals and by the right-wing Independent Socialist Party. But his dictatorship was ineffective and short-lived. It was soon replaced by a "limited democracy" type of government based on the restriction of popular participation, under General Justo.

The year 1930 marked the return of the landed upper class to political power, within a context of international crisis and under the imperative to industrialize. The Prussian training of the army cadres, the increasing impact of fascism on the European continent, and the frictions between Yrigoyen and the armed forces over military appropriations, were all considerations that facilitated the army coup. Moreover, the Argentine army had always been "political": compulsory military service, established in 1901, was designed with political socialization in mind. The army was charged with overseeing elections. In Argentina the draft card and the voter registration card are one and the same documents for males over eighteen years of age. In brief, the Argentine armed forces have always been oriented to "civic action" programs. Internally, politicization was traditionaly intense too: officers' lodges, or secret pressure groups, have always been a feature of army life (Orona, 1965; Potash, 1969, 11–18, 37–38).

Sociologists have discovered somewhat unexpectedly that the Argentine armed forces are not the preserve of the landed elite. The traditional upper class has comparatively little family and class connection with the armed forces with the exception of some elite branches of the service. This was true in 1930, even though General Uriburu had family connections with the landed upper class. The fact remains that the Argentine armed forces are fairly meritocratic in organization, with relatively open recruitment from different social classes. They are a ladder for upward mobility. But this overwhelmingly middle-class composition of the armed forces does not prevent them from pursuing policies which are pro-status quo and anti-popular. They often engage in such policies precisely as representatives of an ambivalent and contradictory middle class (Nun, 1969).

III. THE END OF OUTWARD GROWTH

THE STRUCTURAL CRISIS

Although of unprecedented severity, the Great Depression of the 1930's was not sudden or cataclysmic, turning buoyant prosperity into ruin. In fact the economic position of Argentina—as of most primary producing nations— was very weak and insecure during the 1920's. Both prices and demand for primary commodities had been falling, and the disparity between these prices and those of manufactured goods in world trade was growing wider. Given the insecurity and dependency of its position, Argentina belonged to one of the sectors of the world economy least able to resist the effects of a severe trade depression. Even without the Depression it is difficult to see how in the long run the position of a dependent economy such as Argentina's could have been less critical.

The onset of the Depression accentuated all the weakness of the situation and revealed the shaky basis of the liberal period. Its most obvious manifestation was the fall in the volume and value of international trade. But the main problem in the 1930's was the failure of primary-product prices to recover, and the closely related deterioration in Argentina's terms of trade. The severe reduction in export earnings sharply lowered the purchasing power of the country for imported goods and particularly for manufactured commodities. The share of imports in the total supply of goods fell from 52.9 percent in 1929 to 34.9 percent in 1938 (United Nations, *Economic Survey of Latin America 1949*). The gap left by this reduction of imports began to be filled by home-produced goods. Argentine production, at constant prices, increased by nine percent between 1929 and 1938 while exports fell by 37 percent. The necessity to produce commodities which it was no longer prossible to import reoriented economic activity towards the home market.

Argentina negotiated unfavorable trade treaties in the 1930's, since the Depression weakened her position more than that of the exporters of manufactured goods. Manufacturing countries helped their own balance of payments by protecting domestic agricultural production and this further limited the exports of the primary producers. Britain gave preferential treatment to its primary-producing dominions, Canada, Australia, and New Zealand, in the Ottawa agreements of 1932. In order to regain access to British markets Argentina signed, in 1933, the Roca-Runciman Treaty, which granted the British government import licenses for 85 percent of Argentine beef exports, while Argentina retained only 15 percent. These arrangements tended to divide the Argentine landowning interests. Grains gave way to meats as the most important export product. The stockmen themselves were split into two factions: breeders and fatteners. Fatteners purchased the bred cattle and, owning land closer to the seaports, sold their livestock directly to the meat packers. A stabilized world demand for chilled beef gave them a monopoly control over sales to the export market. This monopoly, reinforced by their control over the Argentine Rural Society, sustained the privileged position of the fatteners among the stockmen and made them the dominant sector of the landed class. Put briefly, the Roca-Runciman Agreement guaranteed Argentina a fixed but reduced share in the British market for meat and bound the British to limit their encouragement of British agricultural producers by subsidies. In return Argentina agreed to stabilize its tariffs on industrial products, to reduce tariffs on some manufactures, and to preserve free entry for fuel. Argentina also reformed its exchange controls so as to facilitate the remission of interest and profits on British-owned investments. It undertook also to defend British-owned transport enterprises (street cars) against competition from automotive transport.

The principal feature of these agreements was the entrenchment of the past and of one class by tightening the bonds of dependency and consolidating the position of the dominant sector of the land-owing class. In other words, privilege was further concentrated at the top and losses were socialized among the rest of the community. It was the beginning of economic and technical sclerosis which cost the Argentine landed bourgeois the first place as competitors in the world market for food and raw materials like wool and linseed. Their policies narrowly followed their immediate class interests. To the lights of these frightened conservatives, their short-sighted efforts were a success. They proved to be a disaster in the long run. They did little to find new markets by attracting new capital and reducing production costs through technological improvement. Argentina in the 1970's is still paying for the trusteeship of its economy to this class in the thirties.

During the decade following 1935, Argentina became an industrial nation. But it changed without becoming different in several important respects. During this period, Argentina drifted in search of an alternative model of growth and modernization to that of outward export expansion. The different attempts proceeded from guesswork and social mending to more conscious planning.

The military-conservative group in power faced an economy seriously affected by the world crisis: exports declined drastically; the prices of produce fell rapidly; unemployment increased; the budget was imbalanced; the state operated with diminished sources of revenue; the *peso* had to be devalued. The government had to engage in a policy of regulating the economy and of financing as well as transferring to the popular strata the heavy losses of the agro-pecuarian producers. The currency was depreciated, and the government fixed minimum prices for grain, assumed control of all operations in foreign exchange, and established a system of import licensing. The conversion of the external and internal debts reduced the state deficit considerably. The transformation of blocked foreign funds into "loans" to the government also contributed to stabilizing the situation. Public works—such as the construction of roads—reduced the impact of unemployment. Financial mechanisms were strengthened and concentrated with the creation of a central bank.

The aims of the conservative coalition in power during the thirties did not go beyond preserving the status quo, yet such a task involved establishing economic controls, and under the umbrella of a controlled economy industry began to grow. Thus the decline of the import capacity of the economy acted as a strong incentive to national industrialization. The process of import substitution led to what has been called an unintegrated industrial economy (Ferrer, 1963, IV)—unintegrated insofar as the process was mostly concentrated on light industry, thus postponing, rather than solving, the problem of economic dependence. Nonetheless, the number of industrial workers began to grow considerably and very rapidly, as did the size and the importance of unions. The landed elite that had indirectly unleashed such process was soon confronted with the demands of an expanding proletariat and with the kernel of what could be labeled a "national industrial bourgeoisie."

Until 1930 industry was subsidiary to the main export sector. After 1930 it began substituting imports and established an important foothold in the economy. Between 1900 and 1930 the proportion of manpower employed in industry remained fairly constant (around 25 percent) compared with 36 percent engaged in primary activities. Major industrial enterprises on a large scale, like the meat-packing industries depended on the export economy. They were not the nucleus of autonomous industrialization. Thus, one should not construe the tensions between ranchers and meat-packers over prices and terms of sale as a class struggle between farmers and industrialists as in, for example, the conflict between the Western agricultural provinces of Canada and the protectionist industrial interests in Ontario and Quebec. The large service and commercial sectors of the Argentine economy were bigger in their use of manpower than agriculture and ranching. This large tertiary sector contained few elements of autonomous growth, for in the main the commercial and service apparatus of society was geared to serving the needs of the dominant agricultural and ranching industry and its beneficiaries. There was a high degree of articulation between these three sectors of the economy until the thirties, with the primary export sector dynamizing the other two. Social conflict took place then less along sectorial lines than along class lines within sectors. In the absence of a clear-cut division between an agrarian and an industrial interest, conflict erupted within sectors, between workers and employers. Thus labor was organized first in the railways, which were big employers of skilled labor and part of the agricultural economy. Conflict was institutionalized in this sector before World War I. Not so in the meat-packing industry, which pursued a policy of paternalism and brutal opposition to the formation of unions. In the commercial sector there was a similar opposition to working-class organizations on the part of employers. For the working class this was a period of anarchist and syndicalist intransigence.

This social and economic constellation changed after 1930. As a response to depression and war, Argentina became an industrial society. By 1944 industrial production constituted a larger proportion of total production than ranching, the production of cereals, and agricultural raw materials. And yet then, as today, these traditional export activities still played as strategic a part in the economy as they did before World War I. Argentina today is still heavily dependent on foreign suppliers for industrial goods and fuel and is still paying for them almost exclusively with exports produced in the rural sector. This peculiar situation indicates that industrialization has not been autonomous, that external dependency has changed but not disappeared, and that the transition from an agrarian to an industrial economy has taken place without anything resembling a social revolution.

Industrialization has taken place on the basis of import substitution. Since the 1930's the proportion of consumer goods in Argentine imports has steadily fallen. But the proportion of capital equipment, steel, and metals has risen to four fifths of all imports. These facts again suggest a profound structural weakness. The flaw of the Argentine industrialization pattern has been known to economists for some time. They have pointed to the fact that Argentine industry is predominantly a consumer goods, "light" industry, which has grown up without making the country less dependent on foreign suppliers. It sustains its growth by relying on the basic industries of the dominant industrial countries. It is a high-cost industry incapable of meeting

international competition, and hence is unable to support its own demand for fuel, raw materials, and capital equipment. On account of
these developments, it is incapable of improving the agro-commercial
industries by inducing a reduction in the cost of export farming and
ranching on which it depends for foreign exchange for its supplies. Thus,
the vicious circle of stagnation is closed.

The stalemated system that is Argentina today stems from an industrialization program tailored to suit the interests of the dominant sector of the landed bourgeoisie. In fact, the original industrial program
of the thirties was not opposed by any powerful social group. Industrialization was part of the defensive strategy of the agrarians who
sought to decrease imports to the level of exports. Industry thus came
into being as a byproduct of their adaptation to less favorable conditions
in the world market. The new economic order was born warped and
its subsequent growth locked in a set of self-reinforcing weaknesses.

Argentine industry was dependent on the export sector for surplus
capital and therefore subject both to the low efficiency of that rural
sector and to fluctuations in world markets. It was also dependent on
the basic industries of the imperialist countries. It was concentrated
in the Littoral and especially around Buenos Aires, thus reinforcing
the dominance of this region over the rest of the nation. The main consequence of industrialization was to redefine the nature of Argentine dependency and to produce a regrouping of social forces, that is, new conflicts
and alliances of social classes.

Industrialization spurred the growth of a large urban proletariat.
The increased demand for labor in the import substitute industries and
a soaring unemployment in the countryside (the world crisis and the
emergency of the United States and Canada as exporters of wheat
had severely damaged Argentine agriculture) combined to produce a
mass exodus to the urban centers. That is why, despite the cessation of
immigration, industrial employment figures showed a steady rise during
the years of world depression, and later during the War. Agrarian
conditions provided a large reservoir of potential workers, and the new
industry attracted them like a magnet. Not only the agrarian crisis led
to internal migrations. Technological development had accentuated an
age-old phenamenon: the crowding out of the small farmer by giant
enterprises technically better equipped. This trend was later accelerated
by the wartime rise of meat prices which led many *estancieros* or ranchers
to prefer using land for grazing instead of leasing it for agricultural
purposes. The shift to grazing before and during the Second World
War added to the surplus of labor in the countryside, since ranching
needs fewer hands. During the 1935 to 1946 period, half a million

persons entered the industrial labor force, an increase of over 100 percent. Large amounts of surplus value were extracted from these workers for investment in industry and services. High agricultural prices in the internal market, by increasing the cost of foodstuffs, further reduced the available income of workers and funneled industrial surplus value to the agrarian elite. This latter aspect brought the interests of the new industrial bourgeoisie into a conflict of somewhat classic proportions with the agrarians. It was a conflict over consumer markets on the surface, and a conflict over the appropriation of surplus value underneath.

At least initially, the protagonists of this conflict were distinct and different social groups. Despite the *estanciero's* marked preference for urban living, few entered the new economic sectors opened up by import-substituting industrialization, though many functioned as urban professionals. The Argentine sociologist Gino Germani comments: "Industrialization was produced outside this group [the landed bourgeoisie]; already during the first phase of industrialization . . . virtually all the *non*-agricultural activity was in the hands of immigrants" (Germani, 1962, 172).

The conflict was aggravated by the Law of Exchange Control introduced by the central bank, which made available to the industrial sector foreign exchange generated by the agrarian export sector. On the other hand, the wage freezes forced upon workers by the conservative governments of the period produced wide discontent among the masses, making them available for political mobilization.

IV. INDUSTRIALIZATION AND SOCIAL CHANGE

PATTERNS OF INDUSTRIALIZATION

We have seen how until the 1920's the Argentine economy was organized in terms of the international division of labor structured by British imperialism. The cattle ranchers were the staunchest defenders of this arrangement within the country. The agro-pecuarian export system did allow, however, the growth of a food industry in order to supply world markets. This was the extent to which the system tolerated industrialization. It was external demand which stimulated the growth of those industries. The combination of abundant raw materials, low costs, and a growing external demand fostered the growth of this subsidiary industrial sector, its fast concentration, and lured foreign capital—British and American—to invest in it. Socially, the economic system was supported by the ranching faction of the landed upper class, British capitalists, and import-export merchants. Politically, the consensus about the system extended to all significant parties, conservative, radical, and socialist alike. Conservatives and radicals defended the agro-pecuarian producers and their markets. Socialists defended consumers and the purchasing power of wage earners and thus were drawn into the prevailing consensus.

This anti-industrial constellation of interests was slowly but steadily subverted by marginal national capitalists emerging from the ranks of the urban middle sectors and immigrants, and by the mounting pressure of international industrial monopolies eager to establish a productive foothold in the country. Capital from these different sources began to flow into new branches of industrial activity.

The national capitalists had the hardest time. The First World War provided some "natural" protection for their incipient industrial establishments. These managed to survive, despite hardships and the open hostility of the dominant class. The industrialists gathered around two organizations: the Argentine Industrial Union (*Unión Industrial Argentina*) and the Argentine Confederation of Commerce, Industry, and Production (*Confederación Argentina del Comercio, la Industria y la Producción*).

On the other hand, American and Continental European capital began to dispute the primacy of British investments in Argentina. It was especially American capital which increased its influence considerably after the First World War. At the end of that war, the United States ranked first among suppliers of Argentine imports. Moreover, in order to secure their position in the Argentine market, American corporations began to make direct, "tariff-hopping" investments. American capital arrived in Argentina to find traditional areas of investment, such as railroads and public utilities, preempted by British capital. On the other hand, the United States was itself a large producer of foods and raw materials which meant that its markets were closed to Argentine produce. The United States economy was, in this respect, competitive vis-à-vis the Argentine economy. American investment flowed mostly into light industry, especially into the production of consumer durables. By the 1920's several subsidiaries of the most important American industrial corporations had already a foothold in Argentina. The Argentine trade balance with the United States yielded then, as always, consistent deficits.

The Argentine agrarian establishment regarded this industrial nucleus with alarm and attempted to thwart it by manipulating fiscal and credit policies. But despite official disfavor, industries managed to survive and even to increase production in the twenties. In brief, the twenties witnessed a modest spreading of industrialization outside the traditional export sector and its related industries. During those years some significant American investments took place as well as certain displacement of British and European goods by American manufactures in the import market. Those trends ran against the best interests of the British and of the Argentine agrarians. The State—operating then with limited autonomy—tried to compromise between these diverse interests. But neither the incipient industrial national bourgeoisie, nor the incoming American corporations, nor the State—controlled at the time by middle-class politicians—challenged the hegemony of the dominant British interests and their landed Argentine allies.

But, as we have already seen, the crisis of 1930 brought about a drastic reduction in the value of Argentine exports on account of import controls instituted in Great Britain. With this came a correlative weakening of the capacity to import manufactures. In short, the neat division of labor and the free trade policies to which Argentina was accustomed went to pieces. Argentina simply could not obtain the amount of manufactured goods from abroad which it had previously imported. To maintain imports would have meant an intolerable trade deficit. To reduce them to the new level of exports meant an equally intolerable retrenchment of consumption. After three long years of waiting for the world capitalist economy to recover, the Argentine ruling class, now firmly entrenched in power by force, decided to launch a program of import substitution through a "contained" national industrialization. In the eyes of this class these were temporary measures in order to weather the crisis and effective only until international trade resumed and with it, Argentina's role as leading agricultural and cattle exporter. This expectation limited industrialization to certain branches of industry and placed it under the auspices of an alliance of classes in which the agrarians remained dominant and the industrial bourgeoisie assumed the role of a junior partner. It was an alliance between sectors of classes rather than between whole classes.

Both the agrarian and the industrial bourgeoisies were internally differentiated on the eve of the crisis. The ranchers were divided, as we have seen, into breeders and fatteners, the former depending on the latter. The industrialists were divided into those investing in so-called "natural" branches (that is, those industries closely tied to the export sector) and "artificial" branches, such as metallurgic industries. During the first years of the Depression, intra-class conflicts erupted, as each of these sectors tried to maintain its position and pass on the brunt of the crisis to other groups. In the end, it was the lower classes that suffered most. Nevertheless, some sectors of the dominant classes, notably the breeders among the agrarians, lost power.

After three years of crisis and sectorial strife, an alliance was formed in 1933 between the cattle fatteners, represented by the Argentine Rural Society, and the industrialists grouped in the Argentine Industrial Union. The economic ministry was put in the hands of a team of ex-Independent Socialists, headed by Federico Pinedo. The class alliance and the ministerial team in power stimulated the diversification of industries and allowed the growth of new branches—especially textiles—in order to replace imports. But this was throughout a controlled process, under the undisputed hegemony of the oligarchy. Room was made for a new class of industrial entrepreneurs, side by side with the landed interests and the older industrial establishments linked to the export economy.

The new industrial bourgeoisie accepted the agrarian definition of the situation and tried to prosper within that framework. Interestingly, this group failed to generate an ideology of its own and to put forth a different program of economic development. In spite of this apparent lack of consciousness and daring, the new bourgeoisie had a definite social identity. Despite inadequate data and conflicting interpretations, the evidence seems to indicate that agrarian wealth played neither a direct nor a decisive role in industrial development and that neither foreign nor domestic monopolies managed to take over the industrialization process of the thirties and forties. Available data shows that concentration in industry remained fairly low during this period (Jorge, 1971, *passim*). In brief, industrialization represented the emergence of a new and distinct social stratum that neither overlapped with the landed bourgeoisie nor was ancillary to foreign monopolies. Import-substituting industrialization took place through the mobilization of urban savings. Entrepreneurial leadership emerged from middle and immigrant sectors. The landed elite had only invested capital in some food and beverage industries in an earlier period but did not participate in the new industrial ventures of the thirties and forties. Foreign capital did develop certain industrial branches but in fact lagged behind the more dynamic national sector and failed to satellize it during those decades. But the new industrial bourgeoisie failed to articulate its own economic designs for the nation. After 1943 it joined a new alliance of classes that culminated with Perónism, but it did not dominate that populist coalition either. Finally, after the fall of President Perón in 1955, as we shall see, it rapidly lost power and was ultimately satellized by foreign corporations, especially by American multinationals which gained a decisive foothold in the economy after 1958.

These vicissitudes raise the issue of the undeveloped or "false" consciousness of the industrial class. Without attempting to provide an exhaustive answer, it would seem that the political impotence and the ideological timidity of the industrial bourgeoisie initially had to do with its overwhelming foreign origins. The Industrial Census of 1935 indicates that 60 percent of all industrial entrepreneurs in Argentina were foreign born. They were mostly concentrated in the new branches of industry—those developed for import substitution. In other words, it was an industrial, but hardly a "national" bourgeoisie. To this fact should be added that traditionally a very low percentage of immigrants to Argentina became naturalized citizens. They thus tended to remain alienated from politics. This feature may help to explain the fact that during the period of industrialization Argentina knew no "party of industry." In this as in other aspects of Argentine social change the resilience of the original agro-pecuarian structure proved to be a decisive limiting factor with long-term political consequences. As new, relatively modern groups—including an industrial bourgeoisie —developed, they were grafted into the agrarian structure but remained socially, politically, and culturally separate. Only gradually did they become interwoven into a closer framework of mutual interdependence. The landed elite—retaining control of the state during a crucial phase of industrialization—impeded the full development and integration of these groups into new institutional frameworks. Furthermore, the earlier political integration of native non-industrial middle sectors during the heyday of agrarian prosperity increased the isolation of the new industrial bourgeoisie from the existing political structures. The so-called middel-class parties, like the UCR were simply not receptive to the new industrial interests.

The textile industries, favored by the local abundance of raw materials, were the fastest growing sector of manufacturing during the thirties. Other industries followed: machinery, electric appliances and rubber tires were developed by foreign capital. The latter's participation in the industrialization process was significant but did not overshadow the mobilization of domestic savings for industrial development. Between 1935 and 1946 the number of industrial establishments grew from forty thousand to eighty-six thousand. National capital flowed into small and medium sized establishments, while foreign capital established larger enterprises. The growth of small- and medium-sized national industries was indeed so massive that throughout this period, industrial concentration remained low on the average (Jorge, 1971, V).

Industrial growth was accompanied by an impressive growth of the working class. The number of workers doubled between 1935 and

1946. Workers thus became the principal occupational category in the forties. These two related processes—the increasing importance of industry and the development of the proletariat—clearly overflowed the expectations and propects of the conservative coalition in power. Official disfavor could not prevent the development of metallurgic industries which were more threatening to the export sector than the textile establishments. A new industrial bourgeoisie with no more than very tenuous links to the landed bourgeoisie, a working class whose ranks were continuously expanding by the incorporation of new workers from the rural areas, and other less strategic groups such as the disaffected rural middle class, the rural proletariat, and even some displaced sectors of the landed classes, formed the ingredients of a new coalition of social forces. This coalition began to take shape during the Second World War and finally found political expression in the populist movement led by Juan D. Perón in the forties. Perónism is incomprehensible without a survey of the patterns of industrialization that developed in the thirties and especially without a study of labor developments during this same period.

TOWARDS A NEW COALITION OF CLASSES

A strong labor movement existed in Argentina already in 1930 when the oligarchy-inspired military coup overthrew the Radical government of Yrigoyen. Thereafter, the industrialization process described above brought thousands of new workers—mostly internal migrants—into the industrial centers of Buenos Aires and the Littoral. The number of unions and their membership went up. The presence of labor organizations which had been established during the years of external immigration, their tradition and experience in labor struggles, provided a base for the mobilization of the new mass of workers and for the articulation of their interests. But there were strains. The labor movement was divided and subjected to continuous repression at the hands of the conservative regimes from 1930 until 1943. Communists, socialists, and syndicalists competed for control over the labor movement and over the leadership of the newly founded trade union congress, the *Confederación General del Trabajo* (CGT). Communists were strong among the metal, textile, and construction workers. Transport workers were organized in more moderate unions. By 1942 the CGT had split into two rival groups. Government controls kept salaries consistently depressed and official repression demoralized the movement.

During the forties, Perónism would unify the working class movement by mobilizing the more recent sectors of the proletariat but also making strong inroads among the older and more established organizations. The "old" and the "new" working classes were more united in the expression of their interests and in their support of Perónism than has been customarily acknowledged by social and political analysts. In fact many of the demands of the working class organizations in the 1930's found continued expression in the labor policies and in the ideology of Perónism.

What took place from 1935 to 1946 was a process of national capitalist accumulation based on the compression of wages and under the political control of a class coalition dominated by landed elements. Perónism represented the vindication of the mass of repressed workers who had born the brunt of a rather "classic" form of accumulation based on the existence of a reserve army of laborers, compressed wages, and political repression (Murmis and Portantiero, 1971, Part II). Productive expansion eventually reduced unemployment, but wages were not allowed to rise and workers' demands went unheeded until 1943, when Perón became Secretary of Labor of a new military regime that seized power from the conservatives and closed the decade of reaction known as *la década infame* or the "infamous decade." In short, the growth of industry resulted in the eventual takeover of government by a populist leader who combined appeals to a long-suppressed but growing working class by promising to bridge the gap between accumulation and distribution in the name of social justice, with appeals to industrial entrepreneurs in the name of national economic development.

It is fruitful to contrast the Argentine experience with other countries —notably Brazil—in which populist regimes outwardly similar to Perónism also attained power. Brazilian populism under Vargas had seized power before the advent of Perón in Argentina. Once in power, the Brazilian populist coalition launched a program of industrialization *with* distribution of income to the workers. The workers were thus firmly tied to the state apparatus. In Argentina, on the other hand, populism gained power after a period of accumulation without redistribution, during which workers, bereft of state protection, created their own organizations. The populist regime had to negotiate labor support first and only after obtaining it did it progressively attempt to control the movement by linking workers' organizations to the state. Nevertheless, the labor movement in Argentina never became an absolute creature of the government, which explains the endurance of Perónist unions after Perón and under strongly anti-labor regimes. The Argentine working-class organizations proved stronger and more autonomous than their counterparts in other Latin American nations. This continued strength of trade unions indicates that what occurred under Perón—as we shall see shortly —was more than just government manipulation of working masses from above. It meant the strengthening of organizations encompassing the majority of the industrial working class—organizations capable of defending the interests of this class after the fall of the populist government. Ultimately it means that economic development could not take place in Argentina disregarding the proletariat: this class had the power to veto any attempt to maximize industrialization while minimizing social change—a favorite strategy of multinational corporations in other countries of the region. The strength of the working class is the other side of capitalist stagnation in Argentina in the latter part of the twentieth century.

The process of industrialization from the mid-thirties until the advent of the Perónist government in 1946 involved the establishment and disestablishment of alliances between different classes and sectors of classes. Six features were of particular import in these developments. First, an initial industrializing alliance in the thirties consisting of the largest cattle interests and industrialists. Second, the agrarian split into a dominant faction composed of cattle fatteners and a subordinate group of cattle breeders. The displaced landowners became the element most strongly opposed to any project of industrialization. Their opposition found political expression in those political parties now excluded from participation (*Unión Cívica Radical* and *Partido Demócrata Progresista*). Third, the growth of a large industrial labor force with new recruits from the rural interior, bereft of political protection, and under classic conditions of labor exploitation produced a union movement independent from the state. Fourth, the development, during the Second World War, of a new set of industries, under the automatic protection afforded by the conflict between the industrial nations. This "new wave" of import substitution under the exceptional conditions of the War gave prominence to new entrepreneurs who had little organization among themselves and who were not represented by the traditional parties. They turned toward the state in search for more insitutionalized protection for their industries as the war came to an end. Fifth, a transformation in the economic role of the state, which increasingly intervened in economic matters and acted as an arbiter between different social classes. The state apparatus gained increasing autonomy during this period. Sixth, a new intervention by the armed forces, this time in favor of a coalition of workers and new industrialists. Thus, a new class coalition was structured after 1943. Three years, Perónism attained power and maintained it for nearly a decade.

Perónism forged an unstable alliance between those sectors of the industrial bourgeoisie in greater need of state protection and the urban proletariat through the medium of the state and military bureaucracies, under the banner of a national developmentalist ideology. Its most

significant feature was the incorporation of the working class movement and its mobilization from above. The military, which captured
the state by means of a coup in 1943, allied itself with recent industrialists in need of protection and vindicated the pent-up demands of
the working class through welfare measures and redistributive policies.
State protection and the enlargement of the consumer market were
conditions *sine qua non* of the continued development of national capitalism. On the other hand, the populist mobilization of working people
was a political expedient designed to buttress the legitimacy of a military regime that had repeatedly failed to win the allegiance of other
social groups, notably the middle sectors. These circumstances lend a
unique historical identity to Perónism and disallow any facile assimilation of this Argentine phenomenon to other social movements of the
twentieth century, especially European facism.

THE ORIGINS OF PERONISM

At this point it may be helpful to return to the historical narrative
from 1930 onward to assess the series of episodes that were a prelude
to Perónism. The revolution of 1930, after having attempted to establish a corporativist system of fascist inspiration, opted for a less extreme solution: the formal restoration of the constitutional regime with
the systematic use of electoral fraud. Short of all-out dictatorship, this
was the only way in which the landed upper class could keep the
middle-class *radicales* out of power. Thanks to such a device, a coalition of conservatives, anti-Yrigoyen radicals, and ex-socialists elevated
General Justo to the presidency, with the support of the army. Justo
managed to institute a political restoration with remarkable skill. Under
his conservative administration a group of politicians who had once
been socialists undertook to revamp the battered agrarian economy
through state controls and intervention. One of the indirect consequences of those measures was, as we have seen, the growth of industry. The set of reforms undertaken by the conservative regime amounted
to a sort of Argentine New Deal the purpose of which was to buttress
the export establishment and secondarily to allow the growth of import-
substituting industries as a way to balance the system. The repeated
recourse to electoral fraud behind a constitutional façade was hardly a
way to legitimate the power of the landed elite. However, they maintained themselves in power for a decade, largely because the center
and left parties did not offer massive opposition. Had the latter done
so, the conservative group in power would undoubtedly have resorted
to direct dictatorship, particularly under international circumstances that
favored authoritarian solutions throughout the world. Behind the po-

litical impotence of the center and left parties stood the inability of the social groups they represented to formulate an alternative economic project for the nation. The *radicales* had become seriously compromised in the political corruption of the conservative regime. The left parties were fearful of provoking a fascist backlash by their actions. The government, on the other hand, attempted to enlarge the basis of its power by stimulating a Catholic renaissance that derived its inspiration from Spanish fascism during the years of the civil war in Spain.

When England turned against the fascist powers, the ideological tension in Argentina abated somewhat. The conservative coalition placed a new man in power. This was Dr. Ortiz, who ascended the presidency thanks to an unprecedented use of violence and fraud in the elections of 1937. Ortiz tried to reincorporate the *radicales* into the political system and gave them the governorship of the province of Buenos Aires through the simple political expedient of allowing honest elections in that province. Thus 1940 seemed to be the year of a return to cleaner democratic politics in Argentina. But democratization was opposed by ultra-conservatives who wanted a more authoritarian system. The latter's interests were favored by the illness of the president, who delegated power in the hands of his archconservative vice-president Dr. Castillo, and died. Castillo soon returned to the political practices of the early thirties. Internationally, he fostered a brand of neutrality that catered to the pro-fascist sentiment of a significant sector of the Argentine ruling circles without, however, alienating British support. This feature of Argentine international relations deserves an explanation. England's benevolence towards Argentine pro-fascist neutrality during the war was based on pure self-interest. It is not difficult to reconstruct the constellation of interests prevailing at the time. Engulfed by the war, England's hold over the Argentine economy weakened precisely at a time when her foodstuff needs were critical to sustain the war effort. British interests feared that if Argentina were to join the Allies, Germany would impede the flow of goods from Argentina to Britain. Germany, on the other hand, increased its investments in Argentina as a way of establishing an imperialist foothold in Latin America. A policy of neutrality thus favored the flow of German capital to the country and the flow of Argentine exports to England. As a consequence, the ruling sector of the Argentine landed bourgeoisie found itself in collusion with both the British and the Axis interests and in conflict with the United States. U.S. attempts to include Argentina in mutual defense agreements and bring her into its own economic orbit failed repeatedly. British and Argentine commercial interests resisted the pressure. War documents recently declassified by the

U.S. National Archives—especially the Churchill-Roosevelt correspondence from 1939 to 1945—reveal that Churchill's reluctance to abide by an economic embargo against the pro-Axis Argentine government was one of the more acrimonious disagreements between the British and the Americans during the War.

As a result of Argentine neutrality, the United States favored Brazil with economic and military aid. The resulting economic and military rivalry between these two South American countries was a leading cause of the Argentine military coup of 1943. As pressures from the United States increased, as the rivalry with Brazil—now favored by the United States—mounted, and as the expected victory of the Axis powers failed to materialize, President Castillo began changing his position near the end of his term. He chose as his successor Dr. Robustiano Patrón Costas, a conservative sugar baron from the northwest who was linked to U.S. interests. The plan was to place Patrón-Costas in power and realign Argentina on the Ally side. The plan failed. The fraudulent and heavy-handed practices of the conservatives had isolated the government from the pro-Ally opposition parties so that it could not now expect their support for a change in policy. The army, on the other hand, was still convinced that the Axis would win the war. The corruption of the conservative civilian regime, the impotence and lack of prestige of the opposition parties, pro-German prejudice, and the power rivalry with Brazil, prompted a military take-over. The officers wanted, by this act, to assure Argentine hegemony over the subcontinent, and wished to launch a program of rigid political control and heavy industrial investments. This bismarckian project was hatched by a military lodge which resembled the Japanese militarist cliques of the same period: the G.O.U. (*Grupo de Oficiales Unidos* or United Officers Corps). In the event of a German victory, this group had fantasies of transforming Argentina into a Latin American sub-Reich. When fascist Germany collapsed in the War, the officers decided that Argentina should become its own Prussia, through domestic repression and foreign expansion. The members of the semi-secret lodge were officers of the rank of colonel, major, and captain, that is, the younger strata of unfulfilled ambitions. The fascist inspiration was unmistakable: in their first public statement they asserted that "as in Germany," their government "would be an inflexible dictatorship" which would "inculcate the masses with the spirit necessary to travel the heroic path in which they will be led." The main instruments of the GOU were General Ramírez, who was minister of war in Castillo's government and General Rawson the commander of the Buenos Aires garrison. General Ramírez ousted President Castillo as the army marched on Buenos Aires on June 4, 1943. General Rawson was proclaimed president, but he only lasted two days because he wished to transfer power to a civilian government. The GOU deposed Rawson and proclaimed Ramírez as the president, thus frustrating the hopes of civilian politicians and establishing a direct and permanent dictatorship.

The 1943 coup was unique in that it represented military autonomy —rule "above politics." The officers set out to construct a sufficiently powerful bureaucratic apparatus, including the agencies of repression, the military and the police, in order to free themselves from the influence of both extreme reactionary and popular or radical pressures in the society. The government was to become separate from society. Such phenomena emerge when there is a general political exhaustion of all classes and factions in society, as Marx showed in his analysis of the class struggles in nineteenth century France. And indeed this was the case with Argentine society in the forties. The new character of military rule emerged in 1943 and 1944; for the first time in Argentine history officers were placed in most administrative and political posts. The constitution was suspended indefinitely and open dictatorship was proclaimed.

But autonomous dictatorship does not last long. It soon finds itself engulfed again by social conflict. If it does not express or instrumentalize a viable coalition of social interests the omnipotence of pure military rule becomes empty and stupid. This is what happened to the officers of the 1943 coup. Isolated from political life, their professional puritanism gave them no guidelines for effective action. Thus, they fell back on the massive generalities of Catonism (Moore, 1966, 491–96): religion, patriotism, and discipline. They attacked professional politicians as grafters, and they persecuted Jews. They brought under church control thousands of children of city workers and middle-class parents who were not among the church's most faithful flock; they spoke of "the movement," the "will of the people," and "national unity," of "social peace" and good morals. But in terms of economic policies and social strategy they moved blindly. In foreign policy they were grudgingly forced to break with the tottering Axis powers. The forced declaration of war on Germany cost Ramírez the presidency, but there was no turning back. Before his replacement, Ramírez had launched vicious attacks against communists, socialists, and Jews. He attacked the unions and placed labor leaders in concentration camps. All political parties were dissolved. Indeed, by October 1943 the officers had managed to punish virtually every class and political grouping in the country, using fascist methods at the exact time when fascism was on the defensive everywhere else. In 1944, when General Farrell assumed power, the

Axis powers were already crumbling and the Argentine middle class became increasingly belligerent against the military regime. It seemed that the days of that regime were numbered—were it not for an episode that had taken place in October 1943, the full significance of which only became apparent a few years later. An officer in the ministry of war, an important member of the GOU, Colonel Juan D. Perón, had asked and obtained the job of running the labor department.

Perón was intelligent enough to realize that the military project could not survive by force alone, isolated from different political groupings and social interests and against overwhelming pressure from abroad. Perón was responsible for ending the assault on the workers' organizations and proceeded to reverse labor policy. He achieved this end with remarkable skill. The unions were well organized and well run when Perón began his work. Despite splits and demoralization after a decade of repression, they withstood the vicious attacks by conservatives and militarists and continued to uphold demands which had been systematically denied by successive administrations since 1930. We have already seen how the working class had borne the full weight of industrial accumulation during the thirties and early forties. By satisfying the pent-up demands of the workers' organizations, Perón easily gained the upper hand over left and center parties which had been rendered impotent by the previous regimes. His approach was eminently reasonable, though opportunist, and the workers' support for Perón was eminently rational. To interpret Perón's appeal as exclusively charismatic, that is, as the irrational attachment of miserable, undereducated, unorganized masses of migrants from the countryside to a Latin *caudillo* is to forget the important role played by older, mature worker organizations and leaders in the initial phase of Perónism. It is my impression that during the initial phase of Perónism there was an objective advance of the Argentine working class as a whole. Under Perón's leadership the Argentine labor movement experienced a phase of liberation and growth before passing under his control in later stages of the regime, when cross-pressures and contradictions turned it into a stagnant and reactionary system.

Perón's first step was to raise the labor department to full ministerial status. He then persuaded his military friends to join with him in meeting some of the trade union leaders. He managed to convince the latter that he meant business when he spoke of satisfying the demands of the working class. He thus obtained the support of a number of leaders and organizations. But many workers were not organized, and many were, because of rapid industrialization, recent arrivals in the Buenos Aires labor market. These were shirtless ones, the *descamisados* about whom

Perón and his companion, Eva Duarte, often spoke. The packing plants, to take an important example, had long resisted attempts at unionizing the workers. The meat workers were subjected to wide wage differentials and to seasonal unemployment. There were many other workers in a similar position, seasonally unemployed, ill paid, and hard to organize. Perón helped them. He got union leaders out of prison and tried to win their support. He organized the unorganized. He opened government posts to union men. In short, he provided many short-run benefits to the workers and added a large welfare dimension to the activities of the state. The support Perón obtained as a result of these measures was not too different from the support of F. D. Roosevelt's social security legislation won from the American poor. Welfarism went deep, and transformed Argentine politics. In 1946 the welfare colonel was able to win the presidency in free elections against a solid block of privilege ranging from large conservative landowners on the right, to the socialist and communists politicos on the left. Perón's success should be understood, however, in terms of his opponents' weakness and serious political mistakes. Perónism came to fill a vacuum created by the debilitation of the different social classes and the weakening of the political fabric in the previous decade. The crisis of the thirties had dealt a serious economic blow to the landed bourgeoisie. It responded to economic weakness with political usurpation, and in so doing, corroded and corrupted the entire political system. On the other hand, industrialization could not be prevented, even though it took place haltingly, was kept contained, and was initially designed as a mere import-substitution device by the agrarians. Industrialization had produced a new bourgeoisie that was politically timid, ethnically segregated, and above all dependent for its prosperity on exceptional international circumstances and on the often reluctant protection of the state. Industry also had given birth to a large urban proletariat—exploited, and repressed, which found its demands unfulfilled and its struggles frustrated. From 1930 to 1935 high unemployment and political repression had weakened the power of the unions. After 1935, rapid industrial expansion reduced unemployment and brought masses of rural migrants into the cities. The union movement began to grow again, but under the severe repression of the conservative regimes, strikes did not produce gains for the workers during this period. These pressures undermined the leadership of socialists and communists in the unions. The General Confederation of Labor (CGT) split into two rival factions in 1942, one controlled by socialists and the other by communists. The frustration of those years finally led workers away from political activity and from union participation. After 1943,

Perón's labor policies offered the workers an opportunity to regroup and advance their position in society.

The political fragmentation and the inconclusive conflict of classes in Argentina had its conterpart in the conflicts between the imperialist powers which impeded any metropolis from controlling the country. World War II exacerbated these trends. In brief, no single class within, and no major power without, could control Argentina. This conjuncture made political action decisive. Perón's strategy was to use the state apparatus in order to forge a new coalition of classes from above that would support a program of national capitalist development.

FROM MILITARISM TO POPULISM

During 1945 the military authorities searched for a constitutional way out from the impasse in which they found themselves. That was very difficult because the different political parties—until recently victimized by the army—were reluctant to respond to the new solicitations of the regime. Their capacity to strike any deal with the military regime was limited by their zealous middle class constituencies, encouraged by the Allied victories in the War, and by the suspicion of the upper classes who were becoming increasingly alarmed at Perón's labor policies. Perón's attempts to improve the lot of the rural workers and to change tenancy regulations were considered an attack on the landed bourgeoisie. Thus, conciliatory moves failed. Negotiations between the military and their civilian opponents broke down and gave way to a frontal clash.

After seeking unsuccessfully to obtain support from traditional parties, Perón launched his presidential candidacy relying almost exclusively on the political forces which he had managed to mobilize from above. These forces, aided by the political mistakes of Perón's opponents, proved sufficient to propel him to power. The military were by then as divided and confused about their own goals as any body of civilian politicians. In August 1945 they lifted the state of siege, trying to placate their opponents. This opened the gates for fairly massive civilian demonstrations—mostly by the middle and upper strata—in favor of the restoration of the constitution and of liberal freedoms. The state of siege was reimposed and repression resumed, at which point an army faction rebelled and marched on Buenos Aires. After some hesitation, they managed to have Perón removed from office and arrested. Not content with the arrest of Perón, civilian politicians demanded the immediate overthrow of President Farrell and the transfer of power to the Supreme Court. Simultaneously, the employer's organizations announced their intention not to give their workers a paid holiday on October 12, 1945, which was traditionally celebrated as Columbus Day. Thus, it became clear that the liberal struggle for constitutional guarantees was at the same time an attack on the proletariat. This was not lost on the workers. When Perón was arrested he was with his companion, Eva Duarte, who immediately rushed to tell union leaders what had happened. Packing-house workers then organized a counter-demonstration. Rioting began on October 15. During the next days, workers from the industrial sub-urbs (Avellaneda and Berisso) began to move into central Buenos Aires. By the 17th they had taken over the city without the opposition of either the police or the local military garrison, which were well disposed to-wards Perón. Nobody knew exactly what to do but there was the feel-ing that this was a turning point. Perón was released from prison and appeared on the balcony of the government house, the *Casa Rosada,* with President Farrell. He gestured in victory to the thousands of workers cheering him in the *Plaza de Mayo.* Then the labor confederation (CGT) declared a general strike in support of Perón. His military opponents were arrested. Perón won the day.

October 17, 1945 was a turning point in Perón's career also. It marked his transformation from a military man of fascist proclivities into a new sort of civilian politician—a democratic populist. From then on he worked for the restoration of the constitution. He retired from the army and accepted the challenge of open elections. He began organizing a new party to give expression to the new coalition of forces behind him. This was the Labor Party which was patterned after its British counter-part. This it not to deny Perón's personal opportunism or his heavy-handed attempts at controlling the working class movement by having his military friends in the government issue special regulatory laws to deal with unions that were cantankerous or by forming parallel rival unions. But the bulk of the working class was solidly behind him. Nor did Perón rely solely upon the workers. He had already won over de-cisive sectors of the armed forces. He now began courting the favors of an institution that had deep roots in Argentine society and reached across class lines: the Catholic Church. He made several concessions to the church—among them his marriage to Eva Duarte and promises of blocking legal divorce and lay education. The bishops—with sound political instinct—began praying for Perón's victory. Perón also estab-lished some rather tenuous links to the traditional parties. He secured a second-rank radical politician, Hortensio Quijano, as his vice-presi-dential running mate.

Arrayed against Perón was almost the entire Argentine Establishment: the Conservative Party and the landed elite, cattlemen and grain farmers of the Littoral, the Industrial Union representing big industrial capital, the middle-class radicals, and even the socialists and communists providing a left-wing embellishment to the conservative conglomerate. It was an establishment coalition parading as a popular front—the *Unión Democrática*. But two ingredients were missing from the conservative coalition: the army and the church. They had joined the new alliance of classes: workers, national industrialists of recent vintage, and scattered middle sectors.

Most observers agree that the election which followed was one of the few free and honest elections in Argentine history. The victory for Perón was clear, if not overwhelming: 1,479,517 votes for Perón-Quijano, the candidates of the Labor Party and 1,220,822 for Tamborini-Mosca, the candidates of the *Unión Democrática*. In the congressional elections the result was even more favorable for Perón. His Labor Party won substantial majorities in the Senate and the Chamber of Deputies. All but one of the provincial governorships went to *Perónista* candidates. There were several amusing episodes in the situation. The American businessman-Ambassador, Spruille Braden, threw himself into the election campaign against Perón, with an enthusiasm worthy of a better cause and sharper judgement. He produced a Blue Book exposing all the political sins of Perón, especially his alleged connections with Nazis and fascists (but carefully deleting the names of fascists who were now opposing Perón). Perón's answer was a Blue and White (the Argentine national colors) book denouncing the imperialist intervention. "Braden or Perón" became one favorite campaign slogan of the Labor Party.

V. POPULISM AND REFORM

ARGENTINA JUSTICIALISTA: THE EQUIVOCAL REVOLUTION

When Perón was elected to the presidency in 1946, he came to power under exceptionally favorable circumstances. He was elected by a majority in open and free elections. His support came predominantly from the urban working class and from sectors of the lower middle class, but not exclusively so, nor was it limited to only one region of the country. Industrialization had already made strides and Argentina had the resources to develop autonomously. There was plenty of money in the banks: the sale of supplies to the Allies during World War II had produced sterling and dollar balances worth fifteen million dollars. International prices of food and agricultural raw materials were then rising relative to industrial goods. Perón's development plans aimed at strengthening and extending basic industrialization, at spreading its benefits throughout the

country, at improving education, renewing immigration, improving social services, and finally attaining an independent "Third World" position, *avant la lettre*, in the community of nations. Yet, despite these
auspicious beginnings, the Perónist revolution failed to materialize. After
ten years of rule the international conjuncture was no longer favorable
to Argentina; her resources had been misapplied and dissipated; her economy was stagnant, her political system more rigid and hidebound. Perón
was ousted from power and his successors did worse. Argentina has since
been underdeveloping at a steady pace. Perón constructed a hybrid
social and political system which he did not run successfully. Those who
inherited that system could neither dismantle it nor run it better than
Perón. The populist facade concealed a tremendous amount of tugging
and hauling among competing interest groups unable to purge each other.
In recent years this stalemated pluralism has increasingly assumed the
character of a latent civil war.

The Perónist victory signalled a change in the balance of social forces:
the working class now formed, together with the army and the church,
the political base of the government and became one of the principal
beneficiaries of post-war prosperity—which lasted until 1949—and of
Perónist policies. The new social policy consisted of welfare measures
and income redistribution organized along semi-paternalistic lines by
Perón and even more sincerely and efficaciously by Eva Duarte de Perón.
This remarkable woman did more than Perón to upset the class structure
of Argentina and to disturb one of its most insidious syndromes—male
chauvinism.

It was above all Evita, as she was called, who presided over the participatory revolution in Argentine politics. She prepared a place for the
uprooted and the excluded in the new social order—or at least made
them feel welcome. Eva Perón was impressively dynamic and beautiful.
She had made her way through a class-bound and male-dominated society from the bottom of economic and sexual exploitation to the top
of political leadership. She was an illegitimate child in a society that
protected the sanctity of marriage by outcasting children born out of
wedlock. She was poor in a society dominated by wealth—a woman
whom males would only reward for the crafty use of beauty. Her life
was bound up with ambition and pride that sought vengeance upon the
masters of superior fortune. Suffering had made her "an enemy of
(bourgeois) society." Her life is fascinating precisely because it embodies the moral essence of an age. She rose above her predestined lot
in a time of social decomposition: she knew how to gain power, how to
use it, now with ruse, now with violence, while championing the cause

of the underprivileged. Twenty years after her death she is still a symbol for the poor and her memory still haunts the bourgeoisie.

THE PHASES AND CONTRADICTIONS
OF NATIONAL POPULISM

Perónism also innovated in matters of economic policy. The mechanisms of control over the economy which Perón inherited from the previous conservative regimes were now used to transfer economic surplus from the primary export sector to the industrial sector. Imports of raw materials and capital goods for industry were kept at low prices. The potential earnings of agrarian exporters were sacrificed in order to finance industrial growth. The state gained increasing control over the economic system through the monopoly of external trade, the nationalization of the central bank, and the concentration in that bank of most reserves from the private banking houses. Railways, telephone and gas companies, and urban transport were all nationalized, thus increasing the capacity of the state to affect the course of economic development. On the other hand, the foreign exchange earnings were spent in the costly compensations to the concerns that were nationalized. A big chunk of earnings accumulated from foreign trade during World War II was invested in the equipment of light consumer industries. By and large, the creation of a heavy industry remained an unaccomplished project. There was limited investment in the infrastructure of transport and public services. A state-sponsored mixed enterprise was set up to produce steel, and the industrial enterprises run by the armed forces were expanded. Even a state-owned aviation industry was set up, but these more ambitious projects did not produce impressive results. Insurance was also nationalized. Although noises were made suggesting the possible nationalization of land, agrarian reform was not instituted. The main export business in grain and meat was not nationalized, but a state marketing agency took control of the export of all major commodities—the Institute for Exchange Promotion (*Instituto Argentino de Promoción de Intercambio*, IAPI)—with power to fix prices to producers and consumers. The differential between the internal and external prices of the meat, grain, and other products that were thus traded gave the government a handsome profit the purpose of which was to facilitate credit to the national industrialists. At the same time the pension system was expanded to all industrial workers, so that 25 percent of the workers' wages (10 percent from the worker and the rest from the employer) was funneled into state pension funds. The pensionable age was set at the low age of fifty-five—more suitable to a post-industrial than to a developing society—and pensions were adjusted to wages at the age of retirement rather than to payments made into pension funds. This pension system eventually extended to rural workers as well.

The relative standing of the working class improved remarkably. Since 1945 Argentina had attained conditions nearing full employment. The marginal work force was being absorbed by industrial expansion. Thus, the solid position of the workers during the first half of Perón's regime was the combined result of a favorable economic conjuncture and of his laborist policy. Workers' earnings rose sharply between the years 1946/ 1947 and 1947/1948, rising 17.7 percent and 11.7 percent respectively. After a new rise in 1949, they stood 24.3 percent above wages in 1945.

Real wages in industry rose much more rapidly than total wages per worker (Silverman, 1969, 244). From 1943 to 1949 labor's share of national income rose from approximately 45 to 59 percent. Most of this shift occurred from 1947 to 1949, reflecting the implementation of new social security programs as well as rising wages (Silverman, *ibid.*, 243). Perón's policies tended to favor the industrial sector. The few available studies indicate that there was a continued rise of entrepreneurial income through 1950. Rentiers (landlords and landholders) and agricultural producers bore the brunt of income redistribution. The rentiers were hit the hardest on account of rent controls and inflation (Silverman, *ibid.*, 243–44). A large proportion of investments went to nonproductive activities which produced, however, high political dividends: housing and public expenditures in social, administrative, and military services. In this way an enormous new complex of interests was created which on one hand supported Perón and on the other constituted a political obstacle to any deepening or radicalization of his "revolution", since that process would of necessity have entailed the sacrifice of immediate rewards to long-term and self-sustained development. In short, the initial political advantage of Perónism became its long-run handicap. Any step toward a serious transformation of the economic order beyond income redistribution and consumer-based industrialization implied tightening the political controls and most likely the transformation of the populist regime into a progressive but more rigid dictatorship. Perón tried on occasion to follow this road, but his moves provoked other supporters—notably the army—to balk. So Perón was confined to reformism—a political formula only suited to times of prosperity. Economic policies became conditional upon the political requirements of populism, and these in turn depended upon prosperity and official largesse. Caught in that circle, Perón became incapable of making sound choices and establishing the priorities which are necessary to make any system effective. Despite five-year plans, the political style of populism made nonsense of plans in general and of the details of their effective execution. As long as the post-war boom lasted, Perón could manage his system by simultaneous and large pay-offs to different groups. Even the much maligned landed oligarchy was not seriously hurt by redistribution and industrial credit. For a while real wages continued to rise and with them popular euphoria. But the Perónist revolution had a serious flaw: nothing really guaranteed its continuation. In this, Perón succumbed to an old Argentine illusion born in a previous epoch of prosperity—the liberal export period—namely, the mirage of endless good fortune, typical of a once-pampered colony. But the lean years arrived in 1950, and Perón was faced with a difficult choice: either to unleash radical social changes, or to preside over the liquidation of his revolution. Either path was fraught with dangers for the regime. Perón chose to move backwards. During his second term as president (he was re-elected in 1952) Perón went conservative. He turned increasingly towards right-wing authoritarianism, but he did not survive his self-imposed Thermidor.

The favorable economic circumstances of the post-war period had allowed Perón to follow haphazard policies which, though inducing mass support, failed to sustain economic development. His populism was not radical enough to change the basic structure of society. His compromises, labelled by some as his economic "bonapartism," were not skillful enough to produce a viable "revolution from above," an Argentine version of bismarckism. After 1948 economic deterioration and political reaction took hold of the regime. Per capita GNP steadily declined. Stagnation set in, at which point Perón frantically attempted to change the direction of his policies. These negative trends set in as a result of economic conditions which were largely beyond the control of the Argentine regime, but they were also caused by policies which stopped short of radical structural reforms.

First, the low prices paid by IAPI to the agricultural producers tended to discourage agricultural production. Acting as a disincentive to agropecuarian productivity, it caused the meat and grain output to decline. The government—in the haste to industrialize—failed to make sufficient foreign exchange available for the purchase of new farm machinery. At the same time, the 1950's witnessed a serious decline of international prices for agricultural products which, coupled with a series of bad droughts in the *pampas* cut export earnings and consequently limited the country's capacity to import. Thus, as the volume of exports declined and the terms of trade moved against Argentina after 1948, the country soon found itself in serious foreign-exchange difficulties. The decline of agriculture was strikingly revealed in 1952 when, after a succession of droughts and bad harvests, Argentina actually had to import wheat from the United States! The problem underlying these difficulties was the regime's decision not to alter the agrarian framework. In the absence of agrarian reform, no incentive had been offered to agricultural production. The country's most strategic productive activities were in fact penalized under the operation of the state trading and multiple-exchange-rate systems, which denied the producers, that is, the landowners, the benefits of high external prices without crippling their capacity to rebound as a pressure group either, and without diversifying agricultural production. In consequence of this, and as a result of the significant rise in the standard of living of the urban masses mobilized by Perónism, a steadily increasing domestic consumption of meat and other foodstuffs inevitably reduced the country's exportable surpluses. The specter of dependency arose once more, even though the *nature* of dependency had changed. The development of consumer goods industries had reduced consumer imports. But the ability to maintain existing industries depended upon the import of indispensable fuels and raw materials and imports of capital goods for industry and transport. As a result of Perón's policies Argentina had an established "light" industry but was not in a position to promote its development without outside aid. One thing then became apparent: the utilization and direction of investment had been Perón's worst blunder. Nearly 74 percent of the total increase in fixed capital had gone into non-productive activities (Silverman, 1969, 251). To give a striking example: between 1945 and 1946, over 50 percent of real investment of the national government was applied to national defense. Between 1947 and 1951 defense expenditures were reduced, but they still represented an extravagant 23.5 percent (Silverman, *ibid*, 252). The cost of living began to rise more rapidly than money wages, so real wages began to decline. At this time, Perón began to rely more on the redistribution of income between industries and occupations, thus reducing wage differentials between skilled and unskilled workers. Political patronage caused wages to rise substantially above output per worker. Government policies resulted in a redistribution of the labor force into the least productive sectors of economic activity. All these developments had serious implications for economic growth: it was simply a failure. At the end of Perón's regime, per capita gross product was only 5.9 percent higher than in 1946. Perón tried to salvage what he could. There was a shift in agricultural policy in the fifties. Perón made friendly gestures toward foreign investors. He began sacrificing the two pillars of the regime: social justice and economic independence. When the internal contradictions of his experiment forced an option between radicalization or reaction, he opted for the latter, but could not escape the political and institutional pressures he had created. Opportunism proved self-defeating. When hard times arrived Perónism revealed its deepest conservative impulses. After all it had attempted to develop a populist labor policy within the institutional framework of capitalism. Laborism had been the strategy of its revolutionary phase. It had provided Perónism with working class support. But it contradicted the requirements of capitalist accumulation which Perón had not once challenged. Perón had now to stabilize the hybrid system he had created: he began instituting repressive controls and freezing the class struggle by setting up corporativist institutions. In brief, he tried to build a power apparatus in order to free himself from the reactionary and radical cross pressures in the society.

Thus, the Perónist administration increased its political control over the country. The supreme court had already been purged in 1947. Later, opinion weeklies had been closed and radio stations had been taken over. Then the government secured from congress the power to mobilize the nation for war, which involved the power to break strikes. These measures amounted to a serious attack on political opponents and constituted a large build-up of presidential power. These early repressive measures had been compensated on the other hand by a large pay-off program: large wage increases for the workers; large budget appropriations for the armed forces; new jobs for political supporters in the new nationalized enterprises; tariff protection for national industrialists. When the economy began to show signs of incapacity to support the strategy of redistribution and pay-offs, when the crisis began to manifest itself in the form of inflation and in the lowering of real incomes, Perón responded by strengthening and extending the political controls. The constitution was reformed—largely to allow the re-election of Perón. The more independent labor leaders were arrested on trumped-up charges. The Labor Party was attacked and a new *Perónista* Party was formed. The labor movement was further bureaucratized; the CGT was made dependent on the leader. In other words, power was centralized and coordinated in the hands of Perón. An Argentine version of the Stalinist "cult of personality" was instituted—balanced only by a generous dose of homespun MacCarthysm: an anti-Argentine activities investigating committee was set up. Despite these features, the regime lacked most of the distinguishing traits of totalitarianism. There were only half-hearted efforts to establish control of the political process, to institute a program of political socialization, to positively control the media. There was increased repression and police brutality but no ubiquitous terror. The regime became stronger and more rigid as time went by, but it was not totalitarian—clearly not a variant of fascist totalitarianism as it is sometimes depicted. In fact some analysts insist that throughout the regime, the relationship between Perón and his followers was basically rational as opposed to the relationship of European fascist leaders to their followers, which is described as irrational (Germani, 1962, 245–52). In short, that Perónism was not "effectively totalitarian" (Silvert, 1967, 362–66). There was censorship, and an atmosphere of intimidation and harassment, but the opposition was not crushed. The presidential elections of 1946 and 1951 Perón was opposed, and most observers agree that the elections were quite free and honest. One thing is clear, however: by the time Perón entered his second term in office (he was reelected in 1951, securing 4.6 million votes against 2.3 million for his radical opponents Ricardo Balbín and Arturo Frondizi) his economic failures began eroding the bases of his support and forced him to become more dictatorial.

In August 1951, a great gathering of Perón supporters proclaimed the candidacy of Perón for a second term as president, and the candidacy of Eva Perón as vice-president. This was an important departure from political norms. Perón's constitutional reform of 1949 allowed the reelection of the president and the candidacy of a woman, for women had been enfranchised due to the efforts of Evita. The conservative flanks of the regime—the army and the church—balked at these prospects. To them, Perón was going too far. The possibility of a woman succeeding to the presidency especially outraged the chauvinism of the officers. They demanded her resignation of the candidacy. Perón bowed to military pressure. Evita was sacrificed. Perón ran for a second term and won the elections. The people were still on his side, but it was the beginning of the end. The economy was stagnant. Almost simultaneously there was a severe drought which revealed how thoroughly Argentina was still dependent on the products of the countryside. In order to feed the people grains had to be imported in the country of wheat. Meat production declined alarmingly. In September 1951 there was a military revolt which was put down partly by pro-Perón officers and partly by the mass mobilization of the workers. Eva Perón contracted cancer and died in July 1952—lucid and fierce to the last. Her funeral produced an outpouring of popular grief as had not been known in Argentina before. Unbeknownst to the mourners, it was also the funeral of Perón's reformist populism. The army was wrought by dissension. The navy was solidly against Perón. There was tension between the regime and ecclesiastical interest since the regime had usurped the church's role in the welfare and charity movements, and the enfranchisement of women was seen with disfavor by the skirted hierarchy. The students also began to move against the regime. By handing over the direction of the universities to incompetent goons, Perón made a serious and rather silly mistake:

he created an opposition among the very people who could have easily and generously supported him.

By 1953 the Argentine economy was in such bad shape that Perón decided to change his economic policy. This period marks the reactionary phase of Perónism. Politically he was not yet in a position to turn the screw on the workers, and to find in stepped-up labor exploitation the funds needed for industrial investment. The landed bourgeoisie and the farmers had been hit hard by drought and by the process of decapitalization to which Perón had subjected them. There was one source of capital to which Perón now turned: American investments. In August 1953 negotiations were opened with Standard Oil of California. Petroleum extraction was now opened to imperialism. Then American and West European firms began taking over major sectors of Argentine industry. With tariff protection now working in their favor, American, German, and Italian firms developed high-cost automobile plants and chemical complexes. The nationalist pretensions of the regime were simply thrown overboard. By 1954 there was a new alignment of forces in Argentine politics. Perón found himself in alliance with the workers —still loyal to him, foreign capitalists, and government office-holders and hangers-on. Against him stood the oligarchy as always, sectors of the army, the church, and increasingly both the industrial bourgeoisie and the urban middle strata. The industrialists found it hard to reconcile their interests with Perón laborism. The middle sectors, which had been outflanked in their quest for power in 1945, were increasingly adopting a pseudo-aristocratic contempt for the plebeian style of the regime. The middle sectors were characterized by false consciousness and political ambivalence. And Perón's unnecessary attacks upon these sectors exacerbated their opposition. Nevertheless, some middle-class organizations began adopting political programs that purported to complete the unfinished work of Perónism: land reform and a transition to socialism. On the other side of the political spectrum, some conservative politicians tried to approach the regime and negotiate with Perón. But Perón chose to free himself from these opposing pressures by beginning to mount corporativist structures in order to control the different social interests —workers, industrialists, and agrarians—from above. Side by side with the docile CGT, a General Economic Confederation (*Confederación General Económica* CGE) was created which grouped capitalists. Then came a CGP, (*Confederación General de Profesionales* or corporation of professionals), a CGU (*Confederación General Universitaria* or University Federation), and even a corporate organization of high-school students, the UES (*Unión de Estudiantes Secundarios*). At the same time, the state ceased to be a champion of the workers and became instead a neutral arbiter in labor disputes. Several strikes were suppressed. By 1954 was clear that Perón's revolution had completed its cycle and was entering a reactionary period. The hybrid system created by Perón was becoming ossified and promised to last indefinitely as a corporative status quo. The opposition was hamstrung and divided. Perón had made his peace with big capital and Argentina was now solidly in the orbit of American imperialism. Yet Perón failed to make the transition to a new conservatism.

Hitherto Perónism had consisted of an uneasy alliance of trade unions and secondary institutions like the church and the army. Prosperity kept them together through a policy of simultaneous and large pay-offs. The economic debacle of the fifties made pay-off impossible and forced instead a different set of political maneuvers that proved fatal to the regime. Perón could not turn against the working class—as the new political situation demanded—without previously weakening the conservative institutions of society: the church and the army. Otherwise he would rapidly become their prisoner. His new political strategy was then to attack the conservative secondary institutions while he kept control of the labor movement and was still popular with the workers; then turn the screw on the wage earners. Such maneuvers, combined with the realignment of Argentina on the American side and the opening of her economy to foreign capital, lured Perón to the prospects of many more years in power as a tamed strongman—a friend of the West. Unfortunately for Perón, his attacks on the secondary organizations backfired. In 1954 he hammered the church with a law making divorce legal, he authorized the reopening of brothels, and downgraded religious holidays—Christmas and Good Friday included—to secondary status. The opposition managed to capitalize on these attacks. In 1955 there were mass demonstrations against the government by middle- and upper-class individuals. Perón took the bait: he replied with further repressive measures. On June 16, navy planes attempted to kill Perón by bombing the presidential house. They only managed to kill several hundred city workers in the heart of the business district of Buenos Aires just after lunch hour. That night several churches in downtown Buenos Aires were burned by Perónist sympathizers. There were rumors that Perón was arming the workers. Perón orchestrated his public resignation on August 31. Masses of workers gathered in *Plaza de Mayo*, asked him to stay in power, and he graciously conceded. But this was the end. In Córdoba the military garrison, under the leadership of General Lonardi, rose against Perón. There were popular demonstrations of support among the middle and upper classes. This time the proletariat was quiescent. The army hesitated at first but did not come to the rescue of the president. Perón boarded a Paraguayan gunboat and was taken into exile.

The Perónist government collapsed as soon as he departed. It was the end of what probably was the first instance of a political phenomenon that later became common throughout the Third World: non-aligned developmentalism in a mixed economy. In Argentina this phenomenon had taken the form of a pseudo-revolution: a coalition of different classes and institutional bureaucracies within a capitalist framework, underwritten by the large funds accumulated by Argentina during exceptional years when the bonds of dependency were relaxed. The alliance collapsed ten years later, when the funds had run out and import substitution could no longer sustain an independent industrialization process. After the fall of Perón, the different components of society turned upon each other in sharp conflicts that to date remain inconclusive—exacerbated by the increasing vulnerability of Argentina to imperialist penetration. After nearly two decades of internal strife and social crisis one secondary organization and one social class have proved durable: the military and the proletariat. Other groups and institutions have been weakened perhaps beyond repair.

When Perón came to power, Argentina had witnessed the slow disintegration of an inherited conglomerate of dependency and misdevelopment, yet still very far from complete. With Perón, many Argentines experienced a momentary sense of liberation, marked by advances in social justice. They were for a moment confronted with the prospect of a society much more open and independent than anything previously known. But they soon began experiencing something else—the unmistakable symptoms of a recoil from that prospect. There was hesitation before the jump, and then a flight backwards. Perónism rode to this jump and refused it. Was it the horse that refused, or the rider? Perón's personal flaws are too great and too many to be dismissed. But the coalition of social interests that supported him and made his experiment possible was fragile and unstable. Perón could not control them. Argentine rulers after him have made the fatal mistake of thinking they could ignore them. Today, other groups are beginning to acquire a new consciousness and new political instruments. These are still far from adequate, and they are not always skillfully handled. Their possibilities have still to be tested. Yet they seem to offer the shimmer of hope in a country wrought by exhaustion and cynicism.

VI. THE NEW DEPENDENCY

THE RESTORATION

At the end of Perón's rule, Argentina was passing through one of the worst economic crises of its history. The failure of the Perónist program of autarkic industrialization, coupled with the policies of mass mobilization and welfarism that had characterized the regime, had left a sequel of inflation and misdevelopment, changing the nature of, but not abolishing, dependency, and reinforcing the pattern of "superstructural" modernization typical of Argentine social change. Perón himself had already been faced with the dilemma of either unleashing a social revolution—a qualitative change in the relations of production—or stabilizing the system he had created through the enforcement of, not only economic, but also social and political, deflation. He had chosen stabilization but failed to survive the strains of the transition. The military leaders that overthrew Perón in 1955 set out to complete with new zest the unfinished task of reaction. The so-called Liberating Revolution of 1955 was designed to contain the class tensions unleashed by Perónist arbitration, to restrict political participation to the "respectable" parties representing the middle and upper classes, and to stabilize the economy by strengthening the traditional export sector, curtailing secondary sources of inflation—wages, public expenditures and services, the state bureaucracy—while simultaneously seeking to attract foreign loans and direct investments.

The program of the regime of 1955 was at the same time a policy of stabilization and one of de-nationalization. Such restrictive and in many ways backward-looking enterprise was fraught with grave risks, for it entailed among other consequences nothing less than the disenfranchisement of the bulk of the urban working class. This was a drastic devolution in the process of political modernization and democratization, and it was accompanied by considerable economic hardships for the lower classes. The program of stabilization in economics and regression in political participation was rendered particularly unrealistic by the liberal commitment of the ruling group to the formal mechanisms of pluralist democracy. Upon the repression of the most significant political phenomenon in twentieth century Argentina—namely, the incorporation of urban and rural masses to the structure of national political participation—the anti-Perónist regime wished to rebuild the old skeleton of pluralism, this time restricted to the parties of the middle and upper reaches of society. This could not but result in political cheating, since by no possible stretch of the imagination could the regime hope to infuse the old parties with representativeness and legitimacy among the large Perónist electorate. This tutored, conservative pluralism of semi-liberal stamp in the long run jeopardized the very stabilizing policies of the government, by making them inconsistent, by fostering a demagogic jostle between unrepresentative parties in a scramble to hoodwink Perónist voters, by strengthening the self-fulfilling prophecy among the military that civilians were corrupt or at best inept in leading the nation, and eventually by generating a cycle of political instability and military intervention that ended with the demise of all liberal semblance *tout court* in 1966. It is therefore possible to treat the decade that ran from 1955 to 1966 as unitary and continuous. Four basic features are worth noting. First, a ruling elite with military and landed upper class components tied to foreign interests. The new coalition agreed on the need to curtail and surpress Perónism, to return to traditional patterns of dependent growth, and to seek foreign aid and investment as a decisive instrument of policy. Second, a defeated Perónist mass, divided and plagued by the inner contradictions of populism, but beginning a "long march" underground. Third, a formal democratic structure of parties of the middle and upper strata. "Restrictive" or repressive pluralism may be adequate descriptive terms for these arrangements. Fourth, an economic strategy designed to dismantle the hybrid system created by Perón, encouraging the export sector and foreign investments and instituting policies of monetary stabilization.

This cursory outline of the socio-political system installed in Argentina after the fall of Perón shows that its various components worked at cross purposes, and especially that, under conditions of restrictive pluralism, economic stabilization could not but generate political turmoil. No wonder then that the main political forces during this period proved unable to develop a common framework or any consensus capable of sustaining a coherent program of economic growth. Government policies were often illegitimate and unrepresentative. Thus, the more the system of restrictive pluralism was corroded by its inner contradictions, the more it became vulnerable to military intervention. And the more frequently military intervention occurred, the weaker the political fabric became. This stalemated pluralism blocked all the ways out of economic stagnation: every one of the potential victims of alternative solutions to the economic impasse—the working class, the middle sectors, the landed bourgeoisie, the industrialists—was still powerful enough to veto the execution of any coherent development strategy.

We have seen how the response to crisis and war had produced an unintegrated industrial system and with it a fragile balance of social forces. Perónism capitalized on these processes and attempted to institutionalize them in a hybrid system. The experiment failed: social equilibrium was not consolidated, and from 1955 onward Argentina entered a period of increased social tension and political confrontations. These strains had deep economic roots, internal as well as international. But other episodes and factors added to the stress: the Cold War and the emergence of Cuban socialism in particular, imposed a new sense of urgency upon the exhaustion of previous political experiments. Not only

the survival of particular governments but the very existence of capitalism and American hegemony were at stake. National and international
interests rapidly moved to stabilize the *status quo*. By the mid-fifties,
the signs of economic decay were unmistakable. Inflation reached intolerable levels. The state could no longer prevent the drift of the economy. The groups in power responded to the critical situation with a set
of neo-liberal policies that clearly betrayed class loyalties. Faced with a
continuous deterioration of the terms of trade, they promoted the concentration of benefits in the export sector, while the other sectors of the
economy moved into recession by virtue of the curtailment of credit and
the application of anti-inflationary policies. The aim was to produce a
rebirth of prosperity through exports and then diffuse that prosperity
through the rest of the system. It simply did not work. Moreover, the
administration of such strong medicine caused unbearable social tensions
which were only assuaged by backtracking and reinstituting state controls and inflationary stimuli. Increased external dependency was one
of the clearest signs of the crisis. Argentina got deeper into debt: the
balance of trade and the balance of payments yielded huge deficits. Its
more complex industrial structure was in even greater need of credit
than the old export structures had been during the period of outward
growth under British hegemony. Without external credit there were
neither raw materials nor essential fuels and parts to keep industry moving. Argentina appealed time and again to the international finance organizations that respond to the directives of North American capitalism.
The International Monetary Fund now called the shots, both directly
by channeling credit and indirectly, by setting the pace of private investments. Thus credits gave temporary respite to the ruling groups of
Argentina. In order to satisfy the pressures of different social classes,
the elite launched periodic inflationary orgies which were subsequently
checked by deflationary brakes and currency devaluations imposed by the
international creditors. But deflationary measures managed to cause recession without necessarily stopping inflation. The stop-go cycle seemed
hopeless. Economic crises were excerbated in the dependent capitalist
system of Argentina precisely when advanced capitalism seemed to have
learned to stabilize its own cycles in the metropolis. Like addicts, the
ruling circles responded to the existing morass with a stronger dosage of
the poison: they pinned their hopes on ever larger flows of metropolitan
dollars and plants. The country was flooded with proposals, plans, and
theories of development. But every one of them was successfully vetoed by
the social sectors that would have had to bear their respective weight.

In 1955 Argentina had reached the full occupation of its potential
labor force, fed from the peripheral regions of the country. Industrial-

ization had placed the manufacturing sector ahead of the agrarian sector in the share of GNP. On the other hand the concentration of industry in the production of consumer goods made it dependent on imports of raw materials, fuels, and capital goods. The stagnation of the agro-pecuarian production and the rise in the internal consumption of that produce had depleted exportable surpluses. The consequence was a steady disequilibrium in the balance of trade. Therefore, any attempt to continue economic growth produced inflation. And policies designed to correct inflation halted growth. When the Perónist administration tried to break that vicious circle by adopting conservative measures (strengthening the export structures, transferring income from urban to rural sectors, appealing to foreign capital, disciplining the labor force), it was overthrown by a military coup. The new regime restored the pre-Perónist political arrangements. The two wings of the new restoration—a liberal conservative faction and a Catholic-fascist sector—agreed on one mistake, namely, to consider that Perónism had died with the fall of Perón. They wished to dismantle the system created by the latter by favoring the policies alrealy instituted by Perón himself in the final hour of his regime. External trade was liberalized and the *peso* was devalued as measures in favor of the primary exporters. Public expenditures were curtailed and workers were denied wage increases. These policies—sponsored by the head of the United Nations Economic Commission for Latin America (ECLA), the Argentine economist Raúl Prebisch—aimed at replenishing the stock of foreign exchange which Argentina needed in order to revamp its mining and industrial structures. But the economic plan was only half-heartedly executed, on account of two main factors. On the one hand, the new economic measures risked popular unrest. Therefore investment was often sacrificed to the maintenance of the wage level for the sake of social peace. On the other hand, the agro-pecuarian interests—who had an important role in the post-Perónist governments—were not disposed to surrender the advantages they had recently obtained for the sake of further industrialization. The net result of economic policy was then to increase the profits of the landed bourgeoisie, to raise the internal prices of foodstuffs, and thereby create more inflationary pressures by raising the cost of living. Development remained an unfulfilled promise.

While the government teams attempted unsuccessfully to dismantle the web of affiliations inherited from the Perónist era, new political groupings wished to operate that system better than Perón had done. The most important of these groups was the left wing of *radicalismo*, led by Arturo Frondizi. Frondizi wanted a renovated *radicalismo* to supersede Perónism. The latter, however, proved more durable than was expected, or wished, by its rivals and would-be heirs. In 1957 the military authorities—under the leadership of the provisional president General Pedro Eugenio Aramburu—called a Constitutional Convention designed to revamp the Constitution of 1953 and scrap the more recent Perónist Constitution of 1949. The elections for the Constituent Assembly revealed the strength of Perónism. The *perónistas* cast over two million ballots representing about 20 percent of those voting. These protest votes took the lead, followed by the votes for the traditional wing of the Radical party (*Unión Cívica Radical del Pueblo*, UCRP). Frondizi and his faction (*Unión Cívica Radical Intransigente*, UCRI) came third. Frondizi was forced to change his political strategy. Instead of replacing Perón he tried to become his ally. He made a secret deal with Perón in which he promised to re-admit the *perónistas* into the political process in return for Perón's support in the presidential elections prepared by the provisional military government for February 1958. The result was an easy victory of Frondizi over his radical rivals. The Perónist support also won for Frondizi the mistrust of the military and the conservatives. As soon as he ascended the presidency, however, Frondizi turned his back on his popular support and sought instead the backing of the industrial sector, which he invited to struggle against the landed interests. Frondizi thus pinned his hopes on leading the national bourgeoisie, and secondarily, the Perónist proletariat, along the path of *desarrollismo* (developmentalism). Despite endless wheeling and dealing, this task proved more formidable than Frondizi had expected. Two considerations were mainly responsible for his failure. On the one hand, the Perónist experience had produced an urban proletariat which was organizationally more advanced than the industrial bourgeoisie. Only sectors of this industrial class had supported Perón, and had done so timidly (Freels, 1968, *passim*). Dependency on state protection and social segregation had kept this class relatively weak in a country in which the traditional hegemony of the landed bourgeoisie had constantly discouraged the investment of capital in industry and induced it into land purchases—the early anti-oligarchic gestures of Perón notwithstanding. The end of Perónism had caused the landed bourgeoisie to rebound politically and to resist the imposition of any sacrifice for the sake of industrial development and integration. This class vetoed different attempts to wrest funds for capital accumulation from the agro-pecuarian sector. Frondizi then, in a classic about-face, turned to foreign monopoly capital to carry forward his plans for industrial *desarrollo*. He signed contracts with foreign oil companies, negotiated credits through the International Monetary Fund, and opened the sluices to the flow of foreign capital into manufacturing, energy production, and public transport. He thus avoided the real problems of internal accumulation and disguised the avoidance with a technocratic ideology of developmentalism. Every major political and economic decision made by Frondizi represented the betrayal of one or more of his previous planks. This maneuvering alienated different sectors of the electorate, multiplied suspicions, and left Frondizi with sheer political ruse as the instrument of government. The tricks did not work: foreign capital left Argentina saddled with enormous debts. After a brief inflationary expansion, growth was halted by a new round of stabilization policies forced upon Frondizi by the zeal of international creditors. Economic austerity provoked the Perónist proletariat into a militant opposition that was met with strong repression. Frondizi's devious and shifting deals with defferent political forces raised the suspicions of the military. His attempted neutrality vis-à-vis the Cuban Revolution enraged the officers who looked to the Pentagon as a Mecca. But it was the durable Perónists who gave Frondizi the *coup de grace*. The provincial elections of 1962 produced unexpected victories for the Perónists who retained the loyalty of one-third of the electorate: they won forty-five of the eighty-six seats up for election in the Chamber of Deputies and ten of fourteen governorships. Meanwhile, the level of violence reached unprecedented proportions: there were guerrilla *focos* in the Northwest and frequent clashes between factions of the armed forces. By allowing *Perónistas* to run, Frondizi was belatedly fulfilling his end of the deal made with them in 1958, but the Perónist victories of 1962 convinced the officers that Frondizi was not worth all the trouble. They ousted him but stopped short of full dictatorship. As a compromise, the military placed Dr. José María Guido, the president of the senate and a colorless politician, in the presidency and instructed him to prepare for new elections.

The Guido administration was marked by two important episodes: the internal conflicts in the armed forces and the acute economic recession produced by the application of the orthodox economic policies sponsored by the IMF. The economic recession forced one third of the available work force to remain idle. At the same time, a new currency devaluation transferred the little prosperity there was into the hands of the agrarians. Political confusion abated temporarily when the armed forces—wrought by serious factionalism as a consequence of their intense participation in politics—decided to retrench and discovered for themselves a new technocratic vocation under the leadership of General Juan Carlos Onganía, who became commander-in-chief of the army. The officers agreed to leave power to an elected civilian government acceptable to the establishment. Under those circumstances, the mantle of power fell this time to the traditional wing of *radicalismo*. Since Perónists were not allowed to vote for their own candidates, the *perónista* wote was dispersed in the presidential elections of 1963. Dr. Arturo Illia, a radical politician from the province of Córdoba, became the new president.

The Illia administration benefited from the expansion of rural production—the effect of economic policies applied since 1955. The activity of the export sector had been kept alive through periodic devaluations of the *peso*. Now, for the first time in several decades, foreign trade yielded positive balances and did so during three consecutive years. The foreign exchange thus obtained was manipulated by the government through a restored exchange control system. These sums however were not large enough to cover the enormous short-term debts inherited from the Frondizi administration. As a result, the Illia government too had to appeal to international creditors, who once more managed to impose on Argentina a program of economic stabilization and austerity that interrupted the process of growth with manageable inflation of the mid-sixties. In brief, during the Illia administration, Argentina saw a temporary respite to the economic malaise but not the end of its troubles. The stop-go cycle of the economy managed to reassert itself in the end.

The political crisis was more serious than the economic difficulties. Just as with Frondizi before, the only hope for the party in power (UCRP) as to concentrate all non-Perónist votes in order to prevent a take-over by a unified Perónist movement in future elections—an event that would have taken place if anti-Perónist opinion remained split in different groupings. But other parties adamantly refused to relinquish their electoral support to the *radicales* in the government. Meanwhile, Perónism was beginning to find support among sectors of the middle class. The latter had opposed Perónism when it became clear that Perón would postpone the satisfaction of its demands in order to attend first to the demands of the industrial proletariat. After the fall of Perón, the middle class did not see those pent-up pretensions fulfilled. Instead, the governments that succeeded Perón increased the privileges of the landed upper class and added a new privileged member to the familiar constellation of Argentine society: foreign monopoly capital. As a consequence of this, sectors of the middle class began to redefine their relationship with Perónism. Thus, Perónism threatened to command an absolute majority in future elections. A return of Perón to power was more than the military could accept, despite the basic unrevolutionary nature of the movement and its leadership. But ten years of anti-Perónist blunders and economic stagnation had produced a peculiar result: Perónism became a treasure-house of myth and legend for many Argentines, providing a source of political inspiration to a younger generation. In these metamorphoses, Perón's regime appeared as a golden age followed by periods of a baser ore in which all manner of greed and deceit broke out while prosperity and loyalty fled.

There were other changes however, which the radical government planned to exploit in its own favor. These had to do with the struggle over the leadership of the Perónist movement. The restoration of 1955 had left many second-rank leaders of Perónism in positions of power and influence in both the unions and the provincial administrations. These leaders wished to institutionalize Perónism and incorporate it in the mainstream of political life as a respectable party in the post-Perónist era. They felt confident that they could accomplish this task by themselves. Their very resilience under hostile, often brutal, governments proved their point. Perón, on the other hand, wished to retain personal control over the movement from his exile in Madrid. He saw the new developments in Argentina as a challenge to his power. He therefore began to sabotage the unity of his own movement as a tactic to retain control. Through a policy of *divide et impera*, Perón pitted different leaders against each other so as to remain the supreme arbiter of the conflicts which he himself instigated. Powerful union leaders and Perónist politicians began to wish they could throw off the yoke of Peróns' personalism. In short, they entertained the prospects of a *Perónismo sin Perón*. They thought that a revamped, tamed, Perónist movement could be accepted as a major political force in Argentina without arousing the ire of the military and the fear of the establishment. Perón countered by sending his third wife—María Estela (Isabel) Martínez de Perón—to Argentina. The government welcomed this move, believing that it could only divide the Perónists further and thereby increase the radicals' own chances in important elections. Isabel Martínez managed, however, to wrest power from local *perónistas* and regroup the movement under the leadership of the exiled strongman. The provincial elections of Mendoza showed this trend very clearly: an obscure candidate sponsored by Perón and his wife easily obtained more votes than the official candidate of the Perónist Party, a seasoned politician of solid local prestige. The lesson was not lost on the military: it became apparent that in the next national elections, Perónism could win—with Perón still at the helm, by proxy.

In June 1966, President Illia was ousted by a bloodless coup. The putsch encountered little if any resistance among the population at large: it had the tacit support of anti-Perónist groups and even the acceptance of some sectors of Perónism that preferred the arbitration of the military to the less productive arbitration of Perón himself. This time the military were unabashed about their intentions: they suspended the constitution, abolished all trappings of liberal democracy, vowed to stay in power *sine die* and called their deed the "Argentine Revolution." Thus the liberal restoration of 1955 came to a precipitous end and nobody rose to defend it.

MONOPOLY CAPITAL AND SOCIAL REGRESSION

During the decade just reviewed, the landed bourgeoisie became once again a dominant political force in Argentina, in conjunction with allied sectors of society. The 1955 experiment was in this sense a second restoration (the first had occurred, as we have seen, in 1930), this time falling upon an industrialized society embittered by the failures of national capitalist development. Since 1943 the landed bourgeoisie had lost the capacity to exercise direct political power, but after the fall of Perón it could still manage to manipulate the apparatus of the state and the armed forces—a stronghold of the middle class—to its own advantage. The second restoration had two objectives: one was to abolish all protection to the accumulation of national industrial capital erected during the populist period. The other was a new economic policy benefiting the agro-pecuarian sector. The first objective was accomplished by dismantling a whole series of institutions created by Perón. The IAPI was abolished; bank deposits were de-nationalized; exchange controls ceased to be enforced; credits to small- and medium-sized industries were cut. The second objective was attained through successive devaluations of the *peso,* which meant massive transfers of resources to the exporters—a regressive redistribution of income in favor of the agrarians. A study of income distribution prepared by the United Nations Economic Commission for Latin America (ECLA) in 1969 clearly reveals the regressive trends in post-Perón Argentina. Detailed statistical estimates were made for three years—1953, 1959, and 1961—so as to observe changes in the characteristics of the distribution. ECLA arrived at the following conclusions:

> . . . the earliest of the three years, 1953, was the one in which the distribution of income was least unequal. In 1959 the overall inequality was much greater. The top 10 percent of all families received over 42 percent of all personal income in the latter year, as compared to 37 percent in 1953, and all other income groups received proportionately less. Even within the top 10 percent it was primarily the upper half of these families which benefited; the shift was almost entirely in favour of the 5 percent of all families at the top of the income scale. (ECLA, 1969, 10)

Commenting on the consequences of post-Perónist policies, the same study goes on to say:

> The net effect was a large shift in income in favour of profits, particularly in the agricultural sector, and the consequent rise in the degree of inequality

noted above. (. . .) The more recent shift in favour of profits and toward greater inequality can to an important extent be regarded as a return to the pre-Second-World-War income distribution. (ECLA, *ibid.*)

It is clear that such policies were antagonistic to the interest of the masses. Under those circumstances, the governments that followed Perón could not hope to retain power in an open system except by corrupting the very principles of democratic rule. They managed this by instituting political proscriptions, betraying electoral promises, making shady deals, trying to accommodate as many sectors of the dominant classes as possible and to deny access to government to the Perónists at the same time. In short, what emerged after the fall of Perón was a *consorteria* to which one could easily apply Pareto's notions of the alternation of elites. When cunning and the art of electoral combinations failed to achieve the principal goal of the restoration, namely, to keep the lid on *peronismo,* civilian governments were felled by military coups. Military regimes in turn became hidebound and rigid, or sometimes threatened —as in 1962—to degenerate into rule by armed factions, at which point they transferred power to new civilian governments, and so on—Ins and Outs, lions and foxes.

The liberal restoration of 1955 failed to return Argentina to the pastoral bliss of 1910. Instead it increased the role of foreign monopoly capital in industry to unprecedented proportions. The new economic sector gained in importance during that period and came to oppose the interests of both the agrarians and the industrialists, and to victimize every class beneath them.

In the sixties, foreign monopoly capital became a powerful political interest group. In 1966 the cluster of interests around foreign corporations saw with pleasure the demise of the civilian government. The economic policies of the Illia administration had been in their own mild way obtrusive to these interests. More generally, the financial and political instability of the restoration decade was incompatible with the objectives of long-range multinational corporate growth. The military coup of June 28, 1966 placed in power a former commander-in-chief of the army, General Juan Carlos Onganía. Since that time, foreign monopoly capital, clustered around large North American subsidiaries, has had decisive influence on the policies of the Argentine state. The new character of dependency under these multinational corporations has drastically modified the contradictions of the society and has exacerbated social tensions to the limit. Whereas during the Perónist period the principal line of cleavage was between the landed bourgeoisie and the nationalist state prone to finance national industrial expansion with agropecurian profits, the new pattern of conflict that developed during the Restoration of 1955–1966 and which emerged full-blown after the 1966 coup, opposes foreign monopoly capital to the popular classes affected by its expansion (Laclau, 1970, 5).

Gone forever were the days of outward growth conjoining the interests of British imperialism with those of the landed oligarchy. Gone, also, were tensions between the agrarians and a nationalist state that protected a weak industrial class and redistributed income in favor of the proletariat. Easy import substitution was exhausted. Autonomous industrial growth had come to a grinding halt for lack of investable resources. The class struggle had reached an impasse. Large North American investments in the industrial sector came to predominate in the economy as a whole. Government rested on the naked use of force. The military regime of 1966 aimed at maximizing satellite industrialization and minimizing social change. The challenge was clear: the Onganía regime undertook to destroy the stalemated equilibrium of social forces, stem the tide of opposition that the destruction of the old order would produce, renovate the economic system with the aid of big monopoly capital, let the latter reconstitute the sundered puzzle of classes, and only then loosen the screws on the community. In short, the aim was to produce a new type of social integration on the basis of a dynamic industrial dependency. Such was the grand project of the self-styled *Revolución Argentina* of General Onganía. Onganía did not, however, calculate the risks. In Argentina, the capacity of monopoly capital to promote a new kind of social integration proved much inferior to its ability to destroy the older equilibrium. It ended up creating mass opposition, narrowing the social base of capitalism, and it promised to rest on increasing, indefinite repression. The response of a wounded community was highly political. It came after three years of insult and injury to economic well-being and political traditions. This response tore at the bland façade of bourgeois society: in May 1969, Argentina witnessed the first of a series of mass urban insurrections led by the industrial working class of the Interior. The masses seized the city of Córdoba in episodes reminiscent of the Paris Commune of 1871. Other cities followed; the revolt became general. The steps leading to these episodes were of probably greater significance than those of the populist outpouring of 1945.

When the military seized power in 1966 they were responding to an immediate political crisis. Whether they were also under pressure from powerful economic interests—big monopoly capital in particular—is hard to know but easy to suspect. In any case, it was foreign monopoly capital that was destined to become one of the main beneficiaries of the regime through legislation and other official measures which allowed transference of ownership and created conditions favoring denationalization of industrial and financial firms in many sectors of the economy (See Table 1).

TABLE 1 Denationalization of the Argentine Economy
Principal Cases 1962–1968

Transferred Firm	Branch	Purchasing Firm	Country
Banco Argentino del Atlántico	Bank	City Bank of N.Y. (Morgan group)	U.S.A. U.S.A.
Banco de Bahía Blanca	Bank	City Bank of N.Y.	U.S.A.
Banco Popular Argentino	Bank	Banco Central Madrid (private)	Spain
Banco Francés del Río de la Plata	Bank	Morgan Guaranty Trust of N.Y.	U.S.A.
Banco Comercial Industrial de Córdoba	Bank	Banco de Santander	Spain
Banco Mercantil de Rosario	Bank	Banco de Santander	Spain
Banco Continental	Bank	Banco de Urquijo	Spain
Banco Holandés Unido	Bank	Algemene Bank Nederland N.V.	Netherlands
Banco Argentino del Centro (Villa Mercedes)	Bank	Banque Armenienne pour L'Amerique et L'Orient	France
Banco El Hogar Argentino	Bank	Banco de Santander	Spain
Banco Internacional de Montevideo	Bank	Bank of America	U.S.A.
Massalin y Celasco	Cigarettes	Philip Morris Int.	U.S.A.
Imparciales	Cigarettes	Reemtsma Fabriken	W. Germany
Particulares	Cigarettes	Reemtsma Fabriken	W. Germany
Piccardo	Cigarettes	Ligget & Myers	U.S.A.
Thompson Ranco	Auto Parts	Thompson Products	U.S.A.
Indeco S.A.	Auto Parts	Federal Mogul	U.S.A.
Suavegom	Auto Parts	Dow Chemical	U.S.A.
Transax	Auto Parts	Ford Motor Co.	U.S.A.
Acinfer S.A.	Auto Parts	Ford Motor Co.	U.S.A.
Argelite S.A.	Auto Parts	Holley	U.S.A.
Beciu S.A.	Auto Parts	Eaton	U.S.A.

TABLE 1 Denationalization of the Argentine Economy
Principal Cases 1962–1968 (cont'd)

TRANSFERRED FIRM	BRANCH	PURCHASING FIRM	COUNTRY
Armetal S.A.	Auto Parts	Bud	U.S.A.
Resortes Argentina S.A.	Auto Parts	Associated Spring	U.S.A.
Resortes Sachs S.A.	Auto Parts	Isringhausen GBM	W. Germany
Agrometal Ingersol	Auto Parts	Borg Warner	U.S.A.
Byron Jackson S.A.	Auto Parts	Borg Warner	U.S.A.
Bendix S.A.	Auto Parts	Bendix	U.S.A.
Proyectores Arg.	Auto Parts	Cibie	France
Salso	Home Appliances	Philips	Netherlands
Protto Hnos. S.A.	Metalwork	Kelsey Hayes Corp.	U.S.A.
IKA	Automobiles	Renault	France
Química Hoechst	Chemical	Hoechst	W. Germany
Duranor	Chemical	Hooker Chemical	U.S.A.
Lepetit	Chemical	Dow Chemical	U.S.A.
Talleres Coghlan	Machinery	Sulzer	Switzerland
COPET	Petro-chemical	Grupo Extranjero Anonimo	
Papelera Hurlingham	Paper	Kimberley Clark	U.S.A.
Fuerte Santi Spiritu	Veterinary Products	Philips	Netherlands
BIROME	Pens	Parker Pen	U.S.A.
Argafer	Ceramics	Philips	Netherlands
Hudson Ciovini	Distribution	Seagram	U.S.A.
Hisina	Synthetic Fabrics	Ducilo	U.S.A.
Banca Bullrich	Investment	Bankers Trust Corp. (Morgan Group 49%)	U.S.A.
Roberts S.A. Finanzas	Finance	Morgan Guaranty International and Baring Bros.	U.S.A.

Sources: El Economista, XVIII, No. 934. Bs.As.: 6–21–68, p. 1. Special Report by Julián Delgado, *Primera Plana*, VI, No. 297. Bs.As.: 9–3 to 9–68, p. 67. *Patria Grande*, I, No. 2, Oct. 1968, p. 7.

The years immediately preceding the coup showed nothing unusual in terms of the traditionally slow growth of the Argentine economy. In fact, as we have seen, there was a somewhat higher rate of growth than usual under the Illia administration. Good harvests and other stimuli to the agrarian sector had strengthened the country's balance of payments. The inflation rate was high—30 percent—but not unusual for Argentina and tolerable in terms of past experience. Politically, however, the situation was far more critical. There were unmistakable signs of instability. The prevalent opinion in the governing party was that, unless the Perónists were somehow incorporated into the political system without unduly rocking the boat, it would not be possible to lead the country toward any kind of consistent development. The participation of Perónists was thus allowed in the provincial elections in 1966, producing Perónist victories in some provinces. These victories were less important per se than as a foreboding of things to come on the national level. Observers began to predict that in the forthcoming elections for congress in March 1967, the Perónists—still under the control of the exiled Perón—would win and thus alter the fundamental power balance. Those prospects produced acute anxiety in military spheres and among establishment groups—the foreign monopoly sector included. The military took power in order to postpone a solution to the political crisis. The solution closest at hand, namely, the incorporation of Perónism on its own terms into the political system, was deemed—perhaps not incorrectly—incompatible with capitalist development, especially with the expansion of foreign monopoly capital. The exercise of unfettered democracy under those circumstances would lead to basic social change possibly beyond the confines of capitalist society. Democratic government was therefore suspended until a vague later date when it was hoped that—in the best tradition of the "free world"—politics would legitimize but not alter the socio-economic system.

The efforts of the military dictatorship were focused on creating the preconditions for monopoly capital expansion. It wished to modernize and streamline the system of dependent industrial capitalism, somehow expecting that the application of the adequate economic measures in that direction would eventually produce a new type of social integration leading ultimately to new forms of political participation. Hence, the overall strategy of the distatorship consisted of three phases, or *tiempos*, as they were called, in this order—*tiempo económico, tiempo social, tiempo político*. The economic plan was executed: foreign monopoly capital took over strategic sectors of the economy with rapidity and precision. But the social phase never was. Instead of a new social integration, the economic takeover produced social dislocation, discontent, and finally massive opposition. Social integration could only mean a better participation of the salaried groups in the share of national income, that is to say, higher real incomes and better levels of employment. But this capitalist utopia was to come after a period of deprivation, during which real wages were lowered and corporate rationalization threw people out of jobs. The official dialectic did not work. For historical reasons which should by now be apparent, the social profile of Argentina is fairly integrated; the working class is characterized by advanced forms of organization and strong feedback capabilities. Therefore, the ruthless expansion of monopoly capital triggered a popular backlash that for a moment reached revolutionary proportions. Thus, the real dialectic of classes shattered the designs of the ruling groups and assigned a very different meaning to the three official *tiempos*: from monopoly capitalist takeover to social dislocation to revolutionary crisis. As a result of these circumstances, during the past few years the military has purged its leading ranks, shelved the former economic plans—at least temporarily—and is frantically searching for a political compromise that can prevent the catastrophe of the *status quo*.

VII. THE CONTEMPORARY CRISIS

DICTATORSHIP AND SATELLIZATION

A detailed chronicle of the *Revolución Argentina* of 1966 is beyond the scope of these pages. Rather, the contours of its different phases will be sketched in terms of economic policies and social response.

The first acts of the military government of 1966 consisted of draconian measures of house-cleaning. Those institutions deemed as obstacles to the economic designs of the ruling circles were simply destroyed. The basic framework of the economic *status quo* was strengthened and there were even some regressive concessions to the agrarian sector. The policies of the government managed to smash a number of institutions— political parties the supreme court the provincial governments the national universities—that constitute the very fabric of bourgeoisie liberalism and the guarantee of juridical defense. Many of these institutions were damaged beyond repair. The CGT was not affected at this stage of the dictatorship. Under the control of A. T. Vandor, leader of the powerful Metalworkers Union, labor organizations adopted a stance of wait-and-see. No coherent economic policy was implemented during the first months of the regime. There were only stop-gap measures designed to rationalize some sectors of the economy and to curb inflation. Thus, an attempt was made to reduce the state deficit, to eliminate bureaucratic featherbedding, to make public services more efficient, making the trains run on time. An isolated effort was made to reorganize the economy of a peripheral province—Tucumán—with disastrous results: massive lay-offs, hunger, popular resistence. The episode was a presage of things to come The Gross Domestic Product declined by one percentage point; inflation continued, and the rate reached a high point of 32 percent during the first year. The relations between the government and labor began to show signs of strain.

The year 1967 marked the beginning of the economic phase of the regime. A new economic minister was in command. This man was Adalbert Krieger Vasena, director of National Lead Company and on the board of ADELA Company, a multinational investment corporation. In addition Alvaro Alsogaray, who had been minister of the economy twice before (during the Frondizi and Guido administrations) became ambassador to the United States. This man was associated with Deltec International Corporation, another multinational firm which had bought out International Packers Limited (a meat producer) and has on its board the Klebergs of the Texas King Ranch (Daniels, 1970, 10; García Lupo, 1969). This team launched a carefully prepared strategy of dependent industrialization based on the expansion of foreign monopoly capital. The paramount goal was, first, to stabilize the economy and within that framework eliminate distortions, increase productive efficiency, and then generate industrial expansion with the aid of foreign capital. The means applied consisted of income, exchange, and fiscal policies. Income policy consisted of a plan designed by large business interests to avoid inflationary pressures to facilitate corporate planning. Salaries were adjusted and then frozen. Social security contributions were reduced. The regime made it clear that hard times lay ahead for labor. The exchange policy was also heavy-handed. The regime produced an over-devaluation of the *peso* designed to "increase confidence" among foreign investors—they could now buy Argentine enterprises with fewer dollars—and to ease the balance of payments situation. The goal of the devaluation was to encourage industrial exports in the long run and to solve the problem of lack of reserves held by the central bank in the short run. To avoid the usual consequence of devaluations—the increase in the income of the agrarian exporters—and land tax was instituted. Fiscal policy in turn aimed at increasing the efficiency of the public sector. There was some large-scale reordering of the railways and the ports. These measures meant, of course, eliminating jobs while increasing the profits of business and using the state to stimulate private foreign investments. Other measures of economic rationalization included a reduction of tariffs, the elimination of rent controls and rural tenancy arrangements, and the modifications of the laws governing credit cooperatives which mobilized the funds of the commercial petty bourgeoisie. Just as the wage freeze repressed the working class, so these other measures were designed to break the economic basis of small and medium enterprises—a rather massive attack on the national and petty bourgeoisies. The unpopular character of these policies was perfectly known to the authorities who were prepared to resist popular pressures by concentrating power in the army and thus guaranteeing the social control necessary for the influx of foreign capital. To the ruling establishment the latter would rush in, restore adequate levels of employment, and create new bureaucratic middle sectors from the scattered fragments of the national and petty bourgeoisies. The workers aristocracy might also eventually benefit from these developments, but the bulk of the proletariat was to remain exploited. On the other hand, the institution of the land tax made it clear that this time the landed bourgeoisie would not be the main beneficiary of reaction: it too would have to bow before monopoly capital. In summary, this was the final satellization of Argentine capitalism. Argentina was supposed to become an industrial dependency in which stabilization is obtained at the expense of capital in the hands of foreign entrepreneurs and their local associates.

The results in the short run impressed the readers of *The Wall Street Journal* and the *Harvard Business Review*: the rate of inflation dropped from 32 percent to about 7 percent in 1967. GNP leaped forward at a rate of 6.6 percent in the same year. The foreign reserve situation was good, the fiscal deficit smaller; wages kept dropping. Argentina was a good spot for investing.

And foreign capital did flow into Argentina after 1967. By contrast to the period of British imperialism, the new imperialism was directed toward industry, accelerating the trend begun in 1955. In the period immediately preceding Onganía, U.S. capital investments in Argentina had already increased from $161 million in 1960 to $617 million in 1965. This flow of capital was less impressive in what it brought in than in what it took over and took out. Statistics reveal a marked discrepancy between the indicators of growth on the one hand and the increased activity of foreign monopoly capital in Argentina, on the other. Between 1960 and 1965, GNP increased at the low overage of 2.8 percent a year, while industrial production grew by a modest 4.1 percent. However, during the same period, sales of branches of U.S. firms in Argentina recorded an increase of no less than 24 percent (Laclau, 1970, 7)! The process of takeover was greatly accelerated during the Onganía regime. By 1968 U.S. investment in Argentina totalled $1,148 million. Economically, this process can be described as one of massive de-nationalization of capital. Socially, it meant the liquidation of small and middle industrialists—the final solution to the national-bourgeois problem. Technically, the new investments were characterized by a high organic composition of capital. The logic of their drive was to increase the weight of constant capital with respect to total capital, that is to say, the part of total capital made up by machines and raw materials, but not in wages, tended to increase with the new advances in mechanization. The upshot was a decline in the capacity of the industrial sector to absorb labor: the marginalization of the working class that had been integrated into the system during a phase of labor-intensive exploitation. The success of governmental policy hinged on the ability to compress wages, marginalize the proletariat, force the national bourgeoisie to sell out, destroy the petty bourgeoisie, and produce on these ruins a renovated economic system controlled by multinational corporations. Since the capacity of the latter to create acceptable occupational levels in a society like Argentina is limited the regime could not promote a cluster of interests sufficiently large to provide a social base for the further expansion of monopoly capital and for the invention of a new political formula. As it was, the military dictatorship saw a rapid narrowing of support and the growth instead of a formidable opposition combining formerly antagonistic sectors of society: an indignant middle class, radical students, a militant proletariat mobilized by the unions. Even the oligarchy showed signs of displeasure at the impact of the plans of the monopolistic military regime. In this way, militarism and monopoly expansion became the unwitting unifiers of groups that previous decades had kept separate. The democratic middle class, the old left, and the student movement had been traditionally estranged from the proletarian masses which began their political experience under the banner of national populism and outside the democratic and socialist traditions. The decade which followed Perónism prepared the ground for transcending those cleavages. The policies implemented after the Restoration of 1955 made the anti-Perónist petty bourgeoisie as much a victim as the Perónist proletariat. Monopolization and denationalization brought these two classes closer together. The military dictatorship of 1966 created further conditions that facilitated their alliance.

When the military regime of Onganía thought that it was reaping the first fruits of its economic policies; when foreign investors began to have confidence in a dictatorship that promised to make Argentina tranquil for capital for decades to come, major urban insurrections broke out in Córdoba, Rosario, and other cities throughout the country, that had world-wide repercussions on account of their unprecedented scale and character. The Argentine working class was fighting back. The main feature of these mass political struggles was the alliance of workers and students with disaffected sectors of the middle class. Something entirely new in Argentina and entirely outside the framework of established practices: the accumulated response to economic hardship and political grievance.

Several factors help to account for the historical radicalization and convergence of the working class and the middle sectors. During the initial period of the restoration of 1955, the middle classes were still part—as they had been in 1945—of the reactionary front. So was the traditional left. Socialists and communists received a share of the spoils after the fall of Perón (mostly university and union posts) while the regime welcomed foreign capital and applied terror to Perónist militants of the working class. *Perónistas* had to work underground and managed to attain a new political consciousness and new skills during those years. On the other hand, the rapid monopolization of industry undermined the economic base of the petty bourgeoisie. It became radicalized. At the same time, unemployment and punitive policies made labor more militant. As bread-and butter unionism failed to produce tangible results, workers were forced to·resort to direct and more political forms of action. They thus began to develop an advanced class consciousness beyond immediate economist demands. These developments took place more rapidly in the cities of the interior, especially Córdoba, where industrialization had taken place after the fall of Perón in the modern, foreign-owned automobile plants, and where the proletariat was less inhibited by past traditions of populist paternalism to assume a radical stance. The bourgeoisie of the interior, on the other hand, was weak, satellized, and dependent on Buenos Aires for maintaining social control. The students of provincial universities were concentrated in compact communities. Recent patterns of urban settlement produced a constant intermingling of students, workers, and the petty bourgeoisie. The latter was offended by the policies of the central government and more generally by the internal colonialism exercised by the capital city vis-à-vis the Interior. Similar situations existed in Rosario, Tucumán, La Plata, and Mendoza. These cities, and the workers within them, became the vanguard of mass opposition to the regime of Onganía.

The radicalization of the middle sectors was unmistakable. With the overthrow of President Illia in 1966, they were prevented from following traditional parliamentary access to decision-making. The economic hardships, the military and police repression, the ideological example of the Cuban Revolution and other events in the outside world, in short, exclusion from power and economic benefits as well as ideological curiosity provoked first splits, then realignments, among different political groupings of the middle classes. Socialists, Communists, Radicals, Social Christians, began dissociating themselves from past attachments, developed new radical sympathies, and eventually took a step that for many of them represents genuine self-criticism: a rapprochement to Perónism.

New forms of struggle emerged in May 1969 during the popular uprisings in the interior—what came to be known as the *cordobazo*. The exhaustion of conventional forms of political expression, the indefinite postponement of a solution to the political crisis that had surfaced in 1966, the economic pinch, the punitive arrogance of the military authorities, led the people to experiment with new and violent forms of protest. Moderate, economist labor leaders were rapidly losing power to more politicized cadres. Young workers seized their factories and took to the streets to fight the police and the troops. They were soon joined by students who had acquired new experience in clandestine activities as a result of the military occupation of the universities in 1966—Onganía's contribution to culture. Students joined workers at the barricades, defended their own neighborhoods in different cities with snipers. The middle classes joined in a supportive capacity. For the first time in Argentine history a classical popular uprising took place, linking the force of the urban proletariat with the middle sectors, the students, and significant sectors of the clergy. The government had to regain the cities by sending in armored columns with air support. Only the unity of the army and the spontaniety, the very surprise, of the revolt, prevented the episode from becoming the revolutionary collapse of the state. Out of these events grew a new sense of power: the belief that the organized uprising of the masses will eventually defeat the apparatus of the state. The events of 1969 were the popular veto to the military's attempt to service the needs of U.S. monopoly expansion at the expense of the community.

The situation of Onganía's government deteriorated. It soon found itself harassed by the liberal-oligarchic opposition on the one hand, and by militant general strikes and guerrilla operations on the other. It reacted violently. A wave of political assassinations swept the country. The union leader Vandor was gunned down at the office of the Metalworkers Union. Former President Aramburu, leader of the liberal Restoration of 1955, was kidnapped from his home and killed. These events detonated another coup by the liberal sector of the army. General Onganía was ousted by a military junta of the three service chiefs, who proceeded to install another general—Roberto Marcelo Levingston—as president in June of 1970.

The new authorities maintained the plans for the expansion of foreign capital. Economic policies remained the same, though capital's confidence in Argentina was shaken. The new economic Minister, Carlos Moyano-Llerena, continued the policies of his predecessor Krieger. But the process of isolation of the dictatorship continued. Urban guerilla actions, student agitation, worker strikes, created a climate of perpetual crisis. The military were forced to change their role. They now devoted their efforts to defusing the powder-keg of the opposition. A new wave of insurrections in 1971 prompted them to try a political solution to the crisis: Levingston was replaced by the Commander-in-Chief of the Army, General Alejandro Lanusee, who saw his task as creating the conditions in which new elections could bring to power a civilian coalition capable of lending some semblance of legitimacy to the *status quo*. The oligarchic-liberal forces represented by Lanusse had to establish a system of alliances with Peronism in the hope of broadening the social base of the regime and allowing dependent capitalism to grow with a measure of public acceptance. It was out of this situation that gradually emerged the decision to hold the general elections in which a Peronist-led coalition, FREJULI (Justicialist Liberation Front) won the presidency. Shortly after taking office, the newly elected President Cámpora resigned and Perón himself, returning to Argentina after eighteen years of exile, won an overwhelming majority in new elections held in September 1973.

CONCLUSION

Political decay, mass violence, the insinuation of novel political elites, are all features of Argentine society since 1969. These phenomena by themselves do not warrant the prediction of a successful overturn of the existing governmental authority and even less the establishment of an alternative state power capable of maintaining itself in existence. But they are unmistakable signs of radical unheaval. No interpretation of present-day Argentina can afford to ignore them, for they are all ingredients of modern revolutions.

The likelihood of revolution in today's Argentina is a question the answer to which is at present inscrutable. But who would have guessed the uprisings of 1969 to 1971? Whoever was equipped to predict the silent role of the urban working class in rocking the foundations of a modern garrison state; to anticipate the union of great masses of the population against military domination and foreign control over the economy? Academics are ill-equipped to discuss revolution. Social scientists exhibit behind their mask of neutrality a profound bias against radical change. The phenomenon of revolution itself defies the rationalist pretensions of the revolutionaries: even at their most successful they ride the whirlwind more than they shape the destinies of societies. Those subjected to the strains of the transition are at best ambivalent: revolutions destroy much that is good as well as much that is bad. On the other hand, if they are not brutally creative, they are nothing—mere revolts which when defeated lead only to greater misery. But the question has to be addressed: the calculus of the price to be paid for revolutionary violence must include that which will be exacted for prolonging the present state of affairs.

The continuation of the present state of affairs in Argentina implies economic stagnation, political persecution—official torture has reached unprecedented levels as of this writing—cultural retrogression, and moral despair. There is certainly much social and political organization which is eminently in need of destruction if Argentina is to develop. The events of recent years have indicated that further mass mobilizations might be able to break up the machine of the state and establish new popular institutions in power. It does not escape the bourgeoisie and the military that this event—even under the likely guise of Peronism—would open the doors to socialism. The official response has two prongs: political *panem et circenses* to distract and defuse the pent-up grievances of vast sectors of the population, and extreme violence (terror) methodically applied to those who have embarked on a course of revolutionary subversion. Tanks, electrical prods, and electoral promises are the means to buttress the institutions which block development: the capitalist state and imperialism.

JUAN EUGENIO CORRADI teaches sociology at New York University. He was born in Buenos Aires in 1943 and was educated in Argentina and the United States, where he completed his undergraduate and doctoral studies in sociology at Brandeis University. He has taught sociology at Cambridge Junior College, Emmanuel College, the New England Conservatory of Music, and the University of Massachusetts in Boston. He is the author of several articles on social change, cultural dependency, and the sociology of knowledge, and co-editor of the forthcoming book *Ideology and Social Change in Latin America*. He is presently Editor for the International Society for the Sociology of Knowledge and is doing research on the impact of mass immigration on Argentine society.

STATISTICS

Argentine Presidents Since 1930

President	Access to Power	Replacement Year	Ended Period	Succeeded by Member of Armed Forces
H. Yrigoyen	1928; free elections	1930	No	Yes
J. E. Uriburu	1930; military coup	1932	does not apply*	Yes
A. P. Justo	1932; fraud	1938	Yes	No
R. M. Ortiz	1938; fraud	1940	No (illness/death)	No
R. J. Castillo	1940; constitutional procedure	1943	No	Yes
A. Rawson	1943; military coup	1943	does not apply	Yes
P. Ramíres	1943; internal coup	1944	does not apply	Yes
E. J. Farrell	1944; internal coup	1946	does not apply	Yes
J. D. Perón	1946; free elections	1952	Yes	Yes (reelected)
J. D. Perón	1952; free elections	1955	No	Yes
E. Lonardi	1955; military coup	1955	does not apply	Yes
P. E. Aramburu	1955; internal coup	1958	does not apply	No
A. Frondizi	1958; elections with proscriptions	1962	No	No
J. M. Guido	1962; military coup and semi-constitutional procedure	1963	No	No
A. U. Illia	1963; elections with proscriptions	1966	No	Yes
J. C. Onganía	1966; military coup	1970	does not apply	Yes
R. M. Levingston	1970; internal coup	1971	does not apply	Yes
A. A. Lanusse	1971; internal coup	1973	does not apply	No
H. J. Cámpora	1973; free elections	1973	No	No
R. Lastiri	1973; constit. procedures	1973	does not apply	No
J. D. Perón	1973; free elections	1977	—	—

* Refers to cases of unconstitutional governments or constitutional but provisional administrations.

399

MILITARY UPRISINGS IN ARGENTINA: 1900–1966.
ORIENTATION AND SUCCESS*

Success   Uprisings in Relation to Popular Movements

	FAVORABLE	OPPOSED	DOES NOT APPLY	TOTAL
Yes	—	8 (2; 17; 18; 20; 21; 26; 27; 31)	2 (13; 28)	10
No	11 (1; 3; 4; 5; 6; 7; 8; 9; 10; 19; 24)	2 (15; 16)	8 (11; 12; 14; 22; 23; 25; 29; 30)	21

*The numbers in parenthesis identify each of the various uprisings until 1966. Since 1966 there have been two successful uprisings and one unsuccessful attempt.

Source: Liisa North, *Civil-Military Relations in Argentina, Chile, and Peru*, Berkeley: University of California, 1966, and Darío Canton, "Las intervenciones militares en la Argentina: 1900–1966," Centro de Investigaciones Sociales. Instituto Di Tella, Buenos Aires, 1967.

Area: Over 1 million square miles. Greatest north-south distance, about 2,000 miles; east-west at widest point, approximately 900 miles.

Population: Over 24 million; some 97 percent classified as of European descent. Population, which consisted mainly of descendants of colonists, was greatly augmented in late 19th and early 20th centuries by waves of immigration from Italy, Spain, and other European countries. Since World War II there has been substantial immigration from neighboring countries. Population projections (in thousands) are as follows:

1975: 26,262
1980: 28,218
1985: 30,107 (Source: CELADE, *Boletín Demográfico*, Año 2, Vol. III, Santiago de Chile, January 1969)

30% of the population is under 14 years of age, 63% is between 15 and 64 years of age. Population increases at a rate of 1.5% per annum. In 1947 less than .5 percent of the Argentine population was classified as Indian.

Urbanization: 72% of the 1965 population. Approximately 60% of the urban population lives in cities of over 100,000. The rural people, living on farms or ranches or in villages with fewer than 2,000 people, account for only 28%, in contrast to the rural population of Latin America as a whole, which amounts to about 60% of the total population.

Capital City: Buenos Aires, with over 33% of total population.

Literacy rate: Estimated at over 90% of the population over 16 years of age. Literacy rates are highest in Buenos Aires and lowest in the Northeast and Northwest. In 1965, 90.5% of the 7–14 age group was enrolled in primary schools, 51.4% of the 15–19 age group was enrolled in secondary schools, and 12.6% of the 20–24 age group was enrolled in institutions of higher learning. However, during 1960–65, only 39.8% of pupils enrolled in primary schools completed their studies.

Birth rate: 21.5 per 1,000 inhabitants.

Death rate: 8.2 per 1,000 inhabitants. (Lower than in the U.S.)

Infant Mortality Rate: 60 per 1,000 liveborn. Generally viewed as the country's most serious health problem. Regionally, the rate varied in 1961 between a low 40 per thousand in the city of Buenos Aires to over 130 in Jujuy Province, in the impoverished Northwest.

Health: Generally good. Physicians and medical facilities concentrated largely in urban areas. Principal causes of death: cancer, heart ailments.

Per capita Gross Domestic Product (1968): $851. Rate of growth: 1.5% per annum (1960–68).

Land tenure:

TABLE 1.1

Rural Holdings Classified According to Size (Percent total rural area)

Five pampean provinces	1914	1960
25 hectares and less	0.7	1.0
26 to 100 hectares	5.1	7.6
101 to 1,000 hectares	32.9	39.9
1,001 to 5,000 hectares	27.5	30.8
5,001 to 10,000 hectares	15.5	10.5
10,001 hectares and more	18.3	10.2
Pampean provinces excluding La Pampa Province		
25 hectares and less	0.8	1.1
26 to 100 hectares	5.8	9.0
101 to 1,000 hectares	35.6	44.4
1,001 to 5,000 hectares	27.0	29.3
5,001 to 10,000 hectares	12.8	8.3
10,001 hectares and more	15.4	5.5
Province of Buenos Aires		
25 hectares and less	0.8	1.1
26 to 100 hectares	4.7	6.8
101 to 1,000 hectares	34.3	43.8
1,001 to 5,000 hectares	30.4	33.8
5,001 to 10,000 hectares	14.4	9.0
10,001 hectares and more	15.4	5.5

Note: one hectare is equivalent to 2.471 acres.

Source: Carlos F. Díaz Alejandro, *Essays on the Economic History of the Argentine Republic* (1970), p. 184, from rural censuses for 1914 and for 1960.

TABLE 1.2

Distribution of Rural Land in Argentina According to Size
and Ownership, 1960
(Percentages of all rural land)

	LESS THAN FAMILY SIZE [a]	FAMILY SIZE [b]	MEDIUM MULTI-FAMILY [c] SIZE	LARGE MULTI-FAMILY SIZE
All Argentina Total	3.4	44.6	33.9	18.1
Exclusively owners	1.4	17.1	20.9	13.6
Sharecroppers and tenants	0.5	6.3	2.4	1.4
Mixed property	0.2	3.2	3.3	1.6
Fiscal lands	0.7	11.2	3.8	0.2
Other forms	0.6	6.8	3.5	1.3
Pampean zone total	3.2	40.7	36.0	20.1
Exclusively owners	1.6	18.7	19.8	13.4
Sharecroppers and tenants	1.0	11.7	6.1	1.8
Mixed property	0.3	6.4	6.6	3.7
Fiscal lands	0.0	0.2	0.1	0.0
Other forms	0.4	3.7	3.4	1.2

a Holdings insufficient to satisfy the minimum needs of a family and not enough to fully utilize productively the labor of the family throughout the year.

b Holdings sufficient to maintain a family at a satisfactory standard of living using the labor of the family and the technical knowledge found in the area.

c Holdings requiring nonfamily labor for full use of the land, but not so much as to require a hierarchical organization based on an administrator. In the pampean zone, for example, multifamily medium units are those using on the average from 4 to 12 workers. The minimum size of multifamily units in the pampean zone fluctuates between 200 and 1,000 hectares.

Source: Comité Interamericano de Desarrollo Agrícola, *Tenencia de la Tierra y Desarrollo Socio-Económico del Sector Agrícola: Argentina* (Washington, D.C.: Unión Panamericana, 1966), pp. 23 and 32. Carlos F. Díaz Alejandro, *Essays on the Economic History of the Argentine Republic* (1970), Table 3.20, p. 185.

Table 1.1 presents the distribution of rural land in pampean provinces according to the size of holdings in 1960 and 1914. Although the size categories directly comparable are rather gross, a trend toward smaller holdings between these years is revealed. Holdings of between 26 and 1,000 hectares show the largest gains.

Table 1.2 presents some of the results of a CIDA study (see source) based on the 1960 census. For that year, it finds that 38% of all rural land was in holdings directed exclusively by owners and was of family size or medium multifamily size. The study puts forth the hypothesis that half of the rural land is exploited inadequately due to land tenure considerations. The study also notes a tendency toward the subdivision of large pampean estates but it asserts that the trend is relatively slow. Inadequate land tenure is made up of minifundia, too small to be efficiently operated (estimated at about 3% of all land); of holdings of appropriate size but with unsatisfactory and unstable tenancy arrangements (20% of all land); and of large estates, latifundia, in which land is not being exploited (35% of all land). Output per hectare declines as the size of the holdings increases, indicating the negative impact of land concentration on rural growth. Furthermore, the existence of multiple unit ownership and artificial subdivisions indicate that land ownership is probably substantially more concentrated than what is indicated by data on holdings. Widespread opinion blames the structure of landholding for the rural stagnation since 1930. Large landholdings and tenancy contracts are considered ill suited for a more intensive exploitation of the soil. Inflation has increased the value of land as a hedge against the erosion of real wealth, thus further immobilizing rural property not used to full capacity. Low and falling land taxes, coupled with higher taxes elsewhere, have strengthened this trend.

Distribution of Income: The data for 1961 show that in over-all terms the distribution was unequal, with a very considerable concentration of income at the top of the scale. The top 5% of all families received 29.4% of all personal income in 1961, and had an average income nearly six times the national average and nearly seventeen times the average of the poorest fifth of all families.

TABLE 1.3

The Distribution of Family Income in Argentina

	1953		1959		1961	
	SHARE OF TOTAL (PERCEN-	INCOME LEVEL (NAT. AVE.	SHARE OF TOTAL (PERCEN-	INCOME LEVEL (NAT. AVE.	SHARE OF TOTAL (PERCEN-	INCOME LEVEL (NAT. AVE.
INCOME GROUP	TAGE)	= 100)	TAGE)	= 100)	TAGE)	= 100)
Lowest 20 percent	7.5	38	6.8	34	7.0	35
Middle 50 percent (21–70)	32.6	65	29.4	59	31.4	63
Upper middle 20 percent (71–90)	22.9	115	21.6	108	22.5	112
Top 10 percent	37.0	370	42.3	423	39.1	391
Top 5 percent	27.3	546	32.1	642	29.4	588

Source: Economic Commission for Latin America, *Economic Development and Income Distribution in Argetina,* New York: U.N., 1969, Table 3, p. 13.

In comparative terms, the over-all inequality, and the concentration at the top of the scale, are less than in most of the rest of Latin America; but this is only an indication of the extreme inequality which exists in the region as a whole. The inequality in Argentina is much greater, for example, than in most of the Western industrial countries. The over-all inequality is largely the result of the concentration of income at the very top, and of considerable inequality among the families which are just below the top; through the middle range of the distribution there is much less inequality, and incomes at the bottom of the scale are relatively high in comparison with other countries. The poorest fifth of all families received 7% of all personal income in 1961, compared to 5% which the same group receives in most other Latin American countries. Combined with the fact that the average income for the country as a whole is one of the highest in the region, this means that the absolute incomes of the poorest groups are high by Latin American standards. In dollar terms, 1% of all families had incomes of less than 500 dollars in 1961; for the lowest income group as a whole the average family income was approximately 890 dollars. In the second income group shown in Table 1.3, the middle half of all families the inequality is relatively small. Income levels at the top of this group are not quite double those at its bottom, ranging from about 45% to about 85% of the national average. For the group as a whole the average income in 1961 was approximately 1,600 dollars per family. Within the top two groups shown in Table 1.3 income rises rapidly, and the inequality is concentrated. At the top of the upper middle group incomes are about 80% above the national average, and the rise is more rapid through the top 10%. Absolute incomes are very high at that level. The top 1% in 1961 had an average income of over 35,000 dollars per family. The large concentration of income in the top decile and in general the rapid rise in incomes toward the top of the scale are common throughout Latin America, but in absolute terms these top incomes in Argentina are well above those of the top groups in most countries of the region. Factors usually cited as contributing to produce relatively high minimum family incomes in Argentina are: a relatively adequate supply of natural resources, especially of land; a low population density; a relatively high ratio of arable to total land; and a low rate of population increase. In broad terms, the over-all inequality can be seen to result principally from differences in income levels of wage and salary earners on the one hand, and of the entrepreneurial group on the other. This split is the major factor in the income distribution in Argentina, overshadowing sectoral, regional, and urban-rural differences. These features suggest the social pervasiveness of the capitalist mode of production in Argentina in three main characteristics: 1) separation of producers from the means of production, 2) concentration of the means of production in a single social class, the bourgeoisie, and 3) the existence of a social class selling laborpower, the modern proletariat.

As Table 1.3 also shows, changes in the distribution of income since 1953 have been regressive. The year 1953 can be considered representative of the late forties and early fifties (the Perón era) during which the share of wage and salary income in the total was substantially larger than it has been in earlier years. The more recent shift has been in favor of profits and toward greater inequality.

Percent of government budget for education: 17.7% (1967).

Foreign trade: From 1948 through 1961 the level of exports had been, on the average, about $1 billion annually. In 1962 total exports began rising by about $100 million a year until they reached the 1966 level, estimated at $1.6 billion. Although total exports rose by about half in the 1962–66 period, there was no significant change in their composition. Farm and stockraising products have traditionally provided at least three-quarters of the value of exports and in some years, as much as 90 to 95%. Manufactured exports rose from 2.6% in 1960 to 5.2% in 1966. Their level remains unimpressive. Because the country is self-sufficient both in food and in most consumer goods, the demand for imports reflects mainly a demand for raw materials and components which fluctuates according to the level of domestic economic activity. In recent years the aggregate value of imports has been approximately $1.1 billion a year. Substitution of domestic manufacture for importation has kept the level of consumer goods imports at between 5 and 10% of total imports. Raw materials and intermediate products for use by industry rose as a percentage of total imports from more than 47% in 1960 to nearly 58% in 1966. Imports of capital goods were about 35% of total imports in the 1960–63 years, a period of heavy imports of new machinery by industrial firms, but fell to about 18% of total imports in 1966.

The most important flow of foreign trade is with the countries of the European Economic Community (EEC), which absorb 38% of exports and furnish almost 25% of imports. Second in importance is trade with the member states of LAFTA, which purchase 15% of exports and supply 20% of imports. Third in importance is trade with countries of the European Free Trade Association (EFTA), which take about 12% of exports and supply 13% of imports. Fourth is trade with the United States, which absorbs about 8% of exports and provides about 23% of imports.

External debt: $2.66 billion at the end of 1966, of which about $1.77 billion was public and just over $890 million was private. Payment of $442 million in 1967 lowered the total somewhat but still left the country with an external debt burden nearly three times its foreign exchange reserves. The country's external credit requirements for 1968 through 1970 were estimated at over $600 million, nearly one-half of the projected surpluses on the balance of trade for those years.

Foreign Investment: the country's largest sources of foreign direct private investment are several hundred United States companies, operating either directly or through licenses; they have total investments amounting to over $1.1 billion, about two thirds of it invested in manufacturing. U.S. investment represents over 55% of all foreign investment (1958–65). British, Italian, West German, French, Belgian, Dutch, and Swiss firms hold investments of importance. Foreign capital, mainly European and U.S., controls 51% of the income of the 50 largest companies (1968). It controls 65% of the market of those companies. Industrial production grows much slower than the activity of U.S. subsidiaries in Argentina, indicating an advanced process of denationalization. Often, industrial stagnation coincided with a sharp growth in sales of U.S. subsidiaries. For instance, in the period 1957–1961, sales of U.S. subsidiaries grew at an annual rate of 23%, while industrial production remained virtually stagnant (0.5%). Dividing the rate of growth in sales of U.S. subsidiaries by the rate of growth of industrial production for the same period gives a rough estimate of the process of denationalization. The index thus obtained for Argentina during 1957–1965 is 5.81, much higher than indices of denationalization for Brazil, Mexico, Venezuela, Canada, South Africa, France, West Germany, Italy, U.K., Japan, Australia, and Philippines. (Source: ECLA, *Estudio Económico de America Latina 1970,* cuadro 29)

Newspapers: In 1968 there were well over 200 significant dailies with an estimated circulation of more than 3 million—roughly one copy to every 3 people over the age of 20. Other periodicals cover a variety of subjects. In 1966 the estimated circulation of 52 of the largest totaled 6.7 million.

Radio: In 1968 the great bulk of the population—an estimated 18.75 million—listened to some 97 radiobroadcasting stations on 7.5 million receiving sets.

Television: In 1968 there were 29 television programing stations and 2 million receiving sets.

Automobiles: 50.8 per 1,000 inhabitants (1967).

Labor: Over 25% of population employed in manufacturing in 1968, when total labor force was estimated at more than 8.5 million.

Industry: Output generates 36% of GNP.

Armed Forces strength: In 1968 —Army: 85,000, three-fourths conscripts serving 1 or 2 years; four army corps; Army Aviation Command. Navy: 35,000, including Naval Aviation Command and marine-type Naval Infantry Corps. Air-Force: 17,000; five operational commands. National Gendarmerie: 11,000 —federal constabulary subordinate to Army. National Maritime Prefecture: 8,000, coast-guard force subordinate to Navy. Police as support for armed forces in internal repression: Federal, 16,000. Provincial forces vary with area and population of each province. Largest: Police of Buenos Aires Province, 18,000.

CHAPTER 4

BRAZIL

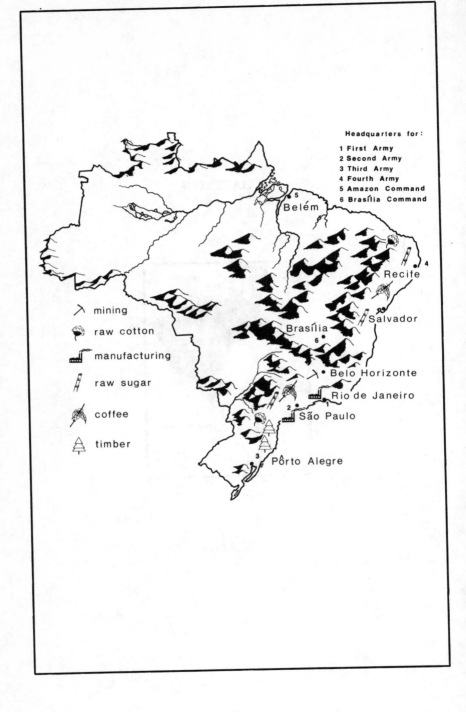

Headquarters for:

1 First Army
2 Second Army
3 Third Army
4 Fourth Army
5 Amazon Command
6 Brasília Command

Belém

Recife

Salvador

Brasília

Belo Horizonte

Rio de Janeiro

São Paulo

Pôrto Alegre

mining

raw cotton

manufacturing

raw sugar

coffee

timber

CONTENTS

BRAZIL

"Militarism is to the army what fanaticism is to religion, what charlatanry is to science, what industrialism is to industry, what mercantilism is to commerce, what Caesarism is to royalty, what demagogy is to democracy, what absolutism is to order, what egotism is to the ego."

(Rui Barbosa, during 1910 presidential campaign in which he was defeated by Marshall Hermes da Fonseca)

"I follow the destiny that is imposed on me. After years of domination and looting by international economic and financial groups, I made myself chief of an unconquerable revolution. I began the work of liberation and I instituted a regime of social liberty. I had to resign."

(President Getúlio Vargas in suicide note of 1954)

"I wanted Brazil for Brazilians and because I had to face and fight corruption, lies and cowardliness, whose only goals are to subject the general needs of the nation to some ambitious groups and individuals from inside and also from outside. However, I feel crushed. Terrible forces came forward to fight me and to defame me by all their means . . ."

(President Jânio Quadros in 1961 letter of resignation)

BRAZIL: THE ORIGINS OF A CRISIS*

BY

THEOTONIO DOS SANTOS

ON STUDYING A DEPENDENT COUNTRY

An examination of Brazil's socio-economic and political structure must be preceded by a discussion of several methodological issues related to the study of a dependent country. The reality of the so-called Third World, and especially of Latin America, cannot be understood outside the context of the European capitalist expansion that changed life in these areas in ways that were absolutely incompatible with the natural development of the native populations. The needs of capitalist Europe determined the nature of these changes. Given their technological, political, and military superiority, the European countries were able to adjust economies to meet their needs, transferring populations (colonizers from Europe to the Third World and slaves from Africa to America) and mobilizing many kinds of capital and resources in order to achieve their goals.

The history of the countries which were affected by this gigantic adventure cannot be understood outside of this context. All the countries had more or less similar experience, and they adjusted to the situation according to their internal possibilities, the composition of locally created forces, and their position in the general system of which they were a part.

The fundamental motive of this international system was to obtain riches and profits for the dominant groups of the central countries. During the colonial period commercial and manufacturing Europe sought precious metals and tropical agricultural products that could not be produced in Europe. During the nineteenth century industrial capitalist Europe bought raw materials for its factories and agricultural products for its urban population. During the twentieth century the United States and Europe needed a market for surplus capital and machines, while continuing to need raw materials, agricultural goods, and some new industrial products.

* Translation by Lois Athey and Marjory Bray

The history of the economies of dependent societies is one of adjustment to those demands or attempts to escape this destiny. Those which adjusted best have, for different historical reasons, experienced substantial economic spurts which, however, failed to produce an indigenous growth process. Rather, the general outcome has been an unfortunate upheaval or decline when the local riches were completely exhausted or when the dominant centers reoriented their demand for such goods.

Even during periods of growth and wealth, the dependent countries were in a disadvantageous position. Intensive exploitation of resources demanded intensive exploitation of workers, forcing them to reach a maximum productivity level, while at the same time they were maintained at low levels of nutrition and inadequate replacement of energy. Specialized production for the international market, intensive exploitation of the work force, and low salaries form a constant trinity of dependency. The necessary complement to this system during the colonial period and at the beginning of the nineteenth century was repression and submission of labor by force.

Despite the fact that the dependent economies were successively dominated by capitalist sectors they did not utilize the most advanced means of production of each period; rather, they employed the most backward work processes. In Europe mercantile capitalism evolved into modern manufacturing, whereas in Latin America slavery and servitude persisted as labor was forced to accept disciplined and dangerous work in the mines or plantations. The Indians of the Andean highlands resisted for years as did those of the Brazilian jungles, and the Negroes imported from Africa, in spite of their unfamiliarity with the region, were able to escape, and sometimes to establish their own villages. This labor group submitted only to armed force. Under these conditions it was absolutely impossible to institute a purely economic coercion and organize a free labor market.

Thus, Latin American capitalist economies developed based on labor systems that were long out of date. Latin America (and the South of the United States until the war of secession) also created wealth that externally served the European bourgeoisie and monarchies and internally the new oligarchy; Latin America also generated class structures and specific policies that we can call dependent. Dependency thus is not a relation whereby a national economy submits to an external economy, but rather a basic relation that *constitutes* and *conditions* the internal structures of the dominated or dependent regions. Dependency implies an economic, social, and political situation in which the structure of societies is conditioned by the needs, actions, and interests of other and dominant nations. This conditioning provides these societies with the framework for their development or for their responses to stimuli produced by the dominant society. The final response is not, however, determined by this situation but rather by the internal forces of the dependent society. It is the character of these forces that explains both their compliant behavior and their degree of conflict with the forces that condition the society.

One must clearly understand that only industrial capitalism, and, to a limited extent, its commercial predecessor of the sixteenth to eighteenth centuries, have been able to create dependent societies. One must differentiate this dependency from a simple relation of interdependence between peoples and nations or even a situation of relative submission in which demands of the dominant nation are sufficiently strong to bring about a fundamental reorganization of the dominant economies, making them structurally dependent.

In order to understand the structures of dependent societies one must first study the world economy. Thus, the following study attempts to analyze Brazil's economic, class, political and cultural structures as they emerge in the context of the development of the world economy. At the same time these structures are analyzed from an historical perspective in order to reveal their true nature and to explain realities that are apparently unexplainable, accidental, or supposed products of national idiosyncrasies, cultural vestiges, or racial origins. We divide our essay according to the major historical stages as reflected in the changing forms of the international capitalist system. However, we devote more attention to the present period.

There are two main reasons why a knowledge of Brazil's socio-economic evolution is of vital importance for an understanding of today's world. First, because in terms of size and population Brazil is today one of the largest countries of the Third World. Her strategic importance is evident by her geographical domination of the Eastern coast of South America, facing Africa, and by the fact that, with the exception of Chile and Ecuador, Brazil has common frontiers with all South American countries. Brazil's modern industrial development has made her a medium-sized force with sub-imperialist aspirations for the South Atlantic. That is, she seeks to become the privileged intermediary for American and European imperialist domination of the region. For all these reasons, Latin American history is and will be greatly conditioned by what happens in this country. In the second place, given Brazil's huge potentialities, her socio-economic evolution has often represented a model of the extreme forms that can occur under imperialist domination and dependent development. When Brazil was a colony, its sugar production held a privileged position and its gold mines played a fundamental role in financing the industrial revolution. At the end of the nineteenth century the nation had a monopoly of the world's coffee supply and during a short period the same held true for rubber. By the middle of the twentieth century Brazil had developed an industrial base with more intensive participation of foreign capital than any other Latin American country. Yet, despite all these opportunities, and its enormous resources and size, in five hundred years Brazil has not been able to break the barrier of dependency and underdevelopment.

This historical fact has always represented a challenge for Brazilian social and political theorists, obsessed by the failure of the "giant eternally asleep in a splendid cradle," as expressed in their national anthem. This existential motivation has led Brazilian social thought to collaborate to a great extent in the creation and polishing of theories of underdevelopment and dependency necessary to explain the Third World's painful situation and to bring about change. In addition, with the creation in the 1950's of an important labor class whose obvious political presence in the country impressed a significant intellectual sector, there developed a radical criticism of the dominant development theories whose inspiration had been predominantly bourgeois. Thus, an analysis of Brazil's historical evolution becomes the elaboration of a correct theory of underdevelopment and dependency as well as a theory of the social revolution which marks the current history of the "Third World."

THE FORMATION OF THE COLONY
THE NATURE OF COLONIZATION

In order to understand Brazil's colonial period, one has to explain the character of mercantile capitalism that led to the maritime discoveries of the fifteenth and sixteenth centuries and colonization thereafter. Expansion of the Iberian peninsula towards Africa, Asia, and subsequently America was led by Portugal. In addition to dominating many of the Atlantic islands, Portugal discovered the maritime route to the Indies, a main objective of the sailing excursions. Portugal's Aviz dynasty constituted the first highly centralized European monarchy, and it set out systematically to reestablish rich commerce with the Indies after the overland route had been cut off by the Arabs. Anticipating French and British absolute monarchies, initiating mercantilism before the rest of the European states, assembling a huge concentration of internal and external capital, compiling and developing the scientific advances and technologies of the era, Portugal and Spain were able to open for the European west a vast economic empire whose last fruits were principally absorbed years later by Holland and England.

This maritime expansion was primarily commercial. The traders reached the rich Hindu commercial center in the Indian ocean and tried to reorient their commerce with Europe from overland routes to a maritime one. Commercial warehouses defended by forts were the first forms of land exploitation. This situation differed, however, in the Canary Islands, in America, and also somewhat in Africa. In these places the traders expropriated the richest areas and carried out a process of absolutely unequal exchange between products of entirely different civilizations (a piece of gold was traded for a European tool without any law of value to regulate such exchange). Over time there grew a need to establish productive centers there under European administration.

The step from pure mercantile relations to colonial production varied according to regional differences. The demand for semi-precious metals and tropical products not available in Europe together with the skills of the colonizers and the technical resources of the era, determined the areas which were colonized. Another factor which conditioned colonial production was the labor force. Wherever there were organized native settlements capable of extracting metals or producing tropical products, the fundamental task was to subdue them and to organize them to work for the colonizer. In trying to destroy ancient native organization or adjust it to the new needs, the colonizers killed millions of Indians. There was a great willingness to experiment with new solutions without considering the historical precedent and consequently a degree of stability was not reached until the middle of the sixteenth century. However, they did try to mobilize vast sectors of the native population to work in the mines or farms without completely destroying a subsistence economy and a minimum communal organization, the latter functioning often as a reserve work force.

In the Brazilian case there was a shortage of labor. Brazilian Indians were too backward to serve as a labor base for a stable rural economy. The initial recourse of the Portuguese was Indian slavery combined with the use of Portuguese outcasts. This proved to be only a limited solution, and thus began a fantastic and terrible historical stage of the removal of the African population to work in America, which expanded and intensified the old Arab slave trade in Africa to an incredible degree. This commerce became one of the most important businesses of mercantile capitalism whose profits were greater than those of other productive activities. As Marx makes clear, slave trade under English control during the eighteenth century was one of the fundamental bases for the original accumulation of capital which led to the modern type of capitalist production.

All labor systems used were of a servile and coercive character, whether they were the organization of Indian communities that paid tribute to the crown, natives that the crown handed over to the *encomenderos* who had the right to exploit mines and lands, or pure and simple slavery of

Africans and sometimes Indians. No free labor market could be created in the colonies in spite of diverse capitalist motivations orienting colonial growth. The principal reason for this situation was the existence of abundant lands whose family or collective exploitation would have been preferred by the laborers had they not been *forced* to work in European or creole mining or agricultural enterprises. The Africans in Brazil demonstrated this preference by escaping from the plantations to form their own communities, the *quilombos,* of which the most famous, Palmares, grew to a large size and existed for over half a century. It established powerful commercial ties with the Northeast cities until its total destruction by Portuguese troops at the end of the seventeenth century.

There were three conditions fundamental to the colonial socio-economic formations. In the first place, colonial societies were a product of the strengthening and expansion of monarchical power that organized and administered overseas areas. The colonial lands, mines, and indigenous populations legally belonged to the monarch. The crown also had a legal monopoly over the right to trade with the colonies. The mercantile bourgeoisie were under the crown's protection and had to pay high tributes for the monarchical concession allowing them to exploit a specific colonial resource or engage in trade when the crown was unable to do so itself. The royal monopoly included access to the indigenous labor force, and this affected colonial socio-economic development: work was necessarily of a servile nature not for traditional reasons but rather because of complete, audacious, and "enterprising" adjustment to the needs of colonial production. The third essential aspect of the colonial socio-economic system was the external determination of the type of production: it had to meet the needs of the European market. During the colonial period Brazil passed through several production cycles, the principal ones being Brazilian timber in the sixteenth century and sugar and gold in the seventeenth and eighteenth centuries. Following a more or less rigid historical continuity a mono-productive economy was maintained, based to a great extent on lands granted by the crown to creole noble families for the purpose of developing huge productive units, employing a slave work force, and fomenting exportation.

THE COLONIAL SOCIO-ECONOMIC STRUCTURE

Let us now turn to a general description of the colonial socio-economic structure and its mono-productive, exporting, *latifundist,* and slave characteristics whose major historical causes we discussed in the preceding section. (The best over-all study of the colonial economy is found in Prado Júnior, 1945.)

The productive structure which formed was conditioned by the European market to which it was oriented. The technology employed, the financial base, and the means of commercialization were profoundly influenced by European practices. Local commerce and technological conditions often were not taken into account, and as a result the colonists were not able to overcome geographic or local climatic difficulties. Production became far-reaching to meet Europe's hungry demand for precious metals and tropical products. Vast regions were devastated; an ecological disequilibrium was produced; native hunting and productive areas were eradicated; new diseases were introduced raising the mortality rate so that over half the Indian population was wiped out in the Americas and almost the entire Indian population was destroyed in Brazil.

The sugar plantation was the basic productive unit of civilization in Northeast Brazil during the sixteenth and seventeenth centuries. The greater part of the sugar production went to the European market. That production was traded by Portuguese merchants who were granted this concession by the Crown. Trade with other countries brought slaves from Africa with the objective of maintaining and increasing production (about 50 percent of the value of exported goods went to pay for the importation of slaves). Trade also meant luxury goods for consumption by the ruling class (from pianos to fashionable clothes or a few books) as well as parts and goods necessary for new investments. To provide for their own food, clothing, and shelter, the exporters had to have a base of local production. In addition to sugar production, there developed cattle and considerable other production for home consumption. To complete the economic picture there developed a small artisan sector, alongside the ports and urban areas (primarily Recife and Olinda) dedicated to commerce and administrative activities. (The two classic studies of this society are those of Freyre, 1936 and 1951.)

During the seventeenth and eighteenth centuries competition in sugar from the Caribbean led to economic decline, but recovery occurred with the discovery of gold in Minas Gerais. Gold in Minas Gerais together with diamond exploitation caused a growth of a wealthy economy in the mountain interior whose power led to the creation of a substantial internal market. Aside from being more specialized than sugar and requiring many other products, mining created a vast administrative apparatus to collect the tax on gold. Mining not only led to the greater development of cattle ranching but also to other agriculture, more extended artisan industry, and an important network of urban services.

As in other parts of Latin America, there was a vigorous industrialization drive during this period. The Crown devised strong sanctions against such activity by closing down any new industry. The levying of a tax on gold caused violent protests and led to the growth of some of the first

Brazilian liberation movements, for example those of Felipe Dos Santos and Tiradentes in the eighteenth century. However, in the eighteenth century the mines were depleted and the gold-based civilization entered a melancholic period of decay. (A comprehensive study of this period is found in Boxer, 1962.)

Within this mono-productive economy that generated supporting economic entities highly sensitive to the fluctations of one commodity, the ruling class was basically dependent on its European matrix. In Europe was located not only the juridical and administrative center but also the commercial and financial centers that controlled the demand for products and supply of slave labor.

At the end of the eighteenth century, however, and at the beginning of the nineteenth, the monopoly exercised over colonial commerce by the Crown and the Portuguese merchants entered a period of sharp decline. The facilities created by the rich commerce and the favorable buying power derived from this commerce, led to the decline of Portugal's internal production, and Portugal became just an intermediary for Brazilian products and European markets. The Portuguese commercial monopoly became a heavy burden on the Brazilian agrarian and commercial bourgeoisie. Contraband traffic somewhat alleviated this situation. The level of industrial development that had been achieved by England put that nation in the best position to offer better prices for Brazilian products, enabling Brazilians to avoid paying not only royal taxes but also intermediate earnings to Portuguese merchants and financiers.

By the beginning of the nineteenth century in Brazil, as in almost all of Latin America, the tendency to trade directly with England allowed Brazil to avoid domination by the Crown and Iberian merchants. Political events transformed this historical trend into a permanent reality. Brazil had very special conditions that oriented this transition. Pursued by Napoleon, Prince Regent Dom João of Portugal fled the court and went to Brazil in 1808 making it the center of the Empire. The British, who not only inspired this act but also guaranteed the success of the royal family's flight, took advantage of the situation by requesting that their products have full access to Brazilian ports. Dom João immediately acceded, creating in effect a real independence of Brazil from Portugal. When King João returned to Portugal in 1821, he left his son as regent of the then United Kingdom of Brazil—indicating a coming independence. Pressured by a strong independence movement and revolutionary republican factions and faced with the reaction of the Portuguese bourgeoisie which wanted to reestablish commercial and political domination over Brazil, the regent himself, Dom Pedro I, declared Brazilian independence in 1822 and began to govern as emperor. After the creation of a liberal monarchy, a crisis period and adjustments soon followed. When in 1831 it was necessary for him to return to Portugal, Dom Pedro resigned from the throne in favor of his son, Dom Pedro II. Civil war continued until 1840 when Dom Pedro reached legal age.

The way in which independence was achieved allowed full control over the new state to be maintained by the ancient rural oligarchy made up of big landowners, and agricultural entrepreneurs, and by the big exporters. They became the nobility of a stable oligarchy with full support from England. The apparently peaceful establishment of the new monarchy (accompanied by an intense crushing of an opposition of small artisans and merchants who had rebelled in the republican movements of 1817 and in the civil war of 1831–1835) also ensured the consolidation of a regime based on slavery that lasted for more than sixty years. For a long time the regime had to rely on slavery because, with an abundance of cultivable land, the labor force preferred to farm on their own when given freedom. A profitable slave trade continued until the middle of the nineteenth century when the British ceased to be interested in this type of trade.

The establishment of a colonial society founded on slavery meant that its dependent character constituted the base of internal production, impeding a full development of internal labor and capital markets. This was in addition to the Crown's monopoly over trade, land, and administration which also impeded capitalist development. Relations of slave production, although modern and situated within the context of world capitalist expansion, hindered capitalist production that would have allowed full development of the country's productive forces. For this reason, the manufactures which developed were based also on the system and thus could not stimulate the growth of large, modern capitalist enterprise. The country experienced important industrial growth only during the second half of the nineteenth century, especially after the abolition of slavery in 1888.

At the same time, the colonial structure created the *latifundio* as the base of the country's wealth. (On the evolution and continued existence of the *latifundio* see Passos Guimarães, 1968.) The *latifundio* was based on a precapitalist form of holding land that was inalienable and the property of the Crown. Independence meant the end of this precapitalist system of land tenure and guaranteed the rural gentry not only possession but also ownership of the land. Legislation was enacted which allowed their conversion into capitalist owners who then had at their disposal an asset which would be sold or used as security for a loan. The *real* beginning of this development took a while, limiting the development of a capital market. By then there was settlement of new agricultural regions and colonization that opened the rural areas to non-nobles and created the base of a more modern society. This modernization process, which created the conditions for Brazil's capitalist development, began only during the second half of the nineteenth century.

MODERNIZATION OF THE EXPORT SOCIETY

The period from political independence in 1822 to World War I was characterized by an expansion of the export economy with a more modern base. At the end of the nineteenth century there emerged an oligarchic-export society that was liberal and authoritarian and solidly linked to British and later to American monopoly capital. The socio-economic changes that occurred during this period of modernization displayed the following fundamental characteristics:

1) Brazilian trade was opened to the world market (especially Great Britain). Commerce was based on the law of value (with unequal relations whose causes are discussed later) and was oriented by the doctrine of *laissez-faire*. The battle between this doctrine and protectionism carried out during this period ended with the victory of the former and a consolidation of the agrarian-export bourgeoisie whose interests were allied with the rapidly rising interests of British imperialism.

2) In spite of a dependence on the slave system until 1888, there were pressures to put an end first to the slave trade and later to slavery itself. By the end of the century Brazil had developed a mixture which included a capitalist wage system and semi-servile relations of labor. The importation of large numbers of European immigrants for the São Paulo coffee region created a new labor market in place of slavery. At the same time, a capital market emerged which freed the nation from its dependency on commerce in slaves and lands.

3) Despite the conservative nature of the ruling class, a consequence of its archaic power bases, the juridical and political super-structure had to modernize and adjust itself to the needs of a liberal-bourgeois society. The adoption of positivism as the basic doctrine of the emerging middle classes, the separation of church and state, and the development of public education, were aspects vital for the adaptation of the super-structure to new economic conditions. However, the economy continued to be agrarian and exporting, since it was unable to overcome its dependent character.

Let us turn to a detailed study of each of these aspects.

EXPANSION OF WORLD TRADE

The decline in gold production at the end of the eighteenth century gave rise to a search for new exports. Cotton, the recovery of sugarcane, and later coffee were the substitutes for trade that had gone through a grave crisis during the first decades of the century. Together with the United States, Brazil was for a while the principal cotton exporter to England (in 1800 Brazil exported 30,000 sacks and the United States 40,000), but she rapidly lost her position (in 1807 she exported 19,000 in comparison to 171,000 sacks for the United States). Brazil's sugar also suffered from strong competition with Cuba. Only during the second half of the nineteenth century did Brazil again experience an important economic growth when coffee came to represent about 60 percent of the country's exports. Brazil achieved an exceptional position in the world market: at the middle of the nineteenth century her coffee exportation accounted for about 50 percent of world coffee; in 1900 this percentage went up to 75 percent. At the beginning of the century there was an important growth in the exportation of rubber from the Amazon region, but later the British moved this industry to other areas. There was also an increase in the export of cacao for making chocolate.

Given the new opportunities in the world market, after 1868 Brazil began to have a favorable balance of trade that allowed her to accumulate a large financial reserve. This reserve was increased even further with the abandonment of the expensive purchase of slaves.

British capital, which during the first half of the nineteenth century had sought to secure partial control of the country by making loans to the Brazilian government and to individuals for financing the balance of trade deficits, changed its relations with Brazil in the second half of the century. Incursions were made into transportation, public utilities, electrical energy, and communications, with the aim of taking advantage of the country's financial reserves generated by the surplus in the commercial balance of payments. This reserve served as a base for the purchase of British railroad equipment, steel, machinery, and other equipment. At the same time the new commercial surplus was also used to import machinery that to a certain degree contributed to industrial development. The capital market began to organize itself, and a banking system was developed. This general climate produced a great deal of euphoria in the dominant classes. They began to develop confidence in the philosophy of economic liberalism as the basis for development.

The coffee monoculture which oriented the country towards the export of agricultural products, was to paralyze Brazil's drive to belong to the new modern industrial era. But it appeared to be the solution for national problems and the best possible path for Brazil's entry into the world market. This situation allowed the agrarian-export oligarchy to develop an ideological and political force which made it become a veritable business, intellectual, and political elite, capable of overcoming all opposition to its domination.

Nevertheless, this oligarchy could not hide its enormous dependence on the British bourgeoisie, which controlled Brazil's coffee commerce as well as provided the modern technology for railroads, ports, communication networks and banks. In the 1860's with surplus capital generated from foreign trade, a Brazilian capitalist, Visconde de Maua, tried to create transportation and mining enterprises with the aid of private bank investments. His failure in the face of international competition and the limitations of an internal slave economy showed how impossible it was for the agrarian-export bourgeoisie* to proceed on its own.

The development of an export economy allowed the bourgeoisie and the urban middle classes to buy foreign manufactured goods at low prices, thus limiting the market for goods produced in Brazil, and undermining the competition of national manufacturing. National industry could develop itself only as a complementary sector dependent on the exporter. However, the highly specialized character of exports destroyed a large part of subsistence agriculture, which stimulated the development of an international division of labor and created a certain degree of internal economic dynamism. Massive food requirements of slaves, skilled peasants, and urban salaried workers had to be satisfied by national agriculture and cattle raising. Thus, the production in these sectors attained a certain level of industrialization as in the case of salted beef in the state of Rio Grande do Sul, milk products in the states in Minas Gerais and Goiás, and improvements in rice and bean cultivation.

The textile, food, and parts industries were stimulated by demands of the salaried urban and rural workers. The continued existence of a slave system would have been a huge impediment to the development of an internal market. With the abrupt abolition of slavery in 1888 industry experienced a sudden spurt, and by the end of the century a relatively important industrial base had been created. In this way national economy achieved a fairly significant degree of specialization which allowed the appearance of a complex class structure at the beginning of the century.

CLASS STRUCTURE

At the end of the nineteenth century the incontestable hegemony of the agrarian-export oligarchy was a quiet and peaceful fact. Growth of the urban middle classes was based on the expansion of the armed forces, the urban zones that grew with the development of commerce, the administrative apparatus that became more and more necessary for control of the economy, and on the creation of an infrastructure of power and transportation for business expansion. Finally, the professional middle classes

---

* Bourgeoisie refers to the middle class whose income derives from commercial and industrial enterprise and whose social behavior and political views are determined or influenced by interest in private property.

grew and gained importance partially due to the newly created school system, and the small businessmen and industrialists began to have increasing influence over the local power structure.

At the same time there was a growth of the urban proletariat composed of railroad workers, port workers, and those of the textile and food factories built during this period. They were mostly Italian immigrants who had come to work in agriculture but had given up this idea because of the high degree of exploitation in that system. The situation of Italian emigrants in Brazil was the object of heavy criticism in the Italian parliament. The debate was to a certain extent led by leftist parties, especially the anarchists, who had a great deal of influence over the emigrant and Italian proletariat.

At the end of the century a salaried proletariat appeared in the rural areas of several regions, for example São Paulo, the state of Rio de Janeiro, part of Minas Gerais, in addition to the proletariat of the Northeast and Rio Grande do Sul. Nevertheless, the majority of the agrarian labor force was composed of peasants in semi-servile conditions or in a mixed salaried-small farmer situation. A great number of these workers were *meeiros* or *parceiros* who, in exchange for the right to cultivate the owner's land, were required to work for him during certain days and in addition to give him part of their products or even animals. Many authors regard such relationships as a form of hidden salary with payment made in goods (see Caio Prado Júnior, 1966). In fact, such relations link the worker to the landowner by the formation of not only economic but also servile ties (which assumed and still assume the form of *compadrazgo*, honor debts, and other forms of dependence). In no way is the *parceiro* a free worker who is the *private owner* of his labor which he sells in a free labor market. He is not salaried; on the contrary, rural and urban salaried relations (and this exists today, to some extent) were affected by those semi-servile relations limiting the development of a capitalist means of production in Brazil.

The other part of the rural work force was and still is composed of a vast population of small property owners (*minifundistas*) who sell their labor and that of their children and relatives during the sugar harvest period. These temporary workers have been (and are today, under different forms, as we shall see) the major component of the rural labor force. They include both small landowners and salaried workers who have one foot in pre-capitalist subsistence agriculture (through occasional sales of their products in a primitive mercantile economy) and the other foot in salaried relations allowing them to buy some of their clothes and other industrial products.

Recently, as a consequence of capitalist development in the countryside, the situation of these groups has deteriorated to such an extent that they are forced to buy agricultural products because their *minifundios* no longer produce sufficient amounts. In addition, they can no longer use the neighboring woods that they had depended on for wood, hunting, and other extra resources. Development of mercantile relations forces them to sell more and more of their produce making them submit to the laws of the market over which they lack control.

We also find the small and medium-sized farmer, landowner, or tenant. This type of peasant existed and still exists today in the south; recently they have been found as far as Mato Grosso and Goiás. They produce most of the modern fruits and vegetables for urban markets and food processing plants. They have also specialized in the cultivation of cereals and in some cases (as in the northern Paraná) even coffee. Many of them belong to German or Japanese colonies which were strongly backed by their governments in their decision to create rich enclaves in Brazil and other countries. They brought their technical and administrative skills to an environment composed of both large highly modernized productive units and completely unprofitable enterprises.

The coffee plantation, the center of economic activity during this period, was not especially concerned with the rational use of land. There was an abundance of land. The coffee magnates, the São Paulo oligarchs, were more interested in commercialization, transportation, and immediate access to information about price changes in the London coffee market than in an improvement of agricultural techniques leading to rational land use. If productivity was high, no one worried about exhaustion of the lands. They moved to other regions or sold the old *fazendas* to new second-class landowners. In addition, the plantations were so large that rarely were there shortages of coffee producing lands.

The coffee cultivators had to worry about very complex problems. They had to import their work force from Europe, specifically from Southern Italy, to insure growth of their plantations. They had to keep close watch over international price controls, and in 1906 forced the government to guarantee a stable coffee price through the Taubaté agreement which required government purchase of surplus coffee stocks in order to regulate the international supply. They had to use their export earnings and even some of their capital surplus to build urban places. They had to keep watch over railroad transportation in the interior and ports and ships on the coast. The coffee oligarchy was much more urban and commercially oriented than agricultural. Its principal representatives were infused with European culture, surrounded by stylish furniture and European paintings, protective of national artists and writers, and responsible for the creation of an academic center such as the Faculty of Philosophy of São Paulo—

a sort of tropical extension of the Sorbonne (so said Claude Levi-Strauss when he visited Brazil during the Second World War). Under these extravagant and refined cosmopolitan cultural surroundings, this oligarchy was able to hide the miserable conditions of peasants who were producing the surplus that fed its leisure. The despicable *jeca-tatu*, idealized at times, ridiculed at others, was the stupid, ignorant, illiterate, miserable human being who produced this enormous wealth, the existence of which he did not have the least idea.

In this way the links were established between an economy of misery and one of opulence whose basic form of division was the extensive and miserable rural life and the refined selective urban environment. This was a mixture of cosmopolitan and provincial, of exquisite culture and massive illiteracy that lacerated and still lacerates Brazil, making it an enormous giant of insoluble contradictions and challenges that are an enigma to those without a dialectic understanding.

New small cities began to reproduce this same structure at the regional level. The large provincial landowners were umbilically tied to the big national oligarchs. In addition, there existed a small provincial bourgeoisie and the extensive miserable peasant class, as well as a small urban proletariat and already some sproutings of a marginal unemployed population. Nevertheless this group was small due to the survival of a natural urban economy that always allowed the poor a small plot for cultivation of a few basic subsistence products. The conditions resulting from an economic crisis of the export sector or natural calamities such as northeastern droughts would break the delicate equilibrium of this provincial economy, forcing people to migrate to urban areas in search of better opportunities. In the first decades of the twentieth century, with the advance of capitalism towards the countryside and the consequent expulsion of enormous rural masses, this migratory process was greatly accentuated.

By the end of the nineteenth century, Brazil's rather complex class structure began to intensify. At the top was the agrarian-export oligarchy, beneath which was the agrarian *latifundist* bourgeoisie which had no direct access to the export sector. In the urban areas there emerged a bourgeoisie based on industry and internal trade and a salaried or professional middle class with a certain degree of access to the power holders who purchased their labor. One also found an enormous agrarian proletariat and semi-proletariat alongside an emergent rural petty bourgeoisie composed of small- and medium-sized landowners or tenants. An industrial proletariat and a semi-proletariat of this service sector also emerged in the cities.

This class structure, in spite of its vertical nature, was sharply divided by the violent opposition between a predominantly pre-capitalist country-side and a highly cosmopolitan urban zone. The violent upheavals of the Brazilan countryside from the end of the nineteenth century to the first decades of the twentieth were not evident in the urban areas. (The most important of these disorders was described in a classic study of Euclydes Da Cunha, 1944.) To some extent, the violent urban disturbances of the 1920's in Brazil would have to take account of rural Brazil.

The institutional and ideological super-structure that was built atop this agrarian-export dependent society was not divorced from the basic forms that give it life.

THE STATE, PARTIES, AND IDEOLOGY

Brazil was the only constitutional monarchy in republican Latin America. Other than its conservative stability, Brazil was not very different from other countries. The same liberal,* elitist, and authoritarian ideology that oriented the *caudillos* of the independence period and the Latin American republics also dominated the Brazilian monarchy and the Empire's political parties. It was the same dominant class that founded the institutional structures and ideologies.

This apparently paradoxical situation derived from the fact that new world liberalism represented the interests of the agrarian-export bourgeoisie and not of the industrial bourgeoisie, as was the case in Europe. On the contrary, Brazilian liberalism served to contain the emergence and development of the industrial bourgeoisie. This conservative and authoritarian liberalism had only to be reconciled with a highly selective electoral college, with the maintenance of servile labor, and with a mini-mum of pragmatism, of empiricism and royal protection for scientific development. Although Dom Pedro II inaugurated the first telephones, his interest in science and the arts was only as one who appreciated them, a dilettante, a consumer. The agrarian-export bourgeoisie was connected to the modern technological world only as passive consumers and not as scientists producing new discoveries.

These conditions did not prevent the appearance, development, and expansion of an utopian socialism of artisan origin that was choked in a violent 1848 to 1850 uprising in Pernambuco. The event was recorded in official Brazilian history only as a small uprising, which did not threaten the central power. Thus was hidden their libertarian, anti-monarchical, and often protectionist nature which was in opposition to the liberalism that crushed artisans and nascent national industry. In Latin America

* Liberalism is a political and economic philosophy that emphasizes individual freedom from restraint, especially by government regulation, and from all arbitrary authority in general.

this alternative of national development toward an internal market flowered only in Paraguay ending in a violent conflict from 1864 to 1870 with the triple alliance of Brazil, Argentina, and Uruguay. Brazil was directly responsible for the genocide of Paraguayans in which about five-sixths of the Paraguayan nation were killed. The Paraguayan war (as it is called in Brazil) like the events in Pernambuco, is an example of an historic episode that helped confirm the important role of the army in national life. With this development, a middle group found its position reinforced although it was kept from power by a creole nobility protected by the monarchy.

The Brazilian movement that waved the republican banner had a clearly positivist* ideological base and was inspired by U. S. federalism. This republican movement sought to solidify the bases of a federal state within a monarchy highly centralized in its juridical forms and highly localized in its regional export-oriented economies. The disappearance of the national slave market in 1888 eliminated one of the important links between the different regions. As a consequence, the different regions turned inward, reinvigorating local and regional life. The republican constitution of 1891 provided juridical means for the functioning of an already entrenched power structure. The export centers, primarily the coffee zone, regained autonomy in order to expand their relations with a growing international market, and thus escaped control of the monarchic centralism.

The Old Republic, which survived from 1889 to 1930, grew out of a conciliation of these regional interests. The basic characteristic of the Old Republic was the "politics of the governors." This consisted of alliances of local political chiefs (the *coroneis*) with state governors and of the governors with officials at the federal level. At the center of the Republic was the group tied to coffee in São Paulo and cattle in Minas Gerais that had overcome the hegemonic tendencies of other regional factions, such as the Southern producers of salted beef. (The best description of this period and the politics of the *coroneis* can be found in Vitor Nunes Leal, 1948 and the best synthesis of facts and sources is in Edgard Carone, 1969.)

The relatively stable agreement among the strong regional interests was based on the army which had established the Republic and continued to be the key to the national unity of regional forces such as had wrecked havoc in the rest of Latin America. Positivism as a social philosophical doctrine, liberalism as an economic doctrine, and federalism as an orga-

---

* Positivism, a philosophy based on principles of Auguste Comte which had impact on Latin America after 1850. According to positivism, the world was ordered rationally and thereby guaranteed progress.

nizing principle were the basis for the economic structure that emerged at the end of the nineteenth century. This involved a long social and economic maturing process.

Other aspects of Brazil's "modernization" included the adaptation of civil law to the needs of a pure, although dependent, capitalism (which was combined with vast sectors of mercantile economy), the separation of Church and State, the reinforcement of the army's professional status and the emergence of public education. These elements made up the superstructure that adjusted itself to the conditions of an expanding national economy and its dependent role within the world capitalist system.

CRISIS IN THE EXPORT ECONOMY AND INDUSTRIALIZATION

The period from the end of World War I until the 1950's was characterized by a definitive crisis in the old export economy and the systematic creation of an industrial expansion backed by a strong nationalistic current. This trend was based on a fluid class alliance that changed over the times because of shifting loyalties. As we will see later, the effort to bring about national development was frustrated at the end of the period, and so was the alliance that backed this policy. The reasons for this failure will appear understandable through a description of the process. The groups that had supported the alliance were trapped between three forces: the national and international elements of the old export sector, the new industrial sector owned by international capital, and the new forces of the working class. Under pressure from the still strong resistence of the decadent export sector, the rapacious ambitions of multinational monopoly capital, and the growing consciousness and organization of the populist movement,* the nationalistic, development-oriented or reformist trend was shown to have no vigor or results. Thus were revealed all its organic weaknesses. We will present a detailed account of the aspects synthesized above.

THE CRISIS OF AN AGRARIAN-EXPORT ECONOMY

The apparently solid agrarian-export economy described previously entered a crisis period at the end of the nineteenth century when the world coffee price began to decline (the average value per sack; £4.09 in 1893, £2.91 in 1896, and £1.48 in 1899). At the same time there was a growth

---

* Populism in Latin America may be defined as a political movement which is opposed to the status quo and is supported by the mass of urban working class and sometimes the peasantry as well as non-working class elements.

of Brazilian coffee production leading to an increase in the world coffee supply.

It was at this point that the coffee bourgeoisie found a solution for the problem that, in fact, halted the crisis only by forcing the Brazilian people to pay for the decline in coffee prices. The 1906 Taubaté agreement set a fixed price for coffee and established means to improve advertising and to control the supply. This was the beginning of a protectionist policy for coffee aimed at stopping the declining trend of prices through national government financial support for regional producers (São Paulo, Minas Gerais, and Rio de Janeiro signed the agreement). Only state intervention could save the coffee economy from the liberal principles upheld until then by the agrarian bourgeoisie.

However, in the long run, the protectionist policy led to an even greater deterioration of world and Brazilian coffee markets. The policy was expensive, forced the state to buy huge coffee stocks, and contributed to a progressive increase in the national debt. In addition, this artificial and very costly fixing of the coffee prices favored producers in other countries and increased international competition leading to a vicious circle that in turn forced increased state intervention. Growing dependence of the farmers on state policies forced them to try and gain control over state affairs; but by making inflation rise and by demanding important national sacrifices, they weakened their position. Thus they were forced to make concessions to and agreements with the new emerging urban classes. At the same time, by forcing a devaluation of the national currency this policy forced a rise in the prices of imported goods and, as a result, favored national industry through a type of indirect protection.

With the 1929 crisis the coffee bourgeoisie suffered a definitive blow. Although they did not lose their important role in national life, they no longer exercised the hegemony they had achieved without great difficulty through the subtle system of political compromises with the governors described earlier. Now the coffee magnates had to content themselves internally with state aid and so-called "confiscation of the exchange earnings" which gave the state through taxation the major portion of export earnings.

In spite of the opinion of some analysts of this period who thought that state financing of coffee revealed the lack of an industrial bourgeois policy, the existence and subtlety of this policy was very clear. The idea behind this policy was the maintenance of the level of coffee production and internal and external earnings thereby generated in order to sell national industrial goods in the internal market and use those earnings to buy raw materials and machinery for national industrial development.

The Brazilian industrial elite was clearly conscious of the need for a protectionist policy. This was also true to a lesser extent of the small and medium industrial sectors who tended to follow the example of their more aware leaders who were grouped together in centers, associations, and, after 1937, in class unions and federations. In a dependent country, where industrial development depends on the capacity to import machinery and raw materials, this consciousness must adjust itself to specific conditions. The essence of the "bourgeois revolution" in these countries, that is the need to accumulate capital for industrialization, implies the necessity to control earnings and use them for investments in local industry. We call this "foreign accumulation of capital." It demonstrates that the establishment of a dependent capitalist system requires the foreign sector. Thus those items which Marx considered the goods of production, such as machines and processed raw materials, were produced in foreign countries. The industrial leaders of that era, especially Roberto Simonsen, had a clear understanding of the problem (Simonsen, 1939).

The crisis of the export sector became acute during the 1920's and all efforts of the rural coffee bourgeoisie to regain control of political power went against the trend of events. The export sector no longer provided the major portion of national income. National income derived from coffee declined from 17 percent to 6 percent between the 1930's and 1950's. Likewise, income generated by agricultural products ceased to be the number one contributor to national income and was replaced by the industrial and service sectors. Agriculture and industry represented 27 percent and 21 percent, respectively, of gross national product in 1947. In 1961 agriculture contributed 22 percent of the G.N.P. while industry was responsible for 34 percent. (The best systematic study of Brazilian data is found in Werner Baer, 1966.)

INDUSTRIALIZATION AS A PROCESS

As we saw earlier, industrialization at the end of the last century and the beginning of the twentieth had tended to complement the export sector. It was the internal market stimulated by the export sector that allowed for industrial development. We have examined other specific aspects of this relation. We showed how this export sector generated income for the importation of machinery and raw materials used by the industrial sector.

However, there were other relations of dependency between the infant industrial sector and the old export structure. The capital that was transferred to industry obviously had to come from the agrarian sector. To the extent that surplus generated in the export sector could not be used to buy imported luxury articles or to capitalize the coffee agriculture, then in decline, one can suppose that this money went directly to investment in industry and services or to the banks which enabled its use by dynamic sectors of the economy. The high rate of labor exploitation in the countryside created an ample economic surplus that was then converted into money, credits, and equities usable in more profitable sectors. In an inflationary system those who lend tend to lose money and those who invest have no reason to fear loans. There are two ways in which inflation worked in favor of industrialization: as a devaluing effect on capital used by businessmen and as a way of increasing the prices of imported goods and thereby stimulating local production.

Under these conditions it was clear that the industrial bourgeoisie would defend policies based on its class interests. This group could never become a radical bourgeoisie. Their slogans could never encompass a radical agrarian reform, an anti-imperialist policy, or a defense of bourgeois democracy. On the contrary, the bourgeois industrial program had to find ways to preserve income derived from the export sector, to control export earnings, to facilitate credit and inflation increases, and to convince the state either to invest or to force international capital to invest in infrastructure (energy; transportation; basic industries of intermediary goods, for example the iron and steel industries) and in the creation of human resources (a national industrial service for the formation of qualified professionals; labor legislation; and social security to lessen labor costs). There was also a need to centralize the government's power, to destroy the Old Republic's federated power bases that encouraged control by the local *coroneis* and regional oligarchies, to reinforce the union and state apparatus, and to create ideological support for the industrial bourgeoisie.

Indeed, the period from 1930 to 1958 was characterized by the adoption (with successes and failures) of these measures. The "New State," directed by Getúlio Vargas after a 1937 coup d'etat and lasting until 1945, was the best example of this type of program. To a lesser extent the liberal alliance that brought Vargas to power in 1930, after a revolution that mobilized wide sectors of the country, especially in the urban areas, also reflected these tendencies. But the movement vacillated and did not break past compromises. The 1937 program was much clearer in its intentions. Even so, some analysts maintained that there was no state hegemony during the period and that therefore all national and external interests were "amalgamated" (as suggested by some Brazilian sociologists) or that this government represented the ambiguous movement of the middle classes that brought it to power in 1930. This position ignored the real meaning of the process. (A presentation of the "amalgamation thesis" is found specifically in Weffort, 1964.)

The fact is that during this period all measures undertaken were to allow a dependent bourgeoisie to create the bases of an industrial society. Two errors led to alternative interpretations. The first mistake was the belief that such a bourgeoisie would defend a classic democratic bourgeois program. In reality it had fought against the liberalism that impeded development. The second error was the belief that the bourgeois class would have a national consciousness. Just as the German bourgeoisie never had the level of consciousness of a Bismarck, so in Brazil, the entire industrial bourgeoisie never arrived at Vargas' level of consciousness, nor that of such economists as Roberto Simonsen or Evaldo Lodi. Nevertheless, these men not only were able to lead the class but also created an entire class apparatus to give a degree of representation to this group and to the small and medium-sized industrialist. Above all they brought about, with obvious concessions, the implementation of a program of economic, political, and social transformations favoring the development of the bourgeoisie as a class.

Brazil failed to become independent, autonomous, democratic-bourgeois or pure capitalist not because it lacked a conscious industrial bourgeoisie, as several studies demonstrate (see an overall treatment of this topic in Cardoso, 1964 and Martins, 1968), but because of the structural impossibility of developing that type of capitalism in the twentieth century. This was virtually impossible in countries with such rigid dependence on the agrarian-export sector, as was the case of Brazil. The Brazilian industrial elite was especially after 1937 aware of the weaknesses of other classes and knew with great subtlety how to mobilize its class to defend its interests and to manipulate the state. The folly of the results was not because the industrial bourgeoisie had no consciousness. On the contrary, because they were a conscious industrial bourgeoisie they wanted to continue along the capitalist road and consequently felt obligated to encourage a dependent industrial development. By staying within a capitalist system, within limits available to bourgeois reformism in dependent capitalist societies, the industrial bourgeoisie only opened the way to today's situation where Brazil cannot overcome underdevelopment or dependency.

The industrialization process in a dependent socio-economic situation takes a different form from that of the dominant capitalist countries. In dependent countries industrialization is not the result of internal technological development, but of imported technology and a productive base externally generated and monopolized. It was not necessary for foreign capital to control the industrial sector as was the case after 1950. Even without direct hegemony of foreign capital, the Brazilian bourgeoisie would have continued to be dependent and to produce dependent development. This is so because Brazil has not been able to create an industrial base independent of royalty payments, of the purchase of American and

European goods, and of exports. Independence would only be possible if it could carry out an authentic agrarian reform and create an internal market sufficiently important to allow development of a national heavy industry.

Industrialization in countries like Brazil not only implies a substitution of imported manufactured goods by locally produced items but also the creation of a new type of commercial relations characterized by the importation of machinery, intermediary products, and processed raw materials (see Maria Conceição Tavares, 1964). However, international capital retains control over the machines, intermediary goods and raw materials allowing foreigners to decide their use. These goods could be sold to the dependent bourgeoisie or kept as a part of foreign capital. The latter alternative would always be preferred when earnings are sufficiently high to pay for the capital invested plus extra earnings or when there is enough financing for the machines to be sold to local subsidiaries. Generally the well-known economic "aids" granted by international and American banks have fulfilled this second function.

There are several considerations that assure increases in the rate of earnings of a scale to pay rapidly for initial investments. The first of these is the low labor wage in dependent countries. The second is the protectionist situation affecting national products that is created by inflation and devaluation of national currencies. This also serves to stimulate industrialization. Help comes from national governments through all types of fiscal exemptions and guarantees of full monopolistic control of the market. Firms of the dominant countries prefer investments in dependent countries rather than the sale of machinery and raw materials to the dependent bourgeoisie. By doing this the foreign companies maintain control over the growing internal market and at the same time guarantee the purchase of their own raw materials, machinery, and intermediary goods. Also this allows them to increase the prices of these products in such a way as to be able to remit abroad the desired amount of dollars, in addition to the normal remittance of profits.

For all these reasons foreign capital found it advantageous to invest in dependent economies. Based on experience during World War II, the industrial bourgeoisie of dependent countries did not believe that international capital wanted to sabotage their national industrial development. Consequently their strategy was to attract foreign capital for productive investments. By the middle of the 1950's the national groups realized that the foreign companies completely accepted their strategy and that it was necessary to reach an agreement with international capital. However, the basis of this agreement, as we shall see, led to the subordination of national to international capital, initiating a new form of dependency.

Industrialization of dependent countries and especially Brazil did not

serve to reinforce a national bourgeoisie but rather led to a denationalization process. In these countries industrialization continued as an instrument for increasing man's control over nature, creating new classes and
social forces, achieving national economic integration, weakening local
power bases, and establishing new types of organization and behavior.
But all these general characteristics acquired a special form and specific
development.

Thus Brazil's dependent industrialization also led to the creation of
specific political and social movements and to a unique ideology. Brazilian
social scientists have faced a difficult problem when trying to define this
uniqueness. Two erroneous analyses ensued. Some sought to define these
peculiarities às radically different from the general laws of capitalist development. For them these factors represented absolutely new phenomena
not foreseen by the social sciences (whether bourgeois or Marxist) of the
developed countries. Others sought to define these peculiarities as the
result of a deviation from a basic model. These peculiarities were considered as special "cases" instead of as significantly important phenomena
that could modify the overall concepts or theory.

Only very recently has light been shed on this problem. Here we refer
to the discovery that these peculiarities are sufficiently important to
compel a redefinition of the concepts and laws concerning the functioning
of capitalism in the socio-economic formations that we call dependent.
These peculiarities lead us to a theory of dependent capitalism which de-
velops alongside and together with a theory of imperialism, that is to
say, capitalism of the dominant (or imperialist) socio-economic formations. Finally, we also see the need to develop a theory of world economic
relations in which these two systems develop simultaneously and con-
temporaneously with a third system, socialism. (A lengthy list of studies
on dependency includes Dos Santos 1968A, 1968B, 70, 71 A and B, Cardoso and Faletto, 1969, and Quijano 1971.) Within this theoretical framework we can explain the unique character of dependent development,
production, accumulation and reproduction. Brazil's industrialization
process must be studied in this way. We must also examine the organizational forms and superstructure that develop in these specific conditions.

THE 1930 REVOLUTION, THE "NEW STATE" (ESTADO NOVO) AND THE NEW INSTITUTIONALIZATION

The alliance of forces that took power in 1930 was composed, on the one
hand, of oligarchic sectors opposed to the hegemony of the São Paulo
coffee magnates, who were trying to save their decaying interests by imposing a certain policy on their allies, and the many middle sectors that
belonged to the lieutenants or *tenentes* movement. This movement mani-

fested itself in the 1920's as a result of urban growth, the deterioration of the hegemony of the agrarian-export oligarchy, and also the crisis of the industrial sectors whose huge growth during the 1914–1918 war was threatened in the 1920's by competition from manufactured products imported after the end of the war. (On the *tenentes* movement see Carone, 1965; and Santa Rosa, 1933.)

The 1920's in Brazil were years of middle-class revolt. During 1922 there was a military attack on the Copacabana Fort by eighteen young military officers. Two years later occurred the São Paulo uprising of Marshal Isidoro and the formation of the so-called Prestes Column that roamed the entire country without being overthrown by the armed forces. These groups formed the nucleus of the *tenentes* leadership that was to create a heroic myth for the middle classes, the petty bourgeoisie, and even the Brazilian workers. Their program was to a great extent adopted by the ANL. This program sought the participation of the middle classes in the old oligarchic political system, primarily through the use of the universal secret ballot without qualifying restrictions. At the same time the *tenentes* vaguely grasped the idea of the "social question" that led them to insist upon a strengthening of federal power. They even attacked the dominant position of foreign capital in the domestic economy.

This program was later to be radicalized by the most important leader of the *tenentes* movement, Luis Carlos Prestes, the leader of the column and a well-known leader throughout the entire country. (On Prestes see Bastos, 1946; and on the Prestes Column see Silva, 1965.) This radicalization was greatly prejudiced by Prestes' joining the Brazilian Communist party. He adopted the program of the Communist Third International, a step that led him to break with many of his military comrades, and he called for the formation of a government of worker and peasant soviets. When Prestes returned from the Soviet Union in 1935 under the aegis of the new Popular Front program (espousing insurrection of the Latin American sector in conflict with the international pacifist doctrine) and formed the ANL (coalition National Liberation Alliance of Aliança Nacional Libertadora), he stirred up the country thus revealing the great force, never before unified, of small bourgeois radicalism with worker support. There was no significant peasant participation in the ANL movement, which might have been mobilized around an agrarian reform program. (There is much documentation on this 1922 to 1935 period in Silva, 1964, 1969 B.)

However, the ANL was late in arriving. The basic political arrangements had been made. The industrial bourgeoisie would not give consistent support to an insurrectional movement led by the Communist party even though Luis Carlos Prestes was its leader. Fascist militias of the Integralist Movement directed by Plínio Salgado and clearly inspired by Nazi-fascism meant that for the first time there were parties organized under specific ideologies operating in Brazil. But the bourgeoisie had already achieved a high level of participation in the Vargas government and the oligarchy preferred to avoid a confrontation. When the ANL forces staged a revolt in 1935 its bourgeois allies did not support the uprising and even betrayed the movement. In 1938, an Integralist uprising was put down by a strongly supported Vargas. Out of the defeat and overthrow of the ANL and the dissolution of the Integralist movement, the New State established itself as an armed regime under a constitution elaborated by Vargas and principally inspired by the corporative state of Benito Mussolini.

The fascist inspiration of the new regime did not correspond, however, to conditions of the era. In spite of extensive common interests between Brazil's bourgeoisie and Germany and Japan, Brazil was forced to join the allied side during the Second World War. Because of the need for mass backing and because of American pressures, Vargas was forced to support democratic ideals and organize the workers. At the same time he took advantage of the war to obtain concessions from the allies, especially the United States, that allowed Brazil to set up a national steel company, the base for a future Brazilian heavy industry.

The "New State" consolidated the various changes initiated by the 1930 Revolution. These can be summarized in four points:

1) A program of industrialization that would create the bases for an advanced capitalism.

2) A program of controlled worker participation, of rules for work conditions and social security, that would attract workers to the cities and serve to keep them on the government's side.

3) A program of administrative reform that would strengthen federal power (while awaiting more favorable political conditions that would allow the government to return to elections in the face of the *latifundistas* who had always controlled the peasant vote), encourage dedication to public service, and rationalize and modernize public administration, thereby eliminating the traditional politicians' clientele relationships.

4) A guarantee to lead the country towards an independent foreign policy and affirmation of national sovereignty and the strengthening of army participation in public administration on behalf of national interests.

POPULISM AND CLASS ALLIANCES

It can be seen that this was a "bourgeois democratic" program, adapted to the specific conditions of a dependent country, both by its negation of the right's anti-communist radicalism and its clear objective of economic development and nationalist affirmation. The Brazilian bourgeoisie, including a competent group of intellectuals, civilian technicians, and military, showed a great deal of sensitivity in understanding the political and institutional instruments necessary for the realization of their goals. The Vargas populism was a manifestation of these concerns. (The content of the populist movement is outlined in two periodicals, the *Boletim del MTIC* and *Cultura Política*.) However, there were also fascist arguments such as the racism displayed in the writing of Oliveira Vianna (1956) and the authoritarianism of Azevedo Amaral (1938).

The leadership of the "New State" was able to give the impression that social security and trade union legislation were gifts from Vargas to Brazilian workers. It was possible to create this myth because a new generation of workers had recently reached the urban areas where they were incorporated in the country's industrial wave while being completely unaware of the revolutionary traditions of the Brazilian labor movement. The popular labor movement had been greatly weakened by the liquidation of the Communist leadership and the earlier failure of the anarchist leadership. Therefore, the concessions made by the head of the "New State" appeared as a truly personal and voluntary act. Vargas' policies encouraged a belief in him as the "father of the poor," the paternal leader of Brazilian workers. Backed by a trade union machinery built from above by men in his confidence, Vargas set up a political machine that would keep him in power until 1945 and that would permit him to run successfully again in the 1950 presidential elections as a candidate of the Brazilian workers' Partido Trabalhista Brasileno (PTB).

Vargas' other political arm, more difficult to control, was the administrative machine that he had set up by appointing federal government "interventors" in the federal states. This machine structured the *coroneis,* or the local *latifundista* chiefs, and the country's industrial bourgeoisie, among whose most outstanding leaders were Roberto Simonsen and Evaldo de Lodi. These forces concentrated themselves in the Partido Social Democrata (PSD). Established by Vargas, the PSD supported him on several occasions, but on others left him alone with the PTB (for example, in the 1950 elections).

Thus the Vargas phenomenon created a new populist political tradition: a personal leadership style exercised in the name of the people around a program of industrial development and very general social justice. Behind this style, populism really represented an alliance of classes between an industrial bourgeoisie that achieved an important, weakly hegemonic place in the government (by way of the bureaucracy, civilian and military technocracy, and a small and select class leadership) and that part of the labor movement which was unable to organize itself, especially the most backward and least organized sectors (the semi-proletariat and unskilled proletariat) under the direction of both the bourgeoisie and workers who were henchmen protected by the government. A large sector of the middle classes (including white collar commercial sector, poorly paid public administration employees, and modern technical professionals) was also drawn into this class alliance either for immediate political objectives or for ideological reasons. Such a front could only be based upon few principles and many techniques of manipulation. It relied on the government apparatus. It employed an electoral machine based on clientelism and corruption as great or greater than that of the Old Republic. (An interpretation of the Vargas period can be found in Ianni, 1965; Vargas' political thought during the "New State" era is found in a collection of his works written in 1938.) This basic situation maintained itself until the 1964 coup. The peasantry, totally ignored up until 1960, thereafter was rapidly and massively incorporated into the front. (A comprehensive history of the period is found in Skidmore, 1967).

The Vargas forces were not overthrown by the fall of the "New State" in 1945 and the reestablishment of a liberal democracy consolidated by the 1946 constitutional assembly. The opposition systematically lost elections until 1960 when Jânio Quadros was elected president, accompanied by Vargas' disciple, João Goulart as vice president. Quadros did not represent the liberal opposition, however, but rather a new type of populism. Moreover, the two Vargas parties of the center-right (PSD) and of the center-left (PTB) remained in power during the period. The PSD candidate, minister of war during Vargas' "New State," Eurico Gaspar Dutra, was president during the period 1945–1950. Vargas returned to power in 1950 as PTB candidate. When in 1955, Juscelino Kubitschek assumed power with Goulart, as vice president, their support from the two parties cemented the PSD–PTB union. In 1961 Quadros came to power with a program that radicalized, to a great extent, the Vargas doctrine (despite its clear eclecticism) but he had as vice president Goulart, which demonstrated the electorate's clear preference for populism. A few months after coming to power and having vacillated between opposing political tendencies, Quadros resigned under strong military and political pressure. Backed by a substantial mass movement, Goulart assumed the presidency. Faced with the opposition of the military chiefs who had formed a provisional government junta, Goulart had to accept, as a condition for avoiding a civil war, a humiliating parliamentary regime that substantially reduced his presidential powers. In 1963 a plebiscite restored these powers and he received the backing of the overwhelming majority of Brazilian people for his program of "structural reforms."

During thirty-four years in power, populism has shown great political vigor and enjoyed mass backing. While we intend to examine the origins of the crisis that overthrew populism, let us first look at the ideological orientations that preceded populism.

NATIONALISM: IDEOLOGY OF INDUSTRIALIZATION

The socio-economic, institutional, and political changes which we have been describing had more or less conscious ideological expressions. Nationalism was the most radical ideological attempt to extend these changes to their ultimate consequences. Its social base, as we see, changed often. In principle it was an ideology of the bourgeoisie and the petty bourgeoisie both of which sought industrialization. Later the monopoly bourgeoisie abandoned that position and adopted the more coherent ideology of "development," which we shall examine in the next section. At the end of the period only the petty bourgeoisie and the labor class backed nationalism, but its content had been radicalized and it had been endowed with a predominately statist and anti-imperialist character.

Since the late nineteenth century, nationalist thought had been created by certain political and social elites. Its elaboration became more and more extensive, gaining wide diffusion among economists, sociologists, scientists, politicians and even philosophers who finally joined to form the Instituto Superior de Estudos Brasileiros (ISEB). This is not the place to study the origin and development of an institute that exercised a fundamental role in Brazilian cultural life, but from a phenomenological viewpoint we shall describe the essence of nationalist thought. The main elaborators of this ideology were Celso Furtado (1959, 1961, 1962, 1964), Guerreiro Ramos (1958, 1961), Helio Jaguaribe (1958, 1962), Nelson Werneck Sodré (1962, 1969), Alvaro Vieira Pinto (1960) and Ignacio Rangel (1957).

There is a fundamental difference between the nationalisms of developed and underdeveloped countries. In developed countries nationalism manifests itself as an instrument of national expansion. In underdeveloped countries it tends to have a defensive character seeking to protect national resources for use in development. This position is necessary because the dominant forces of the developed countries maintain policies contrary to the economic development goals of underdeveloped countries. They are interested in perpetuating the international division of labor between countries producing raw materials (underdeveloped) and countries producing manufactured goods (developed) which permits them to dominate the world.

According to Brazilian nationalist thought two opposed class alliances occur in this situation. One alliance groups together imperialists, the latifundists, and the commercial sectors allied to the exporting group.

The alienated middle classes also support this alliance, both because of their desire for consumption, particularly of imported goods financed by export earnings, and their concern for "moralism" in politics which leads them to stress moral considerations over economic ones. An opposing alliance comprised a nationalist front which espoused development and included an industrial bourgeoisie, the workers, and the technically oriented middle classes interested in economic development.

In principle, the bourgeoisie was responsible for the ideological leadership of the nationalist front. The workers were participants in a capitalist development drive presumably for an increase in the redistribution of income. If the bourgeoisie refused to direct this front, it was necessary to force them to do so. It is important to note that after 1954 the Brazilian Communist Party began to change its political position and to back nationalist positions. The party gave to the bourgeoisie a different role in the broad nationalist and democratic front; according to the party, the laboring class, recognizing possible bourgeois "vacillations," would struggle for leadership of the front.

Whether it was tending toward the right or oscillating toward the left, nationalist thought dominated the overall political movement that fostered a development policy. According to the nationalists, it was above all necessary to combat liberal ideology that opposed the protection of national industry, state participation in the creation of an infrastructure for development, and the imposition of limits on the entry of foreign capital. However there were marked differences between left and right nationalism. Under the influence of the workers and radical sectors of the middle class, the left-wing sector tended to support strong state capitalism in such sectors as petroleum, power, iron and steel; whereas the right-wing sector criticized these activities as excesses.

After 1958, when it was seen that capitalist industrial development could not be implemented without foreign capital, the industrial bourgeoisie substituted for nationalism a new ideology and expression of their class interests known as "developmentalism." This division was evident within the ISEB, when its founder, Helio Jaguaribe, broke with the institute and condemned its sectarian tendencies. His position was very clear: nationalism was an instrument for achieving development. One must analyze the phenomenon of nationalism as the means for achieving the goal of development. It becomes a political enemy when it becomes sectarian against foreign capital in general.

The course of development theory will be discussed later. Here we only wish to demonstrate the internal ambiguity at nationalist ideology and its resulting limitations. These facts reveal as well that the "purification" of nationalism since 1958 is due to its petty bourgeois-radical character and to its worker base. The ideology has been put in the paradoxical position of defending the national bourgeoise whose most economically significant sectors have already passed to the opposition camp, the alliance with international capital, accepting a socially inferior status.

Nationalism favored economic centralization, income redistribution, agrarian reform and a cluster of social changes (mass education and literacy campaigns, for example) and political measures (legality for the Communist party, illegal since 1947, the right to vote for illiterates). These objectives formed an aggregate of goals aspired to by modern intervention-oriented capitalism of a social-democratic nature. This position favored national or autonomous economic development, income redistribution for certain classes and regions, elimination of feudal or pre-capitalist relics, democratization of society and politics, moralization and rationalization of public administration, and the development of education, science and technology.

Nationalist thought sought to recreate the conditions of a contemporary bourgeois society without apparent contradictions. It thus was a vision of the petty bourgeoisie which was peripheral to the modern capitalist system and did not understand the exploitative nature of this system. This utopian or idealistic frame of reference was partly the result of the bourgeois need to mystify its society and partly the consequence of strong petty bourgeois support for this ideology. This utopianism was reflected not only on the level of the state's political economy, but above all in its intent to carry out a third force type foreign policy. This idea was expressed in the doctrine of an "independent foreign policy" that Vargas, Kubitschek, Quadros, and Goulart tried to follow without success. Let us now discuss in more detail the failure of this policy which continued as a consequence of an illusion that was unable to hide itself from contradictions created by social forces at both the national and international levels.

THE CRISIS OF INDUSTRIALIZATION FOR IMPORT SUBSTITUTION AND THE THREAT OF REVOLUTION

INDUSTRIALIZATION AND FOREIGN CAPITAL

Populist nationalism advocated the creation of an independent national economy established on a strong industrial base. In terms of nationalist thought industrialization was associated with national liberation. Imperialism and dependency were seen as characteristic of an agrarian-export economy, while the doctrine of national liberation called for both independence and industrial development oriented toward the internal market.

Reality has proven the extreme falsity of these assumptions. It is true that Brazil's industrialization during the 1930's and 1940's seemed to fulfill nationalist doctrine. But this was the consequence of the capitalist crisis of 1929 and its aftermath, World War II. During that time capital of the dominant countries could not leave its national limits, and during the 30's there was an enormous decline in world commerce. During the Second World War the belligerent countries purchased more food stuffs and raw materials, but their exports were minimal. Under such conditions national capital dominated the internal market, and with the support of the state it provided the bases of industrialization.

The post-war era, however, brought an entirely different situation. In the United States military investments fell sharply and unemployment increased. An enormous capital surplus, which had accrued, was destined for the reorganization of the European and Japanese economies and for the underdeveloped countries. From this moment on there was a substantial increase of American investments in dependent countries and, specifically, in Brazil.

This increase of capital investments was marked by qualitative changes. First, foreign capital penetrated national markets which had been previously controlled and partly defended by powerful foreign exchange barriers. Second, foreign capital stimulated the export of American products, especially so as to protect heavy industry from a threatened recession. Third, foreign investment helped U. S. industries replace their old industrial equipment with modern machinery and thus enabled the United States to assimilate the latest technological advances. Post-war capitalism was constantly revolutionized by rapid technological obsolescence of its installed capacity. The lifetime for its technologies was extremely short, but the export of obsolete machinery to dependent countries alleviated this situation. Additionally, international capital, based in the United States, moved rapidly into dependent countries, and developed new industries and services in order to conquer foreign markets and to use the cheap and abundant labor force.

A first stage of new investment lasted from 1945 to 1950. Between 1950 and 1955 was a time of conflict and indecision, followed by another period from 1955 to 1961 during which investments increased. From 1961 to 1964 adverse reaction to foreign capital brought about another crisis. Between 1964 and 1966 there existed a period in which financial control was extended; and between 1967 and the present, a new period has been initiated with very complex aspects. To assist the reader in easily understanding contemporary Brazil, it is necessary to analyze the movement of capital during these periods.

During the period from 1945 to 1950 foreign capital (almost entirely

American because of European and Japanese economic weakness) established factories for the assembly of finished products. Under government and national industrial pressure other factories were set up for the manufacture of spare parts. At the same time, the U. S. government, as it did in other countries, sent an economic mission to propose a development plan. Through pressure and the provisions of international credit, national governments were encouraged to install a minimum infrastructure while granting concessions for the investment of foreign capital.

Such a program for infrastructure coincided with the interests of national capital, but national capital was also interested in several basic areas already controlled by American capital. This particularly was the case with petroleum. The national bourgeoisie and military and civilian technocrats considered the control of petroleum as essential for national autonomy. This was also the case with control of electrical energy,* communications, iron and steel, and even atomic minerals. According to the U. S. plan, state participation, backed by private capital, would restrict itself to creating the conditions for investment in infrastructure that would allow for an increase in the amount of foreign investment.

Between 1950 and 1955, in the face of growing foreign competition, national capital attempted to build an infrastructure base which corresponded to its own development needs. At that time, however, it was still believed that foreign capital was only interested in the production of exports and national minerals. Despite the fact that during this period foreign capital had begun to penetrate the industrial sector, no one was aware of any specific threat. To the contrary, it was thought that foreign investment in this sector would strengthen national development through the increased productive capacity. Nevertheless, the intense struggle for control of infrastructure and the existing strong nationalist sentiments provoked a conflict that was resolved only during the Juscelino Kubitschek administration.

During this new period national and international capital reached an agreement based on an economic development program that designated the sectors that could be penetrated by foreign capital. In a certain sense, national capital and above all the technocrats in charge of the political economy believed that they had *imposed* certain conditions on imperialism. An aggressive "developmentalist" policy stimulated American and European capital to establish an automobile industry in Brazil, which

---

* Investments in electrical energy were profitable only insofar as they were backed by a substantial state subsidy or were given the opportunity for monopoly exploitation. The U.S. companies sought guarantees for these exceptional conditions until 1960 when they preferred to reach an agreement with the government because this industry had proved to be unprofitable.

would have been impossible without substantial state protection for cars manufactured in Brazil. Other aspects of this "developmentalist" policy were not immediately visible, however. Under the hegemony of foreign capital the creation of an automobile industry, chemical industry, mechanical industry and heavy and light metallurgy in a short five-year period brought qualitative changes within Brazil.

The new industrial sector that developed became the most dynamic area of the national economy. The entire economy had to be reoriented in terms of its technological, organizing and economic leadership. National capital and the technocrats had made an enormous effort through extensive exploitation of the working classes, to establish the base for Brazilian industrialization, with elaborate measures to protect the national market. However international monopoly capital received most of the benefits from this effort, and the national bourgeoisie had to content itself with becoming junior partners.

Between 1961 and '64 there developed a new crisis in the relations between national and foreign capital. Both sides sought to define the new terms of this relation. Under intense popular pressure the Quadros and especially Goulart administrations were anxious that foreign capital submit to a reformist economic development plan. But there was no liberal solution under the new conditions generated by dependent capitalism in Brazil. The strengthening of international monopoly capital had provoked a vigorous economic concentration—a monopolization of the principal sectors which led to an extensive income redistribution favoring the monopoly capital interests to the detriment of the interests of small and medium landowners and above all the labor and lower-income groups.* Consequently, it became difficult to arouse mass support for the continuation of this type of development. (For a general description of this process see Dos Santos 1968 and 1969.)

Foreign capital quickly produced surplus earnings, but there was no possibility for reinvestment in the limited internal market because of the type of income distribution already described above and because of the continued existence of a traditional agrarian structure that kept 50 percent of the population outside the market. The profits earned under highly favorable conditions were more than enough for new investments and at the same time allowed for repatriation of enormous quantities of earnings. These remittances not only compensated for the new capital that entered but also created a "deficit" in the balance of capital funds.

---

* The situation of skilled workers was improved insofar as their number increased, and their standard of living was improved. But these sectors were very aggressive in the struggle to improve their standard of living. They led the worker's movement in economic battles and in promoting reformist nationalism.

This deficit was worsened by the interest due on the growing external debt.

The control exercised by international monopoly capital over the economy was becoming increasingly unpleasant for Brazil. Opposition to this domination became more general, and it became apparent that only a further centralization of political and economic power as well as the use of force could maintain this model of growth. This crisis generated by this conflict was resolved through strengthening the alliance between international monopoly and national capital. This alliance, manipulated by bureaucrats and military and civilian technocrats, eliminated internal dissidence and mass organizations. The military coup of April 1, 1964, that brought Marshal Castelo Branco to power provided the political conditions for the subordination of Brazilian monopoly capital to international monopoly capital.

Such subordination could only be achieved with substantial state participation. The state enacted the economic measures that guaranteed an immediate economic revival with a minimum of reforms. This relative modernization and reformism necessary to attract new foreign investment provoked the almost total ideological disarmament of a sizeable sector of intellectuals on the left, who even generated enthusiastic support for the regime. This was possible principally because the majority of the so-called Brazilian left had been only nationalist and reformist. Its ideals were limited to those of economic development and reassertion of national sovereignty. While the regime did not achieve either of these objectives, its modest and favorable accomplishments neutralized much of the ideological resistance.

From 1964 to 1966 the government was mostly concerned with containing the violent inflation generated by financial speculation, strong monetary pressures derived from the balance of payments deficit, and the issue of paper money. A monetary stabilization program was implemented which lowered production costs, especially as reflected in workers' salaries whose purchasing power was reduced by about 45 percent in scarcely three years. Violent repression was necessary to force this class to accept a decline in their standard of living. A curious aspect of this stage is that foreign capital investments in Brazil were limited during this period. Foreign capital was primarily concerned with using its huge surplus to buy enterprises weakened by the economic crisis and to remit earnings abroad.

Investment of foreign capital was evident again only after 1967 with the beginning of Brazilian economic recuperation. This recovery was achieved by means of an enormous increase in the rate of profit based on a lowering of real wages. In addition there was new confidence in the government because to a certain extent it had been able to straighten out national finances. At the beginning of this period capital investment activated an enormous existing capacity that had been under-utilized during the grave crisis period. At the same time a favorable investment climate and the entry of highly speculative foreign capital produced a substantial amount of stock in giant investment projects.

This general description of the historical aspects of foreign investment in Brazil has enabled us to show the general direction of the process as well as the generation of recurring crises. The investments during the 1945 to 1950 period led to the 1950 to 1955 crisis, while those of 1955–1961 period brought about the 1961 to 1964 crisis. Those of 1967 to 1971 opened the way to a new crisis that we describe below.

THE FAILURE OF NATIONALISM AS AN ECONOMIC POLICY

Nationalism as an economic policy appeared during the 1930's and reached theoretical maturity at the end of the 1940's. The basic aspects of this policy were the following:

1) Control of export earnings to prohibit, on the one hand, the importation of industrial goods that would compete with national products and facilitate, on the other, the importation of machinery and raw materials for national industry. While the mechanisms employed varied greatly, and it is not necessary to pay attention to these aspects here, we must take into consideration the conflict that the nationalist policy generated with the exporting oligarchs.

2) Formation of an infrastructure consisting of state control of energy, transportation, and communications which enabled lower costs for private investors. The consequence of this policy was a conflict with the most backward foreign capital sectors which desired to maintain control of the sources of energy, the mines, and the rest of the national resources. The 1930 revolution had already secured state ownership over the Brazilian subsoil although it had also made several concessions to foreign capital for mineral exploitation.

The bourgeoisie fought to guarantee national ownership of the subsoil and the use of basic national resources. During the second Vargas government (1950 to 1955), national corporations under the control of the state were created for petroleum (Petrobras, studied in Cohn, 1968), electrical energy (Electrobras), iron deposits (Ferrobras), steel, and atomic minerals (Atomibras). Furthermore, a massive plan for the building of highways and other transportation systems was implemented.

3) Direct aid for national industry, through tax exemptions, facilitation of plant installation, maintenance of high prices, low-interest loans (often

these were really gifts because of the rapid loss of value caused by inflation), and state purchases of products. Some industries, such as those in construction, were created and existed almost exclusively at the expense of consumers or with state financing.

It is clear that among all the mechanisms employed, one of the most important was the so-called "administrative corruption" that consisted of an exchange of favors between public bureaucrats who managed the national funds and private individuals who paid a commission in order to receive special benefits. Often the bureaucrat and businessman belonged to the same economic group. Although this practice is very common in all capitalist countries, especially during periods of primary capital accumulation, in countries like Brazil it assumed extreme forms because of the absence of a strong popular movement to check it. On the contrary, in order to subdue the proletariat ideologically, bourgeois populism corrupted its leaders and assimilated them into these same practices. Thus, the struggle against corruption was left to the middle class and oligarchs who benefitted little from this illegal division of the economic surplus created by the workers.

All of these types of aid, including corruption, were quickly adopted by the new foreign companies that arrived in Brazil, and they began to benefit from the system of state aid and concessions to national industry. In addition, foreign companies benefitted from devices designed to attract foreign capital, such as facilities to import goods, tax exemptions, and credit priorities. Not until the end of the 1950's did Brazilian industrialists protest against the excessive nature of these concessions which allowed foreign companies to obtain extraordinarily high earnings to the detriment of national companies.

4) A policy of technical training for workers, guarantees of certain basic rights for the labor force, and social security which attracted the rural labor force to the cities. This movement relieved the landowners of the paternalist responsibilities they had inherited from pre-capitalist structures and created the bases for a modern capitalist economy.

5) A policy of modernization of public services so as to adjust the state apparatus to the needs of capitalist development, a policy which to a certain extent was neutralized by so-called "administrative corruption."

All of these policies were generally applied by very different types of governments, but instead of favoring the development of national capital as was anticipated, they served to open the country's business system to international capital. While nationalist policy "obliged" this capital to invest in the interior of Brazil and to participate in a natonal development plan, international capital also used nationalist policy and the national development plans to create new sources of investments with a high rate of return. Indeed, after 1950 the big international companies had already worked out a more or less defined strategy in this direction.

At the end of the 1950's and the beginning of the 1960's, the Brazilian industrial bourgeoisie, now greatly weakened, was faced with the need to resolve the following dilemma: either abandon the desire for autonomous national development and accept a situation of a dependent bourgeoisie, an inferior partner of monopoly capital; or radicalize its nationalist program establishing direct means of restriction on the entry and exit of foreign capital. Dependent development had created profound problems in the country's foreign economic relations. As we have seen, foreign companies took out more earnings than they invested in the country. At the same time the prices of export products fell, and freight rates and insurance costs for the transport of goods went up. In order to finance the entry of foreign capital and to buy products tied to so-called "foreign aid," Brazil burdened itself with enormous debts owed to the dominant countries, especially the United States. The result of this structural situation was a constant increase in the balance of payments "deficit." In order to pay for this "deficit," new loans were made with interest rates so high that they could no longer be considered "aid." At the end of the period, the interest payment due on foreign debt reached 40 percent of total export income.

At this point the only way to achieve national development would have been to stop this bloodletting by refusing to pay the foreign debt and by limiting or impeding the exit of foreign capital earnings and decreasing the cost of freight rates and insurance through the creation of a national merchant marine. Such a policy was, however, in absolute conflict with that of monopoly capital and the powers that backed it.

As we shall see, through the 1964 military coup, the Brazilian bourgeoisie showed it preferred the road of conciliation: allowing exploitation of the work force and handing over Brazilian mineral wealth to foreign capital in order to increase the country's exports and thus pay a part of the debts. Such a contradictory process led, as we shall see, to a more intensive repetition of the cycles of the earlier crises since there were rises in profit remittances, in the amount of freight rates and insurance (only partly serviced by Brazil), and in the amount of foreign debt. The difficulties of the solution which the bourgeoisie finally adopted, and the complete submission which it implied, led the group to assume leadership of nationalist politics. Finding itself in such a position, the popular movement tended to radicalize its anti-imperialism which in turn forced the majority of the bourgeoisie into support of a policy of agreement with international monopoly capital as manifested in the 1964 coup and the dictatorship that followed. In truth, the alternative of a confrontation could never have been contained within a reformist framework and would have had to have carried the battle to the point of mass power that would have led the country to socialism. Between this path and submitting themselves over to international capital the bourgeoisie had no other alternative.

There were other problems which worsened the overall situation: the huge industrial growth during this period had not been accompanied by a significant increase of internal demand. This was caused by two factors. The first was the highly concentrated, monopolistic character of dependent economic development. The companies which formed during the period sought to satisfy the most significant and concentrated economic demands, those of the high income sectors. Industrial gains were made especially in the growth of sophisticated and technically very advanced consumption, and the creation of the industrial base necessary for this growth. Highly concentrated companies that monopolistically dominated their highly limited market and employed a relatively small labor force created a type of development that excluded the huge popular sectors. This dependent monopoly development brought about an explosive situation in which the contradictions became more and more acute. (For a more complete analyses of this phenomenon that we have labelled the new type of dependency see Dos Santos, 1968.)

Faced with this structural situation the country could select one of two alternatives. On the one hand there existed the possibility of trying to increase the internal market through an agrarian reform that would bring into the market vast peasant groups currently receiving non-monetary payments or very low salaries. There would also have had to be income redistribution benefitting the marginal urban squatter population and wage-earners, most of whom lived in absolute poverty. Such measures, however, led to adverse results. Policies of agrarian reform forced a confrontation with the rural oligarchy and all their urban allies that could only have been won through mass peasant mobilization. This approach also led to a questioning of the principle of land ownership opening the way towards greater agitation against private ownership in general. There are vast latifundiary lands in the Brazilian countryside under capitalist exploitation. The bourgeoisie had to abandon its timid agitations for agrarian reform and back the so-called productive *latifundio*. But, who could stop the widespread peasant movement, born out of the agitation for agrarian reform, which was threatening the system itself? It was therefore necessary to seek another solution to Brazil's huge agrarian problem of more than forty million peasants subsisting in desperate misery in contrast to

the luxury enjoyed by their patrons and the advances of the big and overflowing cities.

The methods of income redistribution which benefitted the wage-earners
led to a fall in profit margins, removing the stimulus for capitalist investment, making the state assume direct responsibility for development of
the productive system. Both national and foreign capital refused to
operate without a high profit margin, and sought other places for their
investments, resulting in a decline in the rate of growth of the gross national product. Only the state could maintain a high investment rate
under these conditions. But this policy of increasing state participation
was contained in the programs of all the mass movements which made
clear that economic development could not at the same time be capitalist
and popular. Socialism as an immediate objective began to be talked
about in Brazil.

The alternative of a reformist policy was no longer available to the
bourgeoisie. It had been converted into an opening for socialism. Given
this situation, the Brazilian bourgeoisie opted for counter-revolution and
joined forces in a strong alliance with international monopoly capital,
latifundiary interests, reactionary sectors of the petty bourgeoisie and the
middle class. The military right, taking advantage of the situation, became the prime movers for the 1964 coup that solved temporarily the
problem of the internal market and international economic relationships.

It is still necessary to describe the bourgeois response to the problem of
the market. Since the bourgeoisie did not intend to augment the internal
market by carrying out an agrarian reform, or to redistribute income in
favor of the wage earners, it had to adopt the following multi-faceted
alternative: First, increase exports diversifying them in the industrial
sector because of the decline in the prices of coffee and primary products;
Second, accentuate the regressive distribution of income in favor of the
upper classes in order to increase consumption of sophisticated products
that would lead to an increase in investments; Third, increase state consumption, especially in the purchase of military goods, create a capital
market that would allow an even greater income concentration in the
hands of monopoly capital, and create mechanisms to subsidize the private sector, increase profit margins, and, consequently, investments.

This plan was passed off as a monetary stabilization policy which reduced workers' real wages, curbed credit (above all for small property
owners), lowered public debt, and decreased imports as a means of reducing the foreign deficit. Such a policy was clearly transitory in order to
permit the recuperation of the rate of profits. We shall describe in detail
this global policy of the bourgeoisie, but first we must look at the repercussions of the crisis in the political and ideological spheres.

THE FAILURE OF NATIONALISM AS AN
IDEOLOGY AND POLITICAL RADICALIZATION

The inability to carry out the program proposed during the 1940's and 1950's led to a profound ideological and political crisis. Nationalism, once a bourgeois ideology, now became an essentially petty bourgeoisie ideology. As we saw, in the 1950's a considerable number of diverse ideologists who espoused independent national development had already rejected a sectarian nationalism to the extent that they preferred economic development to national development. According to them this was a way of attaining development, the maximum objective for mankind in general. They tried to re-embrace liberal bourgeois thought which in principle was cosmopolitan, laissez-faire, internationalist, and modernizing. Few former nationalists could take such a big step, and they consequently looked for intermediate formulas, adapted to the country's situation and the petty bourgeoisie social base that inspired them.

The classic bourgeois liberalism (backed by the old defenders of the international division of labor with a Brazil predominantly agrarian and a rational and technical superiority of foreign capital) was giving way to a cosmopolitan yet modern bourgeois thought. That is to say, a bourgeois thought that recognized the existence of monopoly and the changes it caused, the state's role in capital accumulation and reproduction, and the need for planning and economic intervention. All these ideas were found in the thought of Roberto Campos, at that time Goulart's ambassador in the United States and a collaborator in all past governments as adviser to Quadros, head of Kubitschek's Development Bank, counsellor to Marshal Eurico Dutra and the second Vargas government.

Nationalist thought was also attacked by the left. At the beginning of the 1960's there was a sudden spurt of interest among the Brazilian left in the study of Marxism. Seminar groups began to study Marx's *Das Kapital* and other theoretical books as well as Marxist methodology and analysis of Brazilian reality. This trend was part of a world renaissance of Marxism as a scientific and revolutionary theory. The burst of interest in Marxism was evident not only in the universities, where it did not find expression as a militant doctrine, but also in such new political organizations as the Organization of Revolutionary-Marxist Workers Politics, (Organização Marxista Revolucionária Política Operária—POLOP) that called for a return to classical Marxism in opposition to the policy of bourgeoïs nationalism. In the Brazilian Communist party there was an intellectual renovation, stimulated by the growing ideological struggle.

The left began systematically to attack nationalism for its analysis of the international and national situations and for its political propositions. In the first place, the left attacked the theoretical and methodological premises of nationalism that were based on an assumed perspective which focused on the problems of underdevelopment from the existential situation of being a colony, rather than using an analysis of the world economic system which explained this colonization process and showed its class base. Moreover, the left attacked the nationalist assumption that capitalist development in Brazil had evolved in opposition to a feudal agrarian economy, which allowed national problems to be seen as the result of a pre-capitalist economy when historical evidence showed the incapacity of the existing system to solve those problems. The left also demonstrated that nationalism, in spite of its attacks on North American imperialism, tried to show that capitalism was still the model of the ideal society which could be achieved through development.

In summary, we see that at the end of the 1950's and at the beginning of the 60's developmentalism replaced nationalism as the political thought of the bourgeoisie. Their political thought became more and more anti-Communist and more authoritarian, and it supported administrative and political centralization and a strengthening of the bourgeois state as well as adoption of the economic plan allied with private monopoly capital. At the same time, clearly fascist forces emerged such as the Patrulla Anti-Comunista (PAC), the LIDER, CAMDES and Acción Democrática which formed a rightist parliamentary front. These forces marched together in a demonstration for God, the Family and Liberty that called for the overthrow of the government and the establishment of an armed regime.

At the same time, truly nationalist thought radicalized and took a clearly anti-imperialist position which tended to support state capitalism and basic reforms aimed at the creation of a socialist society. Although up until the 1964 coup this movement continued under predominantly bourgeois leadership, its social bases stemmed more and more from the labor class and from the radical petty bourgeoisie. The centrist core of this movement, headed by the then President João Goulart with the support of the Brazilian Communist Party (Partido Comunista Brasileiro, PCB), continued to emphasize the national-popular aspect of the program, minimizing its anti-imperialist content, basic reforms, and socialist tendencies. Meanwhile the most radical petty bourgeoisie groups led by Leonel Brizola in the South and Miguel Arraes in the Northeast, tried to place greater emphasis on class struggle and radical confrontation, (at a massive rally on March 13, 1964, Brizola proposed the creation of a Constituent Assembly of workers and peasants), and the radicalization of the nationalist program into a movement of national liberation, opposed to imperialism, oligarchy, and monopoly.

The Marxist revolutionary movements on the left, in addition to the

POLOP, were strengthened by the Communist Party of Brazil (Partido Comunista do Brasil, P C do B—the pro-Maoist splinter group of the PCB), the Peasant Leagues that had evolved into the Movimento Radical Tiradentes (MRT—from which there broke off a majority faction of the rebel MRT youth) and the Marxist wing of the leftist Catholic Popular Action (Ação Popular AP). These forces held different positions on the Goulart government and the nature of the revolution. However, there were some common points of agreement. First, they all adopted a clearly defined socialist policy (the PC do B, and the POLOP had a Marxist orientation.) Second, they called for armed confrontation and adopted a critical attitude towards the Goulart government (in the case of the PC do Brasil, there was open opposition to Goulart).

Ideological tendencies polarized. Bourgeois ideology moved further to the right as evidenced by its conciliatory position towards imperialism, its rejection of reformist slogans, its anti-Communist attitude, and above all its support for political authoritarianism. In contrast, nationalist thought became more anti-imperialist, radical reformist, and pro-socialist. These increasingly radical tendencies led to the awareness of the need for a clearly worker-peasant leadership for armed confrontation.

In politics the same dynamics were operating. Existing political parties were polarized and a surge of new political organizations developed. Given the basically undoctrinaire nature of traditional Brazilian political parties, radical nationalist groups began to grow in each of the parties and joined together in parliament to form the National Parliamentary Front (Frente Parlamentario Nacionalista). Its opposition on the right organized a Democratic Parliamentary Front (Frente Parlamentario Democratico).

At the same time various mass movements sprouted as well. One such movement was the workers' Comando General de Trabalhadores which reflected an increase in the political participation of the working classes. There was also the growth of the peasant leagues, peasant associations, and labor unions that held a National Peasant Congress in 1961; the development of the student movement in the universities and high schools reached a combative peak. The military also organized along political and class awareness; there were the nationalist officers group, the National Command of Sergeants, and national associations of corporals and navymen. All these groups joined forces in 1963 in a popular mobilization known as the National Front of Popular Mobilization (Frente Nacional de Movilização Popular) with support from leftist organizations and politicians.

With these new developments in the popular struggle, the class struggle had reached a new level, and the germ of a new power had been sown that would preclude any effort to form a popular nationalist government. The forces allied with the dominant interests rejected any peaceful solution that would have allowed them to regain control of the situation. Thus, groups that had long been conspiring both outside and within the Armed Forces began to act with strong backing from a majority of the ruling class. Groups were formed ostensibly to finance electoral campaigns, such as the Brazilian Institute of Democratic Action (Instituto Brasileiro de Ação Democrática IBAD) which was the subject of a parliamentary investigation. The Institute of Research and Social Studies (Instituto de Pesquisas e Estudos Sociais IPES), an institute for propagandizing and articulating the interests of businessmen who participated in the conspiracy, clearly became involved in contraband, organizing logistic support such as cars, arms, and equipment directly from the factories. These groups adopted more and more intensive fascist mobilization methods culminating in the organization of a massive march for "God, Liberty and the Family" which was the final demonstration of the strength of those planning the coup and the signal for the decisive stages.

The coup was precipitated by a dispute between the Naval Ministry and rebellious sailors, provoked by repressive conditions in the Armed Forces. Since the Goulart administration arrived at a settlement with the sailors which neutral members of the armed forces regarded as breaking the concept of discipline, the *golpista* command decided this was a good time to undertake the prepared coup. The leader of the coup was Goulart's Armed Forces Chief of Staff, Marshal Humberto Castelo Branco. The coup began with a declaration of insurrection by the state government of Minas Gerais in the center of Brazil. Carlos Lacerda, governor of Guanabara and the civilian leader of the movement, declared in an interview that Minas Gerais had the military support of the U. S. government which would send troops through the Rio Doce Valley in support of the provisional government. In fact the American government provided diplomatic recognition for the *golpista* government before it had consolidated. Furthermore, the Central Intelligence Agency (CIA) and even the Federal Bureau of Investigation (FBI) were implicated in the conspiracy as was clearly proven by the publication afterwards of a confidential letter of J. Edgar Hoover and by statements of the then U. S. Ambassador to Brazil, Lincoln Gordon (See the appendix in Skidmore [1967] on American participation in the 1964 military coup).

This is not the place to go into a detailed analysis of the 1964 military coup (we have studied this topic in two of our other books, Dos Santos, 1968 and 1970). Here we have been interested in examining the extent to which the political and ideological process that led to the 1964 coup was a product of a profound crisis that led inevitably to a radical confrontation between the popular movement and dominant classes. This radical confrontation between forces in favor of a socialist revolution and those advocating a reactionary counter-revolution, could not be stopped simply by a strong government based on liberal principles. Let us now turn to a study of the establishment of a reactionary government and events after 1964.

THE CONSERVATIVE REPLY: MILITARY DICTATORSHIP

THE LOGIC OF THE MILITARY GOVERNMENT

The Brazilian army had never before directly governed. It had intervened many times in Brazilian politics, but always as arbiter between the different civilian factions. In 1889 the army took the initiative in overthrowing the monarchy and installing the republican and parliamentary republic. In 1922 junior military officers began an insurrectional movement that in 1930 brought them to power together with many civilian sectors. The Vargas dictatorship that emerged during this period was clearly civilian and evolved to the constitutional assembly in 1934. The sharpening of the degree of political confrontations between 1935 and 1937 led to the emergence of the second Vargas dictatorship in 1937. A new constitution was enacted that set up the clearly dictatorial "New State," inspired by fascist motives but with a different content.

The army overthrew Vargas at the end of 1945 and immediately had the Supreme Court call a new constitutional convention which produced a constitution that lasted until 1964. In 1954 the armed forces participated in the movement against Vargas that led to his suicide. After Vargas' death Vice President Café Filho took over. In 1955 faced with a strong rightist campaign to keep the President-elect, Juscelino Kubitschek, from taking office, the army intervened again overthrowing Café Filho and assuring Kubitschek of the post. In 1961 the military placed strong pressure on President Jânio Quadros, and he consequently resigned. Then three military ministers formed a government coalition to keep Vice President Goulart, who at the time was out of the country, from becoming president. After strong popular pressure, insurrection in two states, and Goulart's agreement to assume the presidency under a weakened parliamentary regime, the military returned power to the civilians.

The period from 1961 to 1964 was very unstable and characterized by a strong polarization. The military was constantly called upon to intervene in favor of one of other of the groups fighting for power. Military groups were formed on the left and on the right. The armed forces was divided not only horizontally into regiments and factions, but also vertically into factions of senior officers and junior officers, sergeants, and recruits.

Meanwhile, during the 1960's the Brazilian and other Latin American armed forces began to modify the concept of their strategic role in politics, a change oriented by the sector dominated by the U. S. government. During this period the idea began to take hold that the fundamental functions of the Latin American armed forces should involve counter-insurgency activity and dedication to "national security." Previously the armed forces had been educated to defend Latin American countries against foreign attack by "Communist Russia."* After the victory of the Cuban Revolution the conception of strategy changed and troops were trained and reorganized to defend the different countries from the "internal enemy": guerrillas, labor unions, students and peasants, all plotting in a psychological and real war against the existing order. Special anti-guerrilla and anti-street demonstration forces were organized. Under the label of counter-insurgency, there was a flourishing of studies on anti-guerrilla warfare, intelligence, psychological warfare, and civic action.

Counter-insurgency doctrine has two basic and complementary aspects: national security and economic development. Lack of national security is caused by underdevelopment which leads to conditions of misery that foment rebellion which the communists use to their advantage. Thus, economic development is the principal means for achieving national security. Up to this point this doctrine was formulated with a hemisphere orientation under the leadership of North America. However, the military in each country makes up its own list of national objectives that are necessary to guarantee security and development. In the case of Brazil, these objectives are related to the international importance of the country in an effort to enter the world of super powers. The unification of these elements in a military doctrine leads the armed forces to the idea that they must govern directly if they are to achieve their objectives.

However, when they carried out the 1964 coup, a majority of the Brazilian armed forces thought that their mission was to clean house so that the country could return immediately to a civilian legalistic path with strong military protection. Long before he came to power in 1964, Castelo

---

* Very few people are aware of the ideological content or of the reality of such expressions as "Communist Russia." The USSR has not been called "Russia" since the fall of the Provisional Government in 1917. Even more ridiculous is the nomenclature "communist," because, if one follows Marxist theory, there is no communist society in existence today.

Branco had warned against military intervention, suggesting that a dictatorship imposed by the armed forces "would enter by force, only be maintained by force, and go out by force" (From Marshal Castelo Branco's archives, cited by Einaudi and Stepan, 1971). Assuming that Castelo Branco intended to remain faithful to his words, one can accept as valid his intention to institutionalize the dictatorship and turn power over to a civilian (in that era Bilac Pinto, president of the Congress, was thought to be his candidate), and this interpretation explains a great many of his political moves. However, at the same time, one can grasp the importance of the Brazilian crisis by realizing that it would have been impossible to institutionalize a regime based on force, as subsequent events showed.

Under a single banner civilians and military were determined to prevent the apparently inevitable social revolution. The old politicians willingly participated in the decision to have the congress elect Castelo Branco president after the overthrow of the Goulart government and the purge of Goulart supporters in Congress. There was intervention in trade unions and peasant and student organizations, expulsion and repression of nationalist military men, as well as violent persecutions, assassinations, and torture of left leaders of the working class. The passivity of the old politicians also allowed for the violent repression of liberals and inoffensive nationalists who had allied with Goulart. The repression was not limited to Goulart's direct collaborators and the left. It was used against the liberal political leaders. First, those who were in some way identified with the Vargas-oriented PSD and PTB, like Kubitschek and Governor Mauro Borges of Goiás State, were deprived of their political rights. Later the government even attacked the civilian leaders of the military movement, such as Adhemar de Barros and Carlos Lacerda.

The military coup of April 1, 1964, was a counter-revolutionary movement that set up the basis for a centralized and clearly repressive state. Power gradually passed to the extreme right groups who now began to reveal their counter-revolutionary nature. The crisis that faced all Brazilians: counter-revolution or revolution, fascism or socialism. This was the dilemma that the majority of the protagonists had not perceived.

Castelo Branco remained in power for two years, from 1964 to 1966. Pressured, on the one hand, by rightist army sectors and, on the other, by old bourgeois politicians, he had to limit his period as head of the new regime, and called for "elections" for a new president to replace him. At the same time he sought to maintain the continuity of his regime by pressuring Congress, purged of all political adversaries, to enact a highly repressive constitution. His successor, Marshal Arturo Costa e Silva also lasted another two years, until 1969. In this period elections were held for governors and congressmen under the new constitution that required a candidate to have a certain ideological position and other references that would guarantee his political acceptability.

This small opening, however, brought new problems. Student, urban worker, and peasant protests reappeared. The military and rightist paramilitary organizations, with protection from the state apparatus, reacted again with repression. Faced with a growing mass movement, a group from the military checkmated parliament by demanding the expulsion of a deputy, Márcio Moreira Alves, who had attacked the government's torturing of political prisoners. However, the Congress reacted in a liberal fashion (backed by military sectors irritated with growing fascism, businessmen, and the U. S. Embassy) and refused to take away Alves' parliamentary immunity, prompting the rightist military in late 1968 to close Congress and force Costa e Silva to sign Institutional Act No. 5 that suspended the very Constitution the regime itself had promulgated.

Thereafter followed a more intensive repression. Congress remained closed for several months and some of the newly elected legislators were expelled; university professors and bureaucrats were removed from their jobs by presidential decree; popular mass leaders were arrested and tortured; and a crackdown was begun against the guerrilla movement that had emerged in 1967. The repression was directed against those who had any relationship, even the most remote, to the revolutionary movement, and also against those who might have come to head the mass opposition (see Alarcón, 1970). Police would sweep indiscriminately through houses, a block at a time. Doormen were obliged to be informers; classroom remarks of professors were reported and so were protests made by public employees. Armed guards were placed in Parties to guarantee tranquility. Everyone was threatened by forced resignation or prison, by torture or death, depending on the judgment of the police and the military men charged with conducting the repression. The police apparatus began to be centrally coordinated under the National Intelligence Service, which operated at the presidential cabinet level with agents at the assistant ministerial level to guarantee an accord between ministerial policy and national security. The police regime that had emerged from 1964 to 1966 and that appeared to lose force from 1967 to 1968 returned now with much more violence and more totalitarian characteristics.

In 1971, the military felt the need to search again for some sort of normalization of the regime. Under enormous restrictions, Congress reopened again; new elections were held with absolute control over the nomination of candidates; several trade union congresses were allowed to be held. But the system vacillated between the need for a certain institutional opening to allow for the continued economic growth which justified the regime and the necessity for impeding the free expression of popular interests. With each new concession there was a new wave of violent repression.

THE BASES OF THE REGIME'S ECONOMIC AND POLITICAL MODEL

Goulart's development program was utopian in that it sought to decrease economic dependency, open new markets, and bring about a significant mass participation without breaking with the system of capitalist production. The other weakness in Goulart's program lay in its contradictory dependence on mass support and foreign investment. As we have seen, a large segment of the mass movement had understood the limits of that policy, even though it prevailed until 1964. The weakest and most critical aspect of this program was the policy against inflation. Inflation had increased because of the balance of payments crisis, the increase in fiscal deficit, and the psychological climate of insecurity and speculation which supplanted many of the normal procedures by which the system had been managed. At the outset there was a price-wage struggle. To stop the inflationary spiral it was necessary to freeze wages or control prices. The first alternative is usually adopted in a capitalist system, thus ensuring high profit rates, and conditions stimulating investments. The second solution, however, is contradictory to the capitalist system. In spite of stimulating an immediate increase in consumption that can serve to employ idle productive capacity, price controls do not result in an increase in investments because in the absence of a wage freeze, salaries continue to rise and (unless there is an even greater increase in productivity) the capitalist's level of earnings is lowered and, therefore, also his desire to invest. The capitalist prefers to hold his money in liquid form or to search for new investment markets abroad. Such a policy of controlling prices results in economic depression if not accompanied by nationalization of the main private companies allowing the state to take the initiative in making investments. Under state control investments could be governed by legislation that leads to planning and socialism.*

During his administration, Goulart constantly vacillated between these two alternatives because he was unwilling to accept the consequences of either. It is clear that the policy of freezing wages requires repressive measures against wage earners, and the policy of price control requires structural reform of the system. (For a more complete discussion of these

* For example, this was the policy followed by the Unidad Popular government in Chile as the way to bring about an immediate recuperation of the economy. With this policy the government was able to achieve a growth rate of nearly ten percent in its first year in power.

two alternatives, and the way they lead to socialism or rightist dictatorship given the conditions of countries like Brazil and the majority of the rest of Latin America with deep structural crises, see Dos Santos, 1970).

After the April 1964 coup, the government decided to resolve this contradiction in favor of private capital. Despite many criticisms (at times even from the bourgeois sectors who did not understand the gravity of the situation) Marshal Castelo Branco backed his Minister of Planning, Roberto Campos, who forcefully implemented a policy of economic recovery for Brazilian capitalism. This policy included the following: First, there was a drastic freezing of salaries so that the average wage lost 40 percent of its buying power over a short period of time. With the adoption of this measure the level of business earnings generally rose immediately. Second, there was a severe reduction of government credits that halted speculative investments and resulted in widespread failure among technologically backward firms. In this way monetary circulation was decreased as were inflationary pressures. Third, the amount of taxes collected was increased through the rationalization of the tax system, action against those who evaded taxes, and the adoption of measures to reevaluate debts to the state so that debtors would not be able to take advantage of inflation. This policy greatly affected the earnings of small- and medium-sized businesses and wage earners. It was complemented by a modernization of public services which included the firing of bureaucrats and a rational streamlining of functions. Thus, in a relatively short time public debts were reduced to a normal level. The Fourth measure undertaken by the government was the adoption of a balance of payments policy aimed at increasing exports (with little immediate success but with better results over the long run) and decreasing imports. This policy was feasible during this period of economic stagnation because there was less demand for imported consumer goods.

It is not difficult to imagine the number of interests affected by these policies. Specifically hurt was the working class whose miserably low standard of living declined further in order to assure the recovery of capitalism. But the small- and medium-sized landowners were also prejudiced and ruined by a policy aimed at the recuperation of the production level of the overall economy through favoring the great modern companies, generally of foreign origin.

Foreign investors did not invest any dollars in the country, however. They preferred to wait for three years, while using part of their internally earned profits not to invest, but to speculate on the failure of national industry. Several companies were bought in this way and, in addition, in 1966 the government allowed speculation without credits. The government permitted the entry of circulating capital from abroad in order to finance the debts of national enterprises, a need caused by the lack of government credit. Thus foreign enterprises began to enter the Brazilian financial market, opening the way to a "takeover" without precedent in the history of world capitalism.

Thus the Castelo Branco government was able to achieve economic recovery, but at the expense of the wage earners and small- and medium-sized landowners. This policy encountered strong opposition among small- and medium-sized landowners, the middle classes, and the politicians who depended on the votes of these groups. The implementation of the policy required strong action against trade unions and student movements, and against the peasant movement especially where there was a rural proletariat that had benefitted during the previous period (for example, the sugar workers of Pernambuco). Opposed to the climate of anarchy prior to 1964, a united dominant class helped the group in power apply their policy, until the opposition was able to unite around the government's war minister and force Castelo Branco to turn power over to Costa e Silva after a grave crisis in which Castelo Branco found himself alone against the heads of the four armies.*

But Roberto Campos' economic policy sought not only monetary stability, but also a new period of investment. To achieve this Campos had to adopt a series of measures designed to encourage investments and to create a market for the goods to be produced. This was not a simple task. The generation of a substantial economic surplus was relatively easy, given the mechanisms generated by the economic depression: the tendency to hold large sums in liquid funds, decreased consumption, lower salaries, and an increase in average productivity. All these aspects tended to lead to the creation of enormous economic profits that in turn enabled industries to make investments.

The principal stimulant in investment was an increase of the profit rate, above all through lowering of salaries. Also, the state sought to orient this investment by granting property tax exemptions for those who invested in specific regions or in government-backed programs. Important mechanisms immediately developed to capture the forced savings so that funds would be at the disposal of the big economic groups. The investment banks, with holdings of national and foreign capital, had full liberty to acquire resources and to carry out direct investments. A large financial market was immediately set up in which new stocks were easily launched. The resulting speculation attracted all Brazilian middle-class savings to the Rio, São Paulo, and Minas Gerais stock markets. Enormous financial investments were created without any real increase in production to sus-

---

* Brazil is divided into several military regions that are grouped together in four regional armies: the South, the Northeast, Central South, and the Central West.

tain them. This market was also opened to foreign capital and conditions were created for foreign banks to operate in Brazil. In effect, there was an effort to transform the city of Rio de Janeiro into the Latin American center for multinational companies.

In this way the Brazilian capital market became integrated into the world financial market in four years and the country became just another pawn in a highly sensitive world financial market. But the resources invested required a material base in the country or the funds would be sent abroad. This could occur rapidly because there are no controls on the internalized movements of capital. Despite the large profit remittances from Brazil there was great interest by international capital in absorbing the excess financial resources by opening new investment areas in the central economies which were in a depressed state and lacked investment opportunities. The situation in Brazil from 1967 to 1971 coincided with the gravest economic recession experienced by the United States since World War II. At the end of that period U. S. economic policy was oriented towards stimulating an economic recovery that was difficult to achieve and would take a long time to mature. If it were successful, this policy would attract large quantities of capital to the United States and lead to an important economic depression in Brazil.

The opening of new markets encountered a serious obstacle at the outset, since the economic "boom" had been achieved by forcing a lowering of real wages, any increase in the real wage level endangered the economic "miracle." After 1967 the new government did not try to stabilize a lowering of the real wage scale and allowed a salary readjustment equal to the rise in the cost of living. The prevention of gains in real wages, the "marvelous wage discipline" described by Roberto Campos, was the foundation for the entire economic structure built by the military dictatorship. It was not a policy that could lead to an expansion of the market or the opening up of new investments. Thus it was necessary to seek other more tortuous routes toward economic growth, to find a market for goods produced by the already installed industry, and above all to give impetus to new enterprises and economic sectors. The so-called "Brazilian miracle" or "model" was based on the proposition that dependent capitalism could find a market for its goods that did not depend on the workers themselves, creators of the country's wealth. This was the path adopted, even though it was at the expense of fundamental liberties, even though it entailed the continued existence of mass poverty, and even though it meant the increase in exploitation of labor and the creation of repressive machinery to ensure the success of this growth "model." Let us now turn to a study of the principal aspects of this "model."

THE BRAZILIAN "ECONOMIC MIRACLE"

The essence of the economic "boom" experienced by Brazil after 1967 was contained in the capacity to raise the rate of profits by *lowering the real value of wages*. This policy was complemented by state intervention designed to raise the level of profits and to stimulate investment, and by the creation of various mechanisms to channel all the surplus generated in Brazil towards the financial system dominated by the big national and foreign companies. The surplus was transferred into different kinds of financial holdings which needed to find investment outlets and markets to stimulate investment. This market was not to be found among the wage earners because their low salaries were the bases for the new investments. The critical problem in this system was that of opening new markets. The economic "miracle" would take place only if these new markets were found.

The political economy which the dictatorship adopted was pursued very efficiently and with a broad understanding of the system's needs. As a consequence, the regime often was classified as a modernizing government which has confused many theoreticians and analysts. In 1964 few Brazilians grasped the real significance of the regime. It was not a regime that would defend old agrarian-export oligarchies allied to the old imperialism. On the contrary, although the military saved these classes from a reformist movement that had classified them as the principal enemy, its objective was to modernize the economic, social, and political structure in such a way as to accelerate the entry of international and national big monopoly capital. The policy of violence and strong-arm tactics did not depend on *caudillos* and the demoralized forces of the old *latifundio,* although these groups were also used, but rather on the modern police and technical armed forces of the contemporary monopolistic state. The regime did not defend the *latifundio*. By raising property taxes on uncultivable lands and limiting the political power of the local chiefs and *coroneis,* it tried to force the big rural landed groups to modernize.

Along with its "modernizing" character, the dictatorship was fundamentally counter-revolutionary in nature. This aspect was revealed through its agrarian policy. By not touching the roots of the *latifundio* system, the regime was unable to create a rural market. The only achievement was to expand this market by opening new agricultural frontiers in Brazil's jungle states (Mato Grosso, Goiás, and the Amazon region). But by not changing the relations of production nor the forms of agricultural land ownership, the regime was unable to create a sufficiently significant salaried worker group to sustain a general increase in consumption. On the contrary, the policy of modernization of the big *latifundios* provoked a large-scale expulsion of the work force that was far in excess of the number of workers absorbed by the new frontier regions.

Thus the dictatorship's agrarian and colonization policies were characterized by two aspects: First, a modernization of rural enterprise that led to an increase in the consumption of fertilizers, agricultural machinery, and production goods while forcing the rural labor force off the land and toward the small cities, thus swelling the squatter settlements. Second, a colonization of new regions that led to an increased demand for construction, an expansion of cultivable lands and therefore an increase in the demand for several products, and the absorption of labor in the infrastructure projects and the new agricultural activities. The colonization process gradually lost its capacity to absorb surplus labor to the extent that the productive activities (basically cattle farming, extractive industries and, especially, mining) of these new regions incorporated very few workers. (To the extent that projects dedicated to infrastructure decrease in their growth rate, it will be difficult to maintain stable settlements, and new social conflicts will tend to emerge.) The creation of new frontiers was an insufficient mechanism for income redistribution and expansion of the market. It was, however, an excellent way to increase investment over the short run, maintaining the country's structures while allowing for the opening of new sources of important earnings.

Another instrument of economic policy readily available to the new regime was the state's civilian and military expenditure. Military consumption became relatively more important during the last few years. How could state consumption patterns be effective when the prevailing policy was to balance the budget? In the first place, there is a shift in expenditures to serve more directly the proposed goals. Second, there was an increase in the collection of taxes because of improvements in the collection apparatus and the attempt to maintain the real value of the fiscal debt through annual readjustment of government debt. Finally, after having achieved a relative degree of stabilization (while maintaining a 20 percent rate of annual inflation), the government issued unbacked paper money to finance state investments and the profitable state industries which continued to produce a surplus. Thus, the state was able to carry out a series of investments and increase the consumption of many products that were essential for the new development scheme.

During the difficult depression years from 1964 to 1966, through its investments in infrastructure, electrical energy, roads and public works, the state had been able to uphold the rate of investment. In addition, the state enterprises in steel, iron mining, petroleum, electricity, telephones, and communications and railroads continued operating with all the requisite intermediate consumption. After 1967, both foreign capital and the state were to make important investments first in heavy petro-chemicals and later in aeronautics. The state also was an investor as well as an important purchaser of naval equipment. New roads were opened to stimulate production in the automobile industry, in a bad state of depression between 1963 and 1966. Military purchases were important for the maintenance and expansion of the heavy mechanical and chemical industry. In 1966 a contract was signed between national industrialists and the armed forces for the creation of an industrial-military complex that would enable the country to pull out of the depression and begin a new growth period. The Vietnam war brought a revival of prices for Brazil's exports. There were also non-military exports for the Vietnam war, while ships, airplanes, arms, munitions, chemical weapons, specialized vehicles, processed foodstuffs and textiles made up a wide gamut of products for the army and growing military police. The army had about three hundred thousand men in uniform and three hundred thousand military police in 1968 (*Frente Brasileño de Informaciones,* [Santiago], November 1971).

Military investments became decisive in the process of capital accumulation. For this to occur in a country not at war nor threatened by a visible enemy required a very strong dictatorship and the justification by the need for internal anti-subversive efforts. Indeed, the anti-popular character of the economic "model" demanded a strong repressive apparatus in order to make itself legitimate. But, at the same time, one must take into consideration that the repressive apparatus becomes a part of the economic "model" itself. Men in uniform become a fundamental element in the fight against unemployment, and it becomes ever more necessary to increase military investments and to intensify the militaristic climate in order to be able to stimulate the system and at the same time to guarantee the working of the "model" of dependent capitalist development. Military and economic aspects complement one another.

But such measures demand, in one form or another, an expansion of state participation either in terms of consumption or investment. This was not to the liking of monopoly capital and was accepted only in the absence of any other alternative. The new leaders of the dictatorship's civilian technocracy, closely associated with the big Paulista* financial and industrial leaders, tried to reactivate the system of credit which favored those with high incomes. At the same time the salaries of technical employees and executives increased, generating an increase in the

---

* São Paulo is the industrial and capital center of the country. This state produces about one-third of total national income despite the fact that her population is approximately 20 percent of the national total. At least two-fifths of the nation's industries are concentrated in this state.

country's median wage level. This accomplished two important objectives: First, an increase in consumption goods requiring advanced technology that led to growth of the most modern industrial sectors. Second, the political objective of winning the backing of the most active sectors of the petty and medium bourgeoisie and the skilled workers who could guarantee a base of support for the system.

With this policy the regime expanded the internal market within the most dynamic industrial sectors, even though the rest of the country was left to fend for itself. Tavares and Serra (1971) studied this aspect of the Brazilian "model" in detail. One can grasp the nature of this "model" by looking at the type of industrial development that took place. While the dynamic industrial sectors had a relatively high growth rate, the so-called traditional industries such as textiles, foodstuffs, clothing, shoes, furniture, beverages, and so forth, grew less than one percent annually between 1962 and 1968 and did not show any appreciable degree of dynamism during the period of recovery between 1969 and 1971.

Thus there was truth in the famous phrase of President Garrastazu Médici, who proclaimed that "the Brazilian economy is doing well, but the people are doing badly." All economic growth achieved by the military regime was at the expense of mass consumption and of a solution for problems of the masses. As a consequence, the social differences between the few who benefitted and the many who did not were exacerbated and the production and consumption of luxury and military goods were increased. Expansion of national and foreign monopoly capital was favored, and the balance of payments problems became more acute as the amount of profits remitted to the system's dominant centers increased. This growth scheme was, however, absolutely insufficient to maintain a reasonable national rate of growth. The multiple reasons can be summarized as follows: First, the policy of increasing state civilian and military consumption collided with the incapacity of the state to increase income, without adopting two counter-productive sources: the issue of paper currency that would lead to a new inflationary spiral, or an increase in taxes on earnings and high income sectors that would be contradictory to the actual model. Second, the expansion of the agricultural frontier reached a limit in at least a few areas with the creation of a mechanized agrarian economy and the growth of cattle raising that employed little labor and showed a diminution of its tendencies to expand. Third, the redistribution of income in favor of the upper middle sectors reached a stable level and to overcome this situation it was necessary to favor redistribution for a greater number of groups of the population. In order to continue feeding consumption the government injected the economic system with a huge dose of credit that in turn began to have inflationary effects. This conspicuous consumption had a demonstration effect on low income sectors and there was a general rise of consumption aspirations among the impoverished majority of the population.

Added to these strongly inflationary factors was the speculative way in which the financial market was created and the obvious limit to its expansion. In essence, the system faced the possibility of an economic crisis.

THE SEARCH FOR AN EXTERNAL MARKET
AND SUB-IMPERIALISM

Brazil also faced economic problems as a consequence of its foreign relations. There was a sharp increase in the remittance of earnings abroad. To attract more capital, controls on profit remittances were eliminated and a variety of investment guarantees gave new preferences to foreign interests over local investors. However, the limited internal market due to lowering of the real wage did not attract the quantity of foreign capital which these policies were designed to stimulate. Moreover, little new capital actually entered Brazil. Foreign firms raised most investment capital locally. Nonetheless, this new "foreign" capital resulted in increased profit remittances and consequently a higher net outflow of capital. Payments for technical services and royalties and for services such as shipping increased. There was a rise in the foreign debt. Also, there was an expanded need to import more raw materials and machinery to maintain an economic boom policy. Because of the limitations of exporting primary products whose prices tend to fall (as is the case of coffee) the country could only maintain its place in the international capitalist system to the extent that it was able to enter into the field of exporting semi-manufactured and manufactured goods and also to market its vast mineral resources.

Thus there was a search for new exports in order to solve two problems. New exports would create foreign exchange to facilitate payment of the foreign debt and profit remittances of foreign capital. They would also provide a market as a substitute for the internal market which could not be developed without a reformist policy which might lead to revolutionary conditions.

In a highly irrational situation, Brazil was able to establish a broad industrial base while not being capable of improving the living conditions of its people. As a consequence of the inexorable laws of dependent capitalist development, Brazil increased its productive capacity mainly for the benefit of international monopoly capital with whom the dependent bourgeoisie, who dominate the country, had cast its lot.

The most paradoxical aspect is that once the industrial base had been built, its growth, under dependent conditions, demanded a massive national effort to place this productive capacity at the service of international monopoly capital which gave the illusion of great economic advances. Just as modernization of the agrarian export economy during the second half of the last century created an appearance of development, broadened the country's productive and technical base, improved the consumption levels of a privileged minority and allowed the misery of the producing groups to exist alongside the enormous wealth of the dominant classes and a certain accommodation of the middle sectors, so too did the reorientation of the Brazilian industrial apparatus towards the international market create an illusion of progress and a broad development process. This earlier development period kept the country from solving its problems and kept the masses in backward conditions and a state of ignorance. An analysis of the new development model that the bourgeoisie tried desperately to implement to save capitalism in Brazil shows that it has led to similar results.

The fundamental assumption of the Brazilian development model since 1964 is that Brazil will take the lead in a new international division of labor within the capitalist world. During the colonial period Brazil produced precious minerals or tropical products in exchange for handicrafts, manufactured goods, and a slave work force. In the nineteenth century new agricultural products and raw materials were exchanged for modern European manufactured goods. With the industrialization process Brazil continued to export primary goods but shifted the type of import to machinery and processed raw materials in order to create a base for traditional industries that employ a relatively large labor force in comparison with the labor required by today's mechanized industries. In the central countries, especially in the United States where labor costs are high, there is less and less interest in these traditional products.

The so-called traditional industries include a large part of agricultural and mineral products exported from the dependent countries and several more elaborate industries such as textiles, shoes, clothing, wood, etc. Taken together these industries affect an important part of the national income, but above all they affect U. S. industrial employment. The underdeveloped countries, especially through UNCTAD (United Nations Conference on Trade and Development), demand that the U. S. government withdraw the high protectionist tariff imposed on importation of these products. The multinational companies are interested in this type of enterprise in the dependent countries, because they can obtain a much higher rate of return than would be the case with similar investments in the United States (where they do not have very direct control over this sector because it is dominated by local capital). Moreover, this type of undertaking opens up new sources of investment abroad. For this reason

UNCTAD is strongly backed by those businesses that sometimes stimulate this type of "nationalism." Thus this position takes on an apparent progressive or even revolutionary content.

Nonetheless, such assumptions underestimate the factors which stand in the way of the achievement of this new division of labor. On the one hand, the production of many of these goods is not limited to the dependent countries; other countries such as Japan participate on a grand scale in this type of competition. For example, in the textile sector Japanese competition can and is liquidating its American counterparts and American capital does not have any control over the Japanese textile industry. In this case, and in many others, if the United States opens the market for these goods, it might provoke the economic failure of important sectors in the United States without American multinational companies being able to take advantage of the situation* through their branches in the selling countries. This stirs up two types of opposition: First, the intensive opposition of the U. S. capitalists of the traditional sector who have been able to mobilize their workers and local middle classes dependent on these industries, creating a protectionist climate in the United States. Second, the milder opposition of certain sectors of international capitalists who think that they must be cautious about opening up the American market to foreign competition. Only a more sophisticated international sector is aware of the need to push a complete opening of the U. S. market in order to achieve penetration in other areas including Japan and the European countries that refuse to allow U. S. capital into certain sectors.

Moreover, with modern world conditions, a series of once advanced sectors are today considered as traditional or semi-traditional. This is the case in the automobile industry, light electronics, machine-tools, that is to say in industries with assembly lines employing large numbers of workers to assemble the final product. In these industries the United States is being surpassed on two levels by Japan and Europe. In the first place, most important U. S. industrial plants were created before the latest advances in automation and their modernization today would create enormous unemployment problems in an economy that has difficulty absorbing labor. In the second place, the well-paid U. S. labor force, is not prepared for quality production, and will eventually be overtaken by Japanese and European competence. Countries such as Brazil can aspire to compete in this sector with some more specialized products.

The multinational companies have decided to transfer the production of manufactured goods to branches in the dependent countries, and Brazil

---

* The apparent contradiction between companies that are both American and multinational is a consequence of the contradictory nature of the reality of these businesses and contemporary capitalism.

is making an effort to place itself in the center of such activity. In some instances, these goods will be exported to the United States and Europe. Brazil already exports auto parts, some machinery, and electronics parts to the United States and Europe and a large part of its exports are products of this type. Automobile engines produced by U. S. firms in Brazil will soon be exported to the United States. There is no doubt that Brazil and other countries on a similar level have a competitive advantage over European and United States industries when it comes to the markets of nearby underdeveloped countries.

To become a satellite producer, an underdeveloped country must have an already established solid industrial base, as is the case of Brazil's industrial center, and an internal market sufficient to justify it. Despite the abject poverty of fifty million inhabitants, Brazil has another forty-two million who receive a reasonable income. In the second place, the country must be willing to give strong backing to an export policy. Once the dictatorship understood the limits of the internal market, it began to emphasize the need to open up an external market. Beginning with the Castelo Branco government Brazil created protectionist mechanisms for national and foreign exporters by granting tax exemptions for exported goods, in the same way as she has made bureaucratic red tape easier and created an "exporting mentality." Third, it is necessary to allow unrestricted remittance of profits obtained from the various enterprises. Fourth, there has to be a government sufficiently strong to force the people to accept the fact that the large productive capacity will alleviate their present state of misery. All these conditions are found in Brazil.

The great export "boom" meant an increase in the value of exported manufactured and semi-processed goods from $270 million in 1967 to almost $1,000 million in 1971. There was also a spurt in the export of minerals, new agricultural products, and beef. Total exports went from $1,500 million in 1967 to $3,000 million in 1971, and were a significant part of the growth in G.N.P. during this period. The possibility that this rate of growth in exports would continue depended, above all, on the ability of the military technocratic group to convince international monopoly capital to back Brazil's aggressive export policy towards the United States, Europe, Africa, and Latin America—a policy that would injure important interests on all sides. Resistance of the United States and other countries to Brazil's effort to export instant coffee, textiles and other products showed that the battle would be fierce. Although it is true that the socialist countries represent important potential trading partners, they have been largely ignored because of the political imperatives of the Brazilian military regime.

The higher echelon Brazilian military leaders operate on the basis of a geo-political model that they are determined to put into practice at any cost. (The concept of sub-imperialism was developed by Marini [1970] and analyzed by other authors including Frias [1967].) The best elaboration of the sub-imperialist concept of Brazil's military leaders was made by its principal theorist, Golberi De Couto e Silva, in his *Geopolítica do Brasil*. According to Couto e Silva, Brazil's continental relationships and position of maritime dominance of the South Atlantic give it a special role within the western world. In exchange for the loan of bases (for example, Fernando de Noronha in Maranhão) that assure strategic control over the Southern Atlantic and a policy of close alliance with the United States, the United States ought to recognize Brazil's hegemony over the Southern Atlantic, including South America and Africa.

This theory was reformulated as a principal goal of the government's 1970–1971 plan which aimed to transform the country into an economic power before the end of the century. Brazil would try to reach this goal by expanding its export sector and by adopting military, political and cultural methods which would bring the nation closer to Latin America and Africa. Thus alliances were signed with all the existing dictatorships of these areas (Portugal and South Africa, Paraguay, Bolivia, and Haiti). Bringing to completion measures initiated under Castelo Branco, his successors have stubbornly maintained a policy of creating an atomic industry. Such aspirations are possible to the extent that the military government can use the country's large uranium reserves and other atomic minerals as a bargaining factor with atomic powers. In spite of North American opposition,* the government has had the support of Germany and Israel whose scientific and technical skills and capital assist in providing the Brazilian military with a power which increases their capacity to apply pressure on their neighbors.

The conditions which we have described reflect a systematic unity: dependent economic development that is monopolistic, concentrated, and exclusive. This development was based on large increases in the degree of exploitation of workers (increase of profit levels based on lowered wages), resulting in much disposable capital for investment, but a restricted internal market. The market was augmented by increases in civilian and above all government military consumption, increases in the incomes of the acquiescent petty bourgeoisie, colonization of new areas, and an aggressive export policy. The consequences of such a policy were

---

* This opposition seems to have been recently weakened with the installation of a big uranium facility in Brazil by Westinghouse and by Nixon's meeting with Garrastazú Médici after Brazil had signed an atomic agreement with Germany's Siemens Corporation. In the Washington meeting Nixon recognized Brazil as a power and the main Latin American ally.

unpopular government by a dominant class, use of force, centralization of power, policy-making by elites with hegemonic aspirations, military support for the expansion of the external market, sub-imperialist ambitions, and a complete opening to foreign capital. This foreign capital supported economic concentration, monopoly, and exclusion of the masses from economic development, thus reinforcing the model of growth.

The instability of the model was evident from the fact that growth was achieved not by overcoming the system's basic contradictions but by accentuating them. Not by responding to consumption demands and making real improvements for the masses, but rather by decreasing their consumption even more. Not by carrying out structural reforms that lead to the creation of a market and production really significant for the people, but rather avoiding structural reform by creating an artificial market for upper income classes which must be maintained by repression. Not by bringing the country out of its dependency, redirecting economic growth to respond to the needs of the population and assuring that the surplus created by labor remained in the country, but rather by turning the country over to foreign capital interests which sent capital abroad and by reorienting the small but significant productive base which had been established during the previous thirty years to serve the external market as the country's people die from hunger.

The type of political policies and outcomes stemming from this model of economic growth are evident. Force must be used to guarantee that workers will accept the low wages, while at the same time a gigantic propaganda campaign is made alleging a "Brazilian economic miracle." There has been increasing illiteracy* at a time when an educational "boom" has prepared skilled workers and technicians for whom jobs are not available. Young persons whose material appetites have been super-stimulated by advertising cannot be re-oriented to higher values by regime without exemplary leaders or ideals. A people who are not under any external military threat must be convinced of the necessity of creating an enormous military industry and apparatus.

The dictatorial government was faced with the following contradictions: unpopularity, restrictive policies, stimulus for a consumer society, a policy of using force, and the need for support for a policy of growth

---

* The government has undertaken literacy campaigns, but never on a scale sufficient to lower the number of illiterates. As the socialist countries have shown, illiteracy can only be rapidly eliminated in underdeveloped countries when there is integrated planning of the socio-economic system which enables the public to participate in massive national literacy campaigns. The Brazilian dictatorship tried to mobilize students in a literacy drive, but it was only able to involve a small number who were ineffective because of the magnitude of the problem.

which undermined the basic interests of the Brazilian masses. The government's inability to achieve institutional stability was a consequence of its class character. This was a government of a dependent bourgeoisie that could not solve the most immediate problems of the people and handed over to military and civilian technocrats the task of saving, at whatever cost, private property in the country. The only political mode of accomplishing this was facism adopted to conditions of a dependent nation.

The alliance of the military with civilian technocrats was formed with complete disregard for either the mass or bourgeois opposition. This was because a government of force was essential for the survival of the bourgeoisie but the bourgeoisie itself was not able to lead such a government and the military believed itself capable of ruling with the help of civilian technocrats. These men interpreted the interests of the dominant class even though some of its members protested. The traditional politicians who were spokesmen for the various classes and social strata were understood as persons to be *consulted* and not as representatives of sectors that would take the initiative in countering the decisions taken by the group in power.

It is evident that these arrangements would lead to several crises. At the outset the group in power was highly unified ideologically and politically. It was a group from the Superior War College plus technical experts who represented the big capital sector, particularly the economist Roberto Campos. His policies (monetary stabilization, free access for foreign capital, setting up the basis for exportation, and the affirmation of the country as a power) have in general remained constant. The dominant class peacefully and willingly accepted the restrictions imposed on them for they were always aware of the masses in the streets and of the force of internal opposition, the popular discontent whose explosive potential they could not ignore.

The group in power thus had a great advantage: the dominant class desired stability far more than anything else. As a result, the conspiratorial intentions of disgruntled elements of the 1964 military coup were paralyzed by the awareness of the violent response that would be made by the group in power if the opposition used the considerable force it had accumulated. The settlement of conflict within the regime was only possible when some military leaders led by the then Minister of War, Arturo Costa e Silva, joined forces against Castelo Branco's group in 1966. Costa e Silva represented a considerable sector of the dominant classes who feared the excessive rigidity of the Castelo administration. As the condition for handing power over to his Minister of War whom he held in great disregard, Castelo Branco demanded the institutionalization of the regime through a constitution. Once in power Costa e Silva allowed remaining professional politicians to recover a degree of political freedom. These politicians had readily backed Costa e Silva. But as anticipated by the most cautious sectors of the dominant class: the regime could not tolerate any opposition. Elections held at this time showed the weakness of progovernment candidates. Conforntation with students, results of labor union elections, and intellectual and artistic expression—in short everything vital in the country showed an violent hatred of the "glorious Revolution" of April 1, 1964. The only support of the government was from fascist organizations financed by decadent landowners and rightist businessmen. It soon became obvious that only force could guarantee existence of the regime and the new repressive wave began in December, 1968.

What was the structure of this regime based on force? The executive was the only authority in the country. The legislators were impotent, unable to take any initiative. At most they fulfilled a consultative function. President Garrastuzú Médici, the highest executive authority, was elected in a highly undemocratic vote held within the armed forces. The candidate with a majority on the first ballot (General Albuquerque Lima) was disqualified, and the high command immediately put forth three new candidates. State governors were named by the president, and the municipal authorities have their positions as a consequence of many diverse situations.

The command of the general staff was the principal deliberative force in the country. The ministers and other authorities still participate in the state security council, a broader but subordinate instrument of decision-making. The National Intelligence Service is the principal mechanism for selecting and controlling the bureaucracy. The secret service of the three branches of the armed forces and the police organizations dedicated to the repression of "subversion" were forces often stronger than those of the ministers, many of whom have "confessed" to the opposition their inability to intervene in security matters.*

---

* One of the most notorious examples was that of the ex-deputy Rubens Paiva, engineer and business executive, who was allied to the legal or tolerated opposition and Brazil's dominant class. He was arrested in his house for unknown reasons and died on the torture table to which he succumbed because of his age. His family was never able to retrieve the body. Both army and police denied his death saying that he had been kidnapped by his "companions" from the police. Neither the cardinal's intervention nor that of high level authorities could bring about a reconsideration of the police decision to maintain this story and not hand over his body. This type of case is repeated daily. See the pamphlet "La dictadura mato a Rubens Paiva" of the *Frente Brasileño de Informaciones* and the *Cuadernos Brasileños* No. 1 "Pena de Muerte en Brasil: de los hechos a la legalidad fascista." An overall study of the

The municipal, state, and federal legislatures functioned very irregularly under constant pressure and it is only at this level that the tolerated "opposition," united in the Movimento Democrático Brasileiro (MDB), have had a restricted tribunal for criticism. Newspapers and magazines were submitted to censure, but above all there is "self-censure," responding to general stipulations issued by the government, military, and police. If a publication went beyond the limit allowed, it was closed, or there were economic sanctions, or editions were withdrawn from circulation. Under such conditions the allowed "opposition" was given no systematic expression in the mass media and could depend only on occasional and circumstantial support from the press. The anti-government guerrilla movements had absolutely no outlet in the press even for publishing their declarations. The only published material available on them is found in police reports.

This regimen of terror was not appreciated by the dominant national classes, especially when some of their children were its victims, nor by the American and European monopoly bourgeoisie who invested in the country. This does not mean, however, that they did not *support* the terrorists in practice even though they did not want to be identified with them. Indeed, they not only supported such policies, they also helped to arrange to finance those who carried them out. The handling of the case of the death squads reveals the reluctance of higher authorities to restrain the activities of those responsible for carrying out the terror. The death squads were police groups dedicated to killing skid row delinquents who would not participate in police control of drug traffic and other illegal activities. A public prosecutor, Helio Bicudo, made public many of the illegal activities and political repression of this police band and implicated the death squad for direct responsibility in drug traffic.* At the height of the inquiry Bicudo was removed from the case and it was put into the hands of the very police groups involved in the crimes being investigated.

In order to conceal from the world the true nature of the Brazilian political system, the ruling class mounted a systematic international press campaign extolling the "Brazilian miracle." This campaign celebrated gross economic gains without analysing their quality and character or whether they were contrary to the interests of the general population. No mention was made to the lowering of real wages, growing poverty, and increasing illiteracy. Even worse, the press tried to justify by these growth

---

tortures is found in Rodrigo Alarcón, *Brasil: Represión y tortura,* Santiago: Editorial Orbe, 1970.

* The poor people killed were usually either members of rival contraband groups or independent elements who refused to give in to control by the death squadron.

rates what it called "police excesses." What were these excesses? According to the data of the Brazilian Information Front, in 1971 there were sentences for some four hundred political prisoners, and another one hundred were killed in the streets and in Brazilian prisons. This type of activity has been revealed in an American Senate Committee hearing, by the Red Cross, and by the OAS Human Rights Committee. These accusations have provoked no reaction from any government. On the contrary, in addition to normal relations, President Garrastazú Médici was invited by Richard Nixon to discuss with him the objectives of his trip to China and USSR, and the U. S. President recognized Brazil as a power that would "lead the way" in Latin America.

The political plan instituted by the Brazilian military gained a strong backing from the economic, political, and even cultural interests of the dominant classes of the world. There was no doubt that there were attempts to *moderate* the repressive characteristics of the regime such as the relative institutionalization achieved in 1969 by returning to Castelo Branco's 1966 Constitution which had been suspended by the Institutional Act No. 5 and implemented on December 5, 1968, under heavy pressure from the military hardline sector. The former planning minister, Roberto Campos, today director of an important investment bank (Invest Bank), formed by powerful international groups wrote in *El Globo* of the superiority of the Brazilian economic model based on "a splendid wage discipline" and compared it with the failure of the Argentine military to hold back workers' wages.

He regarded the inability to create a political model capable of consolidating this economic victory as a definitive weakness. Campos recognized the difficulty of reconciling this "splendid wage discipline" with any form of democracy. However, he argued that opening a legal channel for opposition was less likely to produce a political crisis than not doing so.

Campos' twisted logic glosses over the intrinsic weakness of Brazil's economic growth, that it is limited, threatened by the vagaries of speculative investment, and that it presupposes control of the international market which is itself in crisis. Whatever happens, only a limited liberalization of the political system is possible, and this would scarcely satisfy the Brazilian masses.

The present regime was destined to become more and more fascist through repression, terror, concentration of power in the military and in paramilitary organized groups, restriction of the legislative and consultative organs. This political framework corresponded coherently with the economic system. This did not mean that there were not frequent efforts at liberalization. These led to an awakening of powerful revolutionary desires forcing the dominant class to increase even more its repression.

THE OPPOSITION AND ITS PERSPECTIVE

The military coup of April 1964 completely disorganized the Brazilian popular movement. At that moment the Brazilian left was composed of a group of political forces that were very confused ideologically. The most important group from a historical and functional point of view was the Communist PCB, founded in 1922. It has had a difficult history for it has been underground during most of its existence. It was legalized in 1945, only to be declared illegal again in 1947. In 1958 charges against PCB's leader Luis Carlos Prestes were dropped and the party began an unsuccessful campaign to gain legal recognition, but it was allowed to become active as a semi-public entity. Its influence over the working class increased, and in 1961 it won the leadership of the Brazilian trade union movement in alliance with a new generation of labor leaders of the PTB. The general workers' Comando Geral dos Trabalhadores (CGT) was created, and it began to function semi-officially as a trade union central. The influence of the PCB was not as great in the student movement since the Ação Popular (AP), a left organization with a Catholic base, had won control of the movement at the national level. In the peasant movement, the Peasant Leagues directed by Francisco Juliao's Movimento Radical Tiradentes and other forces of the left predominated. The Communists dominated the less important Union of Farm-Laborers and Agricultural workers (ULTAB). There were many movements in the countryside with confused and even rightist tendencies, especially those groups led by priests and those subsidized with funds from the Agency for International Development and CIA. In the military, PCB had influence among the nationalist officers, but dominant influence among the sergeants and soldiers was held by the radical populist Leonel Brizola and his "groups of eleven" (loosely coordinated cells of eleven people with revolutionary goals operating under Brizola's leadership within a nationalist left orientation). The Política Operária (POLOP) had support within the student movement and had gained a certain influence in the peasant movements and among the urban masses, sergeants, sailors, and workers. The Partido Comunista do Brasil (PC do B), the pro-Chinese faction that split off from the PCB, also had built up support within mass movements.*

* Until 1961 the PCB was called the Partido Comunista do Brasil (The Communist Party of Brazil). This name was one of the reasons why the party was declared illegal in 1947. The term "of Brazil" (do Brasil) meant that this party was the Brazilian section of an international communist party. When the party petitioned for legal recognition in 1958, it proposed to change its name to the Partido Comunista Brasileira (PCB). The faction that split off in 1962 took the old name Partido Comunista do Brasil (PC do Brasil).

One element of the left had a nationalist orientation. It was led by the PCB and included a majority of the Partido Trabalhista Brasileiro and the factions of other parties that made up the Frente Parlamentar Nacionalista (an interparty pact of leftist congressmen). President João Goulart controlled this faction's public position and influence over the masses. The objective of these forces was to form a broad front of workers, peasants and the nationalist bourgeoisie against the foreign enemy, imperialism. According to the PCB, the principal articulator of this position, it was the job of the working class to fight to gain control of this front but this was not a condition for the formation of the front.

On the other hand, there were those who held that the involvement of the national bourgeoisie in imperialism would lead to the downfall of Brazilian politics and advocated the promotion of a workers front which would include laborers, the unemployed, farmers, and the small bourgeoisie both rural and urban. The leader of this group, despite its organizational weakness, was the Política Operária (POLOP) because it was alert to the danger of a bourgeoisie dominated mass mobilization under the ideology of nationalism led politically by João Goulart. This position eventually attracted the most radicalized sectors of the PTB and even the PCB youth, as well as the Movimento Radical Tiradentes (that split into two factions in 1962 and 1963) and sectors of the PC do B. Because it saw the impossibility of the reformist leadership controlling the yearning of the masses for socialism the POLOP understood the probability of a coup and ensuing facism. To forestall these outcomes the group called for formulation of a front that would unite all leftist forces including the PCB which would be separated from Goulart and the other bourgeois sectors that espoused nationalism.

The theoretical correctness of the POLOP position became evident with the 1964 coup. After this date the POLOP's ideas began to exercise a determining role in the evolution of the Brazilian left, but this was not accompanied by an organizational and political base capable of achieving practical results. Between 1964 and 1966 the Brazilian left attempted to adjust itself to the new conditions. A popular offensive emerged during 1967 and 1968, but was repressed in 1969 and 1970. During this period, opposition to the government was divided into three main currents.

1) The legal opposition, under the aegis of the liberal Movimento Democrático Brasileiro (MDB), sought to use its influence to petition the government to let such opposition operate freely. This group offered moderate criticism of the abuses of and attacks on judicial and legislative powers, the regional executive powers, the intellectuals, the university, the labor organizations, and the masses in general. When these outcries led to several attempts at rebellion, these were usually repressed with

drastic measures. In order to survive, the liberal opposition frequently censured itself and limited its programs to very general issues. After the signing of the "Institutional Act No. 5" in December 1968, the liberal opposition was able to survive only after making many concessions under which they agreed to limit their liberal program to the abrogation of the No. 5 Act and a return to the 1966 Constitution. In their 1971 conference a tendency emerged that called for the formation of a Constituent Assembly but this was considered an example of political "infantilism" and was rejected by the leadership of the MDB.

This does not mean that the liberal opposition was totally liquidated. The MDB counted on international backing, above all petty bourgeoisie public opinion, and represented the desires of the middle classes and sectors of the mass movement which wanted to keep the country from becoming totally fascist. The liberal position had to take advantage of situations of political opening which were also necessary for the system's survival. This opposition could not hope to gain power unless an acute crisis developed. Worst of all, this opposition had no program prepared in case it did reach power. Given Brazil's present conditions, a program of structural reforms would have to lead to socialism, so if the liberal opposition supported such reforms it would negate itself and become socialist. Faced with all these vacillations and difficulties, the liberal opposition became weaker and found itself without a base or a clear program.

2) Another sector of the opposition was a movement of underground resistance principally organized around the trade unions and the peasant, student, and mass neighborhood movements. It had a certain political independence from the liberal opposition and tried to build more solid bases of support. As early as 1964 workers, peasants and students tried secretly to organize an underground movement with or without the support or control of a political organization. This organization first appeared with the formation of "Groups of 5" whose objective was to form a resistance movement. Between 1966 and 1968 the student groups were semi-secret and the National Student Union held four clandestine congresses. In a similar fashion worker committees in businesses organized underground, sometimes allied with labor unions, and this activity led to strikes such as that of the bank workers in the industrial cities of Contage and Osasco, São Paulo, and Belo Horizonte, Minas Gerais in 1968. With the exception of the student movement there was no attempt to coordinate resistance at regional and national levels, and this failure greatly weakened the movement. The political organizations which were split into different groups were more interested in organizing their own cells or in recruiting groups for armed action rather than in establishing a strong and united mass underground movement.

3) The third opposition position also dated from 1964 and was represented by a guerrilla movement considered to be the nucleus of the revolutionary army. While this is not the place to discuss the ideas that oriented such movements (on the Brazilian left during the 1964–1971 period see Marini, 1971A), it is necessary to point out that the left was under the influence of the "armed foco" concept.* The force of this concept was so great that it had a strong influence on the orientation of the POLOP between 1964 and 1966. In fact, in 1964 a group of sailors, students, workers, and intellectuals from this organization were arrested in Rio de Janeiro on the eve of their departure for the countryside. Preparations for guerrilla activity continued from 1965 to 1967. During this period there was an abortive armed guerrilla action in the South directed by an army officer and other scattered armed assaults. Later the government apprehended in the countryside a group of ex-sergeants who had been expelled from the armed forces during the 1964 coup.

For the majority of the leftist forces, the guerrilla movement appeared as the only possible form of an armed challenge to the system, but it became more and more difficult to reach the rural areas. Because of these problems the opposition began armed attacks in the cities with the aim of getting hold of resources and material to take to the rural areas. The various politico-military organizations that emerged during this time initiated this struggle without any previous preparation, divided into small groups, without any unifying program and without a national leadership.

Armed actions sprouted in the midst of a monetary mass movement against the government during 1967 and 1968. The situation was favorable because contact with the masses was easy, there were many groups of youths ready to fight, and the repression was not prepared to respond to such a large movement. But instead of taking advantage of these circumstances to build a strong, secret, and armed party, the movements under the inspiration of *foquismo* underestimated clandestine party organization as well as legal struggle.

The first was thought to be an example of bureaucratization. Carlos Marighella, leader of a strong faction that split off from the PCB, refused to unite with his comrades Mário Alves and Jacobo Gorender who had founded the Partida Comunista Brasileiro Revolucionário (PCB-R) under the allegation that there was no need for a new bureaucratic party. The PCB-R itself soon became just an armed group. A large sector that abandoned the Política Operária (POLOP) refused to form a party and divided into two armed organizations the VPR and the COLINA which sought to conduct nation-wide armed actions. The two groups joined in

* A rural guerrilla mobile column, a concept most highly developed by Regis Debray (1967).

1969 to form the VAR Palmares, but self-criticism of the "foco" concept led to another split and a new reorganized VPR. The names of all these organizations are not important here for they were relatively fragile. What is important is that most of the left organizations suffered from "foco" or militaristic splits between 1967 and 1969 (the PCB, the PC do B, the AP and the POLOP) that meant the splitting off of nearly a majority of the members of the organized groups.

What explains this disintegration of organized groups? On the one hand, there was a discrediting of the reformist tendency that the PCB had imposed on the popular movement between 1956 and 1964. Since it failed to recognize the inadequacy of that position, but rather, criticized itself for supposed left deviations, the PCB was unable to respond appropriately to the situation in which the country found itself. On the other hand when the POLOP and other left groups that advocated a revolutionary path showed themselves organizationally and tactically incapable of chan-nelling the revolutionary energies arising in the nation, they laid the bases for their own dissolution.

The mechanical separation between the legal and the clandestine struggles, between the masses and the armed activists, and of the divisions of the left into small groups were the factions that led to a decline in mass participation in anti-government activities that had developed during 1967 and 1968. The broad movement that developed during that period was left without solutions or recourse. Weakened and vacillating, it was an easy target for government repression even though it had once defeated the military police in the streets.

With the mass movement wiped out, censorship increased, legal mass organizations closed, and the clandestine ones repressed, (the dictatorship apprehended eight hundred participants in a national student congress) the repression systematically brought all its force to bear on the guerrilla movement. From this point on the revolutionaries were corralled in the streets of Rio de Janeiro, São Paulo, Belo Horizonte, Porto Alegre and Recife, or surrounded in their rural training camps such as that of the Valle de la Ribiera and those in the interior of Rio Grande do Sul. With heroism and decisiveness they achieved several tactical victories in a com-pletely unfavorable strategic situation. They were able to kidnap the American and Swiss ambassadors, important propaganda acts, and break out of the noose in the Ribiera valley. But hundreds of revolutionaries were killed in the streets or in torture chambers, while the public remained totally uninformed. The organizations were dealt heavy blows, both to their leadership and to their followers.

The years from 1969 to 1971 represented hard setbacks for the left that found itself encircled on all sides and faced with an enormous government publicity campaign to win over public opinion. The government offered as compensations the future benefits that the ongoing economic growth would provide for all. The ideological confusion of the workers was apparent. On the one hand, they watched the regime bring about economic recovery through a miracle in which they did not participate. On the other hand, they saw the left emerge in direct opposition and struggle with the repressive government; but there was no path for their own struggle.

It would seem that the popular forces were in a desperate situation. However, the economic growth sustained during the previous four years began to pose some old problems. Could the external market and that of the upper middle classes guarantee the consumption necessary to maintain the traditional industries that employed the greatest number of workers? Who would buy the products of the industries created by the substantial investments already made? The problem of an internal market reappeared as a problem for Brazilian capitalism. As previously pointed out, only profound reforms of the system could resolve these problems, and the bourgeoisie was still unwilling to adopt these reforms.

Another issue was whether economic growth justified such a strong repression of the entire population. This was another problem for the still important liberal sector. But, above all it was troublesome to the extent that economic development needs an effective and enthusiastic popular collaboration, which was limited by the few material benefits that the system could provide. The repression thus sought to force workers production and to protect the authority of management. This system created deep tensions. The repression itself led to a loss of support from the intellectuals and scientists so necessary for sustained development during a new stage of capitalist accumulation.

Mass movements began to appear again in small strikes, reorganizations of trade unions and student associations; and the liberal opposition tried to break the press censorship. The rural masses of the Northeast demonstrated violent rebellious tendencies by taking over small cities, trains, and regions, and even in other areas there were clashes in the countryside.

It would seem that the reappearance of the mass movement after a short time of quiet revealed its willingness to struggle. In Brazil there was never a civil war which liquidated large sections as was the case in Spain during 1936 to 1939, nor massive military confrontations as in fascist Italy and Nazi Germany. For this reason the Brazilian military regime could not consolidate its fascist characters in an open manner. Perhaps this will be done in a new wave of repressions. The struggle between socialism, as the only popular solution, and fascism, as the only capitalist alternative, will continue, however, to be the key to the Brazilian historical process.

THEOTÔNIO DOS SANTOS is Director of Research at the Centro de Estudios Socio-Económicos of the University of Chile. His research has focused on his native country, Brazil, where he was a professor of sociology at the University of Brasília until the military intervention of 1964. Since that time until the military coup of September 1973, he lived in exile in Santiago, Chile, where he wrote on and researched questions of dependency and imperialism. During the late 1960s he was a visiting professor at the University of Northern Illinois. His recent published writings include: *Socialismo o fascismo, dilema latinoamericano* (Santiago, 1969); *Dependencia y cambio social* (Santiago, 1970), and *La crisis norteamericana y América Latina* (Santiago, 1971). He has also published numerous journal articles of which his "The Structure of Dependence," *The American Economic Review,* LX (May 1970), 231–36, is best known in the United States.

STATISTICS

Physical Data:
Area: 3,286,473 sq. miles
Arable land: 32.3% (including pastures and meadows) (1964)

Demographic:
Population: 95,305,000 (1970)
Birth rate: 40–43 per 1000 persons (1960–'64)
Population Growth Rate: 3.2%
Life Expectancy: 50.8 years (1960)
Ethnic Composition: European 50%; mixed European, Indian, African 40%.
% of population living in cities: 46.3% (1960)

Social:
Literacy Rate: 60.5% (15 years and older) (1960)
Education: 74.2% of the 5–14 year old population (10,217,324 persons) enrolled in school (1964)
    27 students/teacher (primary level) (1968)
    99,924 enrolled in institutions of higher education (1968)
Medical: 4.4 doctors/10,000 persons (1968)
    2.8 dentists/10,000 persons (1968)
    3.4 hospital beds/1,000 persons (1964)
Newspapers: 250 daily newspapers (1969)
    31 daily newspapers circulated per 1000 persons (1967)
Radio: 60 radio receivers/1000 persons (1971)
Television: 72 T.V. receivers/1000 persons (1969)

Government:
Capital: Brazilia
Government Budget: 19,703 thousand million cruzieros (2.465 cruzieros per one U.S. dollar) (1970)
Government Spending: 11% of Gross Domestic Product (1970)

(1970) { 6.1% of government budget spent on education
1.8% of government budget spent on public health
18.0% of government budget spent on defense

History of Government:

Getúlio Vargas   1930–45 (achieved power through revolution and subsequent dictatorship)

Eurico Gaspar Dutra   1945–51

Getúlio Vargas   1950–54

Juscelino Kubitschek   1956–61

Jãnio Quadros   1961 (resigned)

João Goulart   1961–64

Humberto de Alencar Castelo Branco   1964–66 (achieved power through military coup)

Artur da Costa e Silva   1967–69 (chosen by Congress without popular election)

Emílio Garrastazú Médici   1969– (chosen by Congress without popular vote)

Economic Data:

GNP: $29,717,000.00 (U.S. dollars) (1968)

Per Capita GNP: $337.00 (U.S. dollars) (1968)

Growth rate of Gross Domestic Product: 9.0% (1969)

Distribution of Income: The poorest 20% of all income units received 4.2% of the total income earned. The middle 60% of all income units received 37.0% of all income earned. The next wealthier 15% of all income units earned 25.8% of all income earned while the top 5% of all income units received 33% of all income earned.

Size of landholdings (1 ha = 2.471 acres)	% of all farms	% of land
Up to 5 hectares	44.8%	2.4%
5–50 hectares	44.7%	19.0%
50–500 hectares	9.4%	34.4%
Over 500 hectares	0.9%	44.2%

Distribution of Work Force — see next page

Trade Balance: (1970)

export value: $2,807.3 million

import value: $2,792.6 million

Major Trading Partners: (1970)

export to: U.S.A. $669,4 million

Germany $280,9 million

Japan $198,1 million

import from: U.S.A. $924,7 million

Germany $340,7 million

Japan $183,4 million

Source of foreign Exchange by Product: (1969)

    coffee   —41.2% of total exports

    cotton — 7.0% of total exports

    cacao   — 2.5% of total exports

    iron ore— 5.6% of total exports

Foreign Debt: $3,522.2 million (1971)

Service Payments on External Public Debt: 16.6% of Exports of Goods and Services (1970)

Foreign Investment: Central Bank data showed that at the end of 1969 total foreign investment was valued at U.S. 4 billion including 2.4 billion of reinvested earnings. These data showed the U.S. as the largest single foreign investor with U.S. 1.7 billion, France $688.0 million, United Kingdom $466.0 million, Switzerland $249.0 million, West Germany $175.0 million with a balance of 3.3 billion divided among others.

Distribution of Work Force: (1960)

    7.4%—professional, technical, administrative and executive

    7.7%—clerical, sales work

    52.5%—farmers, fishermen, hunters

    .3%—miners, quarrymen

    4.1%—transportation, communication

    14.6%—craftsmen, production workers

    6.4%—service, sport and recreation

    6.0%—workers not classified by occupation

CHAPTER 5

CHILE

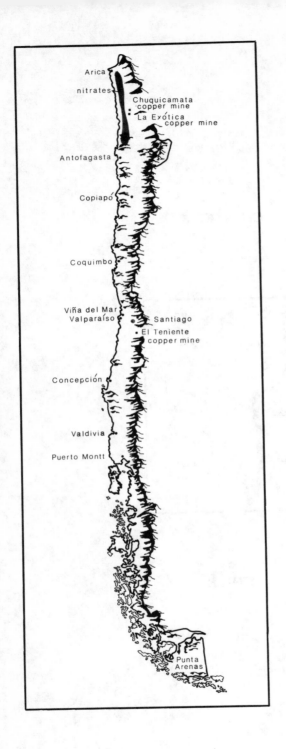

CONTENTS

CHILE

"I met Bolívar one morning,
In Madrid at the entrance to the fifth regiment,
I said, 'Father, are you or are you not, or who are you?'
And he said, looking at the barracks on the mountain:
'I awake each one hundred years when the people wake up.'"

Pablo Neruda (painted as a wall mural in Chile) (NACLA, 1972:9)

"I told Mr. Vaky (State Department Latin American Advisor to Henry Kissinger) to tell Mr. Kissinger Mr. Geneen (President of ITT) is willing to come to Washington to discuss ITT's interests and that we are prepared to assist financially in sums to seven figures. . . . Undercover efforts are being made to bring about the bankrutpcy of one or two of the major savings and loan associations. This is expected to trigger a run on banks and the closure of some factories resulting in more unemployment. . . . Massive unemployment and unrest might produce enough violence to force the military to move."

(Internal ITT Memorandum on the Chilean Situation from Mr. J. D. Neal to Mr. W. R. Merriam, ITT Vice President, dated September 14, 1970)

"The change in the power structure that we are carrying out, the progressive leadership role of the workers in it, the national recovery of basic riches, the liberation of our country from subordination to foreign powers, are all crowning points of a long historical process; of efforts to impose political and social freedoms, of heroic struggle of several generations of workers and farmers to organize themselves as a social force to obtain political power and drive the capitalists from economic power."

(Dr. Salvador Allende, former President of the Republic of Chile, in a speech to the General Assembly of the United Nations, December 4, 1972)

CHILE

BY

MARCELO J. CAVAROZZI

AND

JAMES F. PETRAS

INTRODUCTION*

Chile is one of the few countries in Latin America that has had stable political institutions subject to the electoral process. Unlike other Latin American countries, Chile has had only one period of military-backed government (1924–1931) in the last eighty-two years (Nunn, 1970). Throughout the nineteenth century Chile was ruled alternately by liberal and conservative governments in what one writer correctly referred to as an "oligarchic republic based on the colonial tradition of authoritarianism" (Gil, 1966, p. 88). Nevertheless, Chile has possessed a stable government with an orderly process of political change—unlike her neighbors throughout most of Latin America.

Nineteenth and twentieth century Chile was ruled through a president and congress, both of which were elected. However, the elections were largely or wholly in the hands of privileged property groups. These privileged groups limited the suffrage to property groups (five percent of the adult population actually voted in 1915) throughout the nineteenth century. In the first half of the twentieth century they utilized wholesale bribery, coercive legislation and literacy clauses to limit the effectiveness of non-

---

* This chapter was written prior to the military coup of September 11, 1973. The coup and antecedent developments are analyzed in an appended section. The main body of the chapter, including now ironic references to Chilean political stability has not been altered. (eds.)

elite political parties. In the latter half of the twentieth century elite-oriented parties have given more emphasis to ideological terror by manipulating propaganda symbols through the mass media to distort the image of their opponents among potential lower-class supporters. Thus, while Chile has maintained a stable electoral presidential or parliamentary system throughout most of the twentieth century, the political institutions have not been the product of a mass popular democratic upheaval.

The result of elite management and control of political institutions has been the perpetuation of vast inequalities of wealth, a highly stratified society, great concentrations of wealth, and a judicial and administrative structure tied to propertied interests. Thus, while juridically Chile appeared to resemble a political democracy, the social and economic realities suggest that political freedoms were more formal and less substantive. The effective exercise of political rights was vested in the propertied groups. As one writer has noted, "What we have praised as democracy in Chile since 1920 has amounted to little more than a system in which a small privileged class has been gentlemanly determining, through very limited electoral processes, which of its members would rule the country" (Pike, 1963, p. 296).

Chile's "differences" from the rest of Latin America thus are not to be found in its social structure and economic development which demonstrate many of the same features of inequality, dependence and exploitation as exist in the rest of Latin America. To understand Chile's unique political experience one must examine some factors which, in the nineteenth century, conditioned the emergence of a stable parliamentary political framework as a basis for elite rule.[1]

Nineteenth century Chilean political development was largely the product of several interrelated considerations (Zeitlin, 1968): (1) substantial agricultural and commercial expansion, especially in the period between 1840 to 1870; (2) imperialist expansion leading to the annexation of the rich mining provinces; (3) an "open" ruling class which was capable of absorbing new rising entrepreneurial groups; (4) an effective military-administrative structure capable of exercising social control over the subject population and creating opportunities for economic expansion and growth.

In the post-independence period, unlike many Latin American countries, the Chilean ruling class was composed of entrepreneurs actively involved in the organization of enterprises—with roots in the community. These national entrepreneurs were in a position to exercise authority and

---

[1] Not infrequently political writers confuse the notion of a parliamentary with a democratic form of government. Thus, as in Chile, a parliamentary system based on a fraction of the population was frequently and erroneously referred to as "democratic."

receive the loyalty of the subject population. The ruling elite, while depending on external markets, was nevertheless in control of economic resources and thus appeared to be "legitimate" spokesmen for the "nation" rather than spokesmen for their own class interests. The myth of a "national" leadership and the mystification of the masses (who accepted the elite as their "legitimate" leaders) was further strengthened by the government's program of territorial expansion: extermination of the indigenous population in the south of Chile, and the seizure of their lands—later distributed to "frontier settlers," contributed to the emergence of a "consensual polity."

Cross-class bonds or "national loyalties" were further enhanced by additional Chilean expansionist movements, this time to the north in the 1870's. Chile's imperialist aim during the War of the Pacific (1870's) was clear: seizure of the world's richest nitrate mines at the expense of Peru and Bolivia. The new wealth served to cushion social and political conflicts; patriotism and nationalist pride which emerged from the external military victory served to create a sense of national identity and national-racial superiority. These national-ethnic bonds moderated class cleavages; the economic resources obtained by conquest facilitated a certain degree of class mobility—especially between the middle and upper classes.

Mining and industrial entrepreneurs did not come into conflict with the traditional agro-commercial elite (especially after 1859) ; rather the new and old sectors tended to merge. Kinship ties and social intercourse led to the emergence of a unified ruling class, one in which members from various economic sectors shared overlapping interests. The cross-sectoral alliances foreclosed potential inter-elite conflicts and created a socioeconomic base for the type of bargaining politics which largely describes Chile's multiple-party system.

The ability of the ruling groups to play off against each other was based on one of the most efficient bureaucratic-military organizations in the hemisphere. Elite bargaining and competition in parliament was based on mass exploitation; the means for effective control were largely in the hands of administrators. Vertically organized under the executive branch, the administrators were linked horizonally to the propertied classes—enforcing laws and regulations which promoted business and agricultural propertied interests while restraining dissident reformers through the selective use of the armed forces. Thus, nineteenth century Chilean political institutions, while providing for orderly and peaceful change, public debate, political competition and bargaining, also provided a political facade for elite exploitation of three-fourths of the population.

The dynamic growth of Chile in the early nineteenth century set the groundwork for imperial-expansionist policies (to the north and south). Nevertheless, it was precisely when Chile established itself as a regional power that it began to be penetrated by English capital. The fruits of the War of the Pacific (1879–1883), the rich nitrate and copper mines, were effectively taken over by English and later American capital. The inability of Chile to develop as an autonomous capitalist state despite its initial advantages (national entrepreneurs, infrastructure, and mineral windfall, regional hegemony) foreshadowed the failure of later day efforts at autonomous national-capitalist development in other parts of Latin America.

Chilean dependence was established through foreign penetration of key mining export sectors. Dependence was a late nineteenth century phenomenon linked to the world expansion of British imperialism.[2] The process of foreign penetration did not take place in a backward "traditional" society but in a modernizing, developing agro-commercial society already integrated in the capitalist world-market. With the loss of ownership of the nitrate (and later copper) mines, Chile's dependence on external forces was confirmed; Chile's conversion from an autonomous developing society to a dependent country was completed, despite or perhaps because of its parliamentary political structures. The emergence and strengthening of parliamentary institutions was not incompatible with the conversion of Chile into a dependent state. The one president who attempted to "nationalize" the economy and to limit foreign penetration (Balmaceda) had to turn toward strong executive leadership, suggesting that parliamentary institutions and parties were particularly susceptible to foreign influence.

In summary, while Chile has possessed a long history of parliamentary politics, regular elections, orderly succession of presidents and an elaborate legal-administrative structure, the substantive nature of this political system is largely found in its social relations and economic institutions: a highly exploitative class structure linked to externally controlled economic enterprises.

[2] A comprehensive explanation of how and why Chilean dependence began when it did is beyond the reach of this essay. A theory of dependence must analyze the sources as well as the "character" of dependence, thus giving the concept some specific historical content. This involves focusing on specific elite behavior patterns and decisions as well as the structural determinants of that behavior. André Gunder Frank's (1967) discussion of "dependence" is so general as to embrace all external relations thus losing sight of the important differences between a developing agro-mining economy and a dependent society. Furthermore, his discussion of the "development of underdevelopment" is so vague as to subsume several substantial efforts at economic growth. The open-endedness of Frank's discussion, the lack of historical specificity of dependency thus undercuts any serious analysis of the specific social forces and circumstances and world conditions that produce "dependency."

Chile has been, and still is, a dependent capitalist society. However, Chile's dependent relationship with the imperialist centers has suffered deep transformations throughout the nineteenth and twentieth centuries. After a period of thirty years—from 1830 to 1860—during which the country followed a nationalistic course under the rule of an authoritarian and conservative political elite,[3] the expansion of the international economic system successfully undermined the economic and cultural barriers that had maintained Chile's partial isolation since independence.

Chile's recent economic and political history is an example of how a relationship dependent upon foreign economic and political interests can negatively effect and hence deform a country's socio-economic development. From the last third of the nineteenth century to 1930, Chile was an export-oriented economy, reproducing the pattern that was predominant in Latin America. A foreign-owned economic enclave—mining—constituted the most dynamic sector, thus differing from Brazil or Argentina where the export sector was domestically owned.

The creation and consolidation of import-substituting industries defined the period that extended between 1932 and the late 1950's. An import-substitution process was externally determined, inasmuch as scarcity of foreign exchange made it impossible to buy foreign manufactured articles. However, the development of national industries in Argentina in the 1940's and in Brazil in the early 1950's gave rise to occasional and short-lived economic friction between domestic entrepreneurial sectors and the U. S. and European corporations that sold manufactured articles to Latin America. This was not the case of Chile though. Chile's deformed process of industrial development was not antagonistic to foreign interests. Actually, industrialization was largely carried out with the financial "support" and technical involvement of both U. S. corporations and U. S. governmental institutions.

Foreign capital began to penetrate Latin American internal markets beginning in the late 1950's; it was the reaction of international capitalism to import substitution. Latin American protectionist barriers were overcome through the integration of foreign and domestic resources under the form of monopoly capitalism under U. S. control.

In the case of Chile, the process of foreign penetration started later, during the 1960's, and did not reach the level of penetration that was attained in Argentina, Brazil or Mexico. However, Chilean industrialization based on import substitution has been conditioned and dependent

---

[3] Chile avoided the long anarchic period that followed independence in most Latin American countries. The feud between the two dominant political fractions of the 1820's ended quite early with the victory of the "pelucones" (conservatives) over the "pipolos" (liberals) in the Civil War of 1829.

on U. S. financial support and licensing agreements, thus making Chile as dependent on the United States as the rest of Latin America.

In the first section of this essay we describe the evolution of the two sectors which in turn have constituted the "dynamic" basis of the Chilean economic development from the last quarter of the nineteenth to the twentieth century: the export mining and industrial sectors.

In the second part we analyze Chile's more significant political movements emphasizing, first, the ways in which they have been connected to the interests and ideological orientations of the different social classes and groupings; second, the ways in which they have "mediated" the socio-economic processes relative to each of the forms of economic dependence that we distinguish; and third, the role that the different movements would probably play during the popular government that took power in November 1970.

CHANGING STYLES OF DEPENDENCE

Chilean economic development until 1880 was largely based on agricultural activity, primarily wheat. As was the case under the colonial government, in the post-independence period the expansion of Chilean agriculture was heavily dependent on the demand in world markets, controlled by European commercial capital (Leiva, 1970). During the nineteenth century, a number of important infrastructure programs geared toward the development of commercialized agriculture were successfully implemented: roads, railroads, ports and shipping linking Chilean agriculture to European markets were developed (Amunategui, 1932, pp. 341–42). Most of the agricultural units involved in trade were large landed properties owned by Chileans. European investors were mainly involved in the financial and commercial aspects of the enterprise.

Chilean society, in the first half of the nineteenth century, was made up of a small group of large landowners, a mass of landless peasants and a stratum of urban artisans and businessmen. Chile was a dependent agricultural-commercial capitalist society, not a closed "feudal" society (Frank, 1967). Chilean wheat was not grown primarily for consumption on the large estates in a feudal pattern. Neither the estates nor their owners were economically isolated. Instead, agricultural investors were linked to export markets, operated on the profit principle, and were deeply involved in a variety of financial and commercial activities, and in some cases mining (McBride, 1936: 204). Paternalistic and particularistic social relations, characteristic of feudalism, maintained peasants in optimal conditions for exploitation and profit maximization. The existence of foreign markets for agricultural products provided an incentive for the owners to maximize production while depressing consumption among agricultural workers. But traditional social relations prevented workers from acting collectively through unions to defend themselves. Thus, "feudal" social patterns buttressed the power and authority of the agricultural economic elites who in turn were immersed in capitalist market relations.

The fluctuations in Chilean economic development reflected the changing demand pattern in the world market. As in the colonial period, Chilean economic development was largely determined by decisions made in Europe. The colonial nature of the economy persisted: Chile remained an exporter of raw materials and an importer of finished goods. During the colonial period, Chilean economic changes had been largely determined by decisions made in Europe. The Indian communities—mostly sedentary in the center and the north, and mostly nomadic in the extreme south—were all but wiped out. Men and women were forced into quasi-slavery and serfdom, and the communal lands were expropriated. The *encomienda*—whereby both the land and the labor force attached to it were transferred to *peninsulares* (Spaniards)—and simple land give-aways were used in order to effect the dispossession. The economic life of the colony was oriented to the production of gold and silver in order to meet the economic needs of the Spanish Crown. The precious metals were exported to Spain; the mother country, in turn, controlled the commercial sector of the colony, and banned all industrial activities which could compete with Spanish manufacturers. The colonial pattern persisted after independence: Chile remained an exporter of raw materials and bullion, and an importer of finished goods.[4] Between 1860 and 1875 Great Britain received over fifty-five percent of Chilean exports and provided over thirty-four percent of her imports (Leiva, 1970). Chilean development was not based on the growth of an internal market, linked to the emergence of an industrial capitalist class. Rather its agro-commercial elite promoted a liberal trade policy that perpetuated Chile's economic dependence on industrial imports and agricultural and mining exports. That the Chilean predominant class promoted a liberal trade policy was not fortuitous. From its point of view it was much more convenient to follow the easy course of concentrating on the less risky ventures—i.e. extensive agriculture based on absentee ownership and servitude, and rudimentary mining—rather than to engage in other activities which would have required more initiative and the acceptance of greater chances. The moderate protectionist stand that the Chilean gov-

---

[4] The production of precious metals in Chile never reached level of Peru and Mexico. Thus, the *Capitanía General de Chile* always remained a second-rate colony from the point of view of the Crown.

ernments had adopted before 1860 was replaced by a more liberal policy towards foreign finished goods. This shift coincided with the massive expansion of English goods and capital. The Chilean oligarchy preferred not to antagonize the Englishmen—who as we have seen were buying over half of Chilean exports—and to leave domestic artisan production without any protection.

From the colonial period to the present day this general pattern of economic dependence has prevailed though there have been changes in the particular products which have been involved in the commercial transactions and the pattern of ownership of the export sector. Though agriculture was the predominant economic activity in the first half of the nineteenth century, Chilean entrepreneurs were also busy exploiting mining operations. Annual copper production (the main mining product till the 1870's) increased 2,000 tons during the first thirty-five years (Vergara, 1970). In 1850 copper production rose from 10,500 tons to 45,000 tons; by the 1860's Chile was producing 44 percent of the world's copper (Vergara, 1970). More importantly, the mines were owned and operated by Chilean nationals. Chilean copper production began to decline after 1876 and during the 1890's production was one-half that of the 1870's, largely as a result of increases in production elsewhere (Leiva, 1970). By the 1890's Chile was producing 6 percent of world output.

Nitrate deposits which Chile seized after its successful war with Peru provided a new basis of economic expansion. Nitrate exports jumped from 226,000 tons in 1880 to more than fourteen million tons in 1900 (Leiva, 1970). In the 1870's the nitrate fields were owned by Chileans and Peruvians; by the beginning of the twentieth century the takeover by foreign-firms was complete.

PROPORTION OF CAPITAL IN NITRATES BY NATIONALITY (PERCENTAGES)

	ENGLISH	NATIONALIZED (EUROPEANS)	CHILEANS	PERUVIAN-CHILEANS
1878	13	20	—	67
1884	34	30	36	—
1901	55	30	15	—

Source: Leiva, 1970, p. 22.

English capitalists, largely financed by Chilean bank loans, bought out Peruvian holdings and subsequently expanded their economic position at the expense of the Chileans (Ramírez, 1969, Ch. 3). The taking over of nitrate exploitation by English firms is one of the most paradoxical events of Chilean history. The country fought and won a war in order to take the nitrate fields away from Peru, then turned them over to the English-men. Furthermore, the technology of production was quite simple, and no large investments were required. By the beginning of the twentieth century, control over Chile's main export product was in the hands of English firms who proceeded to export their sizeable earnings to the home country. The nitrate exported to England was processed, and a variety of products were elaborated, thus providing new jobs and more income. It has been estimated that sixty percent of the nitrate earnings remained in England helping that country develop while keeping Chile under-developed. As early as 1881 mining exports amounted to 67 percent of the total while agriculture accounted for less than 15 percent; the propor-tion widened and has not yet been challenged in the twentieth century (Vergara, 1970, p. 21).[5] Thus an enclave—both geographically isolated from the most populated regions, and owned by foreigners—replaced agriculture as Chile's most dynamic economic sector. This change was to have profound consequences during the twentieth century. The long tradition of struggle of the Chilean working class was inaugurated in the *salitreras* (nitrate fields). Miners and nitrate workers constituted for many decades the vanguard of the proletariat. On the other hand, foreign ownership of the most important economic resources allowed for a relative degree of autonomy of the government *vis-à-vis* the domestic oligarchy.

COMPOSITION OF EXPORTS
(IN PERCENTAGES)

	MINING PRODUCTS	AGRICULTURAL PRODUCTS	INDUSTRIAL PRODUCTS
1928–1929	87	10	3
1952–1953	77	12	11

Beginning in the late nineteenth century, U. S. investors began to com-pete with the British for control of Chile's basic wealth. With the rise in demand for copper, U. S. investors, with an initial investment of $2.3 million, in the course of a century accumulated investments totaling over five hundred million dollars, almost exclusively made up of reinvested profits, not new capital (Vera, 1961).

Welcomed and protected by the traditional elite, foreign capital flooded Chile. By the end of the First World War U. S. investment dominated the important mining sector of the economy surpassing the English. In

[5] In 1967 mineral products accounted for eighty-five percent of total Chilean ex-ports. Copper alone accounted for seventy percent and industrial goods only four-teen percent.

1912 U. S. investment was calculated at $15 million, a sum that rose to $451 million by 1928 (Jobet, 1955, p. 209).

Sectors of the non-agricultural economy such as mining, which generated foreign exchange capable of providing capital to make Chile a modern industrial society, were owned by capitalists from the northern industrialized societies who proceeded to skim off the profits. Chile's raw materials were made available to U. S. and European industrial complexes. The equitable distribution of benefits supposed to accrue from this "international division of labor" to both the suppliers of raw materials and the industrial metropolis were not forthcoming. Revenue from the mining sector helped perpetuate the landholding class and strengthened its political and social domination. Taxes on the landed property of the *latifundistas* were eliminated or greatly reduced (Petras, 1969, Ch. 3). The second half of the nineteenth century witnessed a profound transformation of Chile's socio-economic structure, and its complete integration into the international capitalist system. The process of modernization did not involve, though, the displacement of the more "traditional" structures by the "modern" ones. There was a process of accommodation whereby the new (and mostly foreign) groups led the process of expansion of foreign trade without seriously challenging the backward sector based on servile exploitation. The foreign groups who controlled the mining enterprises transferred a fraction of their surplus to the domestic dominant classes in the way of export taxes. The Chilean state, tightly controlled by the landowners of the Central Valley and the large merchants of Santiago and Valparaíso returned in kind through the continuous repression of the militant nitrate proletariat.

First through nitrate and then through copper the Chilean economy was integrated into a world economic system based on the international division of labor which, it was presumed, would last forever. In the Chilean case, the dependent position of providers of raw materials within the world system was thus aggravated by the country's reliance on one single export commodity. This dependence in turn distorted Chile's internal development: the extractive industries towered over the rest of the economy and there was no capital accumulation within Chile. Most of the surplus value derived from nitrate and copper was appropriated by the foreign capitalists, and the rest was transferred to the domestic oligarchy, which did not need to risk these resources in other economic ventures. The result of the alliance was convenient for both the major (and foreign) and the minor (and domestic) partners.

Foreign investors were successful in capturing strategic economic sectors largely because of the support they received from domestic Chilean elites. Once penetrating Chilean society, the foreign mining interests were able to influence domestic elites into taking positions favorable to foreign investment. In 1890 the Chilean National Mining Society, in the course of expressing its approval of a new mining code, stated that "it would contribute to the influx of foreign capital" (Vergara, 1970, p. 36). Even that sector of the Chilean bourgeoisie, directly connected with an industry affected by the foreign presence, did not develop a "nationalist" position, as early as the end of the nineteenth century. The Chilean bourgeoisie preferred the security of being functionaries of U. S. companies, the benefits that accrued to the state from taxation of U. S.-owned mines, and control over the medium and small mines (nitrate and copper) rather than attempt to compete with foreign capital.

One reason for the lack of a "nationalist bourgeoisie" was that most mining entrepreneurs also held important holdings in other sectors of the economy. The participation of Chilean mining entrepreneurs in other economic activity, such as finance and agriculture, which are closely tied to foreign investors and markets, undercut the formation of a nationalist political consciousness. A recent study of the leadership of the National Mining Society found that 52 percent were involved in other types of economic activity, largely agriculture and finance (Vergara, 1970, Ch. 6). Among the top leadership (presidents), sixty-two, or 62.5 percent were involved in other economic activity besides mining—largely finance (Vergara, 1970, Ch. 6). As a result, the overwhelming majority of mining entrepreneurs were members of the Liberal, Conservative, and Radical Parties, whose policies favored the expansion of foreign investment (Vergara, 1970, Ch. 6).

SIGNIFICANCE AND IMPACT OF FOREIGN OWNERSHIP

Frequently it has been argued that foreign investment has a salutary effect on the development of the dependent countries: it brings capital, provides jobs and pays high salaries, and stimulates industrial growth. Rather than bringing capital into Chile, foreign-owned enterprises have served as the most important channel for the de-capitalization of the country. Between 1910 and 1960, U. S. investors remitted over $4,000 million to the United States while the sum total of U. S. investment is less than $1,000 million (Caputo and Pizarro, 1970, pp. 184–85). Thus foreign investment has been a major determinant of Chilean underdevelopment.

While it is true that Chilean copper workers receive a higher salary than the average Chilean worker, it is also true that copper workers are much more productive. Chilean copper workers at the same level of productivity as U. S. copper workers receive one-eighth the hourly salary (Cademartori, 1968, pp. 123 passim). Apart from wages, the living conditions in most U. S.-owned Chilean mining towns is greatly inferior to those of the United States. In sum the intensity of exploitation by U. S. mining firms in Chile is much greater than that found in the United States.

In terms of employment, the increasing mechanization of production has displaced many workers—without providing them with new jobs. In 1945 the U. S.-owned mines employed twenty-five thousand workers and in 1968 they employed seventeen thousand despite a 50 percent increase in productivity (Cademartori, 1968, pp. 123 passim). In addition, much of the machinery is imported from the United States, thus minimizing the impact of the copper industry on the economy. Likewise only a very small fraction of the raw material is processed within Chile. In effect the foreign-owned copper mines and nitrate fields resemble "colonial enclaves," geographically part of Chile but economically an extension of the U. S. economy. Chile's dependence on the United States, rather than promoting development, has served to perpetuate underdevelopment.

In the twentieth century, the Chilean class structure has been shaped by the continuance of the traditional landed elite entwined with emerging urban elites and by a foreign-controlled export sector. Consequently, there developed a middle class which lacked control over major economic resources and utilized the state as its instrument for social mobility and public enterprises (many of which were later turned over to private investors). The lack of an agrarian reform and the high concentration of land ownership generated a large landless peasantry which, for a considerable period in history, was controlled by the landlords but now has become a basis for radical political movements (Petras and Zeitlin, 1970). The exploitation and organization of the great mining centers by foreign capital produced a homogeneous occupational community of miners who have been the most solid basis of socialist and communist support (Petras and Zeitlin, 1970). The decline of the export sector and the expansion of government activity during the world depression of the 1930's and during the Second World War forced the pace of industrialization, creating a substantial industrial proletariat, largely supportive of leftist parties (Petras and Zeitlin, 1970).

THE INDUSTRIAL DEVELOPMENT PROCESS

Dependency of Chile upon the nature and evolution of the international capitalist system has been of overwhelming and omnipresent importance. The development of the country's manufacturing sector could not escape the influence of Western imperialism. The internal characteristics of the sector and the way it related to other economic sectors during the late nineteenth and twentieth centuries were largely determined by the dominant capitalist countries. However, the insertion of Chile's economy in

the world market suffered constant and profound modifications throughout the period. Consequently, the manufacturing sector, though in a
different fashion than other economic sectors, was affected by the quantitative (substantial growth of industrial capacity) and qualitative (from
artisan to manufacturer) changes that took place. The development of
Chile's industrial sector could be subdivided into three periods: 1880–
1932, 1932–1956, and 1956–1970.

THE 1880–1932 PERIOD

During most of this half century the relationship of Chile's economy with
foreign capitalism was established through the nitrate industry which was
controlled by foreign (mainly English) firms. Nitrate producers were
one of the factions of what Chilean historian Claudio Véliz ingeniously
called "La Mesa de Tres Patas" (The Three-Legged Table). They, together with the big landowners of the southern region and the import
firms, constituted the triumvirate which controlled the lion's share of
Chile's economic resources. It should be noted that the country's agricultural sector which exported wheat and flour to California, Australia,
and Europe, started to decay during the late nineteenth century.

Because of the centrality of these three groups, most analysts of Chile's
economic and social processes have tended to assume that industry beyond
the artisan level did not exist before 1930. In adhering to this sort of
interpretation, they unduly underemphasized the importance of pre-1930
industrial production. Since the end of the War of the Pacific[6] textile
and food and beverage industries and sophisticated machine shops acquired considerable importance. Muñoz (1968 p. 16) cites evidence of
English and American consular agents who reported the existence of
plants where railroad cars and even locomotives were being built. The
expansion of railroad lines and nitrate production often made it economic
to build parts and engines rather than to import them and pay considerable transportation costs.

Domestic industrial production, however, did not enter in conflict with
imported manufactured articles and those who wanted to keep imports
cheap—the landowners, importers and miners. Chilean industries complemented, rather than competed with, imports. An example of this
complementarity and of the absence of conflict, was the Sociedad de
Fomento Fabril or the Chilean Manufacturers Association, which was
founded in 1883 by the landholders' association, the Sociedad Nacional
de Agricultura. Véliz was probably right when he pointed out that

[6] The war developed between 1879 and 1882 and pitted Chile against Peru and
Bolivia. Its more important effects were the annexation by Chile of one Bolivian
and two Peruvian provinces and the subsequent appropriation of the nitrate fields,
which were located in the conquered territories, by English nationals.

northern nitrate exporters (as well as southern agrarian exporters and Santiago's importers) ". . . continued buying their clothes in London, providing their women with luxuries in Paris, buying furniture in Italy, tasting French wines and liquors, importing silk, velvet, jewels and glass . . ." (Véliz, 1963, pp. 238–39). He failed, however, to consider the possibility that the consumption of the masses perhaps was not satisfied through imported articles.[7] A recent hypothesis that has yet to be adequately supported suggests that domestic industrial production satisfied to a large proportion the needs of the working classes in cities and nitrate fields. Data has not yet been uncovered to enable us to measure the significance of domestic industrial production before 1914.

When the output levels of the dynamic sectors of the economy (the export- and import-oriented businesses) fluctuated according to the ups and downs of the international market, industrial manufacturers usually were profoundly affected. Sometimes, as during the 1920–21 recession, this meant serious drops of industrial production and innumerable bankruptcies. However, industrial entrepreneurs did not challenge the existing economic structure and the consequences of its functioning. From a purely short-term economic standpoint they behaved rationally in doing so; as long as external conditions remained unmodified, their successful adaptation to the prevailing system was easily accomplished.

THE 1932–1955 PERIOD

Chile's economy was hard hit by the world crisis of the early thirties. Nitrate production, which had already been affected by the development of synthetic substitutes since the First World War, collapsed. Resources derived from exports were reduced to a little over one-ninth in three years, declining from $277.4 million in 1929 to $34.1 million in 1932 (Cademartori, 1968: 214). The capacity to import was thus drastically reduced. As a result the domestic market-oriented manufacturing sector displaced export-oriented mining as the dynamic sector of the economy. Up to 1930 export-oriented mining had been the dynamic element of the economy, its rate of growth and short-term fluctuations determining the growth rate and cyclical ups and downs of the whole economy.

In addition to the shift of the leading economic sector from mining to domestically-oriented industry, significant changes in the composition of the manufacturing sector occurred in the thirties and forties. A whole new set of industries developed, including a steel mill. New lines such as chemicals and metallurgical industries acquired greater importance at the expense of the more traditional production of nondurable consump-

---

[7] Actually, Véliz seems to deny the possibility; he gives as an example—that perhaps should not be taken seriously—the fact that ". . . (their) 'huasos' wore English-made ponchos" (p. 239).

tion goods such as clothing and food processing. (Muñoz, 1968: 160–161). However, these changes did not result in a substantial increase in the growth rate of the economy as a whole.

The qualitative transformation of the Chilean economy in the 1930's and 1940's influenced economic historians and other social scientists to ignore the considerable significance of the manufacturing sector before 1930. It was assumed that the curve of industrial growth experienced a sharp increase (some would say from a value close to zero) after the world crisis. However, recent analyses based on more refined data have tended to disprove that sort of interpretation: Muñoz (1968: 26) found that pre-1930 and post-1930 rates of growth of gross industrial value were similar.

The increasing centrality of the industrial sector has been seen as a cause (sometimes as a consequence) of unavoidable and actual conflict between industrial entrepreneurs and the economically dominant groups. According to this interpretation, industrialists have played the role of leaders—or co-leaders—of the transition "from neo-feudal agriculture to semi-industrial capitalism." [8] John Johnson, from whom the quoted expression was taken, was one of the first and leading exponents of this sort of approach. Its core hypothesis, which was based on the consideration of five Latin American cases—Argentina, Brazil, Chile, Mexico and Uruguay—is overly simplistic: urban middle sectors are modernizing and are democratic and politically moderate, while the landowning elite is traditionalist, authoritarian, and politically reactionary.[9] Johnson advanced the hypothesis that the urban-rural cleavage became critical since the beginning of the process of "economic modernization" that started around 1880. The trend of multiplication and consolidation of pre-existing middle sectors, like professionals, was reinforced by the appearance of merchants, in a first stage, and financial and industrial groups in a second one. One of the major weaknesses of the thesis of "The-Emergence-of-the-Middle-Sectors" is that it erroneously characterizes nineteenth century Latin American socio-economic systems as feudal or semi-feudal. Such an interpretation ignores the relationship to the international economic system, as well as the mercantile background and rela-

[8] Johnson (1958, pp. 43–44) explicitly states that "(middle sectors) had a vital interest in the issue brought to the surface by the transition from neo-feudal agriculture to semi-industrial capitalism . . . the leaders of the middle sectors seized the opportunity to place themselves at the head of the new political amalgams, whose popular bases lay in the lower levels of the social pyramid and more particularly in the urban industrial working groups . . . the new middle sector leadership promised not only economic progress but social democracy."

[9] The more unsophisticated ingredients of the approach show striking coincidences with the political postulates of the Alliance for Progress, established in the early sixties.

tively recent origin of large portions of the landowning oligarchy. Johnson's "original sin," which has been shared by many American and Latin American social scientists,[10] pervades the analysis of the post-1930 import-substitution period. The mistake is to consider the relation between the agro-mining elites and urban industrialists as an antagonistic one. The process, therefore, is pictured as the consolidation of one system at the expense of the other, while both groups should be seen as complementary parts of a relatively integrated system. This later hypothesis refers to long-term structural conditions; the existence of conjunctural conflicts over given economic issues between different sectors of the dominant classes does not contradict it.

We have described some of the weaknesses of the above approach in order to emphasize its association with (or its responsibility for) a number of prevalent myths about the industrialists' economic and political role and the nature and consequences of import-substitution industrialization in Latin America, and more particularly in Chile. The myths deserve closer inspection.

Myth 1: *Industrialization promoted the country's economic growth.* As described above, industrial growth rates before and after 1930 were similar. Therefore the Chilean experience does not provide a suitable test of this myth. However, it may be worthwhile to note that the small changes which occurred in growth rates of industrial value added and per capital income were negatively correlated, the reverse of what this notion would lead us to expect.[11]

Myth 2: *Industrialization made a considerable contribution to income redistribution.* The growth rate of industrial value added in the period from 1915 to 1964 was 4.3 percent. Despite this growth, salaries and wages declined relative to gross value added to the industrial sector,[12]

---

[10] One of the most recent neo-versions of the above mentioned theories is offered by Mamalakis (1969, pp. 9–46).

[11] Approximate average annual rates of increase of per capita income were as follows: (Rates have been determined by the authors upon data supplied by Mamalakis [1965] and CEPAL [1951: 300]).

1915–1924	2.9%
1924–1927	1.8%
1927–1937	2.9%
1937–1945	1.9%
1945–1950	1.3%
1950–1957	1.6%
1957–1964	0.3%

[12] The relative proportion of salaries and wages in relationship to gross value added of the industrial sector was as follows (Muñoz, 1968:195):

indicating greater rather than less inequality in income distribution. Moreover, if we consider the impact that the import-substitution process had upon income redistribution within the whole economy, it is apparent that all the gains made by non-propertied groups went to the upper strata of the working class; i.e. white-collar workers. Pinto (1962, p. 185) gave the following data:

	1940=100	1948	1953
Wages	100	103	107
Salaries	100	109	146
Entrepreneurs' remuneration	100 *	125	160

Within the fourteen year span, the proportion of active population in each economic group remained approximately the same; blue-collar workers 57 percent, white-collar workers 11.5 percent, entrepreneurs (including self-employed) 31.5 percent.

Another Index Of Income Concentration Is Given By The Percentages Of Direct And Indirect Taxes (Ibid, 195)[13]

	DIRECT TAXES	INDIRECT TAXES
1940	43.4%	56.6%
1941	44.5%	55.5%
1942	48.6%	61.4%
1943	51.7%	48.3%
1944	45.6%	54.4%
1945	41.8%	58.2%
1946	39.7%	60.3%
1947	41.5%	58.5%
1948	39.4%	60.6%
1949	36.4%	63.4%
1950	38.5%	61.5%
1951	35.0%	65.0%
1952	37.7%	62.3%
1953	33.9%	66.1%

Myth 3: *Industrialization was the motor force of the country's modernization through the absorption by the manufacturing sector of a sizable proportion of the migrant population' coming from the countryside.* The

1914–1916	.331
1938–1940	.305
1951–1953	.376
1960–1961	.262

[13] Direct taxes supposedly are more likely to tax income on the ability to pay while indirect taxes most commonly are levied on items consumed by those least capable of paying.

percentage of economically active population employed in agriculture, hunting and fishing has been declining since 1940. However, new urban dwellers have not been absorbed by manufacturing industries (Instituto de Economía, 1963, p. 15). Between 1940 and 1960, the proportion of the economically active population in agriculture, hunting and fishing declined by 7.5 percent (from 35 percent to 27.5 percent) while the proportion of the economically active population in manufacturing industries increased by only 0.3 percent (from 16.9 percent to 17.2 percent).

Myth 4: *Industrialization resulted in a reduction of Chile's dependence upon foreign interests.* Chile's process of import substituting industrialization did not increase the country's autonomy: The newly established industries—most of which were always dependent on foreign equipment, licences, and know-how—developed lines of production complementary to, rather than competitive with the economies of the industrialized countries.

Four major factors determined the nature of the process of industrialization:

First, the radical reduction of the amount of foreign exchange that could be spent in buying manufactured goods (during the war years this was coupled with a parallel and drastic reduction of the goods that industrialized countries were prepared to sell the countries that usually provided them with raw materials);

Second, the realization on the part of Chile's industrialists and would-be industrialists that increased levels of protection and substantial state economic support could turn hitherto unattractive ventures into profitable businesses—no matter how inefficient they happened to be if an international scale of comparison were applied;

Third, the "catalyzing" function performed by a small group of *técnicos* —professionals with technical background and orientation—who filled strategic positions in different public agencies, particularly in CORFO (National Development Corporation) which was created in 1939. These *técnicos,* and particularly CORFO's engineers—*los ingenieros de CORFO* —were actually more strongly convinced about the necessity and convenience of industrial development than Chile's industrialists themselves. They not only had the last say about the use to which a large proportion of the resources that were poured into the industrial sector were put, but they also seem to have provided the "industrializing ethos" that the industrial bourgeoisie was clearly unable to articulate by itself;

Finally, the support that American and international banking organizations—the latter also largely controlled by the United States—gave to the programs of economic promotion set forth by the Chilean government during the 1940's.

American economic support and technical assistance were particularly important. Both the projects assisting private manufacturers and the development of the major sectors of the infrastructure were closely tied to the U.S., either directly, as in the case of power and steel, or indirectly as in the case of oil and tire production. The loans contracted by the National Development Corporation with American (public and private) banking institutions, like the Export Import Bank, or international organizations (largely controlled by the United States), like the International Bank for Reconstruction and Development suffered severe restrictions, however. They were always tied to the purchase of American (used or new) goods and equipment. The first loans negotiated with the Eximport Bank

> . . . gave the bank the right to know in advance the type of operations that the National Development Corporation planned to undertake. The (Chilean) agency had to periodically submit to the bank the plans and projects approved by its Board of Directors which would require the bank's financial support, . . . (*Industria*; May 1940)

Conditions were even more astringent in a loan authorized by the Bank three years later: it was understood that the National Development Corporation

> . . . would use (it) to import equipment manufactured, and raw materials substantially produced in the United States; both the equipment and the raw materials *could only be used in projects approved by* Chile's President of the Republic and *the Eximport Bank.* (emphasis added) (*Industria*; April 1943)

Actually, there is no need to overemphasize the fact that during the Radical years both the American government and business tended not to display excessive enthusiasm toward any manifestation of autonomous industrial (or other) development in Latin America. In that sense, to make projects dependent upon the approval of the Eximport Bank would not seem to have provided an altogether auspicious point of departure for this new stage of Chile's industrial growth.

In addition, American loans were probably burdened with even more serious economic and political restrictions. The first series of American loans were connected to the 1942 agreement by which the Chilean government guaranteed a stable price of 12 cents per pound of copper to the United States during the war. Post-war loans of both the Eximport Bank and the IBRD might have constituted a pay-off for President González Videla's sudden, and complete turnabout of 1947. In this action the Communist party was outlawed immediately after occupying three ministerial positions, and the so-called Law for the Defense of Democracy was enacted.[14]

Finally, the involvement of foreign technicians and consulting firms in all of Chile's strategic developmental projects was another consequence of American participation.

THE 1955–1970 PERIOD

Since 1929 industrial production had been growing; this trend came to a halt in 1955. The structural limitations of Chile's economic market, the exhaustion of the easy import-substitution possibilities, and the temporary but severe decline of copper prices, confronted the country with a dilemma: either a radical transformation of the basic features of the socio-economic structure should be attempted, or strict economic measures should be implemented in order to try to mitigate the effects of the most evident contradictions of the system. The second alternative was chosen. The implementation of a rigid and orthodox anti-inflationary plan, which was largely imposed and dictated by the International Monetary Fund, brought about a recession that affected all economic sectors.

The declining trend started to be reversed by the pro-business administration under Jorge Alessandri who took office at the end of 1958. The new government implemented two types of measures in order to revitalize the economy: a credit system designed to subsidize the construction of private housing for middle-income groups; and direct foreign investment through the liberalization of previous restrictions. As a consequence of the new policies (and of the modifications of the conditions of the world market), direct foreign investment increased considerably. Sectoral rates of growth of foreign investment, however, varied greatly while direct investment in mining increased approximately 10 percent from $517 to $586 million between 1960 and 1968; it more than tripled in commerce and manufacturing industries during the same years from $34 to $107 million (Caputo and Pizarro, 1970, pp. 184–85). The shift in the orientation that these figures suggest became even more apparent after 1966. Its effects were significant; it meant that for the first time foreign capital

[14] The case for the first hypothesis is significantly strengthened by the fact that the 12 cents price level resulted in a significant loss for Chile. During the war years, 2,700,000 tons of copper were exported to the United States; since the 1946 price—once the price control was lifted—was 24 cents (24.3 cents as an average between 1946 and 1954), and the Chilean government received 62 percent of the value of copper exports—through the imposition of both a differential exchange rate and an extraordinary tax, the loss amounted to 430 million dollars. (CEDEM, 1969, passim). The argument for the second hypothesis seems less clear-cut, since González Videla was also to make significant, though short-lived, internal political gains thanks to his anti-communist stand.

became interested in Chile's internal market, in domestic consumption of goods produced within the country. Compared to foreign capital in Argentina and Brazil, $107 million was a relatively low figure. It did, however, enable foreign firms to control almost 40 percent of the active stock of private large industrial corporations (Garreton O. and Cisternas J.). This control was obtained at a relatively low cost, considering the amount of resources that were really brought into Chile and it brought considerable benefits to foreign firms. With respect to effective capital investments, Bitar (1970, p. 6) found that between 1960 and 1969—under the new legislation sanctioned by the Alessandri government—$145 million were invested in the industrial sector. While only $28 million was invested by private firms, the bulk was provided by loans of foreign and *domestic* institutions and retentions of earnings. Moreover, foreign firms tended to concentrate their investments in monopolistic or oligopolistic markets. Bitar points out that

> A recent completed study of CORFO analyzes a set of 22 firms with over 50 percent of foreign participation that have been founded in the last eight years. In half of the cases they operate in monopolistic or oligopolistic markets; in 36 percent of the cases they are the leading producers in their respective sectors; i.e., 86 percent of the firms are either completely dominant or leaders in their sectors. (Idem, p. 5)

Aranda and Martínez have made a brief, though vivid, description of the country's economic structure: ". . . a deformed system of monopolistic capitalist relations that pervades the spheres of production, circulation and finance" (Aranda and Martínez, 1970, p. 154). The new leftist government, elected in 1970, has announced some measures that might precede a radical alteration of one of the most important ingredients of that system, its industrial sector: state control of banking deposits; and governmental "orientation" of production in the car industry, in order to increase production of trucks and small cars and stop producing medium-sized large cars.

It seems, however, that these may be the first, but not the last, steps. Further policy measures might be directed towards: nationalizing the country's industrial sector; re-orienting production in order to alter the present situation whereby the most dynamic industrial sectors are producing goods for only 25 percent of the population of the country; and redistributing industrial wealth and establishing mechanisms for the appropriation by workers of productivity increases. Such strategy, if implemented, would without doubt drastically reduce the political power of industrial entrepreneurs and other bourgeois groups. The pattern of Chile's economic development has been closely linked to the fortune of the numerous political forces competing for power. The policies adopted by the parties have significantly affected the emerging socio-economic forces shaping the Chilean economy.

CONTRASTING POLITICAL PERSPECTIVES: THE RADICAL PARTY

The stability of Chile's political system during the present century has been considerable. Except for a comparatively brief period of eight years from 1924 to 1932,[15] constitutional rules have been uniformly observed and every administration has assumed power according to previously existing formal norms. Two political phenomena have largely contributed to this outcome:

First, the fact that the Radical Party, particularly during the period it controlled the presidency, from 1938 to 1952, played both as a "mediatized" political representative of certain bourgeois groups and as a mechanism for the effecting of economic concessions to some segments of the non-dominant classes, specially white-collar workers;

Second, the considerable electoral strength shown by the Right throughout the post-1930 period, which is demonstrated by the fact that the rightist coalition won the 1958 presidential elections and was narrowly defeated by the leftist Unidad Popular or Popular Unity coalition in 1970 when the rightist candidate, Jorge Alessandri, got 34.98 percent of the votes against the 36.30 percent obtained by Socialist, Salvador Allende.

In the following two sections we examine these phenomena paying special attention to those characterstics that may help to explain the present configuration of the Chilean polity.

The Radical party has been usually characterized as the ". . . medium of political expression of the middle class" (Gil, 1966, p. 297). In turn, those who, like Gil, subscribe to this interpretation, attribute the frequent shifts that the party's position on central economic and political issues has experimented, to the basic ambiguity that has supposedly plagued

[15] In 1924, the President, Arturo Alessandri, a member of the Liberal Party who had demagogically pleaded for the support of the urban populace, was ousted from power by the top leadership of the Armed Forces. A year later a clique of young officers led by Colonel Ibáñez reinstated Alessandri in office; however, as soon as Alessandri discovered that Ibáñez wanted to keep a major political role, he resigned. Ibáñez became Chile's strongman, either as the power behind the regime—between 1925 and 1927 or as President—between 1927 and 1931. In July of this last year a popular revolt prompted the Armed Forces to cease supporting Ibáñez. During the following 18 months, one constitutional regime and several de facto governments—including a self-denominated socialist republic—alternated in power until Alessandri reassumed the presidency as the winning candidate of a coalition of the rightist Conservative and Liberal parties and the Radical party.

middle-class ideology. In trying to reveal the class origin of party leaders and followers, these authors have found that they were predominantly middle-class. Without denying the relevance of those considerations, particularly of the social origin of Radical supporters, we will try to supplement that sort of analysis through the consideration of an alternative question: whose interests and ideological preferences were served by party actions during the last forty years? In answering these questions, two aspects, usually ignored by political scientists, are taken into account: that a given political party may perform altogether different functions in different historical periods; and the a priori assumption that there has to be an absolute correlation between class origin of party leaders and groups' interests which are preferentially served by a party should be dismissed.

The Radical party was founded in 1861. In very few years it became (in addition to the traditional Liberal, Conservative and National parties) one of the most active players in the elitist game of Chilean politics. As such it participated in numerous ministerial coalitions before, during and after the Parliamentary Republic was established in 1891 when a feud between President Balmaceda and Congress turned into a civil war. The war ended with the victory of the congressional forces that were supported by the British interests; Balmaceda's increasingly nationalistic policies had started to threaten the interests of foreign capitalists and associated domestic groups. The 1925 Constitution reestablished the presidential system.

However, it was not until 1938 that the Radicals were able to capture the presidency. A change in their tactics affected this outcome. Instead of continuing to perform an important, but non-dominant role within the changing coalitions of the hitherto stable politics of notables, the party became the major partner of an altogether different coalition that included two new political forces, Communists and Socialists.

The pre-1938 record of the party anticipated subsequent development. Its position over basic economic and political issues and the policies it attempted to implement were not antagonistic to the economic interests of Chile's dominant classes—the country's agro-mercantile bourgeoisie and its foreign allies, the British and American firms who consecutively controlled the country's mining sector. In addition to holding key positions in most administrations between 1891 and 1920, the party helped to elect Arturo Alessandri both in 1920 and 1932, and it actually supported Alessandri up to the very moment of joining the Popular Front in 1937. Even after that event Radical leaders were ready to accept Alessandri's offer to join his government; the agreement was blocked by the rightist presidential candidate, Alessandri's own Minister of Finance. Despite their continuous and formal support of free and extended suffrage, the Radicals did not challenge the highly corrupt political system which had favored the persistence of machines, that resulted in the percentage of voter participation in elections fluctuating between 5 and 8 percent of the total population. This sort of behavior was not casual. Actually, Radicals had been marginal to most previous political events that implied some sort of popular mobilization—especially the events surrounding the sanctioning of the 1925 Constitution and the hectic months between July 1931 and September 1932.

Systematic information about the pre-1938 social composition and electoral support of Chile's political parties is lacking. However, two trends are apparent in an examination of the rosters of Radical leaders and congressional representatives: first, the fact that most leaders were professionals, and in this sense the Radical party did not differ from most of the other parties, except the Communists; and second, the comparatively considerable influence of medium and small miners from the provinces north of Santiago and of landowners of the southernmost portion of Chile's central valley. This latter group differed from the aristocratic agrarian elite of the provinces closer to Santiago. They did not belong to the traditional families of Spanish ancestry, their fortunes were more recent, and they usually complained about State indifference toward their fate.

These two inconclusive trends should alert us about the mistake of considering the Radical party as *the* middle-class party, or even as a middle-class party. If we follow strictly the rule of considering the social origin of party leadership as the indicator of what specific class interests and ideological orientations are represented by a given party, we should have to conclude that all Chilean parties with the probable exception of the Communists (whose leaders generally were of working-class origins), are middle-class parties. The syllogism would operate in the following way: Professionals are a sector of the middle class. Most leaders of the Radical (Liberal/Conservative) party were professionals. Therefore, the Radical (Liberal/Conservative) party is a middle-class party.

What we are proposing instead is another, and hopefully more appropriate indicator: party stands on major political and economic issues that have affected asymmetrically the interests of the different social classes and the consequences of the party's concrete actions. Radical leaders were part of a "political class" [16] that initially was not directly tied to the interests of specific social groups. Radicals were a major force —the dominant political force during the 1938 to 1952 period—of a political game that as a whole favored the interests of the hegemonic fraction of Chile's dominant class: the financial and mercantile groups. The "traditional"—and so-called rightist—parties (Liberals and Conser-

[16] Our concept of political class largely overlaps with Aron's notion of "classe dirigeante" (Aron, 1960, p. 267).

vatives and their different factions) were another sector of that political class. The Right was actually very closely intertwined with a previously economically dominant social group, the landed oligarchy of the country's Central Valley. The Radicals access to power was the consequence of Radical landowners replacing the Right—which based most of its political power on the control exerted over the rural population; in this sense, Chile's landed aristocracy as a whole was a political class. The Radical party, however, had an entirely different political clientele, comprised generally of the urban petty bourgeoisie and salaried workers. However, both sectors of the political class similarly favored the interests of the economically dominant class.

The circumstance of considering Radicals as a part of a political class is not to be understood as an assertion of the absolute autonomy of governmental leaders from the dominant classes. Actually the influence of these groups persisted throughout the period; moreover, the many cases of Radical politicians turned into active and prominent entrepreneurs provided a further and quite direct bridge between industrial, commercial, and financial groups on one side and party leaders and governmental officials on the other.

Coincidental with this shift at the political level, external conditions forced a transformation of Chile's economic structure that brought about the expansion of the import substituting industrial sector. As a result of this trend, the industrial faction acquired considerable weight within the dominant bourgeoisie.[17]

We will examine both trends in order to determine the specific effects that the influence of the Radical party had on those processes. At the political level, the nature of the Radical clientele increased considerably the payoffs demanded by non-dominant groups, and more specifically by salaried workers or *empleados* both in the public and the private sector. However, as we have seen when discussing the process of industrialization, the resources required to make effective these concessions were not brought forth by the dominant class. The dominant classes and the *empleados* obtained, both in absolute and relative terms, a higher economic payoff extracted from the rest of the working class, that is the urban and rural proletariat (*obreros* and *campesinos*).

At the economic level, the partial displacement of the Right was highly functional for the consolidation of the trends that were developing. Inasmuch as increasing state regulation and direct economic intervention

[17] Tentative evidences that require further confirmation seem to support Brodersohn's hypothesis that ". . . the dominant sectors (the financial and mercantile bourgeoisie) have pushed the industrialization process . . . They turned to manufacturing activities after the profound crisis of 1929, and even before . . .". (1970, p. 323).

were required, the "modernizing" and statist political philosophy of the Radicals was much more suited to the objective necessities of the changing dominant class than the Manchesterian liberalism and orthodox "free-tradism" of Liberals and Conservatives.

The dominant class obtained important economic benefits during the Radical governments. The inflationary process, that acquired renewed impetus in the early forties, was the central mechanism through which the propertied groups managed to squeeze resources from the working class. Propertied groups, and more specifically, large enterpreneurs, were structurally better equipped than non-propertied groups to adapt successfully their behavior to inflationary pressures. Prices and salaries were continuously competing in an endless race in which salaries were always running behind. Entrepreneurs could resort, and indeed they did resort to direct price increases and tax evasion; in addition, they enjoyed preferential access to the usually liberal credit opportunities.

Market-oriented landowners were, relative to other entrepreneurial groups, in a less than optimal situation. Price controls, when operating, affected mostly prices of staples, and the access of landed groups to credit was increasingly limited during the 1938 to 1952 period. These trends, of course, were partially balanced by the absolute control they kept over the rural working force. Harsh economic exploitation continued to be the rule in the countryside, and the level of rewards remained strikingly low. The absolute absence of attempts to implement an agrarian reform was a characteristic of Radical regimes.

On the other hand, salaries and wages were bound to react to price hikes with at least a time lag of six months. This lag was not insignificant with inflation rates averaging 30 percent per year. Salaries and wages were theoretically to be readjusted each year according to the increases in the cost of living during the previous twelve months. However this practice was not systematically followed. Furthermore, the index of cost of living calculated by the government's statistics agency systematically underestimated actual price increases.

Even more significant was the increase in the level of coercion applied to the urban working class. During the Second World War the sacrifices of the working class, particularly of the non-salaried groups, were rationalized in terms of the contribution that they were making to the country's industrial and overall economic growth. As we have seen, contributions of other social groups were nil, or even negative. After the end of the war, and following the brief honeymoon of the newly elected Radical president, Gabriel González Videla, with the Communist party, energetic labor-repressive policies were enacted. The most important legislation though not the only one, was the 1948 Law of Defense of Democracy, under which the Communist party was banned and scores of Communists and other leftists were sent to a concentration camp in Chile's northern desert. Innumerable trade union leaders at the national and local levels were fired and jailed. A list of Communists in each plant was sent to governmental authorities by the plant owner. Needless to say, every bothersome worker became a "Communist" no matter what, if any, political affiliation he had. As a consequence, bargaining capabilities of the urban proletariat were drastically reduced.

The fifties and sixties saw the end of Radical political hegemony. Through the two decades the party managed to keep a relatively stable number of voters. However, as Chile's electoral population experienced two sizable jumps immediately before the 1952 and 1964 presidential elections,[18] their relative hold over the electorate was consequently reduced. The fact that only as long as the percentage of voting population remained under 10 percent, was Radicalism able to win elections is particularly revealing of the nature of Radical support. The percentage of registered voters who actually voted was relatively stable, it fluctuated between 75.93 percent in 1946 and 86.6 percent in 1952. In a chronically stagnant country such as Chile significant economic individual payoffs in the way of unegalitarian expansion of the social security system and the functioning as an effective spoils system were the only products of election outcomes as long as the proportion of enfranchised population remained low.

However, the Radical party reassumed a relatively prominent role during the 1958 to 1964 presidential period of Jorge Alessandri. This was more evident after 1961 when the rightist parties that constituted the congressional basis of support for Alessandri failed to obtain an absolute majority, and the Radicals became the major partner of a so-called Frente Democrático or Democratic Front. In 1958 and 1964, Radical presidential candidates ran last in the respective elections. The year 1970 found a three-cornered race where the only possibility open to the Radicals was

[18] The number of votes cast in the last seven presidential elections have been the following:

1938	503,871
1942	581,343
1946	631,257
1952	957,102
1958	1,250,350
1964	2,530,697
1970	2,962,748

Gil, 1966, p. 213 and La Nación *Santiago Journal*—(September 6, 1970). Women first voted in the 1952 election. The 1964 increase was due to the reform of registration procedures which took voter registration out from parties' control. The effect of this last reform was particularly noticeable in the countryside.

to choose among the three contenders. The party's official leadership opted for the winning leftist candidate, Salvador Allende. A minor fraction of the leadership—within which the older generation, that had ruled the country twenty years before, participated prominently—formed another party, under the name of Democracia Radical or the Radical Democracy, which threw its support to the rightist candidate, former President Jorge Alessandri.

According to electoral data, Radicals actually gave little support to Allende; the vast majority of the Radical electorate seems to have voted for the other two candidates, probably for Alessandri. An analysis of election returns at the provincial level shows that the correlation between Allende's voting percentages of 1964 and 1970 is 0.99 or the same. This figure strongly suggests that the support given to the winning candidate by the Radical leadership did not increase the number of Allende's supporters.

Despite its probably minimal contribution to the outcome, the Radical party, or what remained of it, obtained a major share in Allende's first cabinet: the ministries of defense, education, and mining. The appointment of an old Radical university professor as minister of defense served to avoid early confrontations with the military establishment. The Minister of Mining was a member of the younger and left-wing generation of the party; he wholeheartedly supported Radical presence in Unidad Popular, even without a Radical filling the presidential candidacy.

At this point, though, it is difficult to predict what will be the role of the party in the Popular Unity government and the effects of its participation. At the worst, and with the help of two other small populist-oriented reformist groups (Social Democratic Party and API) that are part of the UP coalition, Radicalism could attempt to brake some aspects of the program of change that Allende advocated. At the best, Radical presence could provide the government with an aura of moderation that may help to reduce or delay the reaction of hitherto economically dominant groups without detracting from the depth of the revolutionary transformations that are needed.

THE RIGHT

Since 1932 the backbone of the right has been constituted by the Liberal and Conservative parties and their different factions. Until 1966 they frequently coalesced their forces, as in the 1938, 1942, 1952, 1958, and 1964 presidential elections. Occasionally they followed an independent course of action, as in the 1932 and 1946 presidential elections and in all congressional elections. In 1966, partly due to the enactment in 1962 of

a reform bill that proscribed electoral pacts in congressional and municipal elections, Conservatives and Liberals merged to form the Partido
Nacional which is universally identified as rightist in orientation.

There is a second major cause of Chile's record of political stability:[19]
the considerable and persisting electoral strength of rightist parties and
movements during the post-1930 period. If we accept the narrow definition of stability as ". . . periodical renewal of authorities through constitutional elections" (Nun, 1965, 55), it seems correct to assert that " . . . the
army comes to the defense of the threatened sectors and allows for political instability in the defense of a premature process of democratization." (Ibid. 56). Nun equates the threatened sectors to the middle class
as opposed to the threatening sectors, that is, the oligarchy (which im-
proves the mechanisms of political control over the rural masses) and the
working classes. This seems to be a too simplistic and somewhat ambiguous dichotomization. We prefer, rather, to equate the "threatened sectors"
to some factions of the dominant classes, which may or may not, depending on the particular Latin American country under analysis, include
portions of the landed oligarchy.

Despite this qualification, Nun's line of argument seems appropriate,
for it implicitly points to two mechanisms that could prevent the advent
of an unstable political system. The more obvious mechanism is political
exclusion of popular forces from the political process. The second is the
existence of a rightist political movement that could function, more or
less permanently, as an effective electoral alternative. For example, the
threatened dominant classes do not favor unstable political situations
while they are able to win relatively open and non-fraudulent elections.
Chile has provided the only example among the most developed Latin
American countries, where this second alternative has functioned.

Chile has one of the few Latin American rightist political parties that
have survived successfully the extension of suffrage as potential winners
of general elections. From being the most important faction of a minuscule
political class which based its claims to power on a legitimation of political
domination, they have evolved into an adaptive political party which
maintains a strong rural basis and has more recently been able to build
significant urban support. In the 1970 presidential elections, over half
the votes received by the rightist candidate came from Santiago and Valparaiso, the two most populated and largely urban provinces. The capital
itself, Santiago, was carried by Alessandri with a margin of more than
forty thousand votes over Allende. Nationwide Allende led Alessandri by
less than forty thousand votes. Santiago's metropolitan area accounted

[19] We define stability as the constancy of a given set of constitutionally sanctioned patterns of permanence and renewal of governmental authorities.

for 40.43 percent of Alessandri's votes against 35.17 percent of Allende's.

In order to accomplish this evolution successfully, rightist parties had to undergo a radical redefinition of the substratum of their raison d'être and their claims to political power. In pursuing this objective, particularly since the early fifties, the main mechanism has been an "anti-party" stand. Political parties in toto are characterized by the right as the main cause of the country's ills. Radicals are accused of being guilty of the sky-rocketing rate of inflation after 1939 and of promoting governmental inefficiency through the installation of a widespread spoils system.[20] Leftist parties are accused in turn of promoting "disorder"—by pressing for socio-economic reforms for both the urban and rural working class—and making private saving for capital accumulation impossible. In this way, the Right has been able to compensate for the losses suffered in their traditional strongholds—the rural provinces of the country's southern half—through a gradual but persistent build-up of its mass of urban followers. The support of large portions of the urban petty bourgeoisie, small and medium merchants and industrial entrepreneurs for example, and of certain strata of the salaried working class has provided the Partido Nacional with a sizable share of the electorate that has enabled it to survive as a major political force.

The Nacionales have often used a developmentalist phraseology. However, developmentalism has mainly served to mask, sometimes rather unsuccessfully, the central attributes of the party's ideology; especially its anti-Communism and its support of the existing structure. In Chile authoritarianism and fear of change are pervasive among rank and file supporters of the Right.

But to obtain mass support within the framework of a rapidly expanding political system demanded radical tactical changes. Liberals and Conservatives (later Nacionales) were skillful politicians; the alleged political flexibility of Chile's dominant groups was also one of their attributes. The way they adapted to apparently most unfavorable political circumstances was remarkable. Although they were not formally in power after 1938, except for the 1958 to 1964 interlude, they often managed to negotiate from strong positions. They alternatively, and sometimes even simultaneously, exercised a highly flexible policy of opposition and collaboration. In 1939 a Conservative senator, Héctor Rodríguez de la Sotta, stated that the 1938 Popular Front presidential victory was a political

---

[20] That these Right wing denunciations of the Radicals were just political tactical moves is shown by the fact that both the Conservatives and the Liberals actively participated in different Radical governments between 1942 and 1952. Besides, in 1962 the three parties joined to form a Frente Democrático (Democratic Front) to provide congressional support to Alessandri.

cataclysm of irreparable consequences. Three years later, however, rightist parties were already holding ministerial positions. While the Right also lost the subsequent elections of 1942, 1946, and 1952, they came through controlling a large share of political positions during different periods of the presidencies of Ríos, González Videla, and Ibáñez. Jorge Alessandri, the victorious 1958 rightist candidate and chairman of the Confederación General de la Producción y el Comercio, the country's third level entre-preneurial association, was a virtual prime minister (as minister of finance) between 1947 and 1950. The flexible position of the Right was also indicated in 1942 and 1964 when they supported non-rightist can-didates, Carlos Ibáñez and Eduardo Frei. In 1964, the decision paid high dividends, for rightist support enabled Frei to defeat Socialist Salvador Allende. Finally, the Right learned to use and not to dismiss, personalistic and charismatic ingredients in political contests. The last two presidential campaigns of Jorge Alessandri, in 1958 and 1970, leaned heavily on the candidate's supposed personal attributes. Actually, he repeatedly made the point that he was not a party man, that political parties were mostly a nuisance, and that their role should be minimized.

The development of an "anti-party" line within the Right may strengthen further moves toward the support of overtly anti-democratic strategies. Before the 1970 elections two lines could be distinguished among the leadership and ranks of the Nacionales and other minor rightist groups. One sector of the Right was in favor of the observance of consti-tutional rules and relied on the electoral appeal of Alessandri. The second sector, favored by the president of the Nacionales, Sergio O. Jarpa, seemed more inclined to favor a military coup to prevent a leftist victory. The victory of the Socialist candidate promised a reversal of the trend. Actu-ally, some post-elections events—like the assassination of the army's com-mander in chief by a extreme right-wing commando and the refusal of the Nacionales to vote for Allende in the subsequent congressional election where he had already been assured of majoritarian support—suggested the possibility that the bulk of the right-wing would stop supporting the observance of constitutional rules and actively seek a military takeover.

IBANISMO: CHILE'S ABORTED VERSION OF LATIN AMERICAN POPULISM

Though a political phenomenon of the past, an analysis of the character-istics and causes of the failure of Ibañismo may pay considerable dividends in the form of a deeper understanding of Chile's socio-political structure. The remarkable political history of General Carlos Ibáñez extended from 1925 to 1958. In 1925 he led a revolt of young officers which forced a one-year old military junta to return the presidency to the constitutionally elected Arturo Alessandri. After six years of preeminence and some years of exile in Argentina, the general returned to his country in 1938 to become the presidential candidate of the Alianza Popular Libertadora (Liberating Popular Alliance), a movement with Nazi overtones. His participation in an unsuccessful revolt sent him to jail and brought about the withdrawal of his candidacy. After trying to obtain the Front's candidacy for himself, Ibáñez and the Alianza decided to support the Popular Front's candidate, Aguirre Cerda. This support was decisive given the narrow margin of Aguirre Cerda's victory—four thousand votes. According to newspaper reports at least forty thousand persons attended the last Ibañista demonstration in Santiago.[21]

In 1942, he became an independent candidate who eventually was supported by the Right. He survived the pre-electionary period to be defeated by the Radical candidate, Juan A. Ríos. Ibáñez got 204,635 votes against Ríos' 260,034. In 1949, he was elected senator from Santiago, and in 1952 he managed to win the presidency over three other candidates, running as an independent supported by a variety of small political parties—of which the two most important were the Agrario Laborista and the Socialista Popular. Voters failed to give Ibáñez an absolute majority by only 34,000 votes:

Ibáñez	446,439
Matte Larraín (Conservatives & Liberals)	265,357
Alfonso (Radicals & Falange Nacional—later Christian Democratic Party)	190,360
Allende (a faction of the Socialists & the illegal Communist Party)	51,975

The heterogeneous support that brought the presidency to Ibáñez was also a source of the major weaknesses and contradictions of his populist regime.[22] One of Ibáñez' biographers quite accurately summarized the manifold nature of the causes of the general's appeal (Würth Rojas, 1958, 225–26):

[21] The fact that a military supported by a so-called Nazi movement supported a so-called Popular Front demonstrates the inconvenience of the acritical use of conceptual frameworks that correspond to other political contexts in the analysis of Latin American phenomena.

[22] For a classification of the essential characteristics of Latin American populism, see Cavarozzi (1970, pp. 13–14).

"Public opinion was dissatisfied with the performance of political parties; the poor were especially affected by their incapacity to stop the increase in the cost of living and their inaction against speculators. The so-called "pro-order people" were aroused by governmental inaction against unions and workers which . . . had come to constitute an autonomous power within the State. The mass of extreme left wingers and moderate reformists felt strongly against the Law of Defense of Democracy and the concentration camp of Pisagua . . .".

It was impossible to satisfy such divergent and contradictory claims. With the reduction of copper prices immediately after the end of the Korean War there was a sharp reduction of resources derived from exports. The increase of total resources available to the country's economy could have made possible the implementation of redistributing policies favoring the working class without reducing the absolute amount of resources received by the economically dominant groups. Actually this was the policy followed by Ibáñez during the first year of his administration. Ibáñez tried unsuccessfully to function as the arbiter of highly heterogeneous cabinets which included Marxist Socialists like Clodomiro Almeyda as Labor Minister [23] and spokesmen of foreign and domestic private firms like Eugenio Suárez and Oscar Herrera.

The creation in 1953 of the worker's Central Unica de Trabajadores (CUT) could have provided Ibáñez with enough labor support to counteract the weight of entrepreneurial groups. However, the rapidly deteriorating economic situation made a turn to the left impossible. The sort of reformist progressive program that the more leftist components of the Ibañista coalition tried to implement was internally contradictory. The early support of some economic and political reforms for the working class and the attempts at limiting some of the most abusive entrepreneurial practices stood alongside measures like the de-nationalization of the country's steel complex, the frustrated attempt at breaking the U. S. monopoly on the commercialization of copper and the failure to abrogate repressive legislation. (Negotiations to sell copper to Socialist countries were already successfully completed in 1953 when Ibáñez abruptly decided to break them.)

During 1954 continuous cabinet changes resulted in the implementation of a series of short-term and contradictory policies that aggravated the country's financial crisis. The year 1955 marked a turning point: the break-up of the governmental coalition that had started as early as 1953 with the resignation of Socialist ministers affected also the most important remaining pro-government group: the Agrarian Laborist party. While

---

[23] Almeyda, the present Foreign Relations Minister of Allende's government, stayed in the Labor Ministry only 4 months. However, in such brief period of time, he established the necessary conditions for the creation of CUT.

one of its leaders, Rafael Tarud,[24] tried to persuade Ibáñez to break with foreign and domestic entrepreneurial groups, another prominent member of the party, Finance Minister Sergio Recabarren, began secret talks with the International Monetary Fund that finally lead to the hiring of an American consulting firm. The Klein-Saks Mission "recommended" the imposition of a rigid anti-labor stabilization plan during the crest of the inflationary wave in January of 1956. Salaries and wages were frozen, and the ban on importation of foreign manufactured articles was partially lifted. Liberals and Conservatives gave the needed congressional support and a tacit agreement between the Right and Ibáñez enabled the old general to complete his constitutional term in 1958. A last minute turn to the left was Ibáñez' last political gesture. The law of Defense of Democracy was derogated and the General was said to have secretly supported FRAP's presidential candidate, Salvador Allende.

In any case 1958 is an important date of Chile's political history. It signalled the consolidation of an autonomous leftist coalition which favored the road of "peaceful revolution" for the construction of socialism. The reformism of Radicals and Ibáñez populism had exhausted their possibilities and the time of class politics had started. The fact that Allende and Alessandri competed in 1958 and again in 1970 as the two leading candidates is perfectly congruent with this interpretation. Frei's presidency can be seen as the temporary upsurge of a multi-class technocratically-oriented and developmentalist reformism. The PDC 1964 victory was favored by the absence of an effective rightist alternative.

CHRISTIAN DEMOCRACY

During the Alessandri government (1958–1964) the perennial problems plaguing Chilean society continued to manifest themselves: inflation, underemployment and unemployment, economic stagnation and concentration of socio-economic power. However, the degree of politicization and radicalization increased, reaching sectors of the population previously under the control and influence of conservative economic elites. The 1964 election campaign marked an important turning point in Chilean history, for the traditional right-wing parties gave way to the emergence of two political groupings: the Christian Democrats through the Partido Demo-

[24] Tarud, who then became an independent senator and Generalísimo (Supreme Chief) of 1970 Allende's candidacy, was a part-time provincial politician who attempted to use Ibañismo as an instrument for the development of a national industrial bourgeoisie independent from foreign ties. His discretional control of the Consejo Nacional de Comercio Exterior (Foreign Exchange National Council) brought him under the fire of the rightist parties and the industrialists' association.

crata Cristiana (PDC) and the Popular Action Front or Frente de Acción Popular (FRAP), that proclaimed the necessity of structural changes. In the 1964 elections the Christian Democrats won the presidency and set out to reshape Chilean society according to their vision.

Christian Democracy as a political movement competes with the Marxists in its appeal to populist or reform sentiments. At the same time it maintains firm social and economic ties with foreign and domestic entrepreneurial groups. The Christian Democrats orient toward mass organizations that continue to function apart from strictly electoral campaigns. Their socio-economic policies stress increasing production and technical efficiency though redistributive policies are not completely absent.

In practical terms the Christian Democrats attempt to give new vitality to the traditional social structure by building new institutions and mobilizing unused resources around national goals. The ideology of the party stresses "communitarianism"—a notion which is susceptible to a variety of definitions ranging from socialism to corporate capitalism (Silva and Chonchol, 1965 and Castillo, 1963). The PDC contains a variety of political factions which have conflicting social viewpoints. The differences within the PDC have had a very significant impact on the evolution of Chilean government policy and the subsequent development of Chilean political history.

IDEOLOGY AND TENDENCIES WITH THE PDC

The ideology of the Christian Democrats focuses on integration, mobilization, and development. However, these terms have had different meaning for different sectors of the party. One trend within the PDC was largely characterized by its orientation toward the promotion of entrepreneurial groups, a strong bias in favor of "technocratic developmentalism" and corporatist social organization. Another tendency showed a much stronger attraction for populist, reform and redistributive politics. The corporatists tend to favor a society in which there are a plurality of interest groups, each controlled from the top, and in which individuals low in the hierarchy of an interest group (or outside of one) have little opportunity to discuss or resolve issues that might conflict with the policies established by the elites. Corporatism blends modern and traditional values in an attempt to overcome the divisiveness of capitalist society by harnessing pre-capitalist values (family, religion, social obligations) to a modern developmental effort. Technological development and economic growth are perceived as providing the material goods necessary to maintain social solidarity in a hierarchical society. The corporatists believe that labor peace and political stability are necessary to encourage private entrepreneurs to invest in productive activity. The economic and social policy of the corporatists thus depends on the active collaboration and encouragement of private investors.

The populists, on the other hand, place greater stress on the active participation of the poor in the decision-making process, egalitarianism and redistribution of property (especially land), state control of credit and finances. Unlike the conservative corporatist wing of the party, the populists are not averse to working with the Marxist Left on specific issues; the corporatists are more inclined toward "going it alone"—through a strong executive centered government or through working coalitions with the right-wing National Party.

The political division within the PDC to a significant degree is "generational": the leadership group is largely made up by members of Falange Party which split off from the Conservative Party during the thirties. The populist wing of the party is largely composed of the student sector and militants who entered the party in the fifties and sixties. The corporatist leadership of the PDC was made up of, in many cases, the sons of wealthy professional middle-class families (Boizard, 1963, Ch. 15). Under the impact of the world economic crises of the 1930's, these men perceived the need for social adjustment to the problems posed by the emerging urban industrial society. Though they never challenged the hierarchical nature of society, they sought to shift the locus of power from the unproductive landowners toward the new urban industrial and rural entrepreneurial groups. The corporatists sought to pressure traditional high status groups to transfer their skills and wealth to new areas of exploitation, mainly industrial and commercial enterprise. The attractiveness of the West German Christian Democrats to the corporatist wing of the PDC reflects their common outlook: they look toward discipline, authority and *institutionalized* popular movements as the mode of adjusting a hierarchical society to the needs of modern development. In addition to the original Falangists, a considerable number of former followers of the Conservative, Liberal and Agrarian Labor Party (the party of the former President Ibáñez) form the right wing of the PDC. During the period in which the Christian Democrats held the presidency (1964–70), the corporatists, largely led by President Frei, dominated the top executive and administrative posts in the government. In great part the largely conservative policies adopted during the Frei presidency reflected the predominance of the corporatist wing of the PDC in the government.

Members of the populist wing of the PDC held prominent positions, during the first years of the Frei government, in agricultural reform agencies: the Agrarian Reform Corporation or Corporación de la Reforma Agraria (CORA) and the Agricultural Development Institute or Instituto Nacional de Desarrollo Agropecuario (INDAP). The peasant unions which grew rapidly during the 1964 to 1970 period played an important role as a pressure group favoring the rapid expropriation of large landed estates. The friction between the agrarian-populists and the technocratic-corporatists over the extent and rate of social reform led to an important division in the party. In 1968 a section of the populists led by agrarian-reform spokesman Jacques Chonchol split and formed a new organization of social-christian inspiration: the United Popular Action Movement (MAPU) which soon aligned itself with the Marxist parties.

With the departure of the radical populists, the political axis of the party shifted toward the right. However, the moderate populists still maintained sufficient support to nominate Radomiro Tomic as the party's presidential candidate in 1970. In the elections themselves, however, a number of leading conservative Christian Democrats gave only nominal support to the Tomic candidature while significant sectors of the electorate that previously voted for the PDC bolted to the right and voted for Alessandri.

INTERNAL DIVISION IN THE CHRISTIAN DEMOCRATIC PARTY

POPULISTS		TECHNOCRATIC-CORPORATISTS	
RADICALS	MODERATES	MODERATES	RIGHTISTS
↓ (split party 1968) MAPU J. Chonchol, (university students and peasant unions)	Tomic, (peasant unions, university students and middle-class professionals)	Frei, (middle-class, sectors of peasant movement, lower-class women)	J. Velasco Castillo, Pérez Zujovic, J. de Dios Carmona, (business-men and bankers)

SOCIAL BASIS OF PDC ELECTORAL SUPPORT

From 1941 to 1958 the Christian Democrats maintained a position of opposition and negotiation with the dominant political elites. Though generally critical of the Radical Party, the Christian Democrats at least on two occasions accepted ministerial posts—Frei was Minister of Public Works during the Presidency of Ríos in 1945 and Bernardo Leighton was Minister of Education during the González Videla Presidency. From 1941 to 1953 the PDC received less than 4 percent of the total vote; however, with the failure of the Ibáñez government (1952–1958) the Christian Democrats began to grow: in 1957 they received 9.4 percent; in the 1958

Presidential elections 21 percent; in 1963 over 20 percent, more than any of the six other major parties.

In 1964, as the right-wing parties declined, the PDC rose to power. Three factors account for the victory of Frei, the Christian Democratic presidential candidate in 1964. These were the female vote and the influence of the Catholic Church, U. S. interests and the mass media in determining it; the economic and political support of the right-wing parties and the economic dominant class; and the support of a multi-class coalition of urban middle-class, low-paid urban workers in the service sector, isolated tenant farmers still subject to the social pressure of landowners and farm proprietors (Wolpin, 1968).

Frei received 63 percent of the female vote compared to Allende's 32 percent. Almost twice as many women voted for Frei, whose party was identified with the Catholic Church and anti-Communism. Overall, 85 percent of Frei's margin of victory can be accounted for by his strength among women voters. The Christian Democrats were identified with the Catholic Church and drew on the active support of the clergy—who appealed to traditional loyalties and values. At the same time a heavily financed propaganda terror campaign aimed at women was effective in projecting the idea that an Allende victory would result in the destruction of home, family, and nation. U. S. agencies and business groups contributed large sums of money and advisers to the Christian Democratic cause.

In the large urban centers, Valparaíso and Santiago, Frei rolled up a large vote (63 percent) especially among the middle- and lower middle-class and among many of the underpaid, unskilled and unorganized urban workers in the service sector. The vague populist-paternalist program appealed to the less politically active members of the lower class. Outside the big cities Frei gained support from a disparate coalition of social groups: big landowners, middle-class farmers, sectors of the better paid workers in the copper industry and in the provincial towns, among small businessmen and clerks. Right-wing support probably contributed heavily to Frei's vote among the status-conscious, urban middle-class and among the more submissive urban and rural population. The heterogeneous nature of the electoral base of the Frei government was not easily mobilizeable in the post-election period—thus making it difficult for the government to carry out its proposed program. The heterogeneous social base of the PDC—including populist reformers and conservative businessmen more interested in defeating the Socialists than bringing about change —greatly reduced the ability of the government to carry out a far-reaching and coherent reconstruction of society.

POLICIES OF THE CHRISTIAN DEMOCRATS

The policies of the PDC in the areas of social and economic development and their impact on the class structure are much better indicators of the party's orientation than its vague ideological pronouncements. The policy areas of importance which we will briefly consider include: social mobilization among the urban poor and policy toward the industrial labor movement; policy toward national economic development (industry and mines), and; policy toward agrarian reform.

The Christian Democratic government proposed a series of new organizations directed toward "integrating" the "marginal" urban population into society through a program called Popular Promotion. Mothers Centers and neighborhood councils were organized to solve local problems especially those related to the lack of infrastructure. Despite the initial enthusiasm surrounding the inauguration of Popular Promotion it failed to dynamize social development. Functioning within a largely stagnant society, lacking sufficient economic resources, Popular Promotion served to distribute marginal favors while inhibiting the populace from influencing basic decisions which continued to be made by the dominant classes.

Because the government was committed to encouraging private entrepreneurial activity as the basis for economic development, it sought to contain and limit labor's demands, thus offering investors the prospect of a docile, disciplined labor force. The PDC maintained a "hard hand" toward the unionized industrial workers. They used their majority in the Congress and rightist support in the Senate to push through legislation fixing the limit on wage demands; the President used the armed forces to break strikes; the annual cost of living wage increase was far below that proposed by the labor unions. More important, little attempt was made to encourage the massive unionization of industrial workers. On the contrary, the government continually criticized industrial workers for being "privileged," even though many workers lived in conditions greatly inferior to those enjoyed by middle class supporters of the government. The government's commitment to economic development in collaboration with private industry prohibited open support of labor's demands and led eventually to open conflict with labor.

The Christian Democratic policy toward national economic development focused on the expansion of copper production and of manufacturing. The copper policy of the Frei government rejected nationalization of the giant U. S. owned mines in favor of "Chileanization." In exchange for tax concessions and guarantees against nationalization, the PDC law provided that U. S. corporations would agree to increase production from

620,000 metric tons per year to about one million tons and increase the amount of copper refined in Chile from 270,000 metric tons in 1964 to 700,000 tons in 1970. The Chilean government purchased 51 percent of the stock in part of the mining operations and minority holdings in new operations. Management and policy-making still was under strong U. S. influence. The Chilean government, while increasing gross receipts from the increased production of copper, suffered a 16 percent reduction in earnings per ton of copper produced. The price paid by the Chilean government for their shares was considered excessive both in financial terms and in terms of influence in the mining operations. In addition little was done to develop industries which could elaborate products which absorb copper: the copper continues to be shipped to the United States to be processed. Frei's Chileanization program resulted in higher profit remittances per ton of copper produced. As a result in the 1970 elections both Allende, the Marxist, and Tomic, the left Christian Democrat, promised to nationalize the U. S.-owned copper mines and integrate them into Chile's development.

Frei's industrial development policy encouraged the growth of efficient, technologically advanced enterprises. As a result, the expansion of industry did not contribute to the absorption of labor, or lessen the chronic unemployment and underemployment problem. In addition the industrial promotion policy led to a very significant increase in U. S. penetration and control of Chilean industrial enterprises. A study by a leading Christian Democratic economist showed that

> "in the case of copper, while the country was making a serious effort to recover basic resources, at the same time the only two firms which were the biggest manufacturers of copper products passed under foreign control. While the country was recovering the nitrate wealth, a series of nationally owned chemical industries passed into foreign hands. While the country nationalized the electrical services, foreign enterprises were set up to elaborate electrical products." (Biter, 1970, 8–9)

In Chile foreign capital has penetrated the growth sectors of the economy, which have in many cases been originally promoted by the state. During the Frei presidency foreign investment, for example, moved into chemicals, transport industry, electrical machinery, and metal products.

AGRARIAN POLICY OF THE FREI GOVERNMENT

Throughout the 1950's and early 1960's an insignificant faction of the rural labor force was unionized. In 1953 only 1,042 agricultural workers were unionized in fifteen unions; in 1963 there were only 1,500 members in twenty-two unions (Ministerio de Trabajo, Dirección de Estadística, raw data). In the 1964 election the Marxist left and the Christian Democrats both strong advocates of agrarian reform gathered over 95 percent of the vote. When the Christian Democrat Frei took over the presidency in November 1964, there were only 1,658 unionized rural workers in the whole of Chile. Spurred on by the electoral campaign and continuing with increasing militancy afterwards, rural workers began to take direct action. Strikes and work stoppages were occasionally followed by land seizure (Affonso et al., 1970, Vol. II, 7–140). The left wing of the Christian Democrats led by Jacques Chonchol was in charge of the agrarian reform. Under their direction government policy began to change significantly (Chonchol, 1970, 50–87). Government officials in many cases began to take a more positive or at least neutral attitude toward peasant demands; the police were less frequently sent in to defend the interests of the landlords; and more important, Chonchol's INDAP began to actively encourage peasant organization.

The politicization by the left and PDC during the 1964 elections encouraged peasants to make demands; the expression of collective demands and the success in carrying out struggles encouraged the organization of peasant unions. The growth of an active socially conscious peasantry and the competition of different political currents led to the formation of rival peasant trade union confederations (Affonso et al., 1970, Vol I, 65–261). The vast expansion of peasant unions led to increased pressure to accelerate the land reform. The agrarian reform officials, especially Chonchol, began to articulate this demand in government policy-making circles. However, the broad scope of the movement and its increasing militancy conflicted with the policies of the executive. The intentions of the latter were to encourage the gradual unionization of peasants who would present moderate demands, compatible with the time schedule and economic activities of the landowners (not at seeding or harvest) so as not to affect productivity.

THE GROWTH OF PEASANT UNIONS

In 1965, the first year of the Frei government, very little overt organization took place though rural unrest was increasing; in 1966 the unrest and strikes began to coalesce in an organizational way: the number of trade unions increased fivefold: from 2,118 in 1965 to 10,647 in 1966 (Ministerio de Trabajo, Dirección de Estadística, raw data). In 1967 membership in agrarian trade unions increased four and a half times— rising from 10,647 to 47,473 (Ministerio de Trabajo, Dirección de Estadística, raw data). The major impetus for organizing peasant unions came from INDAP and secondarily from the Marxist-led federations. While INDAP lacked experienced peasant leaders, it did have access to government officials in resolving peasant demands, and it was able to neutralize the effects of adverse decisions by local officials of the ministry of labor. While the Christian Democratic agrarian reformers saw peasant agitation and organization as the first step toward a broad transformation of land tenure, President Frei perceived the process as going too fast as well as threatening the "balance" that he wanted to maintain between big landed entrepreneurs and peasants.

> Neither the small, medium or even the large proprietor that is highly productive and maintains good working conditions is threatened (by the agrarian reform). (Mensaje Presidencial al Congreso, 1 de mayo de 1965).

The unionization of the peasants, which the agrarian reformers took to be the *first* step toward a social transformation, Frei perceived as the consequence of a prolonged process of rural education and gradual organization under government tutelage. The executive pressures to slow down government sponsored peasant mobilization began to be applied in 1967; but the agrarian reformers refused to accede and between 1967 and 1968 peasant unionization increased by over 50 percent rising from 47,473 to 76,356 members (Ministerio de Trabajo, Dirección de Estadística, raw data).

By mid-1968 the situation in rural areas appeared to Frei to be getting out of control: Chonchol and his supporters were told to slow down. Despite this pressure as of September 1968 the INDAP-supported trade unions had an absolute majority of the unionized peasantry (52.4 percent), followed by the Marxist-led unions 24.4 percent, and the U. S.-backed pro-Frei Confederación "Libertad" with 23.2 percent (Ministerio de Trabajo, Dirección de Estadística, raw data).

PEASANT MOBILIZATION AND THE SPLIT AMONG CHRISTIAN DEMOCRATS

By the end of 1968 President Frei decided that the unionization process had gone too far; that the peasant unions were engendering too much conflict; that the growth of a militant peasant movement was a threat to the entrepreneurial farmers. In contrast, Chonchol and the agrarian reform wing of the PDC became increasingly aware of the difficulties in carrying out an agrarian reform in isolation from other sectors of the economy; they formulated a strategy which they referred to as the "non-capitalist road to development" and which included the nationalization of banks and credits and increased government control over the commercialization of farm products (Chonchol, 1970, 50–87, interview August 31, 1970). In the meantime the urban economic elites—construction, industry, banking and commerce—were becoming increasingly preoccupied with the militancy in the countryside. They increasingly gave their support to the large landowners association. The Christian Democratic coalition—made up of agrarian reformers and urban capitalists—which had been held together by Frei, then collapsed. Frei was presented with the choice of siding with the economic elites or the agrarian reformers. The choice was never in doubt: Chonchol and a significant part of the left wing departed and formed the MAPU or the United Popular Action Movement.

POLITIZATION AND RADICALIZATION IN RURAL CHILE

Peasant unionism continued to expand. By the end of 1969, 103,043 peasants were unionized, 35 percent above the 1968 level (Fondo de Educación y Extensión Sindical, 1970). The increased pressure of the 1970 electoral campaign and the competition between the candidates for peasant support undoubtedly opened up further opportunities for peasant union organizers to enter the field. If we accept CORA's figures, by the middle of 1970 almost 38 percent of the salaried rural force of 335,000 was unionized in 488 unions (Fondo de Educación y Extensión Sindical, 1970). The growing militancy of the peasants, the increasing activity of the trade-unionists and the promotional activity of agrarian reform officials has increasingly polarized the countryside. The rural labor force has become cognizant of its exploited position in the "traditional" socioeconomic system and has redefined its relationship with the landowners and with the dominant social classes. The rural laboring classes, conscious of their position, have increasingly opted for organizations that could in the short run *improve* their social position and in the long run could *change* the class structure.

In absolute terms the INDAP-organized campesino confederation ("Triunfo Campesino") continued to be the most important with 47,609 members (Fondo de Educación y Extensión Sindical, 1970). However, in terms of the proportion of trade union members, it declined from 52.4 percent in 1968 to 46.7 percent in 1969. The more conservative confederation ("Libertad") decreased slightly from 23.2 to 22.6 percent (Fondo de Educación y Extensión Sindical, 1970). The Marxist-led confederation ("Ranquil") increased from 24.4 to 30.3 percent of the organized peasantry. The large landowner sponsored "United Agrarian Provinces" contained less than one percent. Almost one-half (47 percent) of the increase in peasant union-membership between 1968 and 1969 was accounted for by the Marxist peasant unions—a significant change from the preceding years. The Ranquil peasant union, independent of the Frei government and led by unionists who opposed his policies, showed the greatest gain in 1969. The growth of the left was strongly aided by the incorporation of the left Christian Democrats (MAPU) in the left-wing coalition, Unidad Popular.

The competing confederations concentrated their organizing efforts initially near urban centers, areas of socio-political strength and areas containing concentrations of salaried workers. In recent years, however, the peasant unions have spread to the more distant parts of the country-side, embracing especially rural areas of the south which were previously unaffected. Because of the proximity of the capital and its political-economic resources, the greatest number of organized peasants (13,443) was located in Santiago province (Fondo de Educación y Extensión Sindical, 1970); second was the province of Talca (9,344), long a Christian Democratic and Marxist center of socio-political peasant organization (Fondo de Educación y Extensión Sindical, 1970); third was O'Higgins (8,588) with its mining centers and their radical traditions, which had served to influence and support peasant struggles (Petras and Zeitlin, 1970); fourth was Ñuble, one of the most impoverished and exploited regions which had been swept up in the organizing effort of rural areas, especially in a 1969 wave of land seizures.

INDAP's organizational breakthrough which occurred between 1966 and 1968 extended rural unionism beyond the areas adjacent to socio-political centers to strictly rural areas with little prior history of social struggle. In some areas the establishment of Christian Democratic unions facilitated the entrance of the more radical Socialist and Communist unions; in other cases the initial organizers, once having established their predominance, were able to maintain it. It appears that the Christian Democrats, especially in areas of extreme conservatism, legitimized peasant unionism through their initial efforts. However they had problems in maintaining their influence once the peasant demands began to grow and leftist organizations began to compete for the allegiances of the peasantry.

The major change in Chile during the Frei presidency was not in land tenure but rather in the unionization of the rural wage labor force. The rapid growth of unionism was initially supported by all Christian Democrats. As the movement grew in size and militancy, a division developed as to the goals of the movement. Frei and his supporters perceived the trade union as a pressure group within the traditional structure. The organization of the peasantry was perceived as an instrument to "integrate" them into existing capitalist society—giving them a limited role in determining the terms of their employment by the rural entrepreneurs.

To Chonchol and his supporters the union was an instrument to transform rural society and a substitute for the landowner. Consistent with his past support of a "pluralist" capitalist society (including landowners, bankers and industrialists), Frei never did envision the approach which INDAP proposed. What did change were the young Christian Democrats who, under the impact of peasant organization and struggle, sought to implement the agrarian reform put forth by Frei; and they became increasingly frustrated as they continued to encounter political obstacles put forth by the Frei government. The rebel Christian Democrats were increasingly committed to a general transformation, while Frei became concerned with limiting the structural consequences of mass social organization. The resultant of these contradictory approaches was the successful promotion of a mass peasant union movement and very limited redistribution of land.

LAND DISTRIBUTION DURING 1965–1970

During the period 1965 to 1970 the Frei government expropriated 279 thousand hectareas of irrigated land (Echenique, 1970). By June 1970 the government had expropriated only 17.5 percent of the irrigated land; the large landholders still maintained the great bulk of the best land in the country. During the same period the government expropriated only 12 percent of the non-irrigated land or 3.1 million hectareas (Echenique, 1970). Government statistics do not report the amount of this non-irrigated land that is usable for cultivation. The expropriation program varied considerably from province to province. In Aconcagua 34.8 percent of the irrigated land was expropriated while in O'Higgins only 9.6 percent was taken over (Echenique, 1970).

FAMILY SETTLEMENTS IN THE AGRARIAN REFORM

The Frei government's major failure was in the area of settlement of families on land expropriated through the agrarian reform. In 1964 he promised land to 100,000 proprietors by 1970. By 1967 the figure was reduced to between 40,000 and 60,000. As of July 1970 only 21,105 families received land (Department of Statistics, CORA, August 1970). Of the total peasant population in need of land about 8 percent benefited by the "agrarian reform" and almost 92 percent were excluded.

By 1970 the agrarian reform program was experiencing stiffer resistance from the landowners: CORA officials were assaulted, and landowners armed themselves and prepared to fight against expropriation. This resistance was in contrast to the first years of the agrarian reform which were relatively easy. From the beginning of 1965 to July 1967 land was expropriated under the 1962 agrarian reform law. Most of the expropriations that took place occurred on abandoned farms or farms that were inefficiently operated. Almost one half (47 percent) of the irrigated land expropriated occurred under the old law (Echenique, 1970). Under the

TABLE I

FORMATION OF LAND SETTLEMENT COLONIES
BETWEEN 1965 AND JULY 14, 1970

	1965	1966	1967
Number of land settlement colonies	33	62	151
Amount of land in hectareas	286,839.3	145,616.8	354,847.7
Irrigated land	16,241	17,286.8	47,736.3
Non-irrigated land	270,592.2	128,330	307,111.4
Families benefited	2,061	2,109	4,218

Source: CORA *Reforma Agraria Chilena 1965–1970*
Santiago, Chile, July 1970, p. 45

	1968	1969	1970	Total 1968–70
Number of land settlement colonies	113	209	99	667
Amount of land in hectareas	443,061	1,103,125	328,110	2,661,599.8
Irrigated land	30,136	79,682	22,740	213,828
Non-irrigated land	412,925	1,013,444	305,370	2,437,772
Families benefited	2,915	7,315	2,487	21,105

Sources: Jorge Echenique, *Las expropiaciones y la organización de asentamientos en el período 1965–70,* Universidad de Chile, Santiago de Chile, 1970, p. 21
Department of Statistics, CORA. Raw data for January–July 1970 was provided by personnel.

new law passed in July 1967 the government continued to expropriate land that was not being cultivated efficiently (20 percent of the total holdings expropriated since July 1967) but began to move toward expropriation of other lands. In many cases of expropriation (37 percent) the owners offered to sell their holdings to the government because of the high price which the government was willing to pay (Echenique, 1970). However this option was quickly exhausted and fewer and fewer landowners remained who wanted to sell their *fundos.* Hence the land reform and land settlement process slowed down considerably during 1970. On the other hand the pressure of the *campesinos* and the peasant unions increased and land seizures multiplied during 1968 and 1969. In May 1970 a historic nationwide general strike of peasant unions took place demanding the acceleration of the agrarian reform and an end to the illegal armed resistance of the big landowners.

The peasants and peasant unions increasingly turned toward direct action, radicalizing their demands, and looking toward support from the

Marxist left. Under Frei the promised reforms served merely to raise peasant expectations and to provoke right wing resistance. The Frei government's policy was to create a new middle class entrepreneurial farmer group, alongside the large efficient farm. The trade unions were to serve as tools to improve the living standards of the rest of the *campesinos*. The few thousand *campesinos* who received land experienced a substantial increase in standard of living. The cost of the reform—in terms of payments to the landowners and financing of the post-reform development—strained the limits of the government's commitments. The agrarian reform program of the Frei government created a new stratum of relatively better-off middle-class peasants who now employ labor, mimic the old landowners, and follow their political lead in many cases. Frei also allowed a vast number of landless peasants to be unionized without meeting their basic demands. His policies polarized the countryside and in the process undercut the basis of support for the "centrist" Christian Democrats. The vote of the economically active *campesinos*—largely males— went to the left while the right wing picked up support precisely in the areas where unionism was weak and among small farmers little affected by the new rural organizations.

MALE VOTE FOR PRESIDENTIAL CANDIDATES IN RURAL PROVINCES DURING 1970 ELECTION (EL SIGLO, SEPT. 6, 1970)

	ALLENDE (LEFT)	ALESSANDRI (RIGHT)	TOMIC (CENTER)
Coquimbo	24,859	13,406	11,600
Aconcagua	11,767	8,967	8,879
O'Higgins	24,719	14,350	13,969
Colchagua	9,361	9,345	7,428
Curicó	7,487	5,758	4,510
Talca	15,249	8,476	8,828
Linares	9,758	10,061	7,896
Maule	4,837	4,828	3,337
Ñuble	16,794	15,972	12,987
Bio-Bio	10,998	9,401	6,815
Malleco	8,892	9,910	8,056
Cautin	16,209	26,305	21,295
Valdivia	16,369	14,847	11,851
Osorno	9,074	10,291	8,039
Totals	186,373	161,917	135,490

Allende gained a plurality of the male votes in ten of the fourteen rural provinces while Alessandri captured the remaining four. Tomic was the lowest vote-getter in twelve of the fourteen provinces. The countryside polarized with a significant plurality swinging to the left. The Tomic campaign itself was decidedly more radical than Frei's, for Tomic promised to accelerate the agrarian reform. In other words, the total anti-reform vote in rural Chile amounted to only 36 percent (Alessandri's proportion). It was clear that by 1970 the Chilean countryside was greatly politicized and ready for a rapid and thorough transformation of land tenure, a task which the new Socialist President Salvador Allende faced.

The rural laborers who backed his candidacy were intent on realizing the transformation which Frei promised but never achieved. What was equally obvious, however, was that the landowners were backed by the urban economic elites who stood to lose through government-sponsored nationalizations. Relying on their control over economic institutions, especially banks and factories, they began to apply economic pressure, withdrawing capital and closing enterprises in hope of provoking a crisis and military intervention (*Nación,* Sept. 8, 1970, p. 1). A right-wing coup, however, would be resisted by the great majority of the people (leftist and a section of Christian Democrats) who voted against the right. In a country where the bourgeoisie had long preached obedience to the law and constitution (as it suited their convenience), a right-wing coup could set off a series of conflicts which could lead to a civil war. The military appeared to be divided between those favoring a coup and those who were "constitutionalists." For the right wing and the big landowners time was running out, panic had set in. The agrarian revolution appeared to be imminent.

Thus, the inability of the Christian Democrats to promote *national* development and the increasing penetration of U. S. enterprises, the abortive nature of socio-economic change in urban and rural areas and the hostile posture which the government adopted toward industrial labor led to a decline in PDC support—from 56 percent of the vote in 1964 to 30 percent in 1970. The decision of the right to run a candidate against the Christian Democrats gave the left-wing Popular Unity forces the opportunity to win the 1970 presidential elections—albeit by a narrow margin.

THE LEFT WING IN CHILEAN POLITICS: FROM OPPOSITION TO THE PRESIDENCY

For the first time in history and in 1970, after a half-century of struggle, a Marxist-led popular front achieved a presidential electoral victory. The history of class conflict and working class involvement in Chilean politics, however, dates back to the 1880's and 1890's, when the first massive confrontations between labor and capital took place in the mining areas of the north and south. Out of these early struggles, largely led by anarchists and socialists, emerged the two major working-class parties of Chile, the Communist and Socialist parties, the former in the early 1920's and the later in the early 1930's. In 1932 an uprising by Air Force officers led to the establishment of a Socialist Republic which lasted only ten days, superseded by another civilian/military junta which eventually restored elections and the security of bourgeois property rights. Both the Socialist and Communist parties claim to be Marxist working class parties oriented toward the creation of a socialist society. Both favor a sweeping agrarian reform, nationalization of basic industries, banking and commerce and an anti-imperialist foreign policy. Over the years the leftist parties have participated in electoral and governmental coalitions with parties of the center and even on occasion with right-of-center governments. In the past, political office holding was a vehicle for social mobility. Lower middle-class and working-class leaders have risen into the middle strata via their parliamentary seats. The typical popular leader once gaining office, became more conservative while maintaining few close ties with original followers. The parliamentary process served as a means of containing insurgent groups and perpetuating social rigidity. Thus the two main features of the Chilean politics have been that the industrial working class aligned itself in specific *class* parties and that these parties functioned within the legal-parliamentary framework.

The major event in recent history which shaped the political orientation and growth of the left was the negative outcome resulting from the subordination of the left to middle class-led political coalitions. During the 1930's the left-wing parties gained considerable popular support on the basis of militant activity, eventually trading it off for government positions in the Popular Front, the first left-center coalition. During and immediately after World War II the left-wing parties supported middle-class governments. The results were meagre: agriculture and the newly founded industries remained largely in the hands of the dominant bourgeoisie; social conditions hardly improved; the economy remained heavily dependent on the U. S.-owned mining sector; and inflation continued to undermine wage and salary increases.

THE POPULAR FRONT: THE POLITICS OF COALITION

Chile was badly affected by the world depression. The worst effects were felt by the working classes which had few if any political contacts to obtain relief. The attempts at protest were savagely repressed by the Arturo Alessandri government, and trade unionists were frequently jailed. In this context of economic depression, political repression and social protest, the militant struggles led by the Socialist and Communist parties began to attract a considerable following. Despite severe government opposition, the left substantially increased its political representation in Congress and succeeded in uniting trade union forces in a single confederation. As the 1938 elections approached, the left increasingly represented a major political challenge to the dominant economic elites in power.

Initially the electoral alliance for the 1938 elections was to include only the working-class parties. However, the Communist Party, largely influenced by international considerations, proposed an "anti-fascist" coalition which included the Radical Party. The latter group accepted membership in the Popular Front through an understanding with the Communist Party that the presidential candidate of the Front would be in the hands of the Radical Party. The subsequent victory of the Front enabled the Radicals and Socialists to divide up ministries and to permeate the administrative apparatus of the state. The socialists' long-term revolutionary perspective based on mass organization and struggle was replaced by short-term political advantages—many of them of dubious value to their working-class constituents. The inability of the Socialists to bring about a substantial redistribution in income and land tenure created two sets of interrelated problems: rank and file supporters of the socialists began to express their discontent and to defect from the party; and at the same time conflicts soon led to political divisions, resulting in a number of splits. The Socialist Party's experience with coalition politics considerably weakened its image as a party of change. In contrast, the Communist Party, though supporting the candidates of the Radical Party, refrained from assuming responsibility at the ministerial level and substantially increased its popular following, until 1946.

In 1946 the Communist Party backed the Radical Party's presidential aspirant Gabriel González Videla, who was subsequently elected. The Communists were awarded three minor ministerial positions; however the presence of the Left increased popular demands for change while President González Videla faced pressures from U. S. and Chilean businessmen to put an end to Communist participation in order to receive economic collaboration and aid. González Videla responded by banning the Communist Party and jailing thousands of trade unionists and popular activists on the pretext that they represented a "threat" to internal security and were part of an "international conspiracy." From 1948 to 1957 the Communist Party was outlawed and prohibited from openly participating in the electoral process. Throughout the 1940's the Communist and Socialist parties engaged in bitter struggles which divided the working class and largely benefited the economic elites.

As the 1952 presidential elections approached, a major split-off from the Socialist Party—calling itself the Popular Socialist Party (PSP)—decided to pin its hopes on the "independent" populist candidate Carlos Ibáñez. The PSP hoped to influence Ibáñez in the direction of nationalist and populist policies, as the first step toward a broader transformation. Once again the tactics of coalition with sectors of the bourgeoisie failed to bring results. Instead of nationalist changes, Ibánez liberalized terms for foreign investors, maintained a "hard hand" (*mano dura*) against the trade unions, and accentuated economic inequalities through inflationary policies.

Apart from the Partido Socialista Popular (PSP), the smaller Socialist Party and the Communist Party in 1952 launched Allende as their presidential candidate and gathered little more than five percent of the vote. The government's repression and the fragmentation of the left prevented any serious challenge for power—facts that the left slowly began to realize.

THE TRADE UNIONS AND THE LEFT

The trade unions in Chile embraced approximately 15 percent of the labor force, largely concentrated in the larger industries, mines, and among certain types of employees. In the fifties the socialists and communists were of near equal strength in terms of trade union support. The balance rested with the less important Christian Democratic, Radical and Independent led trade unions. The political rivalries and repression seriously fragmented the trade unions and considerably weakened their capacity to defend the standard of living of the working class. Under the Ibáñez government socialists and communists united their forces, and in 1953 they joined to form a single trade union confederation, the Central Unica de Trabajadores de Chile (CUTCH).

Because of the weakness of the political parties of the Left during the 1950's, the trade unions assumed the leadership of many political struggles. The CUTCH called a series of general strikes of varying success, and ultimately secured the legalization of the Communist Party and the abrogation of the Law for Defense of Democracy which had served to repress opposition to the government. The trade unions thus served to defend the immediate economic interests of its members and to politicize and involve their members in broader movements for social and political change. The overwhelming majority of socialist and communist leaders of the CUTCH who were relatively effective in defending the economic interests of the working class were able to link the trade unions to the left-wing parties. The trade unionists became a firm base of electoral support for the left when it emerged as a unified political force.

THE POPULAR ACTION FRONT AND POPULAR UNITY

The negative results obtained by both the Socialist and Communist parties from their attempts to change Chilean society through coalitions with various representative sectors of the capitalist class finally forced a reappraisal of political strategy. The Socialists covered up their differences sufficiently to form a single party, the Socialist Party. Negotiations between the Socialist and Communist parties, together with a number of smaller political formations, led to the formation of the Frente de Acción Popular (FRAP). In 1958 the FRAP candidate, Salvador Allende, almost won the Presidency, polling 30 percent of the electorate in a four-cornered race and losing by a scant 35,000 out of a total of 1.1 million votes.

In the period from 1958 to 1964, the conservative Alessandri government failed to ameliorate any of the structural defects generating social discontent and political radicalism. Orthodox economic measures to stimulate private investment, a largely symbolic agrarian reform law (designed mainly for external consumption, that is to pay lip service to the slogans of the Alliance for Progress), and the maintenance of vast social inequalities created a public increasingly receptive to reformist and radical ideas. The diverse attempts by different political representatives of the capitalist class (Radicals, Ibañistas and orthodox Conservatives) to provide a solution within the framework of a dependent capitalist society proved to be a failure.

The 1964 presidential elections saw the demise of the older political groups and the confrontation of two new challengers: the FRAP and the Partia Democrata Cristiana (PDC). The PDC promised to carry out a "revolution in liberty" though many of its leaders were closely associated with U. S. and Chilean businessmen. In 1964 the PDC defeated the FRAP, which however obtained almost 39 percent of the total votes and 45 percent of the male votes.

The inability of the Christian Democrats to meet the demands of urban salaried and industrial labor and to carry out a dynamic agrarian reform allowed the socialists and communists to maintain their support of the workers and peasants. The FRAP was expanded to include the Movimiento de Acción Popular Unido (MAPU), (comprised of dissident Christian Democrats), Radicals, and two smaller groups; and the new coalition was renamed Unidad Popular. In 1970, its standard bearer once again was Salvador Allende. The program included the nationalization of major industries, banks, and commerce; a thorough agrarian reform; and a vastly expanded social welfare program. Capitalizing on the division between the right wing and the Christian Democrats, who ran separate candidates, Allende won the presidency in a close contest, gaining 36.2 percent of the votes against 34.8 percent for the rightist Alessandri. Allende scored heavily among male voters (over 40 percent) and gained a plurality in working class and mining municipalities, as well as among the landless peasants and rural workers. To a significant degree, the social basis of Allende's support in 1970 was similar to that which he obtained in 1964, the major difference being that this time the PDC and the right were divided.

THE CHILEAN WORKING CLASS AND THE SOCIALIST ELECTORAL VICTORY OF 1970

For many years U. S. and Latin American sociologists circulated the notion that support for Marxist Socialism was largely a product of the economic backwardness and "traditionalism" of Third World countries; that modern urban industrial cities served to "moderate" the outlook and behavior of the working class—especially the better paid industrial workers. Some sociologists who accepted this view began to speak of "integrated" sectors or classes (including urban industrial workers) and "marginal" classes. The notion of a "bourgeoisified" industrial proletariat even shaped the outlook of left-wing intellectuals who began to speak of a "labor aristocracy" and to look to the peasantry as the sole basis of hope for a revolutionary transformation. The notion that the working class could combine and act as a class in favor of a socialist society against capitalist exploitation and inequality seems to have evaded the eyes of scores of U. S. investigators who claimed to study the lower classes in Latin America. A careful analysis of the political behavior of the Chilean working class refutes the "integration" thesis.

From its formation in 1956, the Marxist-led FRAP directed its political activity toward gaining the support of the working class. The major base of support for the Marxist-led coalition in 1964 and in the 1970 electoral victory was the industrial proletariat employed in the modern urban-industrial centers. As Table I indicates, in 1964 FRAP gained the support of the municipalities (*comunas*) which had the highest concentration of industrial workers. The higher the proportion of industrial workers, the higher the ratio of votes in favor of Allende. The 1970 electoral results suggest that the experience with a Christian Democratic government did not change the workers' political loyalty; on the contrary, the voting ratio of Allende to Alessandri and Allende to Tomic seems to have increased. The presidential voting results suggest that the Christian Democratic "reform" government completely failed to win over the working class as many of its supporters both in Chile and in the United States had hoped. The industrial workers chose to maintain their loyalty with the Marxist candidate and to reject the Christian Democratic alternative.

TABLE I

RELATIVE INDEX OF VOTES BETWEEN ALLENDE AND FREI (1964), ALLENDE AND ALESSANDRI (1970), ALLENDE AND TOMIC (1970). MALE VOTES IN NINE OF THE MOST IMPORTANT CITIES AND TOWNS IN CHILE (PERCENTAGES)

PERCENTAGE OF THE LABOR FORCE IN MANUFACTURING, MINING, & CONSTRUCTION	CITY OR TOWN	ALLENDE VOTES FOR each 100 VOTES FOR FREI (1964)	ALLENDE VOTES FOR each 100 VOTES FOR ALESSANDRI (1970)	ALLENDE VOTES FOR each 100 VOTES FOR TOMIC (1970)
Under 30				
20	Temuco	51 ⎫	78 ⎫	108 ⎫
25	Chillán	113 ⎬ 80*	175 ⎬ 129	225 ⎬ 154
28	Valparaíso	75 ⎭	135 ⎭	129 ⎭
30–35				
30	Viña del Mar	71 ⎫	100 ⎫	130 ⎫
30	Talca	112 ⎬ 100	193 ⎬ 151	194 ⎬ 182
30	Antofagasta	116 ⎭	159 ⎭	222 ⎭
36–40				
36	Valdivia	122 ⎫	173 ⎫	247 ⎫
39	Concepción	95 ⎬ 117	153 ⎬ 208	170 ⎬ 204
39	Talcahuano	134 ⎭	299 ⎭	196 ⎭

*average

TABLE II

RELATIVE INDEX OF VOTES BETWEEN ALLENDE AND FREI (1964), ALLENDE AND ALESSANDRI (1970), ALLENDE AND TOMIC (1970). MALE VOTES IN THE *COMUNAS* (MUNICIPALITIES) OF GRAN SANTIAGO CLASSIFIED BY THE RELATIVE SIZE OF ITS WORKING CLASS (PERCENTAGES)

PERCENTAGE OF THE LABOR FORCE IN MANUFACTURING, MINING & CONSTRUCTION	*Comuna* OR MUNICIPALITY	ALLENDE VOTES FOR EACH 100 VOTES FOR FREI (1964)	ALLENDE VOTES FOR EACH 100 VOTES FOR ALESSANDRI (1970)	ALLENDE VOTES FOR EACH 100 VOTES FOR TOMIC (1970)
Less than 20				
9	Calera de Tango	68	100	70
9	Lampa	89	112	117
13	Providencia	29 } 71*	31 } 80	82 } 105
16	Quilicura	79	108	152
19	Las Condes	42	47	103
20–29				
27	Ñuñoa	59	86	142
30–39				
31	Santiago	67	94	143
32	San Bernardo	92	146	155
35	La Florida	65 } 80	100 } 134	161 } 162
36	Maipú	85	153	171
39	Conchalí	92	168	180
40–49				
43	Puente Alto	104	166	252
45	La Cisterna	90	164	188
46	Quinta Normal	96 } 103	168 } 188	191 } 203
46	Renca	104	193	179
46	Barrancas	122	250	205
50 or more				
51	San Miguel	114 } 121.5	208 } 235	238 } 258
52	La Granja	129	261	277

*average

The Christian Democrats, proponents of a "third way" between socialism and capitalism, found little support for their program among the
class-conscious Chilean working class. No doubt the links between the
Christian Democrats and U. S. and Chilean businessmen weakened their
ability to pass social legislation and economic reforms which would have
redistributed income and increased the participation of the working class
in the industrial system. This suggests that the ability of the Unidad
Popular to maintain itself in political power would depend on its capacity
to meet the demands of the industrial working class for radical anti-
capitalist changes in the urban industrial centers.

The non-working class municipalities continued to give their support
to the Right (Alessandri) and Christian Democrats (see Table II). This
suggested that the political support of the non-Marxist parties (Radicals,
and MAPU) were largely irrelevant in determining the size of the vote
for Allende in the urban centers. In rural Chile, however, MAPU played
a very important role in mobilizing peasant support for Allende. The size
of Allende's vote in the urban industrial centers was largely the result of
the traditional voting behavior of the industrial proletariat. Thus, the
non-Marxist parties were probably over-represented in the seats of government, in relationship to their contribution to the victory of Allende.
Political agreements with the non-Marxist parties, while serving to bolster
the image of a "multi-party government," could work against a coherent
and profound reform program that could sustain the popular support of
the government. The imbalance between the homogeneous social base of
the Allende victory (largely industrial working class socialists and communists) and the politically heterogeneous character of the party leadership could cause serious problems, depending on the constituency which
Allende chose to serve.

The second major basis of support for the Left was the mining sector,
consistent supporters of Marxist political parties for several decades. Even
among the highest paid sectors of the industrial proletariat (copper
workers), Allende received over two and one-half times the vote of Alessandri. Even in the ultra-modern, technologically advanced Chuquicamata mine, Allende received 106 votes for every 100 votes for Alessandri.
The notion of a "workers' aristocracy" hardly serves to explain the behavior of this highly paid sector of the labor force, which may have voted
for the nationalization of the mines knowing full well that it might not
improve their standard of living but would serve Chilean economic
development.

As Table III indicates, the mining workers expressed a high degree of
class solidarity and clearly rejected the non-socialist alternatives and
voted in overwhelming numbers for the socialist Allende. The political

TABLE III

RELATIVE INDICES OF VOTE BETWEEN ALLENDE AND ALESSANDRI AND ALLENDE AND TOMIC (1970). MALE VOTES IN THE MINING CENTERS (PERCENTAGES)

	ALLENDE VOTES FOR EACH 100 VOTES FOR ALESSANDRI	ALLENDE VOTES FOR EACH 100 VOTES FOR TOMIC
Copper Mining Zones		
Chuquicamata	106	301
Potrerillos	232	225
Sewell	406 ⎱ 265*	307 ⎱ 303
El Salvador	319	381
Nitrate Mining Zones		
Iquique	194	258
Pozo Almonte	300	289
Lagunas	130 ⎱ 325	173 ⎱ 337
Toco	412	541
Pedro de Valdivia	591	426
Coal Mining Zones		
Coronel	640	448
Lota	916 ⎱ 794	658 ⎱ 571
Curanilahue	827	608

*average

implications were clear: a social basis for an extensive program of nationalization of mines existed in the sectors of the labor force most intimately involved. An Allende failure to carry out his program of nationalization thus could not be blamed on the lack of political support.

The third major support for Allende's victory was urban working class women. Most observers mistakenly generalized about the conservative voting behavior of Chilean women without taking account of the class differences among women. If we take all the municipalities in greater Santiago which contain 40 percent or more industrial workers (see Table IV), we find that Allende received 119 women votes for every 100 for Alessandri and 147 for every 100 for Tomic.

TABLE IV

RELATIVE INDICES OF VOTES BETWEEN ALLENDE AND
ALESSANDRI AND ALLENDE AND TOMIC (1970). FEMALE
VOTES IN SEVEN WORKING CLASS MUNICIPALITIES
(*COMUNAS*) IN GREATER SANTIAGO (PERCENTAGES)

Percentage of Labor Force in Manufacturing, Mining, & Construction	Municipalities (*Comunas*)	Allende votes for each 100 votes for Alessandri	Allende votes each 100 votes for Tomic
40 or more	Puente Alto La Cisterna Quinta Normal Penca Barrancas San Miguel Granja	119*	147
50 or more	San Miguel Granja	130	203

*average

If we consider the only two municipalities in the capital city of Santiago with an absolute majority of industrial workers (San Miguel and Granja), Allende received 130 women's votes for every 100 for Alessandri and 203 for every 100 for Tomic.

It appears that when modern industrial capitalist economic and social relations penetrate the Chilean household and when strong working class organizations emerge, they have the effect of breaking down the traditionalist beliefs of women and making them available for radical political movements. The social concentration of class-conscious workers, in particular neighborhoods, appears to create a radical political culture which destroys the traditional paternalistic values that have customarily influenced women voters. In other social contexts the lower proportion of women voting for the Left was probably due to the fact that the woman's vote is disproportionately influenced by non-class factors, e.g. the mass media.

From a theoretical viewpoint, the social situation of work in a dependent capitalist society, the experiences that the workers acquire there, the conflicts engendered and the manner of resolving them are the central determinants of the working class vote. The massive support of the Socialist and Communist parties resides in the working class, and this provides, especially when they are politically allied, a cohesive and strategically situated social base that can be mobilized for social and political struggles and change. The Christian Democrats were not able to overcome the immobility of the social situation, in large part because its base was constituted by a heterogeneous mass of individuals with contradictory values and interests. The radicalization of the industrial working class in Chile was largely the result of the failure of Chilean and U. S. capital to generate dynamic development. At the same time the radicalized workers, through their social struggles and political power, provided the Marxist parties with an opportunity to develop Chilean society through socialist policies and institutions.

The Chilean constitution stipulates that Congress must select the president among the top two candidates if no candidate receives an absolute majority. Subsequent to the elections, intense negotiations between the UP and PDC took place. The PDC demanded a series of constitutional guarantees, which in part would guarantee their influence in the Army and public administration and thus place them in a position to limit Allende's power to carry out the reform program of the UP. Allende and his supporters accepted the PDC demands. With strong pressures from UP supporters to carry out his election promises, Allende presented Congress with a series of measures nationalizing banks, copper mines and monopolies. Chile's experiment with a democratically elected socialist government was being watched on all sides: its success or failure would have a very significant effect on the development of the rest of the hemisphere, including the United States.

THE REVOLUTIONARY LEFT: THE MOVEMENT OF THE REVOLUTIONARY LEFT

In 1966 an important extra-parliamentary opposition, the Movimiento de Izquierda Revolucionaria (MIR) appeared. Originally largely based in the student movement of Concepción, it was strongly influenced by the rural guerrilla strategy propounded by the Cuban Revolution. By 1969, however, the MIR initiated a series of successful armed assaults on banks and businesses. Modelling itself on the urban guerrilla strategy and techniques of the Uruguayian Tupamaros, the MIR began to attract considerable support among students and intellectuals. However, the popular base of the MIR was established through its organization of urban slum-dwellers. MIR organized a number of massive land occupations of those without housing (*sin casa*)—establishing "autonomous" settlements, neighborhoods administered and directed by MIR leaders and supporters. The combination of mass base and armed detachments engaged in direct action served to define an alternative route to revolution. During the 1970 electoral campaign the MIR, while not openly supporting Allende, refrained from any action which might have detracted from the campaign. Subsequent to the election, the MIR continued its political organization, mobilizing its support against the attempts by the Right to overthrow the Allende government and at the same time building up popular pressure in order that the Allende government fulfill its promises. Representing the Revolutionary Left, the MIR, stand ready to move its forces into armed action if and when the Allende government failed or was overthrown.

The presence of the MIR as an armed political force partially served to counter-balance the armed conservative forces in Chilean society. Moreover, the possibility existed that if the opposition of the propertied groups exceeded certain boundaries, the revolutionary political position put forth by the MIR might find a favorable response among broad sectors of the forces currently involved in the Popular Unity government.

CONCLUSION

Chile has experienced a variety of political experiments which have sought to develop the economy and improve the standard of living of the population.

The Radicals, representing a conglomeration of relatively privileged non-propertied sectors and factions of the dominant class, successfully created some new industries and social services but were unable to deal with the problems of Chilean dependence on U. S. investors, the concentration of economic power, and the exclusion of the majority of the working classes from the benefits of industrialization. The substantial achievements of social services and industrialization served to buttress the position of the new ruling groups, the urban industrialists and government functionaries.

The Ibáñez government—largely elected on a "nationalist-populist" program—attempted at first to limit the powers of the economically dominant class. Failing that it had reversed itself and sought to come to terms with U. S. and Chilean investors. The Alessandri government had sought to placate the working classes with a low-key program based on open collaboration with domestic and foreign investor groups in the hope of generating sufficient growth to provide additional benefits for lower income groups. The failure of the conservative Alessandri experience provided the background for the victory of the reformist Christian Democratic government of Eduardo Frei. But the incapacity of the Frei government to meet popular demands and put an end to foreign domination led to a general disenchantment. The election of Salvador Allende symbolized the end of a historical period: the repeated failures of reform, conservative and populist governments to direct Chilean society toward a more equitable and dynamic future. It is possible that the election of a socialist president marks a new period in Chilean history: the first attempt to develop the economy through public enterprises, central planning, and mass participation, without the dominant presence of foreign entrepreneurs. An exhaustion of the political solutions within the capitalist framework had been reached. It remained to be seen how successful the new collectivist program would be in overcoming Chile's chronic problems and maintaining popular support.

The electoral victory of Allende in September of 1970 and the successful transfer of power—despite the violent efforts made by the extreme right-wing and the economic impediments devised by the Frei-sector of the Christian Democrats—caused a wave of popular support. So, too, the government's first measures—the distribution of a free liter of milk to all school children, the opening of diplomatic relations with Cuba, China, and other Communist countries and the 45 percent wage increase and price freeze—met with enthusiasm. In the April 1971 elections, the Marxist-led coalition received an absolute majority of the votes cast for the two electoral blocs. During the first year, the Allende government nationalized practically all major mining and financial institutions, a number of major industries, about one-quarter of the large landed estates, and increased control over external commerce.

A great deal was achieved during Allende's first year in office. Although U. S. managers and capitalists left, copper production did not decline. Between January and June 1971, copper production at *Chuquicamata* (the largest mine) reached 142,052 short tons; under Frei in 1970, during a comparable period, 139,632 short tons were produced. The large scale mining concerns (as a whole) produced 331,182 metric tons from January to June 1971, a 9 percent increase over the same period during 1970, when production was 301,138 metric tons.

There were difficulties but, contrary to the image projected by the U. S. media, most important problems had little to do with socialist politics. The major problem was the decline in the international price of copper from a high of eight-five cents per pound to below forty-five cents a pound (for each cent decline in price, Chile lost seven million dollars). The drop in the copper price largely accounted for the decline in foreign reserves. The decline in foreign reserves had more to do with the international market and international corporations than with the efficiency of Allende's government.

Industrial growth was another feature of Chilean economic development during Allende's first year. Manufacturing industry represents nearly a third of national production and, *during the first eight months of 1971, industry increased 7.8 percent over 1970.* This growth occurred in a period when eighty industrial plants (including textiles, cement, and steel) were nationalized or intervened, and the groundwork was being prepared to organize working class participation in management.

The Allende government expropriated over 1,300 landed estates—as much as the U. S. showcase President Eduardo Frei did in six years—and *agricultural production increased by 5.2 percent in 1971* (almost double the growth rate of the Frei government). Despite the vast changes that occurred, the great majority of the reforms took place in a peaceful and orderly fashion. As the production figures suggest, change occurred with a minimum of social dislocation. Part of the success in agriculture was attributed to the government's purchase of banks and control of 80 percent of the credit which it directed, in part, to the land reform beneficiaries. In addition, agricultural growth was promoted by the establishment of a state national distribution firm to aid the peasants on the commercialization of their crops.

The construction industry grew by 9 percent through the building of 83,000 houses, several times the output of the last year of the Frei government. The consumer price index rose 35 percent during 1970 (under Frei). Under Allende through September 1971, it had risen to 13.8 toward a projected figure of approximately 17 percent—half the increase under Frei and the Christian Democrats.

Some shortages persisted under the Allende government. These resulted from extensive hoarding by the rich and middle-class (some basements looked like food warehouses; some freezers resembled meat markets); also there was the common practice of expropriated landowners slaughtering animals—including stud bulls and pregnant cows—to cause the government and people hardships. Nevertheless, the major reason for shortages was the increased purchasing power of the people: beef consumption increased 15 percent, fowls 16 percent, potatoes 55 percent, onions 54 percent, and condensed milk 10 percent. While wages were increased, prices and profits were frozen—as a result, the salaried and wage proportion of the national income increased from 51 percent in 1970 to 59 percent in 1971.

Upon leaving office, the Christian Democrats tried to provoke economic and political chaos: security was lax, capital was allowed to flood out of the country, production was paralyzed, and unemployment soared. The Christian Democrats and Frei hoped that the serious economic crises which they cultivated would lead to the overthrow or downfall of the Popular Unity government. Both their political calculations and their economic sabotage failed: the economy, stimulated by government investment and the increased purchasing power of the masses, began to expand. Unemployment declined from 8.3 percent in December 1970, a month after Allende's inauguration, to 4.7 percent in September of 1971. Labor shortages even developed in some provinces of the country.

In education, at the end of Allende's first year 94 percent of the school age children between six to fourteen, and 35 percent of those between the ages of fifteen to nineteen were in school—a substantial increase over previous regimes.

The government initiated a policy of deficit financing to absorb the unused manpower and resources, to increase the purchasing power of the poor, and to substantially broaden public investment. The increase in public investment compensated in great part for the decline in private and foreign investment. It was projected that in 1972 the government would give greater emphasis to the accumulation process with its base primarily in the internal surplus and in economic cooperation with the communist countries, West Europe, and Japan.

Probably the most popular measure adopted by the Allende government was his decision not to pay compensation in the course of nationalizing the copper mines. Every Chilean school boy knows how many billions of dollars the companies have taken out of the country over the years, and no Chilean has any sense that he owes the U. S. companies anything. On the contrary, many felt that the U. S. companies, not the Chilean government, should assume payment for the 700 million dollar debt incurred by the companies during their expansion period.

At the end of 1971, Chileans (not the U. S. investors) controlled strategic sectors of the economy such as mining, the peasants had received 2.84 million *hectares* of land (about 6.8 million acres), the banks served the public sector and small and medium entrepreneurs. More important, these changes occurred with the maximum of freedom for the opposition. The anti-government coalition of the Christian Democrats and the National Party still controlled the majority of the mass media of the country and spent enormous amounts of time and money financing publicity campaigns to sabotage government programs through public meetings and demonstrations.

The problem in Chile was not lack of freedom but possibly over-permissiveness. Christian Democrats, who shot over thirty miners in a wage dispute in *El Salvador* in defense of their U. S. partners while in the government, now agitated copper workers to double their wage demands against *government-owned mines* at a time when Allende was trying to develop the economy and provide jobs for Chilean workers earning less than one-fifth the salary of the copper workers.

U. S. RESPONSE TO THE ALLENDE GOVERNMENT

U. S. policy toward the democratically elected socialist president was in stark contrast to its policy toward the authoritarian military dictatorship in Brazil—toward the former unmitigated hostility, to the latter lavish praise and aid. The strategy of the U. S. opposition to the Allende government operated on three levels of policy making: an "outsider" strategy, an "insider" strategy, and a regional strategy.

The "outsider" strategy included basically three types of policy moves: symbolic hostility, veiled threats, and overt hostility. Symbolic hostility took the form of not extending to the Allende government the usual courtesies on ceremonial occasions: Nixon snubbed Allende after his electoral victory; the Executive Branch cancelled (over the objection of some military officers) the scheduled visit of the naval vessel *Enterprise* to Valparaiso. These symbolic gestures were meant to pressure the Chilean government and to encourage internal opposition. In fact they strengthened the image of the government as an independent force and alienated sectors of the patriotic lower middle class.

The speeches of U. S. officials regarding Chile's nationalization policies were full of threats of U. S. economic reprisals. The purpose of these speeches was to make other countries aware of possible negative reactions from the United States if they followed the Chilean route. The effect of these speeches was to rally a substantial sector of the Catholic Church in defense of the Allende government. Some churchmen raised the question of the possible justice of *all* underdeveloped countries nationalizing foreign enterprises without compensation.

Overt hostility took mainly economic form: cutting off U. S. loans and credits, while demanding payments on back loans accumulated by previous "friendly" bourgeois governments; cutting off Export-Import Bank loans, specifically blocking Chile's purchase of Boeing airplanes (shifting Chilean purchases to the Soviet Union); shutting Chile off from "international" bank loans (to pressure the Chilean government to meet U. S. corporate compensation demands). The United States could and did manipulate these banks since it has sufficient representation to block any proposed loan.

The "insider" strategy was basically directed toward maintaining and strengthening potential replacements of the Allende government through the selective channeling of resources. Thus, while the United States cut off all development loans, it granted the Chilean military five million dollars worth of credits to purchase military equipment.

In addition, the United States was in constant consultation with the titular leader of the opposition, Eduardo Frei, who made several unpublicized visits to Washington, New York, and curiously enough to the CIA financed Center for International Studies at MIT. The Catholic university stronghold of the right wing received a substantial loan from the IDB—thus increasing its base for anti-government activity.

The regional strategy that U. S. policy-makers began developing before the end of 1971 had two basic ingredients: (1) strengthening Brazil as a counter-revolutionary center and possible source of military intervention, if not directly in Chile, then at least in bordering countries such as Uruguay, if that country decided to go the Chilean route; (2) isolating Chile on its borders—especially with regard to Peru and Bolivia. In part this strategy, early in its development, brought about some immediate payoffs: two days before Chile and Bolivia were to open relations, the U. S. military and embassy (along with Brazil and Argentina) provided logistical support, intelligence reports, and medical supplies to aid the Bolivian army in its overthrow of the national popular Torres government. The United States gained a loyal government in Bolivia led by Hugo Banzer, increased border pressures on Chile, and acquired a passageway from Brazil through Bolivia to Chile. The United States also moved in the direction of closer relations with Peru: there were agreements on most issues which had been pending, especially since the "nationalist" Peruvian military came around to seeing the "need" of foreign investment for economic development. To the extent that U. S.-Peruvian differences narrow, the United States may, in the future, be able to push the Peruvians into a more distant relationship with Chile.

The overall purpose of the U. S. policy-makers—to which their "insider," "outsider," and regional strategies were directed—was to create economic dislocation and provoke a social crisis that could lead to either the overthrow of the Allende government by a civil-military coalition made up of the army, the Christian Democrats, and the extreme right-wing National Party or the discrediting of the government and its defeat in the 1973 congressional elections, thus undercutting the basis for future changes.

In general, the United States had very little success in shaping a hostile environment (with the exception of Bolivia): Argentine-Chilean relations were never better. The Andean countries (Chile, Peru, Ecuador, and Colombia) were working closer together. More important, the internal pressures building up in Argentina, Uruguay, and Colombia were all in the direction of Nationalist-populist and even socialist politics. In addition, the surcharge and other trade restrictive measures alienated bourgeois elites and their governments who felt "betrayed" by their *patron* Nixon. Many members of the Latin elite believed that the U. S. "owners" did have some responsibility and obligations to maintain regarding the upkeep of the client-states. Thus Allende scored a number of diplomatic victories while the U. S. attempt to build a wall of hostile countries around Allende met with little or no sympathy.

U. S. pressures were counter-productive in terms of their impact within Chile and proved to be embarrassing to faithful conservative followers within Chile. In brief, U. S. opposition strengthened national unity behind Allende—it weakened the internal opposition. Middle-of-the-roaders, the Church, and even sectors of the military considered U. S. bullying tactics an affront to their sense of national dignity and perceived Allende as a defender of the national patrimony.

Within the United States, press coverage has distorted events in Chile since Allende took office. Non-facts or opinions of the opposition have been presented without any attempt to provide the government's side. Minor incidents—for example, workers' strikes against employers over wages—were presented as if they were major challenges to the Popular Unity government. Shortages were reported as if they had never existed before in Chile. The U. S. mass media painted a blatantly false picture of growing economic chaos, social disorder, and a sharp decline of popular support. This was exactly the same pattern that the United States had followed prior to and leading up to the 1964 overthrow of the national-popular "Jango" Goulart government in Brazil. In this context, one can only hope that Chile can overcome the tragic difficulties that befall a nation which stands up to the U. S. empire and is forced to go it alone.

EPITAPH FOR A PEACEFUL REVOLUTION*

by Betty Petras and James F. Petras

In many ways Chile in August 1973 resembled Spain, 1936: a popularly elected left socialist government resting on the support of the industrial proletariat and the rural poor; tension and uncertainty rippling through the ranks of the left intelligentsia—waiting, knowing, any day,

* "Epitaph for a Peaceful Revolution" was previously published as "Ballots into Bullets: Epitaph for a Peaceful Revolution," in *Ramparts* vol. 12, no. 4, November 1973. It is reprinted here, with the exception of the final two paragraphs, by courtesy of *Ramparts* and the authors.

any moment, to hear the news that the military garrisons had revolted against the regime and that they would have to respond quickly with arms; the desperation, hysteria and frustration of the shopkeepers, businessmen, and professionals, who were also waiting for the military to move, who everyday prayed for a *golpe* (coup) that would put the *rotos* back in their place, would end "this nightmare" and return Chile to its "rightful owners," *la gente decente*. And out of the slums, enticed by money from right-wing sources and probably the U.S. embassy, hundreds of lumpen were pouring down into the downtown center—the fascist street-fighters of Patria y Libertad who filled the streets with garbage and gunned down anti-fascist truck drivers, racing down the streets bringing desperately needed food to the workers' barrios. Would it be today, tomorrow? Who would start it and how would it end? The questions arose, hung in the air, and remained unanswered. Each day in the early morning dawn the militants dragged themselves to bed after another night of preparedness, another night of "extreme alert" on orders issued from the Central Unica de los Trabajadores (CUT—National Workers Union).

On the morning of September 11, the top military chiefs decided to make their move. A junta was formed which demanded that Allende resign his elected post. The Navy commanders who had recently purged scores of constitutionalist sailors mutinied and seized control of Valparaiso, the port city of Santiago. At this signal, Air Force commanders sent planes to strafe and bomb the presidential palace into submission, while Army units captured the communications network, and Allende remained isolated in the palace where he was soon to die violently.

The military coup was not an isolated act but the culmination of right-wing violence that had raged in recent months. Nor were Allende's final attempts at compromise the first time he had made concessions to the military. For months right-wing terrorist groups had been in the streets—assassinating workers and destroying public facilities. Right-wing truck owners had been holding the Government hostage while shooting truck drivers trying to make deliveries. The Christian Democratic and National Party politicians joined in passing legislation to illegitimize the elected Government. Purges in the ranks of the armed forces and the forcible resignation of loyalist officers prepared the ground for the coup, and Allende accepted it all in the name of compromise, security and reconciliation. He sent his condolences to the widows of the murdered workers, told working-class housewives he sympathized with their problems but lacked the legal instruments to prevent the truck owners from starving the country.

Allende managed in the end to include all the notorious anti-Government military chiefs in his Cabinet—in the hope of preventing a coup. Six parties of the Government coalition condemned the commanders of the Navy for their hideous tortures of constitutionalist enlisted men; Allende disassociated himself from the denunciation, thereby cutting himself off from the only elements in the armed forces who could have saved the people from a bloody massacre. Allende was attempting to conciliate the very people who were to put the gun to his head in a very few days.

Now Allende is dead, trapped in the Presidential Palace where he was placed by millions of Chileans searching for a way out of poverty and exploitation. Allende will always be remembered for the honest effort he made to bring about a more democratic society. His personal bravery and dedication to the cause of social liberation will forever remain a symbol to those Chileans who are emerging to fight against the military dictatorship. For them Allende is not only a symbol of a more just and humane society, but a popular leader of great personal integrity. His final refusal to accede to brute force and his willingness to die rather than surrender will inspire millions of young men and women who carry on the struggle.

How did the military takeover come to pass? During its first year and a half, the Allende Government initiated peaceful but effective change. Large landed estates were expropriated, foreign mines were nationalized, and banks were statified—a measure of social justice long awaited by the Chilean populace. A number of hastily written books and articles were churned out by impressionistic observers hailing "la via Chilena" as a vindication of the electoral path to revolutionary social change. Yet it was too early; the major test was still to come. As the workers and peasants gained power and authority, demands and pressures increased to extend the process to industry, commerce and services. And it became clear early in 1972 that precisely those amorphous strata described by sociologists as the middle classes would not go along even if a majority of the electorate willed it. "Socialism" was barely tolerable if it affected the foreign and agrarian rich. But as workers began to occupy their factories, and to make efforts to equalize salaries and reduce status differences—as the petit-bourgeoisie saw their illusory hopes of someday becoming captains of industry or commerce smashed by the collective action of workers—they turned with a vengeance against the Government.

It was not any particular decline in income, or loss of material goods, that can adequately explain the intensity of feeling with which these petit-bourgeois sectors threw themselves into action. As a matter of fact it is likely that many of these groups have actually benefited materially from the Government's redistributive policies. Yet the mystique of property, mobility and ambition was being profoundly violated. As one pro-Christian Democratic professional in Chile told us, "Our way of life is being threatened. What do I care that I am making more money if the *rotos* are going to have their way." Another middle-sized factory owner exclaimed that, "We are surrounded. In everything we must deal with, there is the Government! We have no security; we will not invest." These Chilean enthusiasts of the democratic marketplace insisted, "*Nobody* wants him!" ignoring the fact that Allende was democratically elected and was still supported by the working class. Such democrats confused their own desire to retain their privileges with those of "everybody." From those whose security had been most fragile before, one heard a continual refrain which contains both plaintive yearning and prophetic understanding: "Chile will never be the same."

POPULAR POWER

In October 1972, the right-wing launched its first major offensive: doctors abandoned hospitals, shops were closed, truck-owners blocked the highways and mobs of middle-class students tried to take over the downtown area. This effort was thwarted as hundreds of thousands of workers occupied their factories and kept them running, set up distribution networks, and prepared for armed combat. The Right extracted some minor concessions from the Government, including military appointees to the cabinet; lost several score factories to the workers; and withdrew, hoping to win in the March 1973 elections what they could not accomplish in the streets during the October days. But in the congressional elections, the Left increased its vote substantially over the 1970 presidential elections. Moreover, the bases of support for both Left and Right were much more homogeneous: in the proletariat quarters, the Left rolled up large majorities, while the Right did the same in middle-class areas. The elections settled nothing; they were a prelude to new and more ominous confrontations.

In June 1973, an abortive right-wing military putsch was defeated by loyalist military officers. The CIA surely must have laughed at the rebels' ineptness: their tanks stopped for stop signs and red lights on their way to seize the governmental palace; mass communication networks were overlooked; and when a tank commander requested petroleum and was refused by the gas station attendant ("There's a gas shortage, you know."), the putschists abandoned the tank. Nevertheless, 21 people were killed before the rebels were put down, and U.S. military advisers must have resolved to correct their "inadequacies" in the future. The well-coordinated uprising of the Chilean armed forces on September 11 was nothing if not a professional operation.

The petit-bourgeois offensive which sought to paralyze the country provoked a historic counter-offensive among the Chilean working class: *Poder Popular*—Popular Power. The very concept was antagonistic to the bureaucratic control of the Government apparatus. "The people are fighting, creating Popular Power," became the new cry.

Factories, stores, offices and farms were occupied, owners and counter-revolutionary managers were expelled, and the workers themselves assumed the administration and defense of the means of production. As *Alerta!*, a daily wall paper of October 1972, proclaimed, "Chile is to be found producing normally from Arica to Magellanes, in the city, in the mines and in the countryside."

The accounts of the initiative and determination with which the workers responded were varied; when the Revlon textile factory was found closed, the workers, all of them women, met, organized, persuaded their vacillating *compañeras*, and single-handedly set the industry operating again. When public transportation halted, workers trudged miles on foot to assume their posts at work. Even the children of the working-class municipality of San Miguel organized to clean the streets of the *miguelitos*, the bent nails scattered by rightists to disable the workers' vehicles.

Networks of direct distribution were established: using vehicles requisitioned from the factories, workers brought their products—dishes, shoes, sugar—straight to the neighborhoods to be sold or exchanged for foodstuffs brought by peasants from the countryside. In the words of a Socialist in Concepcion—both a CUT leader and a leader of an industrial *cordon*—"The potential for Popular Power already exists in the consciousness of the workers. . . . but a large part of converting this into a concrete reality will depend on the vanguards."

What began as a "defensive measure" soon took on a meaning of its own; new forms of class mobilization, organization and struggle emerged. Industrial belts (*cordones industriales*) were organized from below, linking all factories within an area to co-ordinate the workers' resistance to a rightist-military coup. *Comandos comunales* (municipal councils) spontaneously emerged, joining factory workers, neighborhood assemblies, women's organizations, slum settlers—all the popular forces within a geographical area—and providing a vehicle for direct action. These commandos bypassed the traditional Left leadership and the established trade union apparatus, whose capacity for instant mobilization was found wanting.

In describing the success of the cordones, one leader pointed to the fact that, "communists as well as socialists, MAPU, FTR, PR and independents worked together united in the tasks of the cordon." The leaders of these proto-soviets were described by one Allendista as "insolent young men"—aggressively independent young militants whose class instincts distrusted the wheeling and dealing going on in the Moneda (the governmental palace). They trusted in their own power, that of their *companeros* and their workmates. When Allende called on the factory workers to march on the palace to defend the Government against the June putsch, some militants are reported to have told Allende to come to the cordones to be defended.

AUGUST 1973—THE PRELUDE

The cordones and commandos reached their peak in the October 1972 crisis and confrontation; and then, lacking resources and practical tasks, they began to ebb, their members attracted back to the CUT, which organized marches to defend the Government. After initially failing to register the significance of the cordones, the CUT moved to link them more directly to their organization.

The center of the struggle has been in the urban centers, which contain over 70 percent of the labor force. The peasants, while not irrelevant, were an important *auxiliary* force in the struggle between workers and bourgeoisie. The peasants provided logistical support—supplying foods and raw materials.

By August the economy had begun to deteriorate because of the intense social and political conflict. The shortages of essential food items had begun to adversely affect the standard of living in working-class districts—where Government and popular distribution methods failed to function with the efficiency of October 1972. The lack of raw materials had caused important industries to function at less than full capacity, and construction of desperately needed public housing halted as building supplies ran out. Bread lines in working-class sectors were commonplace, while hoarding, black-marketeering and speculation had become a way of life in the *barrios altos*, the upper-income neighborhoods. Run-away inflation rates averaging a 15 percent monthly increase during June, July and August were further dislocating and undermining the economy. Inflation, shortages, and their consequences even more exacerbated the conflict between social classes.

In great part, the deterioration of the economy was the result of the political opposition both internal and external, and not the incompetence and bungling of socialist ideologues, as reported by the U.S. press. Under the pretext of objective reporting, anti-communist journalists like Jonathan Kandell of the *Times* and Norman Gall white-washed right-wing terror, U.S. aggression, and Christian Democratic sabotage, presenting the same picture as the rightist press in Chile: leftists threatening democracy while leading the country to anarchy and chaos. Such reporting created the political atmosphere for the "tragic" but inevitable overthrow of the Government.

In the struggle for control over increasingly scarce resources in a polarized class situation, each side demanded more radical solutions. The workers in the factories insistently sought rationing, workers' or governmental ownership of transportation and retail distribution, and a *mano dura* (hard hand) against the speculators, profiteers and opponents who were sabotaging the economy. Some cordones proposed to seize the trucks of the private owners whose main goal was to bring down the Government; the truck lockout was accompanied by hundreds of rightist anti-Government terrorists incidents, particularly by the fascist Patria y Libertad. Over 500 such attacks between mid-July and August alone were launched against bridges, railroad tracks, power facilities, oil pipe lines, stores, homes and trucks. Meanwhile, the legal opposition parties blocked all reform legislation, used the courts to free terrorists, dispatched the army to disarm factories, prevented any legislation on sanctions against speculation and blackmarketeering, passed a congressional resolution calling on the government to resign because of incompetence, launched impeachment proceedings against members of the Cabinet, and openly urged the military to take over key posts in the Government. In addition, routine sacking of the economy occurred in the private sector (disinvestment and running down of machinery), and bureaucratic sabotage in the public sector.

The intensifying anti-Government activity within Chile was carefully coordinated with U.S. policy designed to further weaken the economy. Loans and credits from public, private and international banks were cut off and shipments of essential parts for U.S.-produced machinery were inexplicably "delayed." On the direct-action front, U.S. financing of opposition activity—especially the truck owners' lockout—was evidenced by the large influx of dollars which recently stabilized for over a month the price of the dollar on the black market.

The U.S. Embassy in Santiago was well-qualified to provide assistance to those plotting against the Government. Ambassador Nathaniel Davis is a veteran with practical experience in eliminating leftists; during his ambassadorship in Guatemala, several thousand working-class and peasant militants were gunned down. Davis surrounded himself with a team of key operatives—"professionals" with long experience in the ways and methods of subversion. Their efforts were cloaked in utmost secrecy; only the results were obvious. Their credentials speak for themselves: John W. Isaminger, political section of the embassy (1942, Army Intelligence; 1951, Intelligence for the Pentagon; operations in La Paz, Guatemala and Washington); Daniel Arzao, Political Council, U.S. Embassy (1943, Army Secret Service; 1951, State Department; 1953, CIA; operations in Phnom Penh, Montevideo, Bogota and Washington); Raymond Warren, office of the First Secretary (1943, U.S. Air Force; 1954, State Department and later CIA; operations in Caracas and Bogota); Frederick Lastrash, First Secretary (1943, U.S. Marines; 1948, Naval Intelligence; 1956, State Department; operations in Calcutta, New Delhi, Amman, Cairo and Caracas); John Tipton, Second Secretary (CIA and State Department; operations in Mexico City, La Paz and Guatemala).

The first specific indication that Washington was involved in the actual preparations for the coup was found in a Reuters dispatch from Washington, apparently leaked by dissident State Department officials. According to the report, Washington knew the time and date of the coup 48 hours before it occurred. An Associated Press dispatch of Sept. 12 observed, "Ties between [the U.S. and Chilean] military establishments seemed to have flourished" over the recent period. There was a large influx of unannounced U.S. officials operating in Chile. The official State Department Foreign Service List listed only 89 functionaries in Chile. Yet a *New York Times* report on Sept. 12 claims there were over 1100, including "dependents."

According to some observers, the coup was probably planned and coordinated by a joint team which included U.S. military personnel and CIA operatives, headed up by U.S. Ambassador Davis, the Chilean military staff, and key political figures, including Eduardo Frei. Once the plan was consummated, Davis flew to Washington the weekend before the coup, reported on final preparations, and obtained further instructions. He then returned to Chile the day before the coup to be on the spot for its execution. The coup thus was neither solely the product of the CIA nor the result of purely Chilean forces, but a combined effort resulting from the shared interests of both the U.S. and the Chilean bourgeoisie and its military allies.

A NATION DIVIDED

A measure of natural dislocation accompanies any transitional period involving fundamental social change: there were administrators directing industries who still lacked the full experience to do so; there was general laxness in disciplining absentee workers; and, as one U.S. technocrat commented, there was an "excess" of democracy in running enterprises. This was in some sense a necessary development. After hundreds of years of exploitation, the workers had a lot to say to each other and a lot to learn as they were the first to admit. But what was most impressive was the way in which the workers were learning to control their destiny: over one-third of the employees in the metal-machinery sector of industry attended training schools to learn new skills; courses in accounting and budgeting (both prerequisites to efficient management) were overflowing; the national plan, including priorities on allocation of resources, was discussed intelligently and freely at workers' assemblies in the plants. The short-term costs of this "excess" democracy were perhaps more visible, but less relevant, than the long-term gain: in this direction, it seemed, lay socialism with a human face. And it was the workers we spoke to who were most aware of their own shortcomings, as well as those of the Government.

Obviously, the economy could not continue performing for long in this way. Yet the deterioration of the economy could not have been resolved in the manner proposed by the Communist Party or Allende. No efforts at increased productivity and planning had a chance to succeed while the question of political power remained undecided. Increasing productivity or controlling inflation would not have occurred as long as the material means to realize these goals were controlled in part by an opposition whose singular goal was the destruction of the Government. For example, this winter (June to August), the Communist Party made a gigantic effort to increase the areas of land to be sown and succeeded—until the truck owners' strike paralyzed the delivery of fertilizers and seeds, as well as leaving peasants with no means to deliver their products to the city. But Allende's complaint that he lacked the "constitutional" means to prevent the destruction of society was no encouragement to the Left—least of all to working-class women who stood three and four hours in line for oil and bread, when it was available. No wonder when thousands of militant proletarian women sought an audience at the Moneda, they demanded the Government confiscate the trucks removed from use by their owners—who had refused all settlement offers, except, as one typical owner put it, "one based on the departure of this Government."

By September there was a great and widening division in Chile—a polarization of class forces in which everyone was almost obligated to take sides. Not everybody on either side was clearly aware of the refinements of underlying ideologies, or all of the consequences inherent in the political position with which they were allied. In part, the lines were drawn according to class loyalties and sentiments—a mixture of social solidarity and antagonism to those who threatened to impose an alien way of life.

For a moment the working class' newly-won role as protagonist of a new society engendered a rejection of all forms of domination and exploitation. Freedom and respect were won in massive confrontations and through years of struggle and study; it is inconceivable that the workers will passively return to the old patterns of subservience and domination. They have experienced freedom and it is likely they will return to capitalism at the end of a bayonet. The industrial proletariat formed the core of socialist politics, but it was not alone. Several hundred thousand unionized peasants and rural workers allied themselves with the Left and provided active support, though their capacity for political mobilization was somewhat more limited. Lastly, there were the *pobladores*, the slum settlers, the urban poor—a large and heterogeneous stratum which was badly mauled by inflation and shortages. Despite the bitterness of empty promises and government vacillation, they were loyal to the revolutionary Left, awaiting the promises of the future.

On the other side of the barricades stood the upper classes and their many allies among the petit-bourgeoisie and lumpenproletariat. Among these amorphous social forces, the truck owners showed themselves to be the most combative and effective. Doctors and dentists were on strike almost continually throughout the year. Nearly all the established "professional" associations had become full-time political vehicles for right-wing politics; lawyers, doctors, dentists and agronomists passed a series of political resolutions up to and including calls for the resignation of the Government. In a state of hysteria and impotence, the doctors expelled Allende from the medical association. In the hospitals of the poor, emergency wards were unattended; women in childbirth, children and old people suffered without medical care; but for the doctors, the defense of their class privilege had priority. All the clap-trap about professional ethics evaporated; what remained was the insolent and gratuitous sneer: "Let the workers go to their Socialist ministers for a cure." Probably the most dangerous classes in Chile were the dispossessed, but physically present and politically active, ex-landowners, ex-industrialists, ex-lawyers for U.S. corporations, etc.—all of whom felt they had nothing to lose and were willing to risk anything, to support any adventure, to recover their property. This stratum provided recruits for the fascist terrorist groups and were probably the warmest advocates of "Plan Jakarta"— physical annihilation of several thousand militants subsequent to a coup.

The depth and pervasiveness of class polarization divided the Church and, to a lesser extent, the Army. There were no "purely professional or non-political organizations in Chile. In the Church hierarchy there were approximately one hundred supporters of "Christians for Socialism" while on the other side, rightist priests were led by one Raul Hasbun, who directed ultra right-wing propaganda over the Catholic University television station. In the middle stood the Cardinal, attempting the impossible—to mediate and reconcile the conflicting forces. In a July exhortation to all Catholics, the Episcopal Council pleaded with both sides to avoid civil war, transform Chile into a modern and progressive society with justice for the poor through profound social change—all through dialogue and prayer.

In the Armed Forces, horizontal divisions replaced vertical ones as class divisions in society became more salient. These divisions were blunted, however, by the incapacity of the Government to offer support and encouragement to the enlisted men who remained loyal. The great majority of Navy and Air Force officers supported the coup against the Government. Largely drawn from the urban middle class, many were willing to tolerate nationalist and agrarian changes but shifted to the right along with their civilian counterparts as the process deepened. Prior to the coup, many officers met frequently with U.S. military advisers in Chile, openly expressing their hostility to the Government and their desire for its demise. Not surprisingly, under the cover of these private house gatherings, U.S. military officials encouraged their Chilean counterparts to act. No doubt the State Department's reported promise to a former official of the Frei Government of hundreds of millions of dollars of direct aid to a Frei-led Government subsequent to a coup, served to convince recalcitrant Air Force officers of the inefficiency of socialism.

Many enlisted men, sons of the popular classes, were against the coup —because of the improvements that accrued to their class of origin as well as the numerous benefits which the Allende government bestowed on the military. Yet the Government worked instead with their officers, men of the Right, without making any effort to link the workers with the ordinary soldiers. Indeed, during the early part of 1973, the generals were still divided between loyalists (about 40 percent for Allende) and putschists (about 60 percent) allied with the Right or in opposition to all political parties. By the end of August, however, the putschists clearly gained the upper hand, forcing the resignation of three loyalists (Prats, Pickering and Sepulveda), and thus further homogenizing the leadership of the Army General Staff in preparation for a coup. The coup was delayed mainly because there was considerable uncertainty among the generals about the degree of support for such a move among conscripts and enlisted men.

While the Armed Forces were deeply divided, the prospects for a successful rightist coup were dim. The Right instead relied on terrorism, combined with pressure inside the military, in attempting to force the Government to resign. The greatest fear among prudent putschists was that the loyalist sectors of the Army would have sufficient support to arm the workers and turn the coup into a civil war, one which the Left could very well win. The right-wing military waited until it had purged its internal opposition before initiating action on more favorable terrain: a unified army against unarmed workers.

The class polarization also deeply affected the Chilean intelligentsia, a group which, in previous periods, commonly expressed concern for the poor and protested against injustice. But by the end of the Government's third year, university professors and even the majority of students allied themselves against the egalitarian aspirations of the working class. Three-fifths of the professors, and over half of the students, elected the anti-government rector of the University of Chile. Over 90 percent of the students are from the middle class; they provided the bodies for the downtown demonstrations, as well as joining ultra-right wing groups. As in Cuba in 1960, and Russia in October 1917, the "idealistic" students suddenly discovered the incompatibility of their class aspirations and a popular revolution.

The "progressive" intellectuals—those who voted for the Left in 1970 —were disoriented by the intensity of the struggle, appalled and exhausted by the shortages, and uncertain of the role they should assume. "The workers don't need us, they act for themselves," were the words of a sociologist. Immersed in their own day-to-day personal problems, they played a marginal role in the workers' struggle. Only a small core of revolutionary intellectuals, and a minority of students, actively participated in the process through disciplined parties and in the day-to-day preparations to resist the coup—recognizing their role as auxiliaries to the workers' organizations.

SMASHING THE DEMOCRATIC MYTH

When Allende was elected in September 1970, a considerable amount of discussion and debate focused on the possibility of Chile following a distinct path toward the construction of socialism; the image projected was of a peaceful transformation of the old structures, utilizing or modifying the existing legal, administrative, military and political institutions. Chile's parliamentary tradition was cited, along with its supposedly non-political professional army, as providing a basis for such peaceful change.

But Chile's parliamentary system was always profoundly anti-democratic. The elected bodies always clearly represented the interests of the ruling classes, while for decades excluding the majority of the lower class from meaningful political participation. This became even more true after 1970, as the system attempted to block any efforts by the working class and peasants to create democratic institutions that reflected their class interests. Congress and the courts were the staunchest opponents of any changes which could have the *cordones* or *comandos* assume any effective legislative power.

The myth of Chilean democracy was also a crucial assumption of Allende's Popular Unity Government. The strategy behind Allende's leadership was that the transition of socialism would be an incremental process; having acquired "part" of the government, the Left through time would gradually gain the other portion and eventually transform governmental office into social power. Unfortunately the historical experience in Chile showed otherwise; even before the coup the peaceful and legal transition to socialism had been brought to a stop. Every institutional road was blocked by the legal and illegal measures adopted by the opposition. The only radical transformations that occurred in the last year were the result of the independent activities of the working class outside of the Government, and in a few instances against the explicit directives of the Popular Unity leadership. For example, almost three-fourths of the industrial firms in the private sector were expropriated because of workers' initiatives, enterprises which the Government had no intention of nationalizing and which at one point Allende and the Communists tried to return to their previous owners—unsuccessfully, because the workers would have none of it.

As a result of the Government's incapacity to meet the obstructionist and illegal challenges of the Right, or the demands of the workers, during the past several months governmental authority sharply declined. Right-wing and working-class actions increasingly defined new areas of power. The Christian Democrats, who a year ago pretended to oppose a military takeover, were insisting the Government be replaced by military officers. Senator Frei, the U.S.'s man in Santiago, refused to criticize the military putsch of June 29, or the continuing rightist terror, while his party's paper appealed to the most retrograde prejudices of the petit-bourgeoisie; on the editorial page of *La Prensa* appeared an article decrying the takeover of Chile by a "Jewish-Communist cell!"

Defying every Government decree, the Christian Democrats and their right-wing allies in the National Party and Patria y Libertad were seeking to assemble a parallel government while goading the military to seize power. In anticipation of September 11, a National Party congressman publicly acknowledged shooting at demonstrators outside of Congress, justifying his action as necessary to defend himself against "Communist dogs." The bourgeoisie openly defied all existing laws which did not suit their interest, all in the name of liberty and democracy. The workers, on the other hand, moved ahead and expropriated factories, attempted to organize themselves for defense, and rejected judicial decisions by bourgeois jurists. The same jurists who freed right-wing bombers and jailed peasant demonstrators were described in the U.S. press as an independent judiciary.

Within the industrial belts, the functioning of workers' defense committees and distributive networks were singularly hampered by the Government's unwillingness to accept a general rationing scheme administered from below. The Chilean workers were aware of the fact that all the expensive restaurants were full of middle-class patrons stuffing themselves with meat and chicken and pisco sours, while they in turn waited in line in hopes of obtaining a bone for soup. The workers' support of Allende was conditional and critical; but lacking any clear revolutionary alternative they pushed ahead, hoping he would rectify his course before it was too late. Despite misgivings about the Government, workers had no illusions what its overthrow would mean. They had already witnessed the barbarous treatment metered out by rightist military officers supposedly searching for arms caches in the factories.

TIME RUNS OUT

In the day-to-day struggle in the barracks, factories and fields, each side tried to gain tactical victories, accumulating forces which would weaken the other side. Each side attempted to impose its own definitive solution to the question of political hegemony; and in the process, each side could have been capable of paralyzing the economy and society. In the middle stood Allende, desperately trying to finish his term in office, appealing first for negotiations with the enemy, and then turning to the workers to defend him against the violent threats of precisely the same people with whom he had proposed a settlement the day before. The institutional noose fastened around Allende's neck by the combined political-military opposition was tightened every day.

First, a *Ley de control de armas* (arms control law) was passed, purportedly to disarm "all" armed groups. Administered by the Army, it resulted in massive searches and raids of factories; workers were herded out in the most humiliating and insulting fashion. Though arms were seldom found, the generals made their point to the workers about what they could expect after a *golpe*. These operations with helicopters and blocked roads were clearly preparations, simulations of a real military takeover.

Throughout July and August, Navy commanders harangued enlisted men against the Government, and then proceeded to arrest those individuals who objected for being "insubordinate." Brazilian-style tortures, such as the forced ingestion of human excretion, were applied to enlisted men who had not responded with enthusiasm to the idea of a coup, to force them to admit that they were plotting subversive action. Meanwhile, to facilitate a harmonious takeover, the Navy officers were purging all anti-coup conscripts and enlisted men, as well as leftist factory workers in munition factories.

In the third instance, the right-wing generals exacted sufficient pressure to oust non-socialist but loyalist General Carlos Prats. Allende, faced with the choice of retiring six rightist Generals and perhaps facing an open military confrontation, or accepting the resignation of Prats, chose the latter. But so doing, he surrounded himself with even more conservative forces, and destroyed one of the few chances the Left had of leading a successful military struggle against the Right.

Along with the attacks on the workers, enlisted men, and loyalist generals, fascist groups stepped up their terrorist assaults against the small number of shopkeepers and truck and bus drivers wanting to go about their business. Workers' leaders such as Oscar Balboa, leader of non-striking truckers, were ruthlessly assassinated, and scores of quietly heroic bus drivers were stoned and shot as they tried to complete their runs. But the Government was unable to offer adequate armed protection, especially with generals sitting in the Cabinet, clandestinely plotting the Government's overthrow.

It was not legality, nor Chile's "democratic tradition," nor Allende's adroitness which restrained for a time the civilian and military *golpistas* from achieving their ends. They were acutely aware of the workers' organizations, their capacity for mobilization, their willingness to fight; they knew, too, that some workers were armed. They were aware of the divisions in their own ranks; they had heard the enlisted men whisper that, "He is the best President we've ever had . . ." And the military officials must have already calculated the costs of the destructive civil war they knew that a *golpe* could provoke. In a textile factory, a young apprentice, a militant socialist, put it nicely: "The military may take over the government, but they can't run the factories—we'd blow them up first."

But time ran out. The petit-bourgeois violently resisted the expansion of workers' power, the socialization of the economy, the proletarianization of the country. The workers were tired of the black market, the shortages and exorbitant prices, the terrorist attacks. As one worker put it, "We lack bread, oil and revolution. We can do without bread and oil, but not without revolution." For many the uncertainty became unbearable; the time came for a definitive answer, and it came from the Right.

MARCELO J. CAVAROZZI is Researcher at the Center for Research in Public Administration, Di Tella Institute, Buenos Aires, Argentina. He has been Visiting Professor at the University of Chile and Lecturer at San Francisco State College. He has published in scholarly journals in Latin America and Europe and is presently doing research on the politics of the Argentine working class and trade unions after 1955.

JAMES F. PETRAS is professor of Sociology at State University of New York, Binghamton. He received his M.A. and Ph.D. from the University of California at Berkeley.

The Western Political Science Association selected Prof. Petras' Ph.D. thesis as the best dissertation in 1968. He is the author of *Politics and Social Forces in Chilean Development* (Berkeley: University of California Press 1969); *Politics and Social Structure in Latin America* (New York, Monthly Review Press 1970); *Cultivating Revolution: The United States and Agrarian Reform in Latin America* (New York: Random House, 1971)—co-authored with Robert LaPorte; *Peasants in Revolt* (Austin: University of Texas Press, 1972)—co-authored with Hugo Zemelman Merino; Professor Petras has co-edited with Maurice Zeitlin *Latin America: Reform or Revolution?* (New York: Fawcett 1968); and co-edited with Martin Kenner *Fidel Castro Speaks* (New York: Grove Press 1969). He has published scores of articles in the major professional journals as well as in political journals in the U.S. and Latin America.

BETTY PETRAS is a Ph.D. candidate in sociology at S.U.N.Y., Binghamton and has published articles and monographs on Chilean society and politics.

STATISTICS

Chile's Presidents since 1932:
    1932–1938   Arturo Alessandri (Liberal)
    1938–1942   Pedro Aguirre Cerda (Radical)
    1942–1946   Juan A. Ríos (Radical)
    1946–1952   Gabriel González-Videla (Radical)
    1952–1958   Carlos Ibáñez (Independent)
    1958–1964   Jorge Alessandri (right-wing Independent)
    1964–1970   Eduardo Frei Montaluo (Christian Democrat)
    1970–   Salvador Allende Gossens (Socialist)

Area: 463,604 square miles
Arable Land: 6.0% (1965)
Population: 9,780,000 (1970)
Birth Rate: 31.9 per 1000 persons (1965–1969)
Infant Death Rate: 71.0 per 1000 infants (1971)
Population Growth Rate: 2.4%
Life Expectancy: 53-6 years (1960–'61)
% of Population Living in Cities: 68.2% (1960)

Literacy Rate: 83.6% (15 years and older) (1960)

Education: 64.4% of 5–14 year old population (1,354,542 students) are
    enrolled in primary school (1969)
    52,937 students are enrolled in institutions of higher education (1968)
    42 students/teacher (primary level) (1969)

Medical:
    5.5 doctors/10,000 persons (1968)
    2.1 dentists/10,000 persons (1968)
    40 hospital beds/1000 (1968)

Newspapers: 53 daily newspapers (1962)
    86 daily newspapers circulated/1000 persons (1962)

Radio: 143 radio receivers/1000 persons (1970)
Television: 51 TV receivers/1000 persons (1970)
Capital: Santiago

Provinces and Population:

Concepíon	539,450
Coquimbo	309,177
Curico	105,839
Linares	171,302
Llanquihue	167,491
Magallanes	73,426
Malleco	174,205
Maule	79,763
Nuble	285,730
O'Higgins	259,724
Osorno	144,088
Santiago	2,436,398
Talca	206,255
Tarapacá	123,064
Valdivia	259,798
Valparaiso	618,112
Antarctica territory	202

Government Budget: 76,418 million escudos ($307 million U.S.) (1972)

Presidents:

1932–38	Arturo Alessandri (Liberal)
1938–42	Pedro Aguirre Cerdo (Radical)
1942–46	Juan A. Ríos (Radical)
1946–52	Gabriel González Videle (Radical)
1952–58	Carlos Ibánez (Independent)
1958–64	Jorge Alessandri (right-wing Independent)
1964–70	Eduardo Frei Moctatuo (Christian Democrat)
1970–	Salvador Allendo Gossenz (Popular Unity)

GNP: 5,316,000 million U.S. dollars (1969)

Per Capita GNP: 610 U.S. dollars

Rate of Growth of GNP: for the years 1967–70, an average annual rate of 2.9%; for 1971, 8.5%

Unemployment: 3.8% (1971)

Distribution of Work Force—See page four

Land Tenure Structure	Units	Land
0–5 hectares	37.0%	0.3%
5–20 hectares	25.0%	1.5%
20–100 hectares	23.0%	5.6%
100–500 hectares	10.1%	11.8%
500–1000 hectares	2.0%	7.3%
Over 1000 hectares	2.2%	73.0%

Trade Balance: (1970)
   export: 1,286.8 million U.S. dollars
   import: 1,208.9 million U.S. dollars

Source of Foreign Exchange by Product:
   78.3% copper
    7.7% iron

    2.0% nitrates

Foreign Debt: 2503.4 million U.S. dollars (public external debt including disbursed and undisbursed funds)

Service Payments on External Public Debt: 18.9% of exports of goods and services

Foreign Investment: The U.S. has 75% of all the investments in Chile. The value is estimated at $788 million.

Distribution of the Work Force: (1960)
    6.8% professional, technical, administrative, executive
   13.8% clerical, sales work
   27.5% farmers, fishermen, hunters, loggers, etc.
    2.3% miners, quarrymen
    3.3% transportation and communication
   26.6% craftsmen, production workers
   13.5% service, sport and recreation
    6.2% workers not classified by occupation

CHAPTER 6

CUBA

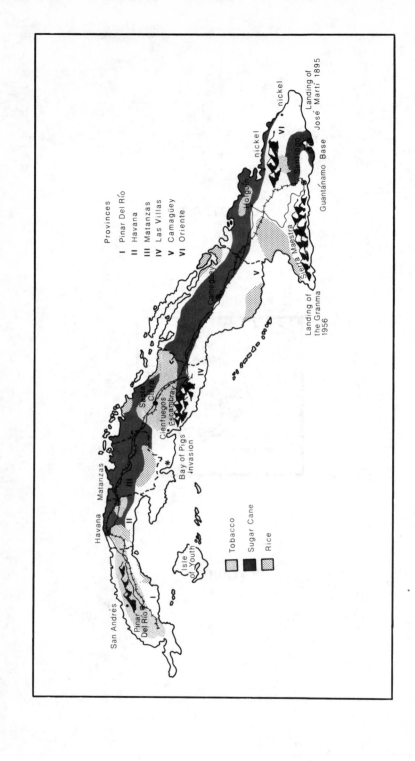

CONTENTS

CUBA

"The fairest island human eyes have yet beheld . . . It is certain that where there is such marvelous scenery, there must be much from which profit can be made." — Christopher Columbus

"If the Christians go to heaven, I do not want to go to heaven. I do not wish ever again to meet such cruel and wicked people as Christians who kill and make slaves of the Indians." — Hatuey, Indian rebel leader, before being burned at the stake in Cuba.

CUBA

BY

DONALD W. BRAY

AND

TIMOTHY F. HARDING

THE CUBAN LIBERATION PROCESS FROM THE INDIANS TO THE 1970's

The Cuban Socialist Revolution took place in a country which was one of the first areas to be subjected to Spanish colonization and the last to win its independence from Spain. Cuba emerged from Spanish control only to be indirectly colonized by the United States via the Platt Amendment, which left Cuba more completely dominated by the United States than any other nation in the "Third World." Poor and underdeveloped though it was, Cuba quite early in its history displayed "the main structural features of a capitalist economy." By the 1950's the nation had a relatively high degree of urbanization, a large organized labor movement, and nearly all of the rural population had been employed directly in the production of export crops. There was more U.S. capital invested in Cuba per capita than in any other country in the third world except the oil-producing countries, and there was a high index of autos per person compared to the rest of the underdeveloped world. But since it did not have a high level of industrialization, Cuba's economy was dominated by sugar exports; moreover, all of the sectors of the Cuban economy were dependencies of foreign banks and other foreign companies. Unlike the situation in mineral-exporting or manufacturing-exporting countries, Cuba's main foreign exchange earner—sugar—was labor-intensive and absorbed a great deal of manpower. The mechanization of sugar cane cutting and harvesting required the designing of special machines which were still not available for wide-scale use fifteen years after the Cuban Revolution.*

The economic transformation of Cuba has involved a gut-wrenching effort through which the loyalty of the comfort-seeker has not been retained. This transformation has been carried out under the nerve-testing threat of U.S. intervention. The Revolution has resolved not to await the achievement of material abundance before undertaking radical social innovations. The degree of change has been awesome and the hemisphere will never be the same because of it.

BACKGROUND TO REVOLUTION

"The fairest island human eyes have yet beheld. . . It is certain thatwhere there is such marvelous scenery, there must be much from which profit can be made." Christopher Columbus.

"If the Christians go to heaven, I do not want to go to heaven. I do not wish ever again to meet such cruel and wicked people as Christians who kill and make slaves of the Indians." Hatuey, Indian rebel leader before being burned at the stake in Cuba.

SPANISH CONQUEST OF THE INDIANS

Many of the indigenous people of Cuba were killed during the Spanish conquest of the island. The rest failed to survive the establishment of an economy based on forced Indian labor used to extract gold and to grow food. Several Indian cultures populated the island at the time of the Spanish conquest, but none of them had such highly developed social systems as the Aztecs, Mayans, or Incas. They had not developed a class system or large numbers of specialized artisans, traders, etc. The Taino Indians who had arrived in eastern Cuba between 1400 and 1460 and

---

* Cuban-Soviet efforts to develop a cane-cutting machine during the 1960's failed because the machines broke down under tropical operating conditions and were not effective when the cane was wind-tangled or the land was uneven. However, a second generation of sugar harvesting combines, the self-propelled "KPT-1," which first came off Soviet assembly lines in significant numbers in 1973, were mechanically perfected and tested to a degree which promised that the mechanization of the Cuban sugar harvest was finally in sight.

were located on the eastern tip of the island, had the most developed technology and besides hunting and fishing, had settled in villages and grew yucca, maize, boniato, pineapple, and tobacco.

After an initial contact with Cuba during Columbus' first voyage, in which the Indians were friendly and hospitable, the Spanish established themselves on Hispaniola. When they returned to conquer Cuba in 1511, some Indian refugees from Hispaniola organized heroic resistance and the conquest became a fierce battle, with the Indians turning to guerrilla warfare under the leadership of Hatuey, and establishing the earliest Cuban tradition of struggle against oppression. Indians who resisted the Spanish were enslaved, a practice condoned at first by the Spanish Church and Crown. Those Indians who remained hospitable were subjected to unprovoked attacks and were often illegally enslaved. Indians were hunted as a sport, and captive Indians were mutilated and fed alive to Spanish war dogs.

The Indians viewed property as communal rather than private. This brought them into immediate and unremitting conflict with the Spanish concept of private ownership and the exploitive system of the *encomienda,* under which the Crown granted the labor power of Indians in a certain area to a Spaniard for a certain period of time. Besides the *encomienda,* the Spaniard received private land grants on which he could employ the labor. The Spaniard in return was supposed to turn the Indians into willing subjects through religious instruction. Laws which protected the Indian were largely ignored. Lands specifically reserved for the Indians were seized by Spaniards. Indians were forced to mine alluvial gold under inhuman conditions. Bartolomé de las Casas reported the death of seven thousand children from famine in a period of a few months when their parents were driven off to work the gold mines. The indigenous life-style did not prepare the Indians for Spanish exploitation. Many Indians preferred suicide and killing their families and children to the nightmare of colonization. Diseases took their toll. There were constant Indian rebellions and raids on Spanish plantations.

With the exception of a few individual clerics, the Spanish Church did little to help the Indians. Bishop Sebastián Ramírez who was "Protector of the Indians" illegally held an *encomienda* of his own. The Church accepted the job of "resocializing" the Indians in the Spanish value system which included legitimizing private property (Spanish) and the Spanish Monarchy which headed both Church and State. Churchman Bartolomé de las Casas, in a passionate outcry against the injustices against the Indians, convinced the Spanish monarchy to take actions to guarantee the survival of a labor force, including abolition of the *encomienda,* but it was too late to save the lives of the Cuban Indians (Las

Casas, 1960). In 1662, of an estimated population of perhaps thirty thousand, some three thousand Indians remained. By 1700 virtually the entire Indian population had disappeared although much of the "white" population was actually *mestizo*. African slaves were imported to replace the Indians.

THE CUBAN ECONOMY UNDER SPANISH RULE

The small gold supply was rapidly depleted along with the Indian population. The main Cuban economic activity then became mounting and supplying expeditions for the Spanish conquest of Mexico, Florida, Central America, and Peru. During the sixteenth century Havana was the leading Spanish port where the Spanish flotillas gathered before returning to Spain. However, as Spaniards left for parts of the Spanish empire where there were more opportunities for enrichment, political hegemony passed from Cuba to the mainland of Spanish America, and the Cuban internal economy declined. Economic activities stagnated during the seventeenth century when pirates, particularly British, raided the Cuban coastal towns. After that Spanish mercantilist policies held back economic development by restricting production in Cuba to products which did not compete with either motherland production or British imports which were supplied to Cuba by Spain. The Spanish failed to develop capitalist production at home, and they relied increasingly on taxation and profit from monopolies in the colonies. The heavy taxes and high interest rates reduced profits and capital formation in Cuba and raised the prices paid for merchandise. The Catholic Church held about one-third of the public wealth. Sugar, tobacco, and cattle production for export developed slowly under tight Spanish government control. The market for sugar was restricted since it all had to enter Spain through Cadiz and Seville. However, with the decline in Brazilian sugar production in the eighteenth century, there began a gradual increase in Cuban sugar exports accompanied by an increased importation of slaves. Nevertheless, the Spanish lavished much more attention on their mainland colonies and Cuban development was much less intensive than, for example, the production of sugar under the French in Haiti. Local resentment of Spanish exploitation grew; Cuban tobacco growers revolted three times against Spanish taxes and restrictions. Smuggling rose rapidly.

The Cuban creoles had their first taste of free trade when in 1762 the British occupied Havana and threw it open to North American commerce. There was an enormous increase in Cuban exports and large numbers of slaves and manufactured goods were imported. The Spanish government found it impossible to reimpose the earlier trade restrictions when the British departed the following year. From then on increasing amounts of sugar were exported to North America and Cuba began to shift from Spanish toward North American domination, a process which ended only with the Cuban Revolution of 1959. The unproductive, dying Spanish imperial system weighed heavily on Cuba, and the creoles uncritically sought to tie themselves to the rising star of British, and later U. S. imperialism. Since the creoles exported agricultural products, they considered cheaper imports of finished goods, lower tax rates, and an increase in creole political representation to be the benefits of moving from the Spanish to the British or U. S. sphere of influence. As Cuba shifted its dependency to countries more economically advanced than Spain, the archaic local production system proved no match for these industrializing powers. The foreign companies began with control of the export of sugar and soon after moved into Cuba and established sugar mills and railroads. The Cuban upper classes were unable to compete with the more financially powerful and technologically advanced investors from abroad. Spain was seen by the Cuban creoles as a decadent and oppressive power. Hispanic culture lost prestige, but there was no national power base or autonomous national elite to lead the building of a Cuban national tradition. So admiration increased for the United States, Britain, and France, and the Cuban upper classes began to assume a truculent inferiority complex. U. S. society was frequently held up as an ideal to be emulated.

During the U. S. independence revolution, privateers from North America plied Cuban ports and trade boomed. In 1784 Spain, in a futile attempt to keep Cuba from shifting its dependence to the United States, reimposed a tight trade monopoly.

The successive revolutionary changes in the United States, Spain, France, Haiti, and the rest of Latin America provided an example for Cuba, but also set the limits on change by frightening the creoles with the spectre of social revolution. The U. S. revolution had greatly expanded the market for Cuban sugar, and there was a dramatic increase in slave importation between 1776 and 1810. Cuba entered the period of Spanish America's independence wars (1810 to 1822) with its population constituted as follows: 44 percent white, 41 percent slave, and 15 percent free colored (some *mestizos* were counted in the white group). With more than half its population slave and free black, Cuba had the highest percentage of Negroes of any country in Spanish America, and that was the principal reason that the creoles in Cuba did not support independence. The creoles wanted to maintain slavery, particularly because of the increase in sugar exports, and they had learned from the Haitian revolution that slaves could achieve their own liberation once a military struggle for independence was underway. There was conflict between the upper caste of creoles, who were either landholders or middle-class professionals, and the Spaniards, who dominated commerce, credit, and administration. But the two groups were bound together by slavery which was more vital to the creoles than to the Spaniards, since the creole landowners profited from working slaves, while the Spaniards were intermediaries with the world market.

In 1809 a rebel movement in Cuba headed by Ramón de la Luz began the struggle against Spanish control which continued until the end of the century. His movement gained support from some free blacks and slaves, but he failed to win support from creole landowners despite promises to respect property. In 1811 another unsuccessful rebel movement was organized by a free black artisan, José Antonio Aponte. During the independence wars in the rest of Latin America, Cuba became a base for the Spanish counter revolution and a haven for counter-revolutionaries. The Spanish Captain General (royal administrator) permitted Cuba to trade freely with the United States in 1810 in violation of orders from Spain. Although in 1817 King Ferdinand VII canceled the liberal Spanish Constitution of 1812, his government granted special privileges to the Cuban upper class so as to retain the support needed to use Cuba as a base for operations against the independence movements in Mexico and South America. These concessions included free trade and the ending of the Crown's tobacco monopoly. In 1820, when the 1812 Constitution was reinstated, Cuban creoles were permitted to elect three deputies to the Spanish Cortes who argued for such reforms as greater autonomy and freedom from trade restrictions. However, in 1823 the Constitution was again revoked, as Spain became part of the reactionary Holy Alliance. The Captain General was given dictatorial powers and Cuban taxes and tariffs were raised in an attempt to compensate for the revenue lost from the rest of Latin America. In response to these conditions, independence movements were organized by small planters in Oriente province who had the highest production costs on the island and who therefore lost their profit margin with the rising cost of sugar production. The movements were also supported by some tobacco farmers, who were not dependent on slavery, and by white middle-class colonists, including intellectuals who had no stake in slavery. Among the rebels were Cuban veterans of Bolívar's army. The groups appealed for support from black Cubans and promised to end slavery. Between 1823 and 1830 several organizations of this type, including the Soles y Rayos de Bolívar, were discovered and the members executed or imprisoned. The large planters did not support these movements, determined as they were to maintain slavery. Their discontent took the form of petitions for "autonomy" within the Spanish empire and reform. Thus the wealthy Cuban creoles chose slavery over nationhood.

Also blocking Cuban independence was the vigorous opposition posed by the United States to Bolívar's plans for liberating Cuba. In 1823 John Quincy Adams, author of the Monroe Doctrine, wrote that the annexation of Cuba to the United States was "indispensable to the continuance and integrity of the Union itself." But since the United States was not then prepared to take the island, it was content to have it remain a colony of Spain, a power which was unable to threaten the United States.

Some concessions were made to the creoles from 1830 to 1834, but then Captain General Miguel Tacón was appointed to Cuba, who treated even the wealthy creoles as disloyal and was widely hated for his repressive ways. Rebellion flared again briefly in Oriente in 1837, but most landowners apparently remained loyal to Spain. After 1835 Britain increased the pressure on Spain and Yankee shippers to end the slave trade, and Cuban slave owners needed Spain to protect slavery from British abolitionists. Sugar prosperity had returned and desire for new slaves made the prospect of moving into the British sphere less attractive for slave owners. There were serious slave revolts in 1841 and 1843; the latter, known as "La Escalera" was actually a conspiracy which was discovered and in the repression thousands were imprisoned and many executed. After these revolts, many Spaniards joined temporarily in proposing annexation to the United States as a way of insuring the protection of slavery, for they feared that the Spanish government would give in to British pressure.

U. S. commercial and diplomatic agents crowded into Cuba; North Americans purchased plantations; sugar companies and banks, using wealthy Cubans as agents, made loans to Cuban landowners in return for guarantees on future crops. Railroads and steam-engines appeared alongside slaves in the sugar fields. As trade with the United States grew, Spanish taxes and administration became ever more repressive to the creoles. Some creoles, unhappy with Spanish domination, sought relief through annexation to the United States. The annexationist filibustering efforts of Narciso López in the 1840's were supported by U. S. pro-slavery groups. The U. S. government favored peaceful purchase of Cuba, but since annexation would have to have been won by struggle against Spain, military attempts by annexationist groups were blocked by the U. S. government, nor did they receive significant support from within Cuba.

In the 1860's the rise of European beet sugar production provoked a critical crisis for the Cuban economy. To compete, Cuban producers would have had to industrialize and to intensify sugar production, but this was incompatible with slavery and Spanish control. Some Spaniards, who monopolized the available capital, introduced modernized mills with which the less efficient creole landowning upper class could not compete.

After creole demands for reform were ignored in 1866, Spanish rule became increasingly repressive as the economy entered a depression. A wide-spread independence conspiracy was organized in the masonic lodges, particularly in eastern Cuba where the profit rate was lowest. The suppression of the slave trade and Oriente landowners' relative lack of capital made slavery a burden in that part of Cuba, and many landowners favored gradual abolition and the introduction of free immigrant labor. Manuel de Céspedes, himself an Oriente landowner, emerged as the leader of an armed insurrection which was supported by other landowners as well as radical professionals, some black freedmen, and some slaves. This phase of the independence struggle, 1878 to 1888, was known as the Ten Years War. Although Céspedes freed his own slaves at the beginning of the war, the movement promised only gradual abolition in an attempt to appeal to Havana province landowners, but they never supported the struggle. Antonio Maceo y Grijales, a mulatto who had been a conspirator, emerged as a brilliant troop commander and guerrilla leader during this period. Maceo had constantly to work against racism within the revolutionary movement. The military necessity of slave support for the rebel movement brought the leaders gradually to an abolitionist position. The outstanding military commander during much of the war was Máximo Gómez, a Dominican volunteer whose brilliant strategic sense provided effective leadership for Maceo's tactics. A fundamental weakness of the movement was the attempt of the upper-class leaders such as Céspedes to win over upper-class support at the expense of mass support. The United States government refused to grant the rights of belligerency to the rebel movement, favoring Cuban independence only if it could be achieved without bloodshed. Despite the unbelievable heroism of the revolutionaries, particularly in the units commanded by Maceo, the fears of social revolution on the part of the upper-class leaders led to internal divisions over program, tactics, and personal prestige which paralyzed the rebel movement in the face of a massive Spanish offensive. In 1878 the revolutionaries accepted a truce.

The Spanish government passed a law in 1879 which provided for abolition of slavery which was finally achieved in 1886. The standard of living of former slaves fell after emancipation and the cost of labor to landowners also fell.

REPLACEMENT OF SPANISH POWER BY THE UNITED STATES

U. S. capital began to enter Cuba to construct larger and more modern mills beyond the Cubans' or Spaniards' reach. The larger mills built tracks to connect them with the main railroads. The price of sugar fell, and small landowners, or those without capital resources to construct railroad spurs onto their properties, went bankrupt or became *colonos,* i.e., suppliers to the large mechanized sugar mills. At the same time most U. S. importers preferred completing the refining of sugar in the United States, blocking integral development of the sugar industry.

The Spanish, not the creoles, had the capital and outlook most akin to that of an entrepreneurial or industrializing class, and even they were rapidly eclipsed after abolition of slavery by the Yankees' greater power, technology, capital resources, and proximity. The Cuban historical experience never permitted the indigenous development of such a class. The U. S. business groups began to substitute for and displace a Cuban bourgeoisie. In the 1950's, Batista's development programs were to assume the existence of an independent entrepreneurial class and fail in its absence.

By the last two decades of the nineteenth century, the planter class and the United States were already inseparably wed. Most U. S. sugar came from Cuba. In 1880, 82 percent of Cuba's sugar exports went to the United States, 5.7 percent to Spain, 4.4 percent to England, and 7.9 percent to the rest of the world. Labor for the sugar fields was recruited in Spain (such Spaniards became small farmers or tenants), and augmented by workers from Haiti and Jamaica. Along with the former slaves, these Caribbean immigrants became part of the labor reserve who worked only a few months a year in the sugar harvest. The cumbersome Spanish administration of the island was an annoyance to the planters and the U. S. businessmen, but both groups feared an independence revolution. As long as the social structure remained intact, the United States could control Cuba through the dependence of the upper class.

The world economic crisis of 1894 focused the grievance of all Cubans upon the obstacles Spain maintained against the two logical alternatives open to Cubans: either a direct link with the U. S. market or the power to diversify the Cuban economy. José Martí, the most articulate representative of Cuban middle-class radical nationalism, who understood the threat to the establishment of Cuban sovereignty posed by U. S. expansionism, fanned the coals of rebellion in Cuba into an open flame in 1896 through superhuman organizing efforts among exiles in the United States. Martí achieved unity without sacrificing the revolutionary program of equality for blacks or eliminating socialist and anarchist labor leaders from the movement. The vast majority of those who fought for independence were black Cubans. The Cuban cigar makers in Florida, mostly under anarcho-sindicalist leadership, provided a seemingly inexhaustible source of funds to finance the revolutionary movement, despite the meagerness of their salaries.

Máximo Gómez and Antonio Maceo returned to Cuba to direct military operations against the Spanish. The Spanish government responded to the guerrilla war with a resettlement policy known as the *reconcentrado* under which all Cubans were ordered to move into garrisoned towns and forbidden to move in the rural districts. Tens of thousands died in the concentration camps in Havana province alone. The revolutionaries retaliated with destruction of economic activities and capital goods and penalties against anyone who violated orders not to trade with or work for the Spanish. Martí joined the guerrillas and died in a skirmish. His death and martyrdom contributed to the unification and strengthening of the movement. Sugar fields and mills were burned by both sides, and U. S. and Cuban sugar interests could no longer hope for "stability and respect of property" under the Spanish, but they feared the policies of a government established by victorious revolutionaries.

In President Grover Cleveland's message to Congress in 1896, he said, "When the inability of Spain to deal successfully with the insurrection has become manifest . . . our obligation to the sovereignty of Spain will be superseded by higher obligations . . ." (Message to Congress, December, 1896). In 1898 Senator Redfield Proctor of Vermont gave an eyewitness report on Cuba to the Senate which was influential in the U. S. Government decision to intervene against Spain. He stressed that Spain could not prevent chaos in Cuba, and the United States Government therefore had to intervene to protect order and property. He also attempted to reassure U. S. property owners who feared that a victory of the independence forces would threaten property rights, arguing that the revolutionary threat was "not so well-founded" (Wisan, 418). The 1896 Republican platform on which McKinley was elected stated that since Spain had "lost control of Cuba" and could not guarantee protection of U. S. property, the United States should "use its influence" to achieve independence for the island (Chapman, 86). The United States declared war on Spain in 1898 and intervened in Cuba with troops on the eve of a successful revolution.

The United States signed the peace treaty with Spain without the presence of the Cuban independence leadership. A key to U. S. military government power in Cuba was the disbanding of the Cuban revolutionary army which was accomplished by the U. S. government providing the money to pay a sum to each soldier for turning in his weapons. Top leaders of the independence forces helped pave the way to complete U. S. control by acquiescing to pacification under U. S. military rule. Upperclass Cubans needed U. S. power to help them maintain their property and political control in the face of revolutionary pressures stirred up by the independence war. General Wood became governor of Oriente province without consulting the provisional government established by the Cuban independence forces. A U. S. military government ruled Cuba until 1902, paving the way for an influx of U. S. investors and Yankee adventurers.

The U. S. Congress had specified that after pacification the United States must "leave the government and control of the island to its people." However, the "Platt Amendment," which the Cubans were forced to incorporate into their constitution as the price for withdrawal of U. S. troops, robbed them of the independence for which they had fought. The Amendment gave the United States the right, among other things, to establish a naval base on Cuban territory and to intervene militarily in Cuba whenever U. S. interests were threatened. Nor could the Cuban Government enter into treaties or contract loans without U. S. permission. Senator Platt, in advocating this new kind of imperialism over annexation, argued that the Cubans "by reason of race and characteristics, cannot be easily assimilated by us . . . Their presence in the American union, . . . could be most disturbing" (Smith, 1963: 128–129). The U. S. intervention and the Platt Amendment aborted the independence movement. Not until the Revolution in 1959 did Cuba really achieve its independence.

Following "independence," U. S. investors descended on Cuba, taking advantage of the post-independence war economic prostration and overwhelming the meager capital resources of the bankrupt creole upper class. U. S. citizens owned one-fourth of the Cuban territory by 1905. With the election of Tomás Estrada Palma in 1902, the U. S. military withdrew and allowed the Cuban upper-class lawyers and businessmen to hold political power in Havana. As a result of the U. S. military intervention, U. S. business presence, and the Platt Amendment, the Cuban government officials were more dependent on U. S. support than on mass political support. The separation of political power from the Cuban people was a source of corruption. The extraordinary corruption of Cuban politics also stemmed from the competition between rival factions of the upper class for control of the government as a source of income since the U. S. controlled the most lucrative private enterprises. One or another group of wealthy Cubans retained power by offering more security to U. S. interests.

Strikes, revolts, and mass unrest began in 1902 and were put down with police and rural guards. After his reelection in 1905, Estrada Palma was faced with massive unrest and resorted to sustaining himself by warning that disorder or revolution would lead to U. S. intervention. According to U. S. government officials William H. Taft (then Secretary of War) and Robert Bacon (Assistant Secretary of State) who were sent to Cuba to investigate, the unexpectedly widespread support for revolt resulted from the government's lack of "moral force," since property was owned by foreigners or Cubans who were not influential politicians. The politicians' lack of prestige and economic power kept them from exerting a stabilizing influence (Taft and Bacon, 1960: 456). When Estrada Palma could no longer maintain order in 1906 in the face of opposition headed by the Liberal Party, he resigned calling for U. S. intervention. The Liberals were not opposed to U. S. intervention. On the contrary, they hoped it would favor them and guarantee that their insurrection would not turn into a popular revolution which they also feared. Estrada Palma's action led to a renewal of U. S. military occupation from 1906 to 1909. The United States landed troops again in 1912, and in 1917 marines were landed once more and they stayed in Cuba until 1923, helping put down strikes and defending property. The U. S. government also imposed an "advisor" on the Cuban Government, General Enoch Crowder, during 1921 to 1923. Crowder essentially managed the financial aspects of the Cuban government.

Representatives of American sugar interests became the leading figures in Cuban public life. Mario G. Monocal, who handled the Hawley sugar interests in Cuba, was elected President in 1912. American groups built twenty-seven new mills in the first twenty years of the republic, and these processed about half of the Cuban sugar production. U. S. imports in Cuba sold more cheaply than before independence because of the absence of Spanish tariffs; the Cubans were prohibited by U. S. political pressure from establishing protective tariffs for national industrial development. U. S. interests benefited from low tariffs by being able to sell more to Cuba and by being able to send sugar and other products produced in Cuba by U. S. companies freely into the U. S. market. These tariff policies maintained by the subordination of Cuba to U. S. interests made national policies to promote development impossible. It was only by changing these power relationships through revolution that development policies became possible.

Political revolts continued. One of the most serious was the 1912 revolt by thousands of black Cubans who had fought in the independence war only to find their situation unchanged. Thousands of black rebels were massacred by the new army established during the marine occupation (1906 to 1909) and expanded by President José Miguel Gómez (1909 to 1913), a fate met by others who chose to challenge the government. The school system and the cultural media cooperated in pacifying the Cubans. The education establishment fell under the control of U. S. universities. Cuban history was written to legitimize U. S. control, and U. S. values were marketed along with U. S. commodities. Cuban national or ethnic culture was never able to develop except for the "mind blowing" escapist culture of rum, dancing, gambling, prostitution, and gangster politics which dulled the sensibilities to foreign domination.

During World War I, sugar beet destruction in Europe drove world sugar prices up, and wealthy Cuban and American companies prospered in what was called the "Dance of the Millions." Tourism became a major factor in the Cuban economy. Inflation kept real wages down. More Haitian and Jamaican cane cutters were imported. When the boom collapsed in 1920, many sugar companies went bankrupt, and U. S. banks took control of the sugar sector. Mills were concentrated into fewer and larger units. By 1926 seven large U. S. companies owned nearly half of the Cuban sugar production.

Gerardo Machado, the sadistic dictator nicknamed "the butcher" who controlled Cuba from 1925 to 1933, faithful servant of U. S. business that he was, nevertheless presided over a gradual nationalization of the Cuban economy. Due to the U. S. tariff wall erected against Cuban sugar during the first years of the depression, the low sugar prices, and the resulting collapse in Cuban trade, some Cuban capital turned toward manufacturing. U. S. companies sold unprofitable sugar holdings to local businessmen (although one-third of the sugar mills and the richest land were still U. S.-owned in 1959). During this period a labor movement, largely Communist-led, developed rapidly, along with a militant student movement. The Communists were in the leadership of textile workers, shoemakers, cigar workers, and teamsters. Machado's goon squads murdered hundreds suspected of opposition. Strikes, mass mobilization, and street fighting brought Cuba to the brink of civil war. The young middle-class opposition leaders later became known as the "generation of the thirties." Machado put down these challenges to the upper class in blood, but when it was clear in 1933 that he could not contain the developing social revolution, even the United States government decided his regime was a liability. Sumner Wells was sent to Cuba as special ambassador charged with preventing a left-wing revolution from replacing Machado.

While the United States was maneuvering for an alternative to Machado, a general strike led by the Communists set off a coup by the senior officers in the Army. This was followed by another coup led by Sergeant Fulgencio Batista and a group of younger officers. Batista placed in power Ramón Grau San Martín, a university professor, physician, and leader of a group of students called the Directorio Estudiantil. During Grau's four months in office, mass mobilization and radicalization continued. Grau passed laws protecting labor and threatened to tax the U. S. electrical company. Workers struck and seized land and factories, proclaiming "soviets" for the first time in Latin America. The United

States refused to recognize Grau, whom Sumner Welles considered "utterly impractical and visionary," and stationed U. S. warships within sight of Havana as a threat. Wells considered that Batista was the only man in Cuba who represented security for commercial and financial interests. At Wells' urging, Batista removed Grau and replaced him with a puppet, leaving Batista himself in effective control. Workers and middle class radicals responded with strikes, but the Army put down the opposition and unions were outlawed. The United States had used its power in support of conservative groups and manipulated the Army and again frustrated a social revolution, this time without needing to use its own military force. The unfulfilled aspirations of 1933 combined with those of 1896 helped generate the Revolution of 1959.

THE PRE-REVOLUTIONARY POLITICAL CONFIGURATION

The time between Cuba's abortive revolution of 1933 and the successful one of 1959 can be divided into three periods. From 1933 until 1944 Batista reigned as strongman over an emerging corporatist[1] coalition. Between 1944 and 1952 two elected civilian presidents, Grau San Martín and Carlos Prío Socarrás, presided over a tenuous parliamentary period. Batista returned to power in 1952 by coup, ruling as a repressive dictator until 1959. "Batista had cast his lot with the conservative pro-American political groups, and his reward was twenty-five years of power" (Smith, 1963: 156). During the inter-revolutionary period four major groups competed for power: the Auténtico party, Batista, conservative groups, and the Communists (MacGaffey and Barnett, 1965: 146).

The genesis of the Auténtico (Authentic Party of the Cuban Revolution—PRCA) party was university-based agitation against the Machado dictatorship which the Directorio Estudiantil helped overthrow in 1933. When Grau San Martín was forced out of the presidency by the United States, the movement went underground, surfacing in 1939 when it was allowed to play a major role in writing the reformist constitution of 1940. It was the main political support for both the Grau and Prío governments.

The politically charged inter-revolutionary period produced one of the most liberal social-democratic constitutions in the hemisphere. However, this idealistic document, an elaborate facade offered to propitiate the legalistic propensities of the righteous and the civic-minded, did not provide the basis for the institutionalization of a parliamentary system founded upon legitimated political parties. By the time of the 1952 coup,

---

[1] Corporatism, a form of organizing society akin to fascism, is characterized by the regimenting of society into organizations such as unions and syndicates which share resources without competing, the government playing the role of compulsory arbiter.

political parties were totally discredited and functioned mainly to support the personal aspirations of their leaders.

The institutional configuration and extra-national pressures were not supportive of a bourgeois, constitutional, parliamentary system. U. S. government officials placed a higher priority on a stabilized business climate than on the development of parliamentarianism. They preferred Batista to the Auténticos, feeling that the parliamentary parties did not provide sufficient guarantees against popular pressures to redistribute income and to develop the economy. The Auténticos were the closest thing in Cuba to a party representing the nationalist elements in the upper and middle classes. The party's trajectory epitomized the opportunistic, corrupt, and vacillating character of those classes. If the establishment of bourgeois democracy is dependent upon a transitional period of stability provided by upper-class control, that function was not discharged by the Cuban elite. The upper class was unconsolidated and did not have at its disposal a strong, loyal Church or military establishment. The Church was marginal to the political process, never recovering the prestige it lost because it had identified with Spain during the 1890's. Batista's astute tactical sense made him more responsive to U. S. pressure than to the less powerful Cuban upper class. Batista replaced the elitist senior officers in 1933 with former low-ranking officers and enlisted men. In 1952 he carried out his coup with captains and lieutenants. Both coups had the effect of preventing a close relationship between the officer corps and the traditional wealthy social elite.

Ideologically related to "Aprista" parties in Peru, Venezuela, and elsewhere, the Auténticos underwent an evolution similar to their foreign counterparts. At first scorned and bruised by the United States, they later accommodated themselves to U. S. economic pre-eminence in their country in exchange for the chance to hold office. Throughout Cuban history, in the absence of economic growth and opportunities for productive private investment for the native upper class, government had been an arena of patronage and self-enrichment. Although graft in Cuba was proportionally small when compared with corruption in the United States, it loomed large in the absence of industrial development. In 1947 when a huge diamond embedded in the floor of the legislative building in Havana was stolen, "Many of the papers declared that it was inevitable . . . because it had been placed in the building where the national legislature, composed of Cuba's leading thieves, met" (Blanksten, 1966: 363). Congressmen were among the chief beneficiaries of the graft-ridden national lottery system. Virtually every public job including school teaching was bestowed through political patronage.

Both Grau and Prío personally plundered the national treasury as their party became a patronage-dispensing apparatus. Their earlier goals of agrarian reform, rehabilitation of the rural population, integrity in government, racial justice, a merit system for government employees, and nationalization of industry were set aside. They did make many concessions to organized labor, but only within the context of the graft-patronage system. By 1959, the "Democratic Left" in Cuba had been thoroughly discredited.

Disenchantment with the Auténticos gave rise in 1946 to a spin-off party called the Orthodox Party of the Cuban People, known as the Ortodoxos, Its founder, Eduardo ("Eddy") Chibás, gained notoriety as a radio commentator who exposed the corruption of the Auténticos. The group claimed to be the true Auténticos. Chibás committed suicide in 1951, but his party had already gained such influence that it was generally expected that its candidate, Roberto Agramonte, would be elected president in 1952, a development forestalled by Batista's coup.

Conservative groups developed three main parties: the Democratic, the Republican, and the Liberal. Their ideologies were quite similar, reflecting upper-class interests and dread of Communism. Their tactics, however, were somewhat different. The Democrats and the Liberals usually supported Batista and his candidates, while the Republicans chose to ally themselves with the Auténticos in 1944 and again in 1948.

The Communist Party of Cuba was founded in 1925 during the Machado dictatorship and although outlawed, played a role in his ouster. In the early 1930's the Communist Party became a major force in the labor movement under the leadership of Blas Roca. Attacking the 1933 Grau government vigorously, the Communists organized rural soviets which assumed temporary control of some land and sugar refineries. In 1935, after the Comintern called for the establishment of popular fronts, the Cuban Communists changed course and unsuccessfully sought an alliance with the Auténticos. From then on the party abandoned a revolutionary role and instead charted its policies in relation to the needs of the Soviet state. Within Cuba, it sought alliances with sectors of the Cuban bourgeoisie, although none of these groups was willing to maintain the alliance for long. Batista modified his regime in 1937 and legalized a Communist front party in exchange for its support; the Communist Party itself was legalized in 1938. Communists took the lead in launching the Confederation of Cuban Workers (CTC) in 1939 and Communist Lázaro Peña became its first secretary-general. At the Communists' suggestion, Batista called the Constituent Assembly which drew up the 1940 Constitution. Communist leader Blas Roca played an important role in drafting the sections of that Constitution guaranteeing workers' rights, and the Communists played a major role at the convention. Support for

Batista during the Second World War from Communist labor leaders was rewarded by his naming two Communists, Carlos Rafael Rodríguez and Juan Marinello, to his cabinet. In 1943 the Communist Party changed its name to the Popular Socialist Party (PSP) which in the 1944 elections supported Batista's candidate, Carlos Saladrigas. After the elections the Communists shifted their support to winning candidate Grau, but in 1947 Grau and his Minister of Labor, Prío Socarrás, renounced them and gradually were able to split the CTC and win most unions away from Communist control. In 1953 Batista declared the PSP illegal, but some Communists were welcomed into Batista's party, the labor movement, and the Labor Ministry.

THE PRE-REVOLUTIONARY SOCIAL SYSTEM

The class system of pre-revolutionary Cuba was composed of bourgeoisie (upper-class capitalists), middle class, workers (including rural workers who were paid wages, such as sugar workers), and peasants, including the *colonos* who grew sugar and supplied it to the mills, the tobacco farmers, and the desperately poor peasantry of the Sierra Maestra mountains of Oriente. However, each social class was divided between those who benefited from their relationship with U. S. business and those who suffered from its effects on the Cuban economy. Most of the upper class (bourgeoisie) were dependent on activities tied to the United States. This included the sugar magnates, large land owners, importers, and real estate men. The commercial middle class of retailers were largely tied to imports of foreign merchandise. Powerful professionals worked for foreign-owned or foreign-oriented firms, or provided services for those whose income was tied to foreign business. An important sector of the working class received higher than average wages from foreign companies, and some of these workers became strongly attached to foreign interests.

In contrast with this U. S. attachment was the small group of nationalist capitalists who owned small plants and stores dependent on government kickbacks. An impoverished lower-middle class group operated fruit, food, and cheap merchandise stands. Workers outside of the foreign sector received lower wages. The poorest workers in Cuba were the rural cane cutters, although sugar was an export sector. They were employed only a few months a year (Boorstein, 1968: 12–14).

Political leaders exercized power on behalf of a mélange of economic groups, but without a secure base in any social class. The upper class was a socially unconsolidated and politically fragmented group of the wealthy. Unlike many other Latin American countries in which there was a traditional landholding upper class, Cuba's bourgeoisie did not own the most valuable land since it was in foreign hands. Association with U. S. economic interests reduced most of the wealthier Cubans to *comprador* status, unwilling to champion economic nationalism and unable to unite around coherent political programs. The fragmentation tendency within the Cuban middle class was to persist after 1959 among those chosing exile in the United States. Repeated efforts to forge integrated counter-revolutionary organizations have been futile (see Fagen and Brody).

While wage workers had experienced substantial trade union activity and their representatives had held ministerial posts in government, labor had not become a poliitcal force sufficiently strong to be a prime mover in national life. Peasants, located mainly in Oriente Province, were a small and politically insignificant part of the lower class. More typical of rural Cubans were seasonally employed sugar workers and small farmers. Both of these groups participated in political bargaining and had received a measure of government protection. The independent farming middle class was largely reduced, by economic crises of the 1920's and 30's into tenants and sharecroppers.

PRE-REVOLUTIONARY POLITICAL INHIBITIONS TO DEVELOPMENT—THE CORPORATIST SYSTEM

Key adjectives to describe the Cuban state before 1959 are "corporatist," "redistributive," "opportunistic," "bureaucratic," and "corrupt" (O'Connor, 1970: 31). More than anyone else, Fulgencio Batista was the architect of the pre-1959 "developing corporatist consensus." The Batista system was a complex of government concessions, controls, and protections for domestic and foreign economic interests. With a combination of coercion, careful organizing, and distribution of available resources, Batista—operating behind the scenes between 1934 and 1940, as President from 1940 to 1944, and as dictator from 1952 to 1958—was able to contain the threat to foreign economic control that national groups such as labor, business, and farmers potentially represented. Fundamental to the whole system was the Law of Sugar coordination of 1937 which established the basic features of the sugar industry. Each grower and each mill were assigned production quotas based on their participation in the 1937 output. Individual growers were paid on the basis of the average sucrose content of all cane ground at their mill. Thus there was no incentive for growers to improve yields through the use of fertilizer, weeding, irrigation, improved types of cane, etc. This cartelization, together with the continued availability of inexpensive rural labor, prevented technical improvements in the sugar industry to the point that yields were only half what they might have been (O'Connor, 1970: 63–64).

Not only the sugar cartel, but virtually every economic sector came under government patronage and control. Economic liberalism was, in effect, universally rejected. The patronage system meant minimum guarantees for some workers and small producers. For example, legislation fixed rent limits for tenant farmers at a maximum of 5 percent or 6 percent per year of the value of the property depending on the size of the plot. This legislation was, however, frequently abused to the advantage of property owners.

Legislation on behalf of trade unionists was profuse, but it had the effect of bringing labor under government control. Under government sponsorship the organized labor movement came to embrace more than half of the work force in the country. As in the case of Vargas in Brazil and Cárdenas in Mexico, the government intervened frequently in strikes, sometimes to enforce worker demands. In large-scale industries, wages, fringe benefits, pensions and job security reached European levels. But the labor movement under leaders like the venal Eusebio Mujal became characterized by corruption, political dependence, bossism, featherbedding, resistance to mechanization, and restriction of access to higher-paying jobs. Worker productivity was one of the lowest in the Americas.

Business groups were similarly interlocked with government. In addition to being the only substantial source of long-term loans for Cuban owned companies, the state provided subsidies, tax concessions, and other benefits to private firms. Political considerations were so vital to business survival that when changes in government occurred, business executives with better connections with the new politicians were often elevated in corporate management.

Intervention by the state to redistribute social and economic advantage took many forms. Perhaps the two most notable net effects of redistributive participation by the state were some leveling of economic fluctuations for organized groups and the furnishing of government jobs for a sizable number of educated members of the middle class who might otherwise have been unemployed. The government itself was the largest employer in the country, hiring people in such excessive numbers that government employment became a kind of social assistance. The impoverished remained impoverished. Insofar as political measures were taken to force departures from the free working of a capitalist market system, these measures largely benefited middle and upper income groups.

Overall, the political economy of Cuba was controlled by a number of organized and monopolistic groups seeking to maintain themselves through government protection. Each group tended to be dominated by the more wealthy persons within it. Each group was largely indifferent to the general public interest.

During his final period of power, from 1952 to 1958, Batista increased government benefits for virtually all sectors of society in an effort to expand industrial and agricultural output. Yet despite some improvement in the economy, opposition to his regime grew steadily, reaching avalanche proportions by the time of his flight on December 31, 1958. Reformist measures could not salvage a fragile social structure emanating from a basically stagnant neo-colonial economy. Furthermore, "Cuba beneath a surface of prosperity was a centre of warring groups of gunmen, policemen, ex-ministers, officers, students, all out for 'supreme power,' none collaborating genuinely with or 'implicated with' each other . . ." (Thomas, 1971: 886).

PRE-REVOLUTIONARY ECONOMIC DISORDERS

By such measures as gross national product per capita Cuba was in 1959 one of the most developed of the underdeveloped nations of the world. However, fundamental shortcomings deformed the economy. First was the extreme under-distribution of benefits in rural areas. A 1956 survey revealed that per capita income in the countryside, including home-grown food, was less than $100 per year. Approximately one-half of Cubans lived in rural areas. The second major defect of the Cuban economy was chronic stagnation. For sixty years before the Revolution there was no lasting gain in per capita income which was $201 annually for 1903–1906 and (in constant prices) $200 per year for the period from 1956 to 1958.

This economic growth impasse resulted in good measure from the nature of the relationships between Cuba and the United States. The degree and manner in which the Cuban economy was *integrated into the U. S. economy* served to maintain the socio-economic status quo and thus to prevent a broad improvement in living conditions for the lower mass of the Cuban population. Among the principal features and consequences of the U. S. embrace were:

First, since the United States was pre-eminent as overseas sugar buyer (in 1960, for example, the United States was assigned 2.3 of a total of 3 million tons exported), and since the quantity of U. S. purchases was established each year by American government officials, sugar production decisions were, in effect, made in the United States.

Second, since sugar dominated the economy (accounting for about 80 percent of total exports while sugar companies controlled 70 to 75 percent of the arable land), and since Cuban participation in the U. S. sugar market together with other export outlets was not growing substantially, the whole economy was not growing.

Third, since U. S. goods were given tariff advantages in Cuba in exchange for quota and price concessions for Cuban sugar sent to the United States, "United States trade penetrated the Cuban market more than the market of any other country." (Sundelsen, 1967: 100) During the 1930 depression decade when such Latin American countries as Chile, Brazil, and Mexico industrialized because of a lack of foreign exchange for consumer goods, Cuban industry stagnated. In 1934, after the overthrow of Machado and Grau San Martín, the United States offered Cuba a Reciprocal Tariff Agreement according to which Cuba would receive an annual quota of sugar in the U. S. market to be sold above the world market price. In return Cuba would not raise protective tariffs against U. S. manufactures. This policy was designed to benefit U. S. sugar importers and U. S. producers in Cuba, but mainly to provide a market for U. S. exports. Therefore Cuba emerged in 1945 with very little more industry than it had in 1930. After the Second World War industrial growth was very slight—3.4 percent between 1950 and 1960 compared to 6.9 percent for Latin America as a whole. In spite of Batista's attempts after 1952, Cuba's industrial development was very limited compared to other Latin American countries given the relatively high buying power of the population and compared to the available resources. The main industries were sugar refining, textiles, tobacco, food processing, rayon, and petroleum refining, nickle refining and cement. Industry absorbed very few of the new workers who entered the job market (Seers, 1964: 286–295).

Fourth, the United States companies also dominated investment in Cuba (a total of approximately $1.5 billion in 1960). "The sugar mills, mines, and almost all the large manufacturing plants in Cuba were foreign enclaves . . . and most of their profits were transferred abroad" (Boorstein, 1968: 4–5). In sum, the economic presence of the United States was of such magnitude that Cuba exercised only marginal control over its economic life. Former U. S. Ambassador Earl E. T. Smith explained to a Senate sub-committee in 1960, . . . "the United States, until the advent of Castro, was so overwhelmingly influential in Cuba that . . . the American Ambasador was the second most important man in Cuba; sometimes even more important than the President."

The Cuban economy did not suffer from a lack of capital investment, although the irregularity of capital investment dependent on the fluctuations in Cuban exports impeded sustained development. The problem was rather that capital invested for the benefit of foreign corporate profit or in the interests of the Cuban upper class did not increase productivity. There was little incentive for an increase in productivity since economic sectors were stagnated at a steady profit rate in non-competing units. Foreign investment tied economic activities ever more closely to production abroad, and native investment concentrated in real estate or the inefficient production of luxury goods protected by political influence. Small-scale subsidiary industries were generally impeded by the importation of finished or semi-finished goods. Exports left Cuba in raw or semi-processed form. Only 22 percent of Cuba's U. S. sugar quota could be exported as refined sugar, so most Cuban sugar continued to be exported in a crude state. Cigars of Cuban tobacco were manufactured mainly in the United States. Mining production was refined abroad. What modern industry there was in Cuba was monopolized by U. S. companies, and based on the importation of semi-finished raw materials and the use of few workers.

Economic development would have required monetary autonomy, the power to modify payment on Cuba's international debt, national control over foreign commerce, national planning, and a radical redistribution of income. However, U. S. business interests required political stability, full payments on loans, laissez faire in commerce and fiscal policy, and the predominance of foreign private and international banks. Given the basic acceptance of U. S. domination, both by Batista and the Cuban bourgeoisie, there could be no economic development, nor would Batista allow the political expression of nationalism. This corporatist system was unable to uplift the lower mass of the population and after 1952 became viciously repressive of those outside the "corporatist consensus." Whatever remained after foreign earnings were distributed was parcelled out to the privileged. With no increase in national income, increasing numbers of people in every sector became dissatisfied and formed a multi-class opposition, the "mirror image" of those in power.

THE GUERRILLA WAR

Those who led the Cuban Revolution grew to adulthood in the context of repeated frustration of national ideals. Martí's aspirations for a worthy and independent Cuba were given brief historical expression during the "100 days" in 1933 to 1934 when President Grau's government defended national interests more effectively than any government since Independence. When the unified activity of the revolutionary generation of the 1930's "ended" and Cuba lapsed into neo-colonialism and corruption, the shameful performance of Grau's Auténticos (1944 to 1952) brought increased disillusionment. Batista's coup which cancelled the 1952 elections and his subsequent dictatorship finally convinced Castro, a group of young Ortodoxos and others that revolution was the only feasible means of bringing national regeneration. "Ours is a generation," said Castro, "to which no one gave a good example."

THE MONCADA ASSAULT

At the time of Batista's return to power in 1952, Fidel Castro was a young lawyer protegé of Ortodoxo leader Eduardo Chibás and a left-wing Ortodoxo candidate for the Chamber of Deputies in the elections cancelled by Batista's coup. As candidate, Castro issued his first political statement, calling for Cubans to struggle to restore the 1940 constitution. Castro later said that he never believed that the platform on which he campaigned could be realized through election, but he felt that if elected he could use the congressional platform to break Ortodoxo party discipline and present a program similar to that later used as the banner of the Moncada barracks uprising in 1953.

After the coup, Fidel wrote a personal letter to Batista asking him to resign, and then initiated a court action against him for violating the constitution by his method of seizing and holding power. He was, in effect, exhausting the possibilities of constitutional opposition while, at the same time, trying to expose the illegality of the regime. Of course, the courts were powerless and unwilling to act against the dictator, but by establishing the lack of legal recourse, Fidel legitimized insurrection as the only way to unseat a dictator who had violated the law. Castro then began to organize action cells, hoping to work with leaders of the Ortodoxo party, in a fight against Batista. However, he soon became disillusioned with party leadership and set out on his own.

Castro gathered a small group around him, mostly workers and lower middle-class Ortodoxo militants. His movement's program at that time included genuine land reform, profit sharing, an increased share of production for sugar farmers supplying the mills, the confiscation of all property illegally seized, the nationalization of utilities, housing reform including cutting rents in half, and educational reform.

They planned the assault on the Moncada and Bayamo barracks in Oriente which took place on July 26th, 1953. The objective was to seize arms and to call for a public uprising in Oriente which would set off a revolution in the whole country. Both attacks failed. Castro's brother, Raúl, who had solicited entry to the Communist Youth earlier the same year, broke that party's discipline and joined his brother in the attack. The 160 participants included six women. Sixty-eight rebels were captured in the first two days and murdered after torture. The treatment became a national scandal, and after the Archbishop of Santiago intervened, those captured later were treated better. The attack was repudiated as "putschist" by the Communists.

Captured with thirty-two others, Castro was tried and sentenced to fifteen years. At the trial, Castro gave his most famous speech, "History Will Absolve Me" in which he extemporaneously developed, with fantastic recall of facts and political theory, an argument for the legality of overthrowing Batista and a basic reform program for Cuba, including a call for elections, press freedom, and civil liberties (Castro, 1961). The economic reforms which Castro proposed had been contained in numerous international bank recommendations which had never been carried out.

Theodore Draper (1962) and others have maintained that after the Revolution, Castro betrayed the promises in this speech because he did not allow the elections and freedom of the press and the agrarian reform went beyond "cooperatives" to collectivization. However, the main thrust of the speech was a promise to carry out a basic redistribution of property and wealth in Cuba, to aid the poorest segments of society, and to establish national sovereignty. Such basic changes were bound to lead to severe conflicts with those trying to maintain their privileges, groups which could count on U. S. support. Any government determined to go ahead with reform would have had to limit the freedom of propertied groups to prevent such changes. In any case, Fidel's understanding of what was necessary to make a revolution changed between 1953 and 1959. The speech was not even particularly anti-United States. As Castro himself later explained, "at the time of the Moncada, I was a pure revolutionary but not a Marxist revolutionary. In my defense . . . I outlined a very radical revolution but I thought then that it could be done under the constitution of 1940 and within a democratic system" (Matthews, 1964: 11). The repression and the trial made Castro a hero.

BETWEEN MONCADA AND THE GRANMA LANDING

In November 1954, Batista staged elections which maintained him in power. There was a sense of economic improvement, partly attributable to an agreement to sell sugar to the USSR. Vice President Nixon and CIA chief Allen Dulles visited Havana, showing U. S. support for the fraudulent regime. In May 1955, Batista released Castro, his brother, and eighteen followers. Batista had been under pressure to release political prisoners, but he also apparently wanted to legitimize his regime after the election by creating a climate of political liberty, even though political activity had been very restricted during the election itself. He felt secure since by this time most of the opposition groups had disintegrated.

Castro met with individuals active in several groups such as the Havana University students, including José Antonio Echevarría, who was later to die leading the 1957 attack on the presidential palace; Santiago University students, including Frank País, later 26th of July leader in Santiago; and the Acción Católica group. When Castro received evidence that he was about to be murdered, he left for Mexico to organize a guerrilla movement. He left behind a nucleus of the new 26th of July movement, including survivors of the Moncada uprising and new recruits from another movement called the Movimiento Nacional Revolucionario. These included Armando Hart Dávalos, Faustino Pérez, Frank País,

Haydée Santamaría, and Melba Hernández. After Castro had left for Mexico in December of 1955, student leaders in Havana headed by José Antonio Echevarría founded the Directorio Revolucionario to fight Batista. This group would remain independent of the 26th of July until after the Revolution took power.

In March 1956, middle-class opposition groups discredited themselves by engaging in a fruitless "civic dialogue" with Batista's government. The Directorio and the 26th of July denounced attempts at conciliation. Castro publicly separated his group from the Ortodoxos in the wake of their discredited attempt at conciliation. The Cuban police increased repression, torturing, mutilating, and killing scores of young workers, students, and peasants, whose corpses were frequently left in roadside ditches as public examples.

Castro's trainees in Mexico were joined by volunteers leaving the Guatemalan reformist regime of Jacobo Arbenz which had been overthrown by the CIA. These included Ernesto "Ché" Guevara, an Argentine medical doctor who had offered his services to the abortive Bolivian revolution before moving on to Peru and Guatemala. Guevara was the most able pupil of guerrilla instructor Alberto Bayo, a veteran from the Spanish Civil War. Three Moncada veterans also joined Castro after working for Arbenz in Guatemala.

ESTABLISHING THE GUERRILLA BASE

Castro set out for Cuba, one step ahead of the Mexican police who were apparently working with the Batista government, on a yacht named "Granma" with eighty-two men of whom twenty-one were veterans of Moncada. Before they arrived, Frank País had led a series of guerrilla raids in Santiago to divert attention from the landing, but coordination with the landing expedition went awry and plans dissolved in confusion. The guerrilla expedition planned to engage in sabotage in Oriente Province to be followed by a call for a general strike. The Granma arrived late, on December 2, at the wrong landing spot, and was sighted by a military plane. Within a few days twenty-four had been killed, and the rest were separated. Fifteen managed to meet, and these formed the nucleus of the rebel army. The rest were dispersed. Dependent on the bandit leader, Cresencio Pérez, Castro and his men learned about hunger and how poor peasants lived and thought. However, they could count on an urban underground organization in Havana and Oriente to supply money and clothing and to organize urban actions.

To attract peasants they paid double for goods, but they were frequently betrayed in those early days by peasants who reported them to the army. Their experience in the countryside was not unlike the first few months of the Bolivian guerrillas headed by Guevara in 1967. The revolutionaries did not know the terrain or even much about the people there. They had to learn. The Sierra Maestra was inhabited by precarious squatters with no educational facilities or other services available to them. They had been terrorized by police and *mayorales* (landowners' armed guards) who never accepted their right to farm the tiny plots they claimed. The Fidelistas attacked military barracks, freed peasant prisoners, and meted out justice to the oppressive *mayorales*. The army evacuated peasants under the threat of massive bombing often using fictitious bombing plans to drive peasants away from their farms, a service to the landowners. The Fidelistas listened to the peasants' complaints and won many of them over to the guerrilla.

Of the original fifteen, only Fidel, Raúl, and Ché Guevara had a university education; the rest were working class. Besides the peasants who joined them, the rest of the recruits were mostly workers or lower middle-class. This was not a middle-class movement, as many have assumed. Nevertheless, their original political strategies were based on urban middle-class Cuban politics including the modalities of electoral maneuvering, gangsterism, and putschism. This pattern of political behavior did not withstand the purifying *guerrilla* experience which severed the leadership's commitment to the anti-Batista middle-class political establishment

In January 1957, Castro arranged for *New York Times* correspondent Herbert Matthews to visit his camp. The subsequent articles in the *Times* were a significant political victory for Castro since Batista claimed the Fidelistas had been eliminated. Castro invited numerous other correspondents to the Sierra Maestra in the next two years as part of his political strategy.

In the spring of 1957, the guerrillas carefully established peasant contacts and lines of communication. They "became firmly convinced of the need for a definite change in the life of our people. The idea of an agrarian reform became crystal-clear, and communion with the people ceased to be a theory and became an integral part of ourselves. . . . Guerrillas and peasants began to merge into a solid mass . . . and we became part of the peasantry" (Guevara, 1968b: 57). This interaction with and dependence on the peasantry clearly changed the thinking of the revolutionary leaders and cadres. Thereafter the peasantry became the group with highest priority in benefiting from revolutionary programs.

EXPANDING THE 26TH OF JULY MOVEMENT

Castro's movement gradually emerged as the principal anti-Batista force. In early 1957, the program of the 26th of July was nationalistic and promised a "total transformation of Cuban life." Within the movement, however, the guerrilla leadership was in control and was more radical than the urban leadership. The Cuban Communists, while admitting Castro's courage, criticized armed action as inappropriate and the July 26th program as insufficiently anti-imperialist. (Later, in 1958, they criticized the Fidelistas for impeding unity by being excessively anti-imperialist. It often seemed that political issues were used by all groups as pretexts for disagreement rather than reflecting substantive differences.) The 26th of July, however moderate it may have appeared in ideology, was the most radical political group in Cuba from 1955 to 1958. A "Civic Resistance" group in Havana set up by Ortodoxo militants and 26th of July organization men and women, became part of the 26th of July, although many of the Resistance members were political moderates and judged the leadership in the Sierra to be too leftist.

The 26th of July urban cadres engaged in revolutionary urban terrorism. Bombs were set to kill police chiefs, a technique used by the resistance in Machado's day. The urban terrorists, under the leadership of the architect Manuel Ray,[2] were of varied backgrounds. Some were of the middle class, but most were workers. The student Directorio group in Havana, which remained independent of the 26th of July, was also active and attempted to assassinate Batista in a March 1957 attack on the presidential palace. Batista's police retaliated by murdering the captured participants as well as many people who were totally uninvolved.

Batista responded to the urban terrorism with purges of the labor movement which were greeted in May with telephone and electrical strikes. Communists who had been tolerated began to be purged partly because Batista had represented the Fidelistas as Communists and was driven to make good on his own rhetoric. This anti-Communist repression coincided with the first tentative efforts by the Communists to approach the 26th of July. Although the 26th of July did not respond, a few weeks later two Communist Youth activists joined the guerrillas.

By mid-1957, many priests in Oriente were active members of the 26th of July. Throughout the guerrilla war the revolutionaries received more support from Catholic Church officials and lay activists than from the Communists, although the Church never officially supported the rebel movement. This undoubtedly affected the relative lack of conflict subsequently between the Church and the Revolution. Nevertheless, the majority of the Church hierarchy, even by 1958, supported neither Batista nor Castro, and sought U. S. support for the creation of a moderate junta which would not tamper with property relations.

Batista's military commander, Francisco Tabernilla, after a few months

[2] After the Revolution was in power, Ray was a cabinet minister; he then left Cuba and headed an anti-Castro counter-revolutionary military organization.

of attempts at military "civic action" to "win the hearts and minds" of the peasants, abandoned such tactics in favor of outright terror against peasants in the guerrilla area. The army evacuated a zone in the Sierra Maestra wherein all persons would be presumed rebels, shot on sight, and bombed freely. In the Sierra, peasants began to feel safer among the guerrillas than in their own homes.

The revolutionaries consistently treated their captives with respect and kindness, in contrast to the brutality used by Batista's troops. This was another way in which they communicated that this was a qualitatively different political movement. They attempted to politicize their prisoners and then released them.

Former President and Auténtico leader Prío Socarrás organized a landing from Miami in May 1957. All sixteen members were captured and shot on arrival. After the failure of this Auténtico action, Castro's organization was recognized by virtually everyone as the main opponent of Batista.

In July 1957, Raúl Chibás, brother of Castro's mentor, Eddy Chibás, and Felipe Pazos, both moderate figures who had joined the July 26th movement, met with Fidel in the Sierra. By this time, Castro's force numbered some two hundred. A *"territorio libre"* had been established with a repair shop, schools, hospital, bakery, shoe factory, and armory. Castro, Chibás, and Pazos issued a manifesto calling for the formation of a liberal-democratic revolutionary front. They promised to hold elections to choose a non-partisan provisional president within a year after defeating Batista. Castro later commented that the document was much less radical than he wished because of pressure from Pazos. It was designed to attract moderate support and to unify the anti-Batista program by promising the type of government that would reassure Auténticos and Ortodoxos. This promise was fulfilled when the rebels established the moderate government headed by Manuel Urrutia and José Miró Cardona after the Revolution took power. The document also asked the United States to suspend arms shipments to Cuba and ruled out in advance a military junta as a substitute for Batista. The economic program included suppression of gambling and corruption, industrialization, and moderate agrarian reform (distribution of unutilized land to the landless and of rented land to tenants and squatters). This document was less radical than earlier statements by the 26th of July leaders, since the movement had gained sufficient prestige to be able to call for unity behind the July 26th banner, and unity could only be achieved with a more moderate position.

After the police assassination of Frank País, rebel underground leader in Santiago, on July 30, 1957, the rebel cadres outside the Sierra organized a long-planned general strike beginning August 1, and lasting a week. The strike was highly successful in Oriente, less so in Havana. It brought further open repression from Batista and a new round of political murders by police, but each act of police terror created new supporters of the rebel movement.

THE UNITED STATES AND BATISTA

The United States openly supported Batista until the spring of 1958. Weapons supplied by the United States to Batista, including bombs, were used against the rebels, and a U. S. military mission remained in Havana until Batista fell. The U. S. government did not want the Fidelista leadership to take power. However, unlike other instances in Latin America, the United States never committed substantial resources to putting down the guerrillas. This may have been because of information such as that from U. S. agent Andrew St. George, who traveled with Castro's forces, to the effect that "Castro was an egomaniac and emotionally unstable but not a Communist." (Thomas, 1971: 938–939, f.n.) However, when U. S. government officials had decided Batista was a liability, and cut off arms and supplies to him, they nevertheless opposed Castro taking power hoping instead for a military junta that would guarantee property.

While Batista's political support deteriorated, the economy remained strong and most business spokesmen clearly felt that high profits justified the repression. Batista and U. S. business and political officials traded compliments. Nevertheless, some affluent people felt that Batista's terror was unnecessary in view of the prosperity. Some wealthy middle-class groups and even one millionaire supported and helped finance the rebel movement, clearly miscalculating the direction it would take.

In April 1957, the new U. S. Ambassador, businessman Earl T. Smith, had arrived in Cuba during a secret turn in CIA policy away from supporting Batista. Smith visited Santiago just after the murder of Frank País and was greeted by a women's demonstration which was brutally repressed by the police. Smith deplored this, and the State Department encouraged him to dissociate himself from Batista's repression.

In September 1957, there was a naval revolt in the city of Cienfuegos, supported and coordinated by the 26th of July cadres outside the Sierra, which held that city for most of a day. As the government recaptured the city, more than three hundred prisoners were shot, and it was claimed that two hundred wounded were buried alive. The CIA had told the military officers involved in the coup attempt that their regime would be recognized if they succeeded and established a military junta to replace Batista. This was the only time the 26th of July movement supported attempts at a military coup.

Ambassador Smith swung around to support of Batista in opposition to the CIA. He felt that the only real alternative to Batista was the rebel movement, which he had come to view as Communist, but most other U. S. officials worked in the Wilsonian tradition for a moderate alternative to Batista as the most secure way of guaranteeing U. S. property and investments. There was general agreement that Castro should not be allowed to take power. The CIA, along with many moderate Cuban opposition groups, hoped for a preventive coup.

Batista's government had been reprimanded by U. S. officials for using U. S.-supplied bombers, tanks, and armored cars in the Cienfuegos revolt in violation of agreements only to use them against "external aggression." In the spring of 1958, this was the justification used when, over the opposition of Ambassador Smith, the United States cancelled arms shipments to Batista except for rockets. At the same time, the United States intercepted an expedition of men and arms which was to leave from Florida to support Castro, although expeditions organized by Prío and the student Directorio Revolucionario had slipped through. Even after the United States ended arms shipments, some U. S. officials continued to identify publicly with Batista, and U. S. investments continued to flow into Cuba. The British continued to sell arms to Cuba.

FINAL MANEUVERING OF OPPOSITION GROUPS

In Miami, in November 1957, some 26th of July representatives including Felipe Pazos joined with most other exile groups to form a Junta of National Liberation headed by Antonio (Tony) Varona. Prío was financing most of the groups involved, with the exception of the July 26th movement. The Junta promised general elections "as soon as possible." When Castro heard of this pact, via the U. S. press, he denounced it as an "outrage," both because Prío had refused to send arms or support for a year, and because the declaration lacked a denunciation of imperialism, did not exclude the setting up of a military junta, and did not give the future president freedom of appointment. Castro thus repudiated Pazos and the others who had acted as July 26th spokesmen. He countered the Junta by announcing that Judge Manuel Urrútia (who had presided at his trial) was his choice for future provisional president. Castro's fundamental disagreement with the other groups was over the issue of whether the 26th of July would control the army and maintain order during the provisional government, and he refused to compromise on this.

Faure Chaumón, a member of the Junta representing the student Directorio Revolucionario, denounced Castro for dividing the Junta and set about organizing an independent invasion of Cuba under Directorio control. Early in 1958, this Directorio expedition of fifteen landed in northern

Camagüey and, after crossing the island, established themselves in the Escambray mountains in southern Las Villas.

In February, the Communist Party declared support for Castro's armed struggle for the first time. Police repression against Communists had become more acute, and this drove local Communists in northern Las Villas into the formation of a small guerrilla organization.

The Sierra leadership called a general strike scheduled for April 9, 1958. This was actually to be an urban uprising. While Castro proposed that the July 26th urban underground cooperate with the Communists (who still had considerable labor support) in organizing the strike, David Salvador, July 26th labor head in Havana, and the other urban leaders refused to involve the Communists in planning the strike. The Communists welcomed the strike tactic as a positive step away from "futile" terrorism, but they were unable to participate actively. The strike was unsuccessful, and the small percentage of workers who struck returned to work in the afternoon of April 9 when they heard a rumor that the strike was organized as a provocation by Batista's police. At least fifty civilians were killed by the police.

Early in 1958, Castro established a counter-government in Oriente and demanded that all highway and railway traffic in Oriente be halted and that all taxes to the Batista government be suspended. Castro's command collected taxes where they could. Anyone remaining in executive office after April 5, 1958 or participating as candidate in Batista's elections called for November was warned that they would be considered guilty of treason.

The impending collapse of the Batista regime led to increasing defections in the Church as well as in the legal and military systems. Members of the Catholic Church hierarchy openly denounced the Batista regime in early 1958, and in March Cuban bishops "called on the government to bring peace through the formation of a government of national unity and on the revolutionaries to abandon sabotage and terrorism" (Thomas, 1971: 982).

Some of Batista's legal officials were refusing to prosecute political prisoners. In 1957 presiding Judge Urrútia declared that some hundred Fidelistas being tried in Santiago should be acquitted. The prosecutor refused to ask for sentence. Several other such instances took place in 1958. On occasion the prosecutors even unsuccessfully attempted to prosecute members of government engaged in murder. Military officers and enlisted men in increasing numbers defected from Batista to the revolutionary forces. In April 1958, Castro made it clear that his movement would reject a military junta taking power and would attack such a government with strikes and military action.

While some centrists joined or supported Fidel's movement when it emerged as the main alternative to Batista, this did not mean they shared the determined radicalism of the Fidelista leadership. They would certainly have preferred a more moderate leadership if any other group had emerged as powerful, but as the 26th of July gained stature the moderate groups appeared increasingly impotent.

In July, Communist leader Carlos Rafael Rodríguez went to the Sierra Maestra after talks between PSP and July 26th leaders. After visiting Raúl Castro, Rodríguez was unable to see Fidel and returned to Havana. In August, Castro reached an agreement with the Communists, but in Havana the July 26th representatives refused to work with the Communists in the labor movement. Carlos Rafael Rodríguez then returned to the Sierra where he remained, but he had little influence on the Fidelista leadership there. A general agreement with the Communists including a labor alliance in Havana was finally reached in October, less than three months before the guerrillas took power.

At a meeting in Caracas, also in July 1958, opposition groups with the exception of the Communists and two factions which sought to run candidates in Batista's November elections, formed a Democratic Revolutionary Civic Front. Urrútia, Castro's choice, was designated president, José Miró Cardona coordinator, and Castro military commander. Castro received more money from Prío, as well as $50,000 from Venezuelan provisional president Admiral Wolfgang Larrazábal and a planeload of arms from Costa Rica.

THE VICTORIOUS CAMPAIGN AGAINST BATISTA

In May 1958, Batista launched an all-out offensive against the rebels in Oriente using seventeen battalions and aerial support. Castro's forces made the government troops pay heavily for their advances and ultimately, even though they were surrounded and had lost most of their territory, they inflicted a decisive defeat on the government. Because of their peasant support, their combat intelligence was far superior to Batista's. Batista's troops fought poorly with low morale, and many deserted. Some were bombed with their own napalm by accident, or because Castro had caused confusion with false radio messages. After a month, most of the troops withdrew again from Oriente. Prisoners taken by government troops were shot unceremoniously, but the rebels treated their 433 captives well, releasing most to the Red Cross. Between April and July 1958, Raúl Castro had established a second front in northern Oriente. By this time, each province had a separate 26th of July command, including workers committees. By August 1958, the war had begun to affect the economy.

An agrarian reform decree, "Law 1 of the Sierra Maestra," was issued in which small farmers who had less than sixty acres would receive additional land up to that amount, and farmers would be guaranteed up to one hundred and fifty acres without fear of expropriation. Lands belonging to the state or Batistianos would be distributed to those entitled to land.

In August, two columns of guerrillas commanded by Guevara and Camilo Cienfuegos were sent to Las Villas province to cut communications in the middle of the island. Cienfuegos, who came from a working-class background, had won the admiration of the guerrillas for his leadership and tactical ability. Cienfuegos absorbed sixty-five Communist-led guerrillas, who had already been operating in Las Villas, and Guevara linked up with the Directorio Revolucionario guerrillas in the Escambray mountains in southern Las Villas. Local July 26th leaders in Las Villas complained that Guevara relied too much on Communists, while Guevara stated that he had some reservations about moderate 26th of July support.

In December, Castro's troops in Oriente took several large towns and decisively defeated the army in that province. In November, Batista had staged the election of his cohort, Andrés Rivero Agüero, who was scheduled to take power in February, but Rivero was so identified with Batista's brutality that the U. S. government would not agree to back him. Ambassador Smith, the CIA, and U. S. business groups in Cuba all agreed to try to replace Batista with a military junta designed to keep Castro out of power, but it was too late.

Guevara in Santa Clara reached an agreement with the Directorio on December 1. Guevara and Cienfuegos were blowing up bridges and interrupting road and rail traffic and communications through Las Villas. They took the offensive on December 18, to the surprise of Batista's army. On December 23, Batista's military chief, Tabernilla, informed the dictator that he thought the war was lost. General Cantillo, the Oriente military commander, met secretly with Castro by helicopter on December 4 and promised that the army would throw out Batista on December 31, in return for Castro not attacking his troops in Oriente. When Cantillo postponed the date, Castro continued to move against Santiago.

On December 28, Guevara attacked the city of Santa Clara in central Cuba. The key element in the city's defense was supposed to have been a train loaded with munitions which was derailed and captured. Thereupon, the army soldiers approached rebel soldiers saying they wanted to stop fighting their own people. Inside the city, the civic resistance groups attacked the police. Three days later air force planes bombed the Guevara-occupied sections of Santa Clara.

On the evening of the last day of 1958, military commanders in Las

Villas and Oriente reported that they could not hold those provinces. Batista resigned and left for the Dominican Republic that very night, along with leading politicians and gambling tycoon Meyer Lansky. The Cuban people began to celebrate. A "government" composed of supreme court justices was ignored. The Army surrendered in Santa Clara and Oriente on January 1.

The CIA provided a bribe to release from prison a Colonel Ramón Barquín, who had led an abortive officers coup in 1956. Barquín took command of the military outside Havana, and U. S. officials hoped that Batista's army would remain intact. Barquín, however, was a secret member of the 26th of July, and he arrested his predecessor Cantillo and immediately phoned Castro for instructions.

Some looting and destruction of property was taking place. A particular target was the Shell Oil Company, because of British arms supplied to Batista. Castro appealed by radio from Santiago for people not to take the law into their own hands. The 26th of July and Directorio forces took over local police stations and amazingly little violence occurred. A general strike called by Castro and the Communists was this time successful.

Guevara and Cienfuegos arrived in Havana on the night of January 1, taking command of the military bases while Directorio leaders occupied the presidential palace. Castro entered Santiago which he announced would be the new capital.

On January 2, the rebel labor organization, headed by 26th of July labor leader, David Salvador, called for mass demonstrations. Rebel committees took over in most unions. Castro moved slowly toward Havana, greeted everywhere by cheering crowds. Directorio leaders, although they were at first given no jobs in the new government, reluctantly released the presidential palace to Urrútia. "The *barbudos,* as they became known, did not drink, did not loot, conducted themselves as if they were saints. No army had ever behaved like this in Havana" (Thomas, 1971: 1033). Castro arrived in Havana on January 8.

THE TRANSITION TO SOCIALISM

THE GUERRILLAS AND THE MODERATES

When the rebel army took power in January 1959, the Revolution was defined as "humanist." The radicalism of Fidel Castro and those close to him was indisputable, but they were more pragmatic than ideological. On January 25, 1959, Castro assured property owners that he did not oppose capitalist enterprise unless it conflicted with Cuban law or interests.

In April he expressed his opposition to dictatorships and Communism, and projected Cuban neutrality in the United Nations. Elections were to be held in two years. The rebel army established a formal government in which moderate professional men predominated. The Communist Party urged moderation, but was not in a position of influence.

Nevertheless, by April 1961, the month of the Bay of Pigs invasion, most Cuban agriculture, industry, commerce, and transportation had been collectivized, Castro had declared the Revolution socialist, the Communist Party (PSP) was closely allied with the government, and Cuba had shifted most of its trade from the United States to the socialist countries. By December 1961, Castro declared that he had become a Marxist-Leninist, "and I shall be a Marxist-Leninist to the end of my life" (Castro, 1962a: 64).

The radicalization of the Revolution has been explained variously as the result of a Communist conspiracy, as a "betrayal" of the Cuban middle class, or as a reaction to the hostility of the United States. The first two theories are erroneous, while the third is only partially correct. The "Communist conspiracy" theory has no factual basis. None of the top rebel leaders was Communist, and the Cuban Communists played no important part in the revolutionary leadership until after the radicalization had taken place. After they were incorporated into the leadership, they played a moderating role.

The rebel movement during the armed struggle was never "middle-class," although many of the leaders had come from the middle class. Most of Castro's followers at Moncada, on the Granma, and in the guerrilla army were from below the middle class. Those who were middle-class were distinguished by their dedication to the freeing of the great majority of the population. Identification with the lower class was not for them an intellectual exercise. In the Sierra the dirt of poverty got under their fingernails to stay. Redemption of the rural poor became their first post-revolutionary goal. In the areas which came under the rebel army control, the distribution of land and the establishment of schools and hospitals bound these peasants and the revolutionary leadership more tightly to each other. Fidel, Raúl, Ché Guevara, and the others were successful guerrillas because they gave up their middle-class behavior, experienced the needs of the peasantry of Oriente, the poorest rural group in Cuba, and became dependent upon them.

The broad appeal of the 26th of July to all opponents of Batista when it was fighting for power was made possible by a contradictory program. For example, it both condemned and supported the pre-revolutionary policy of restricting sugar production. Mechanization of agriculture was denounced and advocated. Manufacturing profits were to be increased by tariffs and decreased by liberal profit-sharing with workers. These contradictions, probably unintended, were the result of appeals to groups with antagonistic interests. The rebel program was designed to appeal to nearly every social class of the Cuban population, since Batista had alienated substantial sectors of all social groups. Although, unlike Batista's coalition, the rebels did not seek the support of the upper class or U. S. business, various July 26th pronouncements had reassured "legitimate" private capital. Once the revolutionaries were in power, however, significant measures were bound to increase the loyalty of some of Castro's supporters and alienate others.

The 26th of July had made a variety of political promises for tactical reasons at different stages in the Revolution. When asked by Matthews about his having gone back on "democratic reforms," Castro said, "Yes, that is true, . . . Every revolutionary movement . . . proposes the greatest number of achievements possible. . . . No program implies the renunciations of new revolutionary stages, of new objectives . . . I told no lies in the Moncada speech. . . That was how we thought at the moment" (1969: 138; see also Lockwood, 1969: 144–145).

In every major revolution the view of the leadership about what was possible and necessary changed during the revolutionary process. This does not mean that the revolutionary leaders had no ideology. In January 1959, they seem to have had a variety of ideologies without a unified doctrine or strategy. Castro, by his own admission, was a radical nationalist aware of Marxism and in a process of transition toward being a Marxist-Leninist Socialist (Castro, 1962a: 46, 64–65). There was apparently a consensus on the intransigency of the leadership toward the United States and privileged groups in Cuba and a determination to act quickly to benefit the vast majority of the population. There does not seem to have been agreement on the form of economic and political organization required to achieve these ends.

Early Relations with Middle Class. Castro did "go back" on certain promises with particular appeal to middle- and upper-class opponents of Batista. There were three types of commitment to the middle class. The first was to retain a democratic electoral framework. The revolutionary leadership was confused about the extent to which basic reforms could be carried within a typical bourgeois-democratic constitutional and electoral framework, partly because they underestimated the power of opposition to fundamental changes. They chose the reforms over the framework. After the Revolution triumphed, there was no popular demand for elections. However, moderates and conservatives knew that money would talk in an election campaign and the upper middle-class politicians could reestablish themselves in power. Thus groups opposed to the fundamental transformations being enacted always called for a return to an electoral system. The second commitment was to retain a capitalist economic framework. The revolutionary leaders failed to foresee the incompatibility of basic reforms with Cuban dependent capitalism. Under the onslaught of reforms designed to help Cuban capitalism, the capitalists themselves defected and Cuban capitalism collapsed, leading to state control. The third and least serious commitment was *tactical*—to share political power with the moderate representatives of the traditional middle class. This commitment was broken when these leaders themselves defected and began to attack the government over such fundamental programs as the agrarian reform and the uncompromising attitude toward the United States. The revolutionary leadership had underestimated the amount of mass support they would have as a result of their leadership of the guerrilla movement. They thought they would have to compromise with the moderates for a long time, but it turned out that to most Cubans such leaders already had little stature.

It was necessary to make compromises with the middle class in order to live up to commitments made to workers and peasants. What differentiated Castro and his associates from earlier leaders with similar programs was his determination to transform Cuba economically, even though the political consequences were that he would have to fight the Cuban upper and middle classes, the United States, and much of the Church, and to ally with the Soviet Union. More than half the "Moncadistas" had died, many after bestial torture, and the surviving revolutionary leaders had repeatedly chanced death and defeated Batista's well-equipped army; they were not over-awed even by the military muscle of the United States. Castro proceeded to mobilize worker, peasant, middle class, and military support with which to withstand the opposition. The leadership acted ruthlessly to transform the multi-class coalition into a class struggle, not because of some prior ideological commitment, but because the groups owning property waged political and economic struggles against the reforms. When they did so, the rebel leaders acted quickly to mobilize the masses and destroy the power base of the property owners.

Unlike all the other political leaders in Latin America who had tried to appeal to elements in each class or divide groups against each other, the Fidelistas developed a class struggle, allying themselves with peasants, workers, and middle class radicals against established bureaucrats, local partners of U. S. business firms, and large sugar, banking, cattle, manufacturing, and commercial interests. The Cuban rebels *alone* of Latin

American leaders were confident of military loyalty during a radical transformation. It was this class struggle which changed the Cuban Revolution after January 1959 into a socialist revolution. It is thus true that the Fidelistas did not lead a socialist revolution against Batista, but they led a movement that set the basis for a socialist revolution.

In addition to the polarization along class lines, a cleavage did develop within classes between those who supported and those who opposed U. S. economic interests. Thus certain workers and union officials who had privileged positions with foreign companies and labor leaders identified with U. S. labor in the "struggle against Communism" tended to side with the United States. The middle class was forced to take sides and split along lines of generation, ideology, and personal identification.

The Polarization of the Middle Class. Much of that old middle class is now located in the United States, but by no means all. (For an analysis of the earlier reasons for leaving Cuba, see Fagen and Brody, 1968.)   In *Inconsolable Memories,*[3] the Cuban novelist Eduardo Desnoyes, (1967) portrays a discontented middle-class man who rejects the Revolution because of how it affects his self-centered goals and patterns of behavior which he refuses to reexamine.   Every aspect of the Revolution which benefits the majority of the population he experiences as a personal annoyance or an invasion of his privacy or freedom, and he wallows in his misery.   Nevertheless, although there are many working-class people in high positions, most of the high government posts and the majority of the middle-level bureaucracy as well as a large number of teaching positions were manned by middle-class individuals who had not been Communists but were nonetheless dedicated to the revolution.   While in revolutionary Cuba a member of the middle class can no longer aspire to certain goals for which he was programed before the Revolution—an unlimited supply of "consumer goods," the accumulation of property, a life of ease, a position of superiority over others, identification with Hollywood and Miami—he can fulfill other middle-class ideals such as sacrifice for the common good, service to the society, caring more about the welfare of others than for himself, security, and meaningful work integrated into a national purpose.   Some frustrated would-be consumers not integrated into the Revolution have contracted what José Yglesias describes as "la enfermedad," in which the sufferer spent all his waking hours worrying about ways to acquire dark glasses, flamboyant clothes and shoes, and the like. (1968)

However, many previously unpoliticized middle-class people who had not suffered from repression were able to identify with benefits made

[3] This novel was later made into the Cuban film *Memorias del Subdesarrollo* (*Memories of Underdevelopment*).

available to the majority. As one Jewish immigrant, who had been a prosperous Havana jeweler until he lost his shop during the Revolution and stayed on as an English teacher, explained to a visiting rabbi,

> Rabbi, we used to have plenty to eat, whatever we wanted, and little children went hungry all over Cuba, just like they do today all over Latin America. We had all we wanted, my wife didn't have to work, she didn't have to stand in line, we didn't have rationing, but the poor went hungry. Today we don't have what we used to, but we have enough, and everybody has enough. Tell me, Rabbi, isn't that what our religion teaches? . . . Rabbi, little girls used to walk the streets of Havana as prostitutes, and teenagers sold themselves to Americans for food and we merchants made money, not from the prostitutes, God forbid, but from the system, from the atmosphere. Today there are no prostitutes, no vice, no Americans, no business. Which is better, Rabbi? . . . Rabbi, people talk about dictatorship now. Do you know what it was like then? Do you know how many people the government shot? How many it arrested? But we were comfortable, we were well off, so we didn't notice. Now there are things I don't entirely agree with, but this government is more fair than you can imagine. And look what it does, Rabbi, with the little we have: look at the schools, the full scholarship students, the child care centers. Look at the chances for the poor to study . . . (Gendler, 1969: 22)

All over Cuba, one meets many professional people who are working harder for less money than they did before the Revolution, but they believe in what they are doing and feel they are contributing to the whole society. "A nationalized small businessman confided . . . that he did not have to fight for a buck anymore, now that he was working for society and not just for himself" (NUC, Cockcroft, 1969: 22).

Most middle-class administrators, technicians, guides, and translators hold more responsible and powerful positions today than they would have held before the Revolution. This shift has occurred because foreigners no longer make the fundamental decisions affecting Cuba, and also because of the emigration of skilled people and the explosion of new services and production. Anyone with skill in Cuba rises rapidly to top positions. The middle class started with greater skills and abilities and those who showed a willingness to work have had little difficulty increasing their expertise through education.

The accommodation of much of the middle class to the Revolution is accompanied by problems coming from prerevolutionary attitudes. In characteristically imperious fashion, many middle-class Cubans believe that it is only they, and not the workers or peasants, who really understand the Revolution, including the need to sacrifice. Thus middle-class revolutionaries criticize poor people who relate to the Revolution in terms of the material benefits it has brought them and are wont to comment about people who "had too much of a working-class background to understand what the revolution was all about" (NUC, Singer, 1969: 15–18).

When poor people complain about the inequalities which have persisted after the Revolution or aspire to consumer goods, they are sometimes accused of having a low level of political awareness.

The U. S. Role in the Radicalization of the Revolution. The radicalization of the Revolution has been explained as a result of U. S. pressure: "The Revolution was waged against the system of power which had existed for six decades. Given the key role of the United States in that power structure, the Revolution inevitably led to conflict between Cuba and the United States" (Zeitlin and Scheer, 1963: 12). The fact that socialist direction was far from the intentions of the Castro leadership, and that both Fidel and Ché *said* that they were responding to the United States in deepening the Revolution, led such analysts as Zeitlin and Scheer and William A. Williams (1963) to conclude that it was the United States which pushed the Revolution to the left.

There is no doubt about U. S. hostility to Castro's taking power and his revolutionary changes. After the attempts of U. S. officials to arrange a military junta to keep Castro from taking power failed, the United States insisted that any expropriated property be paid for in cash. If this admonition had been followed, the revolutionary pledges could never have been fulfilled. U. S. official protests had ominous weight as a result of the history of Cuban-United States relations. In the past such protests had actually been ultimatums frequently followed by some form of intervention. Fidel told U. S. Ambassador Philip Bonsal that there could be no discussion about compensation unless the United States recognized Cuba's sovereign right to expropriate (Castro, 1962a: 25–26).

Immediately after Castro took power there was a severe shortage of capital for industrial and agricultural diversification because his government put emphasis on programs which helped people immediately such as lowering rents and utility rates and raising salaries. In order to achieve Castro's promises of dramatic industrial and agricultural development, Cuba needed short-term aid to overcome the economic problems inherited from Batista and to finance new programs. However, the terms of U. S. aid were well-known because they had been imposed in Chile, Argentina, Bolivia, and Brazil, and they were incompatible with the revolutionary goals. According to Williams, Castro did seek a loan in April 1959, from the U. S.-controlled International Monetary Fund, having eliminated other U. S. credit sources because of their political requirements. Apparently he was turned down because he refused to accept a "stabilization program" which would have paralyzed revolutionary efforts. The United States decided, in the words of Edwin W. Kenworthy of the *New York Times* (April 22, 1959), "to let the Castro Government go through the wringer," of economic pressures until the Cuban government was willing to accept guarantees for U. S. capital and shelve the Revolution in exchange for economic assistance. When Castro responded to these pressures by quickening the pace of the Revolution, U. S. government and private groups cooperated with counter-revolutionaries in sabotaging and terrorist activities, including airplane fire-bomb attacks. The U. S. Senate became a forum for attacks on Cuba by senators and counter-revolutionaries. When Cuba sought to diversify trade by selling sugar to the Soviet Union for oil, the U. S. oil companies refused to refine Soviet oil leading to their expropriation. When the United States cut the Cuban sugar quota in 1960, it forced Cuba into reliance upon the Soviet Union. Diplomatic relations were cut January 3, 1961. By then the United States had placed an embargo on trade with Cuba and was urging other Latin American countries to cut diplomatic and trade relations with Cuba.

The CIA began planning an invasion of Cuba by March 1960 with the support of Vice President Nixon who had spoken with Castro in Washington. By June, armed aerial attacks based in Florida had begun. In April 1961, the U. S.-planned invasion by Cuban exiles landed at Playa Girón (Bay of Pigs) after planes flown by U. S. pilots bombed Havana. It was at this time that Fidel first declared that the Revolution was socialist. After its defeat at Playa Girón, the United States continued to infiltrate terrorists into Cuba and imposed a blockade, pressing the rest of Latin America to isolate Cuba.

There is no doubt that U. S. hostility speeded up the radicalization of the Revolution, but the movement toward socialism cannot be explained by U. S. reaction alone. U. S. pressure after all was designed to moderate the Revolution, as it had in Bolivia, Mexico, and elsewhere. Its effect was the opposite. The radicalization was a result of 1) the attitudes and power base of the revolutionary leadership and their determination to implement basic reforms, 2) the stagnated nature of the pre-revolutionary socio-economic system, and 3) the economic retaliation of entrenched power groups including U. S. businesses in Cuba. Given the first two, the latter actually facilitated the radicalization process.

The movement toward socialism was thus the result of both objective economic conditions and class structure, and subjective political and economic commitments and values on the part of the revolutionary leadership. The foreign dependency, stagnation, monopolization, and unproductivity which characterized the Cuban economy; the enormous technical and capital requirements necessary for the development of any underdeveloped country in the present day; and the absence of a nationalist, autonomous, capitalist class made rapid development of Cuba and a redistribution of wealth to benefit the Cuban masses impossible under capitalism. Only by nationalizing foreign trade, the powerful foreign companies operating in Cuba, and the monopolized private national sector could economic development be effective. In essence, then, development and social equality required socialism. This does not mean, however, that socialism was inevitable in Cuba. On the contrary, the reality of dependency put enormous pressure on any political group in control to conform to the fact of U. S. power. However, the revolutionary leadership was determined to do whatever was necessary to benefit the Cuban workers and peasants; they had the power in the rebel army to do so; and they did not shrink from their goals even when it became evident to them that only under socialist organization could they achieve their aims.

The Eclipse of the Moderates. Although the revolutionaries at first turned formal political offices over to moderates like Provisional President Manuel Urrútia, Prime Minister José Miró Cardona, Foreign Minister Roberto Agramonte, National Bank head Felipe Pazos, real power remained in the hands of Fidel Castro and the rebel army.

The fundamental condition which permitted the implementation of a radical reform program for the first time in Cuban history was destruction of the military establishment which had protected property rights and controlled politics, and its replacement by a rebel army under the complete control of a leadership committed to fundamental change. This was the third time in Latin American history (after Mexico, 1910–1920 and Bolivia, 1952) that the military had been destroyed by a revolutionary force. As the abortive revolutions in Cuban history and the examples of Guatemala in 1954, the Dominican Republic in 1965, and Argentina under Perón demonstrate, it would not have been possible to turn the Revolution into a class struggle without the prior destruction of the pre-revolutionary military. This is why the CIA strived to maintain the armed forces intact after the Cuban Revolution. With armed power in the hands of the rebel army and popular militias, collectivization could not be stopped by sabotage raids from Florida, the CIA-organized invasion, or the economic isolation of Cuba, though these actions made the process more expensive in human lives, productivity, and resources. This new power situation made it *possible* for the regime to dismantle Cuban capitalism and move toward socialism, even though this had not been the original intention of the revolutionary leadership.

The rebel army, not the moderate civilian officials, seized the property of fleeing Batistianos and in March confiscated the land of Batista supporters. The rebel army established the courts in which Batista's henchmen were tried and executed in order to avoid having these same men lynched by mobs in the streets as had happened after Machado's overthrow, or, more recently, after the overthrow of Marcos Pérez Jiménez in Venezuela in 1958. It was the rebel army which carried out the agrarian reform, not the bureaucracy of the former government.

Castro is reported to have had the impossible idea that he "would be content temporarily heading the armed forces and that then he would like to retire to the Sierra Maestra to develop it and to teach" (Matthews, 1969: 81). This contention is supported by letters Fidel sent to close friends in 1959. In 1962, however, Castro implied that the rebel leadership was biding its time watching to see how the moderates performed (Castro, 1962a: 32–33). It is hard to believe that Castro could have trusted the liberals in the government, who had played little or no role in the overthrow, to implement basic reforms. In any case, with real power in the hands of the rebel army leadership, the moderates in the government were unable to hold back the revolutionary program.

Revolutionary laws dealing with the seizure of property of Batistianos, the intervention into companies which had over-exploited workers or broken the law, the cutting in half of rents, and the lowering of mortgage rates were issued in March 1959. These laws and the June agrarian reform law were prepared without the knowledge or cooperation of the "moderates." Such fundamental laws, though reformist capitalist, were clearly designed to help wage earners at the expense of property owners. At the same time however, other government measures were designed to benefit property owners and stimulate business and investment. There was an unsuccessful attempt to attract U. S. tourism. The government measures to stimulate capitalism were based on the mistaken conception that investors constituted an independent and coherent class which would take advantage of government support to replace U. S. economic domination and lead vigorous economic development. But Cuban capitalists viewed the interventions against U. S. and Batistiano property and the agrarian and rent reforms as threats to property in general. Actions designed to encourage small investors at the expense of monopolies were seen as attacks on "private enterprise." Generally it was difficult for Cuban businessmen to see that their own well-being could be separate from that of foreign capital on which they were dependent. Thus when U. S. government officials and business groups attacked revolutionary measures and called them "communist," Cuban groups tended to accept that definition. Undoubtedly the situation *looked* Communist to them, even though such moderates as Felipe Pazos were desperately trying to enlist their support, and the communists during 1959 had no significant power. Once the businessmen and their political representatives were perceived as enemies, the government acted to destroy them. Fidel Castro took Miró Cardona's place as Prime Minister in February 1959. As the moderates in government realized their powerlessness to stop the radical direction of government policy, they either defected or were replaced.

The moderate leaders had no commitment to immediate improvement for poor Cubans. They were interested in conciliating with the United States and conserving capitalism. To them the Revolution had been solely against a political dictatorship. Since the moderates had no independent base of power and were dependent on rebel army support, once they conflicted with the revolutionary leadership they passed from the scene without a struggle. In explaining the defection of moderates, Matthews explains that

> . . . Cuba lost . . . the services of many thousands of civil servants, business-men, bankers, managers, technicians, doctors, lawyers, and the like. It was a grievous loss from which Cuba has not yet recovered, but no one can doubt that in accepting this loss, Fidel Castro saved his revolution. (1969: 139)

The radical turn of the government was probably signalled equally by Castro's insisting on national sovereignty with Ambassador Bonsal and by his resolve to carry out the agrarian reform law to its fullest consequence. Castro had by this time already fallen out with Venezuelan President Rómulo Betancourt, dean of Latin America's "Democratic Left" when, on a visit by Castro to Caracas, Betancourt made it clear that he had chosen to compromise with the United States rather than back Castro's appeal for support against U. S. imperialism. In July, Castro responded to the political crisis provoked by opposition to the agrarian reform by resigning as Prime Minister and issuing a call for mobilized support in order to force the resignation of President Urrutia who had been accusing the government of Communism and refusing to sign the revolutionary laws about which he apparently was not being consulted. After Urrutia resigned, Castro reassumed the premiership and placed Osvaldo Dorticós in the presidency. Ché Guevara replaced Felipe Pazos as head of the National Bank in November 1959.

Old ministries began to be replaced by new organs established by the rebel army. The defection and hostility of the moderate elements led the leadership to call for more active participation by urban workers and peasants, a move which speeded the radicalization.

> The Revolution was consummated with the active support and involvement of the majority of the Cuban working class; the revolutionary government began to implement its social commitments to the peasantry. For both reasons the Cuban Revolution from the beginning took shape as a mass social revolution. . . (Petras, 1970: 111)

The defection of the moderates in the government, which included five cabinet ministers and several diplomatic representatives, was accompanied by attacks on the Revolution by the National Association of Cattlemen, the Tobacco Growers Association, U. S. investors, the Archbishop of Santiago, and the Partido Auténtico. Even rebel army Major Huber Matos was arrested in October 1959 and charged with conspiring with landowners to block agrarian reform. In the face of the opposition from powerful producer and labor groups who were more interested in protecting special privileges than in furthering overall economic development, the government had to be willing to socialize key areas of production and to establish central planning in order to implement reform programs. The transition to socialism, then, was the result of pragmatic solutions to specific problems.

The early important laws of the Revolution were those which provided for seizing the property of Batistianos and the sentencing and execution of criminals from the dictatorship. The rent law, issued in March 1959, was the first law to redefine property relations. It cut rents in half and transformed rent into amortization payments toward purchase. While providing a compensation for former property owners of up to $600 a month, this law essentially expropriated urban dwellings held for income, closing off a source of investment that was particularly important to the middle class, and redistributed the income of those with real estate investments.

THE AGRARIAN REFORM

The agrarian land reform program was the touchstone of the Revolution, for it was this program which provoked the first serious opposition to the government and defection of many of the moderates, and it was in overcoming the obstacles to the land reform that the Cuban leaders entered a process which carried them toward socialism. Land reform had begun during the guerrilla war when the revolutionaries distributed land in the areas they controlled. The first agrarian reform law was promulgated in the Sierra Maestra (Law 3 of the Sierra Maestra). This law implemented the abolition of the latifundios already provided for in article 90 of the 1940 Constitution and called for free distribution of land to those with less than sixty-seven hectares. The rebel leaders had noted the negative effects of dividing up cattle among peasants in the Sierra Maestra, for it led to the slaughter of the cattle. This seems to have influenced Guevara and Castro to favor collectivization as a means of maximizing production. Most rural workers in Cuba were concerned with income and regular employment rather than ownership. In the Sierra Maestra, on the other hand, there was a strong desire for ownership because of the attempt to secure tiny plots against encroachments by private owners. This desire for ownership in that area was respected by the government.

The First Phase. The agrarian reform was carried out in two phases. The first was from 1959 to 1963. Three months after the revolutionaries took power, in March 1959, land belonging to Batistianos was seized, and in May the agrarian reform law was announced and immediately attacked by the sugar mill owners. The law provided for expropriation of all properties larger than 995 acres, with certain exceptions, and provided that cooperatives or small- and medium-sized farms be established. Large properties were to be organized as cooperatives based on intensive production because of the advantages of large-scale production. Renting, tenancy, and share-cropping would be abolished by giving the land to those who worked it. Low interest loans, minimum prices, and new housing were promised for rural workers. The goals of the agrarian reform were to provide farmers an adequate income and to contribute to national economic development by increasing production, which would decrease the need for food imports, increase and diversify exports, and, by increasing the consumption of the rural population, provide an expanded internal market. A National Institute of Agrarian Reform (INRA) was established to carry out the reform, to promote productivity through technology, credit, and the formation of cooperatives, and to develop a government marketing mechanism. The agency was directed to train agricultural experts and cooperative managers and to conduct scientific experiments. It also was empowered to develop rural housing, roads, education, electricity, sanitation, and "people's stores" where rural workers could obtain goods at low prices. INRA was staffed with rebel army officers and it quickly became the most important revolutionary institution.

In June, when the law became official, U. S. business groups complained that the reform was unjust and a "violation of international law," and the U. S. State Department issued a statement that expropriated owners would have to be given prompt and adequate compensation. The United States rejected payment in the form of twenty-year bonds at 4.5 percent interest based on the value placed on these properties by the owners for tax purposes. By late in June, the agrarian reform was well underway in Camagüey Province where 2.3 million acres of primarily large cattle holdings were taken over.

Attacks on the reform and the government were launched by farmer organizations and the major press, as well as by those who had defected from the government and the army. Tony Varona of the Auténtico party attacked the law and called for elections. The PSP joined the attacks on the government in these early months. Communist leaders who were not involved in land distribution because they were not in the rebel army considered the land reform unnecessarily radical. The Communists also clashed with Castro when he urged workers to support a law giving a percentage of their wages to finance the agrarian reform and to postpone wage increases in view of the economic crisis. Communist labor leaders encouraged workers to push for higher wages. In spite of these attacks, there were no attempts by the government to control the press, radio, or television or to retaliate against critics.

Major Pedro Díaz Lanz resigned from the Air Force, accusing the government of being Communist-infiltrated. He then appeared before the U. S. Senate Internal Security Subcommittee to accuse many Cuban officials of Communism. Several of those whom he named as Communists, such as David Salvador, head of the CTC, were actually anti-Communists. The U. S. business community in Cuba also attacked Castro for "flirting" with Communism and even though this charge ignored the real tension between Communists and Fidelistas, the U. S. State Department accepted it as reality. The basic issue for U. S. policy makers was the attitude of the Cuban government toward U. S. property, and the Communist threat was manipulated as a justification for U. S. hostility.

During the first phase of the agrarian reform some six million hectares were expropriated, representing some 50 to 60 percent of Cuba's farm land which had been owned by only 5 percent of its landowners. This land was distributed as sugar cooperatives, collective cattle ranches, and to individual small farmers who had been renters, squatters, or had less than sixty-seven hectares.

When the landowners and their associations reacted to the reform by economic resistance, that is by withholding production, neglecting to plant, failing to supply credit, or, in the case of the cattle ranch-owners, by stepping up slaughter, the INRA responded by speeding up the take-over, so as to safeguard production. The economic resistance and the threat of an agricultural production crisis drove INRA to complete in months a program which Castro himself had expected to take three years.

The cattlemen's association actively resisted the agrarian reform. The large ranchers who feared losing their properties suspended purchase of yearling calves from small property owners, and at the same time speeded up their slaughter rate. In response, INRA seized all large cattle ranches in Camagüey and Oriente so that they could buy yearlings from the small producers and have a place to put them. The alternative would have been to guarantee property rights to the large owners which would have discredited the agrarian reform in the eyes of peasants and owners alike, as such guarantees had done in Mexico. Allowing years of court litigation, as in Bolivia after 1953, would have removed security and incentives from both threatened owners and potential beneficiaries of the agrarian reform. Most of Cuba's largest cattle ranches were seized during 1959 and 1960. While the seizures of 1959 were a result of the production crisis threatened by the announcement of the law, the 1960 seizures resulted from the realization that major private ownership in the cattle industry made planned agriculture impossible.

Economic resistance in other sectors of agriculture took varied forms. Large tobacco farmers refused to prepare the land for the following year's crop, cane farmers failed to plant new seedlings, and other large farmers began to neglect their crops. Again the threat of production crises led to take-overs by INRA.

The expropriation of the sugar plantations did not begin until 1960, after the cattle properties had been seized and the radical direction had been clearly established. The government postponed this crucial aspect of the agrarian reform until after the 1960 sugar harvest for lack of resources to direct production. On July 5, 1960, the United States cancelled Cuba's sugar quota in retaliation for Cuban seizure of the U. S. oil refineries. Cutting the sugar quota probably speeded up the nationalization of sugar mills and plantations, but the seizures had been planned for the July to October period in any event. By the end of 1960, the expropriation of large sugar properties—45 percent of all sugar land—was complete. Cane cooperatives were established on these lands, and the salaried agricultural workers, constituting about nearly all of the affected population, enthusiastically supported these cooperatives. By cultivating unused land and diversifying production, the members of the newly-established cooperatives who had been only seasonally employed, secured year-round employment. Thus they more than doubled their yearly income without increasing their "wage." The *colonos* (small and medium sugar planters supplying the mills of the large sugar plantations) benefited from the agrarian reform provisions which abolished rent on small properties; medium farmers were able to buy more land from the expropriated properties. Nevertheless, the larger *colonos* unsuccessfully opposed the agrarian reform, proposing instead that their share of sugar production be increased, a measure which would have strengthened the pre-revolutionary inefficient and wasteful system of sugar quotas.

With half of the farmland in government hands, the INRA was in a position to rationalize the exploitation of the island's agriculture. It would be necessary to increase greatly the amount of cultivated land to make Cuba self-sufficient in foodstuffs and still export large quantities of sugar. INRA's predominant control of capital, technical aid, and marketing gave its officials considerable control over the remaining independent farmers. O'Connor concluded, "a collectivized agriculture had the air of inevitability, and it is difficult to see how any government determined to accelerate Cuba's economic development could have escaped" the general land politics INRA was compelled to follow (O'Connor, 1970: 105).

Cooperatives and People's Farms. The cattle farms were first directly administered by INRA and then made into collective state farms, *granjas del pueblo,* in contrast to the sugar *centrales* (plantation, including a mill) which were at first organized as cooperatives. Collectivization in the cattle sector was chosen to safeguard production and to avoid the creation of a privileged group of workers. The number of employees on these farms was so small that if the ranches had been organized as cooperatives each worker would have had a much higher income than cooperative members in other sectors of agriculture.

The *granjas* were much larger than the cooperatives and averaged 89.1 hectares per worker compared to 6.6 on the cooperatives. The *granja* workers, like factory employees, received a regular wage. Cooperatives organized on farms producing products other than sugar were soon also transformed into *granjas.*

The early cane cooperatives were run much like the *granjas,* although there was considerable variation between cooperatives in terms of how they were administered. These properties remained undivided as a single production unit. The INRA appointed an administrator to work with the elected cooperative council, but in fact he frequently ran the cooperative, as did the *granja* administrator. Nevertheless, if the cooperative administrator conflicted with the council, the council could and did prevail, and the INRA tended to react by replacing the administrator with someone who was more persuasive. While theoretically the cooperative member received an annual share of production, in fact he was granted a wage of $2.50 a day to see him through the first year. Inadequate accounting made it impossible to calculate the profit, and it was later decided not to distribute profit anyway.

INRA officials preferred the *granjas* form of organization since they had more direct control of planning, technical aid, and resource allocation, even though this control was more potential than real. Many problems arose with the cooperatives, such as their uneven productivity and ability to guarantee earnings, the difficulty of integrating some cooperative production into overall planning, and the disadvantages suffered by workers hired by the cooperatives who were denied benefits of members. Rich and poor cooperatives would lead to increasingly different life styles, something which clashed with the egalitarian aims of the Revolution.

The autonomy of cooperatives made it more difficult to shift people from over-populated productive units to developing areas where labor was short. Most cooperative administrators were deficient in training and experience and needed close interaction with government technicians.

In December 1960, the government began converting the cane cooperatives into *granjas*. The change from cooperatives to *granjas* was well received by cooperative members and was not accompanied by coercion. In the first place the change was not great, and cooperative members seemed to have welcomed the greater security and guarantee of a high income regardless of their individual productivity. Generally the changeover meant an increase in earnings because the wages on the *granjas* had been somewhat higher. According to the government, the cooperative members were working for their own benefit so although they received the land free, they had to repay investments in improvements. Since the *granja* workers were working for the whole society, they received housing and machinery investments free. The INRA thus invested more capital in the *granjas* than in the cooperatives, both because the *granjas* were more directly controlled and because the benefits of production would accrue to the whole society.

On the cooperatives and *granjas,* members were provided with housing, schools, health services, and a retail store. Work to construct the buildings was provided by the rural workers themselves aided by the rebel army. Electricity and other amenities began to transform peasant life, providing a new sense of material well-being, security, community feeling, and confidence in the government. Real income and food consumption increased significantly. The rural poor were clearly the group which experienced more real improvement and owed more to the Revolution than any other group in Cuban society.

The Private Agricultural Sector. Even after the change-over from cooperatives to *granjas,* by the end of 1961, more than half of Cuba's farm land remained in private hands. Private farmers still produced more than the state units in sugar cane, cattle, coffee, and tobacco. Only in rice was more produced in the public sector. Slightly less than half of the privately held land was in small farms of sixty-seven hectares or less, and the rest was left in "medium" farms between sixty-seven and 402.6 hectares. The small private farmers, more than half of them in Oriente province, mostly had received their title or increased acreage as a result of the land reform, since many had been squatters, share-croppers, or renters and had had less than the "vital minimum" of 26.8 hectares. Distribution to small farmers proceeded slowly during 1959 and rapidly during 1960.

During 1960–1961, the government actively courted the support of the small private farmers, attempting to drive a wedge between them and the medium landowners who became increasingly hostile to the Revolution. Credit and machinery were made available to these small holders and they were reassured that they would not be expropriated. In May 1961, the National Association of Small Farmers (ANAP) was organized and farmers with more than sixty-seven hectares were excluded from membership. Credit and supplies of seed, fertilizer, machinery, and know-how were funneled through ANAP. Small farmers were thus bound to the government while medium farmers were alienated, their lands later to be expropriated in 1964. Small farmers were organized into production and credit cooperatives under ANAP, and, although the government encouraged farmers to work in collective arrangements, no coercion was used. The ANAP gradually was in a position to influence the selection of crops to be planted and to bring the small farmer under national production plans. ANAP also oversaw educational, cultural, and social programs. Some ANAP cooperatives evolved toward collective use of the land.

Various methods have been adopted so that the small farms would not be islands of petty capitalism. With the elimination of private distribution channels between 1964 and 1969, the small farmers mainly market their products through government channels. The land can be inherited by a farmer's children, but it can only be sold to the state. It is hoped that as production in the state sector becomes more successful and the services which accrue to farm workers in the state sector become more abundant, private farmers will want to join the state sector. In any case, their children, having benefited from educational and employment opportunities, are not expected to be interested in carrying on the private farming tradition. Rural children in large numbers are studying in urban secondary boarding schools and learning to be fishermen, teachers, and a whole variety of technical specialists including agronomists. Many elderly farmers have turned their land over to the state and received special pensions. In the 1968 Havana Green Belt project, private farms were integrated into a massive production plan which provided the owners with free labor and nearly obliterated the distinction between private and government land.

Still, there has been some hostility toward the government on the part of small farmers, particularly when they have been stirred up by the medium farmers. In the Escambray mountains, small farmers gave some support to a counter-revolutionary guerrilla group which was established in that area after the Revolution. The peasants there had been alienated from the Revolution during the guerrilla phase by the behavior of some of the Directorio revolutionaries in the *Segundo Frente de Escambray*.

After the defeat of the counter-revolutionary guerrillas, these farmers were resettled in Pinar del Rio on a model collective farm.

Diversification. During 1961 and 1962 diversification was emphasized in agriculture, particularly on the cane farms. Part of the intent was to free Cuba from dependence on sugar, and to develop national food production. Sugar was considered the cause of Cuba's foreign domination. Sugar land was plowed under and planted to other crops, while plans to increase sugar yields on remaining cane acreage were designed to maintain the total production of sugar. Under the influence of René Dumont (the French socialist agronomist), livestock farms were to grow crops and crop farms would have livestock.

In 1961, Cuba had its second largest sugar harvest, 6.7 million tons, compared to the previous record of 7 million tons in 1952. This harvest was brought in before diversification and resulted from an optimum combination of available labor, good weather, and the cutting of nearly all standing cane in the absence of artificial quota restrictions. Production of other agricultural products also increased as unused land and unused human resources were put to work.

Although incredibly ambitious production targets were set for most crops, subsequent production did not increase as much as was expected, and in sugar production there was a dramatic decline of 30 percent in 1962, and in 1963, only 3.8 million tons were produced. One reason for this decline was a drought, but other reasons were more significant. Some of the most productive cane land had been plowed under and the projected increases in yield on the remaining sugar acreage were not attained for lack of planning, technicians, labor, and fertilizer.

The diversification plans also went badly in 1962. There was a critical shortage of technically trained supervisory personnel and the rural workers themselves were not equipped by experience to handle the new crops. Planning and administrative confusion contributed heavily to the problems. For example, labor was wasted in preparing seventy-eight thousand hectares for *malanga* (a yam) when there was only seed for half that area. Moreover, there was a severe labor shortage as rural workers were attracted into higher-paid urban construction jobs. Meat production declined because of earlier indiscriminate slaughtering of the herds, while the demand for meat sky-rocketed because of the increased buying power of poor people.

Productivity. It is difficult to measure to what extent lack of incentives or inefficient planning contributed to the production and productivity declines in 1962. Productivity in the state sector was lower than in the private sector, but this could well have been caused by planning mistakes rather than lack of incentive. The most dedicated work applied inappropriately could bring about production declines, and instances of planning mistakes abound in René Dumont's writing. General plans were drawn up which were not adjusted to fit detailed needs. They were based on inadequate facts and diagnoses, and put into effect without consulting the workers in the field or technicians.

In terms of incentive, those who remained small private farmers experienced the least change in work-productivity motivation, since their income still depended on how much they produced. The worker on a *granja* was in a totally new situation. Employment and salary guarantees reduced the material incentives and coercion to work, and there probably was a decline in the number of hours worked per rural worker. There was a change in the nature of agricultural labor, which had been characterized by seasonal unemployment alternating with extreme hardship and long hours of the most difficult kind of work, done by people with the worst housing and health conditions that Cuba had to offer. Naturally when these rural people were given guaranteed salaries, improved housing, health, and education they did not work the way they had been forced to before. Agricultural unemployment was absorbed by year-round employment opportunities on the diversified *granjas*. Cane-cutting and seasonal harvesting and heavy land-cleaning projects were increasingly handled by volunteer workers from urban occupations on special brigades recruited for special tasks or for a limited time.

The revolutionary leaders believed that after centuries of exploitation it was simple justice to guarantee earnings to peasants as a basic right, even if this policy brought productivity problems which would have to be solved later on. Naturally this policy brought broad support from peasants, so that a decline in productivity should not be seen as reflecting opposition to the government. There was no lack of ingenuity by INRA officials or will to cooperate on the part of peasants.

Critics such as René Dumont (1970a, b) felt that Cuba could not afford such high wages and housing expenditures for the rural poor, and that earnings increases should wait for productivity increases and the gradual introduction of intensive methods and machinery. The Cuban insistence on putting "social justice" before increases in production seems to have infuriated many critics.

In the absence of enough trained technicians, those in charge muddled through, frequently failing to make realistic calculations of the cost of alternative methods, not keeping accurate statistics, and not following through on projects initiated. In a situation of scarce resources and labor, each new project interfered with the completion of those already underway. Nevertheless, with all the mistakes that were made, the poorest sector of Cuba, the rural workers, continued to experience an improvement of their living conditions, food consumption, and educational levels during the whole painful period of trial-and-error experimentation. Perhaps the most remarkable success was that the supply of agricultural goods did not fall drastically as the threats of starvation and unemployment were removed as the main motivation for agricultural workers. That the production of some crops declined is less important than that production continued at all in the absence of the coercive incentives which capitalist ideologists assume are universally necessary. Cuba's experiment is particularly significant when compared with the rest of Latin America during the 1960's where food production per capita declined and there was an increase in the misery and deprivation of the rural population.

The Re-emphasis of Sugar. By the end of 1962, failures in the diversification program had led to a new policy direction. It was evident that Cuba would be unable to supply the sugar exports projected in trade agreements already concluded with socialist countries. Sugar production was again to receive primary emphasis, with cattle production in second place. More than two hundred thousand hectares were replanted in cane. Cattle production increases, largely through artificial semination, were to provide large-scale meat exports. Further agricultural diversification was to be postponed until sugar production was up. However, unrealistically high targets were set for other crops such as rice, cotton, and coffee. Agricultural planning was to become more accurate and flexible with more feedback from the individual unit.

The Second Phase of Agrarian Reform. On October 3, 1963, the "second agrarian reform" law was passed, expropriating the medium farmers, those who still owned more than 67.1 hectares or about eleven thousand farms. The two reasons behind this measure were the liquidation of the rural bourgeoisie, many of whom were counter-revolutionaries or engaged in black-market operations, the extension of government control, and the consolidation of state-controlled land which had been scattered in small parcels. The medium farms had at first been more produtive than the state sector, but after nationalization of distribution which lowered sale prices of their crops, such farmers felt less incentive to produce and their total production began to fall. Thus the amount of land directly controlled by the government rose from about half to 70 percent. Small private holders remained with some two hundred thousand farms totaling 30 percent of the land. In 1966, these private owners produced one-third of the sugar, half of the milk, and most of the tobacco, cacao, coffee, fruits, and vegetables. After that time production on state lands of these products increased.

TRANSITION TO SOCIALISM IN INDUSTRY

Somewhat the same trajectory toward public ownership was followed in industry as in agriculture. First the industries belonging to Batistianos was seized. Next the government intervened in companies which were accused of unreasonable rates or failure to pay taxes, such as the U. S.-owned telephone and electrical companies. As the climate for private business became insecure, some companies suspended operations and were taken over by the government to maintain production and avoid unemployment. Then, in July 1960, the foreign oil refineries were seized when they refused to refine imported Soviet oil. Foreign banks were taken over in September. This was followed by a wave of takeovers of plants and mines. Then railroads, ports, movie houses, and hotels were taken over. The government could not turn these properties over to the private sector, since private businessmen had become either enemies of the government or at least uncooperative with official plans.

When the government found itself owning, coordinating, and administering the basic production units in agriculture and industry, socialism had become a fact. Large-scale planning and allocation of capital and resources became necessary just to keep the nationalized sectors operating. While nationalized industry was first handled by a section of INRA, by 1961 the government had to set up three new Ministries of Industry, Internal Commerce, and External Commerce coordinated by a centralized planning agency, Junta Central de Planificación (JUCEPLAN).

By 1961, the general lines of economic policy were to assure a high investment rate to permit a rapid autonomous growth rate, and to achieve a maximum of industrial self-sufficiency using national resources and substituting imports with local production. Parallel to the program of agricultural diversification there was to be industrial diversification. A heavy steel industry was to be established beginning in 1965 as the foundation for truck, tractor, and mechanical industries. A careful national plan projecting growth rates was drawn up in 1961, although it was based on faulty statistics. The economic performance in 1962 showed how unreal these projections were.

Many obstacles to industrialization were removed by policies of the revolutionary government. The agrarian reform and rent reform increased the market by transferring income to the poorest sectors of the population. Nationalization made possible planning and coordination to eliminate waste and to integrate productive capacities with national needs.

However, there were serious obstacles to the development of the newly nationalized industry. Once the United States placed an embargo and blockade on trade with Cuba, Cuban industries, most of which had been integrated into the last stages of production of U. S. corporations rather than into the needs of the Cuban economy, had to either be reorganized or replaced by others which could operate with supplies and parts from other countries, particularly the socialist ones. Production efforts were drained by the constant need to be on guard against attack and the U. S.-sponsored invasion showed the reality of these fears. Workers participated in militia duty.

Another problem faced by Cuba and all socialist countries was how to organize planning so that the nationalized economy functioned efficiently. Because of the lack of experience and trained personnel, planning tended to oscillate between extreme improvization (*"por la libre"*) and mechanical implementation of planning schemes from Czechoslovakia which had little to do with Cuban needs and human capabilities (Boorstein, 1968: 135–140, 152–155). Information on production, costs, markets, and requirements was so sketchy that in the first years effective planning was virtually impossible. The planners themselves were too few and too inexperienced and they tended toward unrealistic centralization combined with de facto anarchy at the local level. Too much confidence in inadequate planning often led to disastrous results. Capital resources and human effort had to be diverted from production to the educational field to provide the technicians, planners, and trained personnel whose skills would only contribute to production years later; in the meantime this vital effort acted as a drag on production. Until an adequate supply of technically-trained revolutionaries was available to man industries and to provide industrial planning, political leaders improvised heroically in the breach.

THE DECLARATION OF SOCIALISM

By April 1961, when Fidel announced, after the bombing attack by U. S. planes, and just on the eve of the Bay of Pigs invasion, that the Cuban Revolution was in fact socialist, he was merely giving a name to what was already a fact. The unsuccessful invasion rallied mass support to the Cuban leadership and to the socialist path they had charted. The result of the invasion was the end of organized resistance within Cuba and the development of Comités de Defensa de la Revolución (CDR) or block committees which increased mass mobilization). It was extraordinary that so many Cubans including revolutionaries with deep anti-Communist sentiments made the transition to socialism so easily. Many explained their own changeover to these writers in such terms as "before, we had no idea what communism was except that everyone said it was bad. Later, when we found out that what we had built was socialism, we knew it was good."

Certain characteristics of Cuban development had facilitated the transition to socialism. One was the recognition by most groups from their own experience that basic structural changes were needed. Batista's corporate system had raised people's hopes and accustomed them to look to the government for solutions. Moreover, only a few wealthy owners were seriously hurt by the transition to socialism. Most medium-sized owners were compensated for any losses they sustained. Opposition was further weakened by the lack of cohesiveness and class solidarity among those who were hurt by the Revolution.

The nationalism which had acted as a common thread while the Revolution was still a multi-class coalition gradually turned into a militant anti-imperialism, binding together rural and urban workers with radical members of the middle class. In the absence of an independent, nationalist capitalist class which could lead development and resist U. S. pressure, the political initiative shifted to the left and radical nationalists in the middle class then helped move the Revolution toward socialism.

THE CUBAN COMMUNISTS, LABOR, AND THE 26TH OF JULY MOVEMENT

The relations between revolutionary leaders and the Communist Party (PSP) were not good in May 1959. Castro formally disassociated himself from the Communists until July 1960, but he became increasingly intolerant of anti-Communist attacks which he perceived as attacks on the Revolution. By October 1959, faced by counter-revolutionary terrorism, attacks from the United States, and the defections of moderate sectors of the 26th of July, all accompanied by accusations that the Revolution had become Communist, the revolutionary leadership began a rapprochement with the Communists and sought Soviet support to sustain the economy. Castro then said he did not believe everything he heard about Communism, since he knew "of the lies that some people are telling about my regime" (Zeitlin and Scheer, 1963: 244; Friedenberg, 1962: 340).

In February of 1960, the Soviet Union extended $100 million in credits to Cuba, and agreed to exchange sugar for oil. The Communist Party gave increasingly uncritical support to the government and Castro helped the Communists win control of the labor movement. Besides opposing anti-communism, Castro had certain positive reasons for bringing Communists into the government. As the revolution became socialist, he needed disciplined administrative cadres. The 26th of July movement as a whole was poorly organized, ununified, and was frequently led locally by leaders who opposed the radical direction of the government and refused to ally with Communists. Castro, having "rushed headlong into nationalization without . . . the rank and file or administrative machine needed . . . ," felt he needed the Communists supposed "keen sense of organization and discipline . . ." (Karol, 1970: 185).

In the labor movement, the 26th of July activists led by David Salvador were opposed to allying with the Communists, as they had shown in their reluctance to ally with the Communists in the Havana underground before the Revolution triumphed. This reluctance had been overruled by the Sierra leadership in late 1958. Most of the 26th of July labor leaders were also ideologically opposed to nationalization of industry and socialism. They fought to retain the privileges and power the union bureaucracies had achieved before the Revolution, hoping to retain a reformed capitalism. There were those who took exception to this position, including Conrado Bequer, head of the powerful sugar workers union who stayed with the Fidelista leadership in the transition to socialism and alliance with the PSP. The anti-Communist July 26th labor leaders did not have enough support to control the labor movement on their own, so they began to ally themselves against the Communists with the remaining labor bureaucrats who had been associated with Batista's labor boss, Eusebio Mujal.

However, Castro had decided that militant anti-Communism could not be tolerated at a time when the Revolution needed support from the Cuban Communists as well as from the Soviet Union. When forced to chose between anti-socialist 26th of July labor leaders and Communists, he chose the Communists. He appealed directly to the workers over the heads of the 26th of July leadership, using as his ally the Communists who still had formidable labor strength. He used his personal influence to help the Communists win control of the CTC and of the Labor Ministry.

At no point did the PSP leadership play a significant leadership role during the transition to socialism or initiate or encourage any aspect of the radicalization of the Revolution. Nor were they in a position to do so. The Communists limited themselves to urging moderation, particularly Cuba's relationship with the United States. PSP leaders were integrated into the government in positions of power only after Castro announced that the Revolution was socialist.

Having announced that the Cuban Revolution was socialist, the rebel leaders set about organizing a revolutionary party. The first stage, beginning in July 1961, involved welding the three revolutionary organizations, the July 26th, the Directorio Revolucionario, and the PSP, into an Integrated Revolutionary Organization (ORI). The second stage, in 1962, was the formation of a United Party of the Socialist Revolution (PURS), which involved organizing a party nucleus in each work center and every locality, and integrating a large number of new cadres into the party. In the final stage, the new party received the name Communist Party of Cuba.

By announcing that the Revolution was socialist, Castro had established his right to control the PSP, as well as to influence revolutionary groups in the rest of Latin America. This position was reinforced when Castro declared in December 1961, that he had become a Marxist-Leninist as a result of his experience in the Revolution. During the end of 1961 and the first months of 1962, Castro went out of his way to support or to avoid criticism of the Communists. Aníbal Escalante, a key figure in PSP leadership, was given the position of organization secretary of the ORI. Escalante used his influence to place his PSP associates in key party and government positions and to disseminate the impression that the most authentic revolutionaries were "old militants" of the PSP. PSP members controlled the formation of the new nuclei of the future PURS, although their separate PSP organization was supposed to have disappeared. Escalante was even consulted on administrative and appointment decisions, bypassing the minister responsible, because of his power in the party and the generally accepted belief that the party was the basic source of power. Despite widespread dissatisfaction with this turn of events, Castro did not allow criticism of the Communists. As a result many able revolutionaries were driven from their positions when they resisted attempts by the Communists to monopolize control of and to impose their views upon various institutions.

Castro's first move against the behavior of Communists within the new party came in early March 1962 when he spoke at a meeting at the University of Havana commemorating the 1957 attack on Batista's palace by the Directorio. He bitterly chastised the old-time Communists for ordering the reader of the political testament of José Antonio Echevarría, leader of the attack on Batista, to omit a reference to his Catholic religious belief. Castro said that attempts at rewriting history would not be tolerated and that "the Revolution must be a school of unfettered thought." "Are we so cowardly, so bigoted in mind, . . . that we have to omit three lines . . . simply because . . . he believed [in God]? . . . In that case we would have to suppress the books of Martí because Martí was not a Marxist-Leninist" (Castro, 1962b: 9).

The next day, Castro compared the despotism of secretaries of the ORI, most of whom were old-time Communists, with that of Batista and his henchmen. Then at the end of March, he launched a full-scale attack on Escalante for "sectarianism" in trying to control the new party. Escalante was allowed to go into exile in Czechoslovakia. Castro complained that members of the July 26th movement who fought in the armed struggle were being dismissed in the new party as politically unprepared, while some of the old-time Communists who were now trying to control the party had been "hiding under their beds" at the time guerrillas were risking their lives. He defined the revolutionary qualification for membership in the new party not as political or ideological credentials, but as qualities of hard work, selfless dedication, and identification with the Revolution and the people's needs. The party nuclei were reorganized with these prerequisites in mind. Workers themselves, the majority of them previously involved in no party, carefully nominated candidates for party membership, and the party nucleus then decided whether to admit them. Castro and other revolutionary leaders went to great pains in the succeeding months to discuss what the qualities of a party member should be. The party's job was not only to politicize and to educate, but to make sure that production was accomplished.

Guevara made a number of speeches in which he criticized the low political consciousness of workers and related it to production failures. At the same time, Guevara, Castro, and others noted that a rise in productivity occurred during and immediately after the U. S.-sponsored invasion. Politicization and therefore the role of the party were seen as crucial in solving production problems, and a vision of the "new man" emerged which was the "man of the perpetual Girón invasion." In the wake of the Escalante controversy, Cuban-Soviet relations were not good, but the Soviet Union was careful not to provoke Cuba.

EDUCATION DURING THE TRANSITION TO SOCIALISM

One of the key symbolic acts of the revolutionary government was to transform the army barracks into schools, including of course the Moncada barracks in Santiago. Education was essential to the revolutionary economic development program. The waste or misuse of potential human skills was a central characteristic of the distorted development Cuba had experienced. It was also vital to the egalitarian, human aims of the Revolution in order to provide equal opportunities for the whole population and to develop a new kind of consciousness in the Cuban people.

Before the Revolution, besides the quantitative lack of schooling available to poorer Cubans, the education system had acted, as it does in all societies, as a control mechanism to sustain the status quo, transmitting values which justified the unequal distribution of property. More than one-fourth of the population never entered school, and the education system functioned as an obstacle course which forced three-fourths of those young Cubans who did start school to drop out before they completed elementary school making only poorer paid and more physically demanding jobs open to them. Educational administration was characterized by graft and corruption. There was no increase in literacy from 1943 to 1959.

On the university level, those who completed school were generally not trained in skills which the country needed for development. The prestigious law school was swollen with students, but the low-prestige agronomy and engineering schools graduated small numbers of students who often could not find productive employment because of the irrational economic structure. As economic development began after the Revolution, the educational gaps loomed as urgent needs.

The Literacy Campaign of 1961. The educational offensive was set off in 1961, which was named the Year of Education. During that year, while industrial and agricultural diversification, planning, and a reorientation of foreign trade were going on, and against the background of the Playa Girón invasion and Cuba becoming socialist, the Cubans engaged in an educational effort which surpassed that of any country in the world up to that time. A massive campaign to eradicate illiteracy was undertaken, which had the additional aim of incorporating the rural poor into the political and economic mainstream. The poor rural Cubans were naturally the most illiterate, and this special effort was another way of showing that their needs had priority. Illiteracy was reduced in one year from an estimated 24 percent to 3.9 percent. The literacy program was the first mass mobilization campaign, and constituted an experiment in the creative use of human energy, highly politicized, to overcome seemingly insuperable problems of underdevelopment.

The brigades of literacy teachers were made up of 286,000 people including one hundred thousand secondary school students who spent from May through October teaching in rural areas, living and working in the homes of the peasants they taught, under the supervision of thirty-six thousand elementary teachers. Some 120,000 workers taught in the campaign in addition to their regular jobs. The campaign was preceded by a census of illiteracy, and the brigade members were themselves trained in a two-week program to use two texts which were designed to politicize in a rudimentary nationalist way. All kinds of special incentives were used, such as concluding the course with the newly-literate student writing a letter to Fidel, and Castro ended the campaign with a rally to welcome back the young teachers at which he gave one of his most moving speeches.

The literacy brigades of secondary students were themselves transformed by the experience of becoming rural teachers. They became "educational guerrillas," in that they lived off the peasantry and provided a service in compensation. They had experiences in the literacy "battle" which instilled in them "guerrilla" mentality of the revolutionary leadership. The "post Moncada" generation which participated in the literacy brigades entered the reformed university knowing not only the ignorance and superstition of the *campesino,* but also his political good sense. They emerged from the experience less oriented toward a soft life, although more appreciative of urban comforts, and "de-privatized," accepting that the public interest had a claim on their private lives (Hochschild, 1970: 56). Thus the peasant and brigadist learned from each other what had been to each Cuba's hidden face, recreating in a less dangerous way the guerrilla experience (Fagen, 1964; Huberman and Sweezy, 1969: 24–26).

During the campaign a bridgadist, Conrado Benítez, was killed by counter-revolutionaries and later the brigades were given his name. In April, the U. S. invasion at the Bay of Pigs heightened the drama of the literacy campaign, for while Cuba was bending every nerve to eradicate illiteracy, the United States was busy trying to destroy the Revolution which made the campaign possible. Symbolically, the brigadists' answer to Playa Girón was to march with giant pencils at their shoulders.

The Reorganization of Schools. Had the revolutionary educational efforts been limited to the spectacular literacy program, it can be assumed that, as in the case of literacy drives elsewhere, the new readers would soon have lapsed again into illiteracy. Literacy itself is only a prerequisite to raising productivity. However, while the 1961 literacy drive was underway, the government was devising a variety of new programs to raise the total educational level of the population. The *batalla del sexto grado* (battle for the sixth grade) was launched in 1962 with the aim of bringing every Cuban to the sixth grade level. Nine-tenths of the rural labor force and six-sevenths of the urban workers were below the sixth grade educational level. The *seguimiento* (follow-up program) took the adults and adolescents who had been reached by the literacy program and carried them through to a completion of the equivalent of the sixth grade.

In rural areas, schools had to be built and staffed so that all children had a school available to them. By 1962, school enrollment of elementary age children had risen from 67 percent to 80 percent. By 1966, virtually all elementary school age children were registered in school. In rural Oriente, Castro made his early dream of establishing a boarding school for rural children in the sparsely populated Sierra a reality when the Camilo Cienfuegos School City began to function. By 1968, more than 160,000 rural children were involved in elementary boarding or semi-boarding schools, which also freed both their parents for productive work.

Most secondary schools before the Revolution were private, and most of these were Catholic. Thus education was a marketable commodity to secure a good position in society available to those who could afford it. All private education was nationalized in 1961, ostensibly as a result of the conflict with the Catholic Church. Castro accused the Church of using the schools to indoctrinate against the Revolution. However, the nationalization of these schools was surely inevitable given the direction of the Revolution. Many of the same teachers stayed on as these schools passed under the control of the Ministry of Education. The changeover in the Hebrew school in Havana, for example, was minimal.

Since rural children had no secondary schools available to them, secondary boarding schools were established for them in Havana mansions abandoned by wealthy families who had left the island. These secondary students were on full scholarship including an allowance. By 1962, secondary enrollment had increased 231 percent over 1958.

After 1962, the minimum educational goal for everyone was raised to ninth grade, and in 1967 it was raised again to the thirteenth grade (one year of technical training beyond completion of secondary school). One of the most impressive expansions was in the field of technical schools (which ran from the ninth through the twelfth or thirteenth grade). These new schools, in which 15,612 were enrolled by 1968, emphasized agriculture, industry, and fishing. Some students were sent abroad on scholarships for special training, particularly to the Soviet Union, and upon their return established new programs in metallurgy, industrial engineering, and other fields.

An impressive effort was made to open the school system to all people regardless of social class or income. Teachers were asked to take on the responsibility of trying to pass *all* their students, and to be sensitive to solving the cause of poor educational performance. Special tests and programs were developed on a massive scale to place children or adults who had dropped out of school, and students were encouraged to accelerate so as to join their age-group as soon as possible. Numerous remedial programs were established for those whose educational advance was blocked by deficiencies. Scholarships at the secondary and university level including full support and an allowance were made available so that parents actually experienced financial relief by having their children study. Adults were bombarded with pressure to become involved in some educational program and it was conservatively estimated that one-third of the labor force was involved in education. Domestic servants (a profession which disappeared after the Revolution) were re-trained to be drivers and bank clerks. *Superación Obrera* and *Mínimo Técnico* classes were established in or near the work place so that workers could raise their technical level and, after meeting the sixth grade level, go on to secondary level education. The Workers' University program prepared workers to enter the technical branches of the university in an accelerated program conducted during paid work time. As rationing was instituted in 1962, students were given priority for clothing and for the food which was supplied in the school lunch rooms and university cafeterias.

A special effort was made to get women involved in education. Nurseries were provided even in rural areas so that mothers could study as well as work. While no one was forced to use a nursery, the demand for them far outstripped the supply and "rationing" takes the form of waiting lists. All careers were open to women, and women numbered about equally with men in such university programs as engineering and medicine which were practically closed to women before the Revolution.

The lack of teachers was a serious obstacle overcome in creative ways with incredible dedication. Before the Revolution, the Ministry of Education had provided teacher sinecures for political appointees who had life tenure and often farmed out their jobs to others at a fraction of the salary. Teachers took no responsibility for the future of their pupils; their job seemed to be to keep the lower class from getting formal education. The dedicated teacher was frustrated. After the Revolution, teachers were called upon to work longer hours at the same pay and only those most dedicated responded. Others left the profession and sometimes the country, but for those who remained there was the satisfaction of heroic participation in the most central battle of Cuban development—*human* development.

A system of rural teacher training at the secondary normal school level was established beginning with a year in a guerrilla-like encampment in the Sierra Maestra followed by two years in a rural school city in the Escambray Mountains in Las Villas and finishing with two years (including practice teaching) in the Makarenko Institute in Havana. As a temporary measure, a "six by six" program was developed in which young students preparing to be teachers alternated six months of teaching with six months of study. Rural teaching methods were slowly developed and teachers were expected to constantly undertake refresher and upgrading courses.

The Universities. The universities, which had been restricted to serving the middle and upper classes, were opened up to all young people through programs which provided full-support scholarships and supplied a variety of avenues around the educational obstacles which had excluded lower-class children. If a student could not qualify for a place in the university upon graduation from high school he could become involved in a work-study program which would bring him into the university at a later date.

Traditional university autonomy, in the past more often violated than not, was replaced with a concept of a university integrated into serving national needs. Students forced the ouster of several professors who opposed the socialist direction of the Revolution. Most of the faculty in prestigious schools such as medicine, law, and architecture resigned. Some former faculty members thrived under the new atmosphere of hard work and integration of their specialty into the over-all push for democratization and development. Faculty members were recruited from the ranks of new graduates, and advanced students also engaged in carefully supervised teaching. Life-time tenure for professors gave way to periodic evaluation by peers and students, and all teachers were expected to engage constantly in seminars to keep improving themselves. Professors were given a heavy work load and required to volunteer for militia duty. A gardener working in the Havana University campus flower beds turned out to be the university president.

The universities were reorganized and tied in with national planning so that it would produce the necessary technical personnel. New schools were established within each university and the number of students increased vastly. However, the law schools were drastically reduced in size, mostly because fewer students saw law as a meaningful career, but also because of revisions in the requirements for a law degree. Education for the professions has been integrated into productive work with the result that the quality of the education has generally improved. Law students, mostly on full scholarship, are required to work mornings in the Ministry of Justice. During their fourth year they serve as advisors in the People's Courts (see Revolutionary Institutions). Upon graduation, doctors and lawyers must spend two years in rural service. Medical and dentistry education includes work in clinics from the first year. Agronomy students analyze soils, while economics and psychology students work together on experimenting in reorganizing assembly lines and on experiments in creating a moneyless society. Journalism students work on national publications, holding their classes in press facilities. Theater and dance students develop plays and ballets as a group and perform them for volunteer labor brigades in rural camps, evaluating their work in discussions with a variety of audiences. Social science students in inter-disciplinary teams do regional studies and studies of companies to evaluate the diverse experiments going on all over the island.

All university students were required to belong to the militia, to spend at least half of their two-month vacation in agricultural work, and to do volunteer labor (without pay) on weekends. Students engage in military training, with the engineering students handling the more sophisticated weaponry.

This kind of education gives a student experience with which to choose a specialty within his profession, and is designed to keep the young professional from developing an elitist attitude. If university graduates have a certain prestige, they are also expected to work harder than others. The gap between school and the "real world" disappears, and the questions of relevancy do not arise. The absence of a university degree is less important than before, since individuals are judged mainly by what they can do. A degree is a prerequisite in medicine and law, but not in other fields.

With all these programs, 27.6 percent of the people in Cuba were studying in some form of organized instruction, compared with an average of 16.8 percent for Latin America as a whole, or 22.6 percent for Costa Rica, the next highest in Latin America (Inter-American Development Bank, 1967: 37).

Ideology and Education. Ideologically, education in Cuba is basically nationalist and Marxist. Historical and economic interpretations in school textbooks are Marxist and nationalist, with an anti-imperialist emphasis. However, in contrast to the nationalism of Mexican textbooks, for example, Cuban ideology stresses a "third world internationalism." The Cubans advocate friendship toward all peoples, and indeed the Cubans, children and adults, are more genuinely friendly to North Americans than any other Latin Americans today. Besides nationalism and anti-imperialism, the education system stresses group identification and idealizes a life of public service. The guerrilla fighter, such as Ché Guevara or Tania Bunke, who died fighting with Ché in the Bolivian struggle, is held up as an ideal of sacrifice. In the broadest sense, all educational material is politicized, but far from considering this propagandizing, Cubans understand politicizing as making material relevant to their national transformation efforts and egalitarian goals. Politicization is designed to motivate students and to prevent alienation which characterizes capitalist society. Plant growth, for example, would be related to real agricultural problems and programs.

At the university level all students, regardless of their field, study Marxist philosophy and economics. There is an explicit attempt to politicize all students in their field of study. Non-Marxist views are also studied, and within Marxist thought the various viewpoints are debated with little sense of orthodoxy, although at times there have been dogmatic tendencies.

Education as Investment. Cuban government planners have allocated a maximum of available resources to education. The expenditure on education in 1967 was four times that in 1956. No other Latin American country has been able to expend a comparable effort on education, both because the pay-off on educational investments is so long delayed compared to current budgetary pressures, and because the social mobility provided by massive educational investments has such revolutionary implications. Cuba alone was able to choose schools and scholarships over unproductive bureaucratic agencies, consumer goods, luxury buildings, and subsidies to the private sector. In 1966 Cuba spent $39 per capita on education or $141.21 per student. Uruguay which had the next highest expenditures on education in Latin America, expended $23.17 per capita or $126.31 per student.

A considerable proportion of the educational "investment" in Cuba, however, takes the form of extra effort and extra time from teachers, workers, students, and technicians. This voluntary input of effort is a result of the people's belief in their society and its leadership and indicates a public commitment to the general society and to future generations. Thus the Cubans not only have a high investment in education, but they also get more education per peso allocated than any other country in Latin America. There is an intense fervor involved in education in Cuba which determines its quality, despite any methodological inadequacies. When educational experts like Ivan Illich despair of any underdeveloped country ever being able to allocate enough capital to "catch up" educationally they omit the incalculable human "capital" available to a mobilized society which believes in its leadership. In any case the educational effort was a huge drain on Cuba's developed economy. In 1972, Castro said that for Cuba to afford to educate nearly the entire population through the thirteenth year, all schools would have to become work centers and all students above the primary level would have to be involved in productive work. Some five hundred student brigades were already involved in building dairies, factories, and dams. Castra projected that in a few years the work performed by students would more than cover the cost of their education.

Education and Planning. The setbacks in agricultural and industrial development in 1962 to 1963 which resulted in part from planning mistakes and inadequate statistics, gave new urgency to education, for it became clear that a highly educated population was a necessity for adequate planning, flexible reallocation of resources, and execution of policies. In 1962, in the economic sector, a controversy developed over whether production could be increased more effectively by moral or by material incentives (See Transition to Socialism, The Economics of Society). Attitudes toward education during the 1961 to 1964 period reflected this debate. The supporters of moral incentives led by Guevara, blamed the failures in production in 1962 to 1963 on insufficient politicization or a lack of revolutionary fervor. Successes against incredible odds were also seen as the result of politicization. They thought the central role of education would be to help create a "New Man," a revolutionary kind of technician who gave selflessly of his energies. This was to be accomplished not only by the values transmitted explicitly, but by the *style* of education: practical field work, participation in production, etc.

Educational Methods. However, while there have been basic changes and enormous expansion in Cuban education, much of the style and method of education continue to reflect pre-revolutionary attitudes. Much of the education for a new man has involved slogans, repetition of phrases such as "We are the Communist Youth and we dedicate our lives . . ." Hero identification has its limitations as a method of building self-reliant "new men." Classroom situations and teaching methods are still generally authoritarian, stress memorization rather than analytical ability, and knowledge rather than understanding. While some might blame the dogmatism on Communist influence, even the Communists reflect pre-revolutionary educational attitudes. For example, groups of children fervently reciting in unison a revolutionary pledge is reminiscent of prayers in the Catholic Church or methods of teaching catechism, which is not to deny the sincerity in either case.

In the rush to prepare new teachers, little emphasis was at first put on new teaching methods. Pre-revolutionary prejudices sometimes creep into education in the form of a revolutionary puritanism. Long hair on boys, short skirts on girls, and other deviations from the norm have been criticized and sometimes suppressed despite objections by some revolutionary leaders. In the name of revolutionary principles, middle-class teachers sometimes reject the culture of poor children and attempt to "civilize" them. At the 1971 Educational Congress one resolution condemned homosexuality and determined that homosexuals could not be teachers. This is justified by pointing out that as a result of repression in the past, some homosexuals formed subcultures which resisted integration into revolutionary society. However, the official government position is apparently that homosexuals per se cannot be revolutionary and are not fit to be educators. These pre-revolutionary attitudes are reinforced by the quantitative expansion of schools, the lack of teachers, and in some cases, their lack of training.

Dogmatic practices often reflect the poor preparation of teachers. Education ministry officials are the first to admit that the quality of education has a long way to go and educational methods are a major focus of their efforts. The 1971 Educational Congress delegates wanted to get rid of the traditional teacher, "one who isn't moved by anything." The new teacher should be full of revolutionary enthusiasm and should work to eliminate the barrier between student and teacher. According to one spokesman at the Congress, if the teacher simply repeats material and expects his students to do the same, then the learning experience becomes empty. Students and teachers are encouraged to criticize one another (Levinson, 1972: 7–9).

The government's insistence on unity, the absence of factions in the Communist Party, the absence of public debate on basic political issues in the press all work against the possibility of dialogue and inquiry in the education system and weaken the schools' ability to develop the critical independence necessary for the "New Man." Nevertheless, there is free discussion, as these authors can attest after participating in and observing seminars in political philosophy at the University of Havana which would have compared favorably with any university in the United States. An observer in Cuban schools reported that children felt free to disagree with authority, though they did not in fact disagree with their authorities. They prized group achievement over individual achievement, although both types of achievement were rewarded. In fostering "emulation" instead of competition, the schools seem to be successful in inspiring high group achievement, rather than the achievement of one individual over another (Wald, 1971: 4–5).

Foreign observers are divided about the amount of scholarship demanded of students. Dumont (Dumont 1970b: 126–27), with his French scholastic traditions, complains that not enough is demanded of scholarship students considering the large quantity of resources invested in them, while Huberman and Sweezy (Huberman and Sweezy 1969: 38) fear that too much work is demanded of them. Our own observation was that an incredible amount of sports and productive labor are combined with a heavy academic program and only high motivation could explain students' ability to survive this program.

Many new aspects of education tend to mitigate the effects of the surviving elitism and formalism. Whatever method is used to teach, since the teacher's job is to now to ensure that all students learn, the traditional techniques are not the arbitrary barrier they once were. The school system no longer functions to track the lower classes into poorly paid activities, but rather to open new opportunities for them. In fact, our interviews suggest that workers preceive the new educational opportunities open to their children as the most important benefit brought by the Revolution.

Grading, testing, and classification still exist as a way of allocating scarce educational resources, though this allocation is more generous and egalitarian than it is in the United States. If a person does not qualify for one program, with effort he can usually reach the same objective by a more circuitous route. There is least tolerance for those who wish to "drop out."

Whatever the style of classroom teaching, much of Cuban education takes place out of the classroom, in productive work, field research, interviews, and through practical experience. Language instruction uses modern oral methods. Besides the field training at the university level, the "School in the Countryside" program takes secondary students and occasionally elementary students to rural encampments for a period of many weeks. Their entire curriculum during that time is related to the rural environment, including science (agriculture) and social studies (the organization of rural production). In 1972 elementary schools were instructed to develop vegetable gardens where all students would work six to ten hours a week as a regular part of the curriculum. This aspect of Cuban education, while it is a result of the shortage of skilled labor and teachers, is also innovative and successful in implanting new values. There is a "guerrilla" atmosphere about education which stresses unpretentiousness, serious dedication, improvisation, and equality between students and teachers. As consciousness on the part of Cubans increases, the question of the teaching methods of revolutionary education will have to be raised.

There is the possibility that after the first generation of revolutionaries is joined by the second generation of technicians that these technicians will form a privileged stratum which would magnify the effects of prerevolutionary attitudes in education. However, the fact that a person is judged mainly on what he can do, and that there are a number of avenues to achieving this practical knowledge, weakens the school system as a control mechanism. As an impediment to the development of a technocracy, Castro has projected the ideal of the whole country becoming a university. Once nearly the whole population is reaching the thirteenth grade level, everyone could simultaneously begin productive work and enter the "university." One would never graduate, but instead work and study intermittently for the rest of one's life. Under this arrangement nearly everyone would be involved in higher education and have similar status.

RELIGION

The Roman Catholics. The Cuban Revolution avoided a serious Church-State struggle of the kind that erupted during the Mexican Revolution, both because the Church was weaker in Cuba and because it followed a more enlightened course. Fundamental characteristics of the

Catholic Church in pre-revolutionary Cuba were: predominance of foreigners (particularly Spaniards) among the clergy, a social base largely limited to the urban upper and middle classes, and weakness of impact upon public life. Cubans were considered the "least Catholic" of Spanish American peoples, although almost all Cubans were nominally Catholic. Yet the Church was an important aspect of society and by the time of the Revolution it boasted over 250 institutions, 72 of which were educational, 128 were centers for convicts, orphans, the impoverished and the aged, and 33 were hospitals and dispensaries. There were more than seven hundred priests.

At the beginning, the triumph of the rebel army was accepted and even welcomed by the Church. Castro, who had received part of his formal education in Catholic schools, did not have strong pro- or anti-religious feelings. The Archbishop of Santiago, Enrique Pérez Serantes, had intervened with Batista to prevent the murder of the survivors of the Moncada assault, and on January 2, 1959, the day after Batista fled, Fidel gave a speech at the Moncada barracks with Archbishop Pérez at his side. A number of priests had engaged in pro-revolutionary activities, some with the guerrillas and others providing medical supplies and hiding places for insurgents. A substantially larger number of active Catholics than Communists participated in the Revolution.

By late 1959, however, conflicts developed between the government and the Church. The Church was, after all, one of the main institutions of the existing social system and its allegiance was to the upper classes, if not Batista. While the Church perceived Communism as the cause of its disenchantment with the Revolution, the real cause was the Church's loss of power within a social revolution. In November, Catholic labor leaders were displaced by Communists in the unions. At the end of the month a National Catholic Congress was organized for the purpose of displaying Catholic solidarity against Communism. One speaker at the congress touched off a demonstration by shouting "Social justice, yes; Communism, no." By this time the revolutionary leadership had decided that anti-Communism was counter-revolutionary, but they tried to reassure the Church that they themselves were not Communist.

A pro-government counter-tendency within the Church was formalized with the organization of *Con la Cruz y Con la Patria* which called for the expulsion of Spanish priests from the country. Also in late 1959, the government unsuccessfully attempted to interest two revolutionary priests, Juan O'Farril and Eduardo Aguirre, in establishing a Cuban Catholic Church.

In May 1960, Archbishop Pérez, having lost his ardour for the Revolution, declared in a pastoral letter that the enemy "is within our gates."

In July a riot occurred outside the Cathedral of Havana after the holding of a mass for the "Victims of Communism." After Archbishop Manuel Arteaga of Havana issued a pastoral letter warning against the "analogies" between Cuba and other socialist countries, priests began in the summer of 1960 to preach counter-revolution from the pulpit. The impact of this activity was confined largely to the cities, since priests were scarce in rural areas.

The showdown between the Church and the Revolution was triggered by the Playa Girón invasion of April 1961. The invaders had carried documents proclaiming "We come in the name of God. . . The only ideology that can vanquish the Communist ideology is the Christian ideology." On May 1, 1961, Castro announced the nationalization of all private schools, most of which were Catholic. In addition, religious teaching was to be confined to churches and foreign priests involved in counter-revolutionary activity were to be expelled. Attacks against foreign priests were resumed in September when a politically motivated religious demonstration led to a riot in which a student was killed. Over one hundred priests precipitously left the island in the wake of the September incidents (Dewart, 1963: 175).

Vatican reaction to these anti-Church measures was restrained. There were no excommunication decrees or severing of diplomatic relations. The Papal Nuncio, Luís Centoz, continued to attend public events in the company of public officials. His successor in 1963 Cesare Zacchi said there was no contradiction between Christianity and the Cuban Revolution, declaring in 1966 "The current relations between Church and State in Cuba are very cordial. There has been no persecution of any sort against the priests, nor have any churches been closed or religious services interrupted" (*Ave Maria*, December 17, 1966: 4).

Counter-revolutionary activity by the Church virtually ended in 1961. Castro made his dramatic gesture on behalf of the right to religious belief on March 13, 1962 at the commemorative ceremony for martyred student leader José Antonio Echeverría. When the young Communist who was reading Echeverría's "testament" deliberately omitted from the text reference to God and religion, Castro was enraged and condemned the action.

The informal ban against foreign Catholic priests ended in 1963 when Castro announced that he had no objection to the introduction of priests from Canada and Belgium, and sixty-five priests entered Cuba in 1964. The Jesuit journal *America* had concluded in 1964 that the mass and the sacraments were "practically as available" as before the Revolution because of the marked increase in the percentage of priests engaged in parish work. A growing understanding between Church and State culminated in 1969 when high Church officials in Cuba proclaimed as a group their objection to U. S. military involvement in Vietnam and denounced the U. S. blockade of Cuba.

The Church continues to receive special concessions from the government. A member of the Central Committee of the Cuban Communist Party is assigned to handle liaison with religious organizations. Food and other items are delivered directly to clergymen, to spare them having to stand in ration lines. The state supplies a modicum of maintenance and construction supplies to the churches.

The Protestants. Protestants were a significant group in Cuba before the Revolution, numbering in excess of 250,000. There were actually more Cuban Protestant ministers than Catholic priests, more Protestant churches and chapels, and an approximately equal Protestant and Catholic attendance at Sunday religious services (Robertson, 1967: I, 1).

Protestants played a key role in the effort to oust Batista whom they associated with corruption, sin, and political tyranny. In a burst of post-Revolution euphoria, Protestants who had been mostly members of the middle class, had their eyes opened to the needs of the poor and the poor responded since "Castro . . . let them [the poor] know they [were] important. And [they then could] believe it when they [heard] the Lord loves them, too" (Robertson, 1967: II, 4). Catholic counter-revolutionaries began their activities before Protestants became counter-revolutionary and therefore the revolutionary government gave preferential treatment to Protestants in the government. However, since the Protestants were "theologically unprepared" for the transcendental changes wrought by the Revolution, they soon dissipated their energies in "evangelism, individual good works, fighting Catholicism, and fearing Communism" (Robertson, 1967: II, 2–4). Since most Protestant ministers were conservative and the Protestant groups were markedly dependent on the United States, the Revolution and Protestantism came to an inevitable impasse which caused most Protestant clergymen to retreat to the United States. The net result was that Protestantism ceased to be an important force in Cuban society. Nevertheless, the 1971 Educational Congress decided to work against the Jehovah's Witnesses, the Evangelical Gideon's Band, and the Seventh Day Adventists because of their opposition to the Revolution.

Jews and Afro-Cuban Cults. Religious freedom is extended to Jewish citizens. Free bus transportation is provided to Jewish children wishing to attend a special school in Havana where religious instruction is available. The state provides special food rations for Jewish religious observances. Cuba maintains full diplomatic relations with Israel. Nevertheless, a considerable proportion of the Jewish community, mostly prosperous middle-class members, left Cuba for the United States. Afro-Cuban religious groups are permitted to function and their dance styles have been given official sponsorship, but adherents of these sects have sometimes been characterized by government officials as prone toward criminal activity.

The future of religion in Cuba eludes analysis. Some observers expect organized religion to fade away. Some Catholics, on the contrary, are convinced that the similarity of revolutionary and primitive Christian goals will in the end strengthen religious faith. The present difficulties of the Church are not seen as fatal. "As history has shown over and over again, where the Church is persecuted she experiences a marvelous renewal of spiritual strength" (*America,* December 12, 1964: 769). One thing is evident. The student priests at the Catholic Seminary in Cuba have gone into the fields and labored with the people. They have grown up with the Revolution. They have been deeply influenced by its social goals. Perhaps if the Church truly becomes a revolutionary Church working closely with the people, it will survive.

THE ECONOMICS OF SCARCITY

Rationing was introduced in Cuba in 1962. There were five reasons for the shortage of food and goods. First, consumption expanded much faster than production, since poor Cubans had more money as a result of lower rents, the eradication of unemployment and underemployment, and the increase in salaries in lower-paid occupations. Second, there was a decline in Cuban agricultural production, including some food products, in the wake of unsuccessful attempts to diversify farms. Third, food and other items which had been imported from the United States were not available after the U. S. economic embargo went into effect. Fourth, the government was determined to maximize investment in order to increase productivity as fast as possible. This investment took the form of imports of industrial and agricultural equipment, with a minimum import capacity left for consumer goods. Fifth, since imports were paid for with foreign exchange (money or credits from abroad), much of the production of meat, vegetables, fruit, and coffee was reserved for export to earn foreign exchange to pay for the imports. The shortages and increased demand brought pressures which could have been relieved either by rationing or by inflation. Inflation constitutes a kind of rationing in that prices rise so that goods are distributed only to those with most money. The Cuban revolutionary leaders, unlike other Latin American politicians in power, were firmly committed to equality, and they met the economic crisis with rationing so that everyone would have equal access to goods.

In the summer of 1963, the Cuban leadership changed the direction of economic development and decided to emphasize sugar exports and agricultural development. After the failures in diversification of agriculture and the fall in sugar exports in 1962, it became clear that Cuba lacked the necessary foreign exchange to set up and supply the new industries which had been projected. Cuba's dependency on sugar before the Revolution had led to an anti-sugar bias on the part of revolutionary leaders which resulted in the reduction in sugar production and an unrealistic attempt to simultaneously diversify agriculture and industry, as if a small island economy could become self-sufficient. When sugar exports declined as a result of a reduction of sugar acreage, crop diversification, and agricultural errors, there was no way to finance the industrial imports. Cuba had accumulated a growing debt with the Soviet Union which could only be repaid with massive exports of sugar. Thus it became evident that initial investment should be concentrated on agriculture, particularly sugar and cattle. Besides sugar, Cuba projected increasing exports of meat, tobacco, coffee, citrus, and vegetables. The leadership also determined to save foreign exchange by growing more food locally. Industry was to be pushed at a slower pace until after 1971. Industries which processed food or served agriculture, such as fertilizer and implements, were to receive priority, as were the nickel, cement, and electrical power industries. The nickel plants at Moa Bay and Nicaro were expanded and integrated so that nickel (now exported as finished metal instead of as concentrated ore) passed tobacco to become the country's second largest export.

By 1964, agriculture, including tractor imports, irrigation, fertilizer, sugar production, forage crops, livestock and the dairy industry received five-sixths of investments and industry unrelated to agriculture received only one-sixth. Agricultural enterprises were grouped into ever larger units specializing in a single product. *Granjas* were grouped into *agrupaciones* and massive projects were developed such as the Banao Plan in southern Las Villas. There, instead of organizing *granjas,* with a permanent resident work force, a unified "plan" system was developed on a scale much larger than any *granja.* Large numbers of men and women town dwellers were brought into barracks (segregated by sex) and enormous fields were cleared, irrigated, and planted in vegetables. Gradually, as production got underway and became mechanized, less workers were needed and they moved on to other rural or urban production centers. Chilean agronomist Jacques Chonchol criticized this method of development as too large to be consistent with adequate incentives and efficiency (Chonchol, 1963: 122–5).

The turn toward sugar and agriculture was partly the result of a desire to establish the maximum independence possible from the Soviet Union.

Castro was angry at the Soviet Union leadership in 1962 when that country withdrew its missiles unilaterally ending the missile crisis (see Cuba and World Affairs). However, between 1962 and 1964 there was a rapprochement with the Soviet Union reflecting the need for Soviet economic and military aid during this difficult economic period. The Cuban leaders accepted the fact that the Soviet Union would not provide unlimited funds for Cuban economic development, and that the sooner the loans were repaid the more independent Cuba would be. They also recognized that the insistence on an independent foreign policy, particularly in relation to revolutionary movements in Latin America, would affect the amount and conditions of the loans contracted. The Cubans signed a long-term commercial agreement with the Soviet Union in January 1964, which provided for selling increasing amounts of sugar to the Soviet Union each year, culminating in an export of 7.5 million tons in 1970. This was expected to require the production of a total of 10 million tons of sugar by that year. Thus the 10 million ton goal for 1970, which was later to become a national obsession, had been set six years earlier.

Once Cuba had committed itself to paying its own way with the Soviet Union, (aside from loans, the only other aid from the Soviet Union was in the form of military assistance which Cuba may or may not have paid for) the revolutionary leaders once again moved toward independence in 1965 by organizing the Tri-Continental Congress in Havana in 1966 and denouncing the Chinese leadership and the Venezuelan Communists in 1966.

THE DEBATE OVER PLANNING: MORAL VS. MATERIAL INCENTIVES

The new agricultural direction of the economy was influenced by the advice of French economist Charles Bettelheim and by the example of the Chinese agricultural retrenchment of 1962 to 1963. Once idle land and resources had been put to work, the emphasis shifted to increases in productivity. A great debate had developed over the means of increasing productivity. One group, supported by Bettelheim and Communist leader Carlos Rafael Rodríguez, pushed for material incentives to get people to work harder, the encouragement of capitalist market mechanisms and profit criteria at the local enterprise level ("market socialism"), and decentralization of planning.

The other group, led by Ché Guevara, believed that productivity and growth depended mainly on workers' political consciousness. Thus, Guevara argued for moral incentives and centralization of planning and control. Centralization was advocated as an essential substitute for the informal controls and local decision-making criteria provided by market mechanisms and material incentives. The dialogue raged in the pages of the journal *Cuba Socialista*. Soviet Union and Czechoslovakian planning advisors pushed for the material incentives "market socialism" position. In 1962, Khrushchev had advised the Cubans to emulate Lenin's New Economic Policy which made temporary concessions to capitalism. Bettelheim argued that Cuba's state of underdevelopment made total planning impossible. Centralized planning, to be most effective, presupposes the access to instant analysis of the comparative costs of alternative methods. This requires advanced computors, accurate data, highly developed communications, and an educated populace. Since he assumed that moral incentives could only work after the economy was highly developed, and since he considered the developmental process largely economic and technical, Bettelheim concluded that Cuba would have to use capitalist market mechanisms, profitability, and monetary incentives to control the economy.

The Guevara group argued that the battle to achieve development would be won only if workers were politicized. Cuban leaders had observed that during the 1961 Girón invasion and the 1962 missile crisis there had been an increase in productivity despite the manpower drain on defense. Guevara concluded that rapid development required the transformation of the Cuban worker into the "New Man" of the "perpetual Girón invasion" who would have a collective identification and would expend a maximum effort because he was needed. The Guevara group was convinced that Cubans would only succeed in building socialism economically and politically to the extent that they changed the behavior and motivation of people.

Guevara's position in favor of centralized planning and against commercial market mechanism predominated by 1964. Centralized budgeting had been adopted in 1963. Guevara's answer to the supposed impossibility of accurate planning in Cuba was to operate Cuba as one gigantic company in which capital was invested wherever needed without calculation of the "profitability" of each enterprise. It was assumed that income of all enterprises would flow back to the government and the profitable enterprises would subsidize those operating at a deficit. If the ability of an enterprise to show profit were used as a criterion for investment, as Bettelheim favored, then growth in the more profitable sectors would keep Cuba underdeveloped. Thus the government's ability to invest in unprofitable but necessary sectors was, for Guevara, a measure of the ability to bring about development (Biedma, 1970: 343–373). Guevara's basic idea was that enterprises, like individuals, should not operate for profit but for general development. The absence of cost accounting in each company would also require less bureaucracy.

Several problems developed under this approach. Over-centralization, inadequate communication, and insufficient personnel tended to inhibit activities at the local level (nails for a farm had to be ordered from Havana) and lower productivity. In the absence of adequate directives, people at the local level had to improvise, leading to "de facto anarchy." With no calculation available, it was difficult for individual units to cut operating costs since they rarely knew if they were operating at a loss and had no basis of comparison. The situation stifled potential growth in production. Guevara's solution was to increase education and political consciousness. With qualified planners and technicians unavailable, leadership had to centralize key policy decisions to a small group. A higher technical and political level in the whole country would mean everyone in Cuba could participate in basic planning decisions.

Cuba was the only socialist country to try the combination of completely centralized planning without cost accounting in each enterprise. When this planning method failed to bring the hoped for results in production, special high-priority projects and plans were added to deal with specific areas of production. These special projects often interfered with regular planning, throwing plans even more out of kilter. For example, trucks needed for construction were used in the Havana Green Belt, or workers needed in a factory were cutting sugar cane. However, there is no guarantee that a "market socialism" model would have produced any better.

During 1964, Castro tried to tread a middle position between moral and material incentives. When Guevara disappeared from Cuba in 1965, the material incentive system which he opposed appeared to have prevailed. The "Socialist Emulation" which was instituted after 1962 was a combination of moral and monetary incentives. A variety of prizes were established for workers who produced most, including cash prizes, and otherwise unavailable items such as trips to Eastern Europe, refrigerators, motorbikes, private automobiles, and houses. Castro in 1965 argued in favor of the necessity for monetary incentives when he said, "We cannot choose idealistic methods which conceive of all men as guided by the concepts of duty . . . [and] expect . . . men to make a maximum effort . . . just because it is their duty, . . ." (Castro, 1965: 8–9) Extra pay was given for overtime work. Nevertheless, national work heroes were held up as examples to be emulated, and while some people won prizes, the honor they received was more emphasized than the material reward. The appliances and automobiles and trips won did not become part of a pattern of goods and income which allowed the worker to change his way of life. At the most, only 20 percent of the labor force participated in competition for these prizes, and "only between 1 and 1.79 percent of the workers were benefitted by the rewards." (Mesa-Lago, 1970a: p. 7)

Increasing amounts of agricultural labor, particularly sugar cane cutting, was done by volunteer urban workers who received no wages. The unavailability of goods (rationing) and the availability of free services had the effect of leveling the buying power of wages. Even the lowest paid workers had an abundance of cash.

In August 1966, Guevara's moral incentive position began to be adopted by the Cuban leadership. Soon after, in 1967, the debate on such fundamental issues no longer appeared in public because *Cuba Socialista, Nuestra Industria,* and other magazines carrying the debate ceased publication. The leadership believed that the low level of ideological maturity of the population rendered public debate on such issues counter-productive. Moral incentives were chosen for both pragmatic and idealistic reasons. The few prizes awarded tended to inspire jealousy rather than more production. The 1965 prizes had not even been delivered by the end of the year. The U. S. embargo and the shortage of foreign exchange meant Cuba did not have enough consumer goods available to inspire large numbers of Cubans to work, particularly since Cubans had been used to U. S. goods (for those who could afford them) and would hardly be impressed by the quality of items from the Soviet bloc. To have spent foreign exchange and capital on consumer goods would have postponed development for some time, and the Cubans were too firmly wedded to establishing equality to provide a large salary differential and sell a few goods at high prices.

Thus when the Cubans espoused Guevara's argument that using moral incentives during the construction of socialism would accelerate the achievement of a Communist society, they were making a virtue of necessity. However, from then on the goal of building communism was considered as important as developing the economy. Moreover, having rejected material incentives, they were still able to avoid forced labor.

Success of moral incentives depended on: first) How politicized the worker was; second) How successful the planning was (a person could hardly expend effort for the common good if his labor was wasted by inadequate planning); third) How technologically or educationally prepared he was; and fourth) How much the worker participated in the decisions controlling his situation. All but the last aspect received concentrated government attention. Decision-making power was concentrated in the hands of a small group, and while this was in line with Guevara's position on centralized planning, the effectiveness of moral incentives was nevertheless limited by the lack of rank-and-file power. The political consciousness of workers was held back by the restrictions on real political debate. Planning errors (partly due to lack of rank-and-file-input) continued to undermine workers' dedication. At least one plant manager concurred that the main obstacles to workers' dedication were administrative blunders which interrupted or wasted production (Reckord, 1971: 76–77). In 1967 there was an attempt to push decentralization. "Production Assemblies" were held in plants and in population centers in which workers evaluated new plans and criticized the execution of old ones. It is not clear why these later became less frequent. Not until 1970 did the need for more worker participation in directing activities again receive official emphasis. During the 1962 to 1966 period, production generally fell far short of plans.

As Cuba turned to moral incentives, and production was seen as a political rather than a technical problem, the new Cuban Communist party, no longer resented as it had been under Escalante, was given the main role in directing and increasing production. The party made the basic decisions on the direction of production and the allocation of resources, and JUCEPLAN and the ministries were left with the job of carrying out the plans. The party also had to mobilize workers at the base level, including volunteer labor, with the help of the mass organizations (see Revolutionary Institutions). The party increasingly selected administrative and technical personnel up and down the line. Thus, in addition to political and ideological orientation, the party took over government and administrative responsibilities.

REFORMING THE BUREAUCRACY

Once mass mobilization by the party was under way, the conservative, wasteful, and privileged bureaucracy was identified as one of the key obstacles to increased production. Corruption, which had been endemic in Cuban society before the Revolution, was rooted out with incredible determination. Right after the rebel army took power a person accused of malfeasance, defined as a counter-revolutionary crime, was subject to the death penalty. In 1966 Castro unleashed a struggle against bureaucracy, although he had been criticizing bureaucratic blocks to productivity since 1962. During this campaign the leadership criticized some bureaucrats for wasting resources, abusing the public, or trying to "pull rank" on technicians and manual workers. Ideal bureaucrats who pitched in with both hands and were dedicated, efficient, and non-self-important, were held up as models. Office staffs were thinned out by transferring bureaucrats to agricultural work, handicrafts, and other sectors.

Despite the continuation of this campaign for several years, the problem of bureaucracy did not disappear. The behavior of the bureaucrat was a survival of a pre-revolutionary cultural pattern in which bureaucrats served the capitalist class indirectly and the chief of state directly. After the Revolution, bureaucrats still owed their jobs to those above them more than those below, since most power was concentrated in the group around Castro. Since bureaucrats did not have the power to change policy or to bypass the centralized hierarchy, their responsibility was narrowed to carrying out directions from above as best they could, a situation which tended to stifle creativity and to encourage paper-pushing. Bureaucrats were "looking over their shoulder," and no amount of humiliation could change that. Thus bureaucrats tended to revert to a negative role whenever the pressure was off.

The plight of the bureaucrat was another result of the failure to give power to the workers instead of the ministries. If bureaucrats felt that they really represented the production workers rather than the government, they would probably change their behavior. However, Cuba had no model for this solution in the socialist countries. The Cubans tended to improvise solutions between the models of pre-revolutionary Cuba and modern-day Socialist practice. The 1967 campaign did succeed in drastically cutting down the number of bureaucrats. More than twenty thousand jobs were eliminated (*Granma Weekly Review*, Oct. 8, 1967: 4). In the Ministry of Education personnel was cut from about 1250 to 250 workers (Sutherland, 1969: 106). Moreover, at the administrative level a new kind of government employee had often emerged, particularly rebel army officers whose identification with the revolutionary leadership and the workers made them free to innovate. In addition, the style of technical training given to future managers and technicians was carefully designed to avoid instilling elitist attitudes in them.

REVOLUTIONARY OFFENSIVE

The execution of Ché Guevara in Bolivia on October 8, 1967 preceded a shift in the course of the Cuban Revolution. By early 1968, a more conservative trend in international policy had emerged along with a dramatic intensification of efforts to increase national production and to heighten the political consciousness of the population. Cuba significantly lessened its support of revolutionaries abroad. The scope and scale of domestic initiatives, officially called the Revolutionary Offensive, was far-reaching enough to invite comparisons with the Chinese Cultural Revolution launched in 1966.

The opening days of 1968 gave a misleading impression of what was to follow. In January an impressive Cultural Congress was held in Havana attended by more than five hundred intellectuals from seventy countries. In addressing the gathering, Fidel praised intellectuals as more revolutionary than many leftist political organizations. He denounced "dogma and petrified thought." There followed in Cuba, however, a period of less open intellectual life.

THE TRIAL OF THE "MICROFACTION"

Late in January, Aníbal Escalante and eight members of the new Communist Party (all of whom had been members of the old PSP), together with twenty-seven others were accused of pro-Soviet activity. This group called the "microfaction" was supposed to have conspired to get the Soviet Union, East Germany, and Czechoslovakia to use economic pressure to change the policies of the Cuban government, to have disagreed with Castro's domestic and foreign policy, and to have organized as a faction. The trial was held in secret but its results and the speech of Raúl Castro testifying for the prosecution were published. The members of the "microfaction" were sentenced to prison terms ranging from three to fifteen years. The first charge to which they were found guilty, violating national security by dealing with a foreign power, was listed in the Criminal Code as a counter-revolutionary crime. However, the second two charges consisted essentially of political opposition within the party which was not officially against the law in Cuba. The prosecution emphasized that organizing a faction was the worst aspect of the group's activity. Thus, while this was not technically a crime, the government made the point that it would not be permitted. It clearly had a chilling effect on political freedom, ironically increasing the power of other former PSP leaders who wished to suppress artists, writers, and others who expressed independent views. The action against Escalante in 1962 had been, on the whole, freedom-promoting, because it was a blow against ideological restrictiveness. Although the "microfaction" was resisting the forward thrust of the Revolution and was treasonously attempting to generate foreign economic pressure against the government, the second Escalante affair appeared in the main repressive because the revolutionary leadership, now secure in power, defined and forbade the active promotion of alternative policies as "factionalism."

At the time of the microfaction trial, the Cuban leadership was apparently quite hostile to the Soviet Union, partly because of differences in foreign policy (the USSR had extended credits to Latin American governments in countries where Cuba was supporting revolutionary movements) and because of resentment over Soviet restrictions on credit to Cuba (a decision reached by the Russians because of the mounting Cuban debt and disagreement over foreign policy). However, the microfaction trial was followed by a period of increasing Cuban-Soviet cooperation as

Cuba went into the Revolutionary Offensive. Some of the reasons for their seemingly abrupt turn of events were ideological, some practical. Growing shortages dictated a more intensive production drive. Continued reliance upon Soviet and other foreign economies for trade and technological support made international revolutionary positions and efforts by Cuba potentially costly to domestic development. Accordingly, Cuban reactions to the international happenings of 1968 were prudent. The Cuban government did not speak out against the repression of French student rebels in May, 1968, presumably so as not to jeopardize commercial relations with France. Cuba accepted the USSR's August invasion of Czechoslovakia as illegal but necessary although Castro did use the occasion to attack the use of material incentives and "market socialism" in the Soviet Union and Czechoslovakia. The Cuban government remained silent after Mexican troops massacred students in Tlaltilco Plaza in Mexico City in October. Castro cautiously praised the military government which seized power by a bloodless coup in Peru in September, making Peru the first Latin American country it had looked upon with sympathy and marking a retreat from the position that only revolutionary armed struggle could overcome imperialism in Latin America.

PROGRAMS OF THE REVOLUTIONARY OFFENSIVE

The Offensive began in March, 1968 with the increased socialization and militarization of the economy. Virtually all remaining small private businesses were nationalized, amounting to 55,636 restaurants, shops, bars, petty manufacturers, etc. These businesses were accused of being centers of black marketing. The take-over was designed primarily to eliminate the economic injustice of private merchants having higher incomes than those of state employees.

To further equalize food distribution, small farmers were forbidden to sell their commodities directly to' consumers, a practice which bypassed the rationing system.

Massive mobilization programs were undertaken to meet agricultural labor deficits, to equalize the performance of hard physical labor, and to raise political consciousness. The Communist Party and military were given increased responsibility for organizing production. Hundreds of thousands of people were recruited by the Labor Confederation (CTC-R) and the mass organizations to do short-term work in agriculture and to prepare for the huge mobilization of labor that would be necessary in the 1969–1970 all-out effort to produce ten million tons of sugar.

An important program launched during the Offensive was the Havana

Green Belt project which sought to transform the area surrounding the capital into a beautiful zone of coffee and fruit trees, vegetables, dairies, and recreational facilities. A majority of the residents of Havana took part in this effort, working without extra pay, in an attempt to help assure their future abundant food supply, and learning firsthand the rigors of agricultural development. Each office in Havana worked with a skeleton staff as personnel were rotated into the fields (Harding and Bray, 1968: 107). The Green Belt was an unqualified sociological success (in furthering revolutionary and socialist consciousness) even if its economic pay-off proved disappointing because of inadequate follow-up and the mineral deficiency of much of the soil surrounding Havana.

An underlying theme of the Offensive was the acceleration of the move toward the elimination of material incentives and selfishness. The practice of accepting tips by restaurant workers was ended. A major campaign was carried out to convert workers to the notion that overtime work was an opportunity to contribute to the general welfare rather than a device to reap extra pay. Workers were encouraged to work overtime without pay and the amount of production demanded during work time increased. In exchange workers renouncing overtime pay were given their full salary upon retirement or in case of job-related disability.

In a move to end once and for all the chronic shortages, economic planners resolved during the Offensive to boost drastically savings and investment which reached thirty-one percent of the gross national product during 1968, and which from 1961 to 1966, had averaged only about nineteen percent of GNP. This decision was presented as calling for collective struggle and heroic levels of work, with increasing hardships in terms of the lack of consumer goods. In this atmosphere, intellectual dissent and political fragmentation were discouraged.

During the energetic swirl of the Offensive, political and life-style deviance were resisted. The flamboyant *Salon de Mai* exhibit of modern painting, which had been brought from Paris in July 1967 to demonstrate that the Cuban Revolution was unthreatened by abstract painters, was closed in 1968. The range of published discussion of public issues was progressively narrowed.

A renewed round of censure was directed against homosexuality which had first been attacked in a systematic way in 1965 when homosexuals were sometimes sent to rehabilitation work camps (UMAP's). Though the UMAP's had been eliminated by the time of the Offensive, the Revolution continued to have particular difficulty in relating to homosexuals. In this case, pre-revolutionary prejudice was strengthened by revolutionary puritanism (McGuinness, 1971: 53).

THE TEN MILLION TON SUGAR CAMPAIGN

The Offensive culminated in the campaign to produce ten million tons of sugar—the major effort to which every activity was related during 1970. The highest production in previous years had been seven million in 1952 and 6.7 in 1961. Production in 1968 and 1969 had been 5.3 and 4.5 million tons respectively. When the almost mystical ten million ton goal was set in 1964, it was assumed that cane-cutting would be mechanized, but the Soviet and Cuban machines had proved too unreliable, so that the 1970 harvest still had to be cut by hand. The expense of producing each ton of sugar over seven million increased almost geometrically. Nevertheless, the Soviet Union, according to Castro, insisted on fulfillment of the agreement made in 1964 which called for Cuba to increase its sugar exports to that country up to a level which required a total production of ten million tons in 1970.

On May 20 and July 26, 1970, in two of the most remarkably candid statements ever made by a national leader, Castro admitted the failure to reach the ten million goal and gave a detailed account of production failures and problems (Castro, 1970a, b). The sugar harvest had fallen 1.4 million tons short of the ten million-ton goal (which still represented, however, the largest harvest in Cuban history, and Castro blamed the failure on the political leadership, including himself: "The administrative apparatus and the leaders of the Revolution are the ones who lost the battle" (Castro, 1970a: 10).

Reasons for not reaching the ten million goal were insufficient organization of the transport of cane, insufficient technical ability, and the absence of needed machinery parts from the Soviet bloc. Key refineries with new machinery were out of production or grinding inefficiently during much of the harvest. It was a costly failure in economic terms. Castro reviewed the damage to the rest of the economy caused by the concentration on the harvest. The effort to produce the ten million tons required such huge investment to expand sugar mill capacity that vital development projects had to be shelved while resources were diverted into sugar. Milk production fell twenty-five percent; steel deliver, thirty-eight percent; cement production, twenty-three percent. To remedy production deficiencies, Castro advocated more worker participation in the control of production and called for a strengthening of the independence of the labor unions which had been allowed almost to wither away.

The failures to produce ten million tons caused a severe drop in morale. The emphasis on moral incentives made the failure a particularly heavy blow. In the absence of individual earning increases the Cubans had been working for the increase in general production available to all; but

when the ten million was not reached and at the same time other production suffered, Cubans had more shortages to face rather than more
abundance. Moreover, the planning mistakes led to an enormous waste
of effort. This is reflected in the complaints of a nurse addressing Castro
at a Labor Confederation meeting in September, 1970:

> It really hurt . . . and you suffered when you realized that nothing could
> be done to avoid all that disorganization. . . . One day we went to Guira to
> harvest potatoes. . . . The people kept telling us "No, not here, over there"
> and when we got over there they'd say "No, not here either; this isn't the place
> assigned to your regional." And, to add insult to injury, all along the way we
> saw people harvesting potatoes, and every time I thought of all the time we
> were wasting and said, "Let's get off here and go to work, man; after all, this
> is Cuba, too, right?" somebody would come over and say, "No, comrades,
> you must work in the place assigned to your regional." Well, by the time we
> started harvesting the potatoes it was real late—too late! They had been
> plowed up three days before, and half of them had rotted. Then, when I
> made up my mind to say something, I was told to keep my mouth shut. But
> I kept telling myself, "All right, someday I'll have a chance to speak to Fidel!"
>   They said to us, "Shut up, that's the way it's got to be." No! It doesn't
> have to be that way! If you tell workers, "Look, comrades, we'll have to walk
> 12 miles to get to the place," they'll do it. But we don't like being fooled;
> workers don't like having the wool pulled over their eyes. (*Granma Weekly
> Review*, September 20, 1970: 8)

THE ANTI-LOAFING LAW

The decline in morale led to a rising absentee rate on the job. While
worker-participation was advocated as one solution for both morale and
planning failures, Castro simultaneously proposed an anti-loafing law to
deal with workers who were idle. Castro made a distinction between
absenteeism as a result of frustration with management ineptitude and
insensibility and absenteeism resulting from generally uncooperative attitudes. Sensitive to criticism that the anti-loafing law was "forcing people
to work," Castro said,

> In a rational and just society, the majority, in defense of its interests, has the
> right and duty to adopt measures to exert pressure on the tiny minority which
> refuses to fulfill its social duty after the hateful right of some men to exploit
> others has been done away with. (Castro, 1970d: 2)

After extraordinarily wide-spread public discussion by the unions and
other mass organizations, the law was put into effect April 1, 1971. The
Cuban leaders said it was not their intent to fill up the jails with loafers,
but rather to have the law act as a deterrent to loafing—specifically to
develop productivity and consciousness. The law did not apply to women.

It required that all able-bodied men either work or go to school, and it established three categories of loafer, from an occasional absentee (without excuse) to a habitual loafer. Penalties ranged from an admonition to a two-year sentence in a rehabilitation work camp. (Ian Kennedy, 1971) Before the law was passed, union representatives complained that the mild sanctions available to the labor councils (lay courts in the factories) were ineffective in discouraging habitual absentees. The government claimed that one hundred thousand people joined the labor force as a result of the law, but it remained to be seen how effective such a measure was, or if the remedy would be worse than the disease.

INTERNAL DISSENT

Following upon the failure of the ten million tons, there was a narrowing of the limits of acceptable criticism both for Cubans and foreign intellectuals (see *Artistic Culture*).

> ... the Cuban regime—caught in the vise-like pressure of the U. S. blockade and economic dependence on Moscow—is making serious concessions to the Kremlin method of dealing with internal dissent, i.e. stifling it with a heavy bureaucratic hand. (Ring, 1971: 21)

CUBAN REVOLUTIONARY SOCIETY

REVOLUTIONARY INSTITUTIONS

Politics in Cuba has a profoundly different form than it does in the rest of the Americas. In the first place, the political and economic spheres are integrated. When Cubans engage in production they are taking part in politics because work activities are the execution of political policies. As Cubans influence the process of production they are consciously performing political acts. Employment is not regarded simply as a means of gaining a livelihood; it is an important way of participating in the political process.

Moreover, politics pervades almost all aspects of life and has as its end the development of well-rounded, fulfilled people living in a sane and cooperative society. Politics addresses itself in a total way to the total person. Individuals in Cuba perceive their everyday efforts as part of a bigger picture of national and international purpose. Youth are socialized to consider the existence of injustice and exploitation anywhere as their concern and their problem. Before dismissing the Cuban political system as "undemocratic," U. S. citizens should ask themselves how meaningfully they are involved in shaping their own society and environment if their participation does not go beyond the occasional casting of a vote for a political candidate. If approval of the government by the people is a basic criterion, the Cuban leadership enjoys more support than any other government in Latin America. If the parliamentary regimes of Latin America are held up as superior to the Cuban way, then one must overlook the privilege-protecting sham that most of those systems really are.

The parliamentary system has been rejected in Cuba. Castro believes that "laws of general benefit" cannot come out of parliaments representing antagonistic interest. "In bourgeois society the interests of the most powerful always prevail." He adds that in those socialist countries which have established parliament, "political power is (in fact) exercised by a party within a revolutionary process." Instead of the parliamentary model, Castro proposes "to convert every citizen into a legislator." He cites true equality as a necessary precondition for "perfect," direct democracy. As a step in the direction of creating direct democracy, Castro says, "We are progressively heading toward mechanisms in which fundamental decisions, all fundamental laws will be discussed by all the workers of the country" (Landau, 1970: 129–133).

To date, the most widely discussed laws in Cuban history have been the 1968 Social Security law and 1971 law against loafing which were the subject of countless public meetings. The Cuban government reports that a number of significant modifications of the draft law (prepared by the Party) resulted from these discussions.

There is an extraordinary degree of public awareness of and interest in international affairs. The Revolution pursues the goal of involving the people in foreign policy by: first, the avoidance whenever possible of secret agreements with foreign nations; second, extensive explanations by leadership of foreign policy measures; and third, wide-spread public discussion of international affairs.

PARTICIPATION

Almost every Cuban has taken some part in and had his life profoundly changed by the Revolution. The character of mass involvement in public life has been direct, epic, and usually not by means of traditional Western organizational forms. Widespread, uncoerced participation in a process of wrenching transformation had been largely made possible by three extraordinary organizational means.

The first is the special, immediate relationship between the revolutionary leadership (particularly Fidel) and the general population. Wherever Fidel and other officials go, discussion and criticism of government policy come easily and naturally from the general citizenry. On the basis of this input from the public, the revolutionary leadership applies pressure upon the bureaucracy which is making demands upon the public. These relationships could be represented thusly:

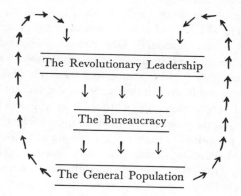

In the absence of formalized avenues of pressure from below on the bureaucracy, this unofficial and sporadic system provides an escape valve, but it also puts an enormous strain on the revolutionary leadership since the same handful of men and women must act as ombudsmen as well as policy-makers and executives. Cuba's small size is one reason this method has been relatively successful.

A second major mode of participation are special national campaigns like literacy and the ten million ton sugar harvest described above.

The Mass Organizations. A third and more systematic mode of participation has been the mass organizations: the Committees for the Defense of the Revolution (CDR) or block committees, the Women's Federation (FMC), the National Association of Small Farmers (ANAP), the Union of Communist Youth (UJC), the Young Pioneers, the militia, and more recently, the Revolutionary Cuban Workers' Confederation (CTCR). Of these, the Committees for the Defense of the Revolution (CDR) have been the most pervasive and consequential.

Nothing has ever existed quite like the Cuban CDR. "Never, not in any classical book of revolutionary theories, has such an institution been mentioned," Castro has said (Fagen, 1969: 102). Conceived primarily as a civil-defense, anti-counter-revolutionary measure, the CDR were organized during the national emergency at the time of the Playa Girón invasion in April 1961, and were given great importance during the

Missile Crisis of 1962. Since then the CDR have assumed a wide variety of functions and attained a membership of more than 4.2 million persons above the age of fourteen by 1973.

The CDR, like all national organizations in Cuba, are organized at the national, provincial, municipal, and neighborhood level, but their most important unit is at the block level: there is a CDR for each side of a city block. Each local CDR is broken down into sub-groups called *frentes* presided over by elected leaders. One *frente* is responsible for public health and has the job of seeing that neighborhood residents receive proper medical assistance and that immunization, rat and insect extermination, and general public health measures are carried out. Another looks after educational needs, encouraging students to stay in school and adults to enroll in educational programs, and resolving problems between pupils and educational personnel. Other responsibilities of CDR *frentes* include the collection and recycling of used materials (stamps, glass, metal, coat-hangers, plastic), patrolling the streets at night unarmed, so that no police are necessary, providing for the repair or improvement of homes, organizing volunteer labor, developing a sense of identity with Vietnamese and other peoples involved in revolutionary struggles, enforcing court sentences of deprivation of liberty, and watching for counter-revolutionary activity. Altogether there are more than fifteen *frentes* in a typical CDR, and they coordinate with all the other organs of government such as the construction, housing, and health ministries. Frequently special tasks are assigned to the CDR like the responsibility for managing all the then remaining small businesses which were nationalized during the Revolutionary Offensive. Women, at least in urban areas, are frequently elected as *frente* leaders. CDR's have their own community education sessions which feature spirited discussions of public issues. Summarizing their "higher-order tasks," one scholar wrote, "the CDR are expected to integrate, to socialize, and to mobilize the masses, to implement revolutionary policies and programs, and to protect both the material and the social resources of the revolution" (Fagen, 1969: 80).

While the CDR may provide some inputs of ideas, opinions, and practices to the government, they mainly implement policies, and it is because they are tied in with national policies of high priority that they are so successful, unlike the numerous "community development" programs elsewhere in Latin America which are ineffective and marginal to national development. In other Latin American countries, program participants are rarely assigned anything *official* to do, nor are they well integrated into a program of national goals. Comprehensive social uplift in the Third World will not result from the disconnected construction of infrastructural sandcastles by means of weak and sputtering community development efforts. In Cuba, not only the government, but also the media, the educational system, and most organized groups have community and national development as their principal tasks, and most people in the country believe fervently that the government leadership is totally dedicated to their best interest and making at least as great a sacrifice as they are. Underdevelopment is under assault from all the institutions and instrumentalities of the society. A preliminary result is that Cuba has become the first country in Latin American history in which virtually the entirety of the population have the advantages of educational opportunity, a nutritionally adequate diet, and a comprehensive medical attention. If a goal of community development is the achievement of public participation in public life, then it must be allowed that Cuba has more of that than any country in the western hemisphere, if not in the world.

In the building of community the CDR's play a more important role than any other institution in the society. It is the CDR's that have been primarily responsible for replacing the isolated, selfish, and privatized life-style of the past with communal attitude. José Yglesias summed up his experience with the CDR in the town of Mayarí, Oriente:

> . . . the right to privacy, the inviolability of the individual, the cult and curse of personal anguish are all based on what seems an indisputable fact: man dies alone. Maybe man neither lives nor dies alone; maybe it is all a cultural attitude. . . The workers and *campesinos* in the CDR's had taken the first steps toward a new cultural attitude. . . They brought a wonderful sanity and healthiness to their organization's pushiness about people's lives: an insistence that the open life—open to the view of one's neighbor—is the natural life of man. I decided that this might well be what would make Mayarí a valley of paradise. (1968: 307)

An intriguing question raised by Yglesias' conclusion is whether privacy and revolutionary community are mutually exclusive. Many of the invasions of privacy in Cuba today are not imposed by the social imperatives of the new order, but are rather the result of open sanction of pre-revolutionary habits of intrusiveness. There is no necessary contradiction between privacy and communal orientation. While a minimum level of material well-being is an essential pre-condition for the enjoyment of any privacy, the CDR's have not always been careful to protect those aspects of private life which do not in any way threaten the achievement of revolutionary goals.

The CDR is the most important institutional means producing the extraordinarily high level of public participation in reshaping the Cuban environment, but they are only one of many dimensions of public involvement. The organization charged with the responsibility for changing the role of women and mobilizing their productive energies is the Federation of Cuban Women (FMC). With a membership of approximately 750,000, the FMC wars against the traditional notions which have stunted the egos and ambitions of females. (See Social Conditions—Women) One of its major accomplishments has been the establishment of an island-wide, but still insufficient, network of child day-care centers to enable women to work outside their homes. Change for women has come slowly and against strong cultural resistance. Only an estimated 150,000 held regular full-time jobs in 1966. Still, the change has been impressive. A U. S. observer summarized the situation:

> Women were visible everywhere: as workers, teachers, administrators, government representatives. They directed important projects and delivered keynote speeches at important events. The landscape of Revolutionary Cuba was not a man's world. No longer were women the janitors, caretakers, and consumers of the society, but its producers and organizers. (Sutherland, 1969: 174–175)

The FMC assumes the responsibility of helping and encouraging women who still work in such occupations as cleaning and waiting on tables to get educational training and be placed in productive jobs. The FMC arranged for women to have preferential hiring.

People's Courts. The Cuban court system includes a new institution, the Popular Courts (*Tribunales Populares*), established gradually between 1966 and 1969, which has become an important vehicle for local involvement in public life. These neighborhood courts are charged with the administration of justice in cases involving petty crimes and disputes. The most common cases involve "public disorder" (fighting, personal quarrels, etc.), thievery, juvenile delinquency, and violations of rationing and health regulations. These courts provide rapid justice—cases are handled within about a month of the accusation. The courts meet in the evening in each neighborhood, each court covering a district with two thousand to six thousand inhabitants. The lay judges, whose only prerequisite is a sixth grade education and membership in a mass organization, are selected by the local section of the Communist Party and the CDR and elected by the community at large. They serve in panels of three, without pay, in addition to their regular jobs. Since they are usually workers without legal training they are given a three-week training course. It is considered "more important that the people know the judges than that the judges know the law" (Berman, 1969: 1335). The judges are advised by an *asesor,* usually a fourth-year law student, who is a liaison with the Ministry of Justice. Appeals from the popular courts are heard by the *asesor* and two other popular court judges. Occasional excess of revolutionary puritanism is supposed to be tempered by the *asesor*; judges have tended to deal harshly with witnesses who introduce hearsay and who are motivated by grudges against a defendant or testify against a person to "make points" with the community. Judges are subject to recall if a complaint against them is validated.

A primary aim of the Popular Courts is educational: to put personal controversies into a political context, to explain new laws, and to legitimize such policies as rationing or health measures. They are well-attended and members of the community participate, either as witnesses or commenting on the case and questioning the judges. The People's Courts are intended to cut through to the sociology of events and persons and to avoid legal technicalities and formalism. The context in which an individual violates the law—e.g. as housing conditions, educational level—is taken into account. Individuals are frequently directed to further their education, or to engage in regular work, even when they are not found guilty. The frequently imaginative sentences, which tend toward leniency and are rehabilitative rather than punitive, include public admonition, restitution of stolen property, indemnization to the injured party, confinement to one's dwelling, restricting the sentenced person from visiting the place (such as a bar) where a disturbance occurred, and sentences to periods in agricultural work camps. Neither fines nor sentences to regular jails are imposed by the People's Courts. Productive work is generally considered the remedy for most deviant behavior.

These courts seem to have attained a maximum of legitimacy. Decisions are rarely appealed, the accused rarely use the lawyers to which they have a right, and local citizens seem to consider the judges part of the community.

> The court's authority . . . is never in question. It is not simply the formal procedure which ensures this, but the whole demeanor of the judges. These three women in their thirties . . . settle to their business with a stern confidence, as if they had the weight of tradition behind them. . . (NUC, Misheloff, 1969: 33)

Although the party has some role in the original choice of judges, who need not be members of the party, the courts seem to be free from political interference. The popular tribunals are a unique institution, different from comparable institutions in other socialist countries.

A second court system with popular involvement, the labor councils (*Consejos de Trabajo*), were established in 1964. These councils are made up of employees in each work place and handle negligences, absenteeism, and minor disputes arising in the production situation.

A special judicial institution, the Revolutionary Tribunals, was established by the rebel army in 1959 and has continued to judge what are defined as "counter-revolutionary crimes." These include counter-revolutionary activity, embezzling or pilfering from government enterprises, and insults to the national flag. These courts are the only ones that can give the death penalty. The judges who serve in panels of three are members of the army chosen by their superior officers. It was the Revolutionary Tribunals which originally judged the Batistianos and which later found the "microfaction" guilty. These courts are quite political and in important trials, Fidel Castro, his brother Raúl, and others of the original guerrilla leadership sometimes appear.

Despite the innovative legal institutions of the Revolution, felonies, divorces, and some other cases continue to be handled by the traditional Cuban court system, the *Audiencias* and the Supreme Court. Except that the lawyers available free of charge to defend accused people are now "revolutionary" lawyers, these courts continue as before. Most of the judges were appointed before the Revolution. Defendants may hire private attorneys if they wish, and 20–30 percent of the attorneys were in private practice in 1968. The government plans eventually to integrate the *Audiencias* (and also the separate traffic courts) into a new court system more on the model of the People's Tribunals with lay judges. The Cuban legal code is based on the 1938 Social Defense Code and the 1940 Constitution. The Code was amended in 1959 when the counter-revolutionary laws were defined. In 1966 a handbook was drawn up to guide the people's tribunals.

Aside from the mass organizations and the Popular Courts, local institutions of government have not developed in a systematic way. In 1965 an effort was launched to decentralize administration, giving birth to regional administrative offices as well as to general town meetings (*asambleas populares*) and a grass roots level of administration (*poder local*). With the Revolutionary Offensive in 1968, there was a downgrading of local administration and local input into planning in favor of the apparent efficiency of national coordination and direction from above. However, the local officials serve as collectors of complaints which they pass up to the leadership. In 1970, there was talk of decentralization; but by 1972, the central government had only fitfully supported the convening of the *asambleas populares* and the establishment of *poder local*. Both concepts were still in an unconsolidated embryonic stage of development. Meanwhile, the pre-revolutionary entities known as municipal councils continued to exist but without much independent authority.

THE PRESS

The press plays a basic role in promoting widespread participation in public life. The emphasis on its mobilization function, however, has left the Cuban press open to charges of neglecting intellectual and cultural give and take.   In 1968 Fidel Castro told American filmmaker Saul Landau "undoubtedly we still have in our press many shortcomings." (1970: 131) A year or so later K. S. Karol summed up the Cuban press:

> After the first wave of enthusiasm when Cuban men of letters had done their best to come to grips with the economic, social, and cultural foundations of their revolution . . . works on contemporary history, economic studies of the period of transition toward socialism, analyses of the new culture and its relationship to the masses became increasingly rare. Theoretical magazines such as *Cuba Socialista,* which used to publish important papers . . . had ceased to appear; others like *Pensamiento Crítico,* now concentrated on foreign authors. The quality of the daily and weekly press seemed to be fast declining. The fact that Cuba was much freer than other socialist countries was poor consolation in these circumstances. (Karol, 1970: 395–396)

The quantitative and qualitative reduction of the Cuban press which Karol noted was documented in detail in 1969 by Carmelo Mesa-Lago. (Mesa-Lago, 1969: 74) One by one the channels through which other than official views could reach the public have been cut off. By 1967 public debate had virtually disappeared from the press which had assumed a government-directed educational function. The newspaper field was largely left to *Granma,* the official organ of the Communist Party which had been founded in October 1965 by the merger of *Revolución* (the organ of the 26th of July Movement) and *Hoy* (the organ of the PSP). With the demise of *Cuba Socialista* and several specialized journals during the 1964–67 period, Castro's speeches became "the main source of statistical information" (Mesa-Lago, 1969: 74).

Although *Granma* was not a forum for the presentation and synthesis of competing policy positions, it did manage to convey in a concise form the basic facts of international events though there was inadequate coverage of ideas and institutions generated in other socialist countries. Most of its space was given over to coverage of the progress and problems of the revolutionary programs. This content made it singularly valuable as a resource for the countless political discussions carried on at various meetings of local units of revolutionary organizations. It became the principal textbook of the ongoing revolutionary process. The use of the press as a text rather than as a forum was justified by the national leadership as appropriate to the existing level of public consciousness. The implication of this position was the assumption that most journalists and intellectuals were on the periphery of the revolutionary struggle.

Castro has always explained the shortcomings of the Cuban press in terms of the lack of good journalists; however, there is evidence that Carlos Franqui's separation from press activities at the time that his newspaper *Revolución* was shut down was the result of a conscious decision not to have a "critical press." The argument was usually that unity was the main necessity and that a critical press was not compatible with unity at the current level of mass political sophistication. How in the absence of real political debate the Cubans were going to acquire political sophistication was not explained.

In a speech in 1971, Jesús Montané, Minister of Communications and a Major in the rebel army from the guerrilla days, expressed guidelines and mild criticisms of press in the following terms:

> One of our main objectives should be to educate through analysis, making use of all arguments in a given situation and presenting the fullest information in the most concise and readable way. Socialism calls for man's understanding to play an essential role in his conduct and motivations. This is why we should never limit ourselves to a mere repetition of slogans, . . . Newsmen should always do work in depth. The newsmen should try to present all the possible slants on a news story, so the reader can judge for himself. The revolutionary press . . . must build, orient, educate and fight. [We will succeed to the extent] that we offer the masses better, broader, more objective, and more analytical information. (*Granma, Weekly Review,* September 19, 1971)

The Cuban press makes no pretense of uncommitted neutrality. Montané describes it as partial, socialist, anti-imperialist, combining "objective information and committed classism." Some of its main functions besides education, are to increase productivity and self-discipline.

LEADERSHIP

During the transition to socialism, the overwhelming majority of the Cuban people continued to support the Revolution and its leadership and to accept socialism and the other policies of government. This has been explained as the product of Castro's charisma. However, the survival of Castro's charisma has depended upon his being identified with a series of policies which directly benefited people, either by improving their standard of living, or by enhancing the quality of their life, their own or their children's opportunities, or by increasing their sense of dignity. Yet each policy which benefited the majority drove a minority into the opposition. For example, the rent reform of 1959 by cutting rents increased the purchasing power of the poorest people. However, it eliminated real estate investment, the speculative dream of many in the middle class. Similarly, the agrarian reform increased the income, living comfort, status, and possibilities of most rural Cubans, but medium landowners (the rural middle class) became insecure and many defected from their initial sympathy.

Fidel. Although Fidel's charisma has been over-emphasized as an explanatory factor in the Cuban Revolution, it remains true that his presence has infused every major development of the Revolution. He has, in addition, participated in countless minor decisions affecting at times even the most inconsequential features of post-revolutionary life. His speaking ability has moved one commentator to describe him as probably the greatest orator of his time (Lockwood, 1970b: 20).

> Fidel differs from other revolutionary heroes in . . . (an) . . . important respect. Whereas Lenin, Trotsky, Debray, Fanon, and Ho most often wrote for party cadres and engaged in internal disputes within the revolutionary movement, Castro invariably addresses himself to the masses of the Cuban people . . . his purpose is always to educate and to raise the level of political awareness. . . . Every speech of Fidel's is a lesson: a clear exposition of policy, analysis, and goals. He speaks often and at length—but is hardly ever demagogic. He speaks because education is the key to the new society. Cuba is an experiment and all the people must participate in it. (Kenner and Petras, 1969: xiv–xv)

When Marilyn and Maurice Zeitlin were doing attitudinal surveys among Cuban workers in 1962, they were puzzled when few respondents named Fidel or Ché Guevara among "three individuals whom you admire very much." The mystery was cleared up when interviewees later explained that the question was worded "aside from personal friends or relatives . . . whom do you admire"; for them Castro and Guevara were considered personal friends (Zeitlin, 1967: 29–30).

The Cuban revolutionary leadership has continuously moved among the people. After ten years of power Castro was spending ninety percent of his time out of his office, often sleeping in tents and riding in jeeps, and he did not plan to change this manner of working. He lives the least comfortably of any chief executive in the world. The omnipresent role of Fidel has generated heated commentary. Observers like Hugh Thomas, K. S. Karol, and René Dumont have charged that Fidel's efforts personally to control too wide a range of decisions is counter-productive, that it discourages managerial initiative and results in ill-advised policies. This view must be weighed against the extraordinary benefits of Castro's leadership. Both the revolutionary leadership and the populace acknowledge that he has earned a place of pre-eminence in the Revolution and that he is capable of inspired vision (Fagen, 1965). His singular status has spared Cuba the kind of feuding among the leadership which has plagued, for example, post-independence Algeria. His unquenchable enthusiasm and energy have bolstered hard-pressed public spirits. Fidel, the personification of the Revolution, is not an abstraction but a ceaselessly traveling reality whom all Cubans see perhaps at least once a year.

His is an important psychological contribution. No matter how work-a-day anyone's efforts may be, they know that these efforts are of personal concern and importance to Fidel. And, curiously, while cabinet ministers and lesser officials may be reluctant to challenge Castro's views, the general population is not.

When Lee Lockwood asked Castro how he felt about being cheered, "Almost like a saviour," he answered.

> The masses bestow upon me a certain quality, perhaps out of necessity, perhaps because it cannot happen in any other way. There is a kind of mechanism in the human mind that tends to create symbols in which it concentrates its sentiments. By transforming men into symbols, they manifest a greater gratitude, they attribute to the individual what is not deserved by him alone but by the many. Often I think of the hundreds, even thousands of men who are working anonymously, making possible all those things for which the people are grateful. Recognition is not divided in an equitable way. It would be an error for any man—I say this sincerely—not to be conscious of this and to believe himself truly deserving of all that recognition and affection. One must have a proper appreciation of the things he has accomplished, but he should never consider himself deserving of the recognition that belongs to the many. I believe that that world be harmful to any leader. (1969: 171)

There is no effort to glorify Castro by naming places after him or by placing his picture in public places. The leadership regards it as undignified to do this for living heroes.

Making decisions without adequate technical depth does mean that Castro has been responsible for certain misguided efforts. But, as he demonstrated in his 26th of July speech of 1970, he is prepared to assume his share of personal responsibility for programs that fall short of their goals. It should also be noted that in some fields, particularly in agriculture, Fidel has more expertise than any other chief executive in the world. Nevertheless, Castor's absence from Cuba for ten weeks on tour of Chile and ten countries of Africa and Europe brought no dislocation of the system in Cuba in 1971–2.

The Communist Party. The heroic and pervasive leadership of Fidel and his guerrilla associates has meant that Cuba probably has the loosest, the least bureaucratized official party of any Socialist country. This circumstance has drawn criticism from Marxists everywhere, particularly in Europe. Nevertheless, the informality of the Cuban Communist Party is in keeping with the personalist style in the politics of Latin America where men—as individual men—often triumph over organization. For the Fidelistas "the traditional bureaucratic Communist Party can be a downright liability, frustrating rather than formenting revolutionary action" (Horowitz, 1970: 9).

With only about seventy-eight thousand members in 1970, the Cuban Communist Party (CCP) was proportionately the smallest among all socialist countries. Fifteen years after the ouster of Batista, the official party had still not held a general organizational congress. Officially beginning to function in 1965, the CCP was the outcome of a process of breaking down and remolding of three organizations, the 26th of July Movement, the Pre-revolutionary Communist Party (PSP) and the Directorio Revolucionario. The CCP passed through two preliminary stages. It was called the ORI between 1961 (when the 26th of July Movement was allowed to fade away) and 1963, and the PURS between 1963 and 1965. By the time it took the name Communist, the "old militants" of the PSP had clearly lost control and most former PSP members had transferred their loyalty to Castro.

In the progression from the 26th of July Movement to the CCP, the revolutionary organizations became more and more rigorous in qualification for membership so that while the present party is relatively small in number, it is an exemplary corps of dedicated persons. Member for member, it is probably the equal or superior of any party in the Socialist third of the world. Predominant among the one hundred person Central Committee, the Politburo, and the Secretariat of the Party are people who participated in the military phase of the Revolution. These are K. S. Karol's "Guerrillas in Power."

Although the CCP is less central to decision-making than the Party is in some other Socialist countries, it does occupy a major place in the Cuban political system. It serves multifold functions described as follows:

1) *Exemplar.* Persons selected for membership by the Party hierarchy must normally be first nominated at their local work center where they must pass the test of a public discussion of their qualifications and character. Only the most dedicated and industrious tend to survive this challenge. Party members are often expected to work a number of hours beyond their regular eight-hour work day without additional pay. Their admirable behavior and commitment are continuously suggestive to the general population.

2) *Recruiter and Appointer.* The Party not only draws talent and dedication into itself, but also plays the key role in discovering and recommending outstanding persons for appointment to administrative positions throughout the government.

3) *Administrator*. Some projects are coordinated by the party itself rather than by government ministries. Examples would be the Havana Green Belt project, the ten million ton sugar harvest of 1970, and many other aspects of the Revolutionary Offensive.

4) *Transmitter and Orienter*. The Party serves as a two-way communication system between the leadership and the base. It takes readings of public opinion and makes them available to leadership at all levels. In this way it discharges a representational and democratizing function. At the same time it also has the function of transmitting decisions and policy orientations from above for local implementation. The performance of this responsibility outweighs its representational function, and it often informally defines the limits within which public issues can be discussed or challenged at the base.

The Armed Forces. Cuba's revolutionary leadership has had a dual military-civilian experience. Original members of the revolutionary armed forces were mostly civilians caught up in a revolutionary process. They have played and continue to play a key role in the development of the new Cuba. Many of the present-day leaders of the country once served in the rebel army. When the Communist Party of Cuba was formally organized in 1965, sixty-eight of the one hundred-person Central Committee were from the armed forces. Since the revolutionary takeover, the core of leadership for government agencies has been supplied by the rebel military, and leading figures such as Fidel continue to engage in military training.

This role duality is one factor which contradicts the assertion that "the Cuban Army has a classically hierarchic structure and hence is basically authoritarian" (Karol, 1970: 543). In their civilian responsibilities, Cuban military men generally conduct themselves in a non-authoritarian manner and this is fed back into the military role. Visitors in Cuba frequently comment on the competence, courtesy, and quiet dignity of rebel army members. Another democratizing influence are the traditions which derive from the guerrilla experience when commanders like Camilo Cienfuegos and Ché Guevara imparted an egalitarian and humanitarian spirit among soldiers of the rebel army.

The Cuban military, while having its own organizational needs and interests, has not been a political force unto itself. There has not developed a military caste nor is there civilian hostility toward persons discharging military duties. Cubans genuinely believe in the need for military preparedness and most regard themselves as participants in a revolutionary struggle.

As a military force the Cuban army surprised the U. S. architects of the April, 1961 "Bay of Pigs" operation who underestimated its capacity to function in a combat situation. Under the field command of Castro himself, the rebel army overcame the attack in a matter of hours, capturing 1,180 prisoners out of a 1,297-man invading force.

The constant need to be on guard against U. S. and exile attack has necessitated a sizable expenditure on national defense: 350 million pesos in 1970 compared with 290.6 million for education (1969), 236.1 million for public health (1969), and 320 million for social security (1970) (Castro, 1970b: 21–22). Total strength of the active units of the armed forces was estimated in 1970 as approaching two hundred thousand with eighty-five thousand reserves. This represented the largest per capita and doubtless most effective armed force in Latin America. Young men are subject to a two and one-half to three-year period of service in the armed forces. However, both sexes may receive military in high schools and technical schools. University students may also satisfy the military requirement while studying. Women may join the military but are not required to enlist. The militia is a 150,000-person adjunct to the regular armed forces. Militia members, all volunteers, serve for about eight hours a week, most notably as guards for public facilities. Women are prominently active in the militia.

The Cuban revolutionary military has always participated in production. Beginning immediately after the Revolution took power, the rebel army units grew their own food, helped construct houses in cooperatives and *granjas,* and later handled heavy land-clearing equipment and crop-dusting planes. Because of its organizational and mobilizational capacities, the role of the military was greatly increased during the Revolutionary Offensive of 1968. It was given the responsibility for certain agricultural undertakings in eastern Cuba and provided eighty thousand soldiers to harvest approximately eighteen percent of the 1970 sugar crop. Such episodes resulted in speculation among foreign observers that the whole production process might eventually be subjected to military discipline. These fears have proved groundless.

POLITICAL-ECONOMIC ADMINISTRATION

Planning. Basic policy decisions are made by the Central Committee of the Party and sometimes by Fidel himself. The elaboration of the policy is assigned to the central planning office (JUCEPLAN) which is responsible for developing yearly and longer range plans for the nation. At times planners have complained that they were not adequately consulted before policy decisions were taken and therefore placed in the position of trying to develop mutually antagonistic or impossible programs

(Latastre, 1968: 29–33). A foreign critic alleged, "As things stand now, many economic decisions involving the expenditure of hundreds of thousands of dollars are still being made without systematic justification" (Leontief, 1971: 21). However, any evaluation of the planning system in Cuba should take into account the political imperatives of a society undergoing a general transformation. In this setting good politics may be bad planning and vice versa. For example, during the 1961 literacy drive, teachers had to be withdrawn from the public schools in the closing period of the campaign to insure its success. One then has to measure the positive political and social value of the dramatically successful literacy effort against the loss of some teachers to their schools for a part of the year. Often there has been a conscious and deliberate avoidance of feasibility studies and elaborate planning because it is feared the findings might lead to pessimism and defeatism. The Revolution has sometimes placed ideas and vision ahead of advanced assurances of success in the belief that a captivating goal will generate its own staff of enthusiasts who will then stretch their own capacities to the degree necessary to achieve the goal in question.

One practical consideration which led to the original impetus for over-all planning of the economy was the foreign trade shift to the socialist countries, especially the USSR. Soviet planners needed Cuban planning to rationalize trade between the two countries. After wooden instruction by Czech planning specialists who often presented principles inappropriate to the Cuban milieu, the Cubans drew up a general plan for 1962. This over-ambitious instrument failed to conform to the economic and human realities of the time. Profiting from these mistakes, the Cubans were able to bring their economy under the control of the plan for 1963. There has been a steady improvement in planning since although a number of major misjudgments and natural disasters have upset the calculations and expectations of JUCEPLAN. Wassily Leontief sums up the positive side of Cuban planning and administration as follows:

> . . . the over-all direction of economic policies is intelligent and aggressively imaginative. . . . So far as the over-all productivity is concerned, the performance of the socialized economy is not inferior and possibly even somewhat superior to that of the communist states in Eastern Europe in the early stages of their development. (1969: 20)

Despite difficulties in planning evidenced by past failures to meet production goals, the probability is that Cuba will generally succeed in achieving a steady rate of development which will in the long run outdistance the development rates of the capitalist economies of other Latin American countries. The surplus created by Cuban labor is no longer sent abroad or wasted on super-consumption for a few, but is being invested at a high rate to create a diversified and productive Cuban economy capable of satisfying the material needs of the people and providing economic independence. The accuracy of planning will doubtlessly increase with experience and with the improving technical education of planners. A basic ground for optimism about Cuba's economic future is the scope and nature of the country's educational system. Latin America as a whole only draws upon the intellectual and technical capacities of that minority fraction of the population in the middle and upper classes because that is generally the portion of society which has access to secondary and university education. If there is a potential scientist or engineer among the lower mass of the people chances are virtually nil that this potential will be developed. Cuba cultivates the capacities of all its pepole. The labor shortage which has impeded growth since 1963 will gradually be overcome by increased mechanization.

In its agricultural sector Cuba is no longer an underdeveloped nation. Land and labor do not lie idle as they did under decisions made by domestic and foreign interests seeking only to maximize profit. Even if the fifteen percent gain in agricultural production per year projected for the 1970's should prove overly optimistic, indications are that Cuba is fast creating a sound and healthy agricultural base. Once agricultural development is secure, industry will emerge as the major emphasis.

The Central Administration. After Prime Minister Castro, the other high-ranking executives are President of the Republic (Osvaldo Dorticós), First Vice-Premier (Raúl Castro), and Secretary-General of Government (Celia Sánchez). In 1972 a ten-member Cabinet Executive Committee was established composed of eight cabinet ministers, Fidel, and President Dorticós. Revolutionary Armed Forces Minister Raúl Castro was designated First Vice-Premier and the seven other ministers were given the rank of vice-premier. After considerable trial and error, those activities which have come to be regarded as sufficiently important to be organized as ministries are: Revolutionary Armed Forces; Foreign Affairs; Interior; Education; Foreign Trade; Internal Trade; Communications; Construction; Transport; Labor; Justice; Public Health; Heavy Industry; Light Industry; Metallurgy and Mining; Food; Sugar Industries; Economic, Technical and Scientific Coordination; the National Bank which functions as a treasury ministry; and the National Institute of Agrarian Reform (INRA) which has ministerial status. In addition to the ministries, there are a number of lesser agencies called National Institutes. These are the Institutes of Hydraulic Resources, Sports, Physical Education and Leisure, Broadcasting, the Cuban Institute of Art and Cinematography

(ICAIC), and the Cuban Institute of Friendship with Peoples (ICAP). Rounding out the list are the National Council of Culture and the Academy of Sciences.

In each enterprise the appropriate ministry appoints managerial personnel, though this function is increasingly influenced by Party recommendations. There has been a gradual transformation in the quality of public administration. Before the Revolution, government work tended to attract the corrupt and unproductive; it repelled the active entrepreneurial type of person. With the disappearance of the private sector and the campaign against bureaucracy, the most effective executives were attracted to administrative positions, but there remained the problem of a severe shortage of skilled administrators because of the loss of such people into exile.

Labor Organization. Until 1970 labor unions were a rather neglected aspect of the Cuban political economy. Theoretically, a full system of unions existed, but they were not a centrally important locus for the generation of ideas and the expression of interests. Special historical and political reasons account for this. Unlike the pre-revolutionary military institutions which were dissolved, the unions were gradually remade. Although Fidel said in May 1959 that the Revolution was bringing effective democracy to the union system and that union leaders would not be picked by the government "but by the free vote of workers in each work place" (Martin, 1971: 28), this pledge was to remain unfulfilled for eleven years.

Castro had personally persuaded union leaders not to call a sugar strike in February 1959 (before the nationalization of the sugar mills), maintaining that the Revolution would be hurt if there were a fall in sugar production and that the workers and the government were essentially one.[4] At the time he characterized the union leaders who insisted on the strike as "demagogues and counter-revolutionaries" but he later commented that this confrontation with the workers whose demands were just, had been one of the most difficult jobs he had ever confronted. Castro used his influence to break the power of July 26th labor leaders who were trying to exclude Communists from top labor positions and give control of the CTC-R to the Communists. After Escalante was expelled in 1962 and PSP "sectarianism" was attacked, union leadership was opened up somewhat to non-Communists.

Nevertheless (according to a Cuban revolutionary writer) these changes did not result in their democratization, and [the unions] continued to use forms

[4] This is the same problem President Allende faced in Chile in 1971 when strikes broke out.

which limited the worker participation. . . The absence of institutionalized procedures, such as periodic assemblies, kept worker participation under control, and thus limited the responsiveness of the union apparatus. (Martin, 1971: 30)

Cubans in 1958 seemed to be considering abolishing the unions altogether. Corruption as a union practice was much more easily eliminated than the idea held by certain privileged "aristocratic" union leaders that union status was a guarantor of privilege. The heads of the telephone, electrical, and port workers were afraid to lose advantages they had won for their members from private companies and the government, but the new government was determined to put into effect for all workers many measures for which unions had traditionally struggled, including elimination of unemployment, health programs, education for workers and their children, rent reduction, better pensions, sick leave, vacations, low cost recreational facilities, abolition of race and sex discrimination in hiring, and free admission to sports events. Moreover, wage demands, traditionally the main focus of union struggles, no longer had the same meaning once programs designed to equalize income had been put into effect.

Although the government felt its interests were identical with those of labor, Guevara said that unions should be allowed to play an independent role, representing the needs of each particular group of workers in relation to the state which, while it *generally* represented workers' interests, could nevertheless ignore the special situation of any particular group of workers. Guevara thought strikes were legitimate, although they would represent "a defeat for the government and the working class," and he gave an example of a strike which had taken place in August 1960 because of a legitimate wage grievance (Zeitlin, 1962: 55). His thinking reflected Lenin's position on unions. However, neither Castro nor those heading the Ministry of Labor or the CTC-R showed any sign of agreeing with Guevara. Castro and the Communist labor cadres seemed to have accepted the view (current in the Soviet Union and Eastern Europe) that the unions should represent the government in enforcing production norms. The Communists from the old PSP accepted this Stalinist view of the role of unions. Nevertheless, in some instances workers did participate in setting production norms and the Cuban reality was far more participatory than a Stalinist stereotype would suggest.

The unions were supposed to arrange housing for members, to alleviate social conditions causing absenteeism, to operate educational programs, and to pressure workers to raise their level of training, but their main responsibility was to get people to work harder, to volunteer for over-time work, and to assure the fulfillment of production plans. All of these functions overlapped with other government organs which had more prestige.

The new Communist Party had the main responsibility for encouraging harder work. Thus it was particularly the Communist Party, which also had an important role in management and organization of production that usurped the role of the unions. The nomination of candidates for union office and the elections were so carefully overseen by the party, and the "old" Communist influence in the CTC-R was so strong, that the union and party leadership were frequently the same, but it was in the party that decisions were made. The most productive workers in each plant, who had been elected as "vanguard workers" (*trabajadores de avanzada*), and formed the pool out of which party members were chosen, began to meet and these meetings took the place of union meetings. The actual participation of most workers in the daily decisions affecting the work place was minimal, although they usually discussed the decisions at some length once they were made. Fidel is reported to have "confessed" in 1968 to K. S. Karol "in sorrow, that he saw no chance of granting the workers the right of self-determination in the near future" (Karol, 1970: 546).

In this situation, the unions tended to disappear, or in the words of a writer in the official magazine *Cuba* unions became "truncated, incomplete, . . . almost a dormant institution." (Martín, 1971: 28). No other mass organization had such a limited life, partly because unions were the only mass organizations to antedate the Revolution. During the Revolutionary Offensive with the extreme pressure to make production more efficient, the unions fell to their lowest position.

In 1969, Carlos Rafael Rodríguez, at that time Minister of Economy without portfolio and member of the party Central Committee, commented that

> the unions are transmission belts for Party directives to the workers but have insufficiently represented the workers to the Party or Revolutionary Government. They cannot merely be instruments of the Party without losing their purpose. Administrators, after all, can be *hijos de putas,* and if they are, the workers must be able to throw them out. (Zeitlin, 1962: 32–43)

Finally in 1970, after the failure to reach the ten million ton sugar harvest goal, Castro said on August 23, "for the immediate future, we must place special emphasis, in the coming months on the question of workers' movement" (Castro, 1970c: 5). Fidel gave as one of the reasons for the failure to meet the ten million ton goal the lack of provision for feedback from workers to administrators, planners, and technicians which would have corrected production bottlenecks before they caused severe damage. On July 26, 1970, he said ". . . We must begin to establish a collective body in the management of each plant. A collective body!" (Castro, 1970b: 31).

On September 2, 1970, Castro told a meeting of the CTC-R that "Even the best administration can not call forth the control, vigilance, militancy and mass energy necessary to overcome problems." (Castro, 1970d: 2). A few days later Castro told a union conference,

> Let us trust our workers and rapidly carry out the elections in all the union sections . . . in a completely free way, in which they put up as candidates whoever the workers want to nominate. . . Let us begin by democratizing the labor movement. If the labor movement isn't democratic it's of no use. (Martín, 1971: 28)

Union elections were held in November 1970. In response to the question of what would happen if workers chose leaders who were not "good revolutionaries," Labor Minister Jorge Risquet answered that such a situation would constitute a "warning, a red light, that it is necessary to improve the work of the Revolution in that work place."

Coinciding with the elections, massive union assemblies were held with complete freedom of discussion in which Fidel and other revolutionary leaders participated. So many complicated problems were brought up in the teachers union meetings that a national educational conference was scheduled for 1971.

Castro considered the new impetus for unions to be a whole new phase of the Revolution, the "democratization" phase. Unions were supposed to become free forums for the expression of ideas, a two-way avenue of communication between government and organized workers. The new roles for unions would require a change in the party and government relationship toward them. The contradictory trend toward more coercion evidenced by the 1971 anti-loafing law and the further restrictions on what was permitted "within the revolution," leaves the future of unionism in Cuba an open question.

SOCIAL CONDITIONS

EQUALITY

Saddled with a pre-revolutionary society of vast inequalities, and aware of the danger of a "new class" of bureaucrats and technicians establishing itself as has occurred in the Socialist countries of Europe, the Cuban revolutionary leadership committed itself to achieving a more equitable society, not one of ". . . those uncultured people who work, and those cultured people who find ways to make them." The Revolution's long range answer to the problem of a privileged class is the development of the worker-intellectual. "In the Soviet Union students *do* practical work. In Cuba workers and students will increasingly *be* the same people." Fidel's "plan" is eventually to have everybody working four hours and studying four hours, in universities built round farms and factories (Reckbord, 1971: 94, 42, 40).

Until such time as the worker-intellectual becomes a real possibility, the Revolution endeavors to eliminate privilege step-by-step. Among measures that have had this objective have been:

The elimination of corruption. The level of official corruption is probably the lowest in the world.

Rationing. Goods in short supply have been successfully rationed on an equitable basis, though the distribution system has been cumbersome.

The universalization of educational opportunity and health care.

The equalization of wages in industry with those in agriculture. This is an important departure from world practice. In both the capitalist countries and in the Soviet Union development capital has, in a sense, come "out of the hide" of rural workers. In Cuba "agricultural wages have been raised to equality with industry"; the same category of job receives the same pay (Bernardo, 1971a: 126). However, there are more higher-paying job categories in urban areas than in agriculture.

> Nowadays some youths have to go (to) the country in order to work, others have to study. The ones who are studying will help the economy as much as the ones who are working. Nevertheless, it would not be fair if the one that you sent to be an engineer earned three times more than the one who had to remain working with a tractor in the field. (Landau, 1970: 139)

Lessening the gap between the quality of life in the capital and in the interior. Before the Revolution resources in most fields from education and entertainment to industry were concentrated in Havana which Fidel described as the macrocephalic head of an underdeveloped body. Revolutionary programs have been designed to reduce the rural-urban imbalance. Havana has a drab look reflecting the refusal to repair and to paint the city until the rest of the country progresses. People have been given the inducements of new housing and better food to move to rural areas. New industrial plants have been concentrated in the interior. Entertainers have been required to spend most of their time touring in rural areas. To prevent the further growth of Havana, empty lots have been planted in coffee and other crops. Even though Havana has lost the night time sparkle depicted in (for example) Warren Miller's novel *Flush Times* (1962), it still presents a more clean and orderly appearance than any other capital city in Latin America.

The effort to equalize all wages. The tendency has been to bring down the highest salaries and to raise the lowest ones. The income scales for new employees has been progressively flattened since 1964. However the new starting salary levels were unequal, ranging from about 95 pesos a month to 450 (a ratio of 4.74 to one). People who had been earning high salaries before, such as physicians and technicians continued to do so, but these salaries were divided into two parts, the new lower salary that a person beginning in the job would earn and the "historic" salary to which they had a right from the past. The "historic" salary would disappear when recipients retired, but in the meantime it was hoped that persons would voluntarily give them up once they were assured that the Revolution would care for their needs and those of their families.

A gradual increase in the distribution of free goods and services which minimizes the effect of income disparity. For students on scholarships, which includes most secondary and university students, all necessities plus a cash allowance are provided. For the general public such items as telephones, funerals, sporting events, medical and education costs are free while nominal city bus fares are optional. Milk for children and day-care centers are also provided gratis, as is most housing. The expectation is that basic food and other needs will be progressively added to the free list as their supply permits until people lose the habit of measuring the satisfaction of human needs in monetary terms. The pilot efforts for the achievement of a "cashless" society are the Isle of Youth and the experimental area, San Andrés, in Pinar del Río Province. The Isle of Youth (formerly the Isle of Pines) is a social laboratory where volunteer young people work without pay and receive goods free. They have planted extensive acreage in citrus (more than has been planted in Israel) and undertaken other agricultural development projects. The work has been organized with the objective of creating a new communal life style. The San Andrés area has been colonized by farmers from the Escambray mountains who were involved with counter-revolutionaries and the non-monetary system there is an experiment in rehabilitation.

A continuing campaign against special privileges. Cubans in high positions have special resources such as use of a government automobile and exemption from standing in ration lines under the general justification of their obligation to work harder than others. Those who abused these limited privileges have often been removed from their positions, however. Certain luxuries like meals in fine restaurants and rooms in sumptuous hotels, prestige houses, antiques, and black market purchases are theoretically more available to those with higher earnings. In practice, recreational facilities and housing are apportioned on an equalitarian basis with most of the formerly private mansions having been converted into public facilities such as schools and museums while exclusive resorts are open to all on a waiting list basis. Most people who frequent luxury establishments seem to be people with humble backgrounds. Everyone who is working appears to have more money that he can practically spend on available goods. Available luxury items are perceived by the poor as more accessible than before and by the formerly rich as no longer reserved to them. For example, as appliances such as refrigerators become available, they are distributed to those who have distinguished themselves in production rather than those who have the highest incomes.

A program of voluntary labor which involves all sectors of the society. A member of the Central Committee of the Party assessed the voluntary labor program in these terms:

> For us equality is good economics as much as idealism. The minute we develop an elite in Cuba, voluntary labour is dead. . . Clearly no man is going to cut cane if the Major is at the beach with his wife and a basketful of fried chicken. (Reckord, 1971: 108)

Pervasive efforts to institutionalize the concept of the "New Man" who is motivated by unselfish goals and prefers communal life over privatism. He is characterized as a person committed to serving his community and humanity at large. He is free of sexism, racism, and capitalist acquisitiveness. In the words of Fidel, he is ". . . a man who will aspire to live in true brotherhood with his equals" (Landau, 1970: 142).

The 1971 law against loafing which makes it difficult for a person to live parasitically, receiving the benefits brought to all by the Revolution without himself contributing. Males who do not work or study are now subject to being compelled to accept work or study assignments. Women are exempted.

LIVING CONDITIONS

Few people have experienced so drastic a change in their lives and in their world as have the Cubans because of the Revolution. In a matter of months, Cuba was transformed from one of the most corrupt and sordid of societies into one in which law-abidingness is the norm. The old Havana was a super brothel. Havana today is socially upright. (Interestingly, the demise of the private automobile has made it the only large city in the world free of troublesome air pollution). Those who knew the old

Havana and its way of life find it difficult to believe that they are visiting the same city today. The magnitude of change in Cuba gives one an altered view of the plasticity—of the transformability—of social forms. The hustler ethic of the past has given way to group concerns and to shared goals. The former acceptance of poverty, gangsterism, ignorance, and suffering have been replaced by a general determination to create a just and healthy society.

A 1969 assessment by a former UN official that seventy percent of the Cuban people "lived better than they did before" the Revolution is essentially true, but needs to be qualified (Quoted in Valdés, 1971: 314). Dramatic victories have been won against poverty and disease, yet some conditions of physical need remain stubbornly unchanged despite heroic efforts to improve them. Whereas urban slums have been largely eliminated, a small portion of rural housing, particularly on small private farms, remained essentially in its "miserable" pre-revolutionary state fourteen years later. Although there has been a general betterment in the area of public health and nutrition, the overall food supply has been slow to grow beyond minimally adequate levels.

Public Health. The Revolution's transformation of health care from a "commodity to be sold" to a "biological right" has produced impressive results attested to by the lengthening of life expectancy from fifty-seven years (1945–1960) to sixty-seven years by 1969. (Valdés, 1971: 334) One writer places the figure at sixty-eight (Butler, 1969). New health facilities have been built throughout the island, almost doubling available hospital beds. The total number of physicians has increased despite the flight of more than two thousand to the United States. The number of graduating physicians which was 335 in 1961 reached 923 in 1969. Some diseases, notably malaria and poliomyelitis, have been eliminated. There has been a marked improvement in the availability of potable water, less in the establishment of sewage systems. Two principal shortcomings of the health system are the shortage of medical supplies and health hazards resulting from remaining sub-standard housing. Still, by such indicators as infant mortality, death during childhood, and control of epidemic diseases, Cuba stands at the head of the Latin American states.

One measure of the degree of humanity in a social system is the treatment of the physically disadvantaged and the insane. By this test, Cuba rates the highest marks in Latin America. There are a variety of high-quality educational programs designed specifically for the handicapped. At the psychiatric hospital near Havana patients are given warm and sympathetic attention (Somers, 1969: 942).

Nutrition. The marked improvement in the nutrition of the Cuban people which the Revolution has brought has not resulted from an increased food supply, but rather from an equitable system of food distribution. Before 1959 more than one-third of the population suffered from malnutrition, and yet a large portion of food was imported. Only four out of one hundred families could eat meat regularly; only two could have eggs. Malnutrition has been overcome through rationing, but the average food allotments are still less than satisfactory to a population which aspires to eat like the upper-middle class before the Revolution. Meat rations during the late 1960's hovered around a weekly ration of three-fourths of a pound per person, fish became increasingly available as an alternative protein source. Much of the diet was made up of starchy items such as rice, plaintain bananas, and a malt soft drink. Milk was almost completely reserved for children. Most aggravating was the bother of having to spend hours in line at food and clothing stores, only to find out sometimes that the awaited item was sold out. Compensating for this are first, that many people (one-fourth of the population) are served free meals in schools, agricultural encampments and factories; second, that most people can afford to supplement their ration allowances by buying meals in restaurants; and third, that extra rations are distributed to persons doing the hardest kinds of work—miners, for example.

Athletics. The improved physical condition of Cubans is one reason why the country has become a leader in the field of sports. International awareness of Cuba's emergence as a major competitor in athletics came suddenly as a result of Cuba's performance at the Pan American Games held in Cali, Colombia in August 1971. While the United States won 218 medals at Cali, Cuba won a surprising total of 105, the next highest number won by a Latin American country being Mexico with 41. Moreover, among the numerous sports in which Cuba defeated the United States were such traditional U. S. favorites as baseball, basketball, and volleyball. A few days later at an Olympic elimination meet in Havana, Cuba again defeated the United States in volleyball.

Castro claimed the Cali victories for all Latin Americans whom the "imperialists have tried to humiliate; have tried to give . . . a feeling of inferiority." (Castro, 1971b: 3). He added, "We don't have the slightest doubt that with the passing of time, all the Latin American countries will have the same conditions that Cuba has today for sports."

Underlying Cuba's upsurge in sports has been a general upgrading of the vigor of the population. Person-for-person they are probably as physically fit as any people on earth. Most of the Cuban population receive regular exercise. The overwhelming majority perform physical tasks in one or more of the following ways: participating in voluntary labor, walking night guard in their neighborhoods as a member of the CDR, serving in the militia, and/or taking part in athletics. There are approximately one million athletes out of a total population of eight million (*Visión*, August 28, 1971: 30). All are amateurs who have other employment.

Castro allowed that coaches and trainers from "sister socialist nations" had played an important role in developing Cuban athletics, ". . . something we're very happy about and very grateful about." He rejected, however, the charge Cuba was using sports as an instrument of politics.

> Really, it's just the other way around—politics is an instrument of sports. That is, sport is not a means but rather an end, like every other human activity . . . that has to do with man's well-being just as education, health, material living conditions, human dignity, feeling and man's spiritual values are all the objectives of politics. (Castro, 1971b: 4.)

At the 1972 Olympic Games in Munich Cubans won 22 medals, more than any Third World country in history.

Housing. Despite the virtual eradication of urban slums and the provision of new housing for persons joining collective farms, the rate of construction of dwellings has been falling behind the overall demand. Perhaps one-half of all dwellings are in need of improvement or replacement. In Havana, before 1971, housing was deliberately not provided in the hopes of encouraging people to move to rural areas where there were chronic labor shortages. To meet the critical housing shortage the government launched a program in Havana in 1971 under which workers formed brigades to build their own homes after regular working hours with materials provided by the state. By 1970 more than half of all homes used electric power (Valdés, 1971: 320).

Consumer Goods. Consumer items are scarce in Cuba, scarce for everyone. A whole range of products which some people take for granted elsewhere, like sunglasses and facial tissues, are hardly available. Private automobiles and even motor scooters are rare and parts must be improvised. Although the clothing rations are meager—two pairs of pants and two pairs of shoes per year—one seldom sees patched garments, and all children seem to have shoes. Almost all essential items are rationed and durable goods like appliances have virtually disappeared from the legitimate market. A black market flourished, partly composed of improvised items such as wooden-soled shoes, the production of which is not actively suppressed.

Private Farmers. The living conditions for the small farmers have improved dramatically, although they are still not completely integrated into the collectivist revolutionary economic system. These improvements included increasing the farmers share of the value of his products by eliminating the middle man, providing unlimited educational and career possibilities for his children, constructing new roads, hospitals, and schools, and making interest-free loans readily available with provisions for canceling repayment in case of drought or other difficulties. Rich farmers have disappeared, but the

> removal of . . . bottlenecks had multiplied the income of peasants from the sale of their crops by more than ten times, an increase which, given the shortage of goods outside the region, is currently absorbed by prestige items produced within the local economy. (NUC, Spalding, 1969: 30)

While small farmers usually supported the government because it improved their general situation, they frequently did not identify with the Revolution. Those who moved away from rural areas were more likely to take on revolutionary attitudes.

Two brothers in a small-farming family in the Sierra Cristal illustrate the divergence of views on this issue. The older one, Jorge, had his own farm while the younger one worked in construction projects. When the younger brother stated that his whole family was working for the Revolution, his farmer brother disagreed.

> I am not working for the Revolution," he argued, "I work the land for myself. The government takes what I sell it, but the land is mine, and the goods I produce on it are my own." His brother demurred, "But if the government asked you to give it your lands, you would." "No," Jorge answered. "I would not give it the land unless I wanted to. (NUC, Spalding, 1969: 31)

Crime Control. The incidence of crime has dramatically decreased since the Revolution. Total crimes recorded in 1960 were 198,107. By 1968 the number had fallen to 96,693. The murder rate dropped from 3.37 per 100,000 inhabitants in 1960 to 1.14 in 1967. Comparable figures for the United States were 4.98 in 1960 and 6.38 in 1967 (*Granma Weekly Review,* May 11, 1969).

There are few police organizations in Cuba: the traffic police; the *Departamento de Orden Pública* which deals with minor crimes such as are handled by the Popular Tribunals; the *Departamento Técnico de Investigaciones* which handles major crimes such as those handled by the Audiencias; and the *Departamento de Seguridad del Estado* which handles domestic and foreign espionage, its cases falling under the jurisdiction of the Revolutionary Tribunals.

Almost all prisoners in Cuba have been given rehabilitation programs. There is still a large number of persons being held for strictly political reasons. Castro admitted in 1965 that there were then twenty thousand political prisoners. The hope of the government is that re-educational programs will eventually lead to their acceptance of the new society. Prison conditions have apparently been steadily improving since the Revolution.

WOMEN

One of the most arresting features of life in the new Cuba is the changing relationship of men and women.

> Pre-revolutionary Cuba assigned three roles to women: man's slave in the home, mother and pleasure object. Life was simple, in a sense. Middle-class girls, after a due amount of chaperoned dating, were turned over by their daddies to husbands—with hymen intact or the deal was off. From then on, life meant four walls and the double standard. (Sutherland, 1969: 171)

Although Ana Betancourt, a champion of women's rights, had distinguished herself among Cuban patriots during the War with Spain, and although Cuban women had won the vote in 1934, ahead of most of Latin America, Cuban women were only in the first stages of emancipation by the time of the Revolution. They were generally assumed to have profoundly different needs and interests than men. Most private secondary schools were sex-segregated, and, as in many societies, at social functions it was common for men and women to form in separate groups as if the sexes had little in common to discuss. Lower-class women had few occupations open to them and were frequently forced into prostitution.

The fact that a drastic change in the status of women has occurred since 1959 is attributable in good measure to the strategic role women played in the revolutionary struggle. Melba Hernández and Haydée Santamaría and four other women took part in the Moncada assault. As the Revolution developed they were joined by many nurses, teachers, organizers and others, some of whom formed a rebel army unit of women combatants. Among the most influential female figures were Vilma Espín who after the triumph of the Revolution became the wife of Raúl Castro and later head of the Federation of Cuban Women (FMC), Celia Sánchez, Fidel's *confidante* characterized by Robert Taber as Fidel's "chief advisor" (Taber, 1961: 91); Haydée Santamaría, wife of Organizing Secretary of the Communist Party Armando Hart, and later president of the influential cultural institute Casa de las Americas; Nora Frómeta, Minister of Light Industries; Elena Gil, secretary to Osvaldo Dorticós and head of the Women's Educational Improvement Plan of the FMC; and

Elena Serra, member of the Central Committee of the Party and director of day nurseries.

These women in particular, operating as part of the key revolutionary leadership, succeeded in making educational and vocational equality for women basic goals of the revolutionary program. They also were responsible for making the child day care center an established feature of Cuban life. The Cuban press contains many stories about the accomplishments of women. For example, *Granma* of February 9, 1969, announces the country's first woman pilot while another article describes an all-woman radio station. The March 30, 1967 issue acknowledges the achievement of a female architect who designed the community of Congre and the May 10 number of 1967 notes the appointment of a 23-year-old woman as the director of a new school.

Policies which have promoted career advancement for women include the selection of women for university training (50 percent of the students in several university schools, including medicine, are women) and appointment of women to administer nationalized companies. When medium and large-sized retail shoe, clothing and hardware businesses were nationalized, the Ministry of Domestic Commerce was directed to select women as administrators of those businesses. Some four thousand administrators were named, and 90 percent . . . [were women]" (Castro, 1963: 4). Similarly when petty commerce was nationalized in 1969 most businesses were taken over by women administrators. Moreover, "Any available job that can be performed by either men or women must be given to a woman if she applies" (Jenness, 1970: 10). Between 1964 and 1970 the number of women in the labor force doubled, approaching a total of six hundred thousand (Purcell, 1971: 15).

Yet legal equality, the availability of contraceptive devices, government-provided inns where unmarried couples can rent rooms by the hour, the easing of divorce, the ending of prostitution and the rehabilitation of prostitutes, the establishment of day care centers, and the appearance of new work and educational opportunities only partially ended the oppression of women. Pre-revolutionary attitudes about women persisted. For example, "Cubans merely smile in disbelief at the idea that men might also have a role in childcare." *Machismo* attitudes among men stubbornly survived. "Cuban women carry guns; . . . but when [they] . . . come home from guard duty, they are expected to cook dinner for their husbands." For Elizabeth Diggs, this contradiction "brings home one of the truisms of women's liberation, that socialism is a necessary but not a sufficient requirement for the equality of women." Ms. Diggs asks about Cuba: "In a society that deplores the idea of exclusive property, why should one person have exclusive rights to the body, time or loyalty of another person?" (NUC, Diggs, 1969: 24–27) The justification given by one Cuban for moving slowly against old sexual attitudes was ". . . too much open encouragement of sexual liberty could make tremendous propaganda for the counter-revolutionaries. Also it would disturb many parents" (Sutherland, 1969: 184).

The image of romantic love portrayed in bourgeois magazines, love which "envelopes two people in a kind of private mist," lives on. However, gradually emerging is a concept of a love which grows out of shared struggle, which does not separate lovers from society, and which is more honest and realistic (Camarano, 1971: 54). Three generations of women were depicted in the Cuban film *Lucía* with the post-revolutionary woman depicted as still having to battle her husband's male chauvinism although he was clearly integrated in the Revolution as a worker. However, while women still have to endure rude stares on the street, openly insulting behavior by men toward women is much less accepted than it used to be, and the Popular Tribunals prosecute men for wife-beating even if the wife withdraws the charge. The political and economic battle for women's rights had largely triumphed; the cultural struggle continued.

RACE

As it still is in all of Latin America, racism was a partially hidden problem in Cuba before the Revolution. Cubans did not in the past want to admit to racist attitudes nor to alter "approved role relations between the races" (Fox, 1971: 22). The Revolution brought racism into the open where it could be examined and attacked. It has proved to be a durable phenomenon, but its material base has been destroyed and the beginning of its ending is underway.

With the virtual extinction of the Cuban Indians and their replacement by African slaves, racism was almost exclusively a black-white issue. Although official figures list less than one-third of the Cubans as black or mulatto, perhaps one-half of the population actually has some "African blood." Unlike the U. S. practice, people are considered "white" with a slight African mixture, and a real social distinction was made between "black" and "mulatto." The system of inter-race relationships that developed in Cuba was in many ways not as harsh as that in the United States. After Independence, whether or not Cubans received elementary education was more a function of place of residence (proximity to cities) rather than race. By 1943 there were 424 black doctors, 560 lawyers, and 3,500 teachers. Yet blacks as a group were clearly on the bottom of the social-economic scale. They did the most undesirable work and were paid the least.

Insofar as Jim Crow-type segregation came to the island, it was mostly as an import from the United States. Spain had not been as racist as the United States which replaced it in the "role of external white mother country" (Sutherland, 1969: 157). Though blacks like Antonio Maceo had played a conspicuous part in the long independence struggle, under U. S. military occupation blacks were prohibited from joining the Havana police force. U. S. businessmen, diplomats, and military men gradually introduced a number of racist practices including segregated beaches, hotels, restaurants, and clubs. The country's more luxurious recreational facilities were effectively "off-limits" to the discernibly black Cuban, a situation that persisted until the Revolution. U. S. companies generally discriminated in their hiring practices, particularly for supervisory personnel, and racism may have been on the increase by 1958.

Cuban blacks as a group did not rally to Castro before 1959 although numerous volunteers were black. "He appeared just another middle-class white radical, with nothing to say to them" (Thomas, 1971: 1122). Three basic explanations are: first, Cuban blacks had their *own* radical tradition of slave revolts and later of providing most of the leadership of the Communist Party. Some black Communist intellectuals had advocated the establishment of an independent black state in Oriente Province in the 1930's. The most famous black Communist intellectual, Nicolás Guillén, was also the most famous poet in Cuba. Second, blacks did not at first rally to Castro because Batista played very effectively upon his own mulatto-Chinese-mestizo racial make-up in appealing to blacks whom he placed in large numbers in his army and police. Third, during the revolutionary struggle Fidel did not make an issue of race. "To read *History will absolve me* would suggest that Castro was addressing a racially homogeneous nation" (Thomas, 1971: 1121).

The Revolution has succeeded in eliminating discrimination in employment and public facilities and in affording equality of education and vocational opportunities for blacks, but many forms of cultural racism have persisted. Blacks have been underrepresented in revolutionary posters, films, and magazines. For example, "In a summer, 1967, issue of *Mujeres*, Cuba's magazine for women, not a single dark face appeared among the forty-eight pages of fashion photographs and drawings" (Sutherland, 1969: 141). Beauty contests (a sexist event at best) continued to reinforce beauty standards which demeaned blacks, and hair-straightening and greater delight in lighter-colored children even among siblings continued to weaken the self-image of blacks. Blacks have noted their disproportionately low representation at the higher levels of responsibility. The government's response has been that this condition reflects past inequities and will be overcome as blacks benefit from the increased opportunities made possible by the Revolution. Black intellectuals have sometimes felt that the Revolution does not give enough attention to the study and propogation of Afro-Cuban culture despite the centers which have been opened for that purpose and despite the government's lifting of the long-standing ban on Afro-Cuban religious ceremonies. The nature of this resentment is suggested by the complaint of a black artist "The ballet is culture, but we are folklore" (Sutherland, 1969: 151). Yet a national puppet theater is based on Afro-Cuban culture, and modern dance has also exalted Afro-Cuban culture. Young revolutionary writers like Miguel Barnet (1968) have continued the tradition of Cuban anthropologist Fernando Ortiz in exploring the black experience.

It is doubtlessly true that the government has not looked favorably upon the emergence of a black cultural nationalism movement and while women have an important national organization, black people do not.

> Why should the Revolution encourage or support movements, the leadership asks, that tend to refragment the population into racial groups when the very purpose of the revolutionary effort is to forge a new Cuban identity . . . above distinctions of race, class, and region? (Fagen, 1970: 22)

The relationship between the U. S. black movement and the Cuban Revolution has often been an uneasy one. Widespread coverage and support of the black struggle in the United States has been given in Cuba. Yet the revolutionary leadership resents discussions by U. S. blacks of post-revolutionary Cuban society in racial terms. Although they denounce racism in the United States, their eyebrows were raised by the racial references made by Stokley Carmichael during his much publicized visit in 1967. They would have preferred him to use class analysis rather than what James Forman has called "skin analysis."

Other U. S. black leaders like Robert Williams and Eldrige Cleaver have had troubled relations with Cuba. After taking asylum in Cuba, Williams left Cuba for China, complaining about Cuban racism. Cleaver had what Lockwood describes as a confusing and difficult time in Cuba before he left for Algeria (Lockwood, 1970a: 11–24). One Cuban explanation is that some U. S. blacks have a vision of liberation which essentially means gaining their share of the material advantages enjoyed by affluent whites in the United States and that they are therefore put off by the sweaty, spartan demands of a Cuban-style forced march for general development. Some U. S. blacks encountered surviving racist attitudes about social and sexual mores. One U. S. black, John Clytus, who spent a considerable time in Cuba concluded in his book *Black Man in Red Cuba* (1970) that Cuba was a "racist hole." This book not only reveals how incompatible the bourgeois values of one U. S. black were with those of the Cuban Revolution, but also the loneliness of an American discovering that the Afro-Cubans are not "soul brothers," but rather the possessors of their own distinct culture. Despite some frictions between U.S. blacks and Cubans, the Revolution has embraced Angela Davis as a major hero figure and Ms. Davis is probably the North American most widely admired in Cuba.

One educated estimate has it that if measured by its arts, "Cuba was over half Negro" (Thomas, 1971: 1123). The fact that all Cubans did to a remarkable degree share in an integrated culture was one reason why there has been such reluctance to acknowledge the existence of racial prejudice and racial oppression. The Revolution's having raised the issue has caused considerable stress and embarrassment for both blacks and whites. A revealing study of Cuban exiles concluded that "Most whites and almost all the blacks and mulattoes in the sample [of exiles in the U. S.] were unprepared [psychologically] for the drastic changes [the Revolution brought] in approved role relations between the races, and found themselves unable or unwilling to live up to the new expectations" (Fox, 1971: 22). Whites were outraged at equal or pro-black hiring practices, labeling them "discriminating" (against whites). Attitudes that black people were inherently less competent were deeply ingrained and totally unconscious. It was not uncommon for blacks who had taken solace in the fact that their blackness was politely ignored to complain that now they felt uncomfortable when people insisted on noticing their blackness. When older people had internalized their blackness as something negative, it is no wonder that they resented the Revolution for making it something they could no longer ignore.

In Cuba some blacks complain because there is no black liberation movement to liberate blacks psychologically. But there is good reason to believe that among younger Cubans racism is rapidly receding. Among nearly everyone the use of the Cuban equivalent of "nigger" has disappeared.

ARTISTIC CULTURE

Perhaps the most sensitive, confusing, and elusive aspect of the Revolution is its relationship with artists and intellectuals. The quantity and quality of artistic expression in Cuba is impressive and René Dumont even complained that too much was being expended on art education, characterizing it sarcastically as "folklore dances . . . in front of a bare cupboard" (Dumont, 1970b: 126).

THE GOVERNMENT AND THE ARTS

The CUBANACAN national art school, a secondary boarding school, has educated students from all kinds of backgrounds from all over the island and will in the future train actors, dancers and students of painting and the plastic arts. There are a variety of organizations which encourage writing and artistic activity, including the Union of Writers and Artists (UNEAC), the National Book Institute, and the internationally-oriented *Casa de las Americas*. The latter, headed by Haydée Santamaría, is respected throughout Latin America for its magazine *Casa* and its prizes in the fields of the novel, short story, poetry, theater, and essay. By the end of the first revolutionary decade, more novels and short stories had been published in Cuba than during the preceding quarter of a century. It is relatively easy for unknown writers to get their works published, even though most of the resources of the Book Institute must be allocated to printing textbooks and technical books (in 1968 about one-eighth of all books published were literary titles). Literary periodicals include *Unión* and *Gaceta* put out by the UNEAC, *Casa,* and the literary journals of the three universities.

There is a vastly expanded audience for literature as a result of the increase in the general education level, politicization of people, and the absence of other uses for cash. The Cubans have become one of the most book-reading people in the world. The publication of books has increased enormously with the Revolution. Before 1959, approximately one million volumes were published in Cuba annually. By 1971 the number exceeded twelve million and officials in the publishing industry estimated that the potential demand for books was about sixty million volumes per year. In any case almost all new books disappeared from store shelves in a matter of a few weeks. The range of imported titles available in Cuba was somewhat broader than those published in other Socialist countries and included such heretical (for the USSR) writings as Kafka and Isaac Deutscher's study of Trotsky. However, the choice of titles inevitable became narrower after 1964, partly because of the scarcity of resources and the need for textbooks, but also because of the constriction of the acceptable area of public discussion.

Important changes took place in the relationship between the artist and society. After the Revolution, culture was made available to all, the revolutionary artist had less need to be alienated from society. "Many artists, when asked what difference the Revolution has made to them personally, said, in effect: 'now we feel needed, as artists and as people'" (NUC, Taylor, 1969: 42). The Revolution aims to break down the class barriers which isolated the old artistic elite. One aspect of this was the "deprofessionalization" of the artist—royalties, profits, and special payment for works of art were eliminated, so that artists receive salaries for work such as teaching or administering in the various government cultural institutes.

Filmmakers work for the Cuban Cinema Institute (ICAIC) which has produced some internationally acclaimed films like *The Death of a Bureaucrat* and *Lucía*. The National Council of Culture maintains twenty-nine professional theater groups (whereas there were only nine in 1959). There are also a number of amateur theater groups which can be found in small towns, schools, and factories. In line with the attempt to equalize country and city, the best artistic performances are made available all over the island including rural labor encampments, with the result that Havana sometimes seems culturally drained.

There are also programs which experiment in making art more meaningful to the majority of the population to whom art was formerly a distant and irrelevant elite exercise. These programs use art to help people better understand and solve social problems. A Havana theatre group went to the Escambray mountain region where they helped people express their immediate local problems through drama, fostering the writing of plays and the formation of drama groups. The *Joven* Theater is made up of a drama group which graduated from CUBANACAN and received a contract as a professional group after completing their two years of "social service." It has used drama to examine the problem of why, ten years after the Revolution, fifteen thousand Cubans still participate in the Sanhazaro religious pilgrimage, traveling on hands and knees, dragging chains long distances, and seeking favors from a saint. The actors concluded that the archaic practices resulted from alienation, which the artists' work could help overcome.

Classical cultural forms also receive extraordinary support and dissemination. The Cuban National Ballet, under the direction of the Cuban Alicia Alonzo who was a leading ballerina in New York City before the Revolution, has reached the pinnacles of artistic perfection according to the rigorous critical standards of French, Soviet, Canadian, and U. S. ballet critics. Miss Alonzo, who is blind, is considered by some to be the world's leading ballerina. The U. S. critics had to travel to Canada to see the Cuban ballet company which has not been allowed to enter the United States.

Cuban groups have done extraordinary experimentation in modern dance, for instance incorporating Afro-Cuban rhythms and the typical posture and walking style of the Afro-Cuban. The National Puppet Theater based in Santiago, working with giant puppets to present Afro-Cuban folk tales and legends, has received international praise.

Poster art has reached a high level; posters stare down at Cubans from everywhere in mod styles exhorting them to emulate Ché, volunteer for work, and raise their level of consciousness.

A surprising amount of U. S. low-grade "popular culture" survives in

Cuba and is taken for granted by Cubans, including old movies on television and old musak tapes played in hotels and even wafting over sugar cane fields. Nevertheless, with all the difficulties in the cultural field, Cuba is developing a new national culture, in contrast to the rest of Latin America (including Mexico where the 1910 Revolution brought a temporary cultural renaissance) where as a part of dependency, what is left of national culture is increasingly giving way to U. S. and European commercial and artistic styles.

CUBAN WRITERS: FOUR "GENERATIONS"

Cuba has a strong literary tradition founded on the towering figure of José Martí, who, besides his role as a revolutionary political figure, was one of the greatest Latin American poets and prose writers, innovating both in content and form. "Beginning with José Martí, and since Cuba became a nation, a search to define 'Cuba's culture' has been going on; the search has always been involved with political struggle and with the relationship of the indigenous Afro-Cuban 'subculture' to the rest of the country" (Salper, 1970: 20).

Writers in Cuba today have been divided into four generations. The first generation began writing around 1925 at the time when the Communist Party was founded and included such Marxists as the novelist Alejo Carpentier (cultural attaché in Paris) and poet Nicholás Guillén (President of UNEAC). Guillén, himself black, wrote "Afro-Cuban poetry." The second generation which began writing in the 1940's included José Lezama Lima who still lives and writes in Havana. It was characterized by "a search for literary refuge in subjectivity and private sensibilities." Few of the third generation which has been called the "generation of the Revolution" participated

in the voluntary struggle . . . : most of them were abroad studying. In pre-revolutionary Cuba, as in much of Latin America today, sons and daughters of the upper-middle class went to European and North American schools. In terms of Cuban cultural consciousness, this resulted in a continual lack of national self-esteem, and a cultural snobbism vis-a-vis Europe and the States: the best way to be recognized in Cuba was to have first been hailed in a foreign country. (Salper, 1970: 21–22)

The most prominent of this generation are Lizandro Otero, a novelist who returned from Paris in 1956 to fight for three years with the Revolution and seems to have completely identified himself with the Revolution; Edmundo Desnoyes, a novelist who returned from the U. S. several years after the Revolution took power and was made head of the National Book Institute; and the poet Heberto Padilla. Desnoyes and Padilla seem to

have begun from a similar existentialist viewpoint. However, when Desnoyes, in *Inconsolable Memories,* (1967) treated middle-class (including
his own) dissatisfaction with and alienation from the Revolution as a
psychological and social problem reflecting negatively on the alienated
person, it was not a criticism of the Revolution. Padilla, on the other
hand, behaved and wrote as if it were the intellectual's responsibility to
be totally dedicated to the Revolution, a duty which included criticizing
openly the Revolution's limitations, such as insensitve bureaucracy, waste,
and privileges granted to revolutionary leaders. His objective was to
strengthen the Revolution, but as economic difficulties mounted and discontent increased, Padilla's opponents in Cuba began to consider his
approach counter-revolutionary.

The fourth or "post-revolutionary" generation, born around 1940 or
later and including the novelist Miguel Bovet, is primarily concerned
with a new cultural consciousness, the creation of the "new man," but
they are continuing a Cuban tradition by investigating Cuba's African
heritage.

THE GOVERNMENT AND FREEDOM
OF ARTISTIC EXPRESSION

The changes in the leadership's attitudes and policies toward writers and
artists reflect the same influences, attitudes, and tensions which have
affected policy in other fields. Factors operating against freedom of expression, even for those who support the Revolution, include: 1) the
difficulties of building socialism in the face of the U. S. blockade and continued overt attacks on the Revolution, 2) the distortions of society as a
result of the experience of underdevelopment, 3) the failures to meet
goals set by the leadership followed by a sense of desperation and a weakening of morale, 4) the dependence, both political and economic, on the
Soviet Union, 5) the need to centralize initiative and decision making
during the transition to moral incentives, 6) the way in which the ebb
and flow of revolutionary forces outside of Cuba affects the leadership's
optimism and ability to take chances, 7) the heritage of a Stalinist attitude
toward art in the minds of former PSP leaders, 8) the theoretical eclectic
empiricism of the non-PSP revolutionary leadership which has fostered
experimentation, but has also led to a tendency to capitulate to Stalinist
attitudes when times are difficult, 9) the failure carefully to analyze the
earlier experience of other socialist countries, 10) the bourgeois background and existentialist cultural alienation of Cubans who qualified as
artistic intellectuals at the time the Revolution took power, 11) the inex-
perience and insecurity of government officials in the cultural field and
the gap between their cultural experience and attitudes (toward, for ex-

ample, abstract expressionism and homosexuality) and those of the artists with whom they were dealing, 12) the impatience of guerrilla leaders with people who are primarily artists, and 13) the lack of agreement between artistic intellectuals and the revolutionary leadership concerning the function of artists in a revolutionary society.

The first policy toward artistic expression between 1959 and 1962 was an uncritical acceptance and support for the artistic production of the first three generations (the fourth had not yet begun to produce). Mainly the third generation of U. S. and European-oriented artists and writers dominated the scene through the weekly cultural supplement *Lunes de Revolución.* They tended toward abstract expressionism, existentialism, and generally *avant-garde* modes of expression in literature and painting. As the PSP members were integrated into the revolutionary leadership some of them, supported by bureaucratic-minded latter-day revolutionaries and people with understandable prejudices against art that was not readily comprehensible to uneducated people pressured for first, the suppression of abstract expressionism, existentialism and *avant-garde* ideas for being decadent and bourgeois and perhaps even degenerate; and second, the official adoption of socialist-realist models for art.

As the old PSP was remolded under the pressure of the Revolution, some Communist intellectuals came out in favor of maximum freedom of expression including the poet Nicolás Guillén. Castro responded by saying that within the Revolution anything was permitted and in June 1961 spoke of

> The artist or intellectual who does not have a revolutionary attitude toward life, but yet is an honest person. . . The Revolution has to understand this reality and therefore it must act in such a way that this sector of artists and intellectuals who are not true revolutionaries find a place to work and create within the Revolution, and so that their creative spirit, even when they aren't revolutionary writers or artists may have the opportunity and liberty to express itself within the Revolution. This means that within the Revolution everything is permitted; against [or outside] it, nothing. (Castro, quoted in Salper, 1970: 19)

At this time there were controversies over specific films and books which were viewed as insufficiently revolutionary or too critical of aspects of the Revolution, but these disputes were generally resolved without resort to total censorship, although the work in question sometimes did not receive distribution.

Later in 1961, *Lunes de Revolución* ceased publication, which was understood as a lessening of influence of the *avant-garde* group. This was a result of several pressures including the growing scarcity of resources, the increase in the power of PSP members of the government, and the war-footing necessitated by U. S. and counter-revolutionary pressures. After Fidel's appeal in 1962 that he Revolution be a "school of unfettered thought" and the denunciation of sectarianism, there was again a greater sense of freedom for writers until 1968. Except when some controversy forced them to deal with what they must have felt was an annoying diversion from the main problems of the Revolution, Fidel and other top revolutionary leaders generally left cultural matters to less important officials not distinguished by their courage and imagination. Cuban artists and writers for the most part avoided or resisted pressures to institute "Socialist realism." Almost every aspect of *avant-garde* art found its expression in Cuban painting, theater, cinema, and writing.

The intellectuals of the third generation had a difficult time figuring out how to relate to the Revolution. Their condition was defined by Ernest Mandel:

> the intellectuals, as a social group, necessarily occupy an ambiguous position. Attracted by the ideals of justice and rationality embodied in the cause of the socialist revolution, the inevitable sacrifices, the continuous efforts, and the "leveling egalitarianism" implied in that same revolution make them pull back. The spirit flies to the aid of the oppressed while the flesh, which is weaker, settles for the not-unimportant material advantages that contemporary capitalist society provides for them. (Mandel, 1970: 801)

Ché Guevara tended to write off the third generation by saying,

> . . . the fault of our artists and intellectuals lies in their original sin: They are not truly revolutionary. . . New generations will come who will be free of the original sin. The probabilities that great artists will appear will be greater to the degree that the field of culture [is] broadened, . . . revolutionaries [are] coming who will sing the song of the new man in the true voice of the people. This is a process which requires time. (Guevara, 1968a: 134)

Leon Trotsky, whose writings on art were printed in *Lunes de Revolución,* wrote in *Literature and Revolution* that the proletariat from their limited cultural experience could not be expected to come up with a full-blown culture and, in the space before a new culture arose after a revolution, the best artistic expression of what was happening in the revolution would come from bourgeois intellectuals who were steeped in artistic tradition. Their distance from the revolution combined with their ability at expression would enable them to best depict the revolution, and, for both artistic and political reasons, they should not be suppressed or forced to become uncritical revolutionaries. Politically they represented even at their most critical, no threat to the revolution, and in fact their freedom would be eloquent testimony that socialist revolution brought more rather than less personal freedom (Trotsky, 1970: 29–62). Hungarian Communist literary critic George Lukács observed after World War II that in a newly established socialist society, critical realism has value in articulating the complexities of the transitional process and in exploring the reaction of those unintegrated into the revolution.

In 1965, during the campaign against homosexuals, many writers and artists were sent to the UMAP detention camps, some just because of their "weird" appearance. The UNEAC reacted by strongly protesting the UMAPS and Castro responded finally by abolishing them. Nevertheless this experience left a serious resentment against those in the government who had established the UMAPS. In 1965 Castro maintained that "I especially am a partisan of the widest possible discussion in the intellectual realm . . . I believe that ideas must be able to defend themselves. I am opposed to the blacklist of books, prohibited films, and all such things" (Lockwood, 1969: 127).

THE PADILLA AFFAIR

In 1968, coinciding with the Revolutionary Offensive, Heberto Padilla won the national poetry prize for a controversial book of poems. Some of the leading figures in the army leadership felt that certain of the poet's allusions were counter-revolutionary and Communist Party officials put pressure on the UNEAC to withdraw the prize. The jury, made up of foreigners and Cubans, refused to change their decision, and Padilla's book was published with a critical introduction by the UNEAC described by critic José Yglesias as "impervious to literary irony, dead to poetry, and quick to quote out of context lines that any readers could see were pro-revolutionary." Yglesias says of articles against Padilla that appeared in the army weekly *Verde Olivo* "It is interesting that although [they] were highly charged with the usual arguments about ivory tower aesthetes . . . the main object of their attack was Padilla, whose work is deeply concerned with the experience of living in a revolution." The jury obviously agreed with Yglesias, and politically supported Padilla in saying,

> The strength of this book, and what gives it its revolutionary significance, lies precisely in the fact that it is not apologetic but critical, polemical, and is connected in its essence to the idea that the revolution is the only possible solution for the problems that obsess its author, . . . (Quoted in Yglesias, 1971: 6)

Padilla lost his job and was without one for more than a year. Finally he appealed directly to Fidel, and was given a teaching job at the University of Havana. Students responded warmly to Padilla as a critic within the Revolution, but the economic crises got worse. In 1971 Padilla was jailed for about five weeks, charged with purveying counter-revolutionary attitudes and associating with anti-revolutionary foreigners.

Leo Huberman and Paul Sweezy observed in 1968 that the economic difficulties and the hard conditions of life, exacerbated by unfulfilled optimistic predictions and promises by the leadership, have resulted in a tendency to lose faith and an erosion of the "ties that bind the masses to their paternalistic leadership." The leadership reasons that the erosion is localized "principally among the intellectuals and professionals. . . It apparently draws the conclusion that the first necessity is to shut these people up before they infect the rest of the population." (Huberman and Sweezy, 1969: 218) These observations proved prophetic. Padilla's arrest took place after the publication of critical books on Cuba written by liberal and leftist European authors: *Cuba, est-il socialiste?* by René Dumont (1970a), *Guerillas in Power* by K. S. Karol (1970), and *Cuba* by Hugh Thomas (1971). All three authors had been granted considerable *entrée* and hospitality by the Cuban government and Dumont, in addition, had served as an influential agricultural advisor on the island.

Englishman Thomas' massive history contained a detailed haughty and almost irrelevant interpretation of the Revolution. Exemplifying his distracted analysis is the interjection while discussing the Revolution's goals "that private ease and entertainment are worth more than all the creeds in the world" (Thomas, 1971: 1430). An interesting observation, but whatever does it have to do with solving the critical development problems of the Third World?

French agronomist Dumont's attribution of the Revolution's shortcomings to the absence of bookkeeping, careful planning, and the excessive interference by Fidel was followed by Polish-French socialist K. S. Karol's indictment of Castro for failing to create a structure of government responsive to the mass and for devitalizing discussion of public issues. Dumont, a cranky cataloguer of everything that went wrong, never seriously analysed the causes of failure. Dumont's and Karol's criticism were especially resented because they were voiced by committed socialists, although with very different viewpoints. Padilla and some other Cuban intellectuals were scored for having reinforced the critical conclusions of Dumont, Karol, and other foreign critics.

Padilla's release from confinement came after he signed a confession, and he then engaged in an hour and a half self-criticism before other writers at a UNEAC meeting. During this spoken confession he denounced several of his fellow writers and they in turn gave self-criticisms. The theme of Padilla's criticism was that he had been objectively counter-revolutionary because of his desire for world literary fame; that he had played the role of persecuted revolutionary critic, magnifying the problems out of proportion and making them public instead of confiding them to the government; and that he generally maintained an egoistic and alienated perspective. Specifically he castigated himself for feeding foreign intellectuals' desire for criticism and being their main source. In the early press version of the written confession Karol and Dumont are identified as CIA agents.

Sixty prominent intellectuals, mostly from Europe and Latin America, all of whom had supported the Revolution in its most difficult periods, appealed to Castro over the Padilla affair not to Stalinize the Revolution. The list included Jean-Paul Sartre, Simone de Beauvoir, most of Latin America's leading novelists, and the Cuban former editor of the newspaper *Revolución* Carlos Franqui who was then in Rome. It then appeared that Castro himself had ordered Padilla's arrest and he responded to the protest (which was not published in Cuba) with scorn:

> You must be raving mad, . . . to think that . . . the problems of this country can be the problems of two or three sheep that have gone astray, that may have some problems with the Revolution because they are not given the right to continue with their poison, their plots and intrigue against the Revolution. . . . Our problems are the problems of underdevelopment and how we can overcome the backwardness in which we were left by you, the exploiters, imperialists, and colonialists; . . . In order for anybody to again win an award, whether national or international, he must be a true revolutionary. (Castro, 1971a: 557–58)

The resolutions of the 1971 Congress on Education and Culture, at which Castro spoke, also attacked the intellectual protesters:

> Those who, with the 'lordlike arrogance' of past days . . . arrogate to themselves the role of exclusive critics while abandoning the scene of the struggle and using our Latin American peoples as themes for their literary creations thereby becoming favorites in bourgeois circles . . . cannot appoint themselves judges of revolutions. . . In Paris, London, Rome, West Berlin and New York these hypocrites find the best terrain for their ambiguities, vacillation and misery generated by the cultural colonialism which they accept and support. All they will receive from the revolutionary peoples is the contempt which the traitor and the deserter merits. (*Intercontinental Press,* June 7, 1971: 535)

These were the same intellectuals Castro had warmly praised at the cultural congress in early 1968 when he contrasted their loyalty to Cuba to Soviet support which he implied was more grudgingly given. In 1971 he seemed to have completely reversed his stand on artistic freedom.

> Sometimes certain books have been printed. The number is not important. As a matter of principle there are certain books of which not a single copy, chapter or page should be published, not even a letter! (Castro, 1971a: 557)

Padilla himself castigated those who protested his treatment, accusing them of being "ferocious enemies of socialism. [Your interests] are in asthetics, Paris gossip, prizes, the theories which were my most odious faults. . . All right, continue to serve the CIA, imperialists, and world reaction" (Padilla, 1971a: 538).

The Mexican prize-winning novelist, José Revueltas, of all the critical intellectuals made perhaps the most telling comments, not from Europe but from the Lecumberri prison in Mexico he had been confined in the aftermath of the 1968 student massacre in Mexico City. Revueltas rejected what he considered to be Padilla's abdication of his critical role. "A writer must raise his voice against the element in a party or a state that resists criticism." Characterizing Castro's remarks about Padilla's imprisonment as "contemptuous and offensive," Revueltas insisted that "This is not an 'insignificant' problem as *compañero* Fidel Castro presented it. . . Unless there is freedom in this sphere, then in essence nothing else can be significant" (1971: 632–633).

Most of the actions and attitudes which Padilla confessed seem to have been things about which Padilla certainly felt guilty, but there is considerable evidence that he successfully struggled against these tendencies. For instance, in the poem "Travelers" he had satirized the bourgeois attitudes of foreign intellectuals who had been guided through Cuba (Padilla, 1971b: 4). José Yglesias asks of the charges against Padilla:

> Are these crimes? Is not writing often an act of egoism which is accompanied by a desire to be published abroad? Padilla had a right to his views and to impart them to whomever he wished. The revolution does not prosecute the counter-revolutionaries living in Cuba who are not shy about complaining to foreigners. (Yglesias, 1971: 4)

Whatever foreigners or agents found out from Padilla was no secret. All the criticized writers did basically support the Revolution and even engaged in volunteer work, although Padilla in his confession said they recoiled against the discomfort of rural labor camps.

The 1971 cultural congress rejected the intellectuals' role as the "critical conscience of society," saying that this was the right of "the people themselves . . . the working class."

> The development of the artistic and literary movement in our country must be based on the consolidation and growth of the amateur movement, aiming at the broad cultural development of the masses, and opposing all elitist tendencies. . . . True genius is to be found among the masses and not among a few isolated individuals. The class nature of the enjoyment of culture has resulted in the brilliance of only a few isolated individuals for the time being. But this is only a sign of the prehistory of society, not of the nature of culture. (*Intercontinental Press*, June 7, 1971: 534–535)

In issuing the call for a mass culture, however, the congress took the hard position that:

> All trends are condemnable and inadmissible which are based on apparent ideas of freedom as a disguise for the counter-revolutionary poison of works that conspire against revolutionary ideology on which the construction of socialism and communism is based. (*Intercontinental Press,* June 7, 1971: 534)

The congress advocated excluding from Cuba those foreign intellectuals whose works and ideology are "opposed to the interests of the Revolution" in order to prevent their negative influence on the new generation.

The Cuban government's stringent attitude toward dissident intellectuals assumes that "recalcitrant artists are one thing and the people another. But if you silence one group it is very likely that you are not listening to the other" (Yglesias, 1971: 8).

Whatever form artistic expression ultimately takes in a socialist society, the current restriction of intellectual freedom in Cuba must be understood in the context of the economic difficulties, the rise of discontent, and the paternalistic style of political control which seems to require in times of difficulty a narrowing of the range of criticism.

CUBA IN WORLD AFFAIRS

With the triumph of the rebel army, Cuba changed overnight from an insignificant actor in world affairs to the most internationally influential country in the history of Latin America. This transformation—a bursting forth of energy, imagination, and courage—caused tension, uncertainty, and disruption. Both the United States and the Soviet Union were perplexed by the sudden emergence of a defiantly independent, hell-bent-for-development nation in the tropical, "fun-loving" Caribbean. The interest of underdeveloped nations everywhere was attracted to the dynamic nature of the change process in Cuba.

In daring to alter the calculus of international affairs so drastically, the Cuban revolutionary government exposed itself to huge risks and challenges. Not only were the Cubans prepared to eject a complex of powerful foreign corporations from their island, they also made known their willingness to assist groups in other Latin American countries who sought to do likewise. This course was as bold as the advance against Batista by the dozen survivors of the *Granma* landing. It demanded an unflagging exercise of nerve and wit and resourcefulness.

Hindsight suggests that the movement of Cuba out of the United States and into the Soviet economic sphere was an inevitable scenario given the radical goals of the Revolution and the predictable U. S. response. The elimination of the U. S. sugar quota left Cuba nowhere to go except to the USSR and the USSR's competition with China for prestige in the Third World left the Soviet Union with little choice but to come to Cuba's assistance. If these events are "obvious" as hindsight, they were always uncertain while they were actually unfolding. This uncertainty—attended by extreme peril—conditioned the Cubans to confront the world with a keen survival instinct and an unsentimental pragmatism.

GENERAL FEATURES OF CUBAN FOREIGN POLICY

During the first fifteen years of the revolutionary government, the following general trends came to characterize Cuban foreign policy.

A protracted state of confrontation with the United States. Termination of diplomatic relations between the United States and Cuba on January 3, 1961 came after almost all U. S. property in Cuba had been nationalized and trade between the two countries had virtually ceased. The price Cuba was made to pay for nationalization of its economy was separation from the U. S. economy. The United States hoped to recover its assets and influence on the island through clandestine sponsorship of military invasion which finally took place at Playa Girón on April 17, 1961. With the defeat of the April invasion the United States concentrated on mobilizing international economic pressures. On September 7, 1961 the U. S. Congress prohibited aid to countries trading with Cuba except under special circumstances. Encouraged by the United States to do so, thirteen countries responded to U. S. pressure and broke diplomatic relations with Cuba. In January 1962, at a meeting of the Organization of American States (OAS) in Punta del Este, Uruguay, the United States succeeded in expelling Cuba from the Organization of American States with the votes of those thirteen nations. The United States was unable to win the votes of Mexico, Bolivia, Uruguay, Brazil, Chile, and Argentina which represented about two-thirds of the territory and two-thirds of the population of Latin America. Early in October President Kennedy ordered closure of U. S. ports to all ships which traded with Cuba.

Meanwhile, the Cuban government was convinced that the United States would organize another invasion, since the Kennedy government had promised an invasion to the Cuban exiles and had begun drafting them into the U. S. army for that purpose. The Cuban leaders sought to prevent this invasion by an arrangement with the Soviet Union to station bombers and offensive missiles on the island. For a summary of the arguments as to whether the missiles were introduced at the suggestion of Cuba or the Soviet Union, see Allison (1971). On October 23, 1962, the U. S. government announced possession of photographic evidence of the presence of offensive missiles in Cuba. There followed the "Cuban Crisis," a Cold War showdown between the United States and the Soviet Union.

Thousands of U. S. servicemen were concentrated in the Southeast of the United States for a possible invasion of Cuba. Curiously, this mobilization coincided with a long-scheduled U. S. amphibious exercise in the Caribbean which had as its objective the seizure of a mythical "Republic of Vieques" which was ruled by a man named Ortsac—Castro spelled backwards. After weeks of negotiation the Soviet Union, without consulting Cuba, agreed to remove its missiles and bombers in exchange for a U. S. promise not to invade the country. Later the United States said that its no-invasion pledge was not binding because Cuba had not allowed on-site inspection to verify the removal of the missiles. The Cuban government had said that it would allow on-site verification if there were U. N. supervision of U. S. bases where Cuban invaders had been trained. The United States rejected this proposal. The Cuban government reiterated five points which it said were essential to a final settlement of the "crisis."

1) Cessation of the economic blockade and other economic pressures exerted by the United States against Cuba.

2) Cessation of subversive activities such as the infiltration of weapons, spies, mercenaries, and saboteurs from the U. S. territory or from elsewhere under U. S. auspices.

3) Cessation of pirate raids from the United States and Puerto Rico.

4) Cessation of violation of Cuban airspace and territorial waters by U. S. aircraft and ships.

5) Restoration of the Guantánamo naval base to Cuba.

President Nixon's "low profile" policy in Latin America decreased the likelihood of a direct U. S. strike against Cuba, but the CIA role remained a question mark. According to columnist Jack Anderson, the CIA continued its efforts after the Playa Girón failure to remove Castro. Anderson claimed to have proof that CIA agents made six attempts to assassinate Fidel, two by poisoning and four by shooting (*The Nation,* May 3, 1971: 547). In addition, there have been periodic small-scale attacks from outside Cuba, all repulsed.

Little inclination to have normal political intercourse with the non-revolutionary regimes of Latin America. Cuba has not attempted to develop links with those hemisphere nations which it considers to be client states of the United States. After ejecting Cuba from the OAS in 1962 the United States succeeded in inducing every Latin American country except Mexico to break relations with Cuba. Even relations with Mexico remained cool and it was not until the nationalistic military seized power in Peru in 1968 that there was another nation in the Americas with which Cuba could identify. Election of socialist Salvador Allende to the presidency of Chile in 1970 resulted in the resumption of relations between Chile and Cuba. Cuba then had a true friend in the hemisphere, but held to its position of not wanting readmission to the OAS so long as that organization remained a "figleaf" for Uncle Sam. In 1972 Cuba announced support of the Omar Torrijos military government of Panama in its effort to regain sovereignty over the Panama Canal, and praised that government for "getting closer to the masses." Cuba proposed a hemisphere-wide aid fund for Panama and pledged its own financial assistance even if other states refused.

Wary but massive economic and technical intercourse with the USSR. The first large trade agreement with the USSR was signed on February 5, 1960 and provided for Soviet purchase of one million tons of Cuban sugar in each of the next five years. With the closing of the U. S. sugar market the Soviet Union became Cuba's leading trading partner, military supplier, and technical advisor. An oft-repeated myth of the U. S. press was that the Soviet Union was subsidizing Cuba at the rate of one million dollars a day. The fact was that Cuba was paying for most of its imports from the USSR with its sugar and other exports. Moreover, the cost of beet sugar production in the USSR was about three times as high as that of Cuban sugar. Thus "Soviet economic policies toward Cuba, centering on the sugar agreement of 1964, are in no sense charity but on the contrary may well yield substantial long run economic benefit to the USSR" (Huberman and Sweezy, 1969: 77). While grateful for the Soviet relationship in the emergency caused by the U. S. economic blockade, the Cubans often complained privately of the stiff terms of Soviet trade agreements.

Heavy economic reliance upon the USSR did not result in dutiful acceptance of Soviet political advice. Within the Cuban Communist

Party the "micro-faction" headed by Aníbal Escalante was sentenced to long jail sentences in 1968 for having conspired to implement Soviet-sponsored policies in Cuba. The Cubans refused to yield to Soviet admonitions to pacify relationships with the United States, to stop encouraging guerrilla warfare in Latin America, and to abandon moral incentives at home. Cuban support for Latin American insurgents was particularly resented by the USSR which was engaged in an unprecedented effort to establish diplomatic and trade relations with the existing governments of Latin America. Moreover, Cuba often denounced the Moscow-oriented Communist parties in Latin America for rejecting armed struggle. In 1962 the Cuban leadership issued the "Second Declaration of Havana" in which a revolutionary strategy of armed struggle was outlined in direct conflict with the Soviet line of peaceful co-existence. The declaration also rejected the assertion of the pro-Soviet Communist parties that the Latin American "nationalist" bourgeoisie was capable of leading a struggle against the United States. The Cubans emphasized that the peasantry would play the primary revolutionary role under the political leadership of the working class, because "the rural population lives in even more horrible conditions of oppression and exploitation; but it is also, with exceptions, the absolute majority sector. " As a result of a mass peasant struggle, "the old order little by little begins to break into a thousand pieces, and that is the moment when the working class and the urban masses decide the battle" (Kenner and Petras, 1969: 102–103). The Latin American Communist Parties which had not participated in any armed revolutionary activity since 1935 continued to oppose guerrilla warfare, as they had in Cuba. Officially they supported the Cuban Revolution, explaining its method of taking power as an "exceptional case," but in their own countries they struggled for the right to participate in elections, supported nationalist sections of the upper class, and pressured for expanded relations with the USSR.

Those commentators who view Cuba as a suppliant victim of Soviet manipulation or who, like K. S. Karol, believe that the Cuban leadership chose subservience to the Soviet Union point to Cuba's failure to denounce the Soviet invasion of Czechoslovakia in 1968. Yet a careful reading of Castro's address on that subject suggests agreement with Lee Lockwood's verdict that it was . . . "primarily an indictment of the Soviet Union's policies and useless to Moscow as an ideological weapon" (Lockwood, 1971: 29).

It is a misunderstanding to equate Cuba's dependence on the Soviet Union with its former control by the United States. The Soviet Union could not supply the same consumer goods, food, and equipment as the United States, but neither did the Soviet Union own the factories in Cuba and take home profits, control the decisions affecting technology and economic priorities, or dominate Cuban cultural life. Thus the Soviet influence did not frustrate Cuban development to the same degree or in the same way that U. S. control did. If a key measure of the negative impact of dependency is its prevention of rapid social change, Cuban "dependency" on the USSR has not impeded profound social and economic transformation. Castro explained in 1972 that Cuba's economic relationship with the USSR was a temporary expedient, that the long-run goal of Cuban planners would be the integration of Cuba into the Latin American economy.

In January, 1973, Cuba won what appeared to be a major concession from the USSR. Interest and payment on the approximately $3 billion Cuban debt (trade deficit) was suspended until 1986 and payment would be spread out for 25 years after that date. Over $300 million in new credits were granted. During 1973, the Cuban leaders pledged more uncritical support of the Soviet Union than ever before.

A troubled relationship with China. As early as December 1959, Cuba and China signed a trade agreement under which China bought fifty thousand tons of sugar. In 1960 several Cuban officials visited China and in July of that year a joint declaration by Cuban and Chinese trade union leaders seemed to give Cuban backing to some aspects of Chinese as opposed to Soviet positions in international politics. Cuba and China established diplomatic relations in September of 1960. Nevertheless, attempting to maintain the friendship and support of both powers, Cuba refused to take sides in the Sino-Soviet dispute long after every other socialist country had declared for one side or the other. In 1965 Castro pointed out the implications of the Sino-Soviet split in weakening the support for North Vietnam, Cuba, and other Third World revolutionary forces. ". . . in the face of an enemy that attacks . . . , there is no justification for division" (Kenner and Petras, 109). He warned that the Cuban Communist Party would not allow the Sino-Soviet split to divide groups in Cuba, although Cuba was the only Socialist country to print the positions of both sides in its press. The main agreement between Cuba and China was over relentless opposition to the United States, in contrast with the peaceful coexistence position of the USSR. But for reasons mostly practical, it was the USSR and not China on whom Cuba came to depend for economic interchange. The USSR had more to offer. A November 1964 Conference in Havana of Latin American Communist parties irked the Chinese because the Cubans agreed to deal with the established, i.e. non-"Chinese" Communist parties of the hemisphere. Then in 1965 Chinese officials in Cuba were accused of attempting to distribute tens of thousands of pieces of propaganda to the Cuban armed forces after they had been specifically warned not to do so. This irritation was followed by a Chinese decision to reduce the volume of their 1966 exports of rice to Cuba to 1964 levels. Faced with a critical rice shortage, Castro accused China of a "criminal act of economic aggression." He went on to criticize Mao for seeking personal deification. Trade between Cuba and China continued at a reduced rate, but Cuba and China remained at arms length until 1971 when China resumed cordial relations in keeping with its more conciliatory posture world wide.

A systematic effort to build relationships with the smaller socialist states. By the end of 1960, Cuba had already established diplomatic relations with Czechoslovakia, Poland, Romania, Yugoslavia, North Korea, and North Vietnam and had signed trade and payments agreements with East Germany, Hungary, and Bulgaria. Later, diplomatic relations were extended to the latter three countries and Mongolia. In 1972 Cuba became a formal participant in the Council of Mutual Economic Assistance (COMECON), the economic organization of the Warsaw Pact nations. Cuba has made an intensive effort to develop commercial and technical relationships with all of the smaller socialist countries, and a substantial level of intercourse with them has been achieved. Cuba identifies more closely with North Vietnam and North Korea than any other countries in the world. Diplomatic relations were also established with the Provisional Revolutionary Government of South Vietnam to whom offers of providing assistance in the form of Cuban military volunteers were made.

A developing role as a leader among Third World nations. Cuba's emerging position of influence in Third World affairs was formalized in January 1966 at the Tricontinental Conference in Havana. At that meeting the Afro-Asian Peoples Solidarity Organization, the organization descendent of the Bandung Conference of 1955, was transformed into the Afro-Asian Latin American Peoples Solidarity Organization (OSPAAL). Havana was chosen as the site of the permanent secretariat of OSPAAL. Cuba was one of the moving forces at the Havana conference and pressed successfully for the position that the USSR and China (members of OSPAAL) "should be both more generous in aid and less demanding in obedience" (Jackson, 1969: 92). At the close of the conference Latin American delegates organized under Cuban initiative a Hemisphere entity known as the Latin American Solidarity Organization (OLAS) also with headquarters in Havana. OLAS held a conference in Havana in July 1967 which was attended by representatives of most of the important revolutionary groups in the hemisphere.

The Cuban sense of responsibility to the Third World sometimes affected domestic decision making. In the late 1960's a lively dispute erupted between Fidel and the Englishman Thomas Preston who until 1969 headed the Cuban Institute of Animal Science. Preston advocated giving priority to the production of beef cattle whereas Castro urged instead stressing milk production. In response to Preston's arguments that raising beef cattle would be "both quicker and cheaper," Castro's answer was

> . . . fresh milk is essential not only for Cuba, but for the Third World, with whom we identify, and which now spends millions importing milk or does without it. Our experience in milk production will be invaluable to that world. Many countries in the Third World already export meat to the developed countries—the tragic colonial pattern of the starving feeding the well fed. Cuba will help break that pattern. (Reckord, 1971: 146–47)

A flexible but steady support of revolutionary groups in Latin America. The Cuban leadership has always understood that the survival and development of the Revolution in Cuba was intimately bound up with the development of revolution in the rest of Latin America. To break out of the economic blockade, to reduce pressure from the United States, and to free themselves of dependence on the Soviet Union, and even to reduce the military posture and to develop democratic forms within the country, the Cubans were dependent upon revolutionary successes in Latin America and the rest of the world. Paradoxically, although Cuban efforts to assist Latin American revolutionaries have met with numerous failures, by 1972 the strength, support, and organization of the insurgents was at an all-time high since the Latin American Underground War began at Moncada fortress in 1953.

Guerrilla warfare in Latin America has evolved through a number of phases, as has Cuban policy toward it. Not long after the triumph of the Revolution, Cuban revolutionaries participated in efforts to overthrow other governments by means of invading groups organized in Cuba. Invasion parties (small groups mostly made up of exiles) departed the island for Panama, the Dominican Republic, Nicaragua, Guatemala, and Haiti. These raiders were ideologically mixed and in the case of the Panama attempt involved the support of the Panamanian upper-class Ambassador to Great Britain, Tito Arias. All of these efforts failed and the practice was abandoned by August 1959. (Szulc, 1967: 80. For a denial that the Cuban Government was involved in these episodes see Zeitlin and Scheer, 1963: 101–102. One legacy of that phase has been that an important leftist movement in the Dominican Republic is named after the date of the unsuccessful invasion of that country, the 14th of June.)

Meanwhile, inspired by events in Cuba, groups of university students throughout Latin America began to act on behalf of revolutionary transformations of their own societies. Underestimating the retaliatory capacity of the military and police, these romantic young people were tragically unprepared for counter-moves by their governments and were almost everywhere defeated. During this early period, which ended about 1963, Caracas, Venezuela was the most notable focus of political combat by students. Aided by counter-insurgency paraphernalia and advisors from the United States, President Rómulo Betancourt ruthlessly smashed the students and postponed for the survivors their dreams of the achievement of a more just society.

Hundreds of students, radical leaders, and intellectuals from many countries visited Cuba during this time. On July 26, 1960, a large number gathered in Havana for the First Latin American Youth Congress. Havana had become the cradle and inspiration of Latin American revolution. When twenty-two Communist parties of Latin America, concerned by Cuban preference for guerrilla groups, gathered in Havana in November 1964, they won from Cuba the assurance that they would not be excluded from Cuban support. In exchange, the Communist parties agreed not to oppose the guerrilla groups who by that time had been largely driven out of the cities and had resumed operations in mountain zones. Thus the Communists worked with guerrilla groups in Venezuela, Guatemala, and Colombia. In the months that followed the Cubans became progressively disenchanted with the Communist parties.

Between the Tricontinental meeting in Havana in January 1966 and the Latin American Solidarity Organization (OLAS) meeting in July 1967, the Cuban government moved staunchly in the direction of preference for armed struggle. The OLAS meeting was dominated by those groups in Latin America who favored or were already engaged in armed struggle and was intended in part as a way of outflanking the Communist parties. The conflict with the Venezuelan Communist Party (PCV) flared into the open. The PCV was in control of one section of the guerrilla Armed Forces of National Liberation (FALN). In 1965 the PCV called for a "democratic peace—a return to legality in exchange for ending the armed struggle" (Kenner and Petras, 1969: 116). FALN leaders Fabricio Ojeda and Douglas Bravo, who was an official in the PCV, believed that the PCV was down playing their activities, starving them financially, and even betraying the guerrillas. In late 1965 Bravo's section of the FALN broke with the PCV and the Cubans sided with them. In 1967 Castro denounced the PCV for abandoning the revolutionary struggle, for deceit, for attacking the Cuban government before other Communist parties, and for demanding that the USSR "virtually break with Cuba." "What will define the Communists of this continent is their attitude toward the guerrilla movement in Guatemala, and in Venezuela."

> . . . the parties that entrench themselves behind the name of communists . . . and believe themselves to have a monopoly on revolutionary sentiment—what they really monopolize is reformism—will not be treated by us as revolutionary parties. And if in any country those who call themselves communists do not know how to fulfill their duty, we will support those who, without calling themselves communists, conduct themselves like real communists in action and in struggle. (Kenner and Petras, 1969: 131–133)

Meanwhile, other important events were unfolding. A French intellectual, Regis Debray, who had spent 1966 in Cuba in touch with its leadership developed a theory of revolutionary warfare based upon the Sierra Maestra phase of the Cuban Revolution. Debray contended that the military leadership of the Revolution should be the political leadership as well, thus rejecting the traditional communist tenet that the party should control the military. He advocated the *foco* or mobile military column which should always avoid the city, a corrosive, dangerous, and baneful influence on revolutionaries. In January 1967 the Cuban *Casa de las Américas* published his book *Revolution within the Revolution?* in 100,000 copies. In May 1967 it was confirmed that Ché Guevara who had disappeared from Cuba in 1965 was in a remote part of south central Bolivia leading a guerrilla force. His capture and subsequent execution on October 8, 1967 (made possible by a U. S. program to train a special Bolivian force, the Rangers, with the specific intent of eliminating Guevara and his group) marked the low point of rural-based guerrilla warfare in Latin America. The Bolivian Communist Party's failure to cooperate with the Bolivian guerrilla movement was an important obstacle to its success. It became apparent that the city was, after all, a more secure environment for the guerrilla than the countryside where counter-revolutionary technology (electronic surveillance, "spy-in-the-sky" satellites, etc.) had left no place to hide. By the time of Ché's death, urban-based guerrillas were already established in Brazil, contesting the rightist military dictatorship which came to power there in 1964, and in Uruguay where the "Tupamaros" were developing a formidable underground force. In Argentina an urban guerrilla force, whose strength was placed in the thousands by 1972, was forming. In Colombia where rural guerrillas had held on despite numerous setbacks, the first major and coordinated urban operations were carried out in October 1971 on the fourth anniversary of Ché's death.

It was this urban phase of the Underground War which appeared to be stronger than any preceding one. It was not the product of Cuban revolutionary theory nor material assistance. In keeping with the Guevarist principle that guerrillas must seize their own weapons, a 1967 observation continued to be true, viz., ". . . there is no evidence that Latin American revolutionaries had recevied direct arms or supplies from Havana" (Szulc, 1967: 84). The victory and survival of the Cuban Revolution was, however, a powerful inspiration and catalyst without which the Underground War would not have achieved its subsequent scope and force.

After the death of Guevara, during the 1968 to 1970 period, the Cubans gave less publicity in their press to guerrilla groups in Latin America, since the news was rarely favorable and Castro had become optimistic about the revolutionary prospects of the nationalist and reformist Peruvian military regime which took power in 1968. Castro took a similar position toward the nationalist military regime of Juan José Torres in Bolivia in 1970 to 1971. The new Cuban stance was denounced by some Peruvian revolutionary leaders and by Douglas Bravo in Venezuela, but it never meant a withdrawal of support for groups involved in armed struggle.

With the coming to power by election of a leftist coalition headed by Marxist President Salvador Allende in Chile in 1970, Castro declared that armed struggle was not a dogma. (At this point Douglas Bravo charged that Cuba was now abandoning guerrilla fighters.) In November 1971, Castro was received in Chile as an official guest of the President, in marked contrast to his visit to Venezuela in 1959 when he had been scorned by President Betancourt for proposing that the two leaders form a common front against U. S. imperialism.

FOREIGN TRADE

Cuban international economic policy has had to deal with certain limiting realities. Geography and history have combined to assign Cuba the role of a trading nation. Traditionally, the value of exports and imports together was greater than half the total value of the gross domestic product. As exporter, Cuba derived most of its earnings from a few basic commodities, especially sugar, tobacco, and nickel. Experience after the Revolution demonstrated that reliance on these exports continued to be the most sensible way to earn foreign exchange.

Considerable economic strains have accompanied the replacement of the United States by the Soviet Union as the country's leading trading partner. Before the Revolution, approximately 75 percent of trade was with the United States. Afterwards, the U. S.-imposed embargo on trade with Cuba resulted in severe economic dislocations and hardships, since Cuban industry, the port system, transportation, technical education, etc. had been geared to U. S. trade.

After the Revolution there was a rapid deterioration of the balance of payments as Cuban imports increased and the exports fell. The balance fell from plus $38.8 million in 1960 to minus $169.6 in 1962. While the socialist countries have become the mainstay of external economic association, the Cubans seek to develop foreign trade and technological relationships wherever possible and feasible. Thus, the Japanese have been the principal advisor on fishing, and supplied machinery in return for one million tons of sugar in 1971; the Italians and French have become major suppliers of agricultural tractors; the Canadians, important in public health; the British in public transportation, overhead irrigations systems, and fertilizer manufacturing; the Spanish as suppliers of fishing vessels, etc. The island has had the benefit of foreign technicians and processes drawn from every corner of the world.

Many factories are being purchased abroad. Foreign engineers help construct these plants and remain in Cuba until they are in operation. The factories are paid for with Cuban exports and when fully purchased their profits accrue wholly to the Cuban economy.

THE MOVEMENT OF PEOPLE

The Exiles. In practice, the United States limits those eligible for entry into the country as political refugees to persons from socialist countries. The first socialist system in the hemisphere therefore produced the first twentieth century Latin American "victims of political persecution" for whom the United States threw open its doors. Cubans responded in large numbers, and by 1972 approximately eight hundred thousand were in exile, mostly in the United States.

It is, of course, impossible to say how many Cubans came to the United States out of simple opportunism because none would admit to such motives. There is an element of truth in the prediction by Castro that if the United States threw itself open to citizens from Latin America in general "it could empty out some of those countries over a week-end" (Lockwood, 1969: 250). It is known that large numbers of Mexican nationals (sometimes estimated as high as one million) illegally reside in the United States. Needless to say, Latin Americans do not move to the United States out of a desire to abandon their Hispanic heritage, but rather mostly because of greater material advantages and social services. In any case, most *gusanos* (literally worms), as the Revolution refers to those who leave, found it extremely difficult to adjust to life in the new Cuba, preferring to try to maintain their pre-revolutionary life-style abroad.

After air service between the United States and Cuba was suspended in 1962, exiles came to the United States via Mexico or Madrid. Beginning in 1965, under an agreement with the Cuban government, the U. S. government financed frequent flights for Cubans between the island and Miami. Before these regular flights ended in 1971 they brought approximately 250,000 additional Cubans to Miami. By 1972 over 300,000 Cubans resided in Miami alone. There they established a version of pre-revolutionary Havana, complete with all manner of Cuban-style businesses, bistros, and even a mini-Mafia. On the whole, the Cubans have done quite well economically in the United States and by 1969 their median income in the Miami area was $6,550 compared to only $5,350 for blacks in the same region. The comparatively rapid economic success of Cuban exiles was subsidized by a special resettlement and welfare program which cost U. S. taxpayers $112 million in 1971 (Burt, 1971: 299–301).

Welfare advantages enjoyed by Cubans often caused resentment among U. S. blacks, Puerto Ricans, Chicanos, and Indians who did not have access to programs of equal coverage. William Clay, a black Congressman from Missouri, led a movement in the House of Representatives to end the Cuba-Miami airlift. In 1971 the House almost voted to end the Cuba flights, but later that year the flights were suspended at the initiative of the Cuban government.

The inflow of Cubans to the United States has been largely peaceful despite some tensions aroused among other minority groups. Although the Cuban immigrants tend to be reactionary politically, their children are adopting more moderate outlooks. One can argue that Cubans in the United States, whatever their politics, continue the ongoing process of Latin people acting as a culturally leavening influence in a Calvinistic society.

There are two obvious effects upon Cuba of the out-migration of about 10 percent of its population. On the one hand, there has been loss of some of the most highly educated and skilled people in the country. On the other hand, the exile outflow is a kind of exportation of the counter-revolution and has vastly reduced the need for the Revolution to resort to coercion at home.

Other Travellers. With the curtailment of the Miami airlift, the movement of people in and out of the island consisted mainly of diplomats, administrators, students, technicians, and voluntary workers. International tourism was negligible. Cuba was expensive for citizens of countries like Canada whose government did not restrict travel there and accommodations were scarce since the best recreational facilities had been given over to workers' use. Cubans were allowed to go abroad for purposes of tourism only in exceptional cases as special rewards for work performance. However, Cubans were sent abroad in substantial numbers to carry out government business, to study, and to do voluntary labor as, for example, groups sent to Peru to do earthquake relief and to Chile to work in social betterment projects.

The United States has striven to keep its citizens and those of other Latin American countries out of Cuba as much as possible. Only a few persons are granted the necessary special permission from the State Department to travel to Cuba on a U. S. passport and no U. S. citizen may go to Cuba without specific approval from the Cuban government. The result is that only a handful of North Americans visit Cuba with the permission of both governments. Much more numerous have been those going without State Department authorization but with invitations from the Cuban government. In 1969 a group totaling 216 U. S. *brigadistas,* as they were called, went to Cuba for two months to help in the historic sugar cane harvest. A second group of 687 and a third of 409 went in 1970; and a fourth group went in 1971, and a fifth in 1972. One reason the United States wants to keep its own young people out of Cuba is to set an example for such prevention on the part of other Latin American countries. What is really "subversive" about Cuba for foreign visitors is how completely the society is being transformed by the Revolution; visitors bring back eye-witness reports which are much more favorable than the news available in the U. S. and Latin American press.

The United States has not allowed non-*gusano* Cubans to come to this country except in connection with U. N.-sponsored activity or U. S. Government-sponsored conferences. In October 1971 a group of nineteen Cuban sugar technicians who had been denied visas to attend a privately sponsored conference on sugar technology held in New Orleans boldly flew into that city in a Cuban airliner. They were detained by U. S. authorities, not allowed to attend the conference, and ordered to leave after two weeks.

REFLECTIONS AND PROJECTIONS

Criticism of the Cuban Revolution comes in manifold forms. One major genre proceeds from those who are simply fond of capitalism, private property, and consumerism. Another is associated with nostalgia for the bawdy, Hemingway-esque good times at the Floridita Bar. Utopian anarchists are put off because the Revolution has not achieved a de-leaderized egalitarianism. Flower children dislike its discipline and rejection of drugs. Many intellectuals and artists say they would not be comfortable working under a mandate "Within the Revolution, anything; outside of it, nothing." Those who love the cosmopolitan nuances of urban life complain of the Revolution's Havana-downgrading rural emphasis. There are Marxists around the world who resent the fact that the Cuban Revolution is so Cuban. Latin American social democrats are vengeful because the Revolution has successfully coped with poverty, illiteracy, and disease when they have failed. There are disgruntled exiles who expected consumer goods for everyone overnight without the necessary years of society-wide mobilization to increase productivity, without the replacement of the privatized life-style; who somehow expected the new administrators to be free of the blemishes and deficiencies imposed by their pre-revolutionary experiences.

Cutting through the entangled growth of critical comment shrouding the Cuban reality, one uncovers a remarkable set of social goals and innovations. These innovations are sufficiently unique—in kind and degree —to compel interest and study by all societies. Among the attention-arresting features of present-day Cuba are the following:

It is probably the country most committed to the early replacement of material by moral incentives.

It has conducted one of the most notable efforts in the world to create a responsive and productive bureaucracy.

It is the first black-white society in the process of eliminating racial injustice through socialism.

It is a world leader in the effort to create more meaningful forms of community life.

It will perhaps be the first Western country to move effectively against meritocracy. Cubans reject the notion that those endowed with greater intelligence should live better than others. This is seen as the tyranny of the more intelligent over the less intelligent.

It is a world leader in involving the public in foreign policy.

It is the first Western society, including the Socialist countries, to undertake development in a form which does not accumulate capital "out of the hide" of the rural population.

The transformation of Cuban life has been guided by idealists for whom efficiency and practicality are not ultimate values. Again and again they have refused to heed the advice of practical persons with experience in remaking societies through socialism. Frequently the consequence of disregarding this advice has been economic failure. But what the Cuban leaders have, in effect, said to the more efficient and affluent socialist governments that emphasize material incentives is *"we don't want your kind of success."* (In 1973, however, Cuba swung back toward material incentives.)

Existing features of socialist countries which the Cubans have rejected are individual materialist motivation, economic decision-making through market mechanisms, and prolonged persistence of class and bureaucratic privileges. These attributes of the Soviet Union and other socialist countries are excused by their advocates as temporarily essential for increasing production until the achievement of sufficient material abundance makes them no longer necessary. The Cuban leadership, however, regards these concessions to pre-revolutionary practices as dangerous and corrosive, asserting that they will only delay the attainment of a society that is classless, moneyless, egalitarian, and brotherly. Fidel Castro has stated the problem in these terms, ". . . Communism certainly cannot be established if we do not create abundant wealth. But the way to do this, in our opinion, is not by creating consciousness through money or wealth, but by creating wealth through consciousness" (Landau, 1970: 127). Refering to the "market socialism" of Yugoslavia, Castro said in 1968 that the suggestion that Cuba implement "a type of tropical Titoism" was "absurd" and "ridiculous" and that "the Revolution could [not] conceivably regress to Rightist positions. . . What we are going to have here is . . . real communism" (Mesa-Lago, 1969–70: 209). Ernesto Guevara championed the notion that aspects of Communism (classlessness, moneylessness, equalitarianism and brotherliness) should be implemented during and not after the stage of socialism, i.e., the stage in which abundance is achieved. Guevara referred to this principle as "the simultaneous construction of Socialism and Communism." The principle has been prominently operative in Cuba and is seen in such policies as the preference for moral over material incentives, voluntary labor, and the effort to make available as many goods and services as possible free of cost at the earliest possible date.

Capitalist and Marxist economists alike, preoccupied as they are with production, have almost all been critical of Cuban attempts to place morality and consciousness on an equal footing with output. But heroic idealism has consistently been a central dynamic of the Cuban Revolution despite other kinds of twists and turns. One of the highest expressions of that idealism was voiced by Castro: "To live in a communist society is to live without selfishness, to live among the people and with the people, as if every one of our fellow citizens were really our dearest brother" (Landau, 1970: 126).

Thus the attainment of goals other than production must be considered in assessing the progress of the Cuban Revolution. There has been a remarkable willingness to undertake radical institutional experimentation. The degree of social transformation that has already occurred makes Cuba seem as different from other Latin American countries' life-style and tone as Mexico is from Denmark. "For Cubans, a world is dying; a world is coming to life" (Matthews, 1964: 16).

Yet, pre-revolutionary habits persisting from what had been essentially a pre-industrial society continue to slow both economic and social development. The educational and political consciousness of the general population has not yet reached a sufficiently high level for the people genuinely to believe that they are capable of governing themselves. Neither does the revolutionary leadership believe that would yet be possible. Moreover, the leadership does not allow independent opposition movements to form either within or outside of the Party. Initiative is encouraged, but always within the framework of national unity and cohesion. One Cuban concluded "This generation needs Fidel's inspiration and the next generation will have technology and good work habits" (Reckord, 1971: 76).

Considering the deep-set social problems and low level of civic culture that existed before 1959, the reluctance of the leadership to allow a multiplicity of political tendencies to be expressed is not surprising. They seem to fear that a premature opening up of the system might be followed by such political and economic dislocations that there would then be no alternative but to resort to forced labor, material incentives, and general coercion.

Whatever the degree of accuracy of this assessment by the revolutionary leadership, and whatever the degree that it might merely be a self-serving analysis, there remain several battles yet to be won in the socio-political arena. Among these are 1) an increased worker participation in management, 2) a system of better safeguarded civil liberties, 3) an acceptance of broader political discussion and intellectual dissent, and the possibility of organizing opposition within a socialist framework, 4) a more democratized Party, 5) a more vital press, 6) the elimination of political prisoners, 7) and the completion of equality for women, blacks, and homosexuals.

Despite the production problems and consumer goods shortages that have persisted since the Revolution, the long range economic prospects would seem to be hopeful. The high levels of current investment in productive capacity and in education should gradually end consumer austerity as Cuba goes on to leave the stagnated economies of most Latin American countries far behind. (In Mexico it took thirty years before the social changes showed up in production increases.)

The Cuban example has altered and will doubtlessly continue to influence the nature of the continental struggle against poverty and imperialism. The Cuban Revolution has firmly anchored the Third-World-wide liberation struggle in the Western Hemisphere.

North American youth, preoccupied with "post-industrial" concerns like sensation, revelation, and private solutions to their problems, sometimes find it difficult to relate to a communal, forced march on behalf of economic development. Some, however, who have gone to Cuba as worker-participants in the Venceremos Brigade have responded enthusiastically. One expressed his reaction to Cuba as follows:

> I felt kind of shameful that I could fuck around with drugs and sort of take advantage of all the leisure and abstraction—what everyone is into in the United States. And it's so easy to get into those things, the cultural diversions, and not do political work. Here you see that the politics penetrates the culture, it's a positive culture, it's something that's moving. You see *"Van"* all over the place. You just get a feeling of motion, that there is positive motion as opposed to the kind of motion going on at home which is really, at this point, about the most decadent, just down-in-the-depths trip. (Levinson and Brightman, 1971: 317)

Cuba has had the courage to dream and to dare, to fail and to push on. Fidel said:

> If we are going to fail because we believe in the capacity of the human being, in the human capacity to surpass oneself, we will fail if it is necessary, but we will never renounce our faith in the human being. (Biedma, 1970: 329–330)

DONALD W. BRAY is Professor of Political Science at California State University, Los Angeles. He earned a B.A. from Pomona College, an M.A. from the University of California, Berkeley, and a Ph.D. from Stanford University. In 1959–60 he did research in Chile as a Fulbright Scholar and subsequently published a number of articles about that country. He also authored "Latin-American Political Parties and Ideologies: An Overview," *The Review of Politics*, January 1967 and the chapter on Uruguay in *Political Forces in Latin America*, Ben Burnett and Kenneth Johnson, eds., Wadsworth, 1968. Dr. Bray has done research in or visited all twenty Latin American countries, his most recent visit to Cuba being in 1968. He has been a visiting professor at the National University of Chile, Notre Dame University, Pomona College, the Universidad Ibero-Americana (Mexico City), the University of California, Riverside, and the University of California, Irvine. Currently he is making films about Latin America.

TIMOTHY F. HARDING is an Associate Professor of History at California State University at Los Angeles. He received his B.A. from Harvard College and his Ph.D. from Stanford University. He studied for nearly two years each in Brazil and Mexico, and has done research in several other countries in South America and the Caribbean, with particular emphasis on Chile, Peru, and Bolivia. He is a specialist on Brazilian labor. He did research in Cuba with Donald Bray in 1968. He has published widely in journals and periodicals and is the author of *The Political Role of the University in Contemporary Latin America* (Latin American Research Monograph, University of California, Riverside: 1968).

STATISTICS

Area: 44,206 sq. miles, 11,452 thousand hectares
Arable Land: 51.5% (including meadows and pastures) (1964)

Population: 8,553,395 (1970)
Birth Rate: 32.2 per 1000 persons (1965–'69)
Infant Death Rate: 39.7 per 1000 infants (1967)
Population Growth Rate: 2.1% (1963–'70)
Life Expectancy: 66.8 years (1965–'70)

Ethnic Composition:
  73% White
  12% Negro
  14% Mixed
  1% Oriental
  (99% of population is born Cuban.) (These figures drastically underestimate the proportion of Cubans with Mixed blood, which in fact
  probably reaches 50%.)

% of Population Living in Cities: 53.4% (1970)
Literacy Rate: 96.1% (1961)
Education: 79.1% of the 5–14 year old age population (1,321,768 per-
    sons) (1965) are enrolled in primary school
  35,490 students are enrolled in higher education (1968–'69)
  30 students/teacher (primary level) (1968)
Medical:
  8.7 doctors/10,000 persons (1968)
  1.9 dentists/10,000 persons (1968)
  4.8 hospital beds/1000 persons (1968)
Newspapers: 9 daily newspapers (1967)
  88 daily newspapers circulated/1000 persons (1967)
Television: 71 TV receivers/1000 persons (1963)
Radio: 159 radio receivers/1000 persons (1970)
Capital: Havana
Provinces and Population:
  Camagüey   785,400
  Havana   2,023,600

Las Villas   1,178,800
Matanzas   447,000
Pinar del Río   555,000
Oriente   2,443,600

Government Spending:

Agriculture, INRA   367.9
Education   219.0
Industry   194.4
Labor   173.8
Administration   143.8
Public Welfare   128.7
Transportation   41.6
Commerce   14.2
Communications   12.9
Total   1,296.3

(1964) in millions of pesos, 1 Cuban peso officially exchanged for $1 in 1963.

Presidents:

Dr. Ramón Grau San Martín   1933
Carlos Hevia   1934
Colonel Carlos Mendieta   1934
Miguel Mariano Gómez   1936
José Antonio Barnet   1936
Federico Laredo Bru   1936
Fulgencio Batista   1940
Dr. Ramón Grau San Martín   1944
Dr. Carlos Prío Socarrás   1948
Fulgencio Batista   1952
Manuel Urrutia   1959
Dr. Osvaldo Dorticós   1959

GNP: 3986 million U.S. dollars (1966)

Per Capita GNP: 511 U.S. dollars (1966)

Distribution of Work Force:

Agriculture   41.9%
Industry   21.1%
Mining   0.5%
Construction   6.9%
Transportation   5.5%
Trade   8.6%
Services & Admin.   15.5%

Land Tenure: There are three forms of enterprise: people's farms owned by the state, the sugar co-operatives composed of former landless workers, and small farms owned by peasants whose output is regulated by the state. The state owned farms produce 80% of Cuba's yields.

Trade Balance: (1970)

export: 234.860 million U.S. dollars
import: 429.090 million U.S. dollars

export to: U.S.S.R. 370.700 million U.S. dollars
China   91.800 million U.S. dollars
Japan   100.600 million U.S. dollars
Spain   31.930 million U.S. dollars

import from: U.S.S.R. 583.600 million U.S. dollars
China   84.100 million U.S. dollars
Italy   64.900 million U.S. dollars

Foreign Exchange: Major Export—Sugar 85%
2nd Major Export—5 to 7% minerals, food stuffs, hides

GLOSSARY

agiotistas: money lenders who made fortunes and had great power during the nineteenth century in Mexico

agrupaciones: an administrative grouping of Cuban collective farms

asambleas populares: Cuban town meetings

asesor: legal advisors to lay judges in Cuban peoples' courts

Atomibrás: state corporation responsible for atomic resources in Brazil

barbudos: "bearded ones," popular name for Castro's guerrillas

braceros: Mexican migrant farm laborer employed in the United States at harvest time

brigadistas: members of special task forces in Cuba, such as the literacy brigades in 1961 or the Venceremos Brigades of volunteer workers from the United States

cefeteleros: coffee growers

campesino: peasant, rural worker

Casa de las Américas: Cuban center for international culture exchange. Also the name of a journal it publishes.

Casa Rosada: The Pink House; the presidential palace in Buenos Aires

caudillos, caudilho: chief, leader; implies high degree of personalism or charisma; military chief, head of a political party or faction, boss

centrales: large sugar mills and adjacent lands owned by the mills in Cuba

charros: cowboys, horsemen

compadresco: concerning the relationship between a godfather and the child's parents

compañero(a): a Spanish approximation of the word "comrade"

comprador: refers to sector of national businessmen dependent upon foreign economic interests—originally trading agents of foreign business groups

confidante: trusted advisor and companion

confradias: "communities"

Con la Cruz y Con la Patria: "With cross and fatherland," pro-Castro Catholic group in Cuba

consejos de trabajo: Cuban courts responsible for cases arising at work places

consorteria: refers to political phenomena which emerged after the fall of the Italian Right in 1876 and which inspired the Italian sociologist Vilfredo Pareto to formulate his theory of the alternation of elites. A loose consortium of patrons, each with their own clienteles to satisfy. The public authorities have the task of accommodating as many sections of the dominant class as possible at the same time. The successful politicians achieve this; those who fail are thrown out of office.

Consulado de Comercio: Chamber of Commerce

cordobazo: refers to the mass urban insurrections of May 1969 and March 1971 in Córdoba and other cities in Argentina

coroneis: colonel; often refers to local political boss or oligarch in rural Brazil

criollo: those of Spanish descent or blood living in the New World

desarrollismo: "Developmentalism." An ideology that stresses the technical aspects of development and modernization, and suppresses the reference to the political control of these processes. In the wake of the failure of bourgeois groups to effect a course of autonomous development, seized by the fear of more radical alternatives, *desarrollismo* represents for these groups a technocratic ideology that neutralizes the implications of the perception of foreign domination over essential productive processes.

descamisados: "The shirtless ones." The term was first used by the well-to-do to belittle the urban masses that assembled in the Plaza de Mayo on October 17, 1945, to demand the release of Perón from arrest by a military group. Perón subsequently seized upon the term as a rallying cry for the common man.

deuda inglesa: "English debt"

diezmos: tithes

Diós es argentino: "God is Argentine." An expression of national self-confidence.

ejidal: from an ejido (or communal landholding)

ejidatarios: communal peasant farmers

ejido: Indian communal landholding

Electrobrás: state corporation responsible for power in Brazil

encomenderos: from encomienda

encomienda: Spanish colonial grant giving right to appropriate labor of native people in specified areas in return for Christianizing them

estancias: Estates. The term refers to big livestock ranches which have been, at least since the early nineteenth century, large-scale units of production for a competitive world market.

estancieros: large livestock producers

Eximibal: Guatemalan subsidiary of International Nickel Co.

fazendas: a large estate, ranch, or plantation

federales: members of nineteenth century party which favored a federal form of government; followers of Rosas or the *caudillos*

Ferrobrás: state corporation responsible for coordination of iron and steel industries in Brazil

finca: plantation, farm

finisterre: "End of the world." A remote region.

finqueros: owner of finca

foco: a guerrilla force serving to focus revolutionary opposition

foquismo: "foco-ism," the advocacy of guerilla "foco" to set off revolution.

frente: committees into which block committees are subdivided in Cuba

Frente de Mujeres: Women's Front

gachupines: native Spaniards controlling Mexico during colonial times

gauchos: Argentina's counterpart of the American cowboys. A *mestizo* group that, during colonial times, came to displace the Indians in the vicinity of the great rivers. As opposed to the latter, they were nominally Christian and lacked a tribal organization. They were well adapted to the environment: unsurpassed horsemen, hunters of cattle, and fierce but poorly organized fighters. Like the Indians they were not easily disciplined as a labor force, but unlike the Indians they were connected economically, politically, and religiously with the Spaniards and Creoles settled in the towns and their environs. They became the means by which the townsmen developed a staple trade based upon production in the hinterland of Buenos Aires. *Gauchos* were an ever-present factor in nineteenth century politics. The transformation of the economy from a commercial-hunting to a commercial-pastoral system based upon privately owned *estancias* worked with wage labor drew workers from *gaucho* ranks and undermined their existence. In the 1870's José Hernandez' epic poem *Martin Fierro* expressed their final agonies in the face of settlement and rationalization on the *pampas*.

golondrinas: Literally, swallows. Seasonal migrants from southern Europe. The harvest season in Argentina came during the winter months in Europe and migrant laborers could, therefore, find employment in the Argentine wheat fields during the slack labor season in their own countries. Gradually, the mechanization of wheat harvesting diminished this international seasonal migration.

golpista: favoring or participating in a military golpe or coup

Granjas = Granjas del pueblo

Granjas del pueblo: peoples (collective) farms in Cuba

gusanos: literally worms. Term applied to disaffected Cuban exiles.

hacendados: owner of hacienda, rancher

hacienda: In Spanish America, an estate of large dimensions raising grains or cattle. Products were consumed locally at the mining centers such as Mexico City or Lima. Amerinds constituted the labor force, dependent, relatively immobile, constrained by a special form of wage labor, debt peonage.

hijos de putas: "sons-of-bitches"

Huelga de Dolores: literally, Strike of Sorrows

jeca-tatu: simple countryman or hillbilly in Brazil

jefe: chief, leader

La década infame: "Infamous decade," referring to the period from 1930 to 1943 in which Argentina was organized by a group of army officers and estate owners, supported by clergymen, bankers, and merchants.

ladino: mixed Spanish-Indian

la nueva burguesía: the new bourgeoisie

latifundia: large landholding

latifundistas: large landholders, plantation owners, large rural property owners

latifundium: Latin; in Spanish, *latifundio*. A large estate. The typical *lati-*

fundio is a property of a certain size owned by one person. This is called the *latifundio geográfico*, to be distinguished from the *latifundio social* which is made up of scattered properties; and from the *latifundio administrativo*, which is a large handholding composed of different properties which are jointly managed but separately owned, usually by close relatives of the main owner.

Litoral: that part of Argentina bordering on the lower Paraná River; the provinces of Buenos Aires, Santa Fe, Entre Ríos, and Corrientes

lombardista: followers of Mexico's ascendant labor leader in 1930's, Lombardo Toledano

machismo: the cult of masculine dominance

malanga: variety of yam

mayorales: enforcers of landlord interests in rural areas before the 1959 Revolution in Cuba

meiero: agricultural worker who receives half of the crop in lieu of wages, or a farm tenant who pays half of his product as rent

mestizos: mixed Indian-Spanish

minifundia: very small landholding

minifundistas: owners of very small landholdings

Mínimo Técnico: on-the-job technical training in Cuba

neo-latifundismo: twentieth-century form of latifundia or monopoly, large landholding agriculture, often legally accomplished by registering sections of the land in names of friends and relatives

oligarquía: The oligarchy. Generally, it is used to refer to a ruling class whose power is ultimately based on the ownership of land.

pampas: Fertile, grass-covered plains which lie in the eastern central region of Argentina. They produce the bulk of the country's pastoral and agricultural wealth and contain two-thirds of the population, sixty percent of the railroads, and four-fifths of the industrial plants.

parceiro: landless agriculturalist who plants or shares

peninsulares: Spanish colonialists

Peronismo sin Perón: Peronism without Perón; refers to unsuccessful attempts to institutionalize Peronism and make it independent from the personal control of the exiled leader after 1955.

pesos: national monetary unit in several Latin American countries. In Argentina, P8.43 equal U.S. $1 as of July 22, 1972.

pistoleros: gunmen

Plaza de Mayo: Historic square in downtown Buenos Aires, flanked by the government palace, the Cathedral, the colonial *Cabildo,* banks, and ministries.

poder local: a decentralizing unit of government administration in Cuba

porteño: person of the port. Resident of Buenos Aires city.

provincianos: those who live in or are from the provinces

quilombo: a fugitive slave settlement in the backlands of Brazil

racime: (a unit of measuring bananas) bunch

rancheros: small or medium-sized farmers, cowboys

ranchos: small or medium-sized private landholding (farm)

reales: monetary units

Revolución Argentina: "Argentine Revolution." The self-characterization of the military regime established after the overthrow of President Illia in 1966.

Río de la Plata: estuary between Uruguay and Argentina

saladeristas: owners of meat-salting plants

seguimiento: program of educational follow-up for adults to complete elementary grades in Cuba

Segundo Frente de Escambray: second guerrilla front established by Directorio Revolucionario in the Escambray Mountains during the Cuban Revolutionary War

Superación Obrera: program of worker education at secondary level in Cuba

tenentes: lieutenants, instrumental in Brazilian revolts of 1922, 1924, and 1930

tiempos: term used by the military authorities during the dictatorship of Onganía to refer to the projected policy phases of the regime

tumultes: spontaneous uprisings of the poor against the wealthy during colonial times

ubiquista: pro-Ubico

unitarios: members of the nineteenth century party which favored a federal form of government: followers of Rosas or the *caudillos*

zonas militares: military zones of Mexico (like states, but for purposes of military authority under the Secretary of Defense)

BIBLIOGRAPHY

INTRODUCTION

Aguilar, Alonso (1965)   *Pan Americanism from Monroe to the Present: A View from the Other Side.* New York: Monthly Review Press.
—————— (1963)   *Latin America and the Alliance for Progress.* New York: Monthly Review Press (Pamphlet Series, 24).
Aldridge, Dan (1969)   "Politics in Command of Economics: Black Economic Development," *Monthly Review,* XIX (November), 14–27.
Allende, Salvador (1972)   "Chile." Washington, D.C.: Embassy of Chile. Speech before the United Nations General Assembly, December 4, 1972.
Almond, Gabriel A. and G. Bingham Powell (1966)   *Comparative Politics: A Developmental Approach.* Boston: Little, Brown and Company.
Anderson, Charles W. (1970)   "Changing International Environment of Development and Latin America in the 1970's," mimeographed.
Bacha, Claire Savit (1971)   "A dependência nas relações internacionais: uma introdução à experiência brasileira." Rio de Janeiro: Masters' Thesis, Instituto Universitário de Pesquisas do Rio de Janeiro.
Baer, Werner (1969)   "The Economics of Prebisch and ECLA." pp. 203–18 in Charles T. Nisbet (ed.) *Latin America: Problems in Economic Development,* New York: Free Press.
Bagú, Sergio (1949)   *Economía de la sociedad colonial: ensayo de historia comparada de América.* Buenos Aires: Ateneo.
Baran, Paul (1957)   *The Political Economy of Growth.* New York: Monthly Review Press.
Baran, Paul and Eric Hobsbaum (1961)   "The Stages of Economic Growth," *Kyklos,* XIV, 234–42.
Baran, Paul A. and Paul M. Sweezy (1966)   *Monopoly Capital: An Essay on the American Economic and Social Order.* New York: Monthly Review Press.
Barkin, David (1972)   "The Redistribution of Consumption in Socialist Cuba," *Review of Radical Political Economics,* IV (Fall), 80–102.
Bell, Daniel (1960)   *The End of Ideology.* Glencoe, Illinois: Free Press.
Bemis, Samuel Flagg (1943)   *The Latin American Policy of the United States.* New York: W. W. Norton.
Bernardo, Roberto M. (1970–1971)   "Moral Stimulation as a Nonmarket Mode of Labor Allocation in Cuba," *Studies in Comparative and International Development,* VI, 6, 119–34.

—— (1971)   *The Theory of Moral Incentives in Cuba.* University, Alabama: The University of Alabama Press.

Bertero, Carlos Osmar (1972)   "Drugs and Dependency in Brazil—An Empirical Study of Dependency Theory: The Case of the Pharmaceutical Industry." Ithaca: Ph.D. Dissertation, Cornell University, 1972. Published as Dissertation Series No. 26, Latin American Studies Program, Cornell University.

Bodenheimer (now Jonas), Susanne (1970A)   "Dependency and Imperialism: The Roots of Latin American Underdevelopment," *NACLA Newsletter,* IV (May–June), 18–27. Also in *Politics and Society* (May 1971), 327–58.

—— (1970B)   "The Ideology of Developmentalism: American Political Science's Paradigm Surrogate for Latin American Studies," *Berkley Journal of Sociology,* 95–137. Republished in Comparative Politics Series (01–015), Vol. II, Beverly Hills: Sage Publications, 1971.

Bonilla, Frank and Robert Girling (Eds.) (1973)   *Structures of Dependency.* Stanford.

Bottomore, T. B. (1964)   *Elites and Society.* Baltimore: Penguin Books.

Cantor, Norman F. (Ed.) (1963)   *The Medieval World: 300–1300.* New York: Macmillan Company.

Caputo, Orlando and Roberto Pizarro (1970)   *Desarrollismo y capital extranjero: las nuevas formas del imperialismo en Chile.* Santiago: Ediciones de la Universidad Técnica del Estado.

Cardoso, Fernando Henrique (1972–1973)   "Industrialization, Dependency and Power in Latin America," *Berkeley Journal of Sociology,* (XVIII).

—— (1972)   "Notas sôbre o estado atual dos estudos sôbre dependência." São Paulo: Centro Brasileiro de Análise e Planejamento (CEBRAP), mimeographed.

—— (1971A)   *Política e desenvolvimento em sociedades, dependientes: ideologias do empresariado industrial Argentino e Brasileiro.* Rio de Janeiro: Zahar Editores.

—— (1971B)   "Teoria da dependência ou análises concretas de situações de dependência?" pp. 25–45 in his *Sôbre teoria e métrodo em sociologia,* São Paulo: Edições CEBRAP.

Cardoso, Fernando Henrique and E. Falleto (1969)   *Dependencia y desarrollo en América Latina.* Mexico: Siglo XXI Editores.

Citizens' Board of Inquiry into Hunger and Malnutrition in the United States (1968)   *Hunger, U.S.A.* Boston: Beacon Press.

Cockcroft, James D., André Gunder Frank and Dale Johnson (1972) *Dependence and Underdevelopment: Latin America's Political Economy.* Garden City, New York: Doubleday and Company, Inc.

Corradi, Juan Eugenio (1971)   "Cultural Dependence and the Sociology of Knowledge: The Latin American Case," *International Journal of Contemporary Sociology,* VIII (January).

Domhoff, G. William and Hoyt B. Ballard (Eds.) (1968)   *C. Wright Mills and the Power Elite.* Boston: Beacon Press.

Dozer, Donald M. (Ed.) (1965) *The Monroe Doctrine: Its Modern Significance*. New York: Alfred A. Knopf.

Easton, David (1957) "An Approach to the Analysis of Political Systems," *World Politics* (April), 383–408.

——— (1953) *The Political System*. New York: Alfred A. Knopf.

Emerson, Richard M. (1962) "Power-Dependence Relations," *American Sociological Review*, XXVII (February), 31–41.

Eyre, S. R. (1971) "Man the Pest: The Dim Chance of Survival," in *The New York Review of Books*, XVII, 8 (November 18), 18 ff.

Fann, K. T. and Donald C. Hodges (Eds.) (1971) *Readings in U.S. Imperialism*. Boston: Porter Sargent Publisher.

Feder, Ernest (1971) *The Rape of the Peasantry*. Garden City, New York: Anchor Books.

Flores, Edmundo (1963) "Land Reform and the Alliance for Progress." Princeton: Center for International Studies (Policy Memorandum 27).

Frank, André Gunder (1972) *Lumpenbourgeoisie: Lumpendevelopment: Dependence, Class, and Politics in Latin America*. New York: Monthly Review Press.

——— (1969A) *Latin America: Underdevelopment or Revolution*. New York: Monthly Review Press.

——— (1969B) "The Underdevelopment Policy of the United Nations in Latin America," *NACLA Newsletter*, III (December), 1–9.

——— (1967A) *Capitalism and Underdevelopment in Latin America: Historical Studies of Chile and Brazil*. New York: Monthly Review Press.

——— (1967B) "Sociology of Development and Underdevelopment of Sociology," *Catalyst*, 3 (Summer), 20–73. Reprinted in his *Latin America: Underdevelopment or Revolution*. New York: Monthly Review Press, 1969, Ch. 2, pp. 21–94.

——— (1966A) "The Development of Underdevelopment," *Monthly Review*, XVIII (September), 17–31.

——— (1966B) "Functionalism, Dialectics, and Synthetics," *Science and Society* (Spring), reprinted pp. 95–107 in his *Latin America: Underdevelopment or Revolution*.

Fromm, Eric (1961) *Marx's Concept of Man*. New York: Frederick Ungar Publishing Company.

Furtado, Celso (1973) "The Concept of External Dependence in the Study of Underdevelopment." Paper to be published in Charles K. Wilbur (Ed.), *Political Economy of Development and Underdevelopment*. New York: Random House, forthcoming.

——— (1970) *Economic Development of Latin America: A Survey from Colonial Times to the Cuban Revolution*. London: Cambridge University Press.

——— (1963) *The Economic Growth of Brazil: A Survey from Colonial to Modern Times*. Berkeley and Los Angeles: University of California Press.

Gil, Federico G. (1971) *Latin American-United States Relations*. New York: Harcourt Brace Jovanovich.

González Casanova, Pablo (1970A) *Democracy in Mexico*. New York: Oxford University Press.

———(1970B) *Sociología de la explotación*. Mexico City: Siglo XXI Editores.

——— (1969) "Internal Colonialism and National Development," pp. 118–39 in Irving Louis Horowitz et al (Eds.) *Latin American Radicalism*. New York: Vintage Books.

Griffin, Keith (1969) *Underdevelopment in Spanish America*. London: Allen and Unwin.

Guevara, Ernesto Ché (1967) *Man and Socialism in Cuba*. Havana: Book Institute.

Gurley, John W. (1970) "Maoist Economic Development: The New Man in the New China," *The Center Magazine*, (May), 25–32.

Hayter, Teresa (1971) *Aid as Imperialism*. Baltimore: Penguin Books.

Hibbert, A. B. (1953) "The Origins of the Medieval Town Patriciate" *Past and Present*, III (February), 15–27.

Hilton, R. H. (1952) "Capitalism—What's in a Name? *Past and Present*, I (February), 32–44.

Hinkelammert, Franz (1970) *El subdesarrollo latinoamericano: un caso de desarrollo capitalista*. Santiago: Universidad Católica de Chile.

Hirshman, Albert O. (1961) "Ideologies of Economic Development in Latin America," pp. 3–42 in his *Latin American Issues: Essays and Comments*. New York: Twentieth Century Fund.

Hobson, J. A. (1965) *Imperialism*. Ann Arbor: University of Michigan Press.

Horowitz, Irving L., Josué de Castro and John Gerassi (Eds.) (1969) *Latin American Radicalism: A Documentary Report on Left and Nationalist Movements*. New York: Vintage Books.

Huberman, Leo and Paul M. Sweezy (1969) *Socialism in Cuba*. New York: Monthly Review Press.

Illich, Ivan (1969) "Outwitting the 'Developed' Countries," *New York Review of Books*, XIII (November 6), 20 ff.

Imaz, José Luis de (1970) *Los que Mandan* (Those Who Rule). Albany: State University of New York Press.

Johnson, Dale L. (1967–1968) "Industrialization, Social Mobility, and Class Formation in Chile," *Studies in Comparative International Development*, III, 7 (Series 033), 127–51.

Johnson, John J. (1964) *The Military and Society in Latin America*. Stanford: Stanford University Press.

——— (Ed.) (1962) *The Role of the Military in Underdeveloped Countries*. Princeton: Princeton University Press.

Jonas, Susanne (see Bodenheimer).

Kaplan, Marcos (1968) "Estado, dependencia externo y desarrollo en América Latina," *Estudios Internacionales*, II (July–September), 179–213.

Kolakowski, Leszek (1968) *Toward A Marxist Humanism: Essays on the Left Today*. New York: Grove Press.

Lambert, Jacques (1959) *Os dois Brasis*. Rio de Janeiro. See also his *Latin*

America: Social Structures and Political Institutions. Berkeley and Los Angeles: University of California Press, 1967.

La Palombara, Joseph (1966) "Decline of Ideology: A Dissent and an Interpretation," *American Political Science Review*, LX (March), 5–16.

Lenin, V. I. (1968) *Imperialism: The Highest Stage of Capitalism.* Moscow: Progress Publishers.

Le Riverend, Julio (1967) *Economic History of Cuba.* Havana: Book Institute.

Levy, Marion (1952) *The Structure of Society.* Princeton: Princeton University Press.

Lipset, Seymour Martin (1963) *Political Man.* Garden City: Doubleday.

López Segrera, Francisco (1972) *Cuba: capitalismo dependiente y subdesarrollo.* Havana: Casa de las Américas.

Lundberg, Ferdinand (1968) *The Rich and the Super-Rich: A Study in the Power of Money Today.* New York: Bantam Books.

Lewis, Gordon K. (1963) *Puerto Rico: Freedom and Power in the Caribbean.* New York: Monthly Review Press.

Magdoff, Harry (1969) *The Age of Imperialism: The Economics of U.S. Foreign Policy.* New York: Monthly Review Press.

Malinowski, Bronislaw (1954) *Magic, Science and Religion and other Essays.* Garden City: Doubleday.

Mandel, Ernest (1968) *Marxist Economic Theory*, Vol. I New York: Monthly Review Press.

Marcuse, Herbert (1968) *One-Dimensional Man: Studies in the Ideology of Advanced Industrial Society.* Boston: Beacon Press.

Marini, Ruy Mauro (1970) *Subdesarrollo y revolución.* Mexico City: Siglo XXI Editores.

Mattelart, Armand, Carmen Castillo, and Leonardo Castillo (1970) *La ideologia de la dominación en una sociedad dependiente.* Santiago: Ediciones Signos.

Merton, Robert (1957) *Social Theory and Social Structure.* New York: Free Press.

Mills, C. Wright (1961) *The Sociological Imagination.* New York: Grove Press. Especially Chapters 1 and 2.

Moore, Russell Martin (1973) "Imperialism and Dependency in Latin America: A View of the New Reality of Multinational Investment," *Journal of Inter American Studies and World Affairs*, XV (February), 22–35.

Murga, F. Antonio (1971) "Dependency: A Latin American View," *NACLA Newsletter*, IV (February), 1–13.

Nichols, David (1972) "Ruling Class as a Scientific Concept," *The Review of Radical Political Economics*, IV (Fall), 35–69.

North American Congress on Latin America (1971) *Yankee Dollar: The Contribution of U.S. Private Investment to Underdevelopment in Latin America.* Berkeley.

Novack, George (1970) "The Permanent Revolution in Latin America," *Intercontinental Press*, VIII (November 16), 978–83.

Nun, José (1967) "Notes on Political Science in Latin America," in Manuel Diegues and Bryce Wood (Eds.), *Social Science in Latin America*. New York: Columbia University Press.

O'Connor, James (1970) *The Origins of Socialism in Cuba*. Ithaca: Cornell University Press.

Organski, A. E. K. (1965) *The Stages of Political Development*. New York: Alfred Knopf.

Parsons, Talcott (1951) *The Social System*. New York: Free Press.

Peña, Sergio de la (1971) *El antidesarrollo de América Latina*. Mexico City: Siglo XXI Editores.

Petras, James (Ed.) (1973) *Latin America: From Dependence to Revolution*. New York: John Wiley and Sons.

—— (1965) "Ideology and United States Political Scientists," *Science and Society*, XXIX (Spring), 192–216.

Petras, James and Maurice Zeitlin (Eds.) (1968) *Latin America: Reform or Revolution?* Greenwich, Connecticut: Fawcett Publications.

Prado Júnior, Caio (1969) *The Colonial Background of Modern Brazil*. Berkeley and Los Angeles: University of California Press.

Pratt, Julius W. (1959) *Expansionists of 1898: The Acquisition of Hawaii and the Spanish Islands*. Gloucester, Massachusetts: Peter Smith.

Prebisch, Raúl (1959) "Commercial Policy in the Underdeveloped Countries," *American Economic Review*, XLIX (May), 251–73.

Quijano, Aníbal (1971) *Nationalism and Colonialism in Peru: A Study in Neo-Imperialism*. New York: Monthly Review Press.

—— (1970) "Redefinización de la dependencia y marginalización en América Latina." Santiago: Centro de Estudios Socio-Económicos (CESO), Universidad de Chile, mimeographed.

—— (1968) "Dependencia, cambio social y urbanización," *Revista Mexicana de Sociología*, XXX, 526–30.

Radcliffe-Brown, A. R. (1957) *Structure and Function in Primitive Society*. New York: The Free Press.

Ray, David (1973) "The Dependency Model of Latin American Underdevelopment: Three Basic Fallacies," *Journal of Inter American Studies and World Affairs*, XV (February), 4–20.

Rhodes, Robert I. (Ed.) (1970) *Imperialism and Underdevelopment: A Reader*. New York: Monthly Review Press.

—— (1968) "The Disguised Conservatism of Evolutionary Development Theory," *Science and Society*, XXXII (Winter), 383–412.

Rostow, Walt W. (1962) *Stages of Economic Growth: A Non-Communist Manifesto*. London: Cambridge University Press.

Ruddle, Kenneth and Mukhtar Hamour (Eds.) (1972) *Statistical Abstract of Latin America: 1970*. Los Angeles: The University of California Latin American Center.

Santos, Theotonio dos (1970A) "Dependencia económica y alternativas de cambio en América Latina," *Revista Mexicana de Sociología*, XXXII (March–April), 417–63.

—— (1970B) *Dependencia y cambio social.* Santiago: Cuadernos de Estudios Socio-Economicos (11), Centro de Estudios Socio-Económicos (CESO), Universidad de Chile.

—— (1970C) "The Structure of Dependence," *The American Economic Review*, LX (May), 231–36.

Schaff, Adam (1965) *Marxism and the Human Individual.* New York: McGraw Hill.

Schmitter, Philippe C. (1972) "Paths to Political Development in Latin America," pp. 83–105 in Douglas A. Chalmers (Ed.), *Changing Latin America: New Interpretations of its Politics and Society,* New York: Proceedings of the Academy of Political Science (XXX, 4), Columbia University.

Schumpeter, Joseph (1955) *Imperialism, Social Classes.* Cleveland and New York: World Publishing Company, Meredian Book.

Sherman, Howard (1972) *Radical Political Economy: Capitalism and Socialism from a Marxist-Humanist Perspective.* New York: Basic Books, Inc.

Silverman, Bertram (Ed.) (1971) *Man and Socialism in Cuba: The Great Debate.* New York: Atheneum.

Staley, Eugene (1961) *The Future of Underdeveloped Countries: Political Implications of Economic Development.* New York: Frederick A. Praeger.

Stavenhagen, Rodolfo (1970) *Agrarian Problems and Peasant Movements in Latin America.* Garden City, New Jersey: Doubleday Anchor.

Stein, Stanley J. and Barbara H. Stein (1970) *The Colonial Heritage of Latin America: Essays on Economic Dependence in Perspective.* New York: Oxford University Press.

Sunkel, Osvaldo (1972) "Big Business and 'Dependencia'," *Foreign Affairs,* Vol. 50, No. 3 (April), 517–31.

—— (1967) "Política nacional de desarrollo y dependencia externa," *Revista de Estudios Internacionales,* I (May).

Sweezy, Paul M. and Charles Bettelheim (1971) *On the Transition to Socialism.* New York: Monthly Review Press.

Szymanski, Al (1972) "Malinowski, Marx and Functionalism," *The Insurgent Sociologist,* II (Summer), 35–43.

Thorson, Thomas L. (1970) *Bio-Politics.* New York: Holt, Rhinehart and Winston.

Torres-Rivas, Edelberto (1969) *Procesos y estructuras de una sociedad dependiente.* Santiago: Ediciones Prensa Latinoamericana.

Tyler, William G. and J. Peter Wogart (1973) "Economic Dependence and Marginalization: Some Empirical Evidence," *Journal of Inter American Studies and World Affairs,* XV (February), 36–45.

United Nations. Economic Commission for Latin America (1970) *Economic Survey of Latin America: 1969.* New York: United Nations.

—— (1950) *The Economic Development of Latin America and its Principal Problems.* New York: United Nations.

United States Senate. Committee on Foreign Relations and Committee on Armed Services (1962) **Hearing, Situation in Cuba,** 87th Congress, Second Session, September 17, 1962, pp. 82–87. Reprinted in *Studies on the Left*, III, 2 (1963), 54–59.

Urquidi, Víctor L. (1964)   *The Challenge of Development in Latin America*. New York: Frederick A. Praeger.

Vaupel, J. W. and Jean P. Curham (1969)   "The Making of Multinational Enterprise." Cambridge: Harvard University Division of Research.

Veliz, Claudio (Ed.) (1965)   *Obstacles to Change in Latin America*. London: Oxford University Press.

Weffort, Francisco Correa (1971)   "Nota sôbre a teoria da dependência: teoria de classe ou ideologia nacional," pp. 1–24 in Fernando Henrique Cardoso *et al, Sôbre teoria e método em sociologia*. São Paulo: Ediçoes CEPRAP.

Weisskopf, Thomas E. *et al* (1972)   "Dependency and Foreign Domination in the Third World," *The Review of Radical Political Economics*, IV (Spring), 1–108. Five articles on Dependency.

GUATEMALA

* Indicates that it is a particularly useful source.

*Adams, Richard (1970) *Crucifixion by Power.* Austin: University of Texas Press.

———— (1968) "El problema del desarrollo político a la luz de la reciente historia sociopolítica de Guatemala," *Revista Latinoamericana de Sociología* (July), 174–198.

Adler, John, Eugene Schlesinger and Ernest Olson, (1952) *Las finanzas públicas y el desarrollo económico de Guatemala.* Mexico: Fondo de Cultura Económica.

Aguilera Peralta, Gabriel Edgardo (1970) "La violencia en Guatemala como fenómeno político," Guatemala: Thesis for Law School, Universidad de San Carlos.

Alexander, Robert (1957) *Communism in Latin America.* New Brunswick, N. J.: Rutgers University Press.

Amaro, Nelson (ed.) (1970) *El reto del desarrollo en Guatemala.* Guatemala: Editorial Financiera Guatemalteca.

Annals of the Cakchiquel and Title of the Lords of Totonicapan (1953), trans. by Adrian Recinos and Delia Goetz. Norman, Okla.: University of Oklahoma Press.

Arevalo, Juan José (1964) *Guatemala, la democracia y el imperio.* Buenos Aires: Editorial Palestra.

Arias, Jorge B. (1962) "Analfabetismo en Guatemala," *Guatemala Indígena* (July–September), 7–20.

Arriola, José Luis (1961) *Gálvez en la encrucijada.* Mexico: Costa-Amic.

Bagú, Sergio (1969) "La economía de la sociedad colonial," *Pensamiento Crítico* 27 (April), 31–65.

Banco de Guatemala (Departamento de Investigaciones Agropecuarias e Industriales (1970) "Estudio preliminar sobre el financamiento del sector industrial."

Batres Jauregi, Antonio (1949) *La América Central ante la historia, 1821–1921.* Vol. II, Guatemala: Tipografía Nacional.

Bauer Paiz, Alfonso (1970) "The Third Government of the Revolution and Imperialism in Guatemala," *Science and Society* (Summer), 146–165.

———— (1969) "A un cuarto de siglo del glorioso 20 de Octubre," *Economía* 21 (July–Sept.) 5–16.

———— (1966) *Destellos y sombras en la historia patria.* Guatemala: Editorial Escolar Piedra Santa.

749

———— (1956) *Cómo opera del capital yanqui en Centroamérica: El caso de Guatemala.* Mexico: Editora Ibero-Mexicana.

Beals, Carleton (1932) *Banana Gold.* Philadelphia: J. B. Lippincott.

Bechtol, Bruce (1969) "Where Men Ride Tigers: The Industrial Landscape of Guatemala." Eugene, Ore.: Ph.D. Dissertation, Department of Geography, University of Oregon.

Beeson, Kenneth (1964) "Indigo Production in the 18th Century," *Hispanic American Historical Review* (May), 214–218.

Behar, Moises (1968) "Food Nutrition of the Maya before the Conquest and at the Present Time." Biomedical Challenges presented by the American Indians, Proceedings of the special session during the 7th meeting of the Pan American Health Organization Advisory Committee on Medical Research, Washington: PAHO (September).

Best, Michael (1969) "Determinants of Tax Performance in Developing Countries: The Case of Guatemala." Eugene, Ore.: Ph.D. Dissertation, Dept. of Economics, U. of Oregon.

Bodenheimer, Susanne (1971) "Crucifixion by Adams," *Berkeley Journal of Sociology* 60–74.

Bodenheimer, Thomas (1971) "Food for Profit," *NACLA Newsletter* (May–June) 8–13.

Britnell, G. E. (1951) "Problems of Economic and Social Change in Guatemala," *Canadian Journal of Economics and Political Science* (November), 468–481.

Bryant, Mavis Anne (1967a) "Agricultural Interest Groups in Guatemala." Austin, Texas: Masters Thesis, University of Texas.

———— (1967b) "Industrial and Commercial Associations in Guatemala" (draft).

Bush, Archer (1950) "Organized Labor in Guatemala, 1944–1949." Hamilton, N. Y.: Colgate University, Latin American Seminar Reports, #2.

Buttrey, Jerrold (1967) "The Guatemalan Military, 1944–1963: An Interpretive Essay." (manuscript)

Calderón Gonzales, Juan Arnoldo (1969) "Endeudamiento externo de Guatemala." Guatemala: Thesis for Facultad de Ciencias Económicas, Universidad de San Carlos.

Cardoza y Aragón, Luis (1965) *Guatemala: las lineas de su mano.* Mexico: Fondo de Cultura Económica.

———— (1955) *La Revolución Guatemalteca.* Mexico: Cuadernos Americanos.

Carter, W. and Fred Goff (1971) "Nickel Imperialism," *NACLA Newsletter* (Jan.), 1–8.

Cehelsky, Marta (1967) "Discontinuities in the Politics of Guatemala: The Liberation Movement of 1954." (draft)

Cohen, Alan (1969) *The Economy of Guatemala 1950–1965.* Guatemala: draft.

Comisión Técnica of the Facultad de Ciencias Económicas, Universidad de San Carlos (1971), "Estudio preliminar sobre incidencias económicas y forma de recuperar por el estado la empresa eléctrica de Guatemala, S. A." *Economía* 28 (April–June), 11–62.

Comité Interamericano de Desarrollo Agrícola (CIDA) (1965). *Tenencia de la tierra y desarrollo socio-económico del sector agrícola.* Washington: Pan-American Union.

Consejo de Economía de Guatemala (1950) *La empresa eléctrica de Guatemala, S. A.: Un problema nacional.* Guatemala: Ministerio de Educación Pública.

Consejo Nacional de Planificación Económica (CNPE), Secretaría General (1970) *Plan de desarrollo, 1971-1975.* Guatemala: CNPE Vol. I.

Contreras R., J. Daniel (1951). *Una rebelión indígena en el partido de Totonicapán en 1820: El indio y la independencia.* Guatemala: Imprenta Universitaria.

Crosby, Alfred (1967) "Conquistador y Pestilencia: The First New World Pandemic and the Fall of the Great Indian Empires," *Hispanic American Historical Review* (August), 321-337.

Crowell, Jackson (1969) "The U.S. and a Central American Canal, 1869-1877," *Hispanic American Historical Review* (February), 27-52.

De Landa, Diego (1937) *Yucatan Before and After the Conquest* (translation of De Landa's *Relación de las Casas de Yucatán,* by William Gates, Baltimore: Maya Society.

Díaz Rozzotto, Jaime (1958) *El carácter de la revolución guatemalteca.* Mexico: Ediciones Revista "Horizonte" Costa Amic.

Dombrowski, John et al. (1970) *Area Handbook for Guatemala.* Washington: Government Printing Office.

Durston, John (1966) "Power Structure in a Rural Region of Guatemala: The Department of Jutiapa." Austin, Texas: M. A. Thesis for University of Texas.

Eisenhower, Dwight D. (1963) *Mandate for Change.* New York: Doubleday.

Fletcher, Lehman et al. (1970) *Guatemala's Economic Development: The Role of Agriculture.* Ames, Iowa: Iowa State University Press.

Flores Alvarado, Humberto (1971) *Proletarización del campesino de Guatemala.* Quezaltenango, Guatemala: Editorial Rumbos Neuvos.

—— (1968) *La estructura social guatemalteca.* Guatemala: Editorial Rumbos Nuevos.

Floyd, Troy (1965) "The Indigo Merchant: Promoter of Central American Economic Development, 1750-1808," *Business History Review* (Winter), 466-489.

—— (1961) "The Guatemalan Merchants, the Government, and the Provincianos, 1750-1800," *Hispanic American Historical Review* (February), 90-110.

Galeano, Eduardo (1969) *Guatemala: Occupied Country.* New York: Monthly Review Press.

—— (1967) *Guatemala, clave de Latinoamérica.* Montevideo: Ediciones de la Banda.

Geyer, Georgie Ann (1966) series of articles in Chicago Daily News (December) on Guatemalan guerrillas.

Gilly, Adolfo (1965) "The Guerrilla Movement in Guatemala," *Monthly Review* (May), 9-40.

Goetz, Delia and Sylvanus Morley, with Adrian Recinos, trans. (1950) *Popul Vuh*. Norman, Okla.: University of Oklahoma Press.

Gordon, Max (1971) "A Case History of U.S. Subversion: Guatemala, 1954," *Science and Society* (Summer), 129–155.

Gott, Richard (1971) *Guerrilla Movements in Latin America*. Garden City, N. Y.: Doubleday.

Griffin, Keith (1970) "Reform and Diversification in a Coffee Economy: The Case of Guatemala." Oxford, England: draft.

Griffith, William (1965) *Empires in the Wilderness*. Chapel Hill: University of North Carolina Press.

Guerra Borges, Alfredo (1969) "El pensamiento económico-social de la revolución de Octubre," *Economía* 21 (July–Sept.), 17–41.

Guzmán Bockler, Carlos (1967) "La enseñanza de la sociología en las universidades de los paises subdesarrollados: El caso de Guatemala." Paper presented to 8th Congreso Latinoamericano de Sociologia, San Salvador.

*Guzmán Bockler, Carlos, and Jean-Loup Herbert (1970) *Guatemala: una interpretación histórico-social*. Mexico: Siglo XXI.

Guzmán Bockler, Carlos, Jean-Loup Herbert, and Julio Quan (1970) "Las clases sociales y la lucha de clases en Guatemala." Draft, for Segundo Seminario Latinoamericano para el Desarrollo.

Hanson, Simon (1968) "The Alliance for Progress: The Sixth Year," *Inter-American Economic Affairs* (Winter), 1–95.

Herbert, Jean-Loup (1967) "Apuntes sobre la estructura nacional de Guatemala y el movimiento de ladinización." Presented to the 8th Congreso Latinoamericano de Sociología, San Salvador.

Herring, Hubert (1968) *A History of Latin America from the Beginnings to the Present*. New York: Alfred A. Knopf Inc.

Hispanic American Report (HAR) various years, 1948 to 1964. Stanford University.

Hoyt, Elizabeth (1955) "The Indian Laborer on Guatemalan Coffee Fincas," *Inter-American Economic Affairs* (Summer), 33–46.

Inman, Samuel Guy (1951) *A New Day in Guatemala*. Wilton, Conn.: Worldover Press.

Instituto de Investigaciones Económicas y Sociales (IIES). Universidad de San Carlos (1969) *Una política para el desarrollo económico de Guatemala*. Guatemala: IIES.

International Bank for Reconstruction and Development (1951). *The Economic Development of Guatemala*. Washington: IBRD.

James, Daniel (1954). *Red Design for the Americas: Guatemalan Prelude*. New York: Day.

Jensen, Amy Elizabeth (1955). *Guatemala: An Historical Survey*. New York: Exposition Press.

Jerez, César (1971) "La United Fruit Co. en Guatemala," *Estudios Centroamericanos* 269 (March), 117–128.

Jones, Chester Lloyd (1940) *Guatemala, Past and Present*. Minneapolis: University of Minnesota Press.

——— (1934) "Loan Controls in the Caribbean," *Hispanic American Historical Review* (May), 141–162.

Karnes, Thomas L. (1961) *The Failure of Union: Central America, 1824–1960*. Chapel Hill: University of North Carolina Press.

Kenyon, Gordon (1961) "Mexican Influence in Central America, 1821–3," *Hispanic American Historical Review* (May), 175–205.

Kepner, Charles and Jay Soothhill (1967) *The Banana Empire*. New York: Russell & Russell.

Krehm, Wilhelm (1957) *Democracia y tiranías en el Caribe*. Buenos Aires: Editorial Parnaso.

La Charité, Norman et al. (1964) *Case Studies in Insurgency and Revolutionary Warfare: Guatemala, 1944–1954*. Washington: American University, SORO.

Lenin, V. I. (1965) *Imperialism, The Highest Stage of Capitalism*. Peking: Foreign Languages Press.

León Aragón, Oscar de (1950) *Los contratos de la United Fruit Co. y las companías muelleras en Guatemala*. Guatemala: Ministerio de Educación Pública.

López, Alvaro (1970) "La crisis política y la violencia en Guatemala," in *Diez años de insurrección en América Latina* (Vol. I). Santiago: Ediciones Prensa Latinoamericana, 77–130.

Lujan Muñoz, Jorge (1968) *Inícios del dominio español en Indias*. Guatemala: Escuela de Estudios Generales, Universidad de San Carlos, Catedra de Cultura 5.

Marina Arriola, Aura (1968) "Secuencia de la cultura indígena guatemalteca," *Pensamiento Crítico* 15 (April), 75–102.

*Martinez Pelaez, Severo (1970) *La patria del criollo*. Guatemala: Editorial Universitaria.

Martz, John (1963) *Justo Rufino Barrios and Central American Union*. Gainesville: University of Florida Press.

——— (1959) *Central America*. Chapel Hill: University of North Carolina Press.

——— (1956) *Communist Infiltration in Guatemala*. New York: Vantage Press.

Mata Gavidia, José (1969) *Anotaciones de historia patria centroamericana*. Guatemala: Editorial Universitaria.

May, Stacy and Galo Plaza (1958) *The United Fruit Company in Latin America*. Washington: National Planning Association.

*Melville, Thomas and Marjorie Melville (1971) *Guatemala: The Politics of Land Ownership*. New York: Free Press.

Molina Chocano, Guillermo (1971) *Integración centroamericana y dominación internacional*. San José, C. R.: Editorial Universitaria Centroamericana.

Monteforte Toledo, Mario (1959) *Guatemala: Mongrafia Sociológica*. Mexico: Universidad Nacional Autónoma de México.

Mosk, Sanford (1955) "The Coffee Economy of Guatemala, 1850–1918," *Inter-American Economic Affairs* (Autumn), 6–20.

Munro, Dana (1964) *Intervention and Dollar Diplomacy in the Caribbean, 1900–1921*. Princeton: Princeton Universiy Press.

——— (1918) *The Five Republics of Central America*. New York: Oxford University Press.

Munson, Donn (1967) "America's Top-Secret Jungle War," *Saga* (November), 18–21, 70–75.

Naylor, Robert (1960) "The British Role in Central America prior to the Clayton-Bulwer Treaty of 1850," *Hispanic American Historical Review* (August), 361–382.

Paredes, José Luis (1964) *Aplicación del Decreto 900*. Guatemala: Universidad de San Carlos, IIES.

Parker, Franklin (1964) *The Central American Republics*. London: Oxford University Press.

Pérez Maldonado, Raúl (1969) *Tales from Chichicastenango* (translated by J. Bebarchi). Guatemala: Unión Tipográfica.

Piedra-Santa Arandi, Rafael (1971) *Introducción a los problemas económicos de Guatemala*. Guatemala: Editorial Universitaria.

——— (1968) "La construcción de ferrocarriles en Guatemala y las problemas financieras de la IRCA," *Economía* 15 (Jan.–March), 5–48.

Pimentel Rodríguez, Alfonso (1969) "Los incentivos fiscales y el desarrollo industrial de Guatemala." Guatemala: Thesis for Facultad de Ciencias Económicas, Universidad de San Carlos.

Rippy, Fred J. (1966) *British Investment in Latin America, 1822–1949*. Hamden, Conn.: Archon Books.

——— (1942) "Relations of the U. S. and Guatemala during the Epoch of Justo Rufino Barrios," *Hispanic American Historical Review* (November), 595–605.

——— (1940) "Justo Rufino Barrios and the Nicaraguan Canal," *Hispanic American Historical Review* (May), 190–197.

Rodríguez, Mario (1965) *Central America*. Englewood Cliffs, N. J.: Prentice-Hall.

——— (1955) "The Livingston Codes in the Guatemalan Crisis of 1837-8." New Orleans: Middle American Research Institute, Tulane University.

Rosenthal, Gert (1971) "The Role of Private Foreign Investment in the Development of the Central American Common Market." Guatemala: draft.

Rubio Sánchez, Manuel (1958) "El Cacao," *Anales de la Sociedad de Geografía e Historia* Vol. XXXI, 81–129.

Sáenz, Vincente (1962) *Rompiendo cadenas*. México: Editorial America Nueva.

Schneider, Ronald (1958) *Communism in Guatemala, 1944–1954*. New York: Praeger.

Senate Foreign Relations Committee (SFRC), U. S. Senate (1971) "Guatemala and the Dominican Republic: A Staff Memorandum." Washington: Government Printing Office. (Sub-Committee on Western Hemisphere Affairs), Dec. 30.

Sloan, John (1970) "Electoral Frauds and Social Change: The Guatemalan Example," *Science and Society* (Spring), 78–91.

—— (1968) "The Electoral Game in Guatemala." Austin, Texas: Ph.D. Thesis, Dept. of Political Science, University of Texas.

Smith, Robert S. (1963) "Financing the Central American Federation, 1821–1838," *Hispanic American Historical Review,* (November), 483–510.

—— (1959) "Indigo Production and Trade in Colonial Guatemala," *Hispanic American Historical Review* (May), 181–211.

—— (1956) "Forced Labor in the Guatemalan Indigo Works," *Hispanic American Historical Review* (August), 319–328.

—— (1946) "Origins of the Consulado of Guatemala," *Hispanic American Historical Review* (May), 150–161.

*Solórzano F., Valentin (1963) *Evolución económica de Guatemala.* Guatemala: Seminario de Integración Social Guatemalteca.

Stein, Stanley J. and Barbara H. Stein (1970) *The Colonial Heritage of Latin America.* New York: Oxford University Press.

Thompson, J. Eric (1954) *Rise and Fall of Maya Civilization.* Norman, Okla.: Universiy of Oklahoma Press.

—— (1942) *Civilization of the Mayas.* Chicago: Field Museum of Anthropology.

Tobar Cruz, Pedro (1959) *Los montañeses.* Guatemala: Ministerio de Educación Pública.

Tobis, David (1971) "United Fruit is not Chiquita." *NACLA* Newsletter (October), 7–15.

Toriello, Guillermo (1955) *La batalla de Guatemala.* Mexico: Cuardernos Americanos.

*Torres Rivas, Edelberto (1971) *Interpretación del desarrollo social centroamericano.* San José, Costa Rica: Editorial Universitaria Centroamericana.

—— (1969) *Procesos y estructuras de una sociedad dependiente.* (Centroamericana). Santiago: Ediciones Prensa Latinoamericana.

Travis, Helen Simon and A. B. Magil (1954) *The Truth about Guatemala.* New York: New Century Publishers.

Ukers, William H. (1922) *All About Coffee.* New York: Tea and Coffee Trade Journal Co.

Unión Patriótica Guatemala (1964) *Guatemala contra el imperialismo, 1954–1964.*

Villamar Contreras, Antonio Marco (1969) "El pensamiento político de la generación revolucionaria de 1944." *Economía* 21 (July–Sept.), 43–62.

Van Aken, Mark (1962) "British Policy Considerations in Central America before 1850," *Hispanic American Historical Review,* (February), 54–9.

Vitale, Luis (1968) "Latin America: Feudal or Capitalist?" in Petras, J. and M. Zeitlin (eds.) *Latin America: Reform or Revolution?* Greenwich, Conn.: Fawcett. 32–43.

von Hagen, Victor (1960) *World of the Maya.* New York: Mentor.

Weaver, Jerry (1970)   "Bureaucracy during a Period of Social Change: The Guatemalan Case." (Manuscript for conference at University of Texas).

Whetten, Nathan (1961)   *Guatemala: The Land and the People.* New Haven: Yale University Press.

Wickiezer, V. D. (1943)   *The World Coffee Economy.* Stanford: Food Research Institute.

Wise, David and Thomas Ross (1964)   *The Invisible Government.* New York: Bantam.

*Wolf, Eric (1959)   *Sons of the Shaking Earth.* Chicago: University of Chicago Press.

Woodward, Ralph Lee (1968)   "The Merchants and Economic Development in the Americas, 1750–1850: A Preliminary Study," *Journal of Inter-American Studies* (January), 134–153.

———— (1966)   *Class Privilege and Economic Development: The Consulado de Comercio of Guatemala, 1793–1871.* Chapel Hill: University of North Carolina Press.

———— (1965a)   "Economic and Social Origins of the Guatemalan Political Parties, 1773–1823," *Hispanic American Historical Review* (November), 544–566.

———— (1965b)   "The Guatemalan Merchants and National Defense: 1810," *Hispanic American Historical Review* (August), 452–462.

———— (1964)   "Guatemalan Cotton and the American Civil War," *Inter-American Economic Affairs* (Winter), 87–94.

Ydigoras Fuentes, Miguel (1963)   *My War with Communism.* Englewood Cliffs: Prentice-Hall.

Young, John Parke (1925)   *Central American Currency and Finance.* Princeton: Princeton University Press.

Zavala, Silvio (1945)   "Contribución a la historia de las instituciones coloniales en Guatemala," *Jornadas* 36.

MEXICO

Acevedor, Lopéz, María Guadalupe and Gilberto Silva Ruiz (1973)   "Análisis de las situaciones de clase de los trabajadores Mexicanos." Unpublished Licenciado Thesis in Sociology, UNAM.

Aguilar, Monteverde, Alonso (1968)   *Dialéctica de la economía mexicana.* México: Editorial Nuestro Tiempo.

————, and Fernando Carmona (1967) *México: requeza y miserio*. México: Editorial Nuestro Tiempo.

Alonso, Antonio (1972) *El movimiento Ferrocarrilero en México 1958–1959*. Mexico: Ediciones Era.

Anderson, Bo, and James D. Cockcroft (1966) "Control and Cooptation in Mexican Politics," *International Journal of Comparative Sociology*, VII, 1: 11–28 (March), reprinted in Irving Louis Horowitz, Josué de Castro, John Gerassi (eds.), *Latin American Radicalism* (1969) New York: Vintage. 366–389.

Ashby, Joe C. (1967) *Organized Labor and the Mexican Revolution under Lazaro Cárdenas*. Chapel Hill, North Carolina; University of North Carolina Press.

Banco Nacional de Comercio Exterior (1968) *México 1968: hechos, cifras, tendencias*. México.

Barkin, David (1973) "The Persistence of Poverty: Economic Growth, Social Stagnation and Political Manipulation in Mexico." Manuscript (available from author, Dept. of Economics, Lehman College, Bronx, New York).

Basurto, Jorge (1973) "Poder politico y movimiento obrero en México," manuscript (available from author, Instituto de Investigaciones Sociales, UNAM, Mexico).

Brandenburg, Frank R. (1964) *The Making of Modern Mexico*. Englewood Cliffs, New Jersey: Prentice-Hall, Inc.

Brown, Lyle C. (1964) "General Lázaro Cárdenas and Mexican Presidential Politics, 1933–1940: A study in the Acquisition and Manipulation of Political Power." Unpublished Doctoral Dissertation, University of Texas, Austin.

Calvert, Peter (1968) *The Mexican Revolution 1910–1914. The Diplomacy of Anglo-American Conflict*. Cambridge: Cambridge University Press.

Carr, Barry (1972a) "Anticlericalism and the Mexican Revolution: A re-interpretation." (occasional paper). St. Anthony's College, Oxford.

———— (1972b) "Labour and Politics in Mexico, 1910–1928." (occasional paper). St. Anthony's College, Oxford.

Castellanos, Rosario, et al. (1969) *La corrupción*. México: Editorial Nuestro Tiempo.

Ceceña, José Luis (1970) *México en la orbita imperial*. Mexico: Ediciones "El Caballito."

———— (1963) *El capital monopolista y la economíca de México*. México: Cuadernos Americanos.

Chevalier, Francois (1967) "The Ejido and Political Stability in Mexico," in Claudio Veliz (ed.), *The Politics of Conformity in Latin America*. London: Oxford University Press. 158–191.

———— (1956) "La formación de los grandes latifundios en México," *Problemas Agrícolas e Industriales de México,* Jan.–March.

Cockcroft, James D., André Gunder Frank and Dale L. Johnson (1972) *De-*

pendence and Underdevelopment: Latin America's Political Economy.
New York: Anchor.

——— (1970) *Economía política del subdesarrollo en América Latina.* Buenos Aires: Ediciones Signos.

Cockcroft, James D. (1968) *Intellectual Precursors of the Mexican Revolution.* Austin and London: University of Texas Press. In Spanish: Mexico, Siglo Veintiuno Editores. S. A.

Comité bilateral de hombres de negocios México-Estados Unidos—Sección Mexicana (1971) *Inversiones extranjeras privadas directas en México.* Mexico.

Córdova, Arnaldo (1973) *La ideología de la revolución mexicana.* Mexico: Ediciones Era.

——— (1972) "El nacionalismo mexicano: un proyecto de dependencia para México," *Punto Crítico* (June), 21–24.

——— (1973) "La transformación del PNR en PRM: el triunfo del corporativismo en México," MS. (available from author, Centro de Estudios Latinoamericanos, UNAM, Mexico).

Cornelius, Wayne A., Jr. (1971) "Nation-Building, Participation, and Distribution: The Politics of Social Reform under Cárdenas," in G. A. Almond and Scott C. Flanagan, eds., (1973) *Developmental Episodes in Comparative Politics: Crisis, Choice, and Change.* Boston: Little, Brown and Company.

Costeloe, Michael P. (1967) *Church Wealth in Mexico: A Study of the Juzgado de Capellanias' in the Archbishopric of Mexico, 1800–1856.* New York: Cambridge University Press.

Couturier, Edith Boorstein (1968) "Modernización y tradición en una hacienda (San Juan Hueyapan, 1902–1911)," *Historia Mexicana* XVIII, no. 1. (July–Sept.), 35–55.

Cumberland, Charles C. (1968) *Mexico: The Struggle for Modernity.* London and New York: Oxford University Press.

Durán, Leonel (1972) *Ideario político de Lázaro Cárdenas.* Mexico: Ediciones Era.

Durán, Marco Antonio (1972) *El agrarismo mexicano.* Mexico: Siglo Veintiuno Editores, S. A.

The Economist Intelligence Unit (1970) *Quarterly Economic Review.* Mexico, Annual Supplement. London: The Economist Intelligence Unit Limited.

Fenster, Leo (1969) "Mexican Auto Swindle," *The Nation* (June 2), 693–697.

Florescano, Enrique (1969) *Precios del maíz y crisis agrícolas en México, 1708–1810.* México: El Colegio de México.

Frank, André Gunder (1971) "Lumpenburguesía: Lumpendesarrollo," MS. Published in earlier forms as "Lumpenburguesia: Lumpendesarrollo—dependencia, Clase y Política en Latinoamerica 1970," Medellín: Editorial Oveja Negra, Caracas: Editorial Nueva Izquierda—Crítica Marxista, 1970; Montevideo: Ediciones de la Banda Oriental, 1971, Mexico: Ed. Era.

——— (1969) *Latin America: Underdevelopment or Revolution.* New York: Monthly Review Press.

García Cantú, Gastón (1971) *Las invasiones norteamericanas en México.* Mexico: Ediciones Era.

Gibson, Charles (1964) *The Aztecs Under Spanish Rule, 1519–1810: A History of the Indians of the Valley of Mexico.* Stanford: Stanford University Press.

Gilly, Adolofo (1971) *La revolución interrumpida.* Mexico: Ediciones "El Caballito."

González Navarro, Moises (1965) "Mexico: The Lopsided Revolution," in Claudio Veliz (ed.) *Obstacles to Change in Latin America.* London: Oxford University Press. 206–229.

González Roa, Fernando, and José Covarrubias (1917). *El problema rural de México.* México: Palacio Nacional.

Grupo Secretaría de Hacienda—Banco de México (1972) *Estadísticas básicas de la inversión extranjera en México.* Mexico: Banco de México (April 7).

Haley, P. Edward (1970) *Revolution and Intervention: The Diplomacy of Taft and Wilson with Mexico, 1910–1917.* Cambridge, Mass.: The MIT Press.

Hernández, Salvador (1973) *Un ensayo sobre el imperialismo norteamericano en México.* Mexico: Cuadernos del Centro de Estudios Políticos, No. 1 (UNAM).

———— (1971) *El PRI y el Movimiento Estudiantil de 1968.* Mexico: Ediciones "El Caballito."

———— (1970) "The PRI and the Mexican Student Movement of 1968: A Case Study of Repression." Unpublished Masters Thesis, Department of Anthropology and Sociology, The University of British Columbia.

Houk, J. T. Dock (1967) *Financing and Problems of Development Banking.* New York.

Humphreys, R. A., and John Lynch (1966) *The Origins of the Latin American Revolutions, 1808–1826.* New York: Alfred A. Knopf.

Katz, Friedrich (1964) *Deutschland, Diaz und die mexikanische Revolution. Die deutsche Politik im Mexiko 1870–1920.* Berlin: VEB Deutscher Verlag der Wissenschaften.

Leal, Juan Felipe (1972) *La burguesia y el estado mexicano.* Mexico: Ediciones "El Caballito."

López Aparicio, Alfonso (1952) *El movimiento obrero en México.* México: Editorial Jus.

Márquez Fuentes, Manuel and Octavio Rodríguez Araujo (1973) *El partido communista mexicano.* Mexico: Ediciones "El Caballito."

Médin, Tzvi (1972) *Ideologia y praxis: política de Lázaro Cárdenas.* Mexico: Siglo Veintiuno Editores, S.A.

Meyer, Jean (1971) *La Christiade: Societé e ideologie dans le Mexique Contemporain,* 5 vols. Thèse de Doctoret d'Etat, Sorbonne. (available from author).

———— (1968) "Los Estados Unidos y el petroleo mexicano: estado de la cuestión," *Historia Mexicana,* XVIII, No. 1, (July–Sept.), 79–96.

Meyer, Lorenzo (1968) *México y Estados Unidos en el Conflicto Petrolero (1917–1942)*. Mexico: El Colegio de México.

Meyer, Michael C. (1970) "The Arms of the Ypiranga," *Hispanic American Historical Review*, L, No. 3, (August), 543–556.

Michaels, Albert L. (1970) "The Crisis of Cardenismo," *Journal of Latin American Studies* (May), 51–79.

——— (1968) "Lazaro Cárdenas y la lucha por la independencia económica de México," *História Mexicana*, 18, No. 1. (July–Sept.), 56–78.

——— (1966) "Mexican Politics and Nationalism from Calles to Cardenas." Unpublished Doctoral Dissertation, University of Pennsylvania.

Nacional Financiera (1970) La economía mexicana en cifras 1970. Mexico: Nacional Financiera.

——— (1969) El Mercado de Valores. (July 7).

——— (1968) Informe Anual, 1967. México.

NACLA (North American Congress on Latin America) (1968) Mexico 1968. New York: NACLA.

Nathan, Paul (1952) "Mexico Under Cárdenas." Unpublished Doctoral Dissertation, University of Chicago.

Navarrete, Ifigenia M. de. (1967) "Income Distribution in Mexico," in Enrique Pérez López et al., *Mexico's Recent Economic Growth*. Austin, Texas: University of Texas Press. 133–172.

Nearing, Scott, and Joseph Freeman (1969) *Dollar Diplomacy*. Monthly Review Press. Earlier Edition (1925). New York: B. W. Huebsch, Inc.

O'Shaughnessy, Edith (1916) *A Diplomat's Wife in Mexico*. New York: Harper.

Parkes, Henry Bamford (1966, 1938) *A History of Mexico*. Boston: Houghton Mifflin Company.

Pena, Moises T. De la (1964) *El pueblo y su tierra. Mito y realidad de la reforma agraria en México*. México: Cuadernos Americanos.

Raby, David L. (1972) "La contribución del Cardenismo al desarrollo de México en las época actual," *Áportes* (October), 31–65.

——— (1970) "Rural Teachers and Social and Political Conflict in Mexico, 1921–1940, with Special Reference to the States of Michoacán and Campeche," Unpublished Doctoral Dissertation, University of Warwick, Coventry (England).

——— (1968) "Los maestros rurales y los conflictos sociales en México, 1931–1940," *Historia Mexicana*, 18, No. 2 (Oct.–Dec.), 190–226.

Rangel, José Calixto (1972) *La pequeña burguesia en la sociedad mexicana, 1895–1960*. Mexico: Instituto de Investigaciones Sociales.

Rebelión y plan de los indios huaxtecos de Tantoyuca, 1856 (1956) México: Editor Vargas Rea.

Reed, Nelson (1964) *The Caste War of Yucatan*. Stanford, California: Stanford University Press.

Reynolds, Clark W. (1970) *The Mexican Economy: Twentieth Century Structure and Growth*. New Haven, Conn.: Yale University Press.

Rosenzweig, Fernando (1965) "El desarrollo económico de México de 1877 a

1911," *El Trimestre Económico*, XXXII, No. 127 (July–Sept.), 405–454.

—— et al. (1965) *Historia Moderna de México. El Porfiriato: la vida económica.* 2 vols. México: Editorial Hermes. *Anuario Estadístico de los Estados Unidos Mexicanos*, 1964–1965 México.

Secretaría de Industria y Comercio. Dirección General de Estadística (1967).

Semo, Enrique (1965) "El gobierno de Obrégon, la deuda exterior y el desarrollo independiente de México," *Revista Historia y Sociedad* No. 2, (Summer).

Shulgovski, Anatol (1968) *México en la encrucijada de su historia.* Mexico: Fondo de Cultura Popular.

Simpson, Eyler M. (1937) *The ejido: Mexico's Way Out.* Chapel Hill, North Carolina: University of North Carolina Press.

Simpson, Lesley Byrd (1941, 1960) *Many Mexicos.* New York: G. P. Putnam's Sons, 1941. Berkeley and Los Angeles: University of California Press, 1960.

Smith, Robert F. (1972) *The United States and Revolutionary Nationalism in Mexico 1916–1932.* Chicago: The University of Chicago Press.

—— (1969) "The Morrow Mission and the International Commission of Bankers on Mexico: The Interaction of Finance Diplomacy and the New Mexican Elite," *Journal of Latin American Studies* I, 2 (Nov.), 149–166.

—— (1967) "Thomas W. Lamont and United States-Mexican Relations," *Harvard Library Bulletin* XV, 1 (Jan.), 49–58.

Solis, Leopoldo (1971) *La realidad económica mexicana: retrovisión y perspectivas.* Mexico: Siglo Veintiuno Editores, S.A.

Stavenhagen, Rodolfo, Fernando Paz Sánchez, Cuauhtemoc Cárdenas, and Arturo Bonilla (1968) *Neolatifundismo y explotación de Emiliano Zapata a Anderson Clayton & Co.* México: Nuestro Tiempo.

Turner, John Kenneth (1910) *Barbarous Mexico.* Chicago: Charles H. Kerr & Company.

United States Department of State (1938) *Foreign Relations, American Republics.*

Various authors (1972) *El perfil de México en 1980.* México Siglo XXI Editores, S.A.

Vaupel, James W., and Joan A. Curhan (1969) *The Making of Multinational Enterprises.* A Source Book of Tables Based on a Study of 187 Major U.S. Manufacturing Corporations. Cambridge, Mass.: Harvard Graduate School of Business Administration.

Vázquez de Knauth, Josefina (1970) *Nacionalismo y educación en México.* México: El Colegio de México.

Whetten, Nathan I. (1948) *Rural Mexico.* Chicago: University of Chicago Press.

Wilkie, James W. (1967) *The Mexican Revolution: Federal Expenditure and Social Change Since 1910.* Berkeley, California: University of California Press.

——, and Edna Monzon de Wilkie (1967) *México visto en el siglo XX, entrevistas de historia oral.* México: Instituto Mexicano de Investigaciones Económicas.

Wionczek, Miguel (1971)   *Inversión y tecnología extranjera en América Latina.*
Mexico: Cuadernos de Joaquín Mortiz.
Wolfe, Eric R. (1969)   *Peasant Wars of the Twentieth Century.* New York:
Harper and Row.
———— (1962, 1959)   *Sons of the Shaking Earth.* Chicago: The Universiy of
Chicago Press.
Womack, John, Jr. (1969)   *Zapata and the Mexican Revolution.* New York:
Alfred A. Knopf.

ARGENTINA

Aparcicio, Francisco y Horacio Difrieri (eds.)   *La Argentina: Suma de geo-
grafía.* 9 vols. Buenos Aires, 1958–63.
Argentina, Dirección Nacional de Estadística y Censos. *General Censuses (Cen-
sos Generales de la Nación) of 1869, 1895, 1914 and 1947.*
———— Dirección Nacional de Estadística y Censos. *Censo Industrial, –1935,*
Buenos Aires, 1936.
———— Dirección de Estadística Social. *Investigaciones Sociales.* Buenos Aires,
1943–45.
———— Dirección Nacional de Estadística y Censos. *Censo nacional minero,
industrial y comercial de 1954.* Buenos Aires, 1954.
———— Banco Central de la República. Memórias. (yearly).
———— Banco de Crédito Industrial. Memórias. Buenos Aires, 1944–56.
———— Banco de la Nación Argentina, Oficina de Investigaciones Económicas.
Revista Económica.
———— Presidencia de la Nación. *Producto e ingreso de la República Argentina
en el período 1935–1954.* Buenos Aires, 1955.
———— *Memória: Gobierno Provisional de la Revolución Libertadora, 1955–
1958.* Buenos Aires, 1958.
Argentina 1930–1960. Buenos Aires: Sur, 1961.
Bagú, Sergio (1952)   *Estructura social de la colonia.* Buenos Aires: El Ateneo.
———— (1949)   *Economía de la sociedad colonial.* Buenos Aires: El Ateneo.
———— (1969)   *Evolución histórica de la estratificación social en la Argentina.*
Instituto de Investigaciones Económicas y Sociales de la Universidad Cen-
ral de Venezuela: Esquema.
Bailey, Samuel L. (1967)   *Labor, Nationalism, and Politics in Argentina.* New
Brunswick: Rutgers University Press.
Belloni, Alberto (1960)   *Del anarquismo al peronismo.* Buenos Aires: Pena
Lillo.
———— (1962)   *Peronismo y socialismo nacional.* Buenos Aires: Coyoacán.

Beyhaut, Gustavo, et all. (1965) "Los immigrantes en el sistema ocupacional argentino," in Di Tella, Torcuato; Germani, Gino; Graciarena, Jorge, et al. *Argentina, sociedad de masas.* Buenos Aires: Editorial Universitaria de Buenos Aires.

Blanksten, I. George (1953) *Perón's Argentina.* Chicago: The University of Chicago Press.

Braun, Oscar (1970) *Desarrollo del capital monopolista en Argentina.* Buenos Aires: Editorial Tiempo Contemporáneo.

Broner, Julio, and Daniel E. Larriqueta (1969) *La Revolución Industrial Argentina.* Buenos Aires: Sudamericana.

Bruce, James (1953) *Those Perplexing Argentines.* New York.

Bunge, Alejandro (1940) *Una nueva Argentina.* Buenos Aires: Kraft.

Burgin, Miron (1946) *Economic Aspects of Argentine Federalism, 1820–1852.* Cambridge, Mass.: Harvard University Press.

Cafiero, Antonio (1961) *5 años después . . . de la economía social-justicialista al regimen liberal-capitalista.* Buenos Aires.

Cantón, Darío (1970) *La política de los militares Argentinos 1900–1970.* Buenos Aires: Siglo XXI.

——— (1969) *Materiales para el estudio de la sociología política en la Argentina.* 2 vols. Buenos Aires: Editorial del Instituto Di Tella.

——— (1968) *El Parlamento Argentino en épocas de cambio: 1890 y 1916 y 1946.* Buenos Aires: Editorial del Instituto Di Tella.

Cárdenas, Gonzalo, et al. (1969) *El Peronismo.* Buenos Aires: Carlos Pérez.

Cardoso, Fernando H. y Enzo Faletto (1969) *Dependencia y desarrollo en América Latina.* Mexico: Siglo XXI.

Ciria, Alberto (1964) *Partidos y poder en la Argentina moderna (1930–46).* Buenos Aires: Jorge Alvárez.

——— et al. (1969) *La Década Infama.* Buesnos Aires: Carlos Pérez.

Cochran, Thomas C., and Ruben E. Reina (1962, 1971) *Capitalism in Argentine Culture.* Philadelphia: University of Pennsylvania Press.

Cortés Conde, Ezequiel Roberto y Gallo (1967) *La formación de la Argentina moderna.* Buenos Aires: Editorial Paidos.

Cúneo, Dardo (1967) *Comportamiento y crisis de la clase empresaria.* 2nd. ed. Buenos Aires: Pleamar.

——— (1965) *El desencuentro argentino 1930–1955.* Buenos Aires: Pleamar.

Cúneo, Niccolo (1940) *Storia del emigrazione italiana in Argentina, 1810–1870.* Milan.

Daniels, Ed. (1970) "From Mercantilism to Imperialism. The Argentine Case," *North American Congress on Latin America (NCLA),* Newsletter, New York and Berkeley, Vol. IV, Nos. 5 and 6.

Delgado, Julián (1968) "Industria: el desafío a la Argentina," *Primera Plana.* Buenos Aires, No. 297, (September 3).

Delich, Francisco J. (1970) *Crisis y protesta social. Córdoba, mayo de 1969.* Buenos Aires: Ediciones Signos.

Díaz Alejandro, F. Carlos (1970) *Essays on the Economic History of the Argentine Republic.* New Haven and London: Yale University Press.

Dieguez, Hector (1969) "Argentina y Australia: algunos aspectos de su desarrollo económico comparado," *Desarrollo Económico* Vol. 8, No. 32, (Jan.–March).

Di Tella, Torcuato (1964) *El sistema político argentino y la clase obrera.* Buenos Aires: Editorial Universitaria de Buenos Aires.

―――― y Tulio Halperin (1969) *Los fragmentos del poder.* Buenos Aires: Jorge Alvárez.

Di Tella, Manuel Guido y Zymelman (1967) *Las etapas del desarrollo económico argentino.* Buenos Aires: Editorial Universitaria de Buenos Aires.

Dorfman, Adolfo (1970) *Historia de la industria argentina.* Buenos Aires: Solar/Hachette.

Eshag, E. and R. Thorp (1965) "Economic and Social Consequences of Orthodox Economic Policies in Argentina in the Post-War Years," *Bulletin of the Oxford University Institute of Economics and Statistics* Vol. XXVII, No. 1, (February).

Fayt, Carlos S. (1971) *El político armado. Dinámica del proceso político argentino 1960–1971.* Buenos Aires: Ediciones Pannedille.

―――― (1967) *La naturaleza del peronismo.* Buenos Aires: Viracocha.

Ferns, H. S. (1969) *Argentina.* London: Ernest Benn Ltd.

―――― *Britain and Argentina in the Nineteenth Century.* London: Oxford University Press.

Ferrer, Aldo (1967) *The Argentine Economy.* Berkeley and Los Angeles: The University of California Press.

―――― et. al. (1969) *Los planes de estabilización en la Argentina.* Buenos Aires: Paidos.

Fichas de Investigación Económica y Social Nos. 1–9. Buenos Aires, April 1964–May 1966.

Fillol, T. R. (1961) *Social Factors in Economic Development. The Argentine Case.* Cambridge, Mass.: M.I.T. Press.

Frank, André Gunder (1969) *Latin America: Underdevelopment or Revolution.* New York: Monthly Review Press.

Freels, John William (Jr.) (1968) *Industrial Trade Associations in Argentine Politics.* Riverside: Ph.D. Dissertation, University of California. Spanish edition, EUDEBA, 1970.

Frondizi, Silvio (1956) *La realidad argentina.* 2 vols. Buenos Aires: Praxis.

Fuchs, Jaime (1965) *Argentina, su desarrollo capitalista.* Buenos Aires: Cartago.

Gambini, Hugo (1969) *El 17 de Octubre de 1945.* Buenos Aires: Editorial Brújula.

Galletti, Alfredo (1961) *La política y los partidos.* Mexico: Fondo de Cultura Económica.

García Lupo, Rogelio (1969) *Contra la ocupación extranjera.* Buenos Aires.

―――― (1967) *La rebelión de los generales.* Buenos Aires: Jamcana.

Germani, Gino (1962) *Política y sociedad en una época de transición.* Buenos Aires: Paidos.

———— (1955)   *Estructura social de la Argentina*. Buenos Aires: Raigal.

Giberti, Horacio (1964)   *El desarrollo agrario argentino*. Buenos Aires: Editorial Universitaria de Buenos Aires.

———— (1961)   *Historia económica de la ganadería argentina*. 2nd. ed. Buenos Aires: Solar/Hachette.

González Trejo, Horacio (1969)   *Argentina: tiempo de violencia*. Buenos Aires: Carlos Pérez.

Gottheil, Julio (1969)   *El compromiso argentino*. Buenos Aires: Paidos.

Halperin Donghi, Tulio (1964)   *Argentina en el callejón*. Montevideo: Editorial Arca.

Hutchinson, Thomas J. (1865)   *Buenos Ayres and Argentine Gleanings*. London.

Ibarguren, Carlos (1955)   *La historia que he vivido*. Buenos Aires: Peuser.

Imaz, José Luis de (1970)   *Los que mandan* (Those Who Rule). Albany: State University of New York Press.

———— (1962)   *La clase alta de Buenos Aires*. Buenos Aires: Editorial Universitaria de Buenos Aires.

International Monetary Fund. International Financial Statisics. (serial).

Irazusta, Julio (1963)   *Influencia económica británica en el Río de la Plata*. Buenos Aires: Editorial Universitaria de Buenos Aires.

Jefferson, Mark (1926)   *Peopling the Argentine Pampa*. New York: American Geographical Society Research Series No. 16, Commonwealth Press.

Jitrik, Noé (1968)   *El 80 y su mundo*. Buenos Aires: Jorge Alvárez.

Jorge, Eduardo (1971)   *Industria y concentración económica* (desde principios de siglo hasta el peronismo). Buenos Aires: Siglo XXI.

Josephs, Ray (1944)   *Argentine Diary: The Inside Story of the Coming of Fascism*. New York: Random House.

Kelly, Sir David (1962)   *El poder detrás del trono*. Buenos Aires: Coyoacán.

———— (1958)   *The Ruling Few*. London.

Kenworthy, Eldon (1967)   "Argentina: the Politics of Late Industrialization," *Foreign Affairs* (April), XLV No. 3.

Kirkpatrick, Jeane (1971)   *Leader and Vanguard in Mass Society. A Study of Peronist Argentina*. Cambridge, Mass. and London: The M.I.T. Press.

Laclau, Ernesto (1970)   "The Argentinian Contest," *New Left Review* No. 62, (July–August).

———— (1969)   "Modos de producción, sistemas económicos y población excedente," *Revista Latinoamericana de Sociología* V No. 2, (July).

Leiserson, Alcira (1966)   *Notes on the Process of Industrialization in Argentina, Chile, and Peru*. Politics of Modernization Series, No. 3, Institute of International Studies, Berkeley, California, University of California.

Levene, Ricardo (1937)   *A History of Argentina*. Chapel Hill: University of North Carolina Press.

Lux-Wurm, Pierre (1965)   *Le peronisme*. Paris: Bibliotèque Constitutionnelle et de Science Politique.

Martínez Estrada, Ezequiel (1942)   *Radiografía de la pampa*. Buenos Aires: Losada.

Martínez, A. B., and M. Lewandowski (1911)   *The Argentine in the Twentieth Century.* London.

Martorell, Guillermo (1969)   *Las inversiones extranjeras en la Argentina.* Buenos Aires: Editorial Galerna.

Magnet, Alejandro (1953)   *Nuestros vecinos justicialistas.* Santiago de Chile: Editorial del Pacífico.

McGann, T. F. (1966)   *Argentina: The Divided Land.* Princeton, N. J.: D. Van Nostrand Co.

Mazo, Gabriel del. (1955)   *El radicalismo. Notas sobre su historia y doctrina, 1922–52.* Buenos Aires: Raigal.

Merkx, Gilbert W. (1968)   *Political and Economic Change in Argentina from 1870 to 1966.* Ph.D. Dissertation, Yale Universiy.

Moore, Barrington, Jr. (1966)   *Social Origins of Dictatorship and Democracy.* Boston: Beacon Press.

Mulhall, E. T. and M. (1863)   *Handbook of the River Plate.* Buenos Aires: Editors of the Standard.

Murmis, Miguel y Portantiero, Juan Carlos (1971)   *Estudios sobre los orígenes del peronismo/ 1.* Buenos Aires: Siglo XXI.

Navarro Gerassi, Marysa (1968)   *Los Nacionalistas.* Buenos Aires: Jorge Alvárez.

North, Liisa (1966)   *Civil-Military Relations in Argentina, Chile and Peru.* Politics of Modernization Series, No. 2, Institute of International Studies, Berkeley: University of California Press.

Nun, José (1969)   *Latin America: The Hegemonic Crisis and the Military Coup.* Politics of Modernization Series, No. 7, Institute of International Studies. Berkeley: University of California Press.

Oddone, Jacinto (1967)   *La burguesía terrateniente argentina.* Buenos Aires: Ediciones Libera, (1st. edition, 1930).

——— (1934)   *Gremialismo proletario argentino.* Buenos Aires: La Vanguardia.

Orgambide, Pedro (1968)   *Yo, Argentino.* Buenos Aires: Jorge Alvárez.

Orona, Juan V. (1966)(a)   *La Revolución del 6 de Septiembre.* Buenos Aires.

——— (1966)(b)   *La logia militar que derrocó a Castillo.* Buenos Aires.

——— (1965)   *La logia militar que enfrentó a Hipólito Yrigoyen.* Buenos Aires.

Ortiz, Ricardo M. (1955)   *Historia económica de la Argentina.* 2 vols. Buenos Aires: Plus Ultra. (2nd. ed.).

Palacio, Ernesto (1960)   *Historia de la Argentina (1515–1957).* 2 vols. 3rd. edition. Buenos Aires: A. Pena Lillo.

Panettieri, José (1969)   *Síntesis histórica del desarrollo industrial argentino.* Córdoba: Macchi.

——— (1967)   *Los trabajadores.* Buenos Aires: Jorge Alvárez.

Panorama de la economía argentina. Buenos Aires, 1957–1966.

Pérez Amuchastegui, A. J. (1965)   *Mentalidades Argentinas (1860–1930).* Buenos Aires: Editorial Universitaria de Buenos Aires.

Perelman, Angel (1961)   *Cómo hicimos el 17 de Octubre*. Buenos Aires: Coyoacán.

Perón, Juan Domingo (1968)   *La hora de los pueblos*. Buenos Aires: Norte.

—— (1963)   *Tres revoluciones militares*. Buenos Aires: Escorpión.

—— (1957)   *La fuerza es el derecho de las bestias. La realidad de un año de tiranía*. Caracas: Garrido.

—— (n.d.)   *Del poder al exilio*. Buenos Aires: Norte.

—— (1952a)   *Política y Estrategia, por Descartes*. Buenos Aires.

—— (1952b)   *Los mensajes de Perón*. Buenos Aires: Editorial Mundo Peronista.

—— (1952c)   *Conducción política*. Buenos Aires: Subsecretaría de Informaciones.

—— (1948a)   *Perón Expounds his Doctrine*. Buenos Aires.

—— (1948b)   *The Argentine International Policy*. Buenos Aires.

—— (1948c)   *Political and Social Situation Prior to the Revolution of 1943*. Buenos Aires.

—— (1948d)   *Social Reform*. Buenos Aires.

Pérón, Eva (1955)   *Historia del Peronismo*. Buenos Aires: Ediciones Mundo Peronista.

—— (1953)   *La razón de mi vida*. Buenos Aires: Escolar, Peuser.

Peronist Doctrine. (Official Publication). Buenos Aires.

Peter, José (1968)   *Crónicas proletarias*. Buenos Aires: Esfera.

Petras, James.   "Peronism," *New Politics* II, No. 2.

Potash, Robert A. (1969)   *The Army and Politics in Argentina, 1928–1945. Yrigoyen to Perón*. Stanford: Stanford University Press.

Primera Plana. Buenos Aires. Weekly.

Puiggros, Rodolfo (1969)   *El Peronismo. Y sus causas*. Buenos Aires: Jorge Alvárez.

—— (1968)   *La democracia fraudulenta*. Buenos Aires: Jorge Alvárez.

—— (1967)   *Las izquierda y el probléma nacional*. Buenos Aires: Jorge Alvárez.

—— (1965a)   *Pueblo y oligarquía*. Buenos Aires: J. Alvárez.

—— (1965b)   *Historia crítica de los partidos políticos argentinos*. Buenos Aires: Argumentos.

—— (1952)   *El proletariado en la revolución nacional*. Buenos Aires: Trafac.

Ramos, Jorge Abelardo (1965)   *Revolución y contrarrevolución en la Argentina*. 2 vols. Buenos Aires: Plus Ultra.

Rennie, Ysabel (1945)   *The Argentine Republic*. New York: The Macmillan Co.

Review of the River Plate (1891–present)   Buenos Aires.

Romero, José Luis (1963)   *A History of Argentine Political Thought*. Stanford: Stanford University Press.

Romero, Luis Alberto et al. (1968)   *El Radicalismo*. Buenos Aires: Carlos Pérez.

Rowe, James (1966)   "Argentina's Durable Peronists: A 20th Anniversary Note,

Part I: Some Preconditions and Achievements," *American Universities Field Staff, Reports Service* XII, No. 2.

Rubinstein, Juan Carlos (1968) *Desarrollo y discontinuidad política en Argentina.* Buenos Aires: Siglo Veintiuno.

Sarmiento, Domingo Faustino (1961) *Life in the Argentine Republic in the Days of the Tyrants.* New York: Collier Books.

Sarobe, José María (1957) *Memorias sobre la revolución del 6 septiembre de 1930.* Buenos Aires: Ediciones Gure.

Sautu, Ruth (1968) "Poder económico y burguesía industrial en la Argentina, 1930–1954," *Revista Latinoamericana de Sociología* Vol. IV, No. 3 (November).

Scalabrini Ortiz, Raúl (1965) *Política británica en el Río de la Plata.* Buenos Aires: Plus Ultra.

——— (1964) *Historia de los ferrocarriles argentinos.* Buenos Aires: Plus Ultra.

Scobie, James R. (1964a) *Argentina: A City and a Nation.* New York: Oxford University Press.

——— (1946b) *Revolution on the Pampas. A Social History of Argentine Wheat, 1860–1910.* Austin: The University of Texas Press.

Sebreli, Juan José (1966) *Eva Perón: ¿Aventurera o militante?* Buenos Aires: Siglo Veinte.

——— (1965) *Buenos Aires: vida cotidiana y alienación.* Buenos Aires.

Silverman, Bertram (1968–1969) "Labor Ideology and Economic Development in the Peronist Epoch," *Studies in Comparative International Development* Vol. IV, No. 11.

Silvert, Kalman H. (1963) "The Costs of Anti-Nationalism: Argentina," in Kalman H. Silvert, ed. *Expectant Peoples.* New York: Vintage Books.

Smith, Peter (1969) *Politics and Beef in Argentina: Patterns of Conflict and Change.* New York and London: Columbia University Press.

Solberg, Carl (1970) *Immigration and Nationalism. Argentina and Chile, 1890–1914.* Austin: The University of Texas Press.

Stein, Stanley J. and Barbara H. (1970) *The Colonial Heritage of Latin America.* New York: Oxford University Press.

Strickon, Arnold (1962) "Class and Kinship in Argentina," *Ethology* I, No. 4 (October).

——— (1960) *Grandsons of the Gauchos.* New York: Columbia University.

United Nations, ECLA (1971) *Estudio económico de América Latina 1970.* E/CN.12/868/Rev. 1. New York.

——— (1969) *Economic Development and Income Distribution in Argentina.* E/CN.12/802. New York.

——— (1964a) *Social Development of Latin America in the Post-War Period.* E/CN.12/660. New York.

——— (1964b) *The Economic Development of Latin America in the Post-War Period.* E/CN.12/659/Rev. 1. New York.

——— (1959) *Análisis y proyecciones del desarrollo económico. El desarrollo económico de la Argentina.* E/CN.12/429/Rev. 1. Mexico.

U. S. Chamber of Commerce in Buenos Aires. *Comments on Argentine Trade.* (Monthly).

Viñas, David (1964) *Literatura argentina y realidad política.* Buenos Aires: Jorge Alvárez.

Walsh, R. J. (1964) *Operación masacre.* Buenos Aires: Continental Service.

Weil, Felix J. (1944) *Argentine Riddle.* New York: The John Day Co.

Whitaker, Arthur P. (1965) *Argentina.* New Jersey: Prentice-Hall.

—— (1954) *The United States and Argentina.* Cambridge, Mass.: Harvard University Press.

BRAZIL

Alarcón, Rodrigo (1970) *Brazil: represión y tortura.* Santiago: Editorial Orbe.

Amaral, Azevedo (1938) *O estado autoritário e a realidade nacional.* Rio de Janeiro: José Olympio Editôra.

Baer, Werner (1966) *A industrialização e o desenvolvimento económico do Brasil.* Rio de Janeiro: Fundação Getúlio Vargas.

Bastos, Abguar (1946) *Prestes e a revolução social.* Rio de Janiero: Editôra Calvino.

Bello, José Maria (1966) *A History of Modern Brazil, 1889–1964.* Stanford: Stanford University Press.

Boxer, C. R. (1962) *The Golden Age of Brazil, 1695–1750.* Berkeley and Los Angeles: University of California Press.

Buarque de Holanda, Sêrgio (1960–1971) *História geral da civilização brasileira.* São Paulo: Difusão Européia do Livro.

Cardoso, Fernando H. (1964) *Empresário industrial e desenvolvimento económico no Brasil.* São Paulo: Difusão Européia do Livro.

—— and Faletto, Enzo (1969) *Dependencia y desarrollo en América Latina.* Mexico City: Siglo XXI.

Carone, Edgard (1969) *A primeira república.* São Paulo: Difusão Européia do Livro.

—— (1965) *Revoluções do Brasil contemporáneo.* São Paulo: DESA.

Cohn, Gabriel (1968) *Petróleo e nacionalismo.* São Paulo: Difusão Européia do Livro.

Couto e Silva, Golbery do (1966) *Geopolítica do Brasil.* Rio de Janeiro: José Olympio Editôra.

Cunha, Euclydes da (1944) *Os sertões.* Several editions. In English: *Rebellion in the Backlands.* Chicago: University of Chicago Press.

Dean, Warren (1969) *The Industrialization of São Paulo, 1880–1945.* Austin: University of Texas Press.

Debray, Regis (1967) *Revolution in the Revolution.* New York: Monthly Review Press.

Frank, André Gunder (1969) *Capitalism and Underdevelopment in Latin America: Historical Studies of Chile and Brazil.* New York: Monthly Review Press.

Freyre, Gilberto (1959) *Ordem e progresso.* Rio de Janeiro: José Olympio Editôra.

—— (1951) *Sobrados e mucambos.* Rio de Janeiro: José Olympio Editôra. In English: (1963) *The Mansions and the Shanties.* New York: Alfred A. Knopf.

—— (1936) *Casa Grande e Senzala.* Rio de Janeiro: José Olympio Editôra. In English: (1946) *The Masters and the Slaves: A Study in the Development of Brazilian Civilization.* New York: Alfred A. Knopf.

Furtado, Celso (1964) *Dialética do desenvolvimento.* Rio de Janeiro: Editôra Fundo de Cultura.

—— (1962) *A pre-revolução brasileira.* Rio de Janeiro: Editôra Fundo de Cultura.

—— (1961) *Formação económica do Brasil.* Rio de Janeiro: Editôra Fundo de Cultura. In English: (1963) *Economic Growth of Brazil.* Berkeley and Los Angeles: University of California Press.

—— (1959) *A operação nordeste.* Rio de Janeiro: Instituto Superior de Estudos Brasileiros.

Graham, Richard (1968) *Britain and the Onset of Modernization in Brazil, 1850–1914.* Cambridge: Cambridge University Press.

Guilherme, Wanderley (1963) *Introdução ao estudo das contradições sociais no Brasil.* Rio de Janeiro: Instituto Superior de Estudos Brasileiros.

Guimarães, Passos, Alberto (1968) *Quatro séculos de latifundio.* Rio de Janeiro: Editôra Paz e Terra.

Ianni, Octavio et al (1966) *Política e revolução social no Brasil.* Rio de Janeiro: Editôra Civilização Brasileira.

—— (1965) *Estado e capitalismo.* Rio de Janeiro: Editôra Civilização Brasileira.

—— (1963) *Industrialização e desenvolvimento económico no Brasil.* Rio de Janeiro: Editôra Civilização Brasileira.

Jaguaribe, Helio (1962) *Desenvolvimento económico e desenvolvimento político.* Rio de Janeiro: Editôra Fundo de Cultura.

—— (1958) *Nacionalismo e desenvolvimento económico.* Rio de Janeiro: Instituto Superior de Estudos Brasileiros.

Leal, Víctor Nunes (1948) *Coronelismo, enxada e voto.* Rio de Janeiro: Editôra Revista Forense.

Leff, Nathaniel H. (1968) *Economic Policy Making and Development in Brazil 1947–1964.* New York: John Wiley and Sons.

Marini, Ruy Mauro (1971a) "La izquierda Brasileña y las nuevas condiciones de la lucha de classes," in Vania Bambirra (editor), *Diez años de insurrección en América Latina.* Santiago: Editorial PLA.

—— (1971b) "El Sub-imperialismo Brasileño." Santiago: Centro de Estudios Socio-Económicos.

—— (1970) *Subdesarrollo y revolución*. Mexico City: Siglo XXI Editores
Martins, Luciano (1968) *Industrialização burguesia nacional e desenvolvimento*. Rio de Janeiro: Editôra Saga.
—— (1935) *Brazil: A Study of Economic Types*.
Oliveira Vianna, F. J. de (1956) *Evolução do povo brasileiro*. Rio de Janeiro: José Olympio Editôra.
—— (1949) *As instituções políticas brasileiras*. Rio de Janeiro: José Olympio Editôra.
Ministerio de Trabalho, Indústria e Comércio (1930–1945) *Boletim do Ministerio de Trabalho, Indústria e Comércio*. Rio de Janeiro: Ministerio de Trabalho, Industria e Comercio.
Normano, J. F. (1945) *Evolução económica do Brasil*. São Paulo: Companhia Editora Nacional.
Paim, Gilberto (1957) *Industrialização e economia natural*. Rio de Janeiro: Instituto Superior de Estudos Brasileiros.
Prado, Júnior, Caio (1966) *A revolução brasileira*. São Paulo: Editorial Brasiliense.
—— (1963) *História económica do Brasil*. São Paulo: Editorial Brasiliense.
—— (1961) *Evolução política do Brasil e outros estudos*. São Paulo: Editorial Brasiliense.
—— (1945) *Formação do Brasil contemporâneo*. São Paulo: Editorial Brasiliense. In English: (1967) *The Colonial Background of Modern Brazil*. Berkeley and Los Angeles: University of California Press.
Quijano, Aníbal (1970) "Redefinición de la dependencia y marginalización en América Latina." Santiago: Centro de Estudios Socio-Económicos.
Ramos, Guerreiro (1958) *A redução sociológica*. Rio de Janeiro: Instituto Superior de Estudos Brasileiros.
—— (n.d.) *A crise política brasileira*. [date and publisher unknown].
Rangel, Ignacio (1957) *Introdução ao estudo do desenvolvimento económico brasileiro*. Salvador: Livraria Progresso, Editôra.
Santa Rosa, Virginio (1933) *El sentido do tenentismo*. Rio de Janeiro: Schmid Editor.
Santos, Theotônio dos (1971a) *La crisis norteamericana y América Latina*. Santiago: Editorial PLA.
—— (1971b) *Dependencia y cambio social*. Santiago: Cuadernos del Centro de Estudios Socio-Económicos.
—— (1970) *Socialismo o fascismo, dilema de América Latina*. Santiago: Editorial PLA.
—— (1968a) "The Changing Structure of Foreign Investment" and "Foreign Investment and Large Enterprise," in J. Petras and M. Zeitlin (editors), *Latin America: Reform or Revolution*. Greenwich, Connecticut: Fawcett Premier Books.
—— (1968b) *El nuevo carácter de la dependencia*. Santiago: Cuadernos del Centro de Estudios Socio-Económicos.
Silva, Hélio (1969a) *1934: A constituinte*. Vol. VII: *O ciclo de Vargas*. Rio de Janeiro: Editôra Civilização Brasileira.

—— (1969b) *1935: A revolta vermelha.* Vol. VIII: *O ciclo de Vargas.* Rio de Janeiro: Editôra Civilização Brasileira.

—— (1968) *1933: A crise do tenentismo.* Vol. VI: *O ciclo de Vargas.* Rio de Janeiro: Editôra Civilização Brasileira.

—— (1967) *1932: A guerra paulista.* Vol. V: *O ciclo de Vargas.* Rio de Janeiro: Editôra Civilização Brasileira.

—— (1966a) *1930: A revolução traída.* Vol. III: *O ciclo de Vargas.* Rio de Janeiro: Editôra Civilização Brasileira.

—— (1966b) *1931: Os tenentes no poder.* Vol. IV: *O ciclo de Vargas.* Rio de Janeiro: Editôra Civilização Brasileira.

—— (1965) *1926: A grande marcha.* Vol. II: *O ciclo de Vargas.* Rio de Janeiro: Editôra Civilização Brasileira.

—— (1964) *1922: Sangue na Areia de Copacabana.* Vol. I: *O ciclo de Vargas.* Rio de Janeiro: Editôra Civilização Brasileira.

Simonsen, Roberto C. (1939) *Evolução industrial do Brasil.* São Paulo: Escola Livre de Sociología.

—— (1937) *História económica do Brasil, 1500–1820.* São Paulo: Companhia Editôra Nacional.

Skidmore, Thomas E. (1967) *Politics in Brazil, 1930–1964.* New York: Oxford University Press.

Sodré Werneck, Nelson (1967) *O que se deve ler para conhecer o Brasil.* Rio de Janeiro: Editôra Civilização Brasileira.

—— (1962) *Formação histórica do Brasil.* São Paulo: Editora Brasiliense.

—— (1946) *Formação da sociedade brasileira.* Rio de Janeiro: José Olympio Editôra.

Stein, Stanley J. and Barbara H. (1970) *The Colonial Heritage of Latin America: Essays on Economic Dependence in Perspective.* New York: Oxford University Press.

Tavares, Maria Conceição (1964) "Auge y declinación del proceso de sustitución de importaciones en el Brasil," *Boletin Económico de América Latina* (Santiago) IX, 1: 1–62.

—— and Serra, José (1971) "El modelo económico brasileño," in *Revista Latinoamericana de Sociología* (Santiago).

Trías, Vivián (1967) *Imperialismo y geopolítica en América Latina.* Montevideo: Ediciones El Sol.

Vargas, Getúlio (1938) *A nova política.* Rio de Janeiro: José Olympio Editôra.

Various Authors (1969) *Brasil en perspectivas.* São Paulo: Difusão Européia do Livro.

Vieira Pinto, Alvaro (1960) *Consciencia e realidade nacional.* Rio de Janeiro: Instituto Superior de Estudos Brasileiros.

Weffort, Francisco C. (1964) *Estado y masas en el Brasil.* Santiago: ILPES.

CHILE

Affonso, Almino; Sergio Gomez; Emilio Klein and Pablo Ramirez (1970) *Movimiento campesino chileno*. Santiago: ICIRA.

Alvárez Andrews, Oscar (1965) *Chile, monografia sociológica*. Mexico: Instituto de Investigaciones Sociales, Universidad Nacional.

Amunategui, Domingo, and Solar (1932) *Historia social de Chile*. Santiago: Editorial Nascimiento.

Aranda and Martinez (1970) *Chile Hoy*. Mexico City. Siglo XXI.

Aron, Raymond (1960) "Classe sociale, classe politique, classe dirigeante." *Archives Europeenes de Sociologie*. 1.

Bitar, Sergio (1970) "La invérsion extranjera en la industria chilena." Mimeographed. Santiago: Instituto de Estudios Internacionales.

Boizard, Ricardo (1963) *La democracía cristiana en Chile*. Santiago: Editorial Orbe.

Brodersohn, Victor (1970) "Sobre el caracter dependiente de la burguesía industrial." In *Chile Hoy*. Mexico City: Siglo XXI.

Cademartori, José (1968) *La Economía Chilena*. Santiago: Editorial Universitaria.

Cámara de Diputados (1938–9) Sesiones extraordinarias.

Caputo, Orlando, and Roberto Pizarro "Dependencia e inversión extranjera." In *Chile Hoy*. Mexico City: Siglo XXI.

Castillo Velasco, Jaime (1963) *Las fuentes de la democracía cristiana*. Santiago: Editorial del Pacífico.

Cavarozzi, Marcelo (1970) "Movimientos políticos en América Latina: Intento de formulación de una tipología." Mimeographed. Buenos Aires.

CEPEL (Economic Commission for Latin America) (1969) Desarrollo social y cambio social en América Latina. New York.

Chonchol, Jacques (1970) "Poder y reforma agraria en la experiencia chilena." *Cuadernos de la Realidad Nacional* Vol. 4. (June), pp. 50–87.

Corporación de Fomento de la Producción (1965) *Geografía Económica de Chile*. Santiago.

Corporación de la Reforma Agraria (1970) *Reforma agraria chilena 1965–1970*. Santiago.

Echenique, Jorge (1970) *Las expropriaciones y la organización de asentamientos en el periodo 1965–1970*. Santiago: Universidad de Chile.

Easton, David (1968) "The Theoretical Relevance of Political Socialization." *Canadian Journal of Political Science*.

Frank, André Gunder (1957) Capitalism and Underdevelopment in Chile and Brazil. New York: Monthly Review Press.

Fondo de Educación y Extensión Sindical, Unidad de Estudios (1970) *Afiliación sindical por confederaciones 1969*. Santiago.

Garréton, O., and J. Cisternas (1969) "Algunas características del proceso de toma de decisiones de la gran empresa. La dinámica de la concentración." Mimeographed. Santiago.

Gil, Federico (1966) *The Political System of Chile*. Boston: Houghton, Mifflin & Co.

Instituto de Economía, Universidad de Chile (1963) *La economía de Chile en el periódo 1950–1963*. Santiago: Universidad de Chile.

Inter-American Committee on the Alliance for Progress (1967) *Domestic Efforts and the Needs for External Financing for the Development of Chile*. DEA/SER/XIV/CIAP. (September).

Johnson, John (1958) Political Change in Latin America. The Emergence of the Middle Sectors. Stanford University Press.

Jobet, Julio César (1955) *Ensayo crítico del desarrollo económico-social de Chile*. Santiago: Editorial Universitaria.

Leiva Lavalle, Jorge (1970)' *El sector externo, los grupos sociales y las políticas económicas en Chile 1830–1940*. Santiago: CESO.

Mamalakis, Markos (1969) "The Theory of Sectoral Clashes." In *Latin American Research Review* 4, (Fall).

—— (1965) "Public Policy and Sectoral Development." In *Essays of the Chilean Economy* by Mamalakis & Reynolds. Homewood, Ill.: Irwin.

McBride, George (1936) *Chile: Land and Society*. New York: American Geographical Society.

Muñoz, Oscar (1968) *Crecimiento industrial de Chile 1914–1965*. Santiago: Universidad de Chile.

North American Congress on Latin America. (1972) *New Chile*. Berkeley: NACLA.

Nun, José (1965) "A Latin American Phenomenon: The Middle Class Military Coup." In Institute of International Studies, University of California, *Trends in Social Science Research in Latin American Studies*. Berkeley: University of California.

Nunn, Frederick (1970) *Chilian Politics 1920–1931*. University of New Mexico: Albuquerque.

Oficina de Estudios para la Colaboración Económica Internacional (1965) *Chile: síntesis económica y financiera*.

Petras, James and Maurice Zeitlin (1970) *El radicalismo de la clase trabajadora Chilena*. Buenos Aires: Centro Editor de América Latina.

—— (1969) *Politics and Social Forces in Chilean Development*. Berkeley: University of California Press.

Pike, Frederick (1963) *Chile and the United States 1880–1962*. Notre Dame, Indiana: University of Notre Dame Press. p. 296.

Ramirez Necochea, Hernán (1969) *Balmaceda y la contrarrevolución de 1891*. Santiago: Editorial Universitaria.

—— *Historia del movimiento obrero en Chile, Siglo XIX*. Santiago: Editorial Austral.

Silva Solar, Julio, and Jacques Chonchol (1965) *El desarrollo de la nueva sociedad en América Latina*. Santiago: Editorial Universitaria.

United Nations, CEPEL (ECLA). (1951) *Estudio económico de América Latina.* New York.

Veliz, Claudio (1963) "La Mesa de Trés Patas." In *Desarrollo Económico* Vol. 3. (April–September) 1–2.

Vera Valenzuela, Mario (1961) *La política económica del cobre en Chile.* Santiago: Universidad de Chile.

Vergara, Diego R. (1970) *Sociedad Nacional de Minería.* Santiago: CESO.

Wolpin, Miles (1968) "La Izquierda Chilena: factores estructurales que dificultan su victoria electoral en 1970." *Foro International* IX. (July–September). 43–68.

Wurth Rojas, Ernesto (1958) *Ibáñez, caudillo engimática.* Santiago: Editorial del Pacífico.

Zeitlin, Maurice (1968) "The Social Determinants of Political Democracy in Chile." In *Latin America: Reform or Revolution?* by James Petras and Maurice Zeitlin. New York: Fawcett.

CUBA

Aguilar, Luis E. (1972) *Cuba 1933: Prologue to Revolution.* Ithaca, N. Y.: Cornell University Press.

Allison, Graham T. (1971) *Essence of Decision: Explaining the Cuban Missile Crisis.* Boston: Little, Brown and Co.

Barnet, Miguel (ed.) (1968) *Autobiography of a Runaway Slave.* New York: Pantheon.

Berman, Jesse (1969) "The Cuban Popular Tribunals," *Columbia Law Review* (December), 1317–1354.

Bernardo, Robert M. (1971a) "Moral Stimulation as a Nonmarket Mode of Labor Allocation in Cuba," *Studies in Comparative International Development* VI, No. 6.

———— (1971b) *The Economics of Moral Incentives in Cuba.* University, Alabama: University of Alabama Press.

Biedma, Patricio (1970) "El socialismo en Cuba," *Cuadernos de la Realidad Nacional* (December), 327–390.

Blanksten, George I. (1966) "Fidelismo and its Origins," *Latin American Politics. 24 Studies of the Contemporary Scene.* Robert D. Tomasek, (ed.) Garden City. N. Y.: Doubleday & Company.

Bonachea, Roland E. and Nelson P. Valdés (eds.) (1972a) *Ché: Selected Works of Ernesto Guevara.* Cambridge, Mass.: MIT Press.

———— (1972b) *Revolutionary Struggles, 1946–1958: Volume I of the Selected Works of Fidel Castro*. Cambridge, Mass.: MIT Press.

———— (1972c) *Cuba in Revolution*. Garden City, N. Y.: Doubleday & Company.

Boorstein, Edward (1968) *The Economic Transformation of Cuba*. New York: Monthly Review Press.

Burt, Al (1971) "Miami: The Cuban Flavor," *The Nation* (March 8), 299–362.

Butler, Willis P. (1969) "Cuba's Revolutionary Medicine." *Ramparts* (May), 6–14.

Camarano, Chris (1971) "On Cuban Women." *Science and Society* (Spring).

Castro, Fidel (1971a) Speech of August 14, *Granma Weekly Review* (August 22).

———— (1971b) "Fidel Castro's Speech on Education, Culture, and Arts." *Intercontinental Press* (June 14).

———— (1970a) Speech of July 26, *New York Review of Books* 21–23. (Sept. 24).

———— (1970b) Speech at meeting of Central Organization of Cuban Trade Unions, September 2–3. *Granma Weekly Review* (September 20).

———— (1970c) Speech of August 23, *Granma Weekly Review* (August 30).

———— (1970d) Speech of May 20, *Granma Weekly Review* (May 31).

———— (1965) "Discurso en el acto de entrega de diplomas a los trabajadores que más se distinguieron en la I Zafro del pueblo," *El Mundo* (July 25).

———— (1963) Speech of January 6, *The Militant*. (February 4).

———— (1962a) *Fidel Castro Speaks on Marxism-Leninism*. New York: Fair Play for Cuba Committee.

———— (1962b) "3 Discursos de Fidel." Havana: Federación Estudiantil Universitaria.

———— (1961) *History Will Absolve Me*. New York: Lyle Stuart.

Chapman, Charles E. (1927) *A History of the Cuban Republic*. New York: The Macmillan Co.

Chonchol, Jacques (1963) "Análisis crítico de la reforma agraria cubana." *El Trimestre Económico* (January–March), 69–143.

Clytus, John (1970) *Black Man in Red Cuba*. Coral Gables: University of Miami Press.

Cuba Resource Center Newsletter (1972) "Exiles." II, No. 4, (July).

Debray, Regis (1967) *Revolution in the Revolution?* New York: Grove Press.

Desnoyes, Eduardo (1967) *Inconsolable Memories*. New York: New American Library.

Dewart, Leslie (1963) *Christianity and Revolution: The Lesson of Cuba*. New York: Herder and Herder.

Draper, Theodore (1962) *Castro's Revolution: Myths and Realities*. New York: Praeger.

Dumont, René (1970a) *Cuba: est-il socialiste?* Paris: Editions du Seuil.

———— (1970b) *Cuba: Socialism and Development*. New York: Grove Press.

Fagen, Richard R. (1970)   "Continuities in the Style and Strategies of Cuban Revolutionary Politics." Unpublished paper.

————— (1969)   *The Transformation of Political Culture in Cuba*. Stanford: Stanford University Press.

————— (1965)   "Charismatic Authority and the Leadership of Fidel Castro." *Western Political Quarterly* XVIII, No. 2 (June).

————— (1964)   *Cuba: The Political Content of Adult Education*. Stanford: Hoover Institution.

Foner, Philip (1962, 1963)   *A History of Cuba and Its Relations with the U. S.* 2 vols. New York: International Publishers.

Fox, Geoffrey E. (1971)   "Cuban Workers in Exile." *Trans-Action* (September), 21–30.

Friedenberg, Daniel M. (1962)   "A Cuban Dialogue." *Dissent* (Autumn), 332–341.

Gendler, Everette E. (1969)   "Holy Days in Havana," *Conservative Judaism* (Winter), 15–24.

Guevara, Ernesto (1968a)   *Ché Guevara Speaks*. George Lavan, ed. New York: Grove Press.

————— (1968b)   *Venceremos! The Speeches and Writings of Ché Guevara*. John Gerassi, ed. New York: The Macmillan Co.

Harding, Timothy F. and Donald W. Bray (1968)   "Urban Farmers: The Green Belts of Cuba." *The Nation* (August 19), 107–109.

Hochschild, Arlie (1970)   "Student Power in Action," *Cuban Communism*. Irving Horowitz, ed. Chicago: Aldine Publishing Co.

Horowitz, Irving L. (ed.) (1970)   *Cuban Communism*. Chicago: Aldine Publishing Company. 3-36.

Huberman, Leo and Paul M. Sweezy (1969)   *Socialism in Cuba*. New York: Monthly Review Press.

Inter-American Development Bank (1967)   *Socio-Economic Progress in Latin America*. Washington, D. C.

Jackson, D. Bruce (1969)   *Castro, the Kremlin and Communism in Latin America*. Baltimore: The Johns Hopkins Press.

Jeness, Linda (1970)   *Women and the Cuban Revolution*. New York: Pathfinder Press.

Jenks, Leland (1928)   *Our Cuban Colony: A Study in Sugar*. New York: Vanguard Press.

Karol, K. S. (1970)   *Guerrillas in Power*. New York: Hill and Wang.

Kennedy, Ian (1971)   Interview, Law School, University of California at Los Angeles. (October 18).

Kenner, Martin and James Petras (eds.) (1969)   *Fidel Castro Speaks*. New York: Grove Press.

Landau, Saul (1970)   "Socialist Democracy in Cuba; an Interview with Fidel Castro," *Socialist Revolution* I, No. 2 (March–April), 128–143.

Las Casas, Bartolomé de (1962)   The Tears of the Indians. Stanford, Calif.: Academic Reprints.

Latastre, Albán (1968) *¿Cuba hacía una nueva economía política del socialismo?* Santiago, Chile: Editorial Universitaria.

Leontief, Wassily (1971) "The Trouble with Cuban Socialism," *The New York Review of Books* (January 7), 19–23.

———— (1969) "Notes on a Visit to Cuba," *New York Review of Books* (August 21), 15–20.

Levinson, Sandra (1972) "Building a Revolutionary Culture: The Education and Cultural Congress," *Cuba Resources Center Newsletter* (New York) (January), 3–14.

———— and Carol Brightman (eds.) (1971) *Venceremos Brigade.* New York: Simon and Schuster.

Lockwood, Lee (1971) *Review of Guerrillas in Power* by K. S. Karol. New York Times Book Review (January 24), 3.

———— (1970a) *Conversations with Eldridge Cleaver.* New York: Dell.

———— (1970b) "An Introduction to Fidel Castro's 26th of July Speech," *New York Review of Books* (September 24).

———— (1969) *Castro's Cuba, Cuba's Fidel.* New York: Vintage Books.

MacGaffey, Wyatt and Clifford Robert Barnett (1965) *Twentieth-century Cuba: The Background of the Castro Revolution.* New York: Doubleday and Co.

McGuiness, Richard (1971) "Cuba and the Sexual Third World," *The Village Voice* (August 19).

Mandel, Ernest (1970) "Intellectuals and the Third World." *Intercontinental Press,* (September 28). Reprinted from *Tricontinental Havana,* (May-June), 801.

Martín, Leonel (1971) "Reestructuración Sindical en Cuba," *Cuba* (International), (April), 28.

Matthews, Herbert L. (1969) *Fidel Castro.* New York: Simon and Schuster.

———— (1964) "Return to Cuba," *Hispanic American Report* (Special Issue).

Mesa-Lago, Carmelo (ed.) (1971) *Revolutionary Change in Cuba: Polity, Economy, Society.* Pittsburgh: University of Pittsburgh Press.

———— (1970a) "Economic-Political and Ideological Factors in the Cuban Controversy on Material versus Moral Incentives." Unpublished paper. (April).

———— (1970b) "The Revolutionary Offensive," *Cuban Communism.* Irving Horowitz, ed. Chicago: Aldine Publishing Co. 73–93.

———— (1969–1970) "Ideological Radicalization and Economic Policy in Cuba," *Studies in Comparative International Development* V, No. 10. 203–216.

———— (1969) "Availability and Reliability of Statistics in Socialist Cuba," *Latin American Research Revew* IV, No. 1. (Spring, Summer). 53–91.

Miller, Warren (1962) *Flush Times.* Boston: Little, Brown and Co.

Montañé, Jesús (1971) Speech at National Press Meeting, *Granma* (Weekly Review), (September 19).

Nelson, Lowry (1970) *Rural Cuba.* New York: Octagon Books.

New University Conference (NUC) (1969) Ethan Singer, James Cockcroft, Elizabeth Diggs, Karen Spalding, Ruth Misheloff, Anna Marie Taylor. *Cuba.* Chicago.

O'Connor, James (1970) *The Origins of Socialism in Cuba.* Ithaca, N. Y.: Cornell University Press.

Padilla, Heberto (1971a) "Padilla Rejects Support," *Intercontinental Press* (June 14), 538.

——— (1971b) "Two Poems," (translated by Paul Blackburn). *New York Review of Books* (June 3). 4–5.

Petras, James (1971) "Socialism in One Island! A Decade of Cuban Revolutionary Government," *Politics and Society* I, No. 2. 203–224.

——— (1970) *Politics and Social Structure in Latin America.* New York: Monthly Review Press.

Purcell, Susan Kaufman (1971) "Modernizing Woman for a Modern Society: The Cuban Case." Unpublished paper. UCLA.

Reckord, Barry (1971) *Does Fidel Eat More Than Your Father?* New York: Praeger.

Revueltas, José (1971) "Padilla's Letter and Fidel's Words," *Intercontinental Press* (July 5), 632–633.

Ring, Harry (1971) "Cuba in '71," *The Militant* (August 6).

Robertson, C. Alton (1967) "The Political Role of the Protestants in Cuba— 1959 to 1962." *Occasional Bulletin,* Missionary Research Library (January, February).

Ruiz, Ramón Eduardo (1968) *Cuba: The Making of a Revolution.* Amherst: University of Massachusetts Press.

Salper, Roberta (1970) "Literature and Revolution in Cuba," *Monthly Review* XX, No. 5 (October), 15–30.

Seers, Dudley (ed.) (1964) *Cuba, the Economic and Social Revolution.* Chapel Hill: University of North Carolina Press.

Smith, Robert Freeman (1963) *What Happened in Cuba: A Documentary History.* New York.

——— (1960) *The United States and Cuba: Business and Diplomacy.* New York.

Somers, Bernard J. (1969) "Pychology and Mental Health Services in Cuba in 1968," *American Psychologist* (October), 940–943.

Súarez, Andrés (1968) *Cuba: Castroism and Communism 1959–1966.* Cambridge, Mass.: MIT Press.

Sundelson, J. Wilner (1967 "A Business Perspective," John Plank, ed. *Cuba and the United States.* Washington, D. C.: Brookings Institute.

Sutherland, Elizabeth (1969) *The Youngest Revolution: A Personal Report on Cuba.* New York: Dial Press.

Szulc, Tad (1967) "Exporting the Cuban Revolution," John Plank, ed. *Cuba and the United States.* Washington, D. C.: Brookings Institute.

Taber, Robert (1961)   *M26: The Biography of a Revolution.* New York: Lyle Stuart.

Taft, William H. and Robert Bacon (1906–1907). *Report in U. S. 59th Congress.* 2nd Session, Ser. No. 5105. House Documents.

Thomas, Hugh (1971) *Cuba: The Pursuit of Freedom.* New York: Harper and Row.

———— (1967)   "Middle Class Politics and the Cuban Revolution," Claudio Veliz, ed. *The Politics of Conformity in Latin America.* London: Oxford.

Trotsky, Leon (1970)   *Leon Trotsky on Literature and Art.* Paul N. Siegel, ed. New York: Pathfinder Press.

Valdés, Nelson P. (1971)   "Health and Revolution in Cuba," *Science and Society* XXXV, No. 3 (Fall), 311–355.

———— and Edwin Lieuwen (1971)   *Revolutionary Cuba: A Research Study Guide (1959–1969).* Albuquerque: University of New Mexico Press.

Wald, Karen (1971)   "The Children of Ché," *The Staff* Los Angeles (September 24), 3–4.

Williams, William A. (1962)   *The United States, Castro and Cuba.* New York: Monthly Review Press.

Wisan, Joseph E. (1934)   *The Cuban Crisis as Reflected in the New York Press. 1895–1898.* New York: Columbia University Press.

Yglesias, José (1971)   "The Case of Heberto Padilla," *New York Review of Books* (June 3), 3–8.

———— (1968)   *In the Fist of the Revolution.* New York: Pantheon.

Zeitlin, Maurice (1970)   "Inside Cuba: Workers and Revolution," *Ramparts* (March), 10 ff.

———— (1967)   *Revolutionary Politics and the Cuban Working Class.* Princeton, New Jersey: Princeton University Press.

———— and Robert Scheer (1963)   *Cuba: Tragedy in Our Hemisphere.* New York: Grove Press.

———— (1962)   "An Interview with 'Che'," *Root and Branch* (Winter), 36–56.

Periodicals

Bohemia

Casa

Cuba (International)

Cuba Resource Center Newsletter, P. O. Box 206, Cathedral Station, N. Y., N. Y. 10025

Cuba Socialista

Granma

Granma (Weekly Review)

Intercontinental Press (New York)

Lunes de Revolución

El Mundo

The Nation

Nuestra Industria
Pensamiento Crítico
Revolución
Verde Olivo
Visión

Films

Cuba: Battle of the 10,000,000 Tons. (New Yorker Films)

Death of a Bureaucrat. (ICAIC, Havana)

Fidel. (New Yorker Films)

Lucía. (ICAIC, Havana)

Memories of Underdevelopment. (Tricontinental Films Center, Berkeley, Calif. and New York)

Report from Cuba. (Indiana University A-V Center, Bloomington, Ind.)

Story of a Battle (Depicts the Literacy Campaign of 1961, Newsreel Films, Los Angeles, Calif. and New York)